# Clinicians' Guide To Adult ADHD

Assessment and Intervention

# Clinicians' Guide To Adult ADHD

## Assessment and Intervention

**Sam Goldstein**
*University of Utah, Salt Lake City, UT*

**Anne Teeter Ellison**
*University of Wisconsin-Milwaukee, Milwaukee, WI*

ACADEMIC PRESS
An imprint of Elsevier Science

Amsterdam   Boston   London   New York   Oxford   Paris
San Diego   San Francisco   Singapore   Sydney   Tokyo

Copyright © 2002, Elsevier Science (USA)

All rights reserved.

No part of this publication may be reproduced or transmitted in any form or by any means, electronic or mechanical, including photocopy, recording, or any information storage and retrieval system, without permission in writing from the publisher.

Requests for permission to make copies of any part of the work should be mailed to: Permissions Department, Academic Press, 6277 Sea Harbor Drive, Orlando, Florida 32887–6777.

Cover photo credit: © *Image 100/Royalty-Free/CORBIS*

Academic Press
*An imprint of Elsevier Science*
525 B Street, Suite 1900, San Diego, California 92101–4495, USA
http://www.academicpress.com

Academic Press
*An imprint of Elsevier Science*
84 Theobald's Road, London WC1X 8RR, UK
http://www.academicpress.com

Library of Congress Catalog Card Number: 2002102336

International Standard Book Number: 0–12–287049–2

PRINTED IN THE UNITED STATES OF AMERICA
02  03  04  05  06  MB  9  8  7  6  5  4  3  2  1

*For Janet, Allyson and Ryan.*

*Thanks to George Zimmar for his editorial assistance and vision in helping us create this text. Thanks also to Kathleen Gardner, as always, for her editorial and technical assistance.*

Sam Goldstein

*This book is dedicated to adults with ADHD. To your courage. To your dignity. To your spirit. For those of you who are still looking for answers . . . I hope the ideas that follow will help.*

*To my husband, Philip. Thank you for all your patience, understanding, and support.*

Anne Teeter Ellison

The great tragedy of science—the slaying of a beautiful hypothesis by an ugly fact. Irrationally held truths may be more harmful than reasoned errors.

*Thomas Henry Huxley*

Although the world is full of suffering, it is also full of overcoming of it.

*Helen Keller*

# Contents

**Contributors** xv

**Foreword** xvii

**Preface** xix

CHAPTER **1** **An Overview of Childhood and Adolescent ADHD: Understanding the Complexities of Development into the Adult Years**
ANNE TEETER ELLISON

Transactional Model of ADHD: Impact of Biogenetic, Neuropsychological, Cognitive, and Psychosocial Deficits 2
Interaction of Neurobiological and Environmental Factors 6
Cognitive and Academic Findings 6
The Developmental Context: Characteristics and Associated Features of ADHD 10
Cumulative Effects of Living with a Developmental Disorder: From Childhood to Adulthood 14
ADHD Risk and Resiliency 15
A Developmental Perspective: Implications for Treatment of ADHD in Adulthood 18
References 19

CHAPTER **2** **Continuity of ADHD in Adulthood: Hypothesis and Theory Meet Reality**
SAM GOLDSTEIN

Introduction 25
Outcome of ADHD in the Adult Years 27

Evaluation   35
Factors Affecting Outcome   37
Conclusion   39
References   39

CHAPTER 3  **Research on Comorbidity, Adaptive Functioning, and Cognitive Impairments in Adults with ADHD: Implications for a Clinical Practice**
RUSSELL BARKLEY AND MICHAEL GORDON

Disorders Comorbid with ADHD in Adults   46
Cognitive Deficits   49
Domains of Adaptive Functioning Examined in Adults with ADHD   55
Clinical Implications   61
Conclusion   66
References   66

CHAPTER 4  **The Assessment Process: Conditions and Comorbidities**
DIANE E. JOHNSON AND C. KEITH CONNERS

Introduction to ADHD in Adulthood: Presentation and Risks   72
Current ADHD Diagnostic Criteria, The DSM-IV   73
Practice Parameters for the Assessment of Adult ADHD   77
Making the Diagnosis of ADHD in Adults   78
Guarding Against Overdiagnosing ADHD in Adults and the Issue of Comorbidity   81
References   82

CHAPTER 5  **Clinical Case Studies**
KEVIN MURPHY

Case one: Assigning the ADHD Diagnosis Incorrectly Can Cause Harm   86
Case two: ADHD or Bipolar Disorder or both?   91
Case Three: ADHD with Comorbid Substance Dependence and Conduct Disorder   95

Case four: ADHD/LD and Test Accommodations for a Professional
    Licensing Exam: Effective Advocacy   99
References   105

CHAPTER 6 **The Clinician's Role in the Treatment of ADHD**
KATHLEEN G. NADEAU

Overview   107
A Multi-level Approach in Treating ADHD in Adults   109
Basic Issues in Treating Adults with ADHD   111
Treating ADHD Across the Adult Life Span   113
The Challenges of the Middle Adult Years   121
Treating Adults with ADHD in Their Middle Years   122
Summary   126
References   126

CHAPTER 7 **Changing the Mindset of Adults with ADHD: Strategies for Fostering Hope, Optimism, and Resilience**
ROBERT B. BROOKS

The Characteristics of Adults with ADHD   128
The Unfortunate Mindset of Adults with ADHD   131
Assessing the Mindset of Individuals with ADHD   135
Coping Strategies: Helping or Exacerbating the Problem?   135
Steps for Changing Negative into Positive Mindsets   138
Concluding Thoughts About Two Men   145
References   146

CHAPTER 8 **A Model of Psychotherapy for Adults with ADHD**
SUSAN YOUNG

Who Are Adults with ADHD and What Are Their Problems?   148
Psychological Therapy   150
Conclusions   158

Appendix 159
References 162

CHAPTER 9 **Pharmacotherapy of Adult ADHD**
JEFFREY B. PRINCE AND TIMOTHY E. WILENS

Introduction 165
Overview of the Neurobiology and Genetics of ADHD 166
Clinical Features of ADHD in Adults 167
Assessment and Diagnosis of ADHD in Adults 168
General Principles of Pharmacotherapy of ADHD in Adults 169
Stimulants in the Treatment of Adults with ADHD 170
Nonstimulant Medications in the Treatment of Adults with ADHD 175
Clinical Strategies for the Pharmacotherapy of ADHD in Adults 179
Combined Pharmacotherapy 181
Summary 182
References 182

CHAPTER 10 **Career Impact: Finding the Key to Issues Facing Adults with ADHD**
ROB CRAWFORD AND VERONICA CRAWFORD

Introduction 187
Barriers to Realistic Career Decision Making 187
Starting Out with a Realistic Picture 189
Reframing and Involvement 192
Client Involvement and Developing Self-Determination 193
The Role of the Professional as Mentor and Facilitator 194
Practical Tools and Strategies for Career Decision Making 196
Gaining Control of the Decision 198
Generating Reasonable Alternatives 200
Living with the Consequences Without Suffering 201
Managing Uncertainties and Assessing Risk Tolerance 202
Conclusion 203
References 204

CHAPTER **11** **What Clinicians Need to Know About Legal Issues Relative to ADHD**
PETER S. LATHAM AND PATRICIA H. LATHAM

Introduction   205
Two Statutes   206
Individual with a Disability   206
Otherwise Qualified   213
The Right to Reasonable Accommodation   215
The Professional's Opinion   216
Conclusion   217
Notes   217
References   218

CHAPTER **12** **Making Marriages Work for Individuals with ADHD**
PATRICK KILCARR

Overview   220
Foundations: Setting the Initial Stages of Therapy   221
Two Therapeutic Approaches   222
Supplemental Interaction Strategies   233
Substance Abuse in the Relationship   236
Assuming Individual Responsibility   238
Summary   239
References   239

CHAPTER **13** **Families and ADHD**
THOMAS W. PHELAN

Introduction   241
Effects of ADHD on Home and Family   242
Parenting and Marriage   245
Good Parenting and Straight Thinking   248
Managing Family Life: What to Do   251
Summary   260
References   260

## CHAPTER 14 Life Coaching for Adult ADHD
NANCY RATEY

Claire's Story 261
What Is Personal Coaching? 262
What Is ADHD Coaching? 262
How Coaching Helped Claire 263
Theoretical Underpinnings of ADHD Coaching 263
The Precepts of ADHD Coaching 265
The Process of Coaching 266
How Does Coaching Work? 267
Distinguishing Coaching from Other Services 272
The Power of Collaboration 273
Coaching Is Never a Substitute for Therapy 274
Issues That Can Complicate the Coaching Process 274
Finding and Choosing a Coach 275
Creating the Right Match 275
Qualities to Look For in a Coach 276
Conclusion 277

## CHAPTER 15 Lifestyle Issues
ARTHUR L. ROBIN

Theoretical Underpinnings 280
Lifestyle Management Model 280
Understanding Strengths and Weaknesses 281
Maximizing Medication 283
Achieving Balance and Establishing Long-Term Goals 283
Planning to Attain Goals: The Day Planner 286
Organizing "Things" 288
Conclusion 290
References 291

**Index 293**

# Contributors

*Numbers in parentheses indicate the pages on which the authors' contributions begin.*

**Russell Barkley** (43), Department of Psychiatry, University of Massachusetts Medical Center, Worcester, MA 01655

**Robert Brooks** (127), Harvard Medical School, McLean Hospital, Belmont, MA 02478

**C. Keith Conners** (71), Department of Psychiatry and Behavior Sciences, Duke University Medical Center, Durham, NC 27705

**Rob Crawford** (187), Life Development Institute, Glendale, AZ 85308

**Veronica Crawford** (187), PART, Glendale, AZ 85308

**Anne Teeter Ellison** (1), Department of Educational Psychology, University of Wisconsin-Milwaukee, Milwaukee, WI 53221

**Sam Goldstein** (25), Neurology, Learning and Behavior Center, University of Utah, Salt Lake City, UT 84102

**Michael Gordon** (43), Department of Psychiatry, State University of New York, Upstate Medical School, Syracuse, NY 13210

**Diane Johnson** (71), Department of Psychiatry and Behavioral Sciences, Duke University Medical Center, Durham, NC 27710

**Patrick J. Kilcarr** (219), Georgetown University's Center for Personal Development, Washington, D.C. 20057

**Patricia Latham** (205), National Center for Law and Learning Disabilities, Cabin John, MD 20818

**Peter Latham** (205), National Center for Law and Learning Disabilities, Cabin John, MD 20818

**Kevin Murphy** (85), Department of Psychiatry, University of Massachusetts Medical Center, Worcester, MA 01655

**Kathleen Nadeau** (107), Chesapeake Psychological Services, Silver Spring, MD 20910

**Thomas W. Phelan** (241), Glen Ellyn, IL 60137

**Jeffrey Prince** (165), Massachusetts General Hospital, Boston, MA 02114

**Nancy Ratey** (261), National Attention Deficit Disorder Association, Wellesley, MA 02482

**Arthur Robin** (279), Children's Hospital of Michigan, Detroit, MI 48201

**John Watson** (xxi) 1759 E. Ski View Dr. Sandy, UT 84092

**Tim Wilens** (165), Massachusetts General Hospital, Boston, MA 02114

**Susan Young** (147), Department of Psychology, Institute of Psychiatry, De Crespigny Park, London, UK, SE5 8AF

# Foreword

Controversy has always accompanied the concept and diagnosis of Attention Deficit/Hyperactivity Disorder (ADHD), both in lay and professional circles. Perhaps resistance to the concept lies in the fact that in some sense the disorder echoes the 19th century concept of a "failure of will," (William James, 1890) or "moral defect," (George Still, 1902). James had postulated that inattention was the root cause of impulsive choices, and Still first described a syndrome of normal IQ children who suffered from a "moral defect." Their unruly behavior, poor school work, and impulsive acts were thought to be the result of a defect in the ability to make correct (moral) choices. It was common at that time to conceptualize psychiatric disorders as the result of excess stimuli overwhelming the sensorium; of distraction leading to impulsive (and hence immoral) behavior.

The continuing controversy and resistance to a medical diagnosis might lie, then, in the persisting belief that the cure for a weak will is moral education, not medicine. If the controversial nature of organicity, minimal brain damage, minimal brain dysfunction, and attention deficit/hyperactivity applies to children, how much more so must be the allegation that it also applies to adults! Here the field is rife with arguments against the diagnosis: hyperactivity disappears in adolescence, onset in childhood cannot be proven, pharmacotherapy is less effective in the adults, disorders of depression, anxiety, sociopathy, borderline personality, and many other psychiatric illnesses account for the putative attentional problems, and so on and on.

Conspiracy theorists harken to some of their favorite explanations for the sudden burst of interest in adult ADHD, such as a collusion among academics, psychiatrists, and drug companies trying to restore income lost with the advent of managed care (if one is to believe one recent FDA maven's assessment). The anti-Ritalin caucus among strident self-appointed "Centers for the Public Interest" and those worried about children "running on Ritalin," now turn their venom on this new-fangled invention of ADULT ADHD as further evidence of moral decline, or of an invented disorder catering to self-diagnosis among those seeking a competitive edge by performance-enhancing drugs.

Now it is surely true that there has been a shameful neglect of clinical and biological research on *adults* with the syndrome of ADHD, with the exception of a few pioneers such as Paul Wender (1979) who very early saw the outlines of a distinctive disorder mirroring that of childhood "MBD". But much has happened in science since those early years when the "brain" part of the syndrome was mere speculation in the absence of hard data. There is now strong evidence for the worldwide prevalence of ADHD in virtually all countries studied. Now there is overwhelming evidence for the strong genetic heritability of ADHD; for anatomic anomalies repeatedly detected by brilliant neuroimaging technologies, including PET, MRI, and fMRI. Alan Zametkin and colleagues (Zametkin, Nordahl and Gross, 1990) opened the doors to this new field with his demonstration in carefully assessed adult probands of ADHD children, finding clear localized differences from normal controls on PET scans. Converging evidence suggests that for many ADHD patients there are dopaminergic defects in receptor or re-uptake mechanisms, particularly in the frontal lobes. Neuropsychological investigations also confirm the presence of persisting defects in executive functions, particularly for working memory, disturbances of time perception, and "forgetting to remember" (meta-memory). Symptomatic studies also detect, as it had previously discovered in adolescents, the emergence of a distinctive failure-related syndrome of low self-esteem, obviously associated with a lifelong history of interpersonal, academic and social failure.

As often happens in emerging sciences, practicing clinicians may advance beyond the known certainties provided by empirical research and clinical trials. Such data are now pouring in, and new compendia of research and practice, such as the recent excellent text by another pioneer, Gabrielle Weiss and colleagues (1999), are springing up to guide both new research and practice.

The current volume takes a comprehensive fresh look at both the clinical and data-related issues surrounding adult ADHD. A wealth of clinical observation and new empirical data are presented here, and will hopefully inform the clinician, researcher, and patient alike, prompting them to put aside controversy in favor of facts, thereby insuring that adult ADHD receives the respect and attention it richly deserves as a disabling condition requiring compassion, informed care, and diligent research, rather than the benign neglect of the past.

C. Keith Conners, Ph.D.
*Professor Emeritus of Psychiatry and Behavioral Sciences*
*Duke University Medical Center, Durham, NC*

## REFERENCES

James, W. (1890). **The principles of psychology**. New York, NY: Holt.

Still, G.F. (1902). The Coulstonian lectures on some abnormal physical conditions in children. **Lancet, 1**, 1008–1012.

Weiss, M., Hechtman, L.T., & Weiss, G. (1999). **ADHD in Adulthood: A guide to current theory, diagnosis and treatment**. Baltimore, MD: The Johns Hopkins University Press.

Wender, P.H. (1979). The concept of adult minimal brain dysfunction. In L. Bellak (Ed.). **Psychiatric aspects of minimal brain dysfunction in adults**. New York, NY: Grune and Stratton.

Zametkin, A.J., Nordahl, T.E., & Gross, M. (1990). Cerebral glucose metabolism adults with hyperactivity in childhood onset. **Archives of General Psychiatry, 50**, 333–340.

# Preface

In the fall of 2000, the wife of one of our adult patients wrote the following:

> Total frustration! That's what I feel like several times a day—or more—I hear, "I can't find my...Have you seen...? Where is my...? If you see my..." He never picks up after himself (dirty dishes, dirty clothes, shaving cream, towels, etc.). I am tired of being the maid. If he uses the remote on the TV or the cordless phone, I have to go find them because he left them somewhere else. I more or less raised our two big girls by myself and now I am more or less raising our little boy by myself. He can't sit still unless golf or football are on TV then he can sit still. So that is all he does at home is watch TV. Please do something for this man because after 20 years of marriage he is making me crazy!

This man's self-report matched his wife's observations. He was well aware of his problems but had long given up hope that there was much he could do about them. The majority of his energy was focused at work, where he had been placed on probation a number of times. In self-report measures he described his difficulty focusing on important tasks and listening when spoken to, his problems with organization, his being forgetful, restless, and, in the last five years, somewhat depressed.

The words of this couple are echoed again and again by the individuals coming to our clinics. Although over the past 50 years the diagnostic category Attention Deficit Hyperactivity Disorder (ADHD) has been considered primarily a childhood condition, the experiences of clinical practice teach that a significant number of children with ADHD appear to carry their impairing symptoms with them into adult life. The significant and pervasive impairments reported day in and day out for children with ADHD has been increasingly demonstrated for a significant portion of this population during their adult years. Though the responsibilities and demands placed upon adults in comparison to children are certainly different, the consequences of these problems—impaired daily functioning—are not. What is it about the condition we today call ADHD that has blinded clinicians until just recently to recognizing that these are problems of life rather than of only childhood? Perhaps their spouses are not as vocal as their mothers, or years of impairment lead those adults with ADHD to suffer in silence, develop dysfunctional coping strategies, or form mindsets to deny the condition or its impact. The self-regulatory problems underlying ADHD are not outgrown. Though symptoms may wax and wane as individuals grow, it is a reasonable conclusion that the majority of inattentive, impulsive, and hyperactive children grow into adults manifesting many of these very same symptoms.

For the general public and perhaps a significant percentage of medical and mental health professionals, it was likely reassuring to believe that the problems caused by ADHD represented a poor fit between some children and their environments. It was likely comforting for parents to hear professionals tell them that not only was this a problem that would be outgrown but that by simply parenting their children differently they could change the condition. Certainly for some, this lead to strong, unwarranted feelings of guilt and to the belief that they were inadequate parents and that their failings had led to this condition. Belief is a powerful ally in the absence of fact. However, over the past ten years the belief that ADHD is just a childhood condition has been increasingly tested. Though for some parts of the lay community and for professionals with "an axe to grind," ADHD is still reported as a condition created by inadequate parenting or, even worse, as an illusion created by the marketing arms of drug companies and psychiatric organizations, the belief that ADHD does not exist or in fact does not cause impairment throughout the lifetime has been tested and the results are clear. A significant number of individuals suffering with this condition in their childhood continue to suffer and lead lives less than their capabilities.

Perhaps another phenomena that has delayed the recognition of ADHD as a lifetime condition has been the history of associating these behaviors only with children. This is not to suggest that adults don't act impulsively or experience difficulty sustaining attention. They most certainly do. But for adults these symptoms historically have been considered to fall clinically within the domains of other conditions, including the DSM-IV Axis II diagnosis of Impulsive Personality Disorder. As far as we are aware, no one has yet to test the theory as to what percentage of adults with this condition demonstrate histories of ADHD. Certainly, as many researchers report including those contributing to this text, individuals with ADHD are at significantly greater risk to develop antisocial, borderline, dependent, and passive aggressive personality styles.

The earliest report of symptoms traditionally related to ADHD is credited to St. John the Baptist. Luke 1:41 cites John describing fetal hyperactivity: "The babe leapt in her womb." There are also allusions in many early civilizations to this symptom as a problem of childhood. The Greek physician Galen was reported to prescribe opium for restless infants (Goodman & Gilman, 1975). Hans Hoffman's description in 1845 of "Fidgety Phil" set the tone that wriggles, giggles, rocking, and swinging were problems of childhood (Papazian, 1995). Interestingly this poem also set the tone for these problems stemming from naughtiness. Naughty children are restricted from Nintendo. Naughty adults, however, are fired or sent to jail. Historically our society has had little empathy for "naughty adults."

The notion of ADHD as a childhood condition was also reinforced by the work of George F. Still in 1902. In describing Still's disease, he suggested that some children have difficulty with moral control because they are unable to internalize rules and limits and exhibit restless, inattentive, and overaroused behavior. Still did not discuss the hypothesized outcome of these children into their adult years. He was, however, quite pessimistic, believing that these children could not successfully transition into adulthood.

Finally, although in the late 1800s and early 1900s symptoms now considered diagnostic of ADHD were recognized as being multicausal, including the result of brain injury, the world outbreak of encephalitis in 1917 and 1918 led to very different outcomes for affected children and adults. Many children who recovered from the encephalitis presented a pattern of restless, inattentive, impulsive, and hyperactive behavior. The adults who recovered, however, did not so present. In extreme cases these adults became extremely catatonic and unresponsive to their environments.

Though the presence, cause, and evaluation of ADHD has been controversial, the issue of treatment for the condition has created by far the greatest controversy. Psychosocial treatments such as cognitive training, once considered promising in directly reducing the symptoms of ADHD, are recognized as at best offering valuable interventions for adjunctive problems related to ADHD. Particularly in adults, problems involving self-esteem, motivation, and the development of an atypical or dysfunctional mindset can be addressed and resolved in counseling.

The greatest volume of literature in the treatment of ADHD has been devoted to the investigation of the direct benefits of psychostimulants and related medications the symptoms of ADHD. A very large, diverse, and scientifically rigorous literature has consistently demonstrated the benefits of psychostimulants for ADHD across the life span (for review, see Greenhill & Osman, 2000). Nonetheless, although stimulants offer excellent short-term symptomatic relief for the problems of ADHD, they have not been demonstrated in the long run to significantly alter the life course for those with ADHD. Thus, from the available, well-controlled research of children with ADHD taking medicine in comparison to those who do not, do not seem to fare significantly better into their adult lives. Outcome as described by multiple researchers appears to be related to the adverse impact of the consequences of living with ADHD. The environmental, educational, social, and familial factors that place all growing children at risk appear to be catalytically driven by the symptoms of ADHD, placing those with the condition at even greater risk. The biopsychosocial nature of ADHD makes it reasonable to conclude that it is the environment more than the direct treatments for ADHD that predict life outcome and course for affected individuals.

We embrace the view of the symptoms of ADHD as catalytic. Place an affected individual in a good context, and ADHD may not represent a significant risk factor. But these symptoms certainly do not represent an asset as far as we believe and can demonstrate. Place them in a child living in a dysfunctional family, exposed to a poor school environment or other significant life stress, and ADHD likely represents a significant risk factor.

In 1988, Carey noted that it was of little importance if one's theoretical orientation toward ADHD saw it as a neurobehavioral phenomenon, lack of fit between individual and environment or even a matter of cognitive style. All three factors must be considered in the intervention process. Recognizing that ADHD is a biopsychosocial disorder affecting individuals differently but consistently throughout their life span shifts the focus from attempting to search for a cure to developing a balance between symptom management and the reduction of immediate problems, all the while building in resilience factors during the childhood years. It is likely that this combination of interventions stands the best chance of leading to positive longterm outcomes for adults with ADHD.

The research literature on this condition during the adult years, or for that matter on the risk factors related to this condition affecting adult outcome during the childhood years, is still very small in comparison to the body of research in this area. Nonetheless, we believe there is a consensus among practitioners that the core symptoms of ADHD affect a significant minority of our population. For affected individuals, this condition represents a poor fit between society's expectations and these individual's abilities to meet these expectations. This condition is distinct from other disorders of childhood and adulthood and can be reliably evaluated and effectively treated. Finally, this condition leads to a high financial cost for society for adults unable to transition into functional life. As Russell Barkley noted in 1991, treatment for ADHD must and will continue to be multidisciplinary and multimodal and, in light of continuing cultural trends and societal expectations, must be maintained throughout the affected individual's life span. Though symptoms and consequences may wax and wane, there is no cure leading to complete recovery.

The first author met John when he was nearly eighteen years of age in 1987. John was the second of his parents' five children. At the time his siblings ranged in age between six and twenty-one years. John's younger brother, David, had recently been diagnosed with Attention Deficit Hyperactivity Disorder. Other siblings had not experienced similar problems. John's history and functioning, despite his advanced intellect and achievement, was consistent for what at that time was referred to as Attention Deficit Disorder with Hyperactivity. In the following year, John participated in counseling focusing on improving relationships with family members and developing a life direction. He subsequently served a two year mission for his church and obtained a college degree. John married and at this writing is the father of two children. He works in a managerial position with a number of siblings in a business started by his father. At 31 years of age John reports that he is happy and satisfied with his life. He continues to take medication for his condition with reported and observed benefits. He participates in intermittent counseling, focusing on specific work, family and life issues as they arise. With the first author, John explored a contribution to this volume focused on sensitizing clinicians on his view of what those who profess to help adults with ADHD must know as well as his personal perception of the factors and forces that have made a positive difference in his life. His words follow.

First, let me start off by dispelling the myth that ADHD is a blessing. It is not. Nor is it an advantage, gift, or desirable in any way. Any professional perpetuating this myth possesses only knowledge derived from textbooks about this condition. Such an individual lacks sufficient understanding and empathy to counsel (much less treat) afflicted individuals. Strong words, because I believe strongly and want to make certain this is understood above all else. Let me expand on this by sharing an experience I had with my therapist.

My therapist has told me on many occasions that I am what every ADHD therapist hopes for in their patients. I have had a very difficult time accepting this. How can someone with my history be the standard for achievement for a class of people? Perhaps my list of "haves" gives some insight into the comment. As he has reminded me I have a loving wife, wonderful children, and a fully functional family that loves me. I have no chemical dependencies, legal or otherwise, nor have I ever. I am financially adequate. I have a degree in marketing, and, subsequently, have a good job in which I do well and find great satisfaction. I am active, and devout in my faith. I am in general a productive reasonably well-adjusted member of society.

All of that sounds really nice. I can hear, "Oh, there's a really together successful guy, by any standard." In that context I will have to gratefully agree. Unfortunately this all belies the issues that don't come up in such a shopping list. I am horribly disorganized, both at work and home. I have a tremendously difficult time completing the tasks before me without succumbing to major tangential distractions. I find it nearly impossible to do simple things that I know are necessary, from getting places on time to completing ordinary daily tasks. My marriage gets strained to near breaking at times due to my inability to stay in a conversation or project reliably. When I do find something that peaks my interest, all else will get pushed aside to make room for it, no matter how trivial it is. Even in print these problems don't appear as dire as they are experienced.

My parents have been amazingly supportive and understanding through the years. This is in contrast to their desperation and frustration. From early on they knew there was a problem, but no one could give them any answers. As a child they sent me to a psychiatrist at a time when it was a financial stretch, only to have him finally conclude that, while there was a real problem, there was nothing that he could do for me! Even when times were the darkest, and my actions brought our family to the brink of chaos, their thoughts were on how to help me. I really didn't understand all the time, effort, and patience that they put into helping me. I was a terror. Not intentionally, I just was quick to react and unaware of my own strength. I could usually pass for several years older than I actually was, and that size coupled with a faulty think-before-you-act chip resulted in lots of bruises and tears for my siblings, and consequently me.

In the end, structure and guidelines in a loving, caring, stimulating environment helped me above all else, due to the limits my parents helped me set and enforce. No single element could do it for me. I required the package. I have come to a point that I think I know *where* the answer lies, but I challenge you the professional to find the answer. I believe the secret to combating ADHD is the building of internalized barriers. An instruction set that *will not* be broken. This is not easy. Pavlovian theory goes out the window with ADHD, as does reason. Even positive and negative reinforcement are of little or no use. That is the dilemma.

In my experience barriers are what insulate and protect someone with ADHD. Unfortunately, those barriers are monumentally difficult to build and enforce. My request of clinicians and professionals who deal with ADHD and like disorders, is to help us (those with ADHD) learn how to construct and be guided by those barriers. Without this understanding, knowledge and insight, all therapy is hit-and-miss and lacks real, long-term efficacy.

This text represents a culmination of over forty-five years of our work in this field. Our publications have included multiple texts (Goldstein & Goldstein, 1990, 1998; Goldstein, 1997; Teeter, 1998), chapters (Goldstein, 1999; Goldstein & Ingersoll, 1993) and research articles on ADHD throughout the life span. One can measure the evolution of a clinical condition by the publication of volumes devoted to specific aspects of the condition. We believe the time has come for a text devoted specifically to the treatment of ADHD in adulthood. Though this text is certainly a work in progress and much research continues to be needed, it is our belief that this text offers a reasoned and reasonable review of the literature, a practical set of clinical guidelines and the observations and insight of respected professionals who have devoted their careers to the scientific research and clinical treatment of this condition. It is our hope that this text will offer professionals a balanced view of promising techniques combined with the skilled application of treatment methods conforming to accepted community standards and the responsible interpretation of clinical science. Knowledgeable, compassionate professionals offer their clients and patients a powerful sense of hope by providing accurate information, understanding, support and most importantly, treatment.

Sam Goldstein, Ph.D.
Ann Teeter Ellison, Ed.D.

## REFERENCES

Barkley, R. A. (1991). **Attention deficit hyperactivity disorder: A clinical workbook**. New York: Guilford press.

Carey, W. B. (1988). A suggested solution to the confusion in attention deficit diagnoses. **Clinical Pediatrics, 27**, 348–349.

Goldstein, S. (1997). **Managing Attention Disorders and Learning Disabilities in Late Adolescence and Adulthood**. New York: Wiley.

Goldstein, S. (1999). Attention deficit hyperactivity disorder. In S. Goldstein & C. Reynolds (Eds.), **Handbook of Neurodevelopmental and Genetic Disorders**. New York: Guilford press.

Goldstein, S. & Goldstein, M. (1990). **Educating Inattentive Children**. Salt Lake City, UT: Neurology, Learning and Behavior Center.

Goldstein, S. & Goldstein, M. (1998). **Managing Attention Deficit Hyperactivity Disorder: A Guide for Practitioners (2nd ed.)**. New York: Wiley.

Goldstein, S. & Ingersoll, B. Controversial treatments for children with ADHD and impulse disorders. In L. F. Koziol, C. E. Stout, & D. H. Ruben, (Eds.) (1993). **Handbook of childhood impulse disorders and ADHD; Theory and practice**. Springfield, IL: Charles C. Thomas.

Goodman, L. S. & Gilman, A. (Eds.). (1975). **The pharmacological basis of therapeutics** ($5^{th}$ ed.). New York: Macmillan.

Greenhill, L. L. & Osman, B. B. (2000). **Ritalin: Theory and practice** ($2^{nd}$ ed.). Larchmont, NY: Mary Ann Liebert.

Papazian, O. (1995). The story of fidgety Philip. **International Pediatrics, 10**, 188–190.

Still, G. F. (1902). The Coulstonian lectures on some abnormal physical conditions in children. **Lancet, 1**, 1008–1012.

Teeter, P. A. (1998). **Interventions for ADHD: Treatment in developmental context**. New York: Guilford press.

# 1

# An overview of Childhood and Adolescent ADHD:

## Understanding the Complexities of Development into the Adult Years

Anne Teeter Ellison

To understand and treat attention deficit hyperactivity disorder (ADHD) in adulthood it is important to view the disorder from a developmental perspective (Teeter, 1998). According to longitudinal studies, a majority of adults with ADHD (70–85%) who were diagnosed earlier in life continue to meet the diagnostic criteria of ADHD into adolescence and adulthood (Barkley, Fischer, Edelbrock, & Smallish, 1990; Biederman, Faraone, Milberger, Guite, et al., 1996; Gittelman, Manuzza, Shenker, & Bonagura, 1985; Ingram, Hechtman, & Morgenstern, 1999; Weiss & Hechtman, 1993). Furthermore, outcome data suggest that ADHD in childhood is a risk factor for significant psychiatric, psychosocial, and college or work adjustment difficulties later in life (Barkley, 1998a; Satterfield & Schell, 1997; Weiss & Hechtman, 1993). Lower educational achievement, felony arrest, substance abuse, early and frequent sexual experimentation, social isolation, and serious driving accidents were found at a higher rate in individuals with ADHD than in a control group (Barkley, Murphy, & Kwasnik, 1996).

In an effort to establish a developmental link for ADHD from childhood into adulthood, this chapter presents an overview of ADHD in childhood and adolescence. First, a transactional model for understanding how biogenetic, neuropsychological, cognitive, and psychosocial factors interact and affect the overall adjustment of individuals with ADHD is advanced. The impact of environmental and cultural factors is also explored. Second, a developmental framework for ADHD is presented in which characteristics and associated features that appear early and persist into adulthood are summarized. Third, risk and resiliency factors are explored in an effort to identify variables that either enhance or impede the adjustment of individuals with ADHD. Finally, issues that impact treatment are discussed.

## TRANSACTIONAL MODEL OF ADHD: IMPACT OF BIOGENETIC, NEUROPSYCHOLOGICAL, COGNITIVE, AND PSYCHOSOCIAL DEFICITS

Tannock (1998) asserts that "ADHD is a paradigm for a true biopsychosocial disorder, raising critical questions concerning the relations between genetic, biological, and environmental factors" (p. 65). Various transactional models of ADHD have explored the interaction of biogenetic vulnerabilities, executive control deficits, and the psychosocial and behavioral manifestations of the disorder (see Teeter and Semrud-Clikeman, 1995, 1997; Teeter, 1998; Barkley, 1997). See Figure 1.1 for a depiction of these interrelated factors.

### Biogentic Findings

Family transmission of ADHD has been supported by a number of studies (Faraone & Biederman, 1994). The rate of ADHD in children of parents with ADHD is higher than for the rate of ADHD in other relatives (Biederman et al., 1995). A parent with ADHD has a 57% chance of having an ADHD child. Adoption studies (Cantwell, 1975), twin studies (Gilger, Pennington, & DeFries, 1992),

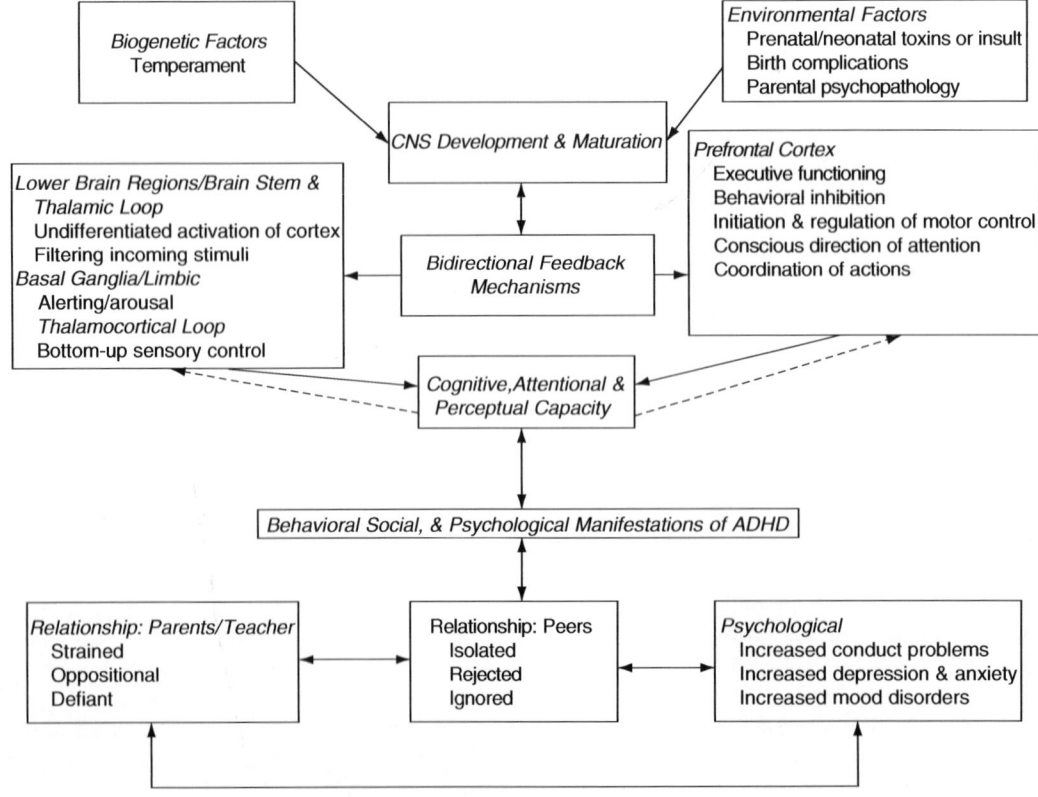

**FIGURE 1.1** Transactional Model for ADHD.

and international adoption studies (van den Oord, Boomsma, & Verhulst, 1994) also have identified strong genetic components of ADHD. Approximately 80% of the inattention-hyperactivity-impulsivity trait is due to genetic factors (Barkley, 1998a). While there is some evidence that extreme scores on this trait increase the genetic contribution, Barkley does indicate that this later point is debatable. Environmental factors account for a much smaller percentage of the variance of the inattention-hyperactivity-impulsivity trait, approximately 6% (Sherman, Iacono, & McGue, 1997; Silberg et al., 1996).

Persistent ADHD—into adulthood—may have a stronger familial etiology than nonpersistent ADHD (Bierderman, Faraone, Keenan, Steingard, Tsuang, 1991)). In their comprehensive genetic study, Faraone et al. (1995) found that boys with ADHD have diverse etiological risk factors, while girls appear to have a stronger familial type with strong heritability factors. Although genetic heritability of ADHD is high, these findings are complicated by the high degree of comorbid conduct, mood, and anxiety disorders found in individuals with ADHD (Biederman, Faraone, Keenan, Steingard et al., 1991).

## ADHD: Advances in the Neurobiological Sciences

Neuroscientists have taken an interest in understanding the neurobiological basis of ADHD. In his overview of lesion and neuroimaging studies, Barkley (1997) indicated that the following regions are involved in executive functions: orbital prefrontal regions for behavioral inhibition; dorsolateral prefrontal regions for working memory; and the right prefrontal regions for inhibition, particularly in the face of distractions. These structures and their functions are critical for understanding the neuroanatomical basis of ADHD.

In a review and analysis of neuroimaging (magnetic resonance imaging, MRI) research, Castellanos (2000) reports that a distributed circuit underlies some of the symptoms of ADHD: "At least in boys, this circuit appears to include right prefrontal brain regions, the caudate nucleus, globus pallidus, and subregion of the cerebellar vermis" (p. 5). Studies have routinely found reduced brain volume, suggesting hypofunctioning, particularly in the cortico-striatal-thalamo-cortical (CSTC) circuits. The CSTC circuit has both excitatory and inhibitory functions, where specific responses are selected and other behaviors are simultaneously inhibited. Pathways in the CSTC circuit are implicated in ADHD. "The fundamental hypothesis motivating neuroimaging investigations of ADHD has been that this neuronal brake does not function optimally, and that such functional deficits should be reflected in relevant anatomic abnormalities" (p. 3). It is important to keep in mind that neuroimaging technology is still evolving, and much of the research has been conducted with small sample sizes and varying methodologies (Castellanos, 2000). It is likely that these circuits have other complex cognitive and motoric functions rather than inhibition. However, there is provisional support from MRI studies that circuits involved with the executive function are linked to ADHD.

Based on adult lesion studies, cognitive neuroscientists postulate three attentional networks. The *orienting/shifting network*, involved with selective attention, is localized in the superior parietal lobules, the thalamus, and the midbrain regions. The *executive network*, involving the anterior cingulate and basal ganglia regions; and the *alerting/arousal network*, involved with vigilance, which is localized in the right frontal lobe, particularly in the superior portion of Brodmann area 6 (Posner & Petersen, 1990; Posner & Raichle, 1994). In her review of neuroimaging studies, Filipek (1996) suggests that there is initial research evidence to support these hypotheses in children. First, young adults (age 24 years) with ADHD did show mild to moderate cerebral atrophy in early studies (Nasrallah et al., 1986). However, young adults in the study had ADHD with comorbid alcohol abuse and received trials of methylphenidate during childhood that could not be ruled out as explanatory factors for the cerebral atrophy. Barkley (1998a) cautions that alcoholism, rather than the ADHD' alone, is likely to account for gross structural atrophy.

Magnetic resonance imaging studies of children with ADHD have revealed narrower right frontal measurements (Hynd, Semrud-Clikeman, et al., 1990), and reversal of the normal left-greater-than-right asymmetry of the caudate region (Hynd, Hem, et al., 1993). A significantly smaller left caudate area accounted for the reversed asymmetry. While Castellanos et al. (1994) did not find caudate asymmetry in their sample of ADHD males who were between the ages of 6 and 19 years, other studies are consistent with the original Hynd et al. asymmetry findings. Filipek et al. (1997) did find smaller left caudate regions in adolescents with ADHD that also resulted in reversed asymmetry of this region compared to normal patterns (left greater than right). To date, inconsistencies focus primarily on which hemisphere is smaller, because there is general agreement across studies that the caudate is smaller (Barkley, 1998a). Filipek et al. (1997) suggest that these inconsistencies most likely relate to methodological differences in the studies, particularly in how the boundaries of the caudate are measured and in the samples that are under study. Barkley (1998a) concludes: "more consistent across these studies are the findings of smaller right prefrontal cortical regions and smaller caudate volume, whether it be more on the right than left side" (p. 168).

Filipek (1996) summarized studies investigating differences in the corpus callosum. In general, these studies reported inconsistent findings in terms of the volume of this region. Early studies reported smaller areas of the genu, splenium, and regions anterior to the splenium (Hynd et al., 1991) and smaller volume in the splenium (Semrud-Clikeman et al., 1994). Others studies found normal volume in the splenium but smaller regions of the corpus callosum, particularly the rostrum and the rostral bodies (Giedd et al., 1994) that connect the premotor and the supplemental motor regions. These smaller cortical areas were correlated to high hyperactivity/impulsivity scores on the Conner's rating scales (see Filipek, 1996, for a review). Again, differences across studies are most likely a result of the different methodologies employed (Filipek, 1996).

## Other Findings of Brain Anomalies in ADHD

In a review of research over the past 25 years, Tannock (1998) reported the following findings. (1) Differences between ADHD and normal controls were found in quantitative encephalograph (qEEG) studies, and while there is little consensus on the precise nature of these abnormalities, studies did show increased slow-wave activity in the frontal lobe and excess beta activity. (2) Event-related potential (ERP) studies revealed altered EEG wave patterns (specifically reduced P3b amplitude), which are related to difficulties in selecting and organizing responses. (3) Greater uptake asymmetry in the left frontal and parietal regions based on SPECT (measures brain glucose metabolism). Further, there may be significant gender differences, where females with ADHD show greater brain metabolic abnormalities as compared to males. Diminished metabolic activity has been found in cerebral glucose metabolism studies using positron emission tomography (PET). Reduced metabolic activity in the left anterior frontal regions was related to the severity of ADHD symptoms in adolescents (Zametkin et al., 1993). Zametkin et al. (1990) also found that adults with ADHD had lowered metabolic activity in the premotor and prefrontal regions of the left hemisphere that are involved with dopaminergic activity. Barkley (1998a) concludes: "This demonstration of an association between the metabolic activity of certain brain regions and symptoms of ADHD is critical to proving a connection between the findings pertaining to brain activation and the behavior comprising ADHD" (p. 166).

## Brain Imaging for the Diagnosis of ADHD

While brain-imaging scans have been useful for investigating the neuroanatomical basis of ADHD, we are not at the point where this technology can be used to diagnose the disorder in individuals. While neuroimaging research has been used for investigating group differences, individuals within groups may vary, so MRI scans are not diagnostic. However, there are reasons to obtain MRI scans for children with ADHD, especially when one of the following is present: significant neurological abnormalities, comorbid psychotic features, atypical symptoms that do not respond to conventional treatment, or one identical twin with ADHD and the other ADHD free (Giedd, 2000).

## Executive Functioning Deficits: Disinhibition

Current research has investigated the disruption of inhibitory mechanisms via frontostriatal circuits for children with different psychiatric and neurodevelopmental disorders. While a disinhibitory model requires further validation, there is sufficient research that supports its basic tenets. Casey (in press) hypothesizes that

> the basal ganglia are involved in suppression of actions while the frontal cortex is involved in representing and maintaining information and conditions to which we respond or act. Developmentally we propose that the ability to support information in prefrontal cortex against information from competing sources increases with age, thereby facilitating inhibitory control. Relevant projections from the prefrontal lobe to the basal ganglia are enhanced while irrelevant projections are eliminated (p. 22).

Deficits in organizing motor behavior, in preparing for motor responses, and in the timing of response execution have been found in children with ADHD (Schachar, Tannock, Marriott, & Logan, 1995). In fact, a number of studies have shown that externalizing behavior disorders appear also to have these deficits, specifically the inability to inhibit, plan, time, execute, modulate, or interrupt motor responses (Mezzacappa, Kindlon, & Earls, 1999). In a study of boys ages 7 to 14 years who were unmanageable in mainstream classroom settings, Mezzacappa et al. (1999) investigated laboratory measures of cognitive and motivational elements of impulse control. Children who were rated higher on externalizing behavior problems also performed more poorly on measures of impulse control. There was an age effect for some children; that is, some behaviors were resolved in adolescence. However, stable deficits were observed in children with externalizing behavior problems on measures of motivational control—the ability to extinguish a previously conditioned response.

In summary, there is sufficient evidence to suggest that ADHD is related to abnormal functioning of cortico-striatal-thalamo-cortical circuits, and prefrontal-striatal regions. ADHD is highly heritable and tends to be genetically transmitted, particularly in cases that persist from childhood to adolescence. Girls tend to have a stronger familial type than boys do. Tannock (1998) suggests that "the most parsimonious interpretation of the findings is that fronto-striatal networks may be involved in ADHD. Abnormalities can occur as a result of alterations in normal developmental processes (e.g., neuronal genesis, migration, synaptic pruning) that may be mediated by genetic, hormonal, or environmental effects or a combination of these" (pp. 83–84). Furthermore, Biederman, Faraone, Keenan, and Tsuang (1991) conclude that strong genetic predispositions interact with psychosocial factors that influence the impact of ADHD. Although it is unlikely that optimal environments make ADHD disappear, it is possible that a "good fit" between the individual and the environment might mediate some of the negative impact of the disorder.

## INTERACTION OF NEURBIOLOGICAL AND ENVIRONMENTAL FACTORS

It is important to note that even though there is strong evidence for a neurobiological basis for ADHD, there are important environmental factors that influence the way in which ADHD is expressed in individuals. Tannock (1998) cautions that

> compromises within an individual's neural substrate are important and necessary but insufficient to understand fully either the current or future level of functioning of an individual. The emergence and manifestation of ADHD and its component symptoms are likely to arise from multiple interacting factors that cannot be understood in isolation. Since most forms of child psychopathology are likely to be attributable to multiple etiologies and their interactions, the incorporation of a developmental-systems perspective will be an important strategy for future research (p. 68).

Environmental theories of ADHD (i.e., poor parenting, cultural tempo, etc.) have little empirical support (Barkley, 1998b). However, Barkley (1998b) suggests that "despite the large role heredity seems to play in ADHD symptoms, they remain malleable to unique environmental influences and nonshared social learning" (p. 64). Environmental factors appear to play a role in the persistence of the disorder, the development of comorbid disorders, and the outcome of individuals with ADHD (Biederman, Faraone, Milberger, Curtis et al., 1996).

Thus, researchers and clinicians should investigate specific environmental factors that interact with biogenetic vulnerabilities in such a way that adjustment is compromised.

## COGNITIVE AND ACADEMIC FINDINGS

### Cognitive-Intellectual Functioning

Longitudinal studies of ADHD in children show that cognitive difficulties and learning disabilities (LD) continue to exist over time (Barkley, 1998a). Decreased intelligence scores (7–15 points) frequently appear in studies, particularly with compromised verbal intelligence, including working memory, digit span, and arithmetic deficits (Faraone et al., 1993; Fischer et al., 1990; Hinshaw, 1992). Even though measures of intelligence may be lower, Stein, Szumowski, Blondis, and Roizen (1995) suggest that ADHD may have a more significant impact on how the child applies his or her intelligence—that is, ADHD may have a more significant impact on adaptive functioning.

Although comorbid LD may account for variations in intellectual abilities for some children with ADHD, Barkley, DuPaul, and McMurray (1990) actually found that children with pure ADHD had lower abilities than children with ADHD plus LD. Hyperactive-impulsive behaviors do affect performance on IQ tests, particularly behavioral disinhibition and executive control deficits. Although it is small, 3–10% of variance in intelligence scores can be accounted for by symptoms of ADHD, especially hyperactivity-impulsivity (Barkley, 1998a). Intelligence may also play a significant protective factor for individuals with ADHD. See later discussion addressing resiliency in adulthood.

### Academic/Work Adjustment

In an investigation of the school and occupational functioning of young adults (18+ years) with ADHD, Hansen, Weiss, and Last (1999) found that they were less likely to graduate from high school than a nonpsychiatric control group. Young adults with ADHD were more likely to have obtained a GED. In a longitudinal study of young children (6–12 years of age) with hyperactivity, Weiss and Hechtman (1993) followed children at age 13 years (5-year follow-up) and at age 19 (10-year follow-up). At follow-up, hyperactive individuals had completed less education, failed more grades, and obtained poor grades in school.

Teens with ADHD frequently do poorly in school and typically do not perform as expected given their intellectual and achievement levels (Barkley, 1998b). Children with ADHD tend to do very poorly (10–30 standard score points) on standardized achievement tests across all academic areas (Fischer et al., 1990; Semrud-Clikeman et al., 1992). In their longitudinal report of children with ADHD, Barkley et al. (1990) and Fischer et al. (1990) found that as many as 46% were suspended from school; 10% dropped out of school; 32.5% were in special education for learning disabilities, 35.8% for emotional disturbance, and 16.3% for speech language disorders. The disturbing aspect of this study was that on average this group had received extensive treatment: 3 years of medication, 16 months of individual therapy, and 7 months of family therapy in addition to 40–65 months of special education (Barkley et al., 1990).

## Psychosocial and Behavioral Findings

According to Erhardt and Hinshaw (1994), children with ADHD have interpersonal problems that are among the most obvious and debilitating, particularly when aggression is present. Social problems range from rejection to isolation and loneliness. Measures of social adjustment also show that young adults with ADHD are more likely to have fathered children than are their non-ADHD counterparts (Hansen et al., 1999): "Perhaps ADHD boys tend to be more sexually promiscuous and/or less likely to use birth control. This finding may indicate that impulsive behavior, one of the hallmarks of ADHD, may continue into late adolescence or early adulthood. These young men may fail to consider the possible ramifications of their actions" (p. 169). The majority of young adults with ADHD in this study also had high rates of psychological problems. They were more likely to seek professional mental health services for these problems than a control group without ADHD. Hansen et al. did acknowledge that the majority of young adults in their study had comorbid disorders (ODD or CD) which may have contributed to their promiscuity or their inability to fully consider the negative consequences of their behaviors. Hansen et al. concluded that in spite of difficulties, they are optimistic about the psychosocial outcome for young adults with ADHD, especially for individuals who receive continued treatment.

In the Milwaukee longitudinal study, hyperactive young adults began having sexual intercourse at an earlier age than a comparison group (age 15 versus 16), had more sexual partners (19 versus 7), and were more likely to have conceived a pregnancy (38% versus 4%; Barkley, 1998a). They were less likely to use contraceptives and more likely to contract a sexually transmitted disease (17% versus 4%) and were more likely to be tested for HIV/AIDS. The Milwaukee study also reported high rates of driving-related difficulties, including license suspensions/revocations (42% versus 28%), accidents where the car was totaled (49% versus 16%), and hit-and-run accidents (14% versus 2%). Driving examiners also rated young adults with hyperactivity to be more distractible and impulsive behind the wheel, which was supported by self- and parent reports of driving skills (Barkley, 1998a).

High rates of other antisocial activities were reported in the Milwaukee study, including: theft, breaking and entering, disorderly conduct, carrying a weapon, assault with a weapon, assault with fists, setting fires, and running away from home (Barkley, 1998a). Other studies have also reported high rates of arrest and incarceration in young adults with hyperactivity (Mannuzza, Gittelman, Konig, & Giampino, 1989; Satterfield, Satterfield, & Cantwell, 1981). In their longitudinal study of Canadian adults, Weiss and Hechtman (1993) did not report these troubling figures. While the majority of adults with hyperactivity do not engage in criminal behaviors, approximately 25% show a persistent pattern of conduct problems that may be related to the presence of comorbid antisocial personality disorder (Barkley, 1998a; Klein & Mannuzza, 1991).

## Behavioral Functioning: Self-Regulation

Self-regulation appears to increase between the ages of 6 and 8 years, and ratings of these behaviors predict impulsivity into adolescence (Olson, Schilling, & Bates, 1999). Laboratory measures of impulsivity were related to teacher and parent ratings of externalizing behavior problems. Girls who were impulsive on laboratory tasks also received high ratings on hyperactivity and delinquency in adolescence (ages 14–17). Children who were able to select delayed rewards at age 8 years had lower rates of hyperactivity in adolescence. While gender differences were not present at age 6 years, by age 8, boys showed more impulsivity. Olson et al. (1999) found that children differ on measures of impulsivity, and these individual differences appear as "traitlike" dimensions of cognitive and behavioral functioning. Longitudinal research on childhood impulsivity is sparse, and these findings are considered exploratory. However, measures of impulsivity and inhibitory control reached significant levels of stability between ages 6 and 8. A significant level of stability was also shown for children's preference for immediate versus delayed reward.

## Cultural Context of ADHD

Prevalence rates of ADHD vary across the world, depending on the classification system employed—the DSM system or the ICD-9, International Classification of Diseases—and the geographical location of the population under study. Barkley (1998a) summarized a series of international studies and reported the following. (1) Anywhere from 2% up to 13.3% (in upstate New York) of children (7–11 years of age) in the United States may be considered. (2) ADHD rates in India are generally higher than those reported in the U.S., where 5.2–29% of children (3–12 years of age) have been diagnosed with ADHD using DSM-III criteria. (3) DSM-III criteria were used in a study in Puerto Rico, resulting in rates of up to 9.5% of children 4–17 years of age. (4) A study of children in New Zealand reported rates of 2–6.7% using DSM- III-R criteria. (5) In a study employing DSM-III and DSM-III-R criteria, 6.1–8.9% of school-age children were identified in China. (6) ICD-9 criteria resulted in rates of 4.2%, 10.9% for DSM-III-R criteria, and 17.8% using DSM-IV for children in Germany. (7) While rates in Canada ranged from 9% of boys and 3.3% of girls, it is difficult to compare these statistics because DSM symptoms were not applied. (8) The Netherlands reported the lowest rates; only 1.3–1.8% of older children (13–18 years) were classified as ADHD. Finally, children (6–17 years of age) of military families have high rates of ADHD, with 11.9–12.2% affected (Jensen et al., 1995). See Barkley (1998a) for a complete review.

Prevalence rates vary depending upon the diagnostic criteria and the inclusion of Predominantly Inattentive Type (ADHD-PI) with Predominantly Hyperactive-Impulsive Type (ADHD-PHI), and Combined Type (ADHD-C; DSM-IV; American Psychiatric Association, 1994). There is great controversy concerning whether the Predominantly Inattentive Type of ADHD, where poorly focused attention and slow information processing is typical, is actually a subtype of ADHD (Barkley, 1998b). Barkley argues that there may be important differences among these subtypes of ADHD and that there may be a different developmental trajectory as well. In cases of the ADHD-PHI or ADHD-C types, hyperactivity may decline with age, and these individuals may no longer meet criteria for diagnosis in the combined or hyperactive-impulsive type. Barkley cautions that we should be careful diagnosing older individuals (where hyperactivity diminishes with age but other ADHD symptoms persist) as ADHD-PI, because they do differ from those who have an early diagnosis of inattentive type. Difficulties with disinhibition underlie the ADHD-PHI and the ADHD-C types but not the ADHD-PI type.

In the United States, controversy over the assessment of ADHD in culturally diverse populations exists. Caution is recommended due to the lack of adequate norms on common rating scales that are frequently used. Reid (1995) investigated the representation of minority children on various measures available for assessing ADHD, and found that only two measures are adequate—the Children's Attention and Adjustment Scale and the Attention Deficit Disorders Evaluation Scale (ADDES). Reid suggests using multimethod approaches, particularly functional approaches, to better assess children from diverse backgrounds. These practices involve behavioral assessment of the problem, intervention planning and implementation, progress monitoring, and intervention revision. "If a child continues to evidence problems related to ADHD—such as difficulties in attention deployment or impulse control—then a diagnosis of ADHD may be indicated" (p. 556).

In a statewide review of children receiving stimulant medication in the Maryland Public Schools, Safer and Malever (2000) data on "nonwhite student groups (black, Hispanic, Asian, and native American) reveal that all have a comparatively lower treatment prevalence for ADHD medication than white students" (p. 537). Based on a review of the literature, Safer and Malever found that black youth do exhibit ADHD features on rating scales at rates similar to white children. Further, cultural factors may explain some of the variation in treatment rates, particularly the low level of stimulant treatment for black high school students. Data from this sample also showed that medication treatment for ADHD was higher in males than in females.

## Gender Differences in Our Understanding of ADHD

In general, boys are more likely to have ADHD than girls, according to DSM-IV (American Psychiatric Association, 1994). The ratio of males to females with ADHD vary depending on the study, where anywhere from 2:1 to 10:1 ratios have been reported, including about 6:1 in clinic-referred samples (Barkley, 1998a). There may be a lot of reasons for these differences, some of which may result from referral biases whereby males are more likely to have aggression and antisocial disorders that prompt referrals than are girls.

In a meta-analysis of gender differences in ADHD, Gaub and Carlson (1997) concluded that there were no gender differences on levels of impulsivity, academic difficulties, social interaction problems, and fine motor functions. Family members did not differ on measures of psychopathology, and parent educational levels did not differ. Intellectual deficits tended to be higher in girls, while hyperactivity levels were lower, and there were fewer signs of aggression, conduct problems, and defiance (externalizing disorders). These differences were dependent on the study samples—clinic versus community. Boys and girls tended to be more similar in clinical samples. In community-based samples, girls with ADHD were less aggressive and had fewer internalizing disorders than males.

In the largest study of girls to date, researchers found that girls showed similar rates of depression (17%), anxiety (32%), and bipolar (10%) disorders that were comparable to earlier studies with boys (Biederman, et. al., 1999). Girls had lower rates of conduct disorders (10%) and oppositional defiant disorders (33%) and had slightly lower intellectual, reading, and math scores (still within normal range) compared to boys. Treatment/interventions needs were also similar for girls and boys with ADHD, including the need for tutoring, special education, counseling, and medication. It will be interesting to determine whether the figures derived in the Safer and Malever (2000) survey of children in Maryland hold up in other states. That is, do girls also receive less medication treatment for ADHD across the country?

## THE DEVELOPMENTAL CONTEXT: CHARACTERISTICS AND ASSOCIATED FEATURES OF ADHD

Let me start out by saying that criteria from present diagnostic systems (i.e., the Diagnostic Statistical Manual–IV) are not adequate for adults (Ingram et al., 1999). (See Chapter 4 for an in-depth discussion of assessment and diagnostic issues for adults with ADHD.) The clinical picture of ADHD varies over time, with some symptoms becoming more or less important depending on the developmental age of the person (Ingram et al., 1999; Teeter, 1998). Table 1.1 summarizes major similarities and differences among adolescents and adults with ADHD and shows how characteristics of ADHD vary across the life span. Also see Goldstein and Goldstein (1998) for a review.

## ADHD Characteristics in Early and Middle Childhood

Early signs of inattention, hyperactivity, and impulsivity in children contribute to difficulties with self-esteem, learning problems, academic difficulties, and underachievement (Barkley, Fisher, Edelbrock, & Smallish, 1990). Psychosocial difficulties often result in peer rejection because of awkward or inappropriate social interactions (Milich & landau, 1989; Milich, Landau, Kilby, & Whitten, 1982). Language difficulties may further contribute to problems in communication, while impulsive, negative, and aggressive behaviors interfere with social interactions. Isolation from peers may further reduce the opportunity to develop effective interaction and coping skills that promote social effectiveness (e.g., frustration tolerance, anger control, negotiation, and compromise).

The academic and learning difficulties that are common for children with ADHD at this age appear related to difficulties with work completion and accuracy rates (Barkley, 1998a) and to poor persistence and motivation on difficult tasks (Milich, 1994). Organizational deficits are frequent (Zentall, Harper & Stormont-Spurgin, 1993), and deficits in self-control result in impulsive, careless mistakes (Teeter, 1998). Off-task, out-of-seat, and noncompliant behaviors also contribute to school adjustment difficulties (Weiss & Hechtman, 1993). An inability to maintain behavioral responses (i.e., poor persistence and vigilance) interferes with classroom behaviors, especially when tasks are repetitive or boring. These difficulties come at a developmental stage when there are more demands on the child and classroom expectations call for sustained attention, effort, and goal directedness. Unfortunately, these demands tap into the very areas that are most difficult for children with ADHD; thus the impact of the disorder can be quite devastating.

Many children with ADHD are exquisitely attuned to the fact that they are not performing up to their peer group, that they are not meeting the expectations of important adults in their lives, and that they are not well liked by their peers. This cycle creates self-doubt and a lack of confidence in one's abilities, which may result in depression. Children at this age may disengage from the learning environment to avoid being humiliated by failure or the negative comments that come from teachers and peers when they "screw up." This withdrawal further exacerbates the learning difficulties that are present, and children at this age may fall hopelessly behind in their academic skills. Because later learning draws on foundational skills, these difficulties may become even more prominent during adolescence. This cycle creates a high risk for school dropout, school failure, and academic underachievement that are common in adolescents with ADHD (Barkely, Fisher, Edelbrock, & Smallish, 1990).

## ADHD and Comorbidity

Children with ADHD are at risk for comobid disorders, including oppositional defiance disorder

(ODD) and conduct disorder (CD) (Barkley, 1998a; Faraone, Biederman, Jettson, & Tsuang, 1997; Eiraldi, Power, & Maguth Nezu, 1997), depression, anxiety, and bipolar disorders (Biederman, Faraone, Mick, Moore, & Lelon, 1996; Perrin & Last, 1996), and reading disabilities (Semrud Clikeman et al., 1992). Furthermore, the severity of ADHD symptoms may predict comorbity (Barkley, 1998a).

## ADHD Subtypes: Comorbidity and Associated Executive Function (EF) Deficits

There is growing evidence that the subtypes of ADHD may have different risk factors associated with the disorder: (1) ADHD predominantly inattentive type (ADHD/PI); (2) ADHD predominantly hyperactive-impulsive type (ADHD/HI), and (3) ADHD combined type (ADHD/C). While hyperactive and inattentive types cannot be distinguished by cognitive deficits alone (Lahey & Carlson, 1992), Barkley (1998a) reports that children with ADHD/C perform more poorly on the Continuous Performance Test and the Wisconsin Selective Reminding Test. Children with ADHD/PI also showed poorer perfomance on the Weschler Coding subtest.

ADHD children who show signs of physical aggression (Sequin, Pihl, Tremblay, Boulerice, & Harden, 1995) and conduct disorders (Giancola, Mezzich, & Tarter, 1998) also appear to have separate risk factors, particularly related to greater executive deficiencies. ADHD children with reading disabilities (RD) also appear at risk for cognitive deficits, including phonological, lexical decoding, rapid naming, and conceptual-reasoning deficits (August & Garfinkel, 1990; Shaywitz et al., 1995). Klorman et al. (1999) also found that children (7½ to 13½ years of age) with ADHD with hyperactivity-impulsivity had deficient EF deficits on tasks requiring planning, working memory, and spatial skills. Paired-associative learning was impaired for a sample of children with ADHD/PI and ADHD/C, according to Chang et al. (in press). Children with ADHD/C had more nonperseverative errors than ADHD/PI, which may reflect attentional problems and acquisition errors (Klorman et al., 1999). Performance on the Wisconsin Card Sort Test did not discriminate groups, while scores on the Tower of Hanoi (TOH) were differentially sensitive, including rule violations. The EF deficits found in the sample of children with ADHD/C were not related to intellectual abilities. But EF deficits were found in the ADHD/C and the ADHD/PI plus RD groups.

## ADHD Characteristics in Adolescence

Unfortunately, research on ADHD in adolescence is sparse. However, even though we have only a handful of studies that address this issue, several are methodologically strong and offer us an excellent picture of the disorder during this stage. Early studies of ADHD explored the extent to which children simply outgrew the disorder over time (Ingram et al., 1999). Weiss and Hechtman (1993) initially found that 25% of children with ADHD could not be differentiated from normal controls in adolescence and that 30% of adults were not significantly different from a control group. Studies suggest anywhere from 43% to 80% of children continue to show ADHD into adolescence (Barkley, Fisher, Edelbrock, & Smallish, 1990; Biederman, Faraone, Milberger, Guite, et al., 1996; Biederman, Faraone, Taylor, et al., 1998; Cantwell & Baker, 1989; Fischer, Barkely, Fletcher, & Smallish, 1993; Weiss & Hechtman, 1993). What is most disturbing about this picture is the growing evidence of the widespread effects of ADHD on all aspects of life—academic, psychosocial, behavioral, and emotional for a majority of individuals. Again, Table 1.1 summarizes major differences among adolescents and adults and shows how characteristics and features of ADHD vary across the life span.

TABLE 1.1  Signs and Symptoms to Look For in Adolescents and Adults with ADHD

| Signs and symptoms | Correlates at developmental stages ||
| --- | --- | --- |
| | Childhood/adolescence | Adulthood |
| Attentional difficulties | Short attention span, not sticking to things; unmotivated, difficulty following instructions in school; can't listen for long, can't remember, everything half finished in home & school; does best with adult supervision; attention most impaired for boring tasks; attention is good for novel & interesting tasks; attention not under "social control"; off-task, restless, vocal behavior during academic tasks | Particularly problematic for college students; other adults may not complain about attention problems—self-select jobs with low demand for constant attention, difficulty keeping mind on reading; concentrates when necessary for 5–10 minutes; rarely sits through a TV show; trouble listening to conversations; interrupts in social interactions; may learn to minimize distractions; misplaces little things (e.g., keys, wallets) |
| Motor problems | Fidgety; drums fingers; kicks feet; restless; overtalkative—"motor mouth"; impaired coordination; poor handwriting; poor eye–hand coordination in sports; soft neurological signs (e.g., clumsy); prolonged reaction times; needs to talk more, move more, & interact with stimulating environment | Many remain hyperactive, fidgety, & restless; uncomfortable sitting still; dislike being inactive; can't relax; rather stand than sit; forced immobility produces anxiety; fidgety and foot movements; "cross-knee" foot jiggle or foot tap; still poor in sports & handwriting |
| Impulsivity | Difficulty delaying gratification; low frustration threshold; impatient; blurts things out in class or interrupts; reckless, with little concern for consequences; acts before thinks; frequent driving accidents; high risk-taking behaviors; teens less likely to use birth control | Greater opportunity to inflict serious self-damage; acts on spur of moment; makes decisions without thinking; little reflection (e.g., quits job, marries or divorces hastily) |
| Emotionality, temper, & mood | Labile moods—dysphoric to overexcited; disruptive disorders when history of early aggression, antisocial problems; unpleasurable stimuli provoke temper; short fuse; may have history of fighting (more typical of conduct disorder); difficulty experiencing pleasure; doesn't seem happy; may be demoralized because of failure, negative feedback from adults, constantly disappointing adults; may have biological factors linked to self-esteem & mood; may engage in sensation-seeking behaviors as teen (e.g., drinking & driving, drug use); ADHD risk for depression & anxiety | Similar lability seen in children; mood shifts, "ups" & "downs" common throughout day; spontaneous roller coaster "ups" are reduced in adults, but "downs" persist; "downs" described as boredom or discontentment; not like major depressive disorder; constantly getting into demoralizing situations because of academic, work, or interpersonal problems; explosive tempers may calm down quickly; always seems irritable; destructive in relationships; anger seems provoked by stimulus. |
| Stress intolerance | Difficulty staying with things under pressure; less tolerant of low-arousal tasks; may be an optimal arousal level | Reports being overactive to normal stress or pressure; inappropriate response to ordinary demands; can't handle things out of the ordinary; describes self as "stressed out," "discombobulated," or "hassled"; anxiety with stress creates problems, and becomes more impulsive, disorganized and less competent |

*Note*: See Goldstein & Goldstein (1998) and Teeter (1998).

In their longitudinal report of symptoms into adolescence, Weiss, Minde, Werry, Douglas, and Nemeth (1971) found that adolescents demonstrated more academic difficulties, significant antisocial problems, and poor self-esteem with continued impulsivity, emotional immaturity, distractibility, and lower hyperactivity. Furthermore, 70% still have ADHD, with significant academic, social, and emotional difficulties (Hechtman, 1999). "Children who also have aggression and/or conduct disorder generally have more negative outcome, and stimulant treatment does not appear to significantly affect this outcome" (Hechtman, 1999, p. 17).

Teens with ADHD have numerous challenging difficulties. To summarize the most prominent aspects of ADHD in adolescence: First, the presence of comorbid disorders becomes a paramount feature and complication for the majority of teens with ADHD. Although young children with ADHD do show high rates of comorbidity (especially LD and ODD), teens with ADHD appear to be highly susceptible to serious psychiatric and emotional disorders as well (Barkley, 1998a; Barkley, Fischer, Edelbrock, & Smallish, 1990). For example, 59% were also diagnosed with ODD and 43% had CD according to Barkley et al. (1990). There appear to be important factors related to the co-occurrence of ADHD with other disorders that need to be addressed in treatment. In a longitudinal study, Faraone et al. (1997) found the following. (1) Relatives of ADHD groups were more likely to have ADHD and ODD than were normal probands. (2) Rates of CD and antisocial personality disorder (ASPD) were related to ADHD + CD probands only. (3) ADHD with ASPD was accounted for by marriages between ADHD and antisocial spouses. (4) ADHD and antisocial disorders occurred in the same relative more often than expected by chance alone. Although Faraone et al. (1997) conclude that ADHD + CD is a familially distinct subtype, they cannot determine whether the familial etiology is genetic or environmental. In general, there was a low probability of ADHD with CD and/or ASPD in relatives for those individual with ADHD and no CD.

Faraone et al. (1997) found that relatives of the ADHD + ODD group had about the same risk for disorders as did the ADHD-only group. The ADHD + ODD group was not that similar to the ADHD + CD group. Furthermore, children with ADHD + ODD who did not develop CD by adolescence were nosologically distinct from those individuals who did develop CD. That is, the ADHD + CD group had earlier onset of ODD and had an increased risk for mood and anxiety disorders, more comorbid psychiatric disorders, and more initial ODD symptoms (Biederman, Faraone, Milberger, Garcia Jetton, et al., 1996). In conclusion, "although a large majority of CD children have prior histories of ODD, many ODD children do not go on to develop CD" (Faraone, Biederman, Jeffson et al., 1997, p. 298).

Second, there may be important differences among children with ADHD who are followed into adolescence versus adolescents who are first referred for ADHD. Comorbid disorders are a challenge at younger ages, but may be even a bigger issue for adolescents. Biederman et al. (1998) hypothesize that teens with ADHD and depression may not receive a diagnosis of ADHD if their symptoms are viewed to be secondary to the depression: "A reluctance to diagnose comorbid conditions could thereby lead to an underdiagnosis of ADHD in adolescence" (p. 306).

In their study of 260 males between the ages of 6 and 17 years, Biederman et al. (1998) found that symptoms and associated features in adolescent ADHD were the same as for ADHD found in younger children. Adolescents with ADHD had higher rates of CD, ODD, mood disorders, and anxiety disorders. Bipolar and substance abuse problems were similar for both the older and the younger groups of ADHD individuals. Family history was significant; that is, adolescents with ADHD had a more remarkable family history of ADHD than did children with ADHD. When ADHD persists into adolescence, there is more likely to be a higher risk factor for familial ADHD. Biederman et al. (1998) caution that it is important for clinicians to pay attention to the age of onset of ADHD when assessing comorbid disorders. "For example, a depressed 5-year-old having subthreshold symptoms of ADHD may be at risk for the full ADHD symptoms in later years. In contrast, because adolescents have passed through the age of risk for ADHD, we will be more confident about negative diagnoses of that disorder" (p. 311). It is critical that clinicians investigate comorbidity in adolescents, due to the risk for suicide in teens with bipolar disorders, conduct disorders, and ADHD (Brent et al., 1988). Finally: "An adolescent with ADHD who presents with acute signs of anxiety, depression, bipolar disorder, or substance abuse will likely receive a diagnosis and treatment for the acute disorder. Although it makes sense to treat the acute condition, that course of action should not deter clinicians from making comorbid diagnosis of ADHD if confirmed by the patient's history and current condition. Once the acute problem has cleared, the ADHD can then be treated as well" (Biederman et al., 1998, p. 312).

Third, ADHD adolescents who also have signs of a social disability (SD) are at a greater risk for mood, anxiety, disruptive, and substance abuse disorders than comparison boys with ADHD and no SD (Greene, Biederman, Faraone, Sienna, & Garcia-Jones, 1997). In this 4-year longitudinal follow-up of boys with ADHD, the presence of SD predicted poor social and psychiatric outcome, particularly substance abuse and CD. Although the etiology of this relationship is not well understood, the construct of social disability needs to be more fully explored. Greene et al. (1997) conclude: "These findings suggest that assessment of social functioning might be useful in identifying subgroups of children with ADHD at very high risk for complicated course and poor prognosis. Such early identification may permit this targeting of scarce societal resources toward those at greatest need to receive services" (p. 764).

## ADHD Characteristics in Adulthood

There is compelling evidence showing that ADHD does not disappear for a majority of adults who have been diagnosed early in life. However, there is evidence that "diagnostic difficulties contribute to a lack of consistency in adult ADHD diagnosis" (Ingram et al., 1999, p. 244).

In their longitudinal study, Weiss and Hechtman (1993) reported high rates of social interaction problems, particularly in male—female relationships. "It should not be surprising then that the greater self-esteem problems of ADHD children noted in adolescence continue and may even worsen as they reach adulthood" (Barkley, 1998a, p. 208). In fact, Hansen, Weiss, and Last (1999) found that young adults with ADHD were more likely to have fathered children, to need mental health services, and to report psychological problems than were control males.

## CUMULATIVE EFFECTS OF LIVING WITH A DEVELOPMENTAL DISORDER: FROM CHILDHOOD TO ADULTHOOD

There is no doubt that a substantial number of children and adolescents continue to show ADHD symptoms into adulthood. How does the presence of chronic symptoms over a lifetime affect adults? There may be a host of factors quite different from those for acute disorders that complicate the treatment of adults with chronic disorders like ADHD. As clinicians and researchers, we need to consider the effects of chronic academic underachievement, loss of social opportunities, and the presence of comorbid disorders that appear to increase with age. These factors complicate the picture of ADHD in adults and suggest the need for multimodal treatment plans to increase the adjustment of adults with ADHD.

Academic underachievement may create a host of adult outcomes that affect the individual's career choices and work enjoyment and satisfaction. Although almost all adults with ADHD are gainfully employed, according to longitudinal studies (Manuzza et al., 1993), they may experience more job stress. Employers do rate adults with ADHD in negative terms on measures of meeting job expectations, getting along with supervisors, working independently, and completing work tasks. Many of these problems appear directly related to their ADHD symptoms, particularly restlessness, impulsivity, and poor concentration. Adults with ADHD have a higher tendency to change jobs and/or to work two jobs to adjust to feelings of restlessness and nervousness that they experience on the job (Borlund & Hechtman, 1976). The good news about the employment picture is that many adults with ADHD own businesses (Manuzza et al., 1993) and are able to select job settings that are more conducive to their unique work styles. However, we don't know enough about the emotional stress that adults with ADHD experience on a daily basis because of problems keeping things organized, staying on top of work demands, keeping emotions in check, and dealing with the pressures of deadlines.

How does social isolation or relationship difficulties early in life affect the development of effective coping skills (i.e., frustration and anger management) that are needed to successfully build meaningful relationships in adulthood? Do individuals with ADHD miss out on important experiences through which one learns the give-and-take of relationships? Do the symptoms of ADHD—emotional reactivity, impulsivity—make social interchanges more emotionally charged and stressful? What is the psychological cost of a history of social isolation in childhood and/or adolescence? These issues should be explored when assessing and treating adults with ADHD.

## ADHD RISK AND RESILIENCY

Some studies suggest that the persistence of ADHD into adulthood is related to comorbidity of other psychiatric disorders, particularly conduct or aggressive disorders (Gittelman et al., 1985; Taylor, Sandberg, Thorley, & Giles, 1991). In an investigation of factors related to early and late remission of ADHD, Biederman, Faraone, Milberger, Curtis et al. (1996) found that only a small percentage of children with ADHD remit in adolescence (15%). About 50% of this group showed remission of symptoms in childhood, and the other half did so in adolescence. Biederman, Faraone, Milberger, Curtis et al. (1996) found that "predictors of persistence were familiality of ADHD, psychosocial adversity, and comorbidity with conduct, mood, and anxiety disorders" (pp. 347–348).

In earlier studies, Faraone and Biederman (1994) found that individuals with familial ADHD may be a subgroup with higher risk factors, including significant reductions in brain metabolic activity (Zametkin et al., 1990) and more neuropsychological impairments (Seidman et al., 1995). It is likely that persistent ADHD triggers a host of family psychosocial adversity as well. Parental psychopathology and first-degree relatives have higher rates of oppositional defiant disorder (ODD), conduct disorder (CD), antisocial personality disorder (ASPD), depression and anxiety disorders (Biederman, Faraone, Mick et al., 1996; Morrison1980). While it is difficult to separate genetic from environmental risk factors in these families, adversity and stress appeared to be significant predictors of persistence (Biederman, Faraone, Milberger, Curtis et al., 1996). These factors most likely interact where biogenetic vulnerabilities combine with family adversity, including conflict, expressiveness, family cohesiveness, low socioeconomic status (SES), large family size parental criminality, maternal mental illness, and severe marital discord, to create poor adult outcome.

Comorbidity of psychiatric disorders is also a significant predictor of persistence of ADHD into adulthood. While evidence of comorbid ODD, CD, and aggression are predictive of poor outcome, Biederman, Faraone, Milberger, Curits et al. (1996) also established a link between persistence and mood disorders (i.e., anxiety and depression). Adults with ADHD also have higher rates of comorbid disorders than do non-ADHD adults (Biederman, Faraone, Mick, et al., 1995). These disorders interact with ADHD to produce a more impaired and persistent form of ADHD. Although children who show early remission of ADHD had lower rates of aggression and CD-related problems, this was not the case for late remission. Early remitters did not differ from late remitters or those with persistent ADHD on presenting symptomology, cognitive and learning deficits, and the need for interventions. However, familial adversity and comorbidity were important factors predicting adult outcome. Children who do not have these risk factors appear to have a more positive outcome.

Lambert, Hartsaugh, Sassone, and Sandoval (1987) found that cognitive and behavioral maturity was a risk factor for later outcome and that the still-hyperactive group in their study (43%) was immature on both dimensions. The residual group (37%) still had persistent learning, behavioral, and emotional problems, but this group was no longer receiving medical treatment for hyperactivity. Although this later group showed signs of behavioral maturity, they did still evidence signs of cognitive immaturity. Both groups required more treatment than the subjects (20%) who showed no problems at follow-up.

Poor adaptive functioning may impact adolescent and adult outcome. Barkley (1998a) states: "Adaptive functioning is frequently used to refer to the child's development of age-appropriate motor skills, self-help abilities (i.e., dressing, bathing, and feeding), personal responsibility and independence (chore performance, trustworthy, use of money, etiquette), and peer relationships" (p. 98). Despite average intelligence, many children with ADHD have low adaptive abilities. Numerous longitudinal and cross-sectional studies report that children with ADHD have poor adaptive abilities compared to age peers (Barkley, Fischer, Edelbrock, Smallish et al., 1990; Greene et al., 1997; Stein, Szumowski, Blondis, & Roizen, 1995). Furthermore, Barkley (1998a) suggests that "the greater this discrepancy between IQ and adaptive functioning, the greater the impairment the ADHD child is likely to experience and the more likely he or she is to experience comorbid disorders" (p. 99). Specifically, Green et al. (1997) found that youth with ADHD with the greatest degree of social or adaptive impairment are more likely to have comorbid disorders at follow-up.

Traumatic events in one's life can also drastically alter the course of ADHD and exert additive risk factors. Weiss (1999) described a case study of a youngster whose ADHD was complicated by a stressful life event:

> Crises in the lives of troubled children are more common than in the lives of healthy children. When they occur they may affect the course of the disorder and its treatment. For example, Willy was an 8-year-old boy treated for ADHD and doing well on a given dose of methylphenidate. One night his father (an adult with ADHD) lost his temper with his son and locked him out of the house. Willy ran away, was picked up by a child molester, and had unfortunate experiences over several days until found by the police. After this episode Willy's course of ADHD worsened, and his normal dose of methylphenidate no longer improved his core symptoms. He also developed an adjustment disorder with anxiety and depression.... [I]t took several years before the child was closer to his previous level of functioning (pp. 3–4).

## Resiliency Factors That Moderate the Impact of ADHD in Adulthood

Which factors help protect or moderate the impact of ADHD? Are there child or adolescent factors that reduce the negative effects of ADHD through the lifespan? Three factors appear to be relevant to these questions: (1) child factors, including the severity of ADHD, the presence of comorbid disorders, and the child's intellectual capabilities; (2) the family environment; and (3) treatment (Ingram et al., 1999).

First, Ingram et al. (1999) suggest that adaptive functioning and coping skills may provide a protective function or may predict poor prognosis or adult outcome. "Individual characteristics such as IQ, comorbidity, oppositionality, aggression,... emotional state, and peer relationships can act singly or in combination to influence the adaptive functioning and outcome" (p. 246). A number of child factors appear to predict outcome, especially antisocial behaviors (Hechtman, 1996), CD and ODD (Satterfield & Schell, 1997), and depression, anxiety, and mood disorders (Biederman, Faraone, Taylor, et al., 1998). Comorbid antisocial behavior disorders are particularly insidious and are associated with higher arrest and substance abuse rates than are found in individuals with ADHD who do not exhibit conduct problems. Biederman and colleagues (1995) found a subgroup of newly referred adults who also exhibited recreational drug and alcohol abuse. Ingram et al. (1999) suggest that this subgroup may be oversampled and may account for some studies that report increased drug and alcohol use in hyperactive youth. Comorbid disorders (e.g., anxiety) need to be considered and addressed when deciding on treatment options, for they do reduce the efficacy of stimulant medication (Pliszka, 1987). Adults who abuse drugs or alcohol also need to address abuse issues separately from treatment for ADHD.

Low IQ is another important factor related to the development of comorbid disorders and treatment outcome in individuals with ADHD. Aman (1996) found that low IQ was related to poor adaptive skills and to impaired functioning over time. There may also be gender differences that are important when considering the effects of cognitive deficits and ADHD; Pearson et al. (1996) found that girls with low IQ (mental retardation, MR) are at greater risk for ADHD than are non-MR groups.

Family factors do affect adult outcome and can serve to buffer the impact of ADHD. In most studies, family risk factors include socioeconomic status (SES), family instability (i.e., divorce and/or separation), parental psychopathy, and alcoholism (Barkley et al., 1990; Biederman et al., 1996; Hechtman et al., 1984; Satterfield & Schell, 1997). Low SES alone does not appear to be the most salient risk factor; it is the accompanying psychological and emotional strain that is placed on families that is more predictive of poor outcome.

There appears to be an interaction between family stability and ADHD, "whereas the families of children exhibiting a more negative outcome deteriorated over time" (Ingram et al., 1999, p. 247). Even though causality cannot be implied, the impact of ADHD on families can be disruptive, while at the same time strong family cohesion and parental support constitute significant resiliency factors for many individuals with ADHD. For case studies see Chapter 5 for examples of how family support can be critical to the overall adjustment of individuals with ADHD.

Finally, treatment issues can also predict adult outcome. To date, there are some significant trends that can be gleaned from studies investigating the effects of treatment on long-term outcome for individuals with ADHD. These are reviewed next.

## Does Early Treatment Affect Adult Outcome?

It is difficult to determine whether treatment per se increases positive outcome for individuals with ADHD. Initial longitudinal studies showed that boys with hyperactivity who received multimodal treatment (e.g., individual and/or group therapy for the child and parent, with stimulant medication) that was designed to meet their individual needs was related to better outcome (Satterfield et al., 1981). On the other hand, in a series of longitudinal reports, Barkley and colleagues (Barkley et al., 1990; Fischer et al., 1990) found that even with the use of extensive educational and mental health treatment, most youth with hyperactivity continue to experience significant academic, behavioral, and social problems in adolescence. In fact, "stimulant medication does not seem to have significantly affected" the educational, psychosocial, and behavioral outcome of ADHD from childhood to adolescence (Hechtman, 1999, p. 24).

Even though social skill deficits appear to be an associated feature of ADHD, social skills training has not proven to be an effective treatment approach to date. "Teaching them additional skills is not so much the issue as is assisting them with the performance of the skills they have when it would be useful to do so at the points of performance where such skills are most likely to enhance the child's long-term social acceptance" (Barkley, 1998b, p. 71).

Although these studies may seem overly pessimistic, there are some encouraging outcomes when looking at individual case studies. In my work with teens and young adults with ADHD, they typically report that they have developed important coping and adaptive skills that helped them become successful either in college or in their jobs. In many instances, these young adults were in therapy or treatment at different times of their lives for different problems. Initially, they and their families sought out and received fairly intensive interventions for academic, behavioral, and/or social problems. Medication in combination with other treatments (e.g., family/parenting, school accommodations, behavioral and psychosocial interventions) did alleviate symptoms of ADHD. However, single treatment approaches did not adequately address all their needs, and therapy at one point in their development did not inoculate them from problems in later stages of life. Early treatment did seem to help them develop coping mechanisms that could be built on for later developmental challenges. Clinicians should prepare adolescents and families for this inevitability—that treatment for ADHD may be a lifelong process. In most instances, the young adults I have worked with have continued to use medication and have continued to learn more about their disorder. They have sought out and received psychological or psychiatric assistance at different times in their life into adulthood and have benefited from appropriate support.

It is possible that we need to think differently about treatment efficacy when it comes to evaluating the effects of interventions on individuals with disorders that create persistent, lifelong problems. We need to adopt a developmental model of treatment where individuals at different stages of life periodically check in with professionals, to develop coping or adaptive skills to get through pressing problems of the moment. In many ways, our therapy/intervention models leave the impression that short-term treatment should provide a buffer through the life span. This perspective is too simplistic and unrealistic for ADHD. We may be setting up unrealistic expectations that treatment in childhood or adolescence will help individuals develop all the adaptive skills needed throughout adulthood. There is little clinical evidence for this, and far too few empirical studies have addressed these issues. We do know that we cannot cure individuals with ADHD, that many of the symptoms are persistent (i.e., impulsivity, inattention, disinhibition), and that when treatments (i.e., medication or other behavioral, psychosocial strategies) are removed, symptoms reappear. What we do know is that the effects of ADHD can be ameliorated when combined treatments are employed, and individuals can develop effective and powerful self-management and adaptive skills.

## A DEVELOPMENTAL PERSPECTIVE: IMPLICATIONS FOR TREATMENT OF ADHD IN ADULTHOOD

First, we need to adopt a developmental perspective when considering ADHD and treatment. There is no evidence that a single treatment approach cures ADHD, nor does early treatment fully mitigate the effects of ADHD over a lifetime. Although symptoms appear to decrease over time in a small number of children with ADHD, they are the exception, not the rule. In fact, the majority of individuals with ADHD in early childhood continue to demonstrate the disorder into adolescence (70–80%) and continue to be symptomatic into adulthood (60%; Ingram et al., 1999). Furthermore, each developmental stage presents its unique challenges and life events that are intensified or complicated by ADHD (Teeter, 1998). Thus, a clinical perspective that considers treatment within a developmental framework is imperative.

Second, clinicians would be wise to look for and foster resiliency factors, including special talents, interests, and experiences, to help mitigate the negative impact of ADHD on adults.

Third, it is unclear whether multimodal treatment (with or without stimulant medication treatment) will prove to be most efficacious for adults. In a two-year multimodal treatment study with children, Abikoff and Hechtman (1996) found medication to be as powerful as combined treatments (e.g., social skills, parenting skills, tutoring, study skills, and medication). The addition of other treatments did not significantly improve outcome, nor were they more powerful than medication alone. However, as Ingram et al. (1999, p. 249) suggest: "The continuation of treatment may be crucial in influencing positive outcome," particularly stimulant medication. Results of the National Institutes of Mental Health (NIMH) multisite study for children (MTA Cooperative Group, 1999) did find that medication and strong behavioral interventions (parent management and a school behavior management system) were effective for treating ADHD for up to 14 months. Children who received medication alone (under the careful supervision of a physician) or a combination of medication with behavioral interventions had reduced symptoms compared to a group receiving behavioral treatments or typical treatments found in the community. It is important to note that in the MTA study, children received careful medication monitoring, which is not typical for community-based interventions. Combined medication and behavioral interventions were very important for reducing other problems that were present in the ADHD group, including anxiety and academic difficulties. We need controlled treatment studies for adolescents and adults to determine which treatments in isolation or combination are most efficacious.

## REFERENCES

Abikoff, H., & Hechtman, L. (1996). Multimodal therapy and stimulants in the treatment of children with attention deficit hyperactivity disorder. In E. D. Hibbs & P. S. Jensen (Eds.). *Psychosocial treatments for child and adolescent disorders: Empirically based strategies for clinical practice*. Washington, DC. American Psychological Association, pp. 341–368.

Aman, M. G. (1996). Stimulant drugs in the developmental disabilities revisited. *Journal of Developmental and Physical Disabilities, 8*, 347–365.

American Psychiatric Association. (1994). *Diagnostic and statistical manual of mental disorders* (4th ed., rev.). Washington, DC: Author.

August, G. J., & Garfinkel, B. D. (1990). Comorbidity of ADHD and reading disability among clinic-referred children. *Journal of Abnormal Psychology, 18*, 29–45.

Barkley, R. A. (1997). *ADHD and the nature of self-control*. New York: Guilford Press.

Barkley, R. A. (1998a). *Attention-deficit hyperactivity disorder: A handbook for diagnosis and treatment*. New York: Guildford Press.

Barkley, R. A. (1998b). Attention-Deficit/Hyperactivity Disorder. In E. Mash & R. A. Barkley (Eds), *Treatment of childhood disorders* (2nd ed., pp. 55–110). New York: Guilford Press.

Barkley, R. A., DuPaul, G., & McMurray, M. B. (1990). A comprehensive evaluation of attention deficit disorder with and without hyperactivity as defined by research criteria. *Journal of Consulting and Clinical Psychology, 58*, 775–789.

Barkley, R. A., Fischer, M., Edelbrock, C. S., & Smallish, L. (1990). The adolescent outcome of hyperactive children diagnosed by research criteria: I. An 8-year prospective follow-up study. *Journal of the American Academy of Child and Adolescent Psychiatry, 29*, 546–557.

Barkley, R. A., Murphy, K. R., & Kwasnik, D. (1996). Psychological adjustment and adaptive impairment in young adults with ADHD. *Journal of Attention Disorders, 1*, 41–54.

Biederman, J. (1998). New data on ADD and girls. *ATTENTION, 4*, 38–40.

Biederman, J., Faraone, S. V., Keenan, K., & Tsuang, M. T. (1991). Evidence of familial association between attention deficit hyperactivity disorder and major affective disorder. *Archives of General Psychiatry, 48*, 633–642.

Biederman, J., Faraone, S. V., Keenan, K., Steingard, R., & Tsuang, M. T. (1991). Familial association between attention deficit disorder (ADD) and anxiety disorder. *American Journal of Psychiatry, 148*, 251–256.

Biederman, J., Faraone, S., Mick, E., Moore, P., & Lelon, E. (1996). Child Behavior Checklist findings further support comorbidity between ADHD and major depression in a referred sample. *Journal of the American Academy of Child and Adolescent Psychiatry, 35*, 734–742.

Biederman, J., Faraone, S., Mick, E., Spencer, T., Wilens, T., Kiely, K., Guite, J., Ablon, J.S., Reed, E., & Warburton, R. (1995). High risk for attention deficit hyperactivity disorder among children of parents with child onset of the disorder: A pilot study. *American Journal of Psychiatry, 152*, 431–435.

Biederman, J., Faraone, S., Milberger, S., Curtis, B. A., Chen, L., Marrs, A., Ouellette, C., Moore, P., & Spencer, T. (1996). Predictors of persistence and remission of ADHD into adolescence: Results from a four-year prospective follow-up study. *Journal of the American Academy of Child and Adolescent Psychiatry, 35*, 343–351.

Biederman, J., Faraone, S., Milberger, S., Garcia Jetton, J., Chen, L., Mick, E., Greene, R., & Russell, R. (1996). Is childhood oppositional defiant disorder a precursor to adolescent conduct disorder?: Findings from a four-year follow-up study of ADHD children. *Journal of the American Academy of Child and Adolescent Psychiatry, 35*, 1193–1204.

Biederman, J., Faraone, S., Milberger, S., Guite, J., Mick, E., Chen, L., Mennin, D., Oulette, C., Moore, P., Spencer, T., Norman, D., Wilens, T., Kraus, L., & Perrin, J. (1996). A prospective 4-year follow-up study of attention-deficit hyperactivity and related disorders. *Archives of General Psychiatry, 53*, 437–446.

Biederman, J., Faraone, S. V., Taylor, A., Sienna, M., Williamson, S., & Fine, C. (1998). Diagnostic continuity between child and adolescent ADHD: Findings from a longitudinal clinical sample. *Journal of the American Academy of Child and Adolescent Psychiatry, 37*, 305–313.

Biederman, J., Faraone, S., Mick, E., Williamson, S., Wilens, T., Spencer, T., Weber, W., Jefton, J., Kraus, I., Pert, J., & Zallen, B. (1999). Clinical correlates of ADHD in females: Findings from a large group of girls ascertained from pediatric and psychiatric referrals. *Journal of the American Academy of Child and Adolescent Psychiatry, 38*, 966–975.

Borlund, B. L., & Hechtman, H. K. (1976). Hyperactive boys and their brothers: A 25-year follow-up study. *Archives of Clinical Psychiatry, 33*, 669–675.

Brent, D. A., Perper, J. A., Goldstein, C. E., et al. (1988). Risk factors for adolescent suicide: A comparison of adolescent suicide victims with suicidal inpatients. *Archives of General Psychiatry, 45*, 581–588.

Cantwell, D. P. (1975). Clinical picture, epidemiology classifications of the hyperactive child syndrome. In D. P. Cantwell (Ed.), *The hyperactive child: Diagnosis, management, current research*. New York: Spectrum.

Cantwell, D. P., & Baker, L. (1989). Stability and natural history of DSM-III childhood diagnoses. *Journal of the American Academy of Child and Adolescent Psychiatry, 28*, 691–700.

Casey, B. J. (in press). Disruption of inhibitory control in developmental disorders: A mechanistic model of implicated frontostriatal circuitry. In R. S. Siegler & J. L. McClelland (Eds.), *Mechanisms of cognitive development: The Carnegie Symposium on Cognition*. (pp.) Hillsdale, NJ: Erlbaum.

Castellanos, F. X. (2000). *Neuroimaging studies of attention-deficit/hyperactivity disorder*. Handout for Meeting on Interdisciplinary Research on ADHD. Developmental Psychopathology and Prevention Research Branch, NIMH. Washington, DC.

Castellanos, F. X., Giedd, J. N., Ekburg, P., Marsh, W. L., Vaituzis, A. C., Kaysen, D., Hamburger, S. D., & Rapoport, J. L. (1994). Quantitative morphology of the caudate nucleus in Attention Deficit Hyperactivity Disorder. *American Journal of Psychiatry, 151*, 1791–1796.

Chang, H. T., Klorman, R. Shaywitz, S. E., Fletcher, J., Marchione, K., Holahan, J., Steubing, K., Brumaghim, J., & Shaywitz, B. (1999). Paired-associate learning in attention-deficit/hyperactivity disorder as a function of hyperactivity-impulsivity and oppositional defiant disorder. *Journal of Abnormal Psychology, 27*, 237–245.

Eiraldi, R. B., Power, T. J., & Maguth Nezu, D. (1997). Patterns of comorbidity associated with subtypes of Attention-Deficit/Hyperactivity Disorder among 6- to 12-year-old children. *Journal of the American Academy of Child and Adolescent Psychiatry, 36*, 503–514.

Erhardt, D., & Hinshaw, S. (1994). Initial sociometric impressions of attention-deficit hyperactivity disorder and comparison boys: Predictions from social behaviors and from nonbehavioral variables. *Journal of Consulting and Clinical psychology, 62*, 833–842.

Faraone, S. V., & Biederman, J. (1994). Genetics of Attention-Deficit Hyperactivity Disorder. In L. L. Greenhill (Ed.), *Child and adolescent psychiatric clinics of North America: Disruptive disorders* (pp. 285–301.) Philadelphia PA: Saunders.

Faraone, S. V., Biederman, J., Chen, W. J., Milberger, R., & Tsuang, M. T. (1995). Genetic heterogeneity in attention-deficit hyperactivity disorder (ADHD): Gender, psychiatric comorbidity, and maternal ADHD. *Journal of Abnormal Psychology, 104*, 334–345.

Faraone, S. V., Biederman, J., Jettson, J. G., & Tsuang, M. T. (1997). Attention deficit disorder and conduct disorder: Longitudinal evidence for a familial subtype. *Psychological Medicine, 27*, 291–300.

Faraone, S. V., Biederman, J., Lehman, B., Spencer, T., Norman, D., Seidman, L. J., Kraus, I., Perrin, J., Chen, W. J., & Tsuang, M. T. (1993). Intellectual performance and school failure in children with attention deficit hyperactivity disorder and in their siblings. *Journal of Abnormal Psychology, 102*, 616–623.

Faraone, S. V., Biederman, J., Wozniak, J., Mundy, E., Mennin, D., & O'Donnell, D. (1997). Is comorbidity with ADHD a marker for juvenile-onset mania? *Journal of the American Academy of Child and Adolescent Psychiatry, 36*, 1046–1055.

Faraone, S. V., Biederman, J., Jeftson, J. G., & Tsuang, M. T. (1997). Attention deficit disorder and conduct disorder: Longitudinal evidence for a familial subtype. *Psychological Medicine, 27*, 291–300.

Filipek, P. A. (1996). Structural variations in measures in the developmental disorders. In R. W. Thatcher, G. Reid Lyon, J. Rumsey, & N. Krasgnegor (Eds.), *Developmental neuroimaging: Mapping the development of brain and behavior* (pp. 169–186). San Diego, CA: Academic Press.

Filipek, P., Semrud-Clikeman, M., Steindgard, R. J., Renshaw, P. F., Kennedy, D. N., & Biederman, J. (1997). Volumetric MRI analysis comparing attention-deficit hyperactivity disorder and normal controls. *Neurology, 48*, 589–601.

Fischer, M., Barkley, R. A., Fletcher, C. S., & Smallish, L. (1990). The adolescent outcome of hyperactive children diagnosed by research criteria: II. Academic, attentional, and neuropsychological status. *Journal of Consulting and Clinical Psychology, 58*, 580–588.

Fischer, M., Barkley, R. A., Fletcher, C. S., & Smallish, L. (1993). The stability of dimensions of behavior in ADHD and normal children over an 8-year follow-up. *Journal of Abnormal Child Psychology, 21*, 315–337.

Gaub, M., & Carlson, C. L. (1997). Gender differences in ADHD: A meta-analysis and critical review. *Journal of the American Academy of Child and Adolescent Psychiatry, 36*, 1036–1045.

Giancola, P. R., Mezzich, A. C., & Tarter, R. E. (1998). Executive cognitive functioning, temperament, and antisocial behavior in conduct-disordered adolescent females. *Journal of Abnormal Psychology, 4*, 629–641.

Giedd, J. (2000). Is brain imaging useful in the diagnosis of attention-deficit/hyperactivity disorder? *ATTENTION, 19*, 19–25.

Giedd, J. N., Castellanos, F. X., Casey, B. J., Kozuch, P., King, A. C., Hamburger, S. D., & Rapoport, J. L. (1994). Quantitative morphology of the corpus callosum in attention deficit hyperactivity disorder. *American Journal of Psychiatry, 151*, 665–669.

Gilger, J. W., Pennington, B. F., Detries, J.D. (1992). A twin study of the etiology of comorbidity: Attention deficit hyperactivity disorder and dyslexia. *Journal of American Academy of Child and adolescent Psychiatry, 31*, 343–348.

Gillis, J. J., Gilger, J. W., Pennington, B. F., & DeFries, J. C. (1992). Attention-deficit hyperactivity disorder in reading disabled twins: Evidence for genetic etiology. *Journal of Abnormal Psychology, 20*, 303–315.

Gittelman, R., Mannuzza, S., Shenker, R., & Bonagura, N. (1985). Hyperactive boys almost grown up. *Archives of General Psychiatry, 42*, 937–947.

Goldstein, S, & Goldstein, M. (1998). *Managing attention deficit hyperactivity disorder in children: A guide for practitioners* (2nd ed.). New York: Wiley.

Greene, R. W., Biederman, J., Faraone, S. V., Sienna, M., & Garcia-Jones, J. (1997). Adolescent outcome of boys with attention-deficit/hyperactivity disorder and social disability: Results from a four-year longitudinal follow-up study. *Journal of Consulting and Clinical Psychology, 65*, 758–767.

Hansen, C., Weiss, D., & Last, C. G. (1999). ADHD boys in young adulthood: Psychological adjustment. *Journal of the American Academy of Child and Adolescent Psychiatry, 38*, 165–171.

Hechtman, L., Weiss, G., Pearlman, T., Asel, R. (1984). Hyperactive as young adults: Initial predictors of adult outcome. *Journal of American Academy of Child Psychiatry, 23*, 250–260.

Hechtman, L. (1996). Developmental, neurobiological, and psychosocial aspects of hyperactivity, impulsivity, and inattention. In M. Lewis's (ed.), Child and adolescent psychiatry: A comprehensive textbook (pp 341–418). Baltimore, MD: Williams & Wilkins.

Hechtman, L. (1999). Attention-deficit/hyperactivity disorder. In M. Weiss, L. T. Hechtman, & G. Weiss (Eds). *ADHD in adulthood: A guide to current theory, diagnosis and treatment* (pp. 17–38). Baltimore: Johns Hopkins University Press.

Hinshaw, S. P. (1992). Externalizing behavior problems and academic underachievement in children and adolescents: Causal relationships and underlying mechanisms. *Psychological Bulletin, 111*, 127–155.

Hynd, G. W., Hern, K. L., Novey, E. S., Eliopulos, R. T., Marshall, R., Gonzalez, M. A., & Voeller, K. J. (1993). Attention deficit-hyperactivity disorder and asymmetry of the caudate nucleus. *Journal of Child Neurology, 8*, 339–347.

Hynd, G. W., Semrud-Clikeman, M., Lorys, A., Novey, E., & Eliopolus, D. (1990). Brain morphology in developmental dyslexia and attention deficit-disorder/hyperactivity. *Archives of Neurology, 47*, 919–926.

Hynd, G. W., Semrud Clikeman, M., Lorys, A. R., Novey, E. S., Eliopulos, D., & Lyytinen, H. (1991). Corpus callosum morphology in attention deficit-hyperactivity disorder: Morphometric analysis of MRI. *Journal of Learning Disabilities, 24*, 141–146.

Ingram, S., Hechtman, L., & Morgenstern, G. (1999). Outcome issues in ADHD: Adolescent and adult long-term outcome. *Mental Retardation and Developmental Disabilities Research Reviews, 5*, 243–250.

Jensen, P. S., Watanabe, H. K., Richters, J. E., Cortes, R., Roper, M., & Liu, S. (1995). Prevalence of mental disorder in military children and adolescents. Findings from two-stage community survey. *Journal of the American Academy of Child and Adolescent Psychiatry, 34*, 1514–1524.

Klein, R. G., & Mannuzza, S. (1991). The long-term outcome of hyperactive children: A review. Special section: Longitudinal research. *Journal of the American Academy of Child and Adolescent Psychiatry, 30*, 383–387.

Klorman, R., Hazel-Fernanadez, L. A., Shaywitz, S. E., Fletcher, J. M., Marchione, K. E., Holahan, J. M., Stuebing, K. K., & Shaywitz, B. A. (1999). Executive functioning deficits in attention-deficit/hyperactivity disorder are independent of oppositional defiant or reading disorder. *Journal of the American Academy of Child and Adolescent Psychiatry, 38*, 1148–1155.

Lahey, B. B., & Carlson, C. L. (1991). Validity of the diagnostic category of attention-deficit hyperactivity disorder without hyperactivity: A review of the literature. In S. E. Shaywitz & B. A. Shaywitz (Eds.), *Attention deficit disorder comes of age: Toward the twenty-first century* (pp. 119–144). Austin, TX: Pro-Ed.

Lahey, B. B., & Carlson, C. L. (1992). Validity of the diagnostic category of attention deficit disorder without hyperactivity. A review of the Literature. In S.E. Shaywitz, B.A. Shaywitz (eds.), *Attention deficit disorder comes of age: Toward the twenty-first century* (pp. 119–144). Auston, TX: Pro-Ed.

Lambert, N. M., Hartsaugh, C. S., Sassone, S., & Sandoval, J. (1987). Persistence of hyperactive symptoms from childhood to adolescence and associated outcomes. *American Journal of Orthopsychiatry, 57*, 22–32.

Mannuzza, S., Gittelman, R., Konig, P. H., & Giampino, T. L. (1989). Hyperactive boys almost grown up: VI, Criminality and its relationship to psychiatric status. *Archives of General Psychiatry, 46*, 1073–1079.

Manuzza, S., Gittelman-Klein, R., Bessler, A., Malloy, P., & La Padula, M. (1993). Adult outcome of hyperactive boys: Educational achievement, occupational rank, and psychiatric status. *Archives of General Psychiatry, 50*, 565–576.

Mezzacappa, E., Kindlon, D., & Earls, F. (1999). Relations of age to cognitive and motivational elements of impulse control in boys with and without externalizing behavior problems. *Journal of Abnormal Child Psychology, 27*, 473–483.

Milich, R. (1994). The response of children with ADHD to failure: If at first you don't succeed, do try, try, again? *School Psychology Review, 23*, 11–28.

Milich, R., & Landau, S. (1989). The role of social status variables in differentiating subgroups of hyperactive children. In L. M. Bloomingdale & J. Swanson (Eds.), *Attention deficit disorder: Current concepts and emerging trends in attentional and behavioral disorders of childhood*, (Vol. 5, pp. 1–16). Elmsford, NY: Pergamon Press.

Milich, R., Landau, S., Kilby, G., & Whitten, P. (1982). Preschool peer perceptions of the behavior of hyperactive and aggressive children. *Journal of Abnormal Child Psychology, 10*, 497–510.

Morrison, J. (1980). Adult psychiatric disorders in parents of hyperactive children. *American Journal of Psychiatry, 137*, 825–827.

Morrison, J., & Stewart, M. (1971). A family study of the hyperactive syndrome. *Biological Psychiatry, 3*, 189–195.

Morison, J. R. (1980). Adult psychiatric disorders in parents of hyperactive children. *American Journal of Psychiatry, 137*, 825–827.

MTA Cooperative Group. (1999). A 14-month randomized clinical trial of treatment strategies for attention-deficit/hyperactivity disorder. *Archives of General Psychiatry, 37*, 1073–1086.

Nasrallah., N. H., Loney, J., Olson, S. C., McCalley-Whitters, M., Kramer, J., & Jacoby, C. G. (1986). Cortical atrophy in young adults with a history of hyperactivity in childhood. *Psychiatry Research, 17*, 241–246.

Olson, S. L., Schilling, E. M., & Bates, J. E. (1999). Measurement of impulsivity: Construct coherence, longitudinal stability, and relationship with externalizing problems in middle childhood and adolescence. *Journal of Abnormal Child Psychology, 27*, 151–165.

Pearson, D., Yaffee, L., Loveland, K., et al. (1996). Comparison of sustained and selective attention in children who have mental retardation with and without attention deficit hyperactivity disorder. *American Journal of Mental Retardation, 100*, 592–607.

Perrin, S., & Last, C. G. (1996). Relationship between ADHD and anxiety in boys: Results from a family study. *Journal of the American Academy of Child and Adolescent Psychiatry, 35*, 988–996.

Pliszka, S. R. (1987). Tricyclic antidepressants in the treatment of attention deficit disorder. *Journal of the American Academy of Child and Adolescent Psychiatry, 26*, 127–132.

Posner, M. I., & Petersen, S. E. (1990). The attention system of the human brain. *Annual Review of Neuroscience, 13*, 25–41.

Posner, M. I., & Raichle, M. E. (1994). Networks of attention. In I. M. Posner & M. E. Raichle (Eds.), *Images of mind* (pp. 153–179). New York: Scientific American Library.

Reid, R. (1995). Assessment of ADHD with culturally different groups: The use of behavioral rating scales. *School Psychology Review, 24*, 537–560.

Safer, D. J., & Malevar, M. (2000). Stimulant treatment in Maryland public schools. *Pediatrics, 106*, 533–539.

Satterfield, J. H., Satterfield, B. T., & Cantwell, D. P. (1981). Three-year multimodality treatment study of 100 hyperactive boys. *Journal of Pediatrics, 98*, 650–655.

Satterfield, J. H., & Schell, A. (1997). A prospective study of hyperactive boys with conduct problems and normal boys:

Adolescent and adult criminality. *Journal of the American Academy of Adolescent Psychiatry, 36,* 1726–1735.

Schachar, R., Tannock, R., Marriott, M., & Logan, G. (1995). Deficient inhibitory control in Attention Deficit Hyperactivity Disorder. *Journal of Abnormal Psychology, 23,* 411–437.

Semrud-Clikeman, M., Biederman, J., Sprich-Buckminster, S., Krifcher, Lehman, B., Faraone, S. V., & Norman, D. (1992). The incidence of ADHD and concurrent learning disabilities. *Journal of the American Academy of Child and Adolescent Psychiatry, 31,* 439–448.

Semrud-Clikeman, M., Filipek, P. A., Biederman, J., Steingard, R., Kennedy, D., Renshaw, P., & Bekken, K. (1994). Attention deficit hyperactivity disorder: Magnetic resonance imaging morphometric analysis of the corpus callosum. *Journal of the American Academy of Child & Adolescent Psychiatry, 33,* 875–881.

Sequin, J. R., Pihl, R. O., Tremblay, R. E., Boulerice, B., & Harden, P. W. (1995). Cognitive and neuropsychological characteristics of physically aggressive boys. *Journal of Abnormal Psychology, 104,* 614–624.

Shaywitz, B. A., Fletcher, J. M., Holahan, J. M., et al., (1995). Interelationships between reading disability and attention-deficit/hyperactivity disorder. *Child Neurology, 1,* 170–186.

Sherman, D. K., Iacono, W., & McGue, M. K. (1997). Attention-deficit hyperactivity disorder dimensions: A twin study in inattention and impulsivity-hyperactivity. *Journal of the American Academy of Child and Adolescent Psychiatry, 36,* 745–753.

Seidman, L. J., Biederman, J., Faraone, S. V., Milberger, S., Norman, D., Seiverd, K., Benedict, K., Guite, J., Mick, E., & Kiely, K. (1995). Effects of family history and comorbidity on the neuropsychology performance of children with ADHD: Preliminary findings. *Journal of American Academy of Child and Adolescent Psychiatry, 34,* 1015–1024.

Silberg, J, Rutter, M., Meyer, J., Maes, H., Hewitt, J., Simonoff, E., Pickles, A., Loeber, R., & Eaves, L. (1996). Genetic and environmental influences on the covariation between hyperactivity and conduct disturbance in juvenile twins. *Journal of Child Psychology and Psychiatry, 37,* 803–816.

Stein, M. A., Szumowski, E., Blondis, T. A., & Roizen, N. J. (1995). Adaptive skills dysfunction in ADD and ADHD children. *Journal of Child Psychology and Psychiatry, 36,* 663–670.

Tannock, R. (1998). Attention deficit hyperactivity disorder: Advances in cognitive, neurobiological, and genetic studies. *Journal of Child Psychology and Psychiatry, 39,* 65–100.

Taylor, E., Sandberg, S., Thorley, G., & Giles, S. (1991). *The epidemiology of childhood hyperactivity.* London: Oxford University Press.

Teeter, P. A., (1998). *Interventions for ADHD: Treatment in developmental context.* New York: Guilford Press.

Teeter, P. A., & Semrud-Clikeman, M. (1995). Integrating neurobiological, psychosocial, and behavioral paradigms: A transactional model for ADHD. *Archives of Clinical Neuropsychology, 10,* 433–461.

Teeter, P.A., Semrud-Clikeman, M. (1997), Child neuropsychology: Assessment and interventions for neurodevelopmental disorders. Allyn and Bacon. Boston, MA:

van den Oord, E. J., Boomsma, D. I., & Verhulst, F. C. (1994). A study of problem behaviors in 10- to 15-year-old biologically related and unrelated international adoptees. *Behavior Genetics, 24,* 193–205.

Weiss, M., Hechtman, L. T, & G. Weiss (1999). *ADHD in adulthood: A guide to current theory, diagnosis and treatment* (pp. 1–48). Baltimore: Johns Hopkins University Press.

Weiss, G., & Hechtman, L. (1993). *Hyperactive children grown up: ADHD in children, adolescents, and adults* (2nd ed.). New York: Guilford Press.

Weiss, G., Minde, K., Werry, J. S., Douglas, V. I., & Nemeth, E. (1971). Studies of hyperactive child VIII: Five-year follow-up. *Archives of General Psychiatry, 24,* 409–414.

Zametkin, A., Gross, M., King, A., Semple, W., Rumsey, J., Hamburger, S., & Cohen, R. (1990). Cerebral glucose metabolism in adults with hyperactivity of childhood onset. *New England Journal of Medicine, 323,* 1361–1366.

Zametkin, A., Liebenauer, L. L., Fitzgerald, G. A., King, A. C., Minkunas, D. V., Herscovitch, P., Yamada, E. M., & Cohen, R. M. (1993). Brain metabolism in teenagers with attention-deficit hyperactivity disorder. *Archives of General Psychiatry, 50,* 333–340.

Zentall, S. S., Harper, G., & Stormont-Spurgin, M. (1993). Children with hyperactivity and their organizational abilities. *Journal of Educational Research, 87,* 112–117.

# 2

# Continuity of ADHD in Adulthood: Hypothesis and Theory Meet Reality

Sam Goldstein, Ph.D.

## INTRODUCTION

In their discussion of ADHD, Weiss and Hechtman (1993) suggest that understanding the continuity of childhood conditions into adulthood is far from simple. The traditional, dichotomous view that childhood conditions are either outgrown or continue to manifest in adulthood in a similar way as in childhood (e.g., intellectual handicap) must be countered by a number of other possibilities. For example, symptoms of a particular condition may persist into adulthood, but changes in adult expectations and lifestyle, as well as the capacity of human beings to develop compensatory strategies, minimize negative impact or, for that matter, even the visibility a condition may have during the adult years. Children with significant large motor delays, for example, often struggle during their childhood years on the playground and in physical education classes. The impact of delayed large motor skills in combination with ADHD has also been suggested as far reaching (Hellgren, Gillberg, & Gillberg, 1994; Rasmussen & Gillberg, 1999). Yet in adults the avoidance of athletic activities may be the only residual effect.

There are also a number of other outcomes for childhood conditions. A condition could in part remit, but the residual symptoms could cause daily functional impairment, or a condition could predispose an adult to certain other kinds of problems. Gradually, over the last 25 years, all of these hypotheses, including acceptance of the continuity of ADHD as an impairing condition throughout the life span, have been considered and examined, and they are now better understood.

The existence of ADHD as a clinically impairing condition is irrefutable (Goldstein & Goldstein, 1998; Barkley, 1997). Though the etiology of the condition and precise symptom profile remain debatable concepts, presenting symptoms and impairing consequences are easily observed and measured. In light of current theories portraying ADHD as a condition of impaired development, it should not be a great philosophical or academic leap to accept the condition as presenting throughout the life span (Goldstein & Goldstein, 1998; Goldstein, 1999; Barkley, 1997, 1998). Yet scientific method requires more than just hypotheses and theory before belief can confidently be described as fact. Though thousands of peer-reviewed studies dealing with ADHD in childhood have been published, the literature still contains fewer than 100 peer-reviewed articles dealing with adult ADHD. The number of studies has been increasing significantly year by year, including the ongoing, reported results from a number of longitudinal studies following children with ADHD into their adult years. Yet, as with any emerging condition, each published study holds the promise of new data, insight, and perhaps a new path to follow with regard to ADHD in the adult years. Time will determine which paths lead somewhere and which are dead ends.

As discussed in the Preface, for now the field of adult ADHD is driven more by trade texts and lay publications than by the availability of scientific literature to guide clinical practice. Even in clinical practice and research, the misunderstanding of the developmental nature of the diagnosis, particularly the fact that a set of childhood-derived symptoms is currently applied to adults, causes misunderstanding and misinformation. For example, in 1996 Hill and Schoener applied the categorical criteria of the DMS-IIIR by reviewing nine prospective studies in which cohorts of children with ADHD were followed up between 4 and 16 years later to determine the number retaining the ADHD diagnosis. The authors subjected the data to nonlinear regression analysis to ascertain the relationship of the condition with chronological age. According to these authors there was an exponential decline over time in the condition. It was suggested that the presence of the condition declined 50% approximately every 5 years. Under this assumption, beginning with a prevalence rate of 4% in childhood, the authors concluded that the estimated rate of adult ADHD ranged from approximately 0.8% at age 20 to 0% at age 40. The study contained multiple methodological problems, but more importantly demonstrated the difficulty of applying childhood criteria to an adult population.

As multiple authors have demonstrated, the number of ADHD symptoms necessary to reach a threshold criterion of a standard deviation and a half between an affected individual and those of similar age decreases with increasing age (Murphy & Barkley, 1996). These authors compared 172 adults with ADHD to 30 adults without ADHD. All had been referred to an adult ADHD clinic. The authors succinctly demonstrated that the issue is not so much meeting symptom threshold, but the experience of impairment relative to others. Those with ADHD demonstrated a specifically greater prevalence of oppositional, conduct, and substance abuse disorders and greater illegal substance use than did the non-ADHD group. Those with ADHD displayed greater self-reported psychological maladjustment, more driving risks, and more frequent changes in employment. Significantly, more individuals with ADHD had experienced a suspension of their driver's license, had performed poorly, quit, or been fired from their job, and had had a history of poor educational performance as well as more frequent school disciplinary actions against them. Multiple marriages were also more prevalent in the group with ADHD.

In the last 15 years, the biopsychosocial nature of this condition across the life span has become increasingly apparent. Epstein, Conners, Erhardt, et al. (1997) demonstrated that adults with ADHD presented with a longer delay when their attention was misdirected with cues in a reaction-time task measuring hemispheric control. Those with ADHD had difficulty switching when misdirected by cues to the right visual field when the target presented in the left visual field. Gansler et al. (1998) administered a battery of neuropsychological tests to 30 adults with ADHD, demonstrating that this population, in comparison to a normal sample, experienced specific problems with the skills necessary to perform test tasks involving visual tracking, auditory attention, and visual continuous performance. Deficits on these tasks suggest problems with executive control, likely linked to a dysregulation of the frontal lobes. This pattern of problems, though not always the consensus reached by other researchers, has provided consistent evidence of deficits in a variety of tasks sensitive to executive function and self-regulation (Jenkins, Cowan, Malloy, et. al, 1998; Holdnack, Noberg, Arnold, Gur, & Gur, 1995).

Readers should consider this chapter a work in progress. Given the nearly exponential growth in interest and peer-reviewed published research dealing with adult ADHD and the time span between the completion of the manuscript for this chapter and the publication of the book, approximately 30–50 additional research studies exploring symptoms, problems, outcome, and, most importantly, treatment of adult ADHD will be published. Nonetheless, the available research suggests a consistent pattern of emerging trends. This chapter will review these trends with regard to various cognitive, emotional, personality, familial, and vocational outcomes for individuals with ADHD. Though some authors have suggested that ADHD may reflect an adapted pattern of skills developed based on an evolutionary model (Hartmann, 1993), the emerging research literature is sobering. Not a single childhood or adult study exists to suggest that those with ADHD hold any type of advantage over individuals without this condition (Goldstein & Barkley, 1998). Further, the increased recognition that ADHD reflects not so much a problem sitting still or paying attention, but rather a problem of self-regulation or self-control, provides a workable hypothesis to explain the myriad problems currently identified for adults with histories of ADHD. This plausible explanation for ADHD postulates that rather than an adapted or evolved set of valuable qualities, individuals with ADHD suffer from weaknesses in the development of efficient self-regulatory and executive functions. These cognitive functions fall on a normal curve, much akin to height and weight. Qualities of ADHD appear to place individuals at the lower tail of an adaptive bell curve for these skills.

Current knowledge of adult ADHD is drawn from a variety of sources, including extrapolation from childhood data, studies of comorbid conditions and their impact on adult outcome, the family studies, longitudinal or long-term follow-up studies, and, finally, research into adult-diagnosed ADHD.

## OUTCOME OF ADHD IN THE ADULT YEARS

The body of literature attesting to the emotional, cognitive, vocational, academic, substance use, and criminal risks of the condition are growing. It has been estimated from available literature that approximately one-third of adults with ADHD progress satisfactorily into their adult years, another one-third continues to experience some problems, while the final third continues to experience and often develops significant problems (for review see Goldstein, 1995; Hechtman, 2000). By combining a number of outcome studies it is reasonable to conclude that 10–20% of adults with histories of ADHD experience few problems. Sixty percent continue to demonstrate symptoms of ADHD and experience social, academic, and emotional problems to at least a mild to moderate degree, and 10–30% develop antisocial problems in addition to their continued difficulty with ADHD and other comorbid problems (Barkley, 1990; Cantwell & Baker, 1989; Gittelman, Mannuzza, Shenker, & Bonagura, 1985; Herrero, Hechtman, & Weiss, 1994; Satterfield, Hoppe, & Schell, 1982; Weiss & Hechtman, 1993). Interestingly, many of these negative outcomes are linked to the continuity, severity, and persistence of ADHD symptoms. There are very limited data to suggest that females at outcome, when controlling for initial presentation, are at less risk for antisocial problems than are males with ADHD (Herrero et al., 1994). It is fair for clinicians to assume that the absence of significant comorbid disruptive behavioral problems during the childhood years is a good predictor of the absence of the development of antisocial disorders in adulthood. Clinicians should be cautioned, however, that the presence of such problems in childhood is not necessarily predictive of antisocial outcome for all cases (Werner & Smith 1998). In their follow-up study, Weiss and Hectman (1993) found only 11% of adults with ADHD to be symptom free, with 79% experiencing some type of internalizing problem and 75% experiencing interpersonal problems. In this cohort, 10% had attempted suicide and 5% were dead from either suicide or accidental injury.

The continuity of the condition in the form of similar symptoms but different consequences has been well demonstrated by Millstein, Wilens, Biederman, and Spencer (1997) in their study of clinically referred adults with ADHD. Ninety-eight percent reported difficulty following directions; 92% reported poor sustained attention; 92% had trouble shifting activities; 88% reported being easily distracted; 80% reported losing things; 70% reported fidgeting, interrupting, and speaking out of turn or not listening.

Arthur Robin and colleagues (Robin, Bedway, & Tzelepis, 1998) demonstrated that beyond the risk of clinical comorbidity and the life impairment, adults with ADHD appear to be at greater risk to develop dysfunctional personality styles. Fifty percent of individuals with ADHD in their follow-up study, in comparison to 5% of normals, demonstrated a personality style characterized by pessimism, helplessness, and disorganization. In contrast, only 44% of those with ADHD, versus 88% of the normal group, demonstrated a personality style consistent with empathy, extroversion, and motivation. In Chapter 3, Russell Barkley and Michael Gordon describe in depth the nature and extent of comorbidity, impairment, and life outcome problems in a longitudinal sample of children followed into adulthood with ADHD. In this chapter a brief overview will be provided describing these vulnerabilities and outcomes.

## Psychological/Emotional

As the number of research studies on adults with ADHD is increasing, the vulnerability of a range of psychiatric problems ADHD correlates with, and may in fact mediate, continues to grow. Mannuzza, Gittleman-Klein, Bessler, Malloy, & LaPadula (1993), in their longitudinal study, reported that at 24 years of age, those with ADHD demonstrated a higher incidence of antisocial personality disorder as well as alcohol and substance abuse. Though these authors did not report a higher incidence of mood or anxiety disorders in this population than in controls, others have. For example, Millstein et al. (1997) reported in their adult sample that adults with the combined type of attention deficit hyperactivity disorder demonstrated a 63% incidence of major depression; 23% dysthymia; 17% bipolar disorder, 11% panic disorder; 12% simple phobia; 21% generalized anxiety disorder; and 7% obsessive/compulsive disorder. Even adults meeting only the inattentive criteria in this study were not immune from fairly similar rates of depression, yet they appeared to experience fewer problems with bipolar and anxiety disorders. The true risk of ADHD in contributing to bipolar illness has yet to be defined. In contrast to Millstein et al. (1997), Sachs and Baldassano (2000) found only eight out of a group of 56 adults with bipolar disorder demonstrating a history of ADHD. Those eight were compared with eight without a history of ADHD. The age of onset of the first affective episode was lower for the subjects with bipolar disorder and ADHD (mean age 12 years) than for those without a history of childhood ADHD (mean age 20 years). Though research on adult females is as sparse as the research on the childhood of females with ADHD, at least one study has demonstrated that 70% of females with adult-diagnosed ADHD experience a history of depression and 62% experience a history of anxiety (Rucklidge & Kaplan, 1997). The incidence of these two conditions in the general population reported in this study, though not insignificant (33% depression, 17% anxiety), is still dramatically less than in the clinical group.

The continuity of this condition into adulthood has been well demonstrated. In 1998 Vitelli studied the relationship between childhood conduct disorder, ADHD, and adult antisocial personality disorder in a sample of maximum security inmates. The results confirmed that childhood conduct disorder and ADHD were significantly related to adult antisocial personality disorders, psychopathy, and impulsivity. The combination of childhood conduct disorder and ADHD appeared to predict significantly worse outcome in regard to problems related to adult violence, substance abuse, and institutional misconduct.

The volume of data describing the emotional and psychiatric risks for individuals with histories of ADHD continues to grow, including recently published studies demonstrating a higher prevalence of anxiety in those with ADHD (Mancini, Van Ameringen, Oakman, & Figueiredo, 1999), panic disorder (Lomas & Gartside, 1999), and even seasonal affective disorder (Levitan, Jain, & Katzman, 1999). These later authors found comorbidity of seasonal affective disorder with adult ADHD to be between 10% and 19%. Specifically they found an apparent relationship between female gender, impulsive symptoms of ADHD, and seasonality.

Symptoms of ADHD have also been found to occur to a higher degree in adults with histories of panic disorder. Fones, Pollack, Susswein, and Otto (2000) reported childhood ADHD features by history occurring in 23.5% of adults with panic disorder; 9.4% satisfied the full DSM III-R and IV criteria, while 14.1% had subthreshold diagnoses. Two-thirds of the panic patients with ADHD indicated persistence of symptoms into adulthood. Though the co-occurrence of ADHD was not reported to influence the clinical pattern of panic, the authors suggested that the comorbidity of ADHD with panic disorder may contribute to adverse social outcome.

## Cognitive Deficits

Comparison studies of neuropsychological testing in a group of adults with ADHD have reported deficits in executive functioning relating to divided attention, visual scanning, and auditory attention (Gansler et al., 1998), speed of processing, and verbal learning (Holdnack et al., 1995). Holdnack et al. demonstrated that adults with ADHD exhibited slow reaction time to target stimuli. Their psychomotor speed was slower relative to controls. These authors also demonstrated inconsistent application of a semantic clustering strategy for those with ADHD memory tasks. Individuals with ADHD appeared susceptible to retroactive interference and item recall inconsistency. In sum, adults with ADHD appear to experience a selective pattern of deficits, revealing slow cognitive processing and significant problems with list learning. Thus, these patterns of selective cognitive weaknesses appear continuous between the childhood and adult years (for review of childhood data, see Chapter 1).

## Academics

The risk of learning disability as well as of lower achievement secondary to scholastic effort is supported by multiple lines of evidence. Those with ADHD appear to significantly underachieve relative to controls (Gittelman et al., 1985; Weiss & Hechtman, 1986; Barkley & Gordon, 2001). Significantly fewer children with ADHD graduate from high school than the general population. Significantly fewer attend college. In the longitudinal studies, only 5% of those with ADHD earned a college degree.

Although the rate of outright learning disability appears to be higher among those with ADHD than in the general population, the lines begin to blur when specific cognitive skills are examined in an effort to explain the academic impairments found in those with ADHD. The most frequently discussed and evaluated deficits relate to those cognitive characteristics referred to as *executive dysfunction* (Denckla, 1994, 1996a, 1996b; Denckla & Reader, 1992). It has been suggested that these impairments over and above intelligence measures and emotional stability indicators best explain why adults with ADHD are often viewed as experiencing learning disability. Denckla (2000, p. 307) suggests that executive dysfunction is the "zone of overlap between ADHD and learning disabilities." From Denckla's perspective these cognitive deficits originate from dysfunction of the frontal lobes or interconnected regions. This impairs a variety of abilities that ultimately affect academic as well as interpersonal relations. As Denckla notes, these problems are endemic but not restricted to populations identified with both learning disability and ADHD, as well as other conditions. Denckla cautions, however, that executive dysfunction is "easier to diagnose than ADHD in adults because adult normed neuropsychological tests and measures are available" (2000, p. 298). Although these weaknesses in some cases are used as markers to explain the underlying deficits of some individuals with ADHD, it is unclear whether they serve as causative explanations, markers, or, for that matter, consequences.

It has also been hypothesized that nonverbal learning disability may overlap with ADHD or the construct of executive dysfunction, because the anterior portion of the right hemisphere is thought to be important in directing self-control and serves an important role in the self-regulatory loop, or the "brain's braking system" (Castellanos, Giedd, Eckburg, Marsh, Kozuch, et al., 1994; Castellanos, Giedd, Marsh, Hamburger, Vaituzis, et al., 1996). The characteristic description of children with nonverbal learning disability may to some extent overlap with symptoms of ADHD, particularly descriptions of being passively inattentive or disorganized. At this time, however, there are no published peer-reviewed studies examining symptom presentation, overlap, or clinical course for individuals with either of these conditions or for those who may suffer from both. Interested readers are referred to Semrud-Clikeman and Hynd (1990) for review of research on nonverbal learning disability. Finally, extrapolating from the available child clinical literature, it is reasonable for clinicians to assume that adults with histories of ADHD are more likely than not to have fallen behind academically, the result not of skill deficit but of lack of practice for proficiency in those subjects requiring repetitive and sustained effort. Thus, academic areas including nonphonetic spelling, execution in written language, math facts, and attention to detail in mathematics may all prove to be areas of weakness in the absence of learning disability for many adults with ADHD.

## Vocational Outcome

Adults with ADHD are less likely to graduate from high school then their peers, less likely to attend college, and even less likely to graduate from college. They are more likely to enter the workforce at a lower level than siblings and less likely to be promoted (Barkley, Fischer, Edelbrock, et al., 1990), though reportedly employed at a rate similar to the population's (Mannuzza, Gittelman-Klein, Konig, & Giampino, 1989; Mannuzza, Klein, Bessler, et al., 1998). They are also likely to experience many more job changes.

The daily lives of adults with ADHD are reported to be fraught with problems that result from faulty self-control, including difficulty with driving. Young adults with histories of attentional problems have been reported to be at greater risk for motor vehicle accident, drinking and driving, and traffic violations. Though to some extent, these outcomes are also contributed to by personal character, gender, and conduct problems as well as driving experience, even after adjusting for these variables, Woodward, Fergusson, and Horwood (2000) found that ADHD during adolescence placed young adults at an increased risk of an injury accident, driving without a license, and other traffic violations. Further, Barkley, DuPaul, and McMurray (in press), in a well-controlled, carefully administered assessment of basic neuropsychological abilities necessary for driving, driving knowledge, decision making, self-ratings, and ratings by others of driving habits and operation of a simulated motor vehicle, confirm that ADHD is associated with a pervasive, multilevel impairment of driving abilities. The group with ADHD, in comparison to a control population, made more errors when rules governing testing performance were reversed. Deficits in multiple areas of driving knowledge and rapid decision making were also evident. During simulated driving, the group with ADHD was more erratic in controlling the vehicle and made many more errors in negotiating simulated driving courses. Both self-ratings and ratings by other indicated that the group with ADHD employed significantly fewer safe driving habits. Further, gender differences and those possibly due to subtypes of ADHD were not found to be significant. Interestingly, Barkley, Guevremont, Anastopoulos, DuPaul, and Shelton (1993) reported that teens with ADHD were also more likely to have driven an automobile illegally prior to the time they became eligible as licensed drivers and were more likely to have their licences suspended or revoked.

Finally, in a prospective follow-up study, Mannuzza, Klein, Bessler, Malloy, and Hynes (1997) followed males with ADHD demonstrating average intelligence for 17 years in their young adult lives. Those with ADHD obtained lower-ranking occupations. These disadvantages were not accounted for by adult mental status. Interestingly, those with ADHD were not unemployed at a rate beyond that of the general population.

## Substance Use and Dependence

In 1990, Shekim reported 34% of a population of 56 adults with ADHD demonstrated alcoholism, while 30% demonstrated drug abuse. An inpatient study was completed by Milin, Loh, Chow, and Wilson (1997) with a clinical sample of 36 adults, many of whom met criteria for a diagnosis of ADHD. Those with symptoms of ADHD tended to be more likely to have a history of alcohol combined with drug use disorders. The authors further reported that symptoms of antisocial personality disorder were far more prevalent in substance abusers with a history of both childhood and adult ADHD than those without this condition. In 1999, Coure, Brady, Saladin, et al. reported histories of substance use in adults in an inpatient setting. In this setting there were significant differences in the percentage of those presenting with ADHD between the substance use disorders groups divided by drug of choice. Of the ADHD subtypes, subjects with combined and inattentive types were significantly more likely to have ADHD symptoms continue into adulthood than the hyperactive/impulsive subtype. Those with cocaine use were more likely to have a history of childhood ADHD when compared to those with alcohol or combined substance abuse in groups.

Wilens, Biederman, and Mick (1998) examined the rates of remission and duration of substance abuse in individuals with histories of ADHD. The duration of substance abuse was over 37 months longer in a population of adults with ADHD versus those without ADHD. The median time to remission was more than twice as long in ADHD as in controls (144 versus 60 months). The authors reported a need to replicate their data but suggested that ADHD is not only a risk factor for the early initiation and a specific pathway for substance abuse but is also associated with longer duration and a significantly slower remission rate.

Finally, the rate of cigarette smoking in adults with ADHD has also been demonstrated as increased relative to the general population (Pomerleau, Downey, Stelson, & Pomerleau, 1995). In a population of 71 individuals with ADHD with a mean age of nearly 34 years, 42% of the males were current smokers, 13% were exsmokers, and 45% had never smoked. Comparative figures for males in the normal population were 28%, 29%, and 42%, respectively. Thirty-eight percent of females in this group with ADHD were current smokers, 31% were exsmokers, and 31% had never smoked, as compared to 23.5%, 19%, and 57.5%, respectively, in the general population. Smokers experienced greater symptoms of ADHD as children than non-smokers and scored higher on measures of childhood and adult psychiatric comorbidity. The authors suggested that smokers with ADHD may need treatment with a stimulant and sustained nicotine replacement therapy before they can actually quit smoking.

## Antisocial and Criminal Behavior

In Weiss and Hechtman's (1986) follow-up ADHD population, 25–45% expressed some antisocial behavior, with the lower figure, 25%, referring to those who were qualified for a diagnosis of antisocial personality disorder. As noted, this increased risk has been reported by multiple researchers (Robin, Bedway, & Tzelepis, 1998; Barkley & Gordon, 2001). Anecdotal reports have long suggested an overrepresentation of ADHD in incarcerated individuals. In 1999 Curran and Fitzgerald examined 55 adult male offenders with a mean age of 26 years referred to a prison psychiatric clinic. Only 9% met the DSM-IV criteria for ADHD, leading to a slightly higher-than-expected prevalence among this young adult prison population. This runs contrary to Eyestone and Howell (1994), who suggest in a population of 100 inmates an incidence of 25% for ADHD. Further, Kapuchinski (2000) suggests, from his experience as a consulting psychiatrist in a prison setting, that a significant number of individuals present or meet the symptom criteria and history for ADHD.

## Symptom Presentation and Definition

In an effort to understand the meaning and course of symptoms of ADHD into adulthood, Murphy and Barkley (1996) collected symptom report data on 720 adults of at least 17 years of age. The adults were obtained by soliciting volunteers from among individuals entering one of two sites of the Department of Motor Vehicles in Massachusetts to apply for or renew their driver's license. These authors constructed two rating scales using the 18 DSM-IV symptom list for ADHD. Each item was rated on a scale of 0 to 3 (rarely or never, sometimes, often, or very often, respectively). Inattention and hyperactive-impulsive symptoms were alternated in their numbered positions listed on the scale. One rating scale was completed based upon self-report over the past six months, while on the second, individuals were asked to report their behavior when they were between 5 and 12 years of age. The authors correlated the data, collecting six scores. The first three were summations of the item scores calculated separately for the inattention, the hyperactive-impulsive, and the total ADHD item list. The second three were symptom counts of the number of positively endorsed items calculated separately within the inattention, hyperactive-impulsive, and total ADHD item list. Creating the symptom counts, the authors considered a symptom as present if the answer given to the item was often or very often (score of 2 or 3). Table 2.1 contains the means and standard deviations for the summary scores for current behavior by age. Table 2.2 shows the means and standard deviations for the number of symptoms endorsed with a 2 or greater for current behavior at each age group. Both tables report the 93$^{rd}$ percentile cutoff for clinical purposes. Tables 2.3 and 2.4 report the summary scores and symptom counts, respectively, for the retrospective recall of childhood ratings. These too are provided separately for each age group and gender, for the authors reported finding significant differences between genders in the recall of these behaviors from childhood.

Murphy, Gordon, and Barkley (2000) extended this work by completing a statistical reanalysis of the original Murphy and Barkley data. In this reanalysis a number of trends were examined. Table 2.5 presents the number of people endorsing each possible number of items at the "at least sometimes" level recalled from childhood. Almost 80%

TABLE 2.1  Means, Standard Deviations (SD), and Deviance Thresholds (+1.5SD) by Age Group for the ADHD Summation Scores for Current Symptoms Collapsed Across Gender

|  | Age | Mean | SD | +1.5SD cutoff | N |
|---|---|---|---|---|---|
| Inattention | 17–29 | 6.3 | 4.7 | 13.4 | 275 |
| Inattention | 30–49 | 5.5 | 4.4 | 11.4 | 316 |
| Inattention | 50+ | 4.5 | 3.3 | 9.5 | 90 |
| Hyper-impulsive | 17–29 | 8.5 | 4.7 | 15.6 | 276 |
| Hyper-impulsive | 30–49 | 6.7 | 4.3 | 13.2 | 309 |
| Hyper-impulsive | 50+ | 5.1 | 3.2 | 9.9 | 93 |
| Total ADHD score | 17–29 | 14.7 | 8.7 | 27.8 | 266 |
| Total ADHD score | 30–49 | 12.0 | 7.8 | 23.7 | 299 |
| Total ADHD score | 50+ | 9.5 | 5.8 | 18.2 | 87 |

Note: From Murphy, K., & Barkley, R. (1996). Updated adult norms for the ADHD Behavior Checklist for adults. *The ADHD Report, 4(4)*, 12–16.

TABLE 2.2  Means, Standard Deviations (SD), and Deviance Thresholds (+1.5SD) by Age Group for Positive Symptom Counts for the ADHD Current Symptoms Collapsed Across Gender

|  | Age | Mean | SD | +1.5 SD cutoff | N |
|---|---|---|---|---|---|
| Inattention | 17–29 | 1.3 | 1.8 | 4.0 | 275 |
| Inattention | 30–49 | 0.9 | 1.6 | 3.3 | 316 |
| Inattention | 50+ | 0.4 | 1.0 | 1.9 | 90 |
| Hyper-impulsive | 17–29 | 2.1 | 2.0 | 5.1 | 276 |
| Hyper-impulsive | 30–49 | 1.5 | 1.8 | 4.2 | 309 |
| Hyper-impulsive | 50+ | 0.8 | 1.3 | 2.8 | 93 |
| Total ADHD | 17–29 | 3.3 | 3.5 | 8.6 | 266 |
| Total ADHD | 30–49 | 2.3 | 2.9 | 6.7 | 299 |
| Total ADHD | 50+ | 1.2 | 2.0 | 4.2 | 87 |

Note: From Murphy, K., & Barkley, R. (1996). Updated adult norms for the ADHD Behavior Checklist for adults. *The ADHD Report, 4(4)*, 12–16.

of the sample endorsed 6 or more of the 18 items as having surfaced during their early lives. Nearly 75% of the sample reported they were currently experiencing 6 or more symptoms of ADHD at least sometimes (see Table 2.6). Murphy et al. point out these data powerfully demonstrate the commonality of some ADHD complaints in the general population that may occur independent of possessing the clinical condition. Further, even when more stringent criteria for symptom frequency are applied, 25% endorsed having at least 6 of the 18 symptoms often or very often during childhood (see Table 2.7). Twelve percent endorsed having at least 6 symptoms often or very often in their current lives (see Table 2.8). The authors further note that almost half of the sample reported that they had failed to give close attention to details or made careless mistakes in their work at least

**TABLE 2.3  Means, Standard Deviations (SD), and Deviance Thresholds (+1.5SD) by Age Group and Gender for the ADHD Summation Scores for Retrospective Recall of Childhood Symptoms**

|  |  | Males |  |  |  | Females |  |  |  |
| --- | --- | --- | --- | --- | --- | --- | --- | --- | --- |
| Scale | Ages | Mean | SD | +1.5SD | N | Mean | SD | +1.5SD | N |
| Inattention | 17–29 | 11.1 | 6.0 | 20.1 | 175 | 8.2 | 5.9 | 17.1 | 99 |
| Inattention | 30–49 | 8.9 | 5.6 | 17.3 | 182 | 7.2 | 6.1 | 16.4 | 133 |
| Inattention | 50+ | 6.1 | 4.0 | 12.1 | 55 | 3.5 | 3.1 | 8.2 | 38 |
| Hyper-impulsive | 17–29 | 10.7 | 6.0 | 19.7 | 174 | 9.0 | 6.0 | 18.0 | 100 |
| Hyper-impulsive | 30–49 | 8.4 | 5.6 | 16.8 | 181 | 6.0 | 5.1 | 13.7 | 135 |
| Hyper-impulsive | 50+ | 5.6 | 3.4 | 10.7 | 55 | 3.3 | 2.7 | 7.4 | 39 |
| Total ADHD score | 17–29 | 21.8 | 11.3 | 38.8 | 173 | 17.3 | 11.4 | 34.4 | 96 |
| Total ADHD score | 30–49 | 17.3 | 10.4 | 32.9 | 177 | 13.2 | 10.8 | 29.4 | 129 |
| Total ADHD score | 50+ | 11.6 | 6.2 | 20.9 | 54 | 6.3 | 4.5 | 13.1 | 37 |

*Note*: From Murphy, K., & Barkley, R. (1996). Updated adult norms for the ADHD Behavior Checklist for Adults. *The ADHD Report, 4(4)*, 12–16.

**TABLE 2.4  Means, Standard Deviations (SD), and Deviance Thresholds (+1.5SD) by Age Group and Gender for the Positive Symptom Counts for the ADHD Symptom Lists for Retrospective Recall of Childhood Symptoms**

|  |  | Males |  |  |  | Females |  |  |  |
| --- | --- | --- | --- | --- | --- | --- | --- | --- | --- |
| Scale | Ages | Mean | SD | +1.5SD | N | Mean | SD | +1.5SD | N |
| Inattention | 17–29 | 3.3 | 2.8 | 7.5 | 175 | 1.9 | 2.7 | 6.0 | 99 |
| Inattention | 30–49 | 2.2 | 2.5 | 6.0 | 182 | 1.7 | 2.6 | 5.6 | 133 |
| Inattention | 50+ | 0.7 | 1.4 | 2.8 | 55 | 0.2 | 0.7 | 1.3 | 38 |
| Hyper-impulsive | 17–29 | 3.1 | 2.7 | 7.2 | 174 | 2.5 | 2.5 | 6.3 | 100 |
| Hyper-impulsive | 30–49 | 2.2 | 2.5 | 6.0 | 181 | 1.4 | 2.0 | 4.4 | 135 |
| Hyper-impulsive | 50+ | 0.9 | 1.5 | 3.7 | 55 | 0.4 | 0.8 | 1.6 | 39 |
| Total ADHD score | 17–29 | 6.4 | 5.1 | 14.1 | 173 | 4.5 | 4.9 | 11.9 | 96 |
| Total ADHD score | 30–49 | 4.4 | 4.7 | 11.5 | 177 | 3.1 | 4.3 | 9.6 | 129 |
| Total ADHD score | 50+ | 1.6 | 2.2 | 4.9 | 54 | 0.5 | 1.1 | 2.2 | 37 |

*Note*: From Murphy, K., & Barkley, R. (1996). Updated adult norms for the ADHD Behavior Checklist for Adults. *The ADHD Report, 4(4)*, 12–16.

sometimes when they were younger. Nearly a quarter of the sample reported these symptoms occurred often or very often. Over a third reported they frequently had difficulty organizing tasks and activities in childhood. A similar percentage lost things necessary for tasks or activities and reported feeling as if they were driven by a motor. As Murphy et al. point out, "these data provide powerful testament to the universality of ADHD symptomatology" (p. 4).

Clinicians should be cautioned that if 10–20% of the normal population endorses symptoms of ADHD, the ADHD diagnosis based largely on self-report in the absence of significant impairment can lead to substantial overdiagnosis. Further, the risk for misjudgment increases, given that according to these data 25% of the population characterized themselves as having had at least 6 symptoms of ADHD during childhood. These data argue against clinicians' making diagnoses in the absence of corroborating data. These authors are undertaking a large epidemiologic study, beginning with a large symptom pool of DSM IV descriptors, complaints, and problem consequences of ADHD in an effort to arrive at a statistically sound set of symptom criteria and a threshold of symptoms as well as impairment in making the diagnosis of ADHD in adults. Recently a very similar pattern of data has been reported with a population of nearly 400 college students (Lewandowski et al., 2000). On the basis of their findings and previous

**TABLE 2.5** Number of People Endorsing Each Possible Number of Items at the "at least sometimes" Level on a DSM-IV Scale of ADHD Symptoms Recalled from Childhood (*n* = 719)

| No. Items endorsed | Count | % | Cumulative |
|---|---|---|---|
| 0 | 19 | 2.64 | 2.64 |
| 1 | 16 | 2.23 | 4.87 |
| 2 | 20 | 2.78 | 7.65 |
| 3 | 18 | 2.50 | 10.15 |
| 4 | 23 | 3.20 | 13.35 |
| 5 | 24 | 3.34 | 16.69 |
| 6 | 34 | 4.73 | 21.42 |
| 7 | 34 | 4.73 | 26.15 |
| 8 | 31 | 4.31 | 30.46 |
| 9 | 46 | 6.40 | 36.86 |
| 10 | 40 | 5.56 | 42.42 |
| 11 | 48 | 6.68 | 49.10 |
| 12 | 56 | 7.79 | 56.88 |
| 13 | 54 | 7.51 | 64.40 |
| 14 | 42 | 5.84 | 70.24 |
| 15 | 45 | 6.26 | 76.50 |
| 16 | 45 | 6.26 | 82.75 |
| 17 | 54 | 7.51 | 90.26 |
| 18 | 70 | 9.74 | 100.00 |

*Note*: From Murphy, K., Gordon, M., & Barkley, R. (2000). To what extent are ADHD symptoms common? A reanalysis of standardization data from a DSM-IV checklist. *The ADHD Report, 8(3)*, 1–5.

**TABLE 2.6** Number of People Endorsing Each Possible Number of Items at the "at least sometimes" Level on a DSM-IV Scale of ADHD Symptoms for Current Functioning (*n* = 719)

| No. Items endorsed | Count | % | Cumulative |
|---|---|---|---|
| 0 | 7 | 0.97 | 0.97 |
| 1 | 11 | 1.53 | 2.50 |
| 2 | 21 | 2.92 | 5.42 |
| 3 | 35 | 4.86 | 10.28 |
| 4 | 36 | 5.00 | 15.28 |
| 5 | 42 | 5.83 | 21.11 |
| 6 | 38 | 5.28 | 26.39 |
| 7 | 59 | 8.19 | 34.58 |
| 8 | 52 | 7.22 | 41.81 |
| 9 | 55 | 7.64 | 49.44 |
| 10 | 59 | 8.19 | 57.64 |
| 11 | 56 | 7.78 | 65.42 |
| 12 | 57 | 7.92 | 73.33 |
| 13 | 57 | 7.92 | 81.25 |
| 14 | 34 | 4.72 | 85.97 |
| 15 | 30 | 4.17 | 90.14 |
| 16 | 28 | 3.89 | 94.03 |
| 17 | 25 | 3.47 | 97.50 |
| 18 | 18 | 2.50 | 100.00 |

*Note*: From Murphy, K., Gordon, M., & Barkley, R. (2000). To what extent are ADHD symptoms common? A reanalysis of standardization data from a DSM-IV checklist. *The ADHD Report, 8(3)*, 1–5.

research, these authors suggest that self-report alone of symptoms of ADHD may be a reasonable initial threshold for assessment but should not be used as confirming criterion.

## EVALUATION

The diagnosis of ADHD in the adult years has been and likely will continue to be a source of controversy. Despite the fact that current etiology theories of ADHD are consistent with a lifetime prevalence for this condition, there is still a tendency to view this as a childhood problem. Faraone (2000) reviewed five domains of the data addressing the validity of the adult ADHD diagnosis, including clinical correlates, family history, response to

**TABLE 2.7  Number of People Endorsing Each Possible Number of Items at the "at least often" Level on a DSM-IV Scale of ADHD Symptoms Recalled from Childhood ($n=719$)**

| No. Items endorsed | Count | % | Cumulative |
|---|---|---|---|
| 0 | 199 | 27.68 | 27.68 |
| 1 | 95 | 13.21 | 40.89 |
| 2 | 68 | 9.46 | 50.35 |
| 3 | 53 | 7.37 | 57.72 |
| 4 | 51 | 7.09 | 64.81 |
| 5 | 37 | 5.15 | 69.96 |
| 6 | 37 | 5.15 | 75.10 |
| 7 | 20 | 2.78 | 77.89 |
| 8 | 21 | 2.92 | 80.81 |
| 9 | 33 | 4.59 | 85.40 |
| 10 | 18 | 2.50 | 87.90 |
| 11 | 10 | 1.39 | 89.29 |
| 12 | 13 | 1.81 | 91.10 |
| 13 | 18 | 2.50 | 93.60 |
| 14 | 11 | 1.53 | 95.13 |
| 15 | 10 | 1.39 | 96.52 |
| 16 | 7 | 0.97 | 97.50 |
| 17 | 12 | 1.67 | 99.17 |
| 18 | 6 | 0.83 | 100.00 |

*Note*: From Murphy, K., Gordon, M., & Barkley, R. (2000). To what extent are ADHD symptoms common? A reanalysis of standardization data from a DSM-IV checklist. *The ADHD Report, 8(3)*, 1–5.

treatment, neuropsychological studies, and long-term outcome. For all five the validity and reliability of this condition in the adult years was confirmed. However, as Murphy (1993) and Barkley and Murphy (1993) point out, given the limited clinical research in adult ADHD, the process of evaluation must proceed with care, caution, and ethics. Clinicians must not only consider the commonality of some of these complaints in the general population, but also possess the skills necessary to recognize when these symptoms may be more characteristic of other conditions related to affect, substance use, personality, depression, or learning disability. In fact, individuals with almost any psychiatric condition and many medical conditions (chronic pain syndrome, traumatic brain injury) endorse many symptoms of ADHD. Medical conditions such as hypo- or hyperthyroidism and even vitamin deficiency can lead to ADHD symptoms as well. The clinician must be sensitive, empathic, and supportive yet also maintain a critical eye and sound clinical judgment. A comprehensive assessment involving developmental and medical history, a review of school performance, employment history, past psychiatric history, and social and marital functioning must all be reviewed and considered. Ideally the clinician should rely on several informants in addition to the patient.

Efforts at arriving at single instrument or battery of instruments to be completed in laboratory settings to diagnosis ADHD have met with little success in childhood or adulthood. There has been increasing recognition that although there are sensitive and specific measures identified based upon

**TABLE 2.8  Number of People Endorsing Each Possible Number of Items at the "at least often" Level on a DSM-IV Scale of ADHD Symptoms for Current Functioning ($n=719$)**

| No. Items endorsed | Count | % | Cumulative |
|---|---|---|---|
| 0 | 220 | 30.56 | 30.56 |
| 1 | 150 | 20.83 | 51.39 |
| 2 | 87 | 12.08 | 63.47 |
| 3 | 66 | 9.17 | 72.64 |
| 4 | 49 | 6.81 | 79.44 |
| 5 | 35 | 4.86 | 84.31 |
| 6 | 28 | 3.89 | 88.19 |
| 7 | 15 | 2.08 | 90.28 |
| 8 | 19 | 2.64 | 92.92 |
| 9 | 16 | 2.22 | 95.14 |
| 10 | 6 | 0.83 | 95.97 |
| 11 | 12 | 1.67 | 97.64 |
| 12 | 6 | 0.83 | 98.47 |
| 13 | 4 | 0.56 | 99.03 |
| 14 | 5 | 0.69 | 99.72 |
| 15 | 1 | 0.14 | 99.86 |
| 16 | 1 | 0.14 | 100.00 |
| 17 |  |  |  |
| 18 |  |  |  |

*Note*: From Murphy, K., Gordon, M., & Barkley, R. (2000). To what extent are ADHD symptoms common? A reanalysis of standardization data from a DSM-IV checklist. *The ADHD Report, 8(3)*, 1–5.

group research, the negative predictive power of these tools, including the continuous performance tests, continues to be poor (Gansler et al., 1998; Corbett & Stanczak, 1999; Lovejoy, Ball, et al., 1999; Jenkins et al., 1998; Epstein, Conners, et al., 1998; Epstein, Conners, Erhardt, et al., 1997).

One hundred and forty-three consecutive referrals to an adult ADHD speciality clinic were evaluated. Thirty-two percent clearly met the diagnostic criteria for ADHD, 32% did not, and another 36% demonstrated ADHD-like features but did not meet full criteria, due to either a lack of childhood history, the presence of complicating psychiatric problems, or a lack of sufficient impairment. Compared with the group that did not meet ADHD criteria, those with clear-cut ADHD demonstrated more frequent histories of learning disability in childhood, less effective reading skills, and weaker performance on a continuous performance test. They also demonstrated higher self-reports for symptoms of ADHD on questionnaires. Individuals in the uncertain group had a higher rate of current substance abuse than either of the other groups. Clinicians must be cautioned when faced with individuals self-referred for ADHD to recognize that the community's perception of adult ADHD may in fact comprise a better description of general psychiatric conditions than of ADHD specifically (Roy-Byrne et al., 1997).

Catz, Wood, Goldstein, et al. (1998) attempted to determine whether a battery of neuropsychological tests could accurately differentiate those with ADHD from those experiencing major depression or dysthymia. None of the neuropsychological measures could distinguish whether faulty performance classified individuals as ADHD or depressed. Clinicians should be cautious that faulty performance on neuropsychological measures, even those purportedly identified as "tests for ADHD," may be associated with conditions other than ADHD.

Walker and Shores (2000) evaluated 30 adults with ADHD, 30 mild psychiatric patients, and 30 controls using a continuous performance test as well as measures of attention, executive function, psychomotor speed, and arithmetic. The group with ADHD performed lower than healthy controls on most measures. However, when compared to the psychiatric group, the performance of the group with ADHD was not significantly lower on any of these measures. Thus, neuropsychological measures may be effective in distinguishing normals from those with impairments but may not allow for finer distinctions within the impaired group. This problem may also present in the use of standardized questionnaires (McCann, Scheele, Ward, & Roy-Byrne, 2000). Because assessment is not the primary focus of this text, interested readers are referred to Goldstein and Goldstein (1998), Goldstein (1995), and Barkley (1998). Faulty performance on neuropsychological measures may not always be within the domain of those suffering from ADHD.

When an evaluation is completed, the clinician must consider the following to make the diagnosis.

1. The symptoms of ADHD have been present since childhood and have been relatively persistent over time.
2. The symptoms should currently exist to a significant degree, causing impairment.
3. This impairment must be observed in multiple life domains, including work, school, social, family, and community.
4. The clinician has carefully considered and ruled either in or out other medical and mental health explanations possibly contributing to symptom presentation and severity and to impairment.

In Chapter 4, Johnoon and Conners provide an overview of an assessment model for ADHD in adulthood.

## FACTORS AFFECTING OUTCOME

Ultimately the life course for any human being is affected by varied and multiple factors. An increasing body of literature operating from a developmental pathways model, however, has increasingly demonstrated that a number of childhood variables can be used to predict, in a general way, risk of adult problems, as well as identifying insulating or protective factors that reduce risk and increase the chances of a satisfactory transition into adult life (for review see Katz, 1997). As a field, researchers dealing with childhood disruptive disorders, including ADHD, are slowly beginning to examine these protective factors. For the time being there are limited data available specific to the population of individuals with ADHD in this regard. It is quite likely, however, that those factors that insulate and protect children from other psychiatric conditions, including disruptive disorders, likely affect those with ADHD. Thus, living in an intact household, above the poverty level, with parents who are free of serious psychiatric problems, consistent in their parenting style, and available to their children appear to be among the most powerful variables at predicting good outcome (for review see Goldstein and Goldstein, 1998).

In long-term follow-up studies, at least 70–80% of adolescents with a previous diagnosis of ADHD continued to meet the diagnostic criteria for the condition, with at least 60% reporting impairing symptoms but fewer meeting the diagnostic criteria during the adult years (for review see Ingram, Hechtman, & Morgenstern, 1999). These authors suggest that the decrease in prevalence is in part due to the developmental nature of the diagnostic symptoms. Prognosis for individuals with ADHD in adulthood appears to be influenced by the severity of their symptoms, comorbid conditions, level of intellectual function, family situations such as parental pathology, family adversity, socioeconomic status, and treatment history.

There is a broader literature available concerning the absence of certain negative factors in predicting outcome. For example, Herrero et al. (1994) demonstrated that females may have less risk simply due to their gender. Subtype differences, specifically children with the inattentive type of ADHD, may also be at reduced risk, for the absence of impulsivity appears to speak to better outcome. In fact, it is hypothesized that problems with self-control are among the best predictors of future outcome when evaluating young children (for review see Barkley, 1997).

Aggressive behavior in general has been found to predict outcome for children with ADHD. Loney, Whaley-Klahn, Kosier, et al. (1983) associated aggression with negative outcome. Hechtman, Weiss, & Perlman (1984) reported that emotional lability was highly correlated with her aggression and predictive of negative outcome, and Fischer, Barkley, Fletcher, et al. (1993) reported that childhood defiance was predictive of later arrests.

Additional negative outcome variables for ADHD include parental psychopathology (Offord, Boyle, Racine, et al., 1992), the presence of conduct and oppositional defiant disorders (Barkley, Fischer, et al., 1990), learning disability (Moffit, 1990), and lower intellect (Hechtman et al., 1984).

Finally, in a recent study, Wilens, McDermott, Biederman, and Abrantes (1999) evaluated a number of treatment variables, including cognitive therapy and medication, in a chart review to predict course and outcome as the result of treatment. On average the individuals studied were treated for nearly a year in 36 sessions. Treatment was associated with significant improvements in ADHD symptoms as well as with a reduction in anxiety and depressive symptoms. Overall global functioning was also reported to improve. Nearly 70% of the adults were considered to be much to very much improved in their ADHD symptoms at the end of treatment. Thus, in the adult literature, in contrast to the childhood literature, treatments designed at reducing symptoms of ADHD during the adult years may in fact lead to better long-term outcome. A number of additional studies appear to support the efficacy of these treatments for adult ADHD. Casteaneda, Levy, Hardy, and Trujillo (2000) found stimulant treatment very effective in 18 of 19 patients with a history of ADHD and cocaine abuse. In fact, long-acting stimulants also appeared to improve recovery, with rare relapses reported. Finally, Cox, Merkel, Kovatchev, and

Seward (2000) report significantly improved driving behavior in adults with ADHD during a medication trial in a study utilizing a driving simulator. Beginning with Chapter 6, the contributing authors provide readers with a framework for developing a multimodal treatment program for adults with ADHD.

## CONCLUSION

The hypothesis concerning the continuity of ADHD into the adult years has become reality. Current theory for the etiology of ADHD is consistent with a lifetime presentation, reflecting developmental rather than a pathological difference between affected individuals and the general population. The consequences of living with the burden of a significantly disabling condition reflecting limited self-control results in demonstrated problems for adults with ADHD. The condition serves as a risk factor, limiting their potential for academic and vocational achievement, as well as acting as a catalyst for comorbid psychiatric and life problems. Though much work remains to be done to understand the developmental course, risk, and protective factors involved in the adult outcome of ADHD, clinicians must increasingly turn their research and clinical attention to the care and treatment of affected adults.

## REFERENCES

Barkley, R. A. (1990). A critique of current diagnostic criteria for attention deficit hyperactivity disorder: Clinical and research implications. *Journal of Developmental and Behavioral Pediatrics, 11*, 343–352.

Barkley, R. A. (1997). *The nature of self-control.* New York: Guilford Press.

Barkley, R. A. (1998). *Attention deficit hyperactivity disorder* (2nd ed.). New York: Guilford Press.

Barkley, R. A., & Gordon, M. (2001). Young adult outcome: Clinical implications. In S. Goldstein and P. A. Teeter (Eds.). *Clinical interventions for adult ADHD: A comprehensive approach.* New York: Academic Press.

Barkley, R. A., & Murphy, K. (1993). Differential diagnosis of adult ADHD: Some controversial issues. *The ADHD Report, 4*, 1–3.

Barkley, R. A., DuPaul, G. J., & McMurray, M. B. (in press). A comprehensive evaluation of attention deficit disorder with and without hyperactivity defined by research criteria. *Journal of Consulting and Clinical Psychology.*

Barkley, R. A., Fischer, M., Edelbrock, C. S., et al. (1990). The adolescent outcome of hyperactive children diagnosed with research criteria: I. An 8-year prospective follow-up study. *Journal of the American Academy of Child and Adolescent Psychiatry, 29*, 546–557.

Barkley, R. A., Guevremont, D. C., Anastopoulos, A. D., DuPaul, G. J., & Shelton, T. J. (1993). Driving-related risks and outcomes of attention deficit hyperactivity disorder in adolescents and young adults: A 3- to 5-year follow-up survey. *Pediatrics, 92*, 212–218.

Cantwell, D. P., & Baker, L. (1989). Stability and natural history of DSM-III childhood diagnoses. *Journal of the American Academy of Child and Adolescent Psychiatry, 28*, 691–700.

Casteaneda, R., Levy, R., Hardy, M., & Trujillo, M. (2000). Long acting stimulants for the treatment of ADHD disorder in cocaine dependent adults. *Psychiatric Services, 51*, 169–171.

Castellanos, F. X., Giedd, J. N., Eckburg, P., Marsh, W., Kozuch, P., King, A., Hamburger, S., Ritchie, G., & Rapoport, J. (1994). Quantitative morphology of the caudate nucleus in attention deficit hyperactivity disorder. *American Journal of Psychiatry, 151*, 1791–1796.

Castellanos, F. X., Giedd, J. N., Marsh, W. L., Hamburger, S. D., Vaituzis, A. C., Dickstein, D. P., Sarfatti, S. E., Vauss, Y. C., Snell, J. W., Rajapakse, J. C., & Rapoport, J. L. (1996). Quantitative brain magnetic resonance imaging in attention-deficit hyperactivity disorder. *Archives of General Psychiatry, 53*, 607–616.

Catz, L. J., Wood, D. S., Goldstein, G., et al. (1998). Utility of neuropsychological tests in the evaluation of ADHD versus depression in adults. *Assessment, 5*, 45–51.

Corbett, B., & Stanczak, D. E. (1999). Neuropsychological performance of adults evidencing attention deficit hyperactivity disorder. *Archives of Clinical Neuropsychology, 14*, 373–387.

Coure, C., Brady, K., Saladin, M., et al. (1999). Attention deficit hyperactivity disorder and substance use: Symptoms, patterns and drug choice. *American Journal of Drug and Alcohol Abuse, 25*, 441–448.

Cox, D. J., Merkel, L., Kovatchev, B., & Seward, R. (2000). Effect of stimulant medication on driving performance of young adults with ADHD: A preliminary double-blind placebo controlled trial. *Journal of Nervous and Mental Disease, 188*, 230–234.

Curran, S., & Fitzgerald, M. (1999). Attention deficit hyperactivity disorder in the prison population. *American Journal of Psychiatry, 156*, 1664–1665.

Denckla, M. B. (1994). Measurement of executive function. In G. R. Lyon (Ed.). *Frames of references for the assessment of learning disabilities* (pp. 117–142) Baltimore: Paul H. Brookes.

Denckla, M. B. (1996a). Research on executive function in a neurodevelopmental context: Application of clinical measures. *Developmental Neuropsychology, 12*, 5–15.

Denckla, M. B. (1996b). A theory and model of executive function. In G. R. Lyon & N. A. Krasnegor (Eds.). *Attention, memory and executive function* (pp. 263–278). Baltimore: Paul H. Brookes.

Denckla, M. B. (2000). Learning disabilities and attention deficit/hyperactivity disorder in adults: Overlap with executive dysfunction. In T. E. Brown (Ed.). *Attention-deficit disorders and comorbidities in children, adolescents, and adults* (pp. 297–318). Washington, DC: American Psychiatric Press.

Denckla, M. B., & Reader, M. J. (1992). Educational and psychosocial interventions. In R. Kurlan (Ed.). *Handbook of Tourette syndrome and related tic and behavioral disorders* (pp. 431–451). New York: Marcel Dekker.

Epstein, J. M., Conners, C. K., Erhardt, D., et al. (1997). Asymmetrical hemispheric control of visual-spatial attention in adults with ADHD. *Neuropsychology, 11*, 467–473.

Epstein, J., Conners, C., et al. (1998). Continuous performance test results of adults with ADHD. *Clinical Neuropsychologist, 12*, 155–168.

Eyestone, L., & Howell, R. (1994). An epidemiological study of ADHD and major depression in the male prison population. *Bulletin of the American Academy of Psychiatry and the Law, 22*, 2–6.

Faraone, S. V. (2000). Attention deficit hyperactivity disorder in adults: Implications for theories of diagnosis. *Directions in Psychological Science, 9*, 33–36.

Fischer, M., Barkley, R. A., Fletcher, K. E., et al. (1993). The adolescent outcome of hyperactive children: Predictors of psychiatric, academic, social, and emotional adjustment. *Journal of the American Academy of Child and Adolescent Psychiatry, 32*, 324–332.

Fones, C., Pollack, M. H., Susswein, L., & Otto, M. (2000). History of childhood ADHD features among adults with panic disorder. *Journal of Affective Disorders, 58*, 99–106.

Gansler, D. A., Fucetola, R., Krengel, M., Stetson, S., Zimering, R., & Makary, C. (1998). Are there cognitive subtypes in adult ADHD? *Journal of Nervous and Mental Disease, 186*, 776–781.

Gittelman, R., Mannuzza, S., Shenker, R., & Bonagura, N. (1985). Hyperactive boys almost grown up: I. Psychiatric status. *Archives of General Psychiatry, 42*, 937–947.

Goldstein, S. (1995). *Understanding and managing children's classroom behavior*. New York: Wiley.

Goldstein, S. (1999). Attention deficit/hyperactivity disorder. In S. Goldstein & C. Reynolds (Eds.). *Handbook of neurodevelopmental and genetic disorders in children* (pp. 154–184). New York: Wiley.

Goldstein, S., & Barkley, R. A. (1998). ADHD, hunting, and evolution: "Just so" stories (commentary). *The ADHD Report, 6(5)*, 1–4.

Goldstein, S., & Goldstein, M. (1998). *Managing attention deficit hyperactivity disorder in children: A guide for practitioners* (2nd ed.). New York: Wiley.

Hartmann, T. (1993). *Attention deficit disorder: A different perception*. Novato, CA: Underwood Miller.

Hechtman, L. (2000). Subgroups of adult outcome of attention deficit hyperactivity disorder. In T. Brown (Ed.). *Attention deficit disorders and comorbidities in children, adolescents and adults* (pp. 437–454). Washington, DC: American Psychiatric Press.

Hechtman, L., Weiss, G., & Perlman, T. (1984). Hyperactives as young adults: Initial predictors of adult outcome. *Journal of the American Academy of Child and Adolescent Psychiatry, 25*, 250–260.

Hellgren, L., Gillberg, C., & Gillberg, I. C. (1994). Children with deficits in attention, motor control and perception almost grown up: The contribution of various background factors to outcome at age sixteen years. *European Child and Adolescent Psychiatry, 3*, 1–15.

Herrero, M. E., Hechtman, L., & Weiss, G. (1994). Antisocial disorders in hyperactive subjects from childhood to adulthood: Predictive factors and characterization of subgroups. *American Journal of Orthopsychiatry, 64*, 510–521.

Hill, J. C., & Schoener, E. P. (1996). Age-dependent decline of attention deficit hyperactivity disorder. *American Journal of Psychiatry, 153*, 1143–1146.

Holdnack, J. A., Noberg, P. J., Arnold, S. E., Gur, R. C., & Gur, R. E. (1995). Speed of processing and verbal learning deficits in adults diagnosed with ADHD. *Neuropsychiatry, Neuropsychology and Behavioral Neurology, 8*, 282–292.

Ingram, S., Hechtman, L., & Morgenstern, G. (1999). Outcome issues and ADHD: Adolescent and adult long-term outcome. *Mental Retardation and Developmental Disabilities Research Reviews, 5*, 243–250.

Jenkins, M., Cowan, R., Malloy, P., et al. (1998). Neuropsychological measures which discriminate among adults with residual symptoms of ADHD and other attentional complaints. *Clinical Neuropsychologist, 12*, 74–83.

Kapuchinski, S. (2000). Examining ADHD's role in incarceration. *Attention Magazine, July/August*, 50–53.

Katz, M. (1997). *On playing a poor hand well*. New York: Norton.

Levitan, R. Jain, & Katzman, M. (1999). Seasonal affective symptoms in adults with residual ADHD. *Comprehensive Psychiatry, 40*, 261–267.

Lewandowski, L., Codding, R., Gordon, M., Marcoe, M., Needham, L., & Rentas, J. (2000). Self-reported LD and ADHD symptoms in college students. *The ADHD Report, 8*, 1–4.

Lomas, B., & Gartside, P. (1999). ADHD in adult psychiatric outpatients. *Psychiatric Services, 5*, 705.

Loney, J., Whaley-Klahn, M. A., Kosier, T., et al. (1983). Hyperactive boys and their brothers at 21: Predictors of aggressive and antisocial outcomes. In K. T. Van Dusen & S. A. Mednick (Eds.). *Prospective Studies of Crime and Delinquency* (pp. 181–206). Boston: Kluwer-Nijhoff.

Lovejoy, D., Ball, J., et al. (1999). Neuropsychological performance of adults with ADHD. *Journal of the International Neuropsychological Society, 5*, 222–233.

Mancini, C., Van Amberingen, M., Oakman, J. M., & Figueiredo, D. (1999). Childhood ADHD in adults with anxiety disorders. *Psychological Medicine, 29*, 515–525.

Mannuzza, S., Gittelman-Klein, R., Bessler, A. A., Malloy, P., & LaPadula, M. (1993). Adult outcome of hyperactive boys: Education achievement, occupational rank, and psychiatric status. *Archives of General Psychiatry, 50*, 565–576.

Mannuzza, S., Gittelman-Klein, R., Konig, P. H., & Giampino, T. L. (1989). Hyperactive boys almost grown up: IV. Criminality and its relationship to psychiatric status. *Archives of General Psychiatry, 46*, 1073–1079.

Mannuzza, S., Klein, R. G., Bessler, A., Malloy, P., & Hynes, M. E. (1997). Educational and occupational outcome of hyperactive boys grown up. *Journal of the American Academy of Child and Adolescent Psychiatry, 36*, 1222–1227.

Mannuzza, S., Klein, R. G., Bessler, A., et al. (1998). Adult psychiatric status of hyperactive boys grown up. *American Journal of Psychiatry, 155*, 493–498.

McCann, B. S., Scheele, L., Ward, N., & Roy-Byrne, P. (2000). Discriminant validity of the Wender Utah Rating Scale for ADHD in adults. *Journal of Neuropsychiatry and Clinical Neuroscience, 12*, 240–245.

Milin, R., Loh, E., Chow, J., & Wilson, A. (1997). Assessment of symptoms of ADHD in adults with substance use disorders. *Psychiatric Services, 48*, 1378–1380.

Millstein, R. B., Wilens, T. E., Biederman, J., & Spencer, T. J. (1997). Presenting ADHD symptoms and subtypes in clinically referred adults with ADHD. *Journal of Attention Disorders, 2(3)*, 159–166.

Moffitt, T. E. (1990). Juvenile delinquency and attention deficit disorder: Boys' developmental trajectories from age 3 to age 15. *Child Development, 61*, 893–910.

Murphy, K. (1993). Issues in the assessment of ADHD adults. *The ADHD Report, 1(1)*, 1–2.

Murphy, K., & Barkley, R. (1996). Updated adult norms for the ADHD Behavior Checklist for adults. *The ADHD Report, 4*, 12–16.

Murphy, K., Gordon, M., & Barkley, R. (2000). To what extent are ADHD symptoms common? A reanalysis of standardization data from a DSM-IV checklist. *The ADHD Report, 8(3)*, 1–5.

Offord, D., Boyle, M., Racine, Y., et al. (1992). Outcome, prognosis and risk in a longitudinal follow-up study. *Journal of the American Academy of Child and Adolescent Psychiatry, 31*, 916–926.

Pomerleau, O. F., Downey, K. K., Stelson, F. W., & Pomerleau, C. S. (1995). Cigarette smoking in adult patients diagnosed with attention deficit hyperactivity disorder. *Journal of Substance Abuse, 7*, 373–378.

Rasmussen, P., & Gillberg C. (1999). ADHD, hyperkinetic disorders DAMP and related behavior disorders. In G. Williams & K. Whitmore (Eds). *A neurodevelopmental approach to specific learning disorders* (pp. 134–156). *Clinics in Developmental Medicine*. London: MacKeith Press/Cambridge University Press.

Robin, A. L., Bedway, M., & Tzelepis, A. (1998). Understanding the personality traits of Adults with AD/HD: A pilot study. *Attention, 4(4)*, 49–55

Roy-Byrne, P., Scheel, L., Brinkley, J., Ward, N., Wiatrak, C., Russo, J., Townes, B., & Varley, C. (1997). Adult attention-deficit hyperactivity disorder: Assessment guidelines based on clinical presentation to a specialty clinic. *Comprehensive Psychiatry, 38*, 133–140.

Rucklidge, J. J., & Kaplan, B. J. (1997). Psychological functioning of women identified in adulthood with attention deficit hyperactivity disorder. *Journal of Attention Disorders, 2(3)*, 167–176.

Sachs, G. S., & Baldassano, C. F. (2000). Comorbidity of attention deficit hyperactivity disorder with early- and late-onset bipolar disorder. *American Journal of Psychiatry, 157*, 466–468.

Satterfield, J. H., Hoppe, C. M., & Schell, A. M. (1982). A prospective study of delinquency in 110 adolescent boys with attention deficit disorder and 88 normal adolescent boys. *American Journal of Psychiatry, 139*, 795–798.

Semrud-Clikeman, M., & Hynd, G. W. (1990). Right hemispheric dysfunction in nonverbal learning disabilities: Social, academic, and adaptive functioning in adults and children. *Psychological Bulletin, 107*, 196–209.

Shekim, W. O. (1990, Spring/Summer). Adult attention deficit hyperactivity disorder, residual state. *CH.A.D.D.ER Newsletter*, 16–18.

Vitelli, R. (1998). Childhood disruptive behavior disorder and adult psychopathology. *American Journal of Forensic Psychology, 16*, 29–37.

Walker, A. J., & Shores, E. A. (2000). Neuropsychological functioning of adults with ADHD. *Journal of Clinical and Experimental Neuropsychology, 2*, 115–124.

Weiss, G., & Hechtman, L. (1986). *Hyperactive children grown up*. New York: Guilford.

Weiss, G., & Hechtman, L. (1993). *Hyperactive children grown up* (2nd ed.). New York: Guilford Press.

Werner, E & Smith, R.S. (1998). Vulnerable But Invincible Publisher: Adams, Bannister & Cox.

Wilens, T., Biederman, J., & Mick, E. (1998). Does ADHD affect the course of substance abuse? *American Journal on Addictions, 7*, 156–163.

Wilens, T. E., McDermott, S. P., Biederman, J., & Abrantes, A. (1999). Cognitive therapy in the treatment of adults with ADHD. A systematic chart review of twenty-six cases. *Journal of Cognitive Psychotherapy, 13*, 215–226.

Woodward, L. J., Fergusson, D. M., & Horwood, J. (2000). Driving outcomes of young people with attentional difficulties in adolescents. *Journal of the American Academy of Child and Adolescent Psychiatry, 39*, 627–634.

# 3

# Research on Comorbidity, Adaptive Functioning, and Cognitive Impairments in Adults with ADHD: Implications for a Clinical Practice

Russell A. Barkley, Ph.D., Michael Gordon, Ph.D.

In this chapter we discuss three aspects of ADHD in adults that have barely edged their way onto the playing field of clinical research. Indeed, only limited data on comorbidity, adaptive functioning, and cognitive impairments have been published in the scientific literature. The late arrival on the scene of data about these three issues says much about the relative infancy of research in the adult ADHD arena. For many years, much of the information available represented little more than extrapolations from the voluminous child literature. When studies involving adults finally emerged over the past decade, they focused primarily on establishing the persistence of ADHD symptoms past adolescence and on medication effects. Fortunately, while the current store of data may not be abundant, it is ample enough to provide some important clinical clues into these aspects of ADHD.

Although the topic of cognitive impairments involves self-evident aspects of functioning, the other two issues are more ambiguous and deserve explicit definition. *Comorbidity* refers to the extent to which other psychiatric disorders co-occur with ADHD beyond that expected by chance alone (the base rates of those other disorders in the general population). Studies of comorbidity therefore address the following question: What other psychiatric disorders commonly join with ADHD? Answers to that question have clinical relevance because they directly inform the assessment process and dictate treatment strategies. For example, if comorbidity is a high likelihood among adults identified with ADHD, the clinician's diagnostic protocol must include strategies for exploring the full range of psychiatric disorders. Without broadband differential diagnosis, the assessment and ensuing treatment plan might address the least impairing component of the client's clinical picture.

*Adaptive functioning* concerns the extent to which an individual can handle routine daily responsibilities that are typical of the average person in the population. It addresses the issue of impairment in a manner somewhat distinct from the DSM-type strategy of establishing symptom counts. An individual can exhibit the requisite number of ADHD symptoms without necessarily demonstrating significant limitations in the management of routine life tasks. Studies about adaptive functioning therefore ask the following question: In what aspects of everyday life are individuals with ADHD likely to be impaired compared to most people? Answers to this question have import not only for the diagnostic process, but also for the deployment of therapeutic efforts, resources, and even legal protections.

Before addressing these topics in detail, we will first elaborate on several overarching issues.

- Our review of the literature includes only those findings derived from scientific study. While workshop presenters and authors of popular literature about ADHD often describe all manner of features and impairments purportedly associated with the disorder, most of those characterizations are based on speculation and clinical experience. Clinical anecdote is a perilous source of information that is vulnerable to error from method artifacts, illusory correlations, and uncontrolled maturational and environmental influences. Referral biases, clinical prejudices, and sampling errors can also grossly distort information derived without the benefit of a scientific method. For instance, many experts in the field have voiced the opinion, based on clinical experience, that ADHD promotes high levels of creativity. However, the scientific literature in no way supports this conclusion. In fact, available evidence intimates no link at all between the disorder and verbal or ideational creativity (Murphy, Barkley, & Bush, in press). Theoretical models also imply an adverse impact of the disorder on certain forms of creativity (goal-directed problem solving or strategy development) (Barkley, 1997a, 1997b). In this instance, as in many others, assertions based on clinical experience fail to withstand scientific scrutiny. Therefore, while empirical studies certainly have their share of limitations, they nonetheless are a more secure source of information in comparison to clinical speculation.

- The reader will notice that the studies we report generally involve two distinct types of clinical samples. The first group consists of individuals who were participants in a longitudinal study of ADHD and, therefore, were identified as symptomatic during childhood. The second brand of studies involves patients who sought treatment during their adult years. While some of these individuals may have had childhood impairment sufficient to warrant a bona fide ADHD diagnosis, the subject inclusion criteria for most of these studies offer no such guarantee. In fact, most of these studies rely entirely (or nearly so) on self-report to document both childhood and current impairment associated with ADHD symptoms. The problem with identifying ADHD based on self-perceptions is that this form of clinical data is notoriously unreliable. For example, we recently reported on how common it is for normal adults to endorse clinical levels of ADHD symptoms in regard to childhood history and current functioning (Murphy, Gordon, & Barkley, 2000). Nearly 80% of the sample endorsed 6 or more of the 18 DSM-IV items as having surfaced "at least sometimes" during childhood. A full 75% reported that they were currently experiencing 6 or more ADHD symptoms at least some of the time. While these percentages decreased when more stringent severity criteria were applied (that is, the symptoms had to be reported as occurring at least "often"), they still were far above what one would expect given prevalence estimates for the disorder. A study by Lewandowski and colleagues (2000) showed similar results for a large sample of college students. These results, in concert with ample evidence that inattention is a nonspecific symptom associated with most forms of mental illness (DSM IV; American Psychiatric Association, 1994), limit confidence in studies for which self-report is the primary basis for subject inclusion. In the least, one should assume that they are more likely than the longitudinal studies to involve subjects who either are relatively well functioning or suffer from other types of psychopathology.

- Subjects in longitudinal studies will differ from clinic-referred adults in other significant ways, most of which would predispose them toward a greater degree of impairment. In addition to being identified much earlier in life, they were also likely brought for evaluation by others concerned about their adjustment. Most clinic-referred adults with ADHD, in contrast, have not been diagnosed previously in childhood and so may have a somewhat milder variant of the disorder. These differences could significantly affect results in studies of comorbidity, adaptive functioning, and cognitive impairment. Therefore, likely differences between the longitudinal and cross-sectional studies in the kinds of subjects they identified may explain many seemingly contradictory findings.

- As we indicated earlier, far less is known about ADHD as it appears in adults than about children or adolescents with the disorder. From what literature exists on the subject, the view is emerging that, while ADHD in adults is qualitatively similar to its childhood variant, it differs in important respects. The more advanced physical, cognitive, social, and educational development of adults accounts for some of these differences. The rest are largely associated with the differences between childhood and adult expectations for independence and self-management. In childhood, the major domains of adaptive functioning are focused on self-care, peer relationships, the educational setting, family functioning, and a slowly progressive level of participation within the larger community (as in clubs, sports, scouts, etc.). By adulthood, these domains have expanded to include occupational functioning, marital functioning, child rearing, sexual activity, driving, financial management, and social contracting (reciprocal altruism or social exchange), among others. Therefore, while the disorder entails consistent types of impairments, their impact will vary across development because of different expectations and demands for adjustment.

- Some of the inconsistencies between the child and adult literature (or among studies in the adult arena) can be ascribed to ecological factors. Adulthood entails the gradual withdrawal of the social "safety nets" provided by parents, relatives, and formal educational systems alongside the increasing demands for personal accountability. Consequently, the adverse effects of ADHD can be greatly amplified and augmented, depending upon context. With these changes, however, also come opportunities for increasingly varied occupational and social niches that adults can self-select into compared to children. This can mask or attenuate some of the impact the disorder may have produced in earlier settings that were compulsory (e.g., school) but are no longer relevant. Because adults are exposed to a much wider diversity of circumstances and life demands, it is easy to understand why studies of adaptive and cognitive functioning produce such varied results.

- Throughout this chapter we review studies that compare adults referred for ADHD with normal or psychiatric controls. On most dimensions, means for the ADHD group will reflect significantly poorer functioning. However, those lower group means do not necessarily indicate that the variable under study is diagnostic or characteristic of the disorder. For example, we will present studies indicating that individuals with ADHD are more likely than others to be issued tickets for traffic (driving) violations. However, this factor is neither sensitive nor specific to ADHD, since many individuals who receive multiple traffic tickets are not ADHD and not all individuals with ADHD have this driving history. We caution against interpreting differences between group means as diagnostic of the disorder because we too often read statements by clinicians that reflect this practice. For example, case reports frequently include statements such as: "The appropriateness of the ADHD diagnosis for Mr. Smith is demonstrated by his long history of traffic violations and automobile accidents, a pattern typical of individuals with ADHD." If Mr. Smith has ADHD, it would be documented by a long and consistent history of global impairment associated with significant impulsive and inattentive behavior. While poor driving may be one consequence of that history, and is certainly consistent with having the disorder, it is not primary evidence for the diagnosis.

- Few of the studies we review include psychiatric controls alongside the ADHD and normal groups. Therefore, differences that emerge between groups of ADHD and normal individuals may be more universal to people with psychiatric disorders than specific to ADHD, per se. Similarly, those studies that compare individuals with ADHD to clinic controls may, in the absence of a normal control group, misinterpret any differences as reflecting the nature of ADHD. In reality, they may say more about the makeup of the individuals with other psychiatric disorders.

## DISORDERS COMORBID WITH ADHD IN ADULTS

The literature on comorbidity makes the distinction between true and artifactual phenomena. In true comorbidity, the presence or severity of one disorder increases the probability for the presence or severity of other disorders. True comorbidity can arise for many reasons (see Angold, Costello, and Erkanli, 1999 for a complete discussion). Two disorders may co-occur more often than by chance alone because both share the same or similar underlying etiologies. For instance, if ADHD shared some genes with major depression, individuals with one disorder might be more likely to manifest the other. Two disorders may also share identical or similar predisposing factors. Disrupted parenting, family turmoil, repeated family stressors, and social disadvantage, for example, are all predisposing factors to both conduct disorder (CD) and major depression, thereby increasing the probability that the two disorders will co-occur. One disorder may itself directly cause or predispose to the other comorbid disorder. For instance, the poor emotion regulation associated with ADHD may create a greater likelihood of displaying anger and hostility when a person is frustrated by others. Such poor emotion regulation may predispose to or directly cause a greater risk for oppositional defiant disorder in ADHD children, especially in the context of disrupted parenting. Finally, an often overlooked source of comorbidity is nonrandom mating among adults with particular developmental or psychiatric disorders. As a case in point, adults with ADHD may be more likely to mate with adults with learning disorders (Biederman, Newcorn, & Sprich, 1991), thereby creating a higher risk for both disorders in any offspring of that mating. These and other factors may help us to understand true comorbidity where it arises in clinical populations.

In clinic-referred samples, comorbidity may be more apparent than real. It can arise as an artifact of referral biases or self-selection factors operating in the flow of patients to a particular clinic or practitioner. Consider the gatekeeping policies of a large managed care or health maintenance organization (HMO) that refers out to psychiatrists or clinical psychologists only those patients with serious psychiatric problems. These specialists will therefore see patients who, simply by consequence of their serious impairment, are highly likely to manifest multiple mental disorders. Any pattern of co-occurrence among psychiatric disorders is more apt to reflect the gatekeeping practices of the HMO, not the footprint of true comorbidity.

Positive or negative self-selection processes can also operate to create pseudo-comorbidity in clinical samples. For example, clinicians who accept only cash-paying referrals will more likely develop a clientele of highly educated and affluent adults with ADHD. Studies based on this sample might conclude that adults with ADHD are more intelligent, entrepreneurial, creative, and successful than the average person. They might also find far less comorbidity than in studies of patients in public sector mental health settings.

## Externalizing Disorders

Children and adolescents diagnosed with ADHD have considerably higher frequencies of comorbid *oppositional defiant disorder* (ODD) and *conduct disorder* (CD) than would be due to chance alone (Angold et al., 1999). This appears also to be true for clinic-referred adults having ADHD. Approximately 24–35% of clinic-referred adults diagnosed with ADHD have ODD, and 17–25% qualify for CD, either currently or over the course of their earlier development (Barkley, Murphy, & Kwasnik, 1996a; Biederman et al., 1993; Murphy & Barkley, 1996b; Spencer, 1997). These figures are well below those reported in studies of ADHD children, particularly studies of hyperactive children, followed to adulthood. In these longitudinal studies, levels of ODD and CD may be double those reported for adults diagnosed with ADHD (Barkley, Fischer, Edelbrock, & Smallish, 1990; Weiss & Hechtman, 1993). Given that CD is frequently a precursor to *antisocial personality disorder*, it is not surprising that 7–18% of adults diagnosed with ADHD qualify for this diagnosis (Biederman et al., 1993; Shekim, Asarnow, Hess, Zaucha, & Wheeler, 1990). And even among those who do not qualify, many receive higher than normal ratings on those personality traits associated with this personality disorder (Tzelepis, Schubiner, & Warbasse, 1995).

Conduct disorder is a strong predictor of substance experimentation and, later, substance dependence and abuse disorders. It is therefore hardly surprising to learn that lifetime rates of alcohol dependence or abuse disorders range between 32% and 53% of adults diagnosed with ADHD. Eight to 32% may manifest some other form of substance dependence or abuse (Barkley et al., 1996a; Biederman et al., 1993; Murphy & Barkley, 1996b; Roy-Byrne et al., 1997; Shekim et al., 1990). Tzelepis et al. (1995) reported that 36% of their 114 adults with ADHD had experienced dependence on or abuse of alcohol, 21% for cannabis, 11% for cocaine or other stimulants, and 5% for polydrug dependence. At the point of their initial evaluation, 13% met criteria for alcohol dependence or abuse within the previous month.

## Affective Disorders

Twenty-four to 43% of clinic-referred adults are diagnosed with generalized anxiety disorder and 52% have a history of overanxious disorder (Barkley et al., 1996a; Biederman et al., 1993; Murphy & Barkley, 1996b; Shekim et al., 1990). These figures are distinctly higher than those found in children. This probably reflects referral bias, as has been found to be the case with clinic-referred children having ADHD (see Barkley, 1998). Studies of community samples of children show that ADHD has only a modest (albeit significant) comorbidity with anxiety disorders (odds ratio of about 1.3; Angold et al., 1999). Studies by Murphy and Barkley (1996b) and Roy-Byrne et al. (1997) found no higher degree of anxiety disorders among their adults with ADHD than occurred in a *clinical* control group of adults seen at the same clinic who were not diagnosed with ADHD, supporting the referral bias interpretation. Furthermore, prevalence of anxiety disorders among adults with ADHD who are relatives of clinically diagnosed ADHD children is relatively low—just 20% (Biederman et al., 1993). Follow-up studies of hyperactive children into adulthood have also failed to find a higher occurrence of anxiety disorders (see Barkley, 1998). Still, clinicians specializing in clinic-referred adults having ADHD must prepare themselves to contend with a relatively high frequency of comorbid anxiety disorders, even if largely the result of referral bias. This may complicate treatment planning, for anxiety has been found in some studies to predict poorer responses to stimulant medications (DuPaul, Barkley, & Connor, 1998), at least in children.

ADHD shows a significant affiliation with *major depression*. Between 16% and 31% of adults with ADHD experience major depression (Barkley et al., 1996a; Biederman et al., 1993; Murphy & Barkley, 1996b; Roy-Byrne et al., 1997; Tzelepis et al., 1995). *Dysthymia*, a milder form of depression, occurs in 19–37% of clinic-referred adults diagnosed with ADHD (Murphy & Barkley, 1996b; Roy-Byrne et al., 1997; Shekim et al., 1990; Tzelepis et al., 1995). A few studies comparing clinic-referred adults with ADHD seen at the same clinic without ADHD have not found a higher incidence of depression among the adults with ADHD (Murphy & Barkley, 1996b; Roy-Byrne et al., 1997). This finding, however, may stem from the fact that depression or dysthymia are often present in clinic-referred adults generally, and so would be higher than normal in these particular control groups.

Some clinical reports have found *obsessive-compulsive disorder* (OCD) to occur in 14% of adults clinically diagnosed with ADHD (Shekim et al., 1990). Others have not found this association. Tzelepis et al. (1995) reported only 4% of their adults met diagnostic criteria for (OCD). Roy-Byrne et al. (1997) likewise reported a 4.3–6.5% prevalence rate, which was not significantly different from their clinical control group. Spencer (1997) recently reported that OCD was somewhat elevated (12%) only among those adults with ADHD having a comorbid tic disorder. The figure for those adults without tics was approximately 2%. OCD therefore does not seem to be differentially associated with ADHD.

A recent study compared 105 young adults (age 18–28 years) clinically diagnosed with ADHD to a community control group ($N = 64$) similar in age and gender representation (Murphy, Barkley, & Bush, 2000). The pattern of comorbid disorders is shown in Table 3.1. As in other studies, this one

**TABLE 3.1 Comorbidity of Clinical Psychiatric Diagnoses (DSM-IV)**

| Clinical disorders | ADHD % | Control % | $\chi^2$ | $p <$ |
|---|---|---|---|---|
| Oppositional defiant | 36.2 | 0.0 | 29.88 | .001 |
| Conduct disorder | 4.8 | 0.0 | 3.14 | NS |
| Major depression | 12.4 | 3.1 | 4.21 | .04 |
| Dysthymia | 21.9 | 1.6 | 13.50 | .001 |
| Any anxiety disorder | 6.7 | 1.6 | 2.30 | NS |
| Antisocial personality | 4.8 | 0.0 | 3.14 | NS |
| Alcohol dep./abuse | 35.2 | 6.3 | 18.19 | .001 |
| Cannabis dep./abuse | 20.0 | 1.6 | 11.94 | .001 |
| Drug dep./abuse | 4.8 | 0.0 | 3.14 | NS |
| Learning disorders | 41.0 | 0.0 | 35.15 | .001 |

*Note*: ADHD = attention deficit hyperactivity disorder; % = the percentage of the group; $\chi^2$ = results for the chi-square analysis; $p$ = probability value for the chi-square if significant ($p < .05$); NS = not significant; dep./abuse = dependence or abuse disorders. Reprinted with permission from Murphy, K. R., Barkley, R. A., & Bush, T. (2000). Young adults with ADHD: Subtype differences in comorbidity, educational, and clinical history. Submitted for publication.

found a higher prevalence of ODD, depression, dysthymia, and substance dependence and abuse, especially for alcohol and marijuana. However, a higher incidence of CD, antisocial personality, and anxiety disorders was not evident in this sample. Such a finding might imply that the comorbidity for those disorders is more likely to occur in clinic-referred adults of older age ranges than that evaluated in this study.

To summarize, adults meeting diagnostic criteria for ADHD demonstrate significant levels of comorbidity for several other psychiatric disorders. Among these, dysthymia and depression may occur quite often (and possibly anxiety disorders). Oppositional defiant disorder (and perhaps CD) occurs among a substantial minority of adults diagnosed with ADHD. Most studies also suggest that antisocial personality disorder, and certainly antisocial activities, occur in a small but significant proportion of adults with ADHD. Less, yet still appreciable, is the level of substance dependence and abuse disorders, particularly for alcohol and marijuana, among clinic-referred adults having ADHD. All of this is to say that clinicians seeing adults with ADHD must be prepared to treat these comorbid disorders in conjunction with those treatments that may be needed for ADHD.

## COGNITIVE DEFICITS

An increasingly popular research focus concerns performance of adults with ADHD on various neuropsychological tests. Interest has been especially high in measures of executive functioning (EF), because these processes are centerpieces for some current theories (Barkley, 1997a) and models (Brown, 2000) of ADHD. However, researchers initially pursued studies of executive functioning based on the longstanding belief that ADHD interferes with prefrontal lobe functioning, which is typically evaluated using EF tasks. Although most of the studies have involved children, some have explored cognitive functioning in adults diagnosed with ADHD. As always, the results have shown general consistencies across development, but with some specific and important differences.

### Intelligence

Most studies have found that children with ADHD have IQ scores that average about 7–10 points lower than control children (see Barkley, 1998). The same pattern does not hold for studies of adults, most of which have found comparable scores across clinic and control groups (Barkley et al., 1996a; Murphy & Barkley, 1996b). Even when group differences have been detected, (Murphy, Barkley, & Bush, in press), mean scores for both groups are still in the normal range or better. For instance, Biederman et al. (1993) found that their adults diagnosed with ADHD had IQ scores significantly below their control groups. However, the mean IQ scores for the ADHD group were generally between 107 and 110. These results do not reflect low IQs in the ADHD group as they do the above-average intellectual functioning of the control groups (mean IQ scores were 110–113). Therefore, the conclusion holds that ADHD in adult populations is likely not associated with general intellectual impairment.

### Executive Functions

Neuropsychologists have expanded the term *executive functioning* to include a wide range of human abilities: inhibition, working memory, resistance to distraction, strategy development, planning and future-directed behavior, flexibility, problem solving, and organization (Lyon & Krasnegor, 1996). At its essence, executive functioning represents a form of social intelligence (Dimond, 1980) or attention to and action toward the future (Denckla, 1996). Barkley (1997a, 2000) has conceptualized the executive functions as those general classes of self-directed actions that humans employ in self-regulation toward the future. They are the actions humans take toward themselves, often covert, so as to modify their own behavior and thereby maximize future, over immediate, consequences. These actions include (1) response inhibition, (2) self-directed sensing (especially visual imagery and private audition), or nonverbal working memory, (3) self-directed speech (the internalization of language), or verbal working memory, (4) self-regulation of emotion/motivation, and (5) self-directed play (flexibility, fluency, and diversity), or reconstitution. Factor analyses of batteries of executive function tests, reviewed by Barkley (1997a), have generally identified factors consistent with this scheme: inhibition, interference control, verbal and nonverbal working memory, emotion regulation, persistence (sustained attention), and fluency.

A literature on the executive functioning of adults with ADHD is beginning to emerge, although it lags behind the far more abundant child literature. We review next those studies that address each major domain of executive functioning as it pertains to ADHD in adults.

## Inhibition, Inattention, and Interference Control

Continuous performance tests have been examined for signs of deficits in inhibition and sustained attention in adults with ADHD. Inattention is often reflected in impaired reaction time, reaction time variability, and omission errors, while impulsiveness may be reflected in commission errors. Studies of children with ADHD often find them to perform continuous performance tasks more poorly than control groups (see Corkum & Siegel, 1993, for a review). Barkley et al. (1996a) found their young adults with ADHD demonstrated more omission (inattention) and commission (impulsiveness) errors on the Conners continuous performance task (CPT) compared to the control group. So did two other studies using this task (Epstein, Conners, Erhardt, March & Swanson, 1997; Seidman, 1997) and studies using other forms of CPTs (Gansler et al., 1998). Roy-Byrne et al. (1997) compared adults diagnosed with ADHD (probable ADHD) to a group having current adult ADHD symptoms without persuasive childhood history (possible ADHD) and to a clinical control group using the Conners CPT. In contrast to the preceding studies, they found that those adults having possible ADHD were significantly poorer on a composite CPT score than the control group, with the probable-ADHD adult group falling between these two groups. Holdnack, Mobers, Arnold, Gur, and Gur (1995) also found poorer CPT performance in adults with ADHD, though in this instance it was on the measure of reaction time only and not omission or commission errors. A study by Kovner et al. (1997) likewise found reaction times on a test measuring the ability to shift response sets in a task to be slower in adults with ADHD ($n = 19$) compared to a control group ($n = 10$). Therefore, some evidence, albeit inconsistent, suggests that adults with ADHD have problems comparable to children with the disorder in the realms of response inhibition and sustained attention.

*Interference control* refers to the capacity to protect ongoing executive functioning, such as working memory, from interference by internal or external distracting events. The Stroop Color-Word Test is often used to assess this aspect of inhibition in children with ADHD; indeed problems with the interference part of the task are among the most reliable findings in children with the disorder (see Barkley, 1997a, for a review). Problems with interference control have been found on Stroop tasks in some studies of adults with ADHD (Lovejoy et al., 1999). Others, however, have not found this to be the case (Corbett & Stanczak, 1999). Differences among the studies in sample sizes, diagnostic criteria for ADHD, and test administration and scoring may account for these discrepancies.

## Working Memory

Matochik and colleagues (Matochik, Rumsey, Zametkin, Hamburger, & Cohen, 1996) compared 21 ADHD adults against the norms provided with the neuropsychological tests on a variety of EF measures, particularly those of verbal working memory. They found that performance of mental arithmetic and digit span on the WAIS-R intelligence test were significantly below normal, as is often the case in children with ADHD. Other studies (Barkley et al., 1996a; Jenkins et al., 1998; Kovner et al., 1997; Lovejoy et al., 1999) also found adults with ADHD to perform more poorly on digit span, auditory addition, and verbal learning tests. These particular tests have been interpreted as reflecting verbal working memory, all of which might imply difficulties with this EF in adults with ADHD. In contrast, tests of verbal learning and verbal memory have generally not been found to be impaired in adults with ADHD compared to control groups (Holdnack et al., 1995; Kovner et al., 1997).

### Flexibility/Fluency

The Wisconsin Card Sort Test (WCST) is frequently employed in neuropsychology to evaluate problem solving and flexibility of responding. Results of research on children with ADHD employing this task are often inconsistent and, in the minority of cases where deficits are evident, effect sizes are relatively small (Barkley, 1997a). Performance on this task was found by Barkley et al. (1996a) to be within the normal range in their ADHD young adults. Others also have not found performance on the WCST to discriminate groups of ADHD adults from control groups (Gansler et al., 1998; Holdnack et al., 1995; Jenkins et al., 1998; Seidman, 1997). Other tests of flexibility or fluency require subjects to generate as many different verbal responses as possible that fall within certain constraints. For instance, the F-A-S test requires participants to generate as many words that begin with each letter as they can within one minute for each letter. A few studies have found adults with ADHD to be impaired in verbal fluency (Jenkins et al., 1998; Lovejoy et al., 1999). Barkley et al. (1996a) compared a small sample of young adults with ADHD ($n = 25$) to a control group ($n = 23$) on measures of verbal fluency and conceptual fluency (object use) and did not find any differences. This inconsistency in findings could be due to low statistical power in the Barkley et al. study. However, discrepant findings across studies are also found in research on children with ADHD (Barkley, 1997a). More research on verbal fluency and conceptual creativity are in order before a more definitive picture of this cognitive domain of EF can be obtained in adults with ADHD.

Barkley et al. (1996a) found that adults with ADHD performed significantly worse on a nonverbal working memory task. On this commercially available toy called the Simon Game, the adult must imitate increasingly longer sequences of tone/color key presses. Other measures of nonverbal working memory have not been used with adults with ADHD, making this yet another area of cognitive functioning in need of greater research with this disorder.

### Response Organization

The Rey-Osterrieth Complex Figure Drawing has been used in neuropsychology to assess both planning and organization. One study used this measure with adults with ADHD and found them to be significantly impaired in accuracy, planning, and neatness as compared to control adults (Schreiber, Javorsky, Robinson, & Stern, 1999). As with other areas of EF research in adults with ADHD, efforts to replicate this finding are required before confidence in the results can be assured.

For the most part, neuropsychological studies of adults with ADHD have employed very small sample sizes, often well below the number necessary for adequate statistical power to detect small to moderate effect sizes (group differences). As a consequence, the failure to find group differences on some measures for which differences in the child ADHD literature have been found may simply be a result of low power. Clearly, future research on the cognitive deficits associated with ADHD in adults will need to employ more adequate sample sizes before a clearer picture of the cognitive impairments associated with the disorder can be obtained. Nevertheless, those group differences that have been observed have been relatively consistent with those EF deficits found in children and adolescents having ADHD.

For example, Murphy, Barkley, and Bush (2001) recently completed a study of the executive functioning of a large sample of young adults with ADHD ($N = 105$) in comparison to a community control group ($N = 64$). These results are presented in Table 3.2. Many of the EF deficits noted earlier were also found in this study. They essentially replicated the findings of earlier studies on EF in ADHD children and extended them to young adults with the disorder, providing evidence of validity of this disorder in the adult age range. Problems in five domains of EF were noted here in the young adults with ADHD, these being response inhibition, poor sustained attention, interference control, and two realms of working memory (verbal and nonverbal).

### Sense of Time

A theory of ADHD developed by Barkley (1997a) strongly suggests that the disorder may interfere with the sense of time, particularly the capacity to hold temporal intervals in mind so as

**TABLE 3.2  Unadjusted Group Means and Standard Deviations for the EF and Olfaction Measures**

| Measure | ADHD group N | Mean | SD | Control group N | Mean | SD | ANOVA F | p (p – IQ) |
|---|---|---|---|---|---|---|---|---|
| *Interference control* | | | | | | | | |
| Stroop interference % | 96 | 52.2 | 37.2 | 64 | 74.0 | 29.4 | 12.04 | .001 (.008) |
| Stroop number completed | 96 | 102.9 | 13.5 | 64 | 110.2 | 5.0 | 11.38 | .001 (.013) |
| Stroop number of errors | 96 | 1.1 | 1.6 | 64 | 0.8 | 1.3 | 0.29 | NS (NS) |
| *Inattention* | | | | | | | | |
| CPT variability of RT | 105 | 13.6 | 11.4 | 64 | 7.5 | 4.9 | 16.21 | .001 (.002) |
| CPT omission errors | 105 | 4.8 | 7.9 | 64 | 1.8 | 3.0 | 6.28 | .13 (NS) |
| WAIS III digit symbol | 101 | 56.6 | 12.0 | 63 | 64.2 | 10.9 | 12.73 | .001 (.015) |
| *Response inhibition* | | | | | | | | |
| CPT hit reaction time | 105 | 399.5 | 267.9 | 64 | 355.1 | 78.6 | 0.74 | NS (NS) |
| CPT commission errors | 105 | 14.0 | 8.1 | 64 | 10.8 | 6.8 | 8.61 | .004 (.007) |
| *Verbal working memory* | | | | | | | | |
| WAIS III digit span | 104 | 16.5 | 3.9 | 64 | 18.0 | 3.7 | 5.25 | .023 (NS) |
| *Nonverbal working memory* | | | | | | | | |
| Simon: longest sequence | 104 | 9.8 | 2.8 | 64 | 11.1 | 3.4 | 10.12 | .002 (.045) |
| *Verbal/ideational fluency* | | | | | | | | |
| COWAT F-A-S Test | 104 | 36.2 | 13.0 | 64 | 40.5 | 8.6 | 10.07 | .002 (NS) |
| Object usage | 105 | 16.9 | 7.2 | 64 | 17.1 | 5.2 | .003 | NS (NS) |
| *Smell identification* | | | | | | | | |
| Smell test error score | 96 | 3.2 | 2.4 | 57 | 2.2 | 1.9 | 5.46 | .021 (NS) |
| Smell test percentile | 96 | 56.7 | 28.4 | 57 | 67.6 | 26.8 | 5.94 | .016 (NS) |

*Note*: ADHD = attention deficit hyperactivity disorder; ANOVA = results for the univariate analyses of variance; $F$ = results of $F$-test; $p$ = statistical probability for the $F$-test if significant (<.05); ($p$ = IQ) = statistical probability for the univariate analyses of covariance using IQ as a covariate if significant (<.05); SD = standard deviation; WAIS = Wecshler Adult Intelligence Scale (3rd ed.); CPT = Continuous Performance Test; RT = reaction time; COWAT = Controlled Oral Word Association Test. Reprinted with permission from Murphy, K. R., Barkley, R. A., & Bush, T. (2001). EFs and olfactory identification in young adults with attention deficit hyperactivity disorder. *Neuropsychology, 15,* 211–220.

to use them to guide behavior. This theory (Barkley, 1997a) stipulates that the psychological sense of time arises chiefly out of nonverbal working memory, though it may be further enhanced by self-speech (as in counting to oneself). *Working memory* (verbal and nonverbal) has been defined as the capacity to hold events actively in mind so as to guide subsequent behavior. This type of memory has been thought to be important for attending to temporal durations that are critical to the timing and timeliness of future directed behavior (Fuster, 1997). Of relevance to ADHD is that working memory and the temporal attention it permits require protection from outside interference by distracting events and so depend on response inhibition, or interference control, to provide that protection (Fuster, 1997). Temporal intervals that are longer than one second and are being used to guide behavior appear to be mentally represented in the dorsolateral prefrontal cortical regions and their interconnections to the basal ganglia (Harrington, Haaland, & Hermanowicz, 1998; Rao et al., 1997; Rubia et al., 1998). In contrast, response timing that may involve intervals of less than one second may be mediated more by the basal ganglia and cerebellum (Mangels, Ivry, & Shimizu, 1998). As applied to ADHD, the theory predicts that the disorder should be associated with deficits in the sense of time because of the disruption that the problem with interference control (inhibition) produces in using working memory to attend to time.

Barkley, Murphy, and Bush (2001) examined time estimation and reproduction abilities in young adults with ADHD and a control group. The participants were presented with six different temporal durations. In one version of the task, they simply had to verbally report the duration of the interval. No group differences were evident on that task. But in the time reproduction task, the adults with ADHD made significantly more errors than the control group on several of the longer time durations. The results, graphically depicted in Figure 3.1, replicate several previous studies of children

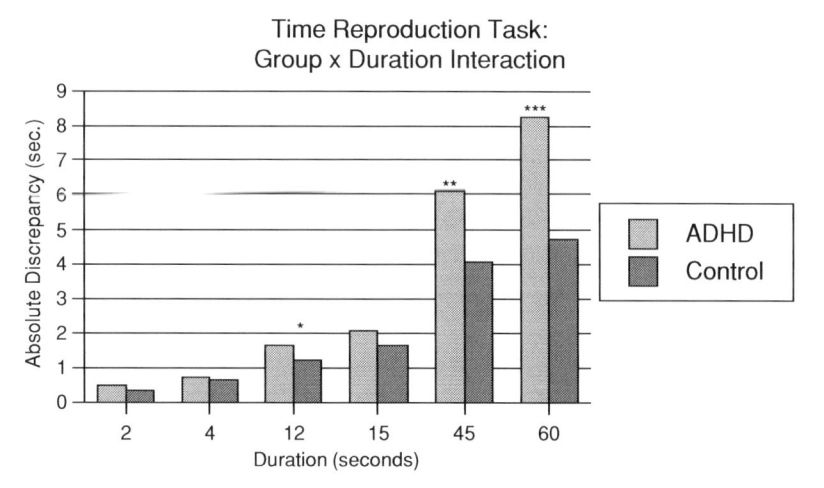

**Figure 3.1** The mean absolute discrepancy scores for each group at each of the sample durations (averaged across two trials). Absolute discrepancy scores reflect the difference between the participant's time reproduction and the sample duration presented expressed as an absolute value. *$p < .05$, **$p < .01$, ***$p < .001$. Reprinted with permission from Barkley, R. A., Murphy, K. R., & Bush, T. (2001). Sense of time in young adults with attention deficit hyperactivity disorder (ADHD). Submitted for publication. *Neuropsychology, 15,* 351–360.

with ADHD (Barkley, 1998). These findings indicate that ADHD interferes with the ability to hold a temporal duration in mind so as to then reproduce the interval. This implies that it is the capacity to use a temporal duration in the guidance of behavior that is most likely the source of the timing deficits evident in those with ADHD. The sense of time is exceptionally important in adult adaptive functioning, given that time deadlines are ubiquitous in adult life. Perhaps these results explain the oft-heard complaint of adults with ADHD that they have a terrible sense of time and are often late for deadlines and other time commitments.

**Emotional Self-Regulation**

The classification of executive functions noted earlier also implies that difficulties with emotional self-control should be evident in adults with ADHD. This is not an area that has been well investigated. Some suggestive evidence that this deficiency exists in adults with ADHD comes from a study by Ramirez and colleagues (1997), who compared college students self-reporting high levels of ADHD symptoms with those who did not. Measures of state and trait anger, inappropriate methods of expressing anger in social contexts, and interpersonal relations were examined. The high-ADHD-symptom group differed significantly from the control group in having higher levels of state and trait anger, more dysfunctional and inappropriate ways of showing anger, and more labile moods of anxiety/depression. They did not report themselves to express emotions with greater intensity or to be more emotionally responsive to external consequences—a finding replicated by Braaten and Rosen (1997) with other college students similarly defined. Yet the parents of participants in the Ramirez et al. study reported their ADHD-like students to have higher levels of anger and poorer methods of expressing it than the parents of control students. This might suggest that young adults with ADHD may underreport the level of their own emotional intensity relative to how others see them. In any case, it would be of great interest to determine if these results could be replicated on clinic-referred samples of adults with ADHD.

**Sense of Smell**

One neuropsychological domain that has been relatively unstudied in children and adults with ADHD is olfactory functioning. Though not an executive function, olfactory identification is mediated by structures within the prefrontal region of the brain nearby those thought to mediate EF. Specifically, olfaction is mediated via the olfactory nerve that courses through the ventral aspects of the prefrontal cortex to the entorhinal cortex. Patients with damage to the prefrontal lobes often experience a diminution either in their olfactory sensitivity or in their capacity to accurately identify common odors (Eslinger, Damasio, & Van Hoesen, 1982; Hamilton, Murphy, & Paulsen, 1999). Substantial neuropsychological research suggests that the prefrontal cortex may be involved in ADHD (see Barkley, 1997a, for a review; also see Seidman et al., 1996). Neuroimaging studies also have shown the prefrontal regions to be significantly smaller and less active in children with the disorder (Castellanos et al., 1997; Filipek et al., 1997; Rubia et al., 1998).

These findings imply that ADHD might be associated with deficits in olfactory identification. The study by Murphy et al. (2001), therefore, included a smell identification test as a means of testing the hypothesis that ADHD may be associated with diminished smell identification. The results confirmed the hypothesis. Nevertheless, the essence of science is replication and the ruling out of alternative explanations for the results. This necessitates that others attempt to replicate these results with adults having ADHD and exclude any competing reasons for these findings. It is possible, for example, that adults with ADHD smoke tobacco more than the normal population, a difference that could adversely affect smell identification.

If this finding of impaired olfaction in adults with ADHD is replicated, it would raise several questions. Is the problem here one of primary olfactory sensitivity or one of being able to label accurately the sensory information being perceived? And to what extent would treatment with stimulant medication reverse either of these impairments?

### Excluding Comorbidity as the Explanation for Deficient Executive Functioning

It is conceivable that the disorders often comorbid with ADHD have some adverse impact on cognitive functioning and so may contribute to or even explain the findings noted above on EF in adults with ADHD. To address this, efforts were taken in the analyses of the foregoing results of Murphy et al. (2001) to demonstrate that the findings were not a function of several comorbid disorders commonly seen in ADHD (ODD, CD, depression). This methodological approach lends greater confidence to the attribution of these EF deficits to ADHD.

## DOMAINS OF ADAPTIVE FUNCTIONING EXAMINED IN ADULTS WITH ADHD

### Self-Care

Little or no research exists on the extent to which adults with ADHD adequately care for their physical and mental health. As yet, researchers have not studied their medical status, physical conditioning, health consciousness, nutrition, hygiene, and efforts at disease prevention. One aspect of self-care that has been explored involves the extent to which adults manage their use of legal psychoactive substances, such as alcohol. An indication that adults with ADHD may have problems with this area of personal care comes from the earlier findings that these adults are more likely to qualify for substance dependence and abuse disorders. Corroborating these clinical diagnoses are the reports of adults with ADHD that they consume more alcoholic drinks per week than do others, that they have gotten drunk more often than others, and that they have been told by others that they drink too much (Barkley, Murphy, DuPaul, & Bush, in press). Similar results are obtained when these adults are questioned about their use of illegal drugs as well. In their study of young adults with ADHD, Murphy, Barkley, and Bush (2001) found that only 11% of the ADHD group felt they were alcoholic (compared to 3% of the control group). However, 29% of the ADHD group had been told by others that they drank too much, compared to just 2% of the control group, and 10% of the ADHD group had been treated for alcohol problems, in comparison to 2% of the control groups. Similar results were obtained for illegal drug use, where 25% of the ADHD group had been told by others that they used drugs excessively (vs. 3% of controls) and 11% had been treated for drug use problems (vs. none of the controls).

It has already been shown that adults with ADHD use alcohol and illegal drugs more than is normal or prudent for health maintenance. If it can also be demonstrated that they smoke tobacco to excess and/or exhibit poorer nutrition, a compelling case could be made that the disorder predisposes these adults to a greater risk of cardiovascular disease and possibly reduced life expectancy.

### Educational Functioning

Adults diagnosed with ADHD are likely to have (or have had) problems in academic functioning sometime during their life course. Approximately 16–40% of clinic-referred adults have repeated a grade (Barkley et al., 1996a; Biederman et al., 1993; Murphy & Barkley, 1996b). Up to 43% have also received some form of extra tutoring services in their academic histories to assist them with their schooling (Biederman et al., 1993). Barkley et al. (1996a) found that 28% of their young adult sample had received special educational services, a figure about half that found in hyperactive children followed to young adulthood, but still higher than normal. Similarly, Roy-Byrne et al. (1997) also found significantly greater frequencies of achievement difficulties in school, grade retentions, and special educational services in adults with ADHD.

The Milwaukee follow-up study of Barkley et al. (1990) has documented substantial difficulties in educational adjustment and attainment in hyperactive children followed to adulthood, as have other follow-up studies (Mannuzza, Gittelman-Klein, Bessler, Malloy, & LaPadula, 1993). For instance, follow-up studies find that 25–35% of these children are retained in grade at least once prior to completion of schooling. At least 60% are suspended from school at least once for disciplinary problems, in comparison to just 18% of a community control group. The rate of frank school expulsion is more than 2.5 times that for control children (14% vs. 5%).

The most troubling finding is that more than four times as many ADHD youth fail to complete a high school education compared to normal teens (37% vs. 9%). The economic impact of this high failure rate alone on the life course and potential economic earnings of individuals with ADHD is staggering. Among those youth with ADHD who do complete high school, their class rankings are significantly below normal (lowest 30th percentile vs. 50th percentile), and their grade point average in high school is a D+ to C− (1.7 vs. 2.6) vs. C+ to B− for normal teens. In the Milwaukee study, only 20% of the ADHD group attempted a college program of any sort, and just 5% (to date) have completed a college degree, compared to 40% or more of normal teens entering college and 35% eventually completing some form of college degree. All of this documents that growing up with ADHD (or hyperactivity) takes a tremendous toll on educational functioning and final educational attainment, the long-term occupational and economic impact of which is enormous. Yet this also supports the point made earlier that subjects participating in follow-up studies may have greater impairment than adults self-referring themselves in adulthood for clinical services, where levels of these various educational outcomes are considerably better.

A history of behavior problems and school suspensions are also significantly more common in clinic-referred adults with ADHD than in clinical control groups (Murphy & Barkley, 1996b). Yet young adults with ADHD seen in clinics are far more likely to have graduated high school (92%) and to have attended college (68%) than are clinic-referred children with ADHD followed to adulthood. In the latter group, the high school graduation rate is only about 64% (Barkley, 1998). Some studies indicate that clinic-referred adults with ADHD may have less education than non-ADHD adults seen at the same clinic or than community control adults (Murphy, Barkley, & Bush, 2001; Roy-Byrne et al., 1997), a finding consistent with adult follow-up studies of ADHD children (Mannuzza et al., 1993). A smaller study, in contrast, did not find this to be the case (Murphy & Barkley, 1996b), perhaps because of low statistical power.

Concerning actual academic achievement skills, adults diagnosed with ADHD perform significantly more poorly on tests of math than control groups (Biederman et al., 1993). Only those adults with ADHD who were relatives of ADHD children were found to be significantly lower on tests of reading in this study. Others have also found clinic-referred adults with ADHD to perform more poorly on reading achievement tests than control groups from the same clinic (Roy-Byrne et al., 1997). Yet the mean scores on both achievement tests in these studies were still within the normal range for these adults with ADHD. Still, these findings are in keeping with studies of children with ADHD, where they are almost routinely found to be below normal in their academic achievement skills (Barkley, 1998). The prevalence of learning disabilities in adults diagnosed with ADHD is well below that found in ADHD children, ranging from 0% to 12% in most studies

(Barkley, Murphy, and Kwasnik, 1996b; Biederman et al., 1993; Matochik et al., 1996).

To summarize, clinically diagnosed adults with ADHD show some of the same types of academic difficulties in their histories as do hyperactive or children with ADHD followed over development, albeit to a milder degree. However, the intellectual levels of clinic-referred adults, as noted earlier, are higher and their likelihood of having academic difficulties is considerably less in most respects than that level seen in children with ADHD followed up to adulthood. This higher level of academic functioning in clinic-referred adults with ADHD makes sense given that they are self-referred to clinics in comparison to children with ADHD. This fact makes it much more likely that these adults have employment, health insurance, a sufficient educational level to be so employed and insured, as well as a sufficient level of intellect and self-awareness to perceive themselves as being in need of assistance for their psychiatric problems. Children with ADHD brought to clinics by their parents are less likely to have these attributes by the time they reach adulthood. They are not as educated, are having considerable problems sustaining employment, are more likely to have had a history of aggression and antisocial activities, and do not seem to be as self-aware of their symptoms as adults having ADHD who are self-referred to clinics (Barkley, 1998).

## Interpersonal Functioning

No studies have examined the interpersonal relationships of clinic-referred adults with ADHD in comparison to control groups. Follow-up studies of hyperactive children in adulthood, however, indicate that interpersonal relationships are problematic and that these formerly hyperactive children have significantly poorer social skills (Weiss & Hechtman, 1993). Only two studies have examined marital functioning in clinic-referred adults having ADHD, and these have been relatively crude in their evaluation of this domain. Murphy and Barkley (1996b) evaluated 172 adults with the disorder and found them to be more likely to have divorced and remarried than control adults. The adults with ADHD also tended to report less marital satisfaction in their current marriages ($p < .08$). Biederman et al. (1993) also found a separation/divorce rate in adults with ADHD approximately twice that found in a control group. These studies suggest that marital functioning is problematic for a significant subset of adults with ADHD and warrants more detailed examination as to the specific difficulties giving rise to this higher level of separation/divorce.

As for general interpersonal functioning, a study of 105 young adults with ADHD (Murphy, Barkley, & Bush, 2000) found them to report significantly higher scores on the interpersonal sensitivity and hostility dimensions of the Symptom Checklist 90—Revised rating scale than did a sample of community control adults. As noted earlier, some research suggests that young adults with high levels of ADHD symptoms may have difficulties with emotional self-regulation, particularly in the management of anger and hostility (Ramirez et al., 1997). Those results were corroborated through parent reports about these same students. Not surprisingly then, Ramirez et al. also found these college students with high levels of ADHD symptoms reported more interpersonal problems than a control group. More research is obviously needed on the specific problems that adults with ADHD may have in emotional self-management and interpersonal functioning.

## Occupational Functioning

Studies of the adult outcomes of hyperactive children (Mannuzza et al., 1993; Weiss & Hechtman, 1993) indicated significantly greater problems in the workplace, significantly lower occupational status, and a greater probability of being self-employed by their 30s than was evident in control groups. Less is known about the occupational functioning of clinic-referred adults with ADHD. In the Murphy and Barkley (1996a) study, adults with ADHD reported having been fired more often from their places of employment than had control adults (53% vs. 31%). The adults with ADHD were also more likely to have impulsively quit a job (48% vs. 16%) and to report having chronic employment difficulties (77% vs. 57%) than had adults in a clinical control group. The ADHD adults also had changed jobs significantly more often than the control group during the same period of time (6.9% vs. 4.6%). Again, as with the interpersonal status of adults with ADHD, the domain of occupational functioning deserves greater research attention than it has received to date. Even so, what little is available suggests that problems in the workplace occur more often in adults with the disorder and may be a substantial reason for their seeking clinical services.

## Motor Vehicle Operation

One area of adaptive functioning that has begun to receive greater research attention is that of motor vehicle driving in teens and adults with ADHD. Clinic-referred teens with ADHD followed over a 3-to 5-year period have been found to have a significantly higher risk for accidents, citations (especially speeding), and license revocations and suspensions than control teens followed over this same period of time (Barkley, Guevremont, Anastopoulos, DuPaul, & Shelton, 1993). They have also been rated by their parents as using less sound driving practices than control adults. More recently, these findings were replicated and extended to young adults with ADHD. In their driving of a motor vehicle, adults with ADHD were more likely to have received speeding tickets, to have received more of them, and to have had more motor vehicle accidents (Barkley, Murphy, & Kwasnik, 1996b; Murphy & Barkley, 1996a). These findings have been replicated in several other studies (Cox, Merkel, Kovatchev, & Seward, 2000; Nada-Raja et al., 1997; Woodward, Fergusson, & Horwood, 2000). A consistent observation has been that adults with ADHD are more likely to have had their licenses suspended or revoked than those in the control groups (24–32% vs. 4%).

A more thorough study of driving risks and behavior was undertaken by Barkley et al., (1996b). They found that young adults with ADHD were more likely to have been involved in crashes that resulted in bodily injuries. They also were rated by themselves and by others as demonstrating significantly less sound driving practices during driving than the control group. The official driving records of these participants corroborated many of these findings. Adults with ADHD had more driving violations on their official records, including speeding tickets, were indeed more likely to have had their licenses suspended or revoked (48% vs. 9%), and to experience such suspensions more often (mean of 1.5 vs. 0.1 episodes). The problems with driving in these young adults could not be attributed to poor driving knowledge, because no differences between the groups were found on an extensive assessment of such knowledge. However, these young adults, when tested on a computer driving simulator, displayed more erratic steering of the vehicle and had more scrapes and crashes while operating this simulated vehicle than did subjects in the control group.

The most thorough assessment of driving performance to date comes from a recently completed study by Barkley, Murphy, DuPaul, and Bush (in press). This project evaluated multiple levels of driving performance and adverse outcomes in a large sample ($N = 105$) of young adults with ADHD in comparison to a community control group. These levels included basic cognitive functions necessary for driving, driving knowledge and rapid decision making, driving performance (on a simulator), actual driving behavior (self- and other ratings), and history of adverse driving events (self- and DMV reports). Findings similar to those presented earlier concerning adverse outcomes (accidents, citations, speeding, etc.) were obtained in this study. These are set forth in Tables 3.3 and 3.4. Furthermore, this study showed that the young adults with ADHD had difficulties in basic cognitive abilities that are a prerequisite for safe driving (motor coordination, reaction time, motor inhibition, sustained attention). In their decision making during high-risk driving situations, the ADHD group also demonstrated significantly poorer performances, evaluated using a videotaped test of multiple high-risk driving scenarios.

Unlike many other domains of adaptive functioning, there is sufficient research available now to unequivocally indicate that ADHD poses substantial driving risks in young adults. These adults are impaired across multiple levels of driving performance relative to control adults. Important now is to investigate the degree to which medications, and other treatment approaches, may be able to reduce these significant problems with driving performance.

## Sexual Behavior

We were unable to identify research that examined the sexual functioning of clinic-referred adults with ADHD. Fortunately, some follow-up studies of hyperactive children in adulthood have evaluated aspects of sexual activity. In the Canadian longitudinal study (Weiss & Hechtman, 1993), sexual adjustment problems were reported by as many as 20% of the ADHD group in adulthood

TABLE 3.3  Negative Driving Outcomes (Categorical Answers) from the Driving History Interview and the Official DMV Driving Record

| Measure | ADHD group N | ADHD group % Yes | Control group N | Control group % Yes | $\chi^2$ | p |
|---|---|---|---|---|---|---|
| **Self-reported history:** | | | | | | |
| Drove illegally before licensed to do so | 105 | 63.8 | 64 | 40.6 | 8.63 | .003 |
| Ever ticketed for traffic violations | 105 | 83.8 | 64 | 68.8 | 5.27 | .021 |
| Ever had parking ticket | 105 | 47.6 | 64 | 39.1 | 1.18 | NS |
| License suspended or revoked | 105 | 21.9 | 64 | 4.7 | 9.05 | .002 |
| Had a vehicular crash as driver | 105 | 72.4 | 64 | 67.2 | 0.51 | NS |
| Ever received a speeding ticket | 105 | 79.0 | 64 | 64.1 | 4.57 | .032 |
| Ever ticketed for reckless driving | 105 | 9.5 | 64 | 0.0 | 6.48 | .010 |
| Ever ticketed for driving while drunk | 105 | 4.8 | 64 | 0.0 | 3.14 | NS |
| **Official DMV record:** | | | | | | |
| Ever ticketed for traffic violations | 105 | 80.0 | 64 | 60.9 | 7.29 | .007 |
| Licensed suspended or revoked | 105 | 35.2 | 64 | 20.3 | 4.25 | .039 |
| Had a vehicular crash as driver | 105 | 41.0 | 64 | 29.7 | 2.17 | NS |
| Ever received a speeding ticket | 105 | 63.8 | 64 | 50.0 | 3.13 | NS |
| Ever ticketed for reckless driving | 105 | 1.9 | 64 | 0.0 | 1.23 | NS |
| Ever ticketed for driving while drunk | 105 | 5.7 | 64 | 1.6 | 1.73 | NS |

*Note*: ADHD = attention deficit hyperactivity disorder; $N$ = total sample size per group used in the analysis; % Yes = percentage of each group responding affirmatively to this question; $\chi^2$ = results of the chi-square; $p$ = probability value for the chi-square if significant ($p \leq .05$); DMV = Department of Motor Vehicles. Reprinted with permission from Barkley, R. A., Murphy, K. R., DuPaul, G., & Bush, T. (in press). Driving knowledge, competence, and related cognitive abilities in teens and young adults with attention deficit hyperactivity disorder. *Journal of the International Neuropsychological* Society.

TABLE 3.4  Group Means and Standard Deviations for the Dimensional Scores from the Driving History Interview, Official DMV Driving Record, and Driving Performance Rating Scales

| Measure | ADHD group N | Mean | SD | Control group N | Mean | SD | t | P < |
|---|---|---|---|---|---|---|---|---|
| **Self-reported history:** | | | | | | | | |
| Total tickets for traffic violations | 88 | 11.7 | 20.6 | 44 | 4.8 | 3.2 | 3.07 | .003[a] |
| License suspensions or revocations | 105 | 0.5 | 1.26 | 64 | 0.1 | .21 | 3.57 | .001[a] |
| Vehicular crashes as driver | 105 | 1.9 | 2.4 | 64 | 1.2 | 1.1 | 2.55 | .012[a] |
| If so, at faults in vehicular crashes | 75 | 1.3 | 1.2 | 43 | 0.9 | 0.8 | 2.43 | .017[a] |
| Damage caused in 1st crash ($) | 105 | 3055.3 | 7095.8 | 64 | 1119.1 | 1983.8 | 2.63 | .010[a] |
| Speeding ticket | 88 | 3.9 | 5.2 | 44 | 2.4 | 1.5 | 2.55 | .012 |
| Tickets for reckless driving | 88 | 0.2 | 0.6 | 44 | 0.0 | 0.0 | 2.75 | .007[a] |
| Tickets for driving while drunk | 88 | 0.7 | 0.3 | 44 | 0.0 | 0.0 | 2.16 | .033 |
| Parking tickets | 88 | 6.3 | 16.8 | 44 | 1.8 | 2.3 | 2.46 | .016[a] |
| **Official DMV records:** | | | | | | | | |
| Tickets for traffic violations | 105 | 5.1 | 8.4 | 63 | 2.1 | 2.4 | 3.45 | .001[a] |
| License suspensions or revocations | 105 | 1.1 | 2.2 | 63 | 0.3 | 0.7 | 3.34 | .001[a] |
| Vehicular crashes as driver | 105 | 0.6 | 0.8 | 63 | 0.4 | 0.7 | 1.33 | NS |
| Speeding ticket | 105 | 1.6 | 2.0 | 63 | 1.0 | 1.2 | 2.46 | .015 |
| Tickets for reckless driving | 105 | 0.1 | 0.2 | 63 | 0.0 | 0.0 | 1.35 | NS |
| Tickets for driving while drunk | 105 | 0.1 | 0.4 | 63 | 0.1 | 0.1 | 1.28 | NS |
| **Driver performance scale:** | | | | | | | | |
| Self-ratings of performance | 105 | 50.5 | 5.6 | 63 | 55.2 | 3.7 | −6.51 | .001[a] |
| Other ratings of performance | 96 | 48.7 | 6.7 | 63 | 53.0 | 5.3 | −4.47 | .001[a] |

*Note*: ADHD = attention deficit hyperactivity disorder; all results reported are for *t*-tests except for five measures, the analyses of which employed analysis of covariance. T = Results for the *t*-test; p = statistical probability for the *t*-test if significant (<.05); SD = standard deviation; DMV = Department of Motor Vehicles. [a]Indicates that this group difference remained significant after statistically controlling for a group difference in IQ score. Reprinted with permission from Barkley, R. A., Murphy, K. R., DuPaul, G., & Bush, T. (in press). Driving knowledge, competnece, and related cognitive abilities in teens and young adults with attention deficit hyperactivity disorder. *Journal of the International Neuropsychological Society*.

(versus 2.4% for the control group). However, the authors did not specify the nature of these adjustment problems. In the ongoing Milwaukee follow-up study, participants were questioned in late adolescence and early adulthood (mean age 20 years) about their sexual activities. Preliminary results indicated that the hyperactive group began having sexual intercourse at an earlier age than the control group (15 vs. 16 years.) and had more sexual partners in their lives (19 vs. 7). The hyperactive young adults were less likely to use contraception. Not surprisingly, these young adults were more likely to have conceived a teenage pregnancy (38% vs. 4%), and were more likely to have contracted a sexually transmitted disease (17% vs. 4%). While many more in the hyperactive group had been tested for AIDS/HIV (54% vs. 21%), none had tested positive. Compared to the control participants, the hyperactive subjects in the Milwaukee study were no more likely to experience sexual dysfunction (impotence, painful intercourse, failures to achieve orgasm, etc.).

These findings indicate a relatively high-risk sexual lifestyle among the formerly hyperactive children on reaching late adolescence and young adulthood. Given that the pattern of findings from follow-up studies in other domains of functioning have largely been replicated in clinic-referred adults, though to a lesser extent, the findings reported here for sexual activity intimate that similar problems may occur among adults clinically diagnosed with ADHD. If replicated, they would certainly suggest the need for some preventive sexual counseling in the adolescent and young adult years of individuals having ADHD.

## Unstudied Domains

As we indicated at the outset of this section, many central aspects of daily functioning have not been studied. These include child rearing, the management of household responsibilities (cooking, cleaning, shopping, etc.), time management more generally, and financial management. And certainly far more needs to be done in the domains of marital and interpersonal functioning and sexual behavior, given the strong suggestion in follow-up studies that these domains are likely to be affected by clinical levels of ADHD in adulthood. Efforts should also be made to study the specific impairments that may be occurring in employment settings for adults with ADHD as well, given the dearth of information available to date on this important domain of adult adaptive performance.

Our clarion call for research in the area of daily adaptive functioning reflects more than our particular need for empirical tidiness or completeness. Hard data concerning the impact of ADHD on managing routine tasks are absolutely central to solid identification and treatment. After all, if ADHD is anything, it is a disorder of routine task management. What characterizes people with ADHD is that they cannot handle the quotidian aspects of their lives as well as most others. Their impairments are therefore evident not just in challenging environments, but when they must cope with the commonplace. Indeed, someone moves from having ADHD-like characteristics to actually warranting a diagnosis when he (or she) fails at everyday life maintenance. If more information were to become available about these domains of daily adaptive functioning, it would allow the field to develop an understanding of ADHD that went beyond symptoms lists, to a full appreciation for the impact of those symptoms on functioning.

## CLINICAL IMPLICATIONS

Current research on ADHD in adulthood, while admittedly limited, nonetheless has specific implications for clinical management of the disorder. Indeed, data of the sort we have reviewed form some of the key underpinnings for prudent diagnostic and treatment strategies. Because the general management of ADHD has been extensively covered elsewhere (see Murphy, 1998; Murphy & Gordon, 1998; Wilens, Spencer, & Biederman, 1998), we will not delve fully into that topic here. Instead, we will simply highlight some of the clinical issues we feel our research review has raised.

**ADHD is associated with global impairment in functioning.** The research we have cited paints a picture of ADHD that leaves little doubt about its harmful effects on adjustment. In every major realm of functioning, individuals with this disorder show demonstrable limitations. It is a testament to the disorder's impact that it affects such a wide swath of human activity at all developmental levels (see Spencer, Biederman, Wilens, & Faraone, 1994). These data therefore cast serious doubt on the skeptic's view of ADHD as somehow inconsequential or trivial. The extant scientific literature provides entirely too much evidence of global impairment to justify a dismissive attitude toward this problem. In essence, the ability to attend and exert self-control is fundamental to healthy adjustment. When individuals fall at the extreme, abnormal end of the continuum for these traits, they will inevitably struggle in most life circumstances as compared to other people. The reader should keep in mind, however, that the research also speaks against a romanticized construal of ADHD as somehow advantageous or adaptive. We cannot find one research study that suggests a benefit associated with having this disorder (see Barkley, 1998, for further discussion). While individuals with ADHD are not irrevocably destined for gross maladjustment, they are a uniquely vulnerable group. In fact, the evidence for global impairment is so strong that it brings into serious question the notion that someone can be ADHD just in narrow slices of functioning. For example, some clinicians have told us that otherwise high functioning patients met criteria for ADHD because of narrow limitations in circumscribed aspects of test taking or job performance. Judging from the data we have reviewed (especially involving individuals identified during childhood), ADHD is unlikely to make surgical strikes in narrowly focused domains of a person's adjustment. The far higher probability is that the disorder will launch a general assault on an individual's coping abilities.

**The impairments associated with ADHD extend beyond inattention and impulsiveness.** The concept of executive functioning provides a model for understanding the broad impact of ADHD-type symptoms on adjustment. While ADHD individuals will inevitably manifest problems of poor self-control and distractibility, they will also demonstrate other, associated neuropsychological deficits that have significant deleterious effects. Among the most important are problems with nonverbal and verbal working memory. In essence, working memory is a form of attention to the future. Virtually all domains of major life activities require planning, forethought, and otherwise remembering what needs doing and when it needs to be done. It is not so much that adults with ADHD do not know what to do. *It is that they cannot do what they know when it would have been important to remember to do so.* Given that working memory is essential to a sense of time, timing, and timeliness of behavior toward the future, ADHD may be creating a form of time blindness or future myopia. The data on EF also have implications for treatment: Teaching skills, conveying information, or giving insight into the nature of one's problems would not be a sufficient treatment approach for ADHD. What individuals with ADHD need most are accommodations in the natural settings at key points of performance. The object of treatment is therefore to help them show what they know where and when it is most effective for them to do so.

**While clinicians should understand the role of executive functioning in ADHD, they should not regard tests of executive functioning as sensitive or specific to the disorder.** Major domains of daily adaptive functioning probably reflect the extent of the disorder and its degree of impairment better than will cursory, short-term observations in clinical settings or neuropsychological testing. Executive functioning, and especially working memory, involves the cross-temporal organization of behavior—the linking together of events, possible responses, and their likely consequences over large gaps in time among these various contingency arrangements. Current tests of executive functions are not up to the task of assessing these complex functions. Although the tip of this iceberg (impulsivity) might be gleaned from psychological testing, the adverse impact of ADHD on executive functioning and the cross-temporal organization of behavior are not so easily evaluated. Even though studies of groups of adults with ADHD may find differences between their means and those of a normal control group, those group differences do not establish those scores as diagnostic. For clinical diagnosis, the critical issue for the EF tests is their positive and negative predictive power. In studies examining the utility of neuropsychological tests for childhood ADHD, the power has generally been found to be too low to justify reliance on them for clinical diagnosis, especially if they are interpreted independent of real-life, clinical information (see Gordon & Barkley, 1998). In the adult literature, too few sophisticated studies of EF tests are available to even judge their diagnostic utility. Therefore, we suggest that clinicians focus far more on the extent to which the disorder is interfering with the management of daily responsibilities in major domains of adaptive functioning, since these domains: (a) are likely to reflect the major social purposes of executive functioning; (b) are a large part of the reason the adult with ADHD has sought clinical services; and (c) are critical to even determining whether or not a true disorder is present.

**Comorbidity is commonplace and requires attention during assessment and treatment planning.** Perhaps the most clinically meaningful finding of all those we presented in this chapter concerns the extent of comorbidity associated with ADHD. In at least 70% of cases, an individual with ADHD will have at least one other psychiatric disorder. Oppositional defiant disorder, conduct disorder, major depression, antisocial personality, and substance abuse disorders appear more often in adults with ADHD than would be expected from population prevalence estimates. The implications for management are significant because they establish a compelling rationale for designing a broad-based diagnostic protocol that explores issues beyond those associated with ADHD. If an evaluation focuses only on ADHD-related concerns, the chances are high that the clinician will miss other disorders, some of which may have even greater negative impact on functioning than ADHD. Our suggestion is that clinicians assume a high probability of comorbidity for any particular patient and plan both diagnosis and treatment accordingly (see Gordon, 1995). A comprehensive clinical picture will ensure that the individual with ADHD receives all the treatments required, not just those indicated for ADHD alone. In fact, some comorbid disorders may adversely influence the responding of these adults to standard ADHD therapies. As previously noted, high levels of anxiety have been found in some studies to be associated with poorer stimulant drug responding, at least in children with ADHD. This implies that clinicians seeing adults with ADHD be cognizant of this possibility. Further consideration of antianxiety or antidepressant medications may be in order for this comorbid subset of adults with ADHD.

**For treatment planning, adopt a chronic disability perspective.** For most individuals, ADHD will be a chronic, life-long disability that will require far more than brief evaluation and a short-term intervention. As with all chronic disabilities, clinicians will have to program for ongoing monitoring and reintervention if they expect to manage symptoms and preclude more serious secondary complications from emerging. A thriving practice specializing in ADHD in adults will quickly find itself filled with repeat clients who may need to be followed and treated periodically for years. The nature of this particular psychiatric beast ensures that clinicians and patients will settle into a long haul of ongoing assessment, monitoring, reconsideration of lifestyle choices and medication strategies, and effective problem solving.

**Occupational and educational accommodations are highly likely.** The studies we reviewed indicate that ADHD in adults interferes with educational functioning and eventual levels of educational attainment. Those older teens and young adults with bona fide ADHD who beat the odds and gain admission to college will inevitably require accommodations if they hope to manage inherently high demands for attention, persistence, and executive functioning (see Gordon & Keiser, 1999, for a discussion of these accommodations and the documentation that will necessitate). Medication may be of substantial benefit to the adult with ADHD in both college and occupational settings. Many cases, however, will require additional accommodations in view of the limited time course during which medications can be used each day and the fact that a sizable minority (20%) may not respond positively to these medications. Clinicians unaccustomed to advising clients on these accommodations and related issues must develop a network of professional colleagues who are more expert at doing so if they are to provide a more comprehensive treatment package for these young adults.

The same will be true for the management of problems in occupational functioning as well. Young adults may require advice and even occupational assessment to assist them with finding the most appropriate occupation and employment setting in view of their ADHD and comorbid disorders or cognitive deficits. Older adults frequently require assistance with personal and work organization, time management, and office interpersonal skills. Developing a regional network of specialists in occupational counseling or time management and personal/work organization would seem to be advisable for clinicians that frequently evaluate adults with ADHD.

**Problems with driving demand clinical intervention.** Driving is of major importance to most of the general adult population; indeed the capacity to maintain gainful employment may be predicated on this domain of functioning in many regions. It is also an area in which inhibition, resistance to distraction, reaction time, motor coordination, and the executive functions are exceptionally important. Deficiencies in these areas, commonly seen in adults with ADHD, can be life threatening to both those adults and to other drivers around them. The available research is more than adequate to demonstrate that ADHD interferes with many different levels of safe motor vehicle operation. The disorder predisposes to a significantly greater risk of adverse driving outcomes (accidents, citations, and license suspensions/revocations). Clinicians must review this domain of functioning with their clients having ADHD and, where appropriate, make necessary recommendations for either limiting driving privileges, increasing supervision of independent driving, or even placing the adult with ADHD on stimulant medication for the management of their driving risks. Although there is a relative absence of research on the effectiveness of stimulants for the management of driving performance problems, a small pilot study has demonstrated improved performance on a driving simulator in adults with ADHD (Daniel Cox, personal communication, February 2000). In view of this, the fact that stimulants are well known to improve inhibition, reaction time, motor control, and the potentially life-threatening consequences of not treating the adult driver having ADHD, all argue forcefully that serious consideration be given to providing stimulants during motor vehicle operation.

**Health considerations may be an issue.** Although the topic has been little studied, findings to date suggest that adults with ADHD may have more health, lifestyle, and even frank medical difficulties than the normal population. This would be evident simply from knowing that they use alcohol and illicit drugs (and probably tobacco) more often than does the normal population. Given the poor self-regulatory abilities indicated in the disorder, it is not difficult to imagine that these deficiencies could also adversely impact the individual's nutritional, exercise, hygiene, and other regimens that influence their health status. This entire area of adaptive functioning requires far more research before specific recommendations can be proffered on an empirical basis. Meanwhile, clinicians will certainly need to attend to the possibility that the adults seen in their clinical practice with the disorder may be in need of treatment for substance dependence and abuse as part of the treatment package. It is further suggested, though, that clinicians be aware of the larger realm of possible health-related difficulties that may arise in adults with ADHD and perhaps inquire about them as part of the initial evaluation.

**Marital counseling could be in order.** Admittedly, much more research needs to be conducted on the nature, degree, and specific domains of marital difficulties that arise in cohabiting with a partner that has ADHD. For now, all we know is that adults with ADHD are twice as likely to have marital separations or divorces and tend to report being less satisfied in their marriages than adults in various control groups. This is enough to suggest that clinicians may want to screen for these problems in the initial evaluation and be prepared to provide referrals to marital therapists in their geographic region for a significant minority of adults with this disorder.

**Counseling on sexual activities and contraception may be advisable.** Research is lacking on whether or not problems exist in the sexual practices or contraceptive use of clinic-referred adults with ADHD. As we indicated, however, longitudinal data raise concern for hyperactive children upon reaching adolescence and adulthood. Nearly 40% of these teens and young adults had been involved in a teen pregnancy—a 10-fold increase in such risk. And four times as many (16%) had already contracted a sexually transmitted disease. At a minimum, such findings should serve to encourage clinicians to discuss sexual behavior along with contraception and disease prevention measures with teens (and their parents) and young adults with ADHD.

**ADHD Predominantly Inattentive Type has garnered scant research attention and therefore remains somewhat of an unknown.** The reader may have noticed that we have reviewed few studies relevant to the adaptive functioning, comorbidity, and cognitive impairments associated with ADHD Predominantly Inattentive Type. The fact is that, despite the increasing popularity of this diagnosis in adult populations, precious little empirical data are available to draw any conclusions about the key aspects of management. Only the studies noted earlier by Barkley, Murphy, and Bush (2001) and Murphy et al, (2001) made any effort to examine for subtype differences among their adults with ADHD in driving, executive functioning, sense of time, and comorbidity. Surprisingly, few differences were evident, save comorbidity for antisocial outcomes.

These findings are quite inconsistent with the more abundant literature on ADHD subtypes in children. Those results indicate that individuals classified with the Predominantly Inattentive Type of ADHD, compared to subjects with Combined Type, are more likely to show symptoms of daydreaming, staring, passivity, hypoactivity, sluggish information processing, and difficulties with focused attention. (Barkley, 1998; Milich, Ballentine, & Lynam, 2001). Children with the Inattentive Type have far less comorbidity for ODD and CD and may be more passive in social interactions with peers (unlike children with Combined Type, who are generally more aggressive, intrusive, and hence rejected). Some research suggests that Inattentive ADHD may be less responsive to stimulant medications than the Combined Type, although this finding requires further replication.

This pattern of distinctive attributes for the Predominantly Inattentive Type has led some investigators to call for considering this type of ADHD as actually a separate disorder entirely, if more carefully defined (Barkley, 1998; Milich et al., 2001). Symptoms of daydreaming, sluggish cognitive tempo, lethargy, and hypoactivity would be prominent in their differential diagnosis relative to ADHD Combined Type.

Research on the inattentive variant of ADHD is especially difficult to evaluate in adolescents and adults because samples become progressively contaminated due to two factors. The first relates to the natural life history of the disorder: Some individuals who once qualified for the Combined Type diagnosis fall out of that category and into the Inattentive one because, as is so often the case, they are not as hyperactive as they were during childhood. Therefore, the ADHD Predominantly Inattentive Type subject pool can become tainted by Combined Type dropouts, i.e., people who are somewhat less physically overactive and impulsive than they once were but still have all the central clinical features and history of the Combined Type subgroup. Failure to distinguish these now-subthreshold Combined Types from the more distinctive Inattentive Types (who have sluggish cognitive tempos and were never clinically impulsive) will result in clinical and research confusion. It therefore does not surprise us that research to date has failed to detect differences between Inattentive and Combined Type subgroups.

The other factor that cannot help but muddy the diagnostic and empirical waters in this domain concerns failure to rule out other psychiatric disorders before settling on an ADHD Predominantly Inattentive designation. While early-appearing, chronic, and pervasive impulsive/hyperactive behavior usually falls within the province of ADHD, inattentive behavior is far more nonspecific. Unless the study involves a credible process by which other psychiatric disorders are ruled out, the resulting subject pool will inevitably contain individuals whose inattention stems from anxiety, depression, substance abuse, or schizophrenia or from any number of other psychiatric or learning conditions (see Gordon & Barkley, 1999, for a more complete discussion). Therefore, until more extensive and compelling research emerges about the Inattentive subtype of ADHD in adults, we counsel caution in overinterpreting the research literature and, indeed, in assigning this diagnosis. Further, we recommend that clinicians exploring this diagnosis for any particular client focus on the distinctive symptoms associated with the Inattentive Type ADHD, that is staring, daydreaming, mental fogginess, sluggish processing of information, social passivity, hypoactivity, and a dearth of impulsiveness. Other possible psychiatric and educational explanations must also be ruled out.

## CONCLUSION

In this chapter we reviewed empirical findings about the psychiatric comorbidity, cognitive deficits, and impaired domains of adaptive functioning in adults with ADHD. The results, though still relatively sparse, depict ADHD as a disorder that cuts a wide swath across the various domains of major life activities in which adults must demonstrate self-sufficiency. The literature highlights difficulties in educational, occupational, interpersonal, and marital functioning as well as specific deficits in motor vehicle operation. Follow-up studies of hyperactive children in adulthood have also indicated heightened risks for teen pregnancy and sexually transmitted disease. All of these findings suggest that managing the responsibilities of daily adult life can be challenging for adults with ADHD. Some of these impairment domains may well stem from the disorganization and time blindness associated with deficient executive functioning.

We reviewed a host of implications for the clinical assessment and management of adults with ADHD that flow logically from the empirical findings. However, recommendations based on this literature must remain relatively general, given the absence of research on the more specific or molecular aspects of the functional impairments that exist within each of these domains of major life activities. The exception is motor vehicle operation, which has been fairly thoroughly investigated. Nevertheless, clinicians must be cognizant of those various difficulties likely to be occurring in clinic-referred adults with ADHD so as to consider them in the formulation of effective treatments for the disorder, its comorbidities, and associated adaptive impairments.

## REFERENCES

American Psychiatric Association (1994). *Diagnostic and statistical manual of mental disorders—Fourth Edition (DS—IV)*. Washington, DC: American Psychiatric Press.

Angold, A., Costello, J., & Erkanli, A. (1999). Comorbidity. *Journal of Child Psychology and Psychiatry, 40*, 57–88.

Barkley, R. A. (1997a). *ADHD and the nature of self-control*. New York: Guilford Press.

Barkley, R. A. (1997b). Behavioral inhibition, sustained attention, and executive functions: Constructing a unifying theory of ADHD. *Psychological Bulletin, 121*, 65–94.

Barkley, R. A. (1998). *Attention deficit hyperactivity disorder: A handbook for diagnosis and treatment* (2nd ed.). New York: Guilford Press.

Barkley, R. A. (2000). Genetics of childhood disorders: XVII. ADHD, Part I: The executive functions and ADHD. *Journal of the American Academy of Child and Adolescent Psychiatry, 39*, 1064–1068.

Barkley, R. A., Fischer, M., Edelbrock, C. S., & Smallish, L. (1990). The adolescent outcome of hyperactive children diagnosed by research criteria, I: An 8-year prospective follow-up study. *Journal of the American Academy of Child and Adolescent Psychiatry, 29,* 546–557.

Barkley, R. A., Guevremont, D. G., Anastopoulos, A. D., DuPaul, G. J., & Shelton, T. L. (1993). Driving-related risks and outcomes of attention deficit hyperactivity disorder in adolescents and young adults: A 3–5-year follow-up survey. *Pediatrics, 92,* 212–218.

Barkley, R. A., Murphy, K. R., & Bush, T. (2001). Time perception and reproduction in young adults with attention deficit hyperactivity disorder. *Neuropsychology, 15,* 351–360.

Barkley, R. A., Murphy, K. R., DuPaul, G. J., & Bush, T. (in press). Driving knowledge, performance, and adverse outcomes in teens and young adults with ADHD. *Journal of the International Neuropsychological Society.*

Barkley, R. A., Murphy, K. R., & Kwasnik, D. (1996a). Psychological adjustment and adaptive impairments in young adults with ADHD. *Journal of Attention Disorders, 1,* 41–54.

Barkley, R. A., Murphy, K. R., & Kwasnik, D. (1996b). Motor vehicle driving competencies and risks in teens and young adults with ADHD. *Pediatrics, 98,* 1089–1095.

Biederman, J., Faraone, S., Spencer, T., Wilens, T., Norman, D., Lapey, K. A., Mick, E., Lehman, B. K., & Doyle, A. (1993). Patterns of psychiatric comorbidity, cognition, and psychosocial functioning in adults with attention deficit hyperactivity disorder. *American Journal of Psychiatry, 150,* 1792–1798.

Biederman, J., Newcorn, J., & Sprich, S. (1991). Comorbidity of attention deficit hyperactivity disorder with conduct, depressive, anxiety, and other disorders. *American Journal of Psychiatry, 148,* 564–577.

Braaten, E. B., & Rosen, L. A. (1997). Emotional reactions in adults with symptoms of attention deficit hyperactivity disorder. *Personality and Individual Differences, 22,* 355–361.

Brown, T. (2000). *Attention deficit disorder and comorbidities in children, adolescents, and adults.* Washington, DC: American Psychiatric Press.

Castellanos, F. X., Giedd, J. N., Marsh, W. L., Hamburger, S. D., Vaituzis, A. C., Dickstein, D. P., Sarfatti, S. E., Vauss, Y. C., Snell, J. W., Lange, N., Kaysen, D., Krain, A. L., Ritchhie, G. F., Rajapakse, J. C., & Rapoport, J. L. (1996). Quantitative brain magnetic resonance imaging in attention-deficit hyperactivity disorder. *Archives of General Psychiatry, 53,* 607–616.

Corbett, B., & Stanczak, D. E. (1999). Neuropsychological performance of adults evidencing attention-deficit hyperactivity disorder. *Archives of Clinical Neuropsychology, 14,* 373–387.

Corkum, P. V., & Siegel, L. S. (1993). Is the continuous performance task a valuable research tool for use with children with attention-deficit-hyperactivity disorder? *Journal of Child Psychology and Psychiatry, 34,* 1217–1239.

Cox, D.J., Merkel, L., Kovatchev, B., & Seward, R. (2000). Effect of stimulant medication on driving performance of young adults with ADHD: A preliminary double-blind placebo controlled trial. *Journal of Nervous and Mental Disease, 18,* 230–234.

Denckla, M. B. (1996). A theory and model of executive function: A neuropsychological perspective. In G. R. Lyon & N. A. Krasnegor (Eds.), *Attention, memory, and executive function* (pp. 263–277). Baltimore: Paul H. Brookes.

Dimond, S. J. (1980). *Neuropsychology: A textbook of systems and psychological functions of the human brain.* Boston: Butterworths.

DuPaul, G. J., Barkley, R. A., & Connor, D. (1998). Stimulants. In R. A. Barkley (Ed.), *Attention deficit hyperactivity disorder: A handbook for diagnosis and treatment* (2nd ed., pp. 510–551). New York: Guilford Press.

Epstein, J. N., Conners, C. K., Erhardt, D., March, J. S., & Swanson, J. M. (1997). Assymetrical hemispheric control of visual-spatial attention in adults with attention deficit hyperactivity disorder. *Neuropsychology, 11,* 467–473.

Eslinger, P. J., Damasio, A. R., & Van Hoesen, G. W. (1982). Olfactory dysfunction in man: Anatomical and behavioral aspects. *Brain and Cognition, 1,* 259–285.

Filipek, P. A., Semrud-Clikeman, M., Steingard, R. J., Renshaw, P. F., Kennedy, D. N., & Biederman, J. (1997). Volumetric MRI analysis comparing subjects having attention-deficit hyperactivity disorder with normal controls. *Neurology, 48,* 589–601.

Fuster, J. M. (1997). *The prefrontal cortex: Anatomy, physiology, and neuropsychology of the frontal lobe* (3rd ed.). Philadelphia: Lippincott-Raven.

Gansler, D. A., Flucetola, R., Krengel, M., Stetson, S., Zimering, R., & Makary, C. (1998). Are there cognitive subtypes in adult attention deficit/hyperactivity disorder? *The Journal of Nervous and Mental Disease, 186,* 776–781.

Gordon, M. (1995). *How to operate an ADHD clinic or subspecialty practice.* Syracuse, NY: GSI Publications.

Gordon, M., & Barkley, R. A. (1998). Tests and observations. In R. A. Barkley (Ed.), *Attention deficit hyperactivity disorder: A handbook for diagnosis and treatment* (2nd ed., pp. 294–311). New York: Guilford Press.

Gordon, M., & Barkley, R. A. (1999). Is all inattention ADD/ADHD? *The ADHD Report, 7*(5), 1–8.

Gordon, M., & Keiser, S. (1999). *Accommodations in higher education under the Americans with Disabilities Act.* New York: Guilford Press.

Hamilton, J. M., Murphy, C., & Paulsen, J. S. (1999). Odor detection, learning, and memory in Huntington's disease. *Journal of the International Neuropsychological Society, 5,* 609–615.

Harrington, D. L., Haaland, K. Y., & Hermanowicz, N. (1998). Temporal processing in the basal ganglia. *Neuropsychology, 12,* 3–12.

Holdnack, J. A., Moberg, P. J., Arnold, S. E., Gur, R. C., & Gur, R. E. (1995). Speed of processing and verbal learning deficits in adults diagnosed with attention deficit disorder. *Neuropsychiatry, Neuropsychology, and Behavioral Neurology, 8*, 282–292.

Jenkins, M., Cohen, R., Malloy, P., Salloway, S., Johnson, E. G., Penn, J., & Marcotte, A. (1998). Neuropsychological measures which discriminate among adults with residual symptoms of attention deficit disorder and other attentional complaints. *The Clinical Neuropsychologist, 12*, 74–83.

Kovner, R., Budman, C., Frank, Y., Sison, C., Lesser, M., & Halperin, J. M. (1997). *Neuropsychological testing in adult attention deficit hyperactivity disorder: A pilot study.* Submitted for publication.

Lewandowski, L., Codding, R., Gordon, M., Marcoe, M., Needham, L., & Rentas, J. (2000). Self-reported LD and ADHD symptoms in college students. *The ADHD Report, 8(6)*, 1–4.

Lovejoy, D. W., Ball, J. D., Keats, M., Stutts, M. L., Spain, E. H., Janda, L., & Lanusz, J. (1999). Neuropsychological performance of adults with attention deficit hyperactivity disorder (ADHD): Diagnostic classification estimates for measures of frontal lobe/executive functioning. *Journal of the International Neuropsychological Society, 5*, 222–233.

Lyon, G. R., & Krasnegor, N. A. (1996). *Attention, memory, and executive function.* Baltimore: Paul H. Brookes.

Mangels, J. A., Ivry, R. B., & Shimizu, N. (1998). Dissociable contributions of the prefrontal and neocerebellar cortex to time perception. *Cognitive Brain Research, 7*, 15–39.

Mannuzza, S., Gittelman-Klein, R., Bessler, A., Malloy, P., & LaPadula, M. (1993). Adult outcome of hyperactive boys: Educational achievement, occupational rank, and psychiatric status. *Archives of General Psychiatry, 50*, 565–576.

Matochik, J. A., Rumsey, J. M., Zametkin, A. J., Hamburger, S. D., & Cohen, R. M. (1996). Neuropsychological correlates of familial attention-deficit hyperactivity disorder in adults. *Neuropsychiatry, Neuropsychology, and Behavioral Neurology, 9*, 186–191.

Milich, R., Ballentine, A. C., & Lynam, D. R. (2001). ADHD Combined Type and ADHD Predominantly Inattentive Type are distinct and unrelated disorders. *Clinical Psychology: Science and Practice, 8*, 463–488.

Murphy, K. R. (1998). Psychological counseling of adults with ADHD. In R. A. Barkley (Ed.), *Attention deficit hyperactivity disorder: A handbook for diagnosis and treatment* (2nd ed., pp. 582–591). New York: Guilford Press.

Murphy, K. R., & Barkley, R. A. (1996a). Attention deficit hyperactivity disorder in adults. *Comprehensive Psychiatry, 37*, 393–401.

Murphy, K. R., & Barkley, R. A. (1996b). Prevalence of DSM-IV symptoms of ADHD in adult licensed drivers: Implications for clinical diagnosis. *Journal of Attention Disorders, 1*, 147–161.

Murphy, K. R., Barkley, R. A., & Bush, T. (2001). Executive functions in young adults with attention deficit hyperactivity disorder. *Neuropsychology, 15*, 211–220.

Murphy, K. R., Barkley, R. A., & Bush, T. (2000). Young adults with ADHD: Subtype differences in comorbidity, educational, and clinical history. Submitted for publication.

Murphy, K. R., & Gordon, M. (1998). Assessment of adults with ADHD. In R. A. Barkley (Ed.), *Attention deficit hyperactivity disorder: A handbook for diagnosis and treatment* (2nd ed., pp. 345–371). New York: Guilford Press.

Murphy, K. R., Gordon, M., & Barkley, R. A. (2000). To what extent are ADHD symptoms common? A reanalysis of standardization data from a DSM-IV checklist. *The ADHD Report, 8(3)*, 1–4.

Nada-Raja, S., Langley, J.D., McGee, R., Williams, S.M., Begg, D.J. & Reeder, A.I. (1997). Inattentive and hyperactive behaviors and driving offenses in adolescence. *Journal of the American Academy of Child and Adolescent Psychiatry, 36*, 515–522.

Ramirez, C. A., Rosen, L. A., Deffenbacher, J. L., Hurst, H., Nicoletta, C., Rosencranz, T., & Smith, K. (1997). Anger and anger expression in adults with high ADHD symptoms. *Journal of Attention Disorders, 2*, 115–128.

Rao, S. M., Harrington, D. L., Haaland, K. Y., Bobholz, J. A., Cox, R. W., & Binder, J. R. (1997). Distributed neuronal systems underlying the timing of movements. *The Journal of Neuroscience, 17*, 5528–5535.

Roy-Byrne, P., Scheele, L., Brinkley, J., Ward, N., Wiatrak, C., Russo, J., Townes, B., & Varley, C. (1997). Adult attention-deficit hyperactivity disorder: Assessment guidelines based on clinical presentation to a specialty clinic. *Comprehensive Psychiatry, 38*, 133–140.

Rubia, K., Overmeyer, S., Taylor, E., Brammer, M., Williams, S., Simmons, A., Andrew, C., & Bullmore, E. (1998). Prefrontal involvement in "temporal bridging" and timing movement. *Neuropsychologia, 36*, 1283–1293.

Schreiber, H. E., Javorsky, D. J., Robinson, J. E., & Stern, R. A. (1999). Rey-Osterrieth Complex Figure performance in adults with attention deficit hyperactivity disorder: A validation study of the Boston Qualitative Scoring System. *The Clinical Neuropsychologist, 13*, 509–520.

Seidman, L. J. (1997, October). *Neuropsychological findings in ADHD children: Findings from a sample of high-risk siblings.* Paper presented at the annual meeting of the American Academy of Child and Adolescent Psychiatry, Toronto.

Seidman, L. J., Biederman, J., Faraone, S. V., Milberger, S., Seiverd, K., Benedict, K., Bernstein, J. H., Weber, W., & Ouellette, C. (1996). Toward defining a neuropsychology of ADHD: Performance of children and adolescents from a large clinically referred sample. *Journal of Consulting and Clinical Psychology, 65*, 150–160.

Shekim, W., Asarnow, R. F., Hess, E., Zaucha, K., & Wheeler, N. (1990). An evaluation of attention deficit disorder—residual type. *Comprehensive Psychiatry, 31(5)*, 416–425.

Spencer, T. (1997, October). *Chronic tics in adults with ADHD*. Paper presented at the annual meeting of the American Academy of Child and Adolescent Psychiatry, Toronto.

Spencer, T., Biederman, J., Wilens, T., & Faraone, S. V. (1994). Is attention-deficit hyperactivity disorder in adults a valid disorder? *Harvard Review of Psychiatry, 1*, 326–335.

Tzelepis, A., Schubiner, H., & Warbasse, L. H. III (1995). Differential diagnosis and psychiatric comorbidity patterns in adult attention deficit disorder. In K. Nadeau (Ed.), *A comprehensive guide to attention deficit disorder in adults: Research, diagnosis, treatment* (pp. 35–57). New York: Bruner/Mazel.

Weiss, G., & Hechtman, L. (1993). *Hyperactive children grown up*. New York: Guilford Press.

Wilens, T., Spencer, T. J., & Biederman, J. (1998). Pharmacotherapy of adult ADHD. In R. A. Barkley (Ed.), *Attention deficit hyperactivity disorder: A handbook for diagnosis and treatment* (2nd ed., pp. 592–606). New York: Guilford Press.

Woodward, L.J., Fergusson, D.M., & Horwood, J. (2000). Driving outcomes of young people with attentional difficulties in adolescents. *Journal of the American Academy of Child and Adolescent Psychiatry, 39*, 627–634.

# 4

# The Assessment Process: Conditions and Comorbidities

Diane E. Johnson, Ph.D., C. Keith Conners, Ph.D.

This chapter focuses on the assessment process for adults who are seeking a diagnosis of attention deficit hyperactivity disorder (ADHD). At the present time there are no laboratory tests to confirm the diagnosis of ADHD. The diagnosis is based on a compilation of information that includes a developmental/medical/family/school history and risk assessment, review of diagnostic criteria (symptom presence and impairment assessment), differential diagnosis of common co-occurring disorders, and ratings scales from significant others and parents (American Academy of Child and Adolescent Psychiatry, 1997). The authors of this chapter are both affiliated with the Attention Deficit Disorder Program at the Duke Child and Family Study Center at Duke University Medical Center. The Duke Child and Family Study Center is a subspecialty clinic that integrates mental health research and empirically based clinical services to children and their families. The Attention Deficit Disorder Program is involved in research and clinical services for ADHD across the life span, from early preschool identification and intervention to assessment and treatment of ADHD in adults up to the age of 64 years. This chapter stems from our knowledge of empirically based assessment procedures as well as our experience in assessing hundreds of adults with and without ADHD. This is intended to be a source for clinicians who want to better understand how to identify ADHD in their practice as well as a tool for researchers who continue to struggle with diagnosing adult ADHD.

The chapter contains five sections: (1) an introduction to adult ADHD and our risk model that sets the stage for discussing assessment issues; (2) a description and discussion of the current ADHD diagnostic criteria as published by the American Psychiatric Association's *Diagnostic and Statistical Manual for Mental Disorders, Fourth Edition* (DSM-IV; American Psychiatric Association, 1994); (3) a description of empirically based practice parameters for the assessment of adult ADHD as published by the American Academy of Child and Adolescent Psychiatry (American Academy of Child and Adolescent Psychiatry, 1997); (4) a description of our clinical procedures within a medical university setting for making the ADHD diagnosis in adults; and (5) a discussion of how to guard against overdiagnosing ADHD in adults and dealing with issues of comorbidities inherent in this population.

## INTRODUCTION TO ADHD IN ADULTHOOD: PRESENTATION AND RISKS

Although Wender (1995) very early noted the importance of ADHD in adults, for the most part the notion that ADHD can persist into adulthood is relatively new and remains controversial in the public opinion polls. Most of the research on adult ADHD has occurred within the past decade, in contrast to 50 years of childhood ADHD research. Adult ADHD research has focused on identification, prevalence rates, comorbidity, and use of medication for treatment. What is striking about research on adult ADHD is the lack of continuity in the identification of the disorder across the various studies, due in part to changing diagnostic criteria, differing diagnostic criteria within the United States compared to Europe, as well as a lack of consistency in what constitutes adult ADHD (Conners & Erhardt, 1998). In the past decade, there has been a proliferation of self-help books, documentaries, and television programming (Waid, Johnson, & Anton, 1997) and an exponential increase in the prescription of psychostimulants for adults (Sallee, 1995). "These developments have not been without controversy as the validity of the diagnosis of ADHD, particularly in adults, has been questioned" (Waid, Johnson & Anton, 1997, p. 393). Adding to the complexity, for clinician and researcher alike, is the high rate of comorbidity of ADHD with a number of psychiatric conditions, including learning disabilities, mood and anxiety disorders, conduct/antisocial personality disorders, and substance-related disorders (Biederman, Newcorn, & Sprich, 1991; Biederman et al., 1993; Milberger, Biederman, Faraone, Murphy, & Tsuang, 1995).

While research has focused on identification, comorbidity, and treatment, the impact of ADHD on adult academic and occupational outcomes and functioning in interpersonal areas is less studied. It is believed that the pattern of academic/occupational and interpersonal difficulties associated with ADHD is similar across the life span. ADHD is now believed to be a chronic, lifetime disorder that exacts a considerable toll on those suffering from it as well as on the families of those who must care for them (National Institute of Health, 1998). Several other chapters in this text describe in more detail the complexities and morbidity of ADHD in adulthood; however, a brief overview will set the stage for discussing issues of assessment. Although as many as 40% of children with ADHD may no longer be symptomatic by young adulthood, several long-term studies have demonstrated that a significant proportion of those with ADHD end up with serious emotional, interpersonal, social, and economic limitations. These include risks of death by misadventure, driving accidents, teenage pregnancy, sexually transmitted diseases, alcohol and other substance abuse, and academic underachievement. In addition, profound impairment of self-esteem and personal identity are frequent sequelae in adults with a childhood history of ADHD (NIH, 1998). Adults with ADHD, as a group, compared to adults without ADHD, tend to be less educated, have more work-related difficulties, more often quit or are laid off from jobs, hold lower-status jobs, have more social skills difficulties, have elevated rates of divorce, separation, and marital dissatisfaction, and have higher rates of gambling, depression, and alcoholism (NIH, 1998). These outcome data play an important role in the assessment of ADHD, as we will discuss further in this chapter.

There are a host of complaints and observations in adults with ADHD that must be considered in the assessment process. Adults with ADHD often complain that they have rapid, brief mood shifts or a hot temper (Sallee, 1995; Ward, Wender, & Reimherr, 1993). In fact, hot temper was one of Wender's cardinal criteria for the diagnosis in adults. Due to a lifetime of failures associated with ADHD, they often present with low self-esteem, feelings of inadequacy, stress intolerance, and feelings of being chronically overwhelmed. They may report an inability to relax, restless sleep, or an excessively active lifestyle. There can be a lifelong history of not living up to their potential, difficulty keeping jobs or sustaining relationships, and a disorganized and inefficient approach to school or work (Sallee, 1995). They may report requiring absolute deadlines in order to complete tasks, multitasking difficulties, misjudging how long it takes to do things, failing to plan ahead, or having to do things right away lest they forget. In interview sessions, you may note disorganization in answering open-ended questions, disinhibition, distractibility, or constant purposeless motion of extremities.

How does an adult end up with ADHD, comorbidity, and/or the complaints and observations just noted? Modern conceptions of disease emphasize that diseases are best conceptualized as an accumulation of risks (Conners & Erhardt, 1998). There are a host of pathogens that require certain factors in the host before the disease will manifest, as well as protective factors that operate in the host to ward off the disease. While etiology is discussed in detail in another chapter, it is an important assessment issue that should be noted briefly. Conners and Erhardt (1998) describe in detail a host of risk factors, both potentially causal as well as protective, that play a role in the expression of ADHD. One of these risk factors is genetics. Although no single marker for genetic transmission has been located, a comprehensive review of the neurobiological literature strongly suggests genetic and biological explanation for ADHD (Zametkin, 1989). Metabolic and nutritional factors have been suggested since 1929 in childhood ADHD, and although comprehensive reviews of the role of nutrients, food additives, and sugar indicate a limited relationship with the etiology of ADHD, there is current evidence suggesting a complex intertwining of nutrition, exposure to environmental toxins such as lead, and other risk factors (Conners & Erhardt, 1998). Another suspected risk factor discussed in Conners and Erhardt's review is temperament, where it has long been suspected that normal variations in temperament can dispose one to problems with ADHD. Other risks include medical risks, such as pregnancy and delivery complications, early illnesses or injuries, slowed development, and environmental stress (Hartsough and Lambert, 1985). The actual amount that these risks may contribute to the expression of ADHD is not known; however, an analysis of these risks is important in the assessment process, as we will discuss further. An important therapeutic contribution of a risk assessment is the implicit communication to the patient that attention to modifiable risks (e.g., parenting style, educational opportunity) plays an important role in the expression of the disorder (Brooks & Goldstein, 2001).

## CURRENT ADHD DIAGNOSTIC CRITERIA, THE DSM-IV

Wender and colleagues (Wender, 1995; Ward, Wender, & Reimherr, 1993) were the first to develop specific criteria for the diagnosis of ADHD in adults, known as the Utah Criteria. The Utah Criteria (Ward, Wender, & Reimherr, 1993) emphasized that adult ADHD is a continuation of a childhood disorder, with attentional difficulties *and* consistent motor hyperactivity continuing into adulthood, a consideration of differential diagnoses (excluding ADHD if major psychopathology), and the recognition of associated features of marital instability, academic and vocational difficulties, substance abuse, and atypical responses to psychoactive medications, to name a few. Today, the Utah Criteria are rarely, if ever, utilized in the United States as a diagnostic and research tool. They have been replaced, most recently, by the American Psychiatric Association's (1994) latest version of the *Diagnostic and Statistical Manual of Mental Disorders, Fourth Edition* (DSM-IV; APA, 1994). Before discussing the DSM-IV criteria for ADHD, it is important to note that the European diagnostic criteria, the *International Statistical Classification of Diseases and Related Health Problems, Tenth Revision* (ICD–10; World Health Organization, 1992) have evolved into criteria that are quite similar. Conners and Erhardt

(1998) provide further discussion of these two instruments.

The DSM-IV is a categorical diagnostic system, meaning that the result is either inclusion or exclusion, the person either has ADHD or does not. Hinshaw (1994) notes that the ultimate aim of any categorical diagnostic scheme is to identify subgroups that are homogeneous with respect to pathogenesis, symptom presentation, family history, course, and treatment response. While a DSM-IV diagnosis is required in order to obtain treatment for ADHD, the assessment procedure should also encompass dimensional measures of ADHD, such as rating scales, which are discussed later in the chapter. This section focuses on the categorical diagnosis of ADHD as specified in the DSM-IV. The diagnostic criteria are presented, along with comments regarding how to determine whether or not a criterion is met. Keep in mind, though, that the DSM-IV criteria create the potential for both overdiagnosis and misclassification.

ADHD is located in the DSM-IV (APA, 1994) under disorders *Usually First Diagnosed in Infancy, Childhood, or Adolescence*. Each disorder has a diagnostic code (a four- or five-digit number). The DSM-IV currently classifies three subtypes of ADHD: (314.00) ADHD, Predominantly Inattentive Type, (314.01) ADHD, Predominantly Hyperactive-Impulsive Type, and (314.01) ADHD, Combined Type. ADHD, Predominantly Inattentive Type is what was formerly known as Attention Deficit Disorder, or ADD. The DSM-IV also identifies a fourth ADHD diagnostic category, (314.9) ADHD, Not Otherwise Specified (NOS). ADHD, NOS is used for disorders with prominent symptoms of inattention or hyperactivity-impulsivity that do not meet full criteria for ADHD. Also, for individuals (especially adolescents and adults) who currently have symptoms that no longer meet full criteria, "In Partial Remission" should be specified.

In order to be classified ADHD by DSM-IV, five diagnostic criteria must be met (APA, 1994). These criteria follow, along with comments related to adult ADHD.

**A. *At least six of nine symptoms of inattention and/or at least six of nine symptoms of hyperactivity-impulsivity have persisted for at least 6 months to a degree that is maladaptive and inconsistent with developmental level*.** The nine inattentive symptoms [with our developmentally appropriate adult examples included in brackets] include the following.

1. Often fails to give close attention to details or makes careless mistakes [e.g., accuracy is sacrificed for speed, fails to check over work, not good with detailed work].
2. Often has difficulty sustaining attention [cannot keep mind of a single activity for long periods, long conversations with friends are difficult to follow, fun activities like watching sports are difficult to track].
3. Often does not seem to listen when spoken to directly [others complain that the mind appears to be elsewhere, people call the person "spacey" or "not there," people repeat the individual's name to get his or her attention].
4. Often does not follow through on instructions and fails to finish things [needs deadlines to get things completed, is unable to follow through on multiple commands given at once, jumps from task to task].
5. Often has difficulty organizing tasks and activities [does not plan ahead, depends on others for order, has a poor sense of time, is often late, is inefficient, makes lots of lists that are not used],
6. Often avoids, dislikes, or is reluctant to engage in tasks that require sustained attention [procrastinates, delays detailed work like filing taxes].
7. Often loses things [is absent-minded, loses keys, wallet, organizers, lists].
8. Often is easily distracted cannot filter out unnecessary noise, has a difficult time refocusing after being interrupted, daydreams].
9. Often is forgetful [forgets to schedule or use organizer, has others help remember, returns

home during the day to retrieve forgotten items].

The nine hyperactive-impulsive symptoms include the following.

1. Often fidgets [cannot sit still, bites nails, taps feet and fingers].
2. Often leaves seat [difficulty staying seated through a television program or lecture, likes to do active things].
3. Often runs about or climbs excessively [feels internal restlessness].
4. Often has difficulty playing or engaging in activities quietly [talks during movies, talks loudly in restaurants, has difficulty moderating speech volume].
5. Often is "on the go" [is always moving, is unable to relax].
6. Often talks excessively [takes a long time to get a point across, people complain that they cannot get a word in].
7. Often blurts out answers [says things without thinking, rarely hears the end of others' sentences, "sticks foot in mouth" frequently].
8. Often has difficulty awaiting turn [is impatient in lines and traffic, more so than others].
9. Often interrupts or intrudes on others ["steps on peoples' toes", violates others' space/ boundaries, is called intrusive].

The examples in brackets are taken from the Conners Adult ADHD Diagnostic Interview for DSM-IV (CAADID; Conners, Epstein, & Johnson, 2001). Criterion A brings up several diagnostic issues related to ADHD in adulthood. First, these inattentive and hyperactive-impulsive symptoms represent a set of behaviors that every human exhibits from time to time. Everyone forgets things, interrupts others, or gets distracted (Murphy & Barkley, 2000). These symptoms also present differently across the life span. The DSM-IV criteria do not allow for such symptom variation and, thus, the clinician must be sensitive to the adult presentation of these childhood-based symptoms. March, Wells, and Conners (1995) discuss developmental differences in ADHD symptoms across the life span. In adults, ADHD may present as disorganization, poor concentration, not finishing things, procrastination, impulsivity, affective dyscontrol, anxiety, substance abuse, and antisocial behavior.

Secondly, the DSM-IV is not adjusted for developmental changes in the number of symptoms. There is some question as to whether or not six or more symptoms must be present in adulthood to accurately diagnose ADHD. Murphy and Barkley (1995), in a study of 467 adults with ADHD, found that the number of symptoms needed to accurately diagnose ADHD, with a 93% confidence level, declined significantly over time. The authors were able to accurately categorize 30- to 49-year-olds with only four of nine symptoms; for adults 50+ years of age, only three of nine symptoms were required; and interestingly, in 17- to 29-year-olds, only four of nine inattentive and five of nine hyperactive-impulsive behaviors were required. However, the current diagnostic criteria require the six or more symptoms, and if medicolegal or research considerations require a formal diagnosis, one should not deviate from the DSM-IV criteria. Hopefully, future revisions in the DSM will address some of these concerns.

**B. Some hyperactive-impulsive or inattentive symptoms that caused impairment were present before age 7 years.** This criterion is also controversial when diagnosing ADHD in adulthood, for at least two reasons. First, it is very difficult for many adults to document when symptoms first presented and impaired their functioning. Retrospective memory may not be accurate, and there may be no collateral informants to corroborate early childhood history. Second, because the criterion states that some symptoms were present and impaired functioning before the age of 7 years, it is unclear whether or not the adult has to meet full childhood criteria for ADHD in order to continue to meet criteria in adulthood. In research studies of adult ADHD, it is more common for there to be documentation of a childhood diagnosis of ADHD as well as a current diagnosis of ADHD. However, the way the criteria are written, as long as some symptoms were present that impaired functioning before age 7 years, a diagnosis of ADHD may be met. Requiring a specific age of onset for ADHD is controversial and may also be addressed in future revisions of the DSM.

*C. Some impairment from the symptoms is present in two or more settings (e.g., at school or work and at home).* It is essential when applying the DSM categorical scheme that impairment be determined. This means that even if the person has six of nine inattentive and/or six of nine hyperactive-impulsive behaviors that have persisted for at least 6 months and with an onset prior to the age of 7 years old, *they do not count unless the symptoms result in significant life impairment in more than one domain of functioning.* ADHD is not just the presence of inattention or hyperactivity; it is the presence of these symptoms to the point that they are impairing functioning. Impairment is different than symptom presence. For example, avoiding tasks requiring sustained attention is the symptom, the impairment from this avoidance may include not paying bills or taxes on time and being penalized, or, in the workplace, being passed over for a promotion because time lines are not met. For adults, impairment settings might include school (college functioning), work (occupational performance), home (conducting daily life activities, marital adjustment, or parenting), or social (friendships, sports, or club activities). Examples of impairment in academic functioning, then, may include receiving lower grades because assignments are not completed and turned in by deadline, chronic lateness or missing classes due to disorganization, or avoiding taking required courses because the subject requires concentration and attention that the person has difficulty maintaining. Unfortunately, the DSM-IV provides no operational guidelines for determining impairment, nor does it provide a complete list of settings.

*D. There must be clear evidence of clinically significant impairment in social, academic, or occupational functioning.* As already stated with criterion C, the DSM-IV provides no operational guidelines for determining clinically significant impairment. What is required here is that one domain of functioning be *clinically* significantly impaired. An example of this may be that the person has continuously lost jobs or dropped out of school (as opposed to receiving poor work performance reports or lower grades) or fails to maintain friendships (as opposed to having difficulties with relationships). Other domains of impairment may include functioning within the home and intrapersonal functioning (sense of self-efficacy and self-esteem). Low self-esteem itself is common among many well-functioning adults. But when self-esteem is lowered to the point that there is demoralization, depression, lowered vocational effort, or constant and inhibiting self-criticism, then impairment is present.

*E. The symptoms do not occur exclusively during the course of a pervasive developmental disorder, schizophrenia, or other psychotic disorder and are not better accounted for by another mental disorder (e.g., mood disorder, anxiety disorder, disassociative disorder, or a personality disorder).* This criterion is also perhaps the most challenging in assessing the adult with ADHD. Issues of differential diagnosis, comorbidity, and the effects of the natural aging process make this criterion particularly difficult. With regard to comorbidity, the same diagnoses that are common in childhood ADHD are believed to be common in adult ADHD, and the adult with ADHD is more likely than not to have a comorbid psychiatric condition (Biederman, Newcorn, & Sprich, 1991). In cases of adult ADHD, it is believed that depression co-occurs in 15–75% of cases, anxiety in 25% of cases, antisocial personality disorder in 30–50% of cases, substance use in 30–50% of cases, and learning disabilities in anywhere from 10% to 90% of cases (Biederman, Newcorn, & Sprich, 1991). In this regard, the clinician must determine not only if ADHD is present, but also if psychiatric conditions co-occur as well.

The differential diagnosis of ADHD in adulthood is difficult not only due to comorbidity, but due to a host of other conditions that may also include attention or organizational deficits (Waid, Johnson, & Anton, 1997), thus presenting as ADHD but in actuality not ADHD (i.e., misclassifying another condition as ADHD). Other such psychiatric conditions may include, but are not limited to, substance intoxication or withdrawal, intermittent explosive disorder, borderline personality disorder, posttraumatic stress disorder, mental retardation, bipolar disorder, Tourette's disorder, major depression (with agitation), and adjustment disorders. Medical conditions could include head injury, hyper-/hypothyroidism, multiple sclerosis, epilepsy, stroke, dementia, hepatic or renal insufficiency, vitamin deficiency states, sensory deficits (such as hearing loss), drug side effects, stroke, and frontal, parietal, or temporal tumors, to name a few (for review see Waid, Johnson, & Anton, 1997). In addition to psychiatric or medical conditions, other causes for inattention or organizational deficits may include the normal aging process, environmental stress, and age-appropriate high activity levels (Waid, Johnson, & Anton, 1997).

## PRACTICE PARAMETERS FOR THE ASSESSMENT OF ADULT ADHD

In 1997, the Journal of the American Academy of Child and Adolescent Psychiatry (AACAP) published practice parameters for the assessment and treatment of children, adolescents, and adults with ADHD. These guidelines may be obtained via the Academy of Child and Adolescent Psychiatry's Web site at *www.aacap.org*. These ADHD practice parameters are the only ones published for adults to date. These practice parameters were developed by the Work Group on Quality Issues with AACAP and are based on an exhaustive review of the literature, providing empirically based guidelines for assessment. These practice parameters also include treatment planning and treatment, but these aspects of the guidelines are beyond the scope of this chapter. In general, the practice parameters for an adult ADHD evaluation, as specified by AACAP, requires a complete psychiatric assessment, including: (a) an interview with the patient to obtain a developmental history, psychiatric history and past treatments, present and past DSM-IV ADHD symptoms, impairment history (including the domains of school, work, family, and peers), differential diagnosis of alternate and/or comorbid DSM-IV disorders, an assessment of strengths, talents, and abilities, and mental status examination; (b) standardized rating scales completed by the patient's parent (where available); (c) medical history; (d) family history; (e) interview with significant other or parent, if available; (f) physical evaluation (if not completed within the past year); (g) school information; and (h) referral for additional evaluations if indicated (such as psychoeducational, neuropsychological, or vocational evaluations).

The practice parameters (AACAP, 1997) provide this additional information for the clinicians. ADHD is often missed in adults, particularly if the disorder was not identified when the patient was a child. As we have witnessed as well, adults often seek evaluation and treatment after the child has been diagnosed and the parent recognizes the symptoms. Adults with undiagnosed ADHD in childhood may have been missed because either some comorbid condition clouded the picture (e.g., a chaotic school or comorbid anxiety) or they were extremely bright or compliant, had consistent discipline at home, an accommodating school team, or interpersonal charm that allowed the child to cope with symptoms of ADHD enough so as to not be impaired. This is particularly true of the ADHD, Predominantly Inattentive Type (AACAP, 1997). Thus, the clinician must be trained in assessing the adult from a developmental perspective, looking for childhood underachievement or labeling such as being undisciplined, unmotivated, or "spacey" (AACAP, 1997). Since adults with ADHD may possess limited insight into their difficulties and may be poor reporters, relying on current information from spouses, significant others, or employers, as well as retrospective reports from parents, is important. School records and past psychiatric reports can make a major contribution to the assessment, as can a medical history and recent physical examination. Psychological testing or neuropsychological testing may be indicated but is not necessarily required (AACAP, 1997). This multimodal assessment has been advocated and examined in the childhood ADHD literature for several years (Conners & Erhardt, 1998). As Conners and Erhardt note, "The major problem with these multi-level assessments is how to integrate information across informants and domains in such a way that the needs of both diagnosis and treatment formulation are served" (p. 505).

The AACAP (1997) practice parameters indicate that standardized rating scales may be useful. We find that they are helpful and important tools when used in conjunction with the categorical diagnostic system of the DSM-IV (APA, 1994). Rating scales provide an alternative method of establishing how symptoms fit together, how prevalent the symptoms are in the normal population, and what level of a specific dimension is statistically abnormal. Thus, for example, one can examine the construct of inattention across a normative sample and determine how frequent a person's inattention is compared to age- and gender-matched peers. The advantages of this dimensional measurement is that it is cost effective and covers a broad range of behaviors, the dimensions are empirically derived, quantitative information is obtained for group comparisons and measures of change, and, as just noted, normative comparisons with age- and gender-matched peers is obtained.

## MAKING THE DIAGNOSIS OF ADHD IN ADULTS

In our Attention Deficit Disorder Program, a clinical practice located in a university medical school, we have applied the AACAP practice parameters (1997) in the following ways. When an adult calls for an assessment appointment, we send them a packet of materials that must be completed and returned to our clinic before we schedule an appointment. We request that the identified adult call and discuss this appointment; we do not accept parents or spouses calling in for their loved ones. We have found that contact with the identified person results in better compliance and follow-through. The assessment packet is mailed to the individual, or the person may pick it up if so desired, in an attempt to collect as much "free" information ahead of time for which the patient is not billed. The packet contains a cover letter with an explanation of the assessment visit, a request to discontinue any psychostimulant ADHD medication the day of the visit with their physician's approval, a request for any past records from school, psychological or medical evaluations, and/or work reports, and directions to the clinic. The assessment packet contains the following three assessment instruments: a developmental history, self- and collateral rating scales, and a parent rating scale.

A detailed developmental history form that requires written responses or endorsements is included. This history form begins with gestational information and ends with current adult information. With regard to childhood and childhood risk factors, the history form includes questions about family of origin, gestational risk factors, delivery risk factors, temperament risk factors, developmental risk factors, environmental risk factors, medical history, academic history, psychiatric history, and family history. With regard to adulthood, the history form includes questions about educational/academic history, occupational history, social/interpersonal history, health history, psychiatric history, comorbid psychiatric screening questions, substance use, and current environmental stressors.

The history form we developed is our attempt to create a comprehensive developmental history for diagnosing adult ADHD. The Conners Adult ADHD Diagnostic Interview for DSM-IV (CAA-

DID; Conners, Epstein, & Johnson, 2001) is an empirically based structured interview that aids the process of diagnosing ADHD. The Interview is divided into two parts, administered separately. The first part, which can be administered as either a clinical interview or a self-report questionnaire (as we use it), is the developmental history questionnaire. Having the patient complete the questionnaire ahead of time is less time consuming for the clinician, allows the patient to gather information from others if necessary, and allows the patient to break the task into smaller sections if necessary. Whether the patient completes the history form beforehand or in the waiting room, the history form takes about 45–60 minutes to complete. As a clinical interview, it can take much longer, since open-ended questions are difficult to answer and fatigue increases distractibility.

Also included in the packet is an adult ADHD self-report rating scale and an adult ADHD collateral rating scale. Both scales rate current frequency of ADHD and ADHD-related behaviors. While there are several rating scales on the market and/or published in the literature, we use the Conners Adult ADHD Rating Scales (CAARS; Conners, Erhardt, & Sparrow, 1999). These instruments provide reliable and valid assessment of ADHD-related symptoms across clinically important domains (home, work, and interpersonal functioning), discriminate between clinical and nonclinical groups, allow for multimodal assessment (self-report and significant other's report), have short forms for research settings, are linked to the DSM-IV (APA, 1994) diagnostic criteria, and have parallel structure with the Conners Parent and Teacher Rating Scales—Revised, which are used in making childhood ADHD diagnoses. The CAARS-Self and-Other Rating Scales are based on a large normative database of 2,000 adults. These scales are easy to administer and score. Additionally, patients have benefited from being educated about their ADHD symptoms in relation to other same gender age mates. The CAARS-Other Rating Scale allows us to gather information on current symptom presence if a significant other is not available at the time of the assessment or by telephone follow-up. It has been our experience that many adults have difficulty bringing a significant other with them to the assessment appointment due to issues of conflict or confidentiality.

The third and final measure included in the packet is a parent rating scale to be retrospectively completed by the parent or a person who knew the adult as a young child. That rater must be older than the adult being assessed by at least several years. While several childhood ADHD Parent Rating Scales exist, we use the Conners Parent Rating Scale—Revised, Long Form (CPRS-R:LF; Conners, 1997). However, we use the scale in a different manner than it is currently marketed. We change the instructions of the instrument so that it requires the "parent" to rate the adult offspring's ADHD behaviors based on when their child was between the ages of 7 and 15 years. There is no normative data to score the CPRS-R as a retrospective report; however, standard scoring provides a parent rating of retrospectively reported childhood behaviors along several dimensions, including: Oppositional, Cognitive Problems/Inattention, Hyperactivity, Anxious-Shy, Perfectionism, Social Problems, and Psychosomatic. These scores can be compared to how parents currently rate their children, providing some dimensional information about externalizing and internalizing childhood behaviors. Also, embedded in the measure are the 18 DSM-IV diagnostic symptoms useful in determining early childhood diagnostic criteria.

Underreporting of childhood ADHD symptomatology has been well documented (Wender, Reimherr, & Wood, 1981; Barkley, Fischer, Edelbrock, & Smallish, 1991). Wender and colleagues (1981) found poor agreement between the recollections of adult patients and those of their parents of ADHD symptoms during childhood, with parental recall being a more valid measure as well as a better predictor of treatment response. Biederman and colleagues (Biederman, et al., 1993; Biederman,

Faraone, Knee, Munir, & Tsuang, 1990), on the other hand, have demonstrated that a reliable and valid clinical diagnosis of childhood ADHD can be made based on self-report.

Once the packet is returned, the patient is called and an appointment scheduled. The rating scales are scored before the appointment and put in the clinical chart with the developmental history form. A reminder call the week before and sometimes the day before is helpful. Once the adult arrives for the assessment appointment, but before the person sees the clinician, she or he is asked to complete a computerized version of the Structured Clinical Interview for DSM-IV Axis I Disorders (SCID; First, Spitzer, Gibbon, & Williams, 1997). This computerized diagnostic interview requires that the patient answer yes/no questions related to the past and current presence of a variety of psychiatric disorders, including mood, anxiety, substance-related, psychotic, somatization, and eating disorders. While this instrument can be administered as a paper-and-pencil interview, in the clinic we have found it more time and cost effective to administer the interview via computer and then to follow up during the clinical interview. The patient can usually complete the diagnostic screen within 30 minutes.

We sometimes ask the person also to complete a computerized Axis II (personality disorders) diagnostic screening interview. However, since we have found that the personality disorder questionnaires often overdiagnose individuals, we usually evaluate Axis II disorders as part of the clinical interview. It is often difficult to determine in one session whether or not a person has a personality disorder, especially when the person is presenting with Axis I symptoms. Thus, past psychological/psychiatric treatment records are often helpful.

Once the SCID findings have been printed, the clinician reviews the findings, along with the history form and rating scales. The clinical interview includes a review of the previously completed history form (e.g., in the case of our clinic, the Conners Adult ADHD Diagnostic Interview for DSM-IV, Part I). In reviewing the history questionnaire, we ask for additional information about positive responses as well as observe the patient's response style. Next, we follow up on the computerized DSM-IV Axis I questionnaire and, if completed, the Axis II diagnostic screening. The final part of the diagnostic interview is the completion of Part II of the Conners Adult ADHD Diagnostic Interview for DSM-IV (Conners, Epstein, & Johnson, 2001). The interview guides the clinician through the DSM-IV criteria. It provides the clinician with commonly reported examples of the 18 ADHD symptoms in childhood and adulthood, prompts for the pervasiveness of the symptoms across the life span, and contains operationalized guidelines that aid the clinician in assessing domains of impairment, due to ADHD, in childhood and adulthood. Thus, the CAADID can also be used to assess ADHD in children and adolescents.

It is important to note that there are a variety of other structured interviews and rating scales available to the clinician. Formats for such interviews have been published by Barkley (1990) and Mannuzza and Klein (1987). Other adult ADHD rating scales include the Brown Attention-Deficit Disorders Scales (Brown, 1995), the Patient Behavior Checklist (Kane, Mikalac, Benjamin, & Barkley, 1990), and the Wender Utah Rating Scale (Ward, Wender, & Reimherr, 1993).

No other information or testing is completed routinely, but an assortment of tests or information may be necessary. If the person is overdue for a physical, especially if a medical condition is present or changing, one may be requested prior to conceptualizing the person's difficulties in a final formulation. We may request to speak to a parent, spouse, coworker, or treatment provider in some cases, or we may request further neuropsychological or vocational assessment. We would obtain a signed release before contacting anyone. We do not routinely complete a neuropsychological battery on these adults because the literature does not support that any testing in and of itself is conclusive. However, the results and observations of a continuous performance test (CPT) are often helpful. Within two to three hours of the person's arriving at the clinic, feedback is given to the individual, with referrals as necessary. An explanation of ADHD is given to the person in a multimodal presentation (charts and pictures as well as verbal explanations) and questions are answered. A packet of psychoeducational materials is given to the adult with ADHD that includes a variety of resources (books, Web sites, local organizations), information about ADHD and treatment options, educational rights of the person with ADHD, and strategies for coping with ADHD. A written report is generated that documents the assessment. This report is mailed to the patient following the visit.

In an effort to translate the information in this chapter to practice, it may be helpful to review other adult ADHD assessment protocols, such as Murphy & Gordon's (1998) published protocol from the University of Massachusetts.

## GUARDING AGAINST OVERDIAGNOSING ADHD IN ADULTS AND THE ISSUE OF COMORBIDITY

Murphy (1994) notes that diagnosing ADHD in adults is not an exact science. There is no single neurological or psychological test or test battery that can conclusively determine whether or not an adult has ADHD. The very limited amount of controlled research on adult ADHD, the lack of reliable and valid rating scales, and the fact that almost everyone at times experiences some of the symptoms of ADHD make overdiagnosis a concern. Murphy goes on to report that liberally diagnosing ADHD in adults can have significant social, academic, vocational, and/or legal implications and can potentially undermine the efforts of those who do have the disorder. By way of summary, we might reemphasize the points made by Murphy (1994, pp. xxx, 3–4):

> Remember that ADHD is a neurobiological disorder characterized by developmentally inappropriate levels of sustained attention, impulsivity, and hyperactivity with a childhood onset.

It is chronic and pervasive and causes significant impairment in functioning. There should be evidence that the person meets DSM-IV criteria and there should also be no lengthy period of remission from the symptoms without an explanation (such as no symptom impairment for the two years the adolescent was in military school due to environmental modifications).

ADHD does not have an onset in adulthood.

> Keep the primary symptoms of inattention, impulsivity, and hyperactivity in the forefront.

Secondary symptoms such as procrastination, chronic lateness, or underachievement do not, in and of themselves, indicate ADHD. Murphy (1994), as well as others, have noted that it is not uncommon for parents of ADHD children to present for assessment because they were aware of the genetic and familial component of ADHD, and not necessarily because they were troubled by symptoms.

> Beware of adults who may be looking for 'performance enhancement.'
> Beware of adults who may have something to gain by securing an ADHD diagnosis,

whether it is to qualify for special accommodations on professional licensing examinations or to obtain stimulant medication for recreational use.

> Pay careful attention to other diagnoses that may account for the symptoms,

especially depression, anxiety, substance abuse/dependence, or antisocial personality disorder.

In conclusion, assessing the adult for ADHD is not an exact science, and one must rely on one's clinical experience and expertise in discerning whether or not the person's complaints of inattention and/or hyperactivity-impulsivity are the result of continuing ADHD symptoms from childhood, another psychiatric or medical condition, or simply the natural result of the aging process. The field of adult ADHD is only one decade old, and further research is needed in the areas of assessment and treatment.

It has been our clinical experience that providing an accurate diagnosis of adult ADHD, particularly in adults who were not identified with ADHD in childhood, can be therapeutic in and of itself. These individuals often report immediate relief once they have a framework in which to explain their lifelong difficulties academically, at home, socially, and/or personally. After a lifetime of believing that they are unintelligent, unmotivated, lazy, or inexplicably different from others, the diagnosis may be welcomed. They will need to further educate themselves about ADHD and to discuss treatment options. Sometimes, mixed with relief are overwhelming feelings of sadness or anger because so much time has passed without ADHD being identified. In order to accurately provide information to patients, clinicians must remember to abide by the DSM-IV diagnostic criteria and to uphold the AACAP practice parameters, which represent the only published guidelines for assessing adult ADHD to date. We believe that comprehensive self-education is the prerequisite to effective self-management by the adult with ADHD. It is the responsibility of clinicians to provide accurate diagnosis, education, support, and treatment as a critical foundation for both.

## REFERENCES

American Academy of Child and Adolescent Psychiatry. (1997). Practice parameters for the assessment and treatment of children, adolescents, and adults with attention-deficit/hyperactivity disorder. *Journal of the American Academy of Child and Adolescent Psychiatry, 36*(Suppl. 10), 85S–121S.

American Psychiatric Association. (1994). *Diagnostic and statistical manual of mental disorders* (4th ed.). Washington, DC: American Psychiatric Press.

Barkley, R. A. (1990). *Attention deficit hyperactivity disorder: A handbook for diagnosis and treatment.* New York: Guilford Press.

Barkley, R. A., Fischer, M., Edelbrock, C. S., & Smallish, L. (1991). The adolescent outcome of hyperactive children diagnosed by research criteria. III. Mother–child interactions, family conflicts and maternal psychopathology. *Journal of Child Psychological Psychiatry, 32*, 233–255.

Biederman, J., Faraone, S. V., Knee, D., Munir, D., & Tsuang, M. T. (1990). Retrospective assessment of DSM-III attention deficit disorder in non-referred individuals. *Journal of Clinical Psychiatry, 51*, 102–107.

Biederman, J., Newcorn, J., & Sprich, S. (1991). Comorbidity of attention deficit hyperactivity disorder with conduct, depressive, anxiety, and other disorders. *American Journal of Psychiatry, 148*, 564–577.

Biederman, J., Faraone, S. V., Spencer, T., Wilens, T., Norman, D., Lapey, K. A., Mick, E., Lehman, B. K., & Doyle, A. (1993). Patterns of psychiatric comorbidity, cognition, and psychosocial functioning in adults with attention deficit-hyperactivity disorder. *American Journal of Psychiatry, 150*, 1792–1798.

Brooks, R., & Goldstein, S. (2001). *Raising Resilient Children.* New York: Contemporary.

Brown, T. E. (1995). *Brown Attention-Deficit Disorders Scales.* San Antonio, TX: Psychological Corp.

Conners, C. K. (1997). *Conners' Parent Rating Scales—Revised.* North Tonawanda, NY: Multi-Health Systems.

Conners, C. K., Epstein, J., and Johnson, D. (2001). *Conners' Adult ADHD Diagnostic Interview for DSM-IV (CAADID).* North Tonawanda, NY: Multi-Health Systems.

Conners, C. K., & Erhardt, D. (1998). Attention-deficit hyperactivity disorder in children and adolescents. In A. S. Bullack & M. Hersen (Eds.), *Comprehensive clinical psychology, 5* (pp. 487–525). New York: Elsevier Science.

Conners, C. K., Erhardt, D., & Sparrow, E. (1999). *Conners' Adult ADHD Rating Scales.* North Tonawanda, NY: Multi-Health Systems.

First, M. B., Spitzer, R. L., Gibbon, M., & Williams, J. B. W. (1997). *Structured Clinical Interview for DSM-IV Axis I Disorders—Clinician Version.* Washington, DC: American Psychiatric Press.

Hartsough, C. S., & Lambert, N. M. (1985). Medical factors in hyperactive and normal children. *American Journal of Orthopsychiatry, 55*, 190–201.

Hinshaw, S. P. (1994). *Attention deficits and hyperactivity in children.* Thousand Oaks, CA: Sage.

Kane, R., Mikalac, C., Benjamin, S., & Barkley, R. A. (1990). Assessment and treatment of adults with ADHD. In R. A. Barkley (Ed.), *Attention deficit hyperactivity disorder: A handbook for diagnosis and treatment* (pp. 613–654). New York: Guilford Press.

Mannuzza, S., & Klein, R. G. (1987). *Schedule for the assessment of conduct, hyperactivity, anxiety, mood, and psychoactive substances (CHAMPS).* New Hyde Park, NY: Children's Behavior Disorders Clinic, Long Island Jewish Medical Center.

March, J. R., Wells, K., & Conners, C. K. (1995). Attention-deficit/hyperactivity disorder: Part I. Assessment and diagnosis. *Journal of Practical Psychiatry and Behavioral Health,* 219–228.

Milberger, S., Biederman, J., Faraone, S. V., Murphy, J., & Tsuang, M. T. (1995). Attention deficit hyperactivity disorder and comorbid disorders: Issues of overlapping symptoms. *American Journal of Psychiatry, 152,* 1793–1799.

Murphy, K. (1994). Guarding against over-diagnosis of ADHD in adults. *ADHD Report, 2,* 3–4.

Murphy, K., & Barkley, R. A. (1995). Preliminary normative data on DSM-IV criteria for adults. *ADHD Report, 3,* 6–7.

Murphy, K., & Barkley, R. A. (2000). To what extent are ADHD symptoms common? A reanalysis of standardization data from a DSM-IV checklist. *ADHD Report, 8(3),* 1–5.

Murphy, K. R., & Gordon, M. (1998). Assessment of adults with ADHD. In R. A. Barkley (Ed.), *Attention-deficit hyperactivity disorder: A handbook for diagnosis and treatment* (2nd ed., pp. 345–369). New York: Guilford Press.

National Institute of Health. (1998). *Diagnosis and treatment of attention deficit hyperactivity disorder.* NIH Consensus Statement 16, pp. 1–37. Washington, DC: U.S. Government Printing Office.

Sallee, F. (1995). *Attention-deficit/hyperactivity disorder in adults.* Champaign, IL: Grotelueschen Assocs.

Waid, L. R., Johnson, D. E., & Anton, R. F. (1997). Attention-deficit hyperactivity disorder and substance abuse. In H. R. Kranzler & B. J. Rounsaville (Eds.), *Dual diagnosis and treatment: Substance abuse and comorbid medical and psychiatric disorders* (pp. 393–425). New York: Marcel Dekker.

Ward, M. F., Wender, P. H., & Reimherr, F. W. (1993). The Wender Utah Rating Scale: An aid in the retrospective diagnosis of childhood attention deficit-hyperactivity disorder. *American Journal of Psychiatry, 150,* 885–890.

Wender, P. H. (1995). *Attention deficit hyperactivity disorder in adults.* New York: Oxford University Press.

Wender, P. H., Reimherr, F. W., & Wood, D. R. (1981). Attention deficit disorder ("Minimal brain dysfunction") in adults. Archives of *General Psychiatry, 38,* 449–456.

World Health Organization (1992). *International statistical classification of diseases and related health problems* (10th Rev.). Geneva: Author.

Zametkin, A. J. (1989). The neurobiology of attention-deficit hyperactivity disorder: A synopsis. *Psychiatric Annals, 19,* 584–586.

# 5

# Clinical Case Studies

Kevin Murphy Ph.D.

Differential diagnosis of Adult ADHD is a complex and formidable challenge, for a number of reasons. (1) The symptoms of ADHD are core symptoms of human nature that we all experience at times (Murphy & Gordon, 1998). It is not necessarily pathological to occasionally experience inattentiveness, impulsivity, forgetfulness, or disorganization. (2) As we are all aware by now, most adults with ADHD also have comorbid psychiatric conditions that can complicate the assessment process and influence treatment decisions. Disentangling ADHD from other psychiatric diagnoses, such as mood and anxiety disorders, substance abuse, and situational/environmental stressors, can be a difficult challenge for even the most seasoned diagnostician. (3) The term *clinically significant impairment* means different things to different people. How inattentive or impulsive does one have to be to meet the threshold for a clinical diagnosis? Measuring impairment and quantifying when a patient's symptoms cross over the line into *abnormal* involves a certain degree of subjectivity and clinical judgment. Obtaining a consensus among professionals on just where this standard lies on the impairment continuum is an ongoing challenge and a source of significant controversy.

(4) The diagnosis of ADHD in adulthood hinges heavily on childhood history, which can be difficult to obtain. In addition, reliance on self-reported memories of childhood symptoms may be vulnerable to inaccuracy, distortion, and incompleteness. (5) The increased awareness and popularity of the disorder, combined with the paucity of scientific research to date, has resulted in much folklore, myth, and misconception about adult ADHD among both patients and professionals. What we know about this disorder from results of sound empirical research is still extremely limited.

With these cautions in mind, the main purposes of this chapter are (1) to illustrate some of the more common challenges that arise in the assessment of Adult ADHD, (2) to discuss how these challenges were conceptualized and resolved, (3) to describe the rationale for the assessment/treatment decisions rendered, and (4) to underscore the importance of doing a credible and thorough assessment. I have chosen actual case examples of patients treated at the UMASS Adult ADHD Clinic in an effort to impart practical clinical information to clinicians interested in learning more about the nuances of assessing and treating Adult ADHD. These cases have been chosen to highlight important and useful "in the trenches" wisdom and are representative of the range of assessment and treatment issues that clinicians will likely wrestle with in practice. It is my hope that through these clinical cases, practitioners will not only gain a greater appreciation for the complexity of issues they will encounter in assessing and treating adult ADHD, but also learn to think more critically and intervene more effectively.

## CASE ONE: ASSIGNING THE ADHD DIAGNOSIS INCORRECTLY CAN CAUSE HARM

Susan was an attractive 20-year-old single college sophomore referred by her mother (a social worker) for further evaluation of an attention deficit hyperactivity disorder that had been diagnosed by her pediatrician the previous year. They were seeking a more comprehensive evaluation and a second opinion on the ADHD diagnosis. Susan reported long-standing problems with inconsistent concentration, easy distractibility, forgetfulness, restlessness, fidgeting, and disorganization that dated back to early childhood. These symptoms caused a great deal of frustration and a feeling that she was not working up to her full potential. Her mother consulted with Susan's pediatrician after Susan reported having unexpected difficulty studying and getting her work done during her freshman year of college. She had trouble listening to class lectures, daydreamed, had great difficulty remembering what she read, was physically restless, and could not seem to stay seated for an entire class. Her mother recognized these symptoms as being consistent with ADHD and wanted to determine (1) if ADHD was causing these problems and (2) what could be done about them. The pediatrician diagnosed ADHD and prescribed Ritalin, which Susan found helpful.

So far, on the face of it this sounds very much like the prototypical set of ADHD symptoms we so routinely hear from patients. Almost all adult ADHD evaluations have some of this sort of "face validity" to them, especially with respect to self-reported symptoms. But as you will see, clinicians need to go well beyond simple symptom endorsement to make a valid diagnosis. Does this person have ADHD? Why or why not? Is there enough information here to reliably establish the disorder? Are there any other psychiatric disorders that might better account for the symptoms? What other kinds of information would you need to have before you could be more certain of the diagnosis? Even if she has ADHD, are there any comorbid conditions that can also be identified?

Let's take a closer look at the details of this case. On what basis was the initial ADHD diagnosis made? The pediatrician's 1 1/2-page report was based on a single 30-minute meeting with Susan and her mother. Here are selected passages from the pediatrician's actual report copied verbatim.

> Susan is a 19-year-old young woman who is referred for evaluation in the ADHD Clinic. Susan's mother, who accompanied her to the visit, said that she had noticed that she was always fidgety and considered her energetic and "flakey" at times. She noted she has a tendency to misplace things and forget things. Susan herself reports being easily distracted when she is trying to concentrate on her work or studying. She had maintained good grades through high school, but had a difficult time in college this year. During the school year, she on one occasion took a friend's Ritalin and found that she was very focused for studying when she took it.
>
> Subsequently, a family friend who is a physician gave her a prescription for Ritalin, sustained release, 20 mg, which she took on an as-needed basis for school projects and for studying and found it helpful. She has not had any side effects as far as anorexia or sleep problems when taking the medicine.
>
> As she has been growing up, Susan has suffered no serious illnesses and has never required hospitalization. She has had some minor trauma, but none with neurological sequelae.
>
> Developmentally, Susan met her early milestones of motor and language development at appropriate times. She also developed independence skills appropriately and had done well academically through most of her school years. Susan's mother feels that Susan's father may have had some similar problems as they are encountering in Susan. No one else in the family is known to be affected. Her general physical examination was normal, and she appears to be in good general health.

I feel that Susan's symptoms are consistent with adult attention deficit disorder and she has had a positive response to Ritalin. I therefore provided her with further prescription for Ritalin of 20 mg sustained-release, which she will now use on a daily basis in the morning before class. She will use a second tablet later in the day as needed for course work or studying. I will see Susan back in approximately 3 months' time, depending on her school schedule, to find out how things are going and to give her further prescriptions if appropriate.

Dr's signature

Unfortunately, this type of an evaluation is not at all uncommon. For a variety of reasons, including the constraints of managed care, clinicians often do not have the time, training, or resources to conduct the kind of comprehensive evaluation that is necessary to accurately diagnose ADHD. This pediatrician's thinking probably went something like this: She and her mother are self-reporting all the right symptoms, which they say have been evident since childhood, and she has responded positively to her friend's Ritalin. She probably has ADHD, so why not treat her with medication in an effort to help? What's the harm? As you will see, misdiagnosing someone with ADHD can have negative consequences and may not be just a benign mistake.

I will now provide more of the history and details of this case that emerged from my more thorough evaluation of Susan. My evaluation included a comprehensive diagnostic interview with Susan and her mother, current and retrospective versions of the ADHD Rating Scale completed by Susan and her mother, and some testing, which was primarily for research purposes. The testing included an intellectual screen (Shipley), the Wide Range Achievement Test, the Nelson Denny Reading Test, the SCL-90-R, and the Conners Continuous Performance Test. Another critical aspect of my evaluation was inspection of her past school records, including her kindergarten record, elementary and middle school report cards, high school and college transcripts, and prior achievement test scores. Her mother brought in some of these records, and the rest were obtained through the mail with a signed consent accompanying Susan's request that her records be sent to our clinic.

## Relevant History

Susan's developmental and health histories were normal and unremarkable. She had no mood, behavior, or temperament problems as a child and had no problems with peer relationships. She had no prior psychiatric difficulties or treatment until her freshman year of college, when she sought some brief counseling for low-grade depression symptoms. She denied any history of anxiety symptoms, suicidal ideation, psychosis, or eating disorders. She has had several summer jobs and reported no history of any vocational impairment. However, what became apparent over the course of the assessment was that she was having some problems with substance abuse. She had been using marijuana on a daily basis since eleventh grade and had been using alcohol regularly since then as well. On the Young Adult Self-Report Form she indicated she had been intoxicated 65 out of the past 90 days, had used marijuana every day, and had also experimented with other drugs on occasion. Susan stated her substance use may have affected her motivation, but denied that it was affecting her academics because of how well she had done historically in school. Although her mother knew Susan had used alcohol and tried marijuana, she had no idea of the extent of her abuse. Other symptoms Susan described included never feeling satisfied, feeling indecisive about her future, restless sleeping, feeling unfocused and lazy, feeling like she does not fit in with her peers, and fearing that she would never find a special boyfriend that she could connect with. She added that she tended to hang out with friends who did a lot of partying because she found other peers who were more serious about school to be boring.

## School History

Susan had completed her sophomore year at a large midwestern college. She had always performed exceptionally well in school (A's and B's) and was always in accelerated and gifted classes. Her college GPA was 3.8, and she graduated near the top of her high school class. She never repeated a grade, was never considered a discipline/behavior problem, had no problems with peer relationships, and consistently did her homework. Her early school report cards documented no history of academic or behavior problems. To the contrary, her report cards were filled with teacher comments showing her to be a cooperative, conscientious, well-mannered, attentive child who was well liked by her classmates and a pleasure to have in class. Other quotes taken directly from her records included "effort is outstanding, citizenship is exemplary, mature, responsible, self-motivated, enthusiastic, and fine attitude." In short, her overall school history demonstrated absolutely no evidence of the types of symptoms or impairment that typically accompany ADHD.

## Testing/Rating Scale Results

Susan's overall testing results also showed no evidence of neurological dysfunction or attention problems, nor any impairment in learning. Her Shipley results yielded a composite score at the 92nd percentile, corresponding to the superior range of intelligence. On the Wide Range Achievement Test Susan scored at the 88th percentile in reading, the 75th percentile in spelling, and the 98th percentile in arithmetic (achieving a very rare perfect score on this subtest). On the Nelson Denny Reading Test Susan scored at the 83rd percentile in reading comprehension and at the 54th percentile in reading rate. Results of the Conners Continuous Performance Test were in the normal range. All of her prior standardized achievement test scores were in the above-average to superior ranges. Her SCL-90 scores showed moderately elevated scores on the Depression and Interpersonal Sensitivity scales.

Interestingly, despite an objective history wholly unsupportive of having ADHD, Susan endorsed 10 of the 18 symptoms of ADHD for both current and childhood functioning on the ADHD Rating Scale. Her mother endorsed 8 of the 18 ADHD symptoms for current functioning and 7 during childhood. So, although the history of functional impairment was not at all consistent with a developmental disability, both the patient and her mother saw Susan as exhibiting a significant number of ADHD symptoms throughout her life. Surprising? Not at all. Our data from a previous study (Murphy, Gordon, & Barkley, 2000) demonstrated just how common it is for normal adults to endorse ADHD symptomatology across the life span. In our community sample of 719 "normal" adults surveyed at two Department of Motor Vehicle offices in central Massachusetts, almost 80% reported experiencing six or more ADHD symptoms "at least sometimes" during childhood, and nearly 75% reported they were *currently* experiencing six or more ADHD symptoms "at least sometimes." Large percentages of adults identify with at least some of the symptoms of this disorder; far fewer actually meet full DSM-IV diagnostic criteria. As we have repeatedly emphasized in prior publications (Murphy & Gordon, 1998; Gordon & Murphy, 1998; Murphy & Barkley, 1996), diagnosing ADHD requires much more than simple symptom endorsement.

Does Susan have ADHD? Here is a summary of the major reasons why, according to DSM-IV, she does not meet criteria for ADHD.

1. It is quite clear she did not meet criteria for ADHD as a child, which is required to receive the diagnosis as an adult. There is no indication in her history that she experienced developmentally deviant problems with attention, self-control, or hyperactivity/impulsivity.
2. Her school history was not at all reflective of the typical kinds of ADHD symptoms/impairment that usually accompany ADHD. For example, she was always in gifted/accelerated classes, graduated 13th in her high school class, and had a 3.8 GPA in college. Further, her objective school records clearly

demonstrated she suffered no significant academic impairment historically and was a consistently high achiever who required no special help or accommodations to succeed.
3. She has experienced no significant impairment in work, social, or daily adaptive domains and clearly does not meet the impairment criteria required for a DSM-IV diagnosis.
4. Her symptoms appear to be better explained by a combination of other factors, including her chronic and daily marijuana use, alcohol abuse, and general personality factors.

## Feedback Session

I chose to directly and emphatically explain to Susan and her mother all of the reasons why she did not have ADHD. I received permission from Susan to discuss the substance abuse issues with her mother present. In a rather forceful and unequivocal manner, I told Susan that I believed the substance abuse was affecting her moods, academics, motivation, and overall functioning more than she was probably aware. I strongly recommended she eliminate or at least drastically reduce her alcohol and marijuana use and, if she was unable to accomplish this on her own, to seek professional help immediately. I pointed out and emphasized her extraordinary package of strengths and how unfortunate or even tragic it would be if she allowed her substance abuse to compromise or ruin her future. Now was the time to wake up and stop the progression into substance dependence—before it was too late. My tone was quite passionate, for I felt strongly that what happened in this feedback session could have huge implications on her future. Her outcome could go either way, and I believed that challenging her to make some critical lifestyle decisions, offering some strong guidance, and magnifying her impressive strengths just might help her set sail in the right direction.

Next, I recommended Susan discontinue her use of Ritalin, because there was no compelling need or reason to continue. It was apparent that Susan was operating under the illusion that ADHD was her primary problem and was conceptualizing all of her difficulties in ADHD terms. This prevented her from focusing on the core issue she really needed to be addressing—the substance abuse. She later admitted that the Ritalin was probably just helping her rebound from hangovers—activating her so she could study with less trouble. In her head, she attributed her academic success in large part to the medication and in that sense had come to rely on it. I was convinced that Susan was capable of excelling at school without the use of the medication (provided the substance abuse was under control) and believed it would be helpful to her in the long run to realize she could succeed on her own merits.

I also recommended Susan give some thought to spending more time with a different peer group, one that might have more in common with her regarding academics and future career potential. She had been hanging out with the wrong crowd at school, which was likely not helping her situation. It was also suggested she seek some individual counseling aimed at improving her self-esteem and interpersonal satisfaction, exploring/clarifying her personal, career, and academic goals, helping her reduce or eliminate her substance abuse, and for ongoing encouragement and motivation to stay on a positive track.

Although I had hoped that my evaluation and feedback had had a positive impact on Susan, it was not until several months later that I learned more about her outcome. While eating lunch in a local restaurant, I suddenly felt someone tapping my shoulder. I turned around and saw Susan's mother. With tears in her eyes she grasped my hand and told me how grateful and thankful she was for my efforts at "setting Susan straight." She went on to say that Susan had cut way back on her partying, had immediately stopped taking the Ritalin, had developed some new and healthier friendships, seemed more confident and self-assured, and was continuing to excel in school. She still did not have the boyfriend she wanted, but this was no longer the travesty that she had viewed it as before. The fear that had been so evident in her mother's face during our evaluation had been replaced with relief and gratitude.

What are some of the lessons/key points this case teaches us?

1. It illustrates the importance and value of obtaining early objective historical records. Her paper trail of school report cards was indisputable proof that she did not have ADHD as a child. Without this sort of data, it would have been far more difficult to reliably establish the absence of a childhood onset of symptoms/impairment. It is crucial to keep in mind that ADHD is a *developmental* disability with a *childhood onset* that typically results in a *chronic* and *pervasive* pattern of impairment in school, social, work, and daily adaptive domains. Persons with bona fide ADHD will usually leave a trail of evidence in their wake as they go through life that is a testament to their developmentally deviant problems with attention, self-control, and/or hyperactivity. Where there is no impairment, there is no disorder. When historical records offer no compelling record of impairment, it is difficult to justify an ADHD diagnosis.

2. It demonstrates the pitfalls of relying solely on self-reported symptoms and impairment. The pediatrician based the diagnosis exclusively on self-reports from Susan and her mother. Again, virtually all adult ADHD assessments have some "face validity" to them. Our challenge as clinicians is to move beyond the surface and make sure we thoroughly explore the key questions that are at the heart of a credible ADHD evaluation. Ideally, adult ADHD evaluations should strive to gather as much evidence as possible to address these key questions:
   a. Are the symptoms of inattention, impulsivity, and overactivity clearly evident?
   b. Is there objective evidence that these symptoms cause significant impairment in school, work, or social domains and in daily adaptive functioning?
   c. Have these symptoms been present since childhood? If not, is there a plausible explanation as to why the symptoms did not cause significant impairment until later (i.e., early treatment, accommodations, tutors, special school placement)?
   d. Have the symptoms been an enduring and consistent feature of this person's behavior over time and across situations? If not, are there convincing reasons for the inconsistencies?
   e. What evidence is there that the symptoms are not due solely to insufficient effort or motivation, poor vocational match, or transient situational or environmental circumstances/stressors?
   f. Is the symptom picture better explained by some other psychiatric or medical diagnosis?
   g. Is there evidence that other psychiatric conditions may coexist with the ADHD symptoms, and how would this affect the treatment plan?

3. It shows us never to assume that a previous professional's diagnosis is valid. It is always preferable to conduct your own independent and objective evaluation with an open mind, attempting to address as many of the key issues listed earlier as possible with whatever resources are available to you.

4. It illustrates that a positive Ritalin response is not diagnostic of ADHD. In fact, most anyone who tried using a stimulant would report feeling more attentive and focused. The fact that Susan reported being able to study and focus better while on Ritalin in no way establishes that she has ADHD.

5. It shows the importance of clinician's having a repertoire that includes being able to explain convincingly and effectively how and why the patient does not have ADHD and what other diagnosis may better explain their problems.

6. It reminds us to make sure we apply the full DSM-IV criteria (including the requirement for "clinically significant impairment") as opposed to accepting self-perceptions of ADHD-like complaints as sufficient for establishing the disorder.

7. It informs us of the potential harm that mislabeling someone as ADHD can cause. Had Susan gone on believing that her problems were due to ADHD, this would have prevented or further distanced her from addressing her real problem. Her substance abuse would have continued to progress, she would have continued taking medication that was not necessary, her parents' angst would have continued, and she would have continued to attribute her success to something other than herself, which would have further eroded her self-esteem. Moreover, if she ever requested academic or workplace accommodations in the future under the Americans with Disabilities Act and was required to submit documentation in support of her disability, it is highly unlikely she would be able to substantiate either a diagnosis or a disability.

## CASE TWO: ADHD OR BIPOLAR DISORDER OR BOTH?

(A version of this case was originally published in the Clinical Grand Rounds section of the *ADHD Report*, Vol 6, No. 1, pp. 14–16, and is reprinted by permission of Guilford Press). The patient was a 37-year-old married male who was self-referred to our clinic. His daughter had been diagnosed with ADHD and while attending a local CH.A.D.D (Children and Adults with Attention Deficit Disorder) meeting he discovered that ADHD was now being recognized and treated in adults. He had been diagnosed with hyperactivity as a child and had continued to experience problems with concentration, distractibility, following tasks through to completion, school performance, and maintaining successful employment. A review of his history indicated he had experienced longstanding ADHD symptomatology beginning in early childhood that had continued to plague him throughout his life. His developmental history was unremarkable in that he experienced no major temperament problems as a child and reached all of his major developmental milestones at age-appropriate times. However, he did indicate experiencing problems with peer relationships as a child and was often ridiculed and physically beaten by his peers. He had no history of any past or present significant health problems. His first marriage lasted seven years and ended in divorce. He was married to his second wife for ten years and had a 9-year-old daughter who had been recently diagnosed with ADHD. His father had an eighth-grade education, and the patient suspected that his father also had ADHD and learning problems.

## Past Psychiatric History

The patient came to our clinic with an established diagnosis of bipolar disorder. He had been taking lithium 1800 mg per day for the previous eight years. He had been hospitalized on two occasions at a Veteran's Administration Hospital, which was where he received his bipolar diagnosis. Both he and his wife never believed this was an accurate diagnosis, wanted a second opinion, and wanted to explore ADHD as a possible alternative explanation for his longstanding problems.

The patient had been diagnosed with hyperactivity in the sixth grade and was put on Ritalin for two years, with excellent results. He apparently stopped taking the medication after his doctor moved away and he could not find another doctor to prescribe for him. He was told he was too old to take Ritalin and would outgrow his symptoms. From the ninth grade on, he went untreated and continued to have ongoing problems with self-control, academics, and peer relationships. He had been hospitalized in two different VA hospitals for depression and anxiety symptoms in the past. The first hospitalization occurred after he was informed he had a terminal disease, which he later learned was not true. His "depression" disappeared immediately after this good news was confirmed and he was discharged. The second hospitalization occurred after a loud argument with his ex-wife when he was under the influence of alcohol. He was agitated and verbally abusive and a neighbor called the police, who escorted him to the VA Hospital for evaluation. He reported using alcohol and marijuana while in the service but denied any current use or abuse. Thorazine was prescribed during his second hospitalization, which he took only once due to negative side effects. He denied ever having any delusions or hallucinations, manic episodes, or obsessions/compulsions. He described himself as extremely impulsive, disinhibited, argumentative, and hyperactive.

## School History

The patient graduated from high school and attended several colleges over a 13-year period but was unable to complete a degree. He described a history of problems with school, including inconsistent performance and grades, distractibility, impulsivity, poor concentration, poor reading comprehension, hyperactivity, and peer relationship problems beginning in early elementary school. He had a history of performing below his potential in school, and his teachers always thought he could do better. He was placed in remedial reading classes during his earlier school years and stated he never was able to do homework. He had great difficulty sitting still, focusing, and sustaining his effort and concentration long enough to get anything done. School had always been a source of great frustration for him, and he never understood why he was not able to achieve up to the level of most of his peers.

## Vocational History

The patient estimated he had worked at well over a hundred different jobs in his adult life. He routinely held four or five part-time jobs at a time and would replace jobs as fast as he lost them. He needed constant variety and became easily bored with most of his jobs. He estimated that he had been fired from at least 50 jobs in the past and had impulsively quit at least another 25. Most of his jobs were in the electronics and manufacturing fields. He had chronic problems with getting along with coworkers and especially authority figures and bosses. He always had great difficulty conforming to rules, was often late, and did what he wanted to do instead of what he was supposed to do. While in the service he had great difficulty following the rules and regimentation and was given an abrupt general discharge under honorable conditions after numerous reprimands.

## Assessment Results

A summary of his results indicated that both he and his wife endorsed 16 of the 18 symptoms of ADHD currently. He endorsed the same number of symptoms for when he was a child. Intellectual assessment yielded an IQ in the above-average range, and his performance on the Wide Range Achievement Test indicated average to above-average skills in math, spelling, and reading. Clearly, there was a marked difference between his measured intelligence and his history of poor school performance. A careful review of his history suggested that he had never met full criteria for mania and had never met criteria for a major depression. There appeared to be little evidence to support a diagnosis of bipolar disorder. Although he did experience several periods of episodic depression, they were associated with situational precipitants and tended to resolve suddenly when circumstances changed. In short, there seemed to be little symptomatology in his history that would support a diagnosis of bipolar disorder and many indications of long-standing symptoms consistent with ADHD. Further, both he and his wife indicated lithium was not at all helpful. In fact, he indicated he had taken his lithium only sporadically for much of the past eight years due to his ambivalence about the bipolar diagnosis. It was also not clear that he had ever experienced a true manic episode. His wife of 12 years stated that she had never seen him exhibit manic symptoms, and she also doubted the bipolar diagnosis.

## Treatment Decisions and Discussion

This case illustrates some of the difficulties in differentiating the hyperactive/impulsive symptoms of ADHD from a mild form of bipolar disorder. In most cases, the vastly different symptomatology between ADHD and classic bipolar I is not difficult to distinguish. For example, the markedly elevated mood, grandiosity, pressured speech, decreased need for sleep, hypersexuality, reckless spending, and in some cases psychotic symptomatology associated with a true manic episode are quite distinct from ADHD. However, it can be much more difficult to differentiate ADHD from a milder form of this mood disorder, such as bipolar II, hypomania, or cyclothymia, where there is considerable symptom overlap with ADHD. In this case, the evidence supporting an ADHD diagnosis included the following:

1. The patient and his wife endorsed a sufficient number of DSM.III-R symptoms.
2. He had received a diagnosis of hyperactivity during childhood.
3. He had a positive response to Ritalin for two years during childhood.
4. Despite his above-average intelligence, he had a longstanding history of poor/uneven school performance.
5. He had a longstanding history of peer relationship problems.
6. He had problems maintaining consistent employment that appeared to be related primarily to severe impulsivity, hyperactivity, and oppositionality.
7. ADHD was present in the family bloodlines (daughter diagnosed and father suspected of having ADHD).
8. His overall history was more suggestive of a chronic and pervasive pattern of ADHD-like impairment, which clearly began in early childhood, not the wide and cyclical mood swings, episodic bursts of productivity, grandiosity, insomnia, pressured speech, and excessive activity level/ reckless behavior associated with bipolar disorder.

On the other hand, evidence supporting a possible bipolar disorder included the following:

1. Periods of episodic depression symptoms in the past.
2. Periodic explosive temper outbursts that may have resembled the agitation and mood lability of a mood disorder.
3. The patient had been prescribed 1800 mg of lithium per day for the past eight years and had not experienced a major depression or manic episode since being on the drug.
4. He had been hospitalized on two previous occasions and diagnosed as having bipolar disorder.
5. His pattern of working several part-time jobs simultaneously and the sheer number of jobs, terminations, and impulsive quits could plausibly be viewed as stemming from hypomanic behavior.
6. He spent money impulsively (often on hobbies or "toys" that he quickly got bored with) that created a significant financial hardship for his family.

In our opinion at the time, there was more evidence to support an ADHD diagnosis than a bipolar diagnosis. A detailed feedback session was conducted with the patient and his wife reviewing the reasons for both the ADHD diagnosis and the possibility of the bipolar diagnosis. The patient and his wife agreed with the ADHD diagnosis and expressed a strong desire to pursue treatment for ADHD. An informed consent discussion was conducted with the patient and his wife outlining the possible risks and benefits associated with treating him for ADHD. Since we could not reliably predict the outcome or guarantee a positive response, it was pointed out that if he did have a form of bipolar disorder and was treated with a dopamine agonist such as Ritalin, there was a possibility of precipitating a manic episode. Once he understood the potential risks and benefits and our informed consent discussion was documented, we proceeded with treatment.

We began by gradually tapering his lithium dose over several weeks until the lithium was discontinued altogether. Over the course of this withdrawal period the patient's mental status was monitored closely to ensure that his mood remained stable. No evidence of manic symptoms emerged, so a Ritalin trial of 5 mg TID three times a day was started. He tolerated this well, reported no side effects, and reported an increased ability to focus and concentrate. After one week, his dose was increased to 10 mg three times a day. He continued to respond extraordinarily well with no appreciable side effects, and his dosage was increased to 15 mg TID and eventually to 20 mg TID. At no point in his treatment did he ever display symptoms of mania or a major depression. The Ritalin produced an immediate and dramatic improvement in this patient's day-to-day functioning.

Although we were not completely sure at the time whether he had ADHD alone or ADHD with a comorbid mood disorder, several clues emerged that suggested we were not treating a mood disorder.

1. The patient had never believed the lithium was beneficial at any dose level.
2. No noticeable change in his mental status or moods occurred over the course of the lithium withdrawal.
3. Ritalin even at low doses produced dramatic and ongoing improvement in all aspects of his life.
4. Ritalin did not induce any manic-like symptoms.
5. No history of bipolar or mood disorder was present in the patient's family bloodlines, but there was a positive family history of ADHD (daughter and possibly his father).
6. He remembered having a poor response to a tricyclic antidepressant during his first hospitalization.
7. His overall improvement has continued for nine years, with no evidence of depression or mania.

The combination of going off the lithium, getting back on Ritalin, education about the disorder, and some supportive counseling improved his life in a most profound way. His accomplishments since beginning treatment for ADHD included the following.

1. He not only completed his undergraduate degree, but continued on to earn a Masters degree, graduating with honors.
2. He currently has one job, and the revolving-door pattern and problems with temper and impulse control at work have markedly improved.
3. His moods are more stable, and he is able to control his temper to a much greater degree.
4. He is far less impulsive, is able to think ahead and anticipate consequences more effectively, and is more financially secure since gaining better control over his impulsive spending habits.
5. His marriage is more solid and stable, and as a result of his improvement he and his wife agreed to have another child.

It has now been almost nine years since his adult ADHD diagnosis, and he continues to do extraordinarily well. He continues to take Ritalin 20 mg three times a day and remains stable in his work and family life.

## Parting Comments

This case again illustrates the importance of a thorough assessment and history taking when evaluating for adult ADHD. On the face of it, it is understandable how someone with his prior history and behavior could have been viewed as having bipolar II disorder or cyclothymia. Unfortunately, this patient struggled for years with a misdiagnosis of bipolar disorder and ineffective treatment. Another lesson evident from this case (as also mentioned in Case One) is not to automatically assume that a previous diagnosis from another professional is valid. It is always preferable to perform an independent and objective assessment and to gather your own data in support of your diagnostic conclusions as opposed to merely accepting another professional's opinion. Accepting the previously established bipolar diagnosis as valid and failing to consider ADHD as a possible explanation for his difficulties would have been most unfortunate for this patient.

Although this patient still experiences ADHD symptoms, they have become far less disruptive, and the overall quality of his life has been dramatically improved. The components to his treatment and successful outcome included not just stimulant medication, but education about the disorder, supportive counseling, a supportive wife, making appropriate vocational and educational choices, and a lot of hard work.

## CASE THREE: ADHD WITH COMORBID SUBSTANCE DEPENDENCE AND CONDUCT DISORDER

(A version of this case was originally published in the Clinical Grand Rounds section of The *ADHD Report*, Vol. 8, No. 3, pp. 14–16, and is reprinted with permission of Guilford Press). Most clinicians are well aware that adolescents with ADHD and comorbid conduct problems and substance abuse are among the most difficult individuals to treat successfully. They present special and enormously difficult challenges and frustrations to parents, educators, and professional treatment providers. Some of the common issues these teenagers face include lack of understanding and denial of their disability, fear of being stigmatized and not being accepted, low self-esteem, treatment compliance issues regarding medication and counseling, acceptance of their disability and learning not to devalue themselves because of it, peer group influences, problems with the law, and struggles with parents around autonomy/independence/maturity issues.

Although research studies indicate the outcomes for this group are generally quite poor compared to teens with ADHD who do not have conduct or substance abuse problems, it is essential that all of us—parents, teachers, and professionals—not give up on them. Scientific studies report findings based on group data, not on any one individual. It is important to remember that group data do not dictate the outcome of any one individual. It is therefore essential that we identify and assist those with ADHD/CD/substance abuse, because underneath their problems they can, in some cases, be skilled, capable, productive people who contribute significantly to society if properly treated.

The main purpose of this case is to convey the message that no one is hopeless and that even those with the poorest prognosis can sometimes defy the odds and turn things around. It is hoped that patients with similar profiles can glean hope from this story and that clinicians will be reinforced never to give up on these most challenging cases.

### Background Information

I began seeing J when he was 16 years old. He had been diagnosed with ADHD, conduct disorder, and polysubstance dependence a year earlier at the UMASS Child ADHD Clinic. He had a longstanding history of school/learning problems, disruptive and aggressive behavior, impulsivity, and severe attention difficulties beginning in very early childhood. These problems led his mother to pull him out of public school after first grade and homeschooling him until the eighth grade. He began drinking alcohol at age 12 and shortly thereafter began abusing marijuana, acid, and crack cocaine. His attempt at public high school failed, and he ended up dropping out of school in ninth grade.

J immediately began having problems with the law and had been in jail and juvenile detention centers several times before his 16th birthday for charges including auto theft, breaking and entering, assault and battery, and various drug charges.

One of J's favorite things to do was to engage in fistfights. He loved the rush and excitement of a good fight and actively sought them out. His idea of fun on a Saturday night was to throw rocks at police cars because he "loved the chase." J's biological father (whom he never knew) had a history of alcohol and drug abuse, behavior problems resulting in expulsion from high school, antisocial behavior, and incarceration. J seemed destined for a similar fate.

By the tender age of 17, J had already experienced five inpatient hospitalizations for substance dependence, was thrown out of several others for rule infractions, attended several other court-mandated outpatient treatment programs, was well known to all the local police, and had served significant jail time. He could not seem to follow through with anything. Many professionals involved in his treatment figured he would either be dead or permanently incarcerated by the time he was 21. He could not stay clean from drugs, would continually relapse after brief periods of sobriety, had a violent temper, hung around with the wrong people, had never worked at a competitive job, had no formal education, and was a source of intense frustration to his treatment providers. At least one of his doctors labeled him as "hopeless" and "did not want to waste any more time on him."

## Initial Treatment Attempts

Despite this clinical picture, there was something about J that I found engaging and likable. I did not find him to be the intractable antisocial personality-disordered person that others had. Underneath his hard exterior was a charisma of sorts, an engaging spirit and personality, a great deal of "street smarts," and a dry sense of humor. It seemed that a part of him wanted to find a way to turn his life around, but he just didn't know how or where to begin. I began my work with him by focusing on his most pressing problem—his substance abuse. I was desperately trying to influence him to acknowledge his substance abuse problem and to work at maintaining sobriety. If he could remain clean for even a brief period, it might allow us to pursue a stimulant medication trial to concurrently treat his underlying ADHD symptomatology and curb his severe impulsivity. I also attempted to educate him about ADHD to help him understand its relationship to some of his current and past problems. I tried to instill hope that if he could get clean and we could treat his underlying ADHD, he would see significant improvements in his life. Unfortunately, at that time he was not able to understand or accept the ADHD piece, and he continued to struggle with sobriety and the law. Consequently, he was not able to achieve a degree of sobriety/stability that would have allowed us to safely medicate him for ADHD. Nevertheless, I hoped I had at least planted some seeds and stimulated him to begin thinking in a positive direction.

## Later Course

I continued to offer supportive counseling to J, but he eventually moved out of the area and I lost touch with him for several years. In the meantime, we began treating his mother for ADHD and she responded beautifully to Ritalin. I did not see J again until several years later. His mother had kept me abreast of his progress, which turned out to be truly remarkable. In short, despite some setbacks and struggles, J was able to find a way to turn his life around and sustain a positive direction in a way that no one thought possible. Today, at age 24, J is drug free, takes Ritalin on a regular basis, has maintained successful and steady employment as a chef, has stayed out of legal trouble, and appears to have a good chance at a bright future. How did someone with such a poor prognosis accomplish all of this? I asked J to sit down with me and discuss the factors that contributed to his unlikely and impressive turnaround. He gladly agreed, and here is what he told me.

## Factors in His Turnaround

**Getting clean from drugs.** This was the foundation that allowed other positive events to occur in his life. He finally realized he had lost control and could not continue his familiar pattern and that his drug use was always associated with big trouble. He had been exposed to a great deal of substance abuse education in his prior inpatient and outpatient treatment but had not been ready to make the life changes required to succeed. With some added maturity and a growing realization that his way was not working, he decided he must begin to make some serious changes. J made a conscious decision that he wanted to live and be straight. With his reputation and history, to have any chance of making it he felt he had to make a fresh start elsewhere. He moved away from his hometown (and the people, places, and influences that helped keep him stuck) and went to a resort area, where he knew a friend who got him a dishwashing job. He began attending Alcoholics Anonymous and Narcotics Anonymous meetings and cut ties with all the negative influences and people from his past.

**He began taking Ritalin.** After witnessing his mother's dramatic improvement while on Ritalin, J decided he had nothing to lose by trying it. He noticed an immediate improvement in his ability to focus, sustain his effort and concentration, and slow down. His impulsive temper was improved (but not cured), and he seemed to have generally better self-control. Although he did not respond quite as dramatically as his mother had, there was clearly a marked improvement in his overall functioning. He stated there is absolutely no way he would be able to perform his current job as a chef without the Ritalin. His current dose is 20 mg four times a day, and he, his mother, and his girlfriend realize it is, and will continue to be, a key to his future success.

**He found a supportive, straight, and healthy girlfriend who genuinely cared about him.** This was a new experience for J. She apparently saw the good in him and made it quite clear she would not be a part of his life if he chose to use drugs. She was bright, responsible, and hard working, seemed to understand and accept him, and has been a distinctly positive influence on J. It was indeed fortunate that he met her when he did, because at any other time in his life their relationship would never have happened. She provided some much needed structure and encouragement, they had a lot of fun together, and she believed in him. J also helped her in many ways, and they became best friends. They have begun to live together and are learning how to adjust to each other's style and personal habits. So far, it seems to be going reasonably well.

**He found a job situation that "fit" him, which allowed him to experience success.** After working as a dishwasher and paying his dues for a while, J was offered a chance to start working as a prep cook, which he immediately excelled at. He loved the hands-on aspect of the job, the fast pace and excitement, the varied responsibilities, the physical movement required, and the opportunity to move to different resort locations periodically when the need arose. For example, he got to work in the kitchens at Steamboat Springs, Colorado; Deer Valley, Utah; Key Largo, Florida; and Glacier National Park. He was transferred frequently enough so that he never was bored. He worked long hours, worked weekend nights, which helped him stay clean and out of trouble, and began learning as much as he could about the culinary trade. He made it a point to be polite and respectful to his bosses, and before long it became apparent that he was talented and highly valued. For the first time in his life he was having success in a competitive job, and he began making good money. His self-esteem continued to improve. He began assuming more and more responsibility and eventually found himself in a head chef position supervising a staff of 33. His quick temper still interfered on occasion, but his overall performance was excellent.

**Taking up karate.** Coinciding with his new life was a decision to study karate. Since he always loved to fight, he was a natural, and it soon became his passion. He loved the philosophical part as much as the physical, and he eventually earned a black belt. It taught him self-discipline at a time when he greatly needed it, and the structure and commitment it required was also therapeutic. He competed in and won several tournaments and also became a karate teacher himself. His success resulted in his gaining some much needed self-respect and self-confidence. Between his work, the karate, and his girlfriend, he had little time or energy left to find any trouble.

**His mother.** Despite seeing her relatively infrequently and a history of ups and downs with her, J always knew his mother loved him, saw the good in him, and was behind him. Although he often got angry with her (and especially his stepfather), he always respected her and knew she would never give up on him. It was comforting for him to know that deep down, no matter what kind of trouble he was in, she would always be there and would never abandon him. She was the one constant in his life when everything else seemed so unstable and chaotic. She helped him out of numerous jams, and as he has matured, J has gained more and more respect for his mother. In retrospect, J has come to realize how important she has been and continues to be to him. No one is more proud of where he has come to today, and his mother has always been his number-one fan.

**Luck.** It never hurts to have some luck, and J has experienced his share of good fortune. He could have been killed or seriously injured in numerous situations and seems to have been in the right place at the right time on many occasions. Given the experiences and places he has been in the past and what could have been, he is the first to admit that he is indeed fortunate to be where he is today. On the other hand, to some extent he has also made his own luck. Armed with his good social skills and street savvy, J has made his own breaks by taking charge of opportunities that have come his way and capitalizing on them.

**Social skills.** J may have little formal education, but he has a Ph.D. in street smarts and social intelligence. He has always been "cool," knows how to talk to and get along with all kinds of people, is likable and funny, and knows how to create opportunities for himself. He respects people who also show him respect, makes friends easily, and has made significant strides in learning how to reach out and be a friend to others. His interpersonal style and ability has clearly contributed to his current success and will no doubt continue to be a valuable asset in the future.

## Current Status and Future Goals

J continues to stay clean of drugs but does drink alcohol on occasion. Although he realizes the safest course is complete abstinence, his use of alcohol has stayed largely under control in recent years. He has a full-time job as a chef in yet another resort location, is living successfully with his girlfriend, is physically active with his karate, has no current problems with the law, and is taking his medication consistently. He is considering pursuing his GED and may even consider furthering his education in the future. Although his course has been anything but smooth and linear and he has had his share of setbacks, J has managed to overcome huge odds and turn his life in a positive direction. He seems to enjoy life now and can actually see a future for himself. Although the jury is still out on his long-term outcome, his attitude, motivation, and determination to stay on a positive track bodes well for his future.

## Conclusion

Despite the generally poorer outcomes of those adolescents with comorbid ADHD, conduct disorder, and substance abuse, some, like J, do go on to achieve satisfactory outcomes. We need to strive to better understand the variables that are correlated with positive outcome and keep working at bringing them about. Clinicians can play a powerful role in helping these adolescents learn ways to overcome their problems, by instilling hope, reducing discouragement and demoralization, and fostering a belief that they *can* be successful in school, work, and their future lives. They need to understand that they have a treatable condition and that they have some power, control, and responsibility over how effectively they learn to manage it.

## CASE FOUR: ADHD/LD AND TEST ACCOMMODATIONS FOR A PROFESSIONAL LICENSING EXAM: EFFECTIVE ADVOCACY

Attention deficit hyperactivity disorder has become an increasingly popular basis for seeking test accommodations under the Americans with Disabilities Act. The ADA is an *antidiscrimination law* whose goal is to ensure *equal access* and to level the playing field for individuals with disabilities (Gordon & Murphy, 1998). It serves to protect people who are otherwise qualified to perform the essential functions of a job from being discriminated against solely on the basis of a disability. More specifically, the ADA states that to be considered disabled, a person must be "substantially limited (not mildly or trivially) in a major life activity" compared to the "average person in the general population." Consequently, persons who demonstrate uneven performance or relative weaknesses in select areas that do not amount to a "substantial limitation" in a major life activity compared to most people are not considered disabled and are therefore not eligible for accommodations under the law. What do these words mean and what relevance do they have to mental health professionals? How do we apply these principles to real-life cases?

If you are not exactly sure, you are not alone. In fact, most mental health professionals who submit documentation on behalf of examinees are uninformed about the legislative intent of the ADA and unfamiliar with the fundamental principles inherent in the ADA (Gordon & Murphy, 1998). This is not especially surprising given that (1) the law is only ten years old and its impact on higher education has begun to surface only relatively recently, and (2) continuing education training opportunities on the subject are not readily available.

But perhaps the largest source of error lies in our confusing special education laws (such as the Individuals with Disabilities Education Act, or IDEA) with antidiscrimination laws (such as the ADA). Most clinicians are familiar with the IDEA, which is a special education law that dictates that children who underachieve due to a disability are entitled to remedial services that correct or circumvent deficiencies (Gordon & Murphy, 1998). A major goal of the IDEA is to facilitate success or a positive outcome. Its spirit and intent are consistent with how most clinicians and advocates have been trained—to do whatever it takes to help students optimize their performance and reach their goals. However, a critical distinction between IDEA and ADA that is so often misunderstood is that this notion of creating conditions to facilitate success really has nothing to do with the ADA. Again, the ADA is intended to guarantee *equal opportunity* or *equal access*, not a successful outcome. Where the goal of the IDEA is to facilitate learning and optimize student achievement, the ADA is *outcome neutral* and addresses the responsibility of institutions to ensure that otherwise-qualified individuals are not discriminated against on the basis of a disability. Failure to understand this fundamental difference between these two laws is the source of much confusion, anger, and heartache among both students and their clinicians.

Not only this, but due in part to some recent precedent-setting cases (*Price v. National Board of Medical Examiners*, 1997; *Gonzalez v. National Board of Medical Examiners*, 2000) and some recent Supreme Court decisions (*Sutton v. United Airlines*, 1999; *Murphy v. United Parcel Service*, 1999; *Albertson's v. Kirkingburg*, 1999), the term *disability* is becoming more narrowly defined. The documentation requirements not only to adequately substantiate a diagnosis, but to demonstrate that a person's degree of impairment is sufficient to rise to the level of a disability, are quite rigorous and not commonly understood by the average diagnostician. *Standard diagnostic/testing reports done in the course of routine practice almost always fall short of what is required to substantiate a disability.* Clinicians must build a compelling case based on a history of clinically significant functional impairment (preferably with prior objective records and not simply self-reported memories) that shows the person is substantially limited in a major life activity in comparison to most people in the general population. This is a difficult standard to meet, especially in graduate school environments, where most people, simply by virtue of being accepted into these highly competitive environments, are functioning at a higher level than the "average" person. In short, the high-stakes issues surrounding ADHD, test accommodations, and the ADA are contentious ones that are poorly understood by most mental health professionals.

This case illuminates and explains many of the concepts and key issues diagnosticians need to understand to substantiate a diagnosis and to establish a *disability* as this term is defined under the law. It will also point out some of the common mistakes mental health professionals make in their documentation efforts. My hope is that after digesting this case, clinicians will be better equipped to handle similar cases, better able to apply these principles in a fair and objective manner, and thereby be more effective clinicians/advocates.

## Background Information

Tom was a 24-year-old single white male referred by his parents. He had experienced problems with concentration, distractibility, impulsivity, and school/learning problems beginning in early childhood. His developmental history was mostly unremarkable, with the exception of being delayed in talking. He was not able to combine words so others could understand him until age 4. His mother described him as extremely active, always on the go, impatient, disorganized, and a bit overbearing at times. He had no significant health problems. Both of his sisters had been diagnosed with ADHD, and Tom suspected his paternal grandmother also had it.

## Past Educational and Psychiatric History

Tom first saw a mental health professional during second grade due to poor school achievement. Despite a WISC-R Verbal IQ of 107, Performance IQ of 109, and Full Scale IQ of 109, his Core evaluation report from 1978 recommended he be held back in second grade, described him as distractible and having problems with reading, and documented a diagnosis of dyslexia. This was based on school records, parent input, and testing results that showed him to be functioning two years below grade level in reading. This educational testing report clearly spelled out the nature of his problems and described the types of errors he made (letter reversals, b–d consonant confusion, poor oral reading not yet developed at the preprimer level, sequencing errors, substitutions, random guessing, poor word recognition, and distractibility). It provided a sound rationale for the diagnosis of reading disorder/dyslexia and also described some early indications of ADHD symptomatology. The report also made recommendations that logically flowed from the nature of the impairment. These included daily one-to-one reading instruction, tutoring, varying the pacing of material and teaching style, use of multisensory teaching techniques for phonics and sight word learning, ongoing informal assessments of progress, and reevaluation in one year's time. Future evaluations and testing continued to validate the ongoing nature of his problems and the types of interventions, accommodations, and compensatory strategies he utilized. For example, his documentation indicated he had been receiving resource room assistance five times a week for reading, spelling, and auditory memory throughout elementary school, had worked extensively with tutors on organizational strategies, on proactive planning, and on completing long-range assignments, and had received tutoring in algebra and foreign languages after failing both in high school. He had also decided early on to learn to type using a word processor and to use spell-check due to his poor handwriting and severe spelling problems (also well documented).

Tom provided another report from a psychologist he saw in tenth grade that summarized all of his prior evaluations and validated his ongoing and continued functional impairment. It also described additional details, including problems with self-esteem arising from his school problems, his anger at having been labeled with a disability and his difficulty accepting this, and his resentment at having to spend so much time with tutors and in resource rooms. This report spelled out a series of recommendations that included extended time on tests, private tutoring, waiving his high school's foreign language requirement, encouraging him to use spell-check, grammar-check, and a word processor, and exploring colleges that have a reputation for understanding and accommodating students with his types of challenges. Further, it documented his parents' desire for him to attend a year at Landmark School (a special school for students with ADHD and/or LD) to consolidate his skills before taking on the challenges of college. Again, this psychologist's report clearly explained the longstanding nature of his problems, included concurrent validation of his difficulties from multiple sources (several prior testing reports, school records and report cards, input from parents and tutors, and scores from prior standardized achievement tests), and provided a rationale for the suggested accommodations that made good intuitive sense and logically flowed from Tom's history of functional impairment.

## Rationale for Comorbid ADHD Diagnosis

Despite many of his past records describing ADHD-like symptomatology, Tom had never been diagnosed with ADHD. His problems had always been conceptualized as purely learning disabilities. Although I agreed that his primary problems were in the realm of learning disabilities, I also felt there was ample evidence of comorbid ADHD that could be contributing to his academic and social difficulties. The evidence for the possible existence of ADHD included the following.

1. Tom endorsed 13 of the 18 symptoms of ADHD for current functioning and 15 of the 18 symptoms for childhood functioning.

2. His mother also endorsed 15 of the 18 ADHD symptoms for both current and childhood functioning.

3. His school report cards documented a consistent pattern of ADHD symptomatology and impairment throughout his school history, including excessive talking, distractibility, inconsistent effort, not working up to potential, problems with conduct and self-control, being unprepared for class, and trouble completing homework.

4. His distractibility, forgetfulness, restlessness, and disorganization had interfered in his prior work history, resulting in inconsistent performance reviews. He was bored easily and had great difficulty doing what he termed mindless and repetitive work. He also had problems with listening, interrupting, impatience, and losing things frequently, both in school and in work situations. He vowed he could never do a job where he was required to sit at a desk

all day. After a few trials doing office-type work, he ended up doing landscaping during summers because it offered some variety, was movement oriented and less restrictive, and was outdoors.

5. From a genetic standpoint, ADHD is known to be highly heritable and familial, and several members of Tom's immediate and extended family also had documented ADHD.

6. The diagnostic interview with both Tom and his mother supported an early-appearing, chronic, and pervasive pattern of impairment in attention and self-control separate from his more discrete learning/reading problems. There was also ample evidence that these symptoms were continuing to cause significant current impairment in his adult life in school and work domains.

7. My diagnostic interview carefully ruled out other possible explanations for his symptoms before concluding ADHD was an appropriate diagnosis. He denied significant problems with depression, anxiety, substance abuse, mania, or psychosis, and no environmental or situational stressor appeared to better account for his problems.

8. A Ritalin trial produced a dramatically positive response. He was more focused, less restless, and able to sustain his effort and study productively for longer periods, and his grades improved significantly while on the medication. Moreover, his parents and girlfriend validated and were astonished to see the vast improvements in his self-control, follow-through, ability to listen and not interrupt, and overall behavior.

9. In short, although I thought the LD problems were responsible for the lion's share of his academic problems, I believed that ADHD was also contributing, and the combination of the two made school a particularly difficult and frustrating experience for Tom.

## Later School/Psychiatric History

At the time he saw me, Tom was a third-year law student and was planning to request the accommodations of extended time and the use of a word processor on his upcoming Bar exam. In addition to the objective records already described, he was able to produce documentation of his SAT scores (340 verbal, 390 math the first time, and 410 verbal, 350 math the second time, both with extended time), class rank in high school (135 out of 256), undergraduate transcripts (2.3 GPA and verification he had received services through the Students with Disabilities Office), and written verification that he had been granted accommodations in past educational and testing environments. We also gathered his prior intellectual assessment results, which consistently showed him to be functioning in the above-average range of intelligence (most recent WAIS-R results were Verbal IQ 119, Performance IQ 112, Full Scale IQ 118). It was quite obvious that Tom was much brighter and had more ability than his rather mediocre paper trail would suggest. He described his struggles in college and law school and the perseverance and methods he employed to work around his weaknesses. He continued to seek tutoring and a proofreader, maximized his use of technology (word processor, spell-check, Palm Pilot), and got to know all of his professors, who ended up respecting his impressive strengths, his work ethic, and his resilience.

## Personal Qualities

Another aspect of his history that played an important role in his ability to cope so successfully was his vibrant personality and can-do attitude. It was quite clear from comments on his school records that teachers recognized his many strengths. He was viewed as intelligent, upbeat, articulate, and ambitious. He was also very good-looking, likable, and "politically astute," which made teachers more inclined to cut him some slack and overlook his weaknesses. Tom told me he felt that having to work so hard to overcome his challenges would prepare him to compete effectively in the professional world. His motivation, intense desire to succeed, and upbeat attitude allowed him to truly believe he could become a successful lawyer in spite of his problems. He did not dwell on his areas of weakness or use them as excuses—he found a way to work around them and spent more time developing his strengths. He did not overreact to setbacks. Instead, he learned from them and developed concrete plans to offset them. I could not help being impressed with his character and the way he approached his problems. In short, Tom was always willing to put the necessary time and effort in to do the best he possibly could and refused to let obstacles derail him.

## Initial Request for Accommodations on the Bar Exam

Tom continued to receive accommodations for extra time and the use of technological supports throughout law school. Although it was an ongoing struggle, he made it through. When it came time for the Bar Exam, he simply completed the rather brief application for test accommodations (requesting extra time, use of a word processor and spell check) and assumed they would be granted without question. He assumed wrong. His request for accommodations was denied because he had failed to provide adequate objective documentation that substantiated his diagnoses, and he had not demonstrated that he was substantially limited in a major life activity compared to the average person in the population. Tom was understandably shocked and angry and immediately asked me to advocate for him because he knew it would be near impossible for him to pass without the accommodations he had come to rely on.

I asked him to gather all his prior records together and explained the high "burden of proof" required to be considered disabled under the law and how special education laws like IDEA differed from antidiscrimination laws like the ADA. I forwarded copies of Tom's original school records and past evaluation reports (which should have been sent in the first place) along with the following letter to the Dean of his Law school:

> Dear Dean Jones:
> The purpose of this letter is to advocate for Mr. Tom and request that you grant his request for accommodations on his upcoming Bar Exam. He is requesting both a computer word processor and extended time. Tom informed me recently that his previous request for these accommodations had been denied. I would like to offer the following documentation to substantiate his diagnoses and provide information to demonstrate that his request is both legitimate and reasonable.
>
> I evaluated Tom on (date of service) and found that he met criteria for Adult Attention Deficit Hyperactivity Disorder (314.01). He also has a longstanding learning disability (dyslexia), which is well documented and has resulted in significant academic struggles for him. He began receiving resource room and special education services in second grade and continued them throughout his school history. He has a history of significant weaknesses in reading, auditory processing, spelling, foreign languages, handwriting, and algebra. Tom has been granted special accommodations, including extended time and use of a computer throughout his high school, college, and law school curriculum and has come to rely on this as an essential support for him to demonstrate his true knowledge. I have included copies of *all* his prior evaluations and test reports to substantiate his longstanding history of both LD and ADHD symptomatology and impairment. To deny him this request now, after he has become accustomed to using the computer and having extra time, would be unfairly penalizing him, in my opinion.
>
> Tom informed me that the consultant that assists you in determining eligibility for special accommodations wanted to see additional documentation that better substantiated an early onset of symptoms, ongoing functional impairment stemming from his disability, and current impairment. The enclosed documents should be more than sufficient and Tom regrets that he did not include them in his original request for accommodations. I am aware of the high "burden of proof" necessary to substantiate both a diagnosis and a disability. I am also confident that this documentation will clearly demonstrate that he has the necessary history, evidence of chronic and pervasive functional impairment, and a history of prior treatment/accommodations to justify that he is substantially limited in the major life activity of learning.

I understand that on the face of it Tom does not come across as someone with significant learning disabilities or ADHD. He is intelligent, verbally skilled, makes a nice presentation, and has no outward or obvious signs of any disabilities. However, his problems are real and well documented and continue to interfere in his functioning. He has done an extraordinary job of coping with his challenges and is an excellent role model for others who are struggling to overcome similar problems. He deserves a lot of credit for his perseverance and willingness to face these kinds of academic struggles, which, to say the least, do not come easy for him.

Tom will need to use computer technology and employ all of his compensatory strategies when he becomes a lawyer. He has always been willing to do whatever it takes to succeed. I urge you reconsider your previous decision on the basis of the strength of the enclosed documentation. Thank you for your time and consideration of this matter.

Sincerely,
Kevin Murphy, Ph.D.
Chief, Adult ADHD Clinic
University of Massachusetts Medical Center

## Outcome

After submitting the supporting documentation and letter, Tom was granted his requested accommodations and passed the Bar Exam on his first attempt. He is currently a successful attorney in the investment banking industry in a large northeastern city.

## Keys to Appropriate Documentation and Effective Advocacy

What were the reasons Tom was granted accommodations? The following points are crucial to keep in mind when evaluating the adequacy of documentation for ADA level accommodations requests.

1. He provided a compelling paper trail documenting ADHD and LD symptomatology from early on in childhood that had continued to cause significant impairment in his life presently. Hence, he adequately substantiated a *childhood onset* and *current impairment* with hard data.

2. His documentation showed that the DSM-IV criteria for ADHD and LD had been applied and provided a sound rationale for the diagnostic conclusions supported by data from multiple sources (diagnostic interviews, testing, objective historical records, parent input)—*not merely self-report*.

3. He provided data to indicate he had been undergoing standard treatments for LD and eventually ADHD since childhood (tutors, academic and test accommodations, behavioral strategies, special education, resource room assistance, and medication).

4. His documentation offered sufficient data to validate that he experienced *developmentally deviant* and *clinically significant impairment* arising from his learning problems and ADHD. For example, he had severe problems learning to read, was recommended to be held back in second grade, required tutors throughout his school history, failed several classes and consistently struggled in school despite above-average intelligence, and had great difficulty regulating his behavior as evidenced by the pervasive teacher comments on his report cards.

5. There was a logical connection between the nature of his impairment and the accommodations he was requesting. All too often, a costly mistake diagnosticians make is to infer that if their client has a diagnosis of ADHD (or LD), then this alone should automatically entitle them to any and all possible accommodations regardless of whether the accommodation has any relevance to their particular history of functional impairment. *This is not true*. A mere diagnostic label is insufficient to justify accommodations. Clinicians must remember that accommodation requests need to be tailored to each individual's unique set of circumstances, need to logically flow from the history of functional impairment, and need to be supported by the history of academic struggles—ideally by objective records rather than only self-report.

6. He provided compelling evidence to indicate that extended time and use of a word processor were

appropriate accommodations to ease the impact of his disabilities and that he had benefited from them historically. The data supplied indicated that given the nature of his impairment, he would be at a distinct disadvantage without those accommodations. Indeed, his use of those accommodations was well documented for many years, and he had come to rely on them to demonstrate his knowledge. The quality of his earlier records showed that denying those accommodations in his case would have been unfairly penalizing him on the basis of his disabilities.

7. He provided data from multiple sources (self and parent interview, prior assessment reports, objective school records, past standardized testing scores, narratives from past treatment professionals and tutors) that demonstrated concurrent validation regarding the nature and degree of his problems. His diagnosticians did not simply recite a barrage of test scores as if some testing algorithm alone could substantiate a disability. This is another common error that many clinicians make. They oftentimes rely almost exclusively on or overemphasize testing results as the basis for an ADHD diagnosis—instead of gathering a comprehensive history, as was done here. There is no test or battery of tests that can reliably diagnose ADHD. It is critical to build a case based on documenting long-standing patterns of inadequate adjustment and not simply pointing out relative weaknesses on selected subtests as if this is proof positive of ADHD. And bear in mind that someone with superior overall intelligence whose worst scores on a testing battery are still average would likely not be considered disabled, because they would not be viewed as sufficiently deviant from the average person. In other words, an intraindividual discrepancy alone is not adequate to substantiate a disability; there must be associated evidence that the person's functional ability is impaired to a significantly greater degree than most people in the general population.

8. His current and prior diagnosticians documented that they had ruled out other possible explanations for his problems before concluding that ADHD (or LD) was the appropriate diagnosis. This is another common error of omission. Clinicians should always indicate they have considered and ruled out the range of other possible reasons for the symptom picture, such as mood and anxiety disorders, substance abuse, family/marital problems, and a situational/environmental stressor. Failure to do this leaves doubt as to what may be causing the impairment—since all of these possibilities can result in ADHD-like symptoms.

## Conclusion

The area of academic/test accommodations and ADHD is in dire need of more high-quality research. Critical questions, such as how much extra time is appropriate for various disabilities, how various disabilities impact people in testing situations, and what types of accommodations are appropriate for whom, need to be further explored before we can draw any data-based conclusions on these issues. In the meantime, if clinicians wish to optimize their advocacy efforts for students with ADHD or LD, it is strongly recommended they adhere to the principles suggested here and build a solid case for the diagnosis as well as providing a defensible rationale for the requested accommodations.*

---

*For a more detailed discussion of the ADA and test accommodations/documentation issues, including a sample report, see Gordon and Murphy (1998) and the additional references at the end of this chapter.

## REFERENCES

Barkley, R. A., & Murphy, K. R. (1993). Guidelines for a written clinical report concerning ADHD adults. *The ADHD Report, 1*(5).

Gordon, M., Barkley, R. A., & Murphy, K. (1997). ADHD on trial. *The ADHD Report, 5*(4), 1–4.

Gordon, M., & Murphy, K. R. (1998). Attention deficit hyperactivity disorder (ADHD). In M. Gordon & S. Keiser (Eds.),

Accommodations in higher education under the Americans with Disabilities Act (ADA): A no-nonsense guide for clinicians, educators, administrators, and lawyers (pp. 98–129). New York: Guilford Press.

Gordon, M., & Murphy, K. R., & Keiser, S. (1998). Attention deficit hyperactivity disorder (ADHD) and test accommodations. *The Bar Examiner, 67*(4), 26–36.

Murphy, K. R., & Barkley, R. A. (1996). Prevalence of DSM-IV symptoms of ADHD in adult licensed drivers: Implications for clinical diagnosis. *Journal of Attention Disorders, 1*(3), 147–161.

Murphy, K. R., & Gordon, M. (1996). ADHD as a basis for test accommodations: A primer for clinicians. *The ADHD Report, 4*(6), 10–11.

Murphy, K. R., & Gordon, M. (1998). Assessment of adults with ADHD. In R. A. Barkley (Ed.), *Attention deficit hyperactivity disorder: A handbook for diagnosis and treatment* (rev. ed., pp. 345–369). New York: Guilford Press.

Murphy, K. R., Gordon, M., & Barkley, R. A. (2000). To what extent are ADHD symptoms common? A reanalysis of standardization data from a DSM-IV checklist. *The ADHD Report, 8*(3), 1–5.

*Albertsons v. Kirkingburg*, 527 U.S. 555, 119 S. Ct. 2162, 144 L.Ed.2d 518 (U.S. 1999).

*Murphy v. United Parcel Service, Inc.*, 527 U.S. 516, 119 S. Ct. 2133, 144 L.Ed.2d 484 (U.S. 1999).

*Sutton v. United Airlines, Inc.*, 527 U.S. 471, 119 S.Ct. 2139, 144 L.Ed.2d 450 (U.S. 1999).

*Gonzalez v. National Board of Medical Examiners*, No. 99–1931, (6th Cir.) (2000).

*Price v. National Board of Medical Examiners*, 966 F. Supp. 419, 425 (S.D. W.Va. 1997).

# 6

# The Clinician's Role in the Treatment of ADHD

Kathleen G. Nadeau, Ph.D.

## OVERVIEW

In this chapter I will describe the gradual evolution I have undergone as a clinician, over the past dozen years, as I increasingly specialized in treating adults with attention deficit hyperactivity disorder. This evolution was influenced by my observation that many of the therapeutic approaches in which I had been trained were much less effective in working with adults with ADHD. My orientation shifted from a focus on "psychological" issues to a focus on "neuropsychological" issues. It became clear that some of the approaches used in cognitive rehabilitation with individuals suffering from much greater neurological challenges could be appropriately adapted for use with adults with ADHD. At the same time, it became evident to me that some of the structures and supports that were helpful for children with ADHD could be modified for adults by shifting emphasis from educational issues to vocational issues. Because we are treating adults with difficulties in practical, everyday functioning, we need to develop specific skill sets, as clinicians, for which we have received little or no prior training. After outlining the theoretical underpinnings of the therapeutic approach that I have gradually developed, I will illustrate its practical applications through the discussion of several clinical cases.

Like many other clinicians who currently treat adults with ADHD, I worked for many years as an eclectic but traditionally trained psychotherapist. I used a combination of approaches, including psychodynamic, insight-oriented techniques, cognitive-behavioral therapy, and family systems theory, among others. I was taught, as most of us were, to offer no directives or advice and to allow the client to set the pace and select the focus for each session. My role was supportive, passive, interpretive, and sometimes challenging of the client's attitude or beliefs, but never directive or prescriptive. The common belief among most schools of psychotherapy was that there was some neurosis, inner conflict, or learned attitude that underlay dysfunction in daily life. Once this psychological determinant was addressed, the individual would quite naturally begin to behave in a more constructive, "healthy" manner in his or her daily life and relationships.

I was taught to believe that the individual would take up healthier modes of living when "ready" and not before. My role was to help the client achieve this state of "readiness," not to suggest, direct, or influence the mundane details of daily life. In fact, therapists generally relegated a focus on "practical" issues to other, less highly trained professionals—counselors, career consultants, and the like. Our focus was on "deeper," more important "psychological" issues, disdaining a superficial "environmental cure." Changes in partners, places of employment, or regions of the country were considered escapist efforts that were doomed to failure because "psychological" problems would follow the client wherever we went.

At the same time that I worked with adults using these widely espoused methods, I began to work with an increasing number of children with ADHD. Following the passage of laws mandating that services be provided for children with special needs from ages 2 to 21, the number of parents seeking diagnosis and treatment of ADHD for their children increased dramatically. Finally, the schools were required to provide services and support. There was suddenly a strong incentive to seek an ADHD diagnosis in order that children could benefit from the programs and services being developed.

In my work with parents and children with ADHD, I played a variety of roles: diagnostician (administering psychological and psychoeducational testing), therapist (focusing on social and interpersonal issues of children with ADHD), family therapist (working with parents and children to develop more workable daily routines and problem-solving strategies), and educational consultant (attending school meetings with parents as complex individual educational plans (IEP's) were developed to meet the needs of each individual student. I interfaced with tutors, neurologists, pediatricians, child psychiatrists, educational specialists, sensory integration specialists, vision specialists, and any other professionals whose specialty touched on some condition commonly associated with ADHD. These children had complex needs that could be met only through a variety of services. My role evolved beyond therapist to treatment coordinator, developing and coordinating wrap-around treatment programs for these children.

A few short years later, children whom I had first encountered at age 8 or 9 were in high school, approaching college. It became essential that I work with such students and their families to identify colleges that could provide good support services. For those who weren't attending college, my focus was on helping them to make good choices of vocational training or to find "ADHD-friendly" entry-level employment. For those high school students heading to college, it became evident that these young adults needed much guidance to make an appropriate choice of a college major that was compatible with their strengths and interests. Personality testing, interest testing, and career guidance were essential. However, it was my experience that when these students were referred to career counselors or career centers, they often could not find anyone experienced in the special needs and concerns of young adults with ADHD. Career testing and guidance became, by necessity, an important part of the growing set of therapeutic skills that I found necessary in order to effectively treat adolescents and young adults.

Meanwhile, parents of children with ADHD self-identified and sought treatment for adult ADHD issues. Many of these parents struggled with adult versions of the very same sorts of challenges that befell their children: self-esteem issues and relationship difficulties, impulse control, difficulty developing and maintaining habits, disorganization and forgetfulness, and difficulty reaching their potential in the world of work. Paralleling the school challenges faced by children, adults faced similar challenges in the workplace: difficulties with deadlines and with completing long-term projects, difficulties expressing themselves succinctly either verbally or in writing, problems with details and paperwork. And because continuing education is a necessity for many of us as our careers evolve or change, adults with ADHD must often face daunting educational challenges that more directly parallel the challenges that children with ADHD must meet in the classroom. They, too, needed assistance in learning how to manage their ADHD patterns on a daily basis. But unlike their children, they did not have a parent at home to help them implement and consistently practice the new patterns they were attempting to develop.

Increasingly, adults who had been unable to find a therapist experienced in diagnosing and treating adults with ADHD contacted me. Often they had sought treatment from a psychiatrist or psychologist whose response was that he or she "didn't believe in" adult ADHD. Unfortunately, ten years later such a response is still not uncommon, but even those who acknowledge ADHD in adults are often prone to misdiagnose ADHD as anxiety, depression, or bipolar disorder, misinterpreting ADHD symptoms. Such diagnoses of depression and/or anxiety may be not incorrect but, rather, incomplete, because they overlook underlying or comorbid ADHD.

Even when the diagnosis of ADHD is made correctly, the treatment approaches, aside from the prescription of stimulant medication, are often ineffective, and sometimes potentially destructive. Many psychotherapists, it seems, have simply transferred their generic bag of psychotherapeutic tricks to the treatment of adults with ADHD, making psychodynamic interpretations, approaching the psychotherapy session in an unstructured and nondirective fashion, and focusing primarily on improving self-understanding and self-esteem. In the worst cases, psychotherapists interpret ADHD-driven behaviors from a psychological rather than neurocognitive perspective. Viewed through psychological lenses, lateness is an expression of passive aggression, impulsivity is a function of immaturity, and compulsive talking and drivenness are evidence of bipolar disorder. A psychodynamically oriented clinician may persist in interpreting lateness and/or forgetting as resistance to treatment, never suggesting to the client techniques that can help develop better on-time habits or reminder systems. Psychotherapy with adults with ADHD is ineffective when it ignores the need for structure in the therapy session; worse, though, is the potentially destructive psychotherapy that blames the client, attributing his neurologically based patterns to dark, negative psychological forces.

## A MULTI-LEVEL APPROACH IN TREATING ADHD IN ADULTS

The challenge for the psychotherapist is to sort through the layers of personality traits, of psychic conflicts, and of neurologically based patterns and to approach each of these in ways that can effectively address them. The effective psychotherapist of individuals with ADHD needs to take a broad perspective rather than use a single theoretical lens through which he or she interprets all behaviors.

In working with an adult with ADHD, it is essential never to lose sight of the to need treat the client on multiple levels simultaneously. ADHD is a condition that has a primary neurological basis with secondary psychological features, and exists, very commonly, alongside complicating coexisting psychiatric disorders that must be addressed as well if treatment for ADHD is to be effective.

### Neurocognitive Psychotherapy

First, the therapist must always remember that ADHD is primarily a neurobiological condition that affects behavior and emotions. To address the neurobiological aspect of ADHD, we can borrow very appropriately from cognitive rehabilitation models, using those theoretical underpinnings to design a treatment program. Typically, cognitive rehabilitation treatment models approach the rehabilitation of a neurologically impaired individual via a multidimensional method:

- Improving cognitive function
- Developing internal and external compensatory strategies
- Restructuring the physical and social environment to maximize functioning

**Improving Cognitive Function**

In treating ADHD, the most powerful and immediate intervention to improve cognitive function is the use of psychostimulant medication. Improved cognitive functioning can also be supported, secondarily, through improved sleep patterns, regular exercise, improved nutrition, and reduced stress. The clinician should consider all of these strategies to be appropriately within her or his domain, engaging the collaboration of other professionals as needed.

**Developing Internal and External Compensatory Strategies**

The second component of cognitive rehabilitation is to develop internal and external compensatory strategies. Teaching compensatory strategies is highly useful in working with an adult with ADHD and should appropriately be a major focus of therapy. In my therapy with patients, I refer to such strategies under the umbrella of "learning how to *take charge of ADHD*."

**Restructuring the physical and Social Environment**

The third prong of this cognitive rehabilitation approach is that of restructuring the physical and social environment to maximize functioning. In my work with adults, I speak about this environmental restructuring in terms of *creating an ADHD-friendly environment*. Social restructuring involves educating family members and significant others, as well as making proactive choices to live among, socialize with, and work among individuals who are more aware of the individual's strengths and less critical or intolerant of his ADHD patterns. Physical restructuring involves changing aspects of the client's physical environment to minimize the challenges of ADHD. This might entail changing to a less stressful job, moving to shorten a stressful commute, moving from a single-family home to a townhouse to lessen the stressful maintenance demands of a larger home, or organizing and uncluttering the home to promote more efficient, orderly daily routines for the family.

We commonly use all of these techniques when working with children with ADHD. We work, through coaching, tutoring, teaching therapist and parent support, to enhance the child's executive functions of planning, self-monitoring, remembering, and following through on homework and extracurricular projects. We help the child to begin to develop compensatory strategies: making lists, writing down reminders, using day planners to record homework assignments and activities. And we actively work to make his or her social and physical environments more ADHD friendly through careful selection of school, of classroom teacher, of playmates, and of extracurricular activities. Most therapists can transfer these approaches fairly easily to 18- or 20-year-olds. But with older adults, we may forget the neurobiological underpinnings of the challenges they face and assume that they are, or *should be*, capable of doing such things for themselves, without the least guidance or suggestion from the therapist!

## Addressing Secondary Psychological Issues

In addition to addressing cognitive functioning, it is critical to address the secondary emotional symptoms of ADHD. By the time an individual has struggled with ADHD for many years, there is a secondary but very significant set of issues, including low self-esteem, demoralization, a sense of shame and self-blame, as well as anxiety and depression that result from the chronic stress of living with ADHD.

Many adults have engaged in more traditional psychotherapy for years. They have known that "something was wrong," but neither they nor their psychotherapist knew that the "something" was related to ADHD. Often, such traditional psychotherapy has been helpful in dealing with destructive early childhood experiences, trauma, or depression. However, even when such issues have been dealt with effectively, these adults are left with a feeling of being out of control in their daily lives, overwhelmed by issues that others deal with more evenly. In the worst cases, adults seek treatment for ADHD having been damaged by previous psychotherapy. Such individuals, prone to feelings of shame and self-blame, have had these feelings strengthened through the destructive process of having their neurologically driven behaviors interpreted psychologically. The psychotherapist has, in effect, endorsed their self-blame, implying that they could stop their disorganization, lateness, forgetfulness, and general underfunctioning if they effectively addressed their psychological issues.

## Treating Comorbid Conditions

To complicate the situation further, ADHD is typically one of a cluster of issues that must all be addressed in order for treatment to be effective. Individuals with ADHD frequently suffer from high-incidence conditions such as learning disabilities, anxiety, and depression, as well as low-incidence conditions such as obsessive-compulsive disorder, bipolar disorder, posttraumatic stress disorder, chemical dependencies, eating disorders, and Tourette's syndrome, among others. For a certain subset of adults with ADHD, comorbid childhood oppositional defiant disorder has evolved into a conduct disorder and finally into an antisocial personality disorder.

ADHD exists along a continuum from mild to severe and can be found in highly intelligent, high-functioning individuals (although this may come at a great cost), as well as among very dysfunctional individuals who have struggled with unemployment, substance abuse, and repeated encounters with the judicial system. Because the treatment of adult ADHD is in its infancy, the majority of those seeking treatment fall into the more educated, higher-functioning end of the spectrum. There is enormous need, however, to treat the great numbers of adults with ADHD who are in prison, who are on unemployment roles, or who are chemically dependent. A broad array of clinical skills and extensive training and experience across a spectrum of disorders is required to treat this disorder that is so commonly embedded in a spectrum of related disorders.

## BASIC ISSUES IN TREATING ADULTS WITH ADHD

## Structuring the Psychotherapy Session for Adults with ADHD

It may be helpful to think of the therapy session as a microcosm of the issues that are faced in the days, weeks, and months in the life of an adult with ADHD. Just as structure, compensatory strategies, and reminders are needed in daily life, they are also needed within the therapy session. The therapist, to be most effective, needs to have her "therapist's ears" attuned to unspoken feelings and unexpressed issues, guiding the client to deal with important issues that may not be in the forefront of the client's mind as he comes to the session. But at the same time, the therapist should always be aware of the difficulties experienced through lack of structure. Unlike with other sorts of clients, it is rarely most productive to allow the client to ramble or free-associate. In fact, rambling associations are exactly what the client needs to combat in order to remain effectively focused on the conversation or activity at hand!

Memory difficulties are commonly reported in adults with ADHD. There may be no real sense of continuity from session to session without added structure from the therapist. Audiotaping sessions can be extremely helpful. Clients may tape their session and then review it repeatedly while driving their car during the week. If taping is not done, notetaking is essential. Clients should be encouraged to purchase a spiral notebook dedicated to their therapy sessions, in which they should write key issues that are discussed and issues that occur to them during the week that they want to bring up in the subsequent session, and in which they record "homework assignments." It can even be helpful to have a supply of such notebooks on hand to provide to new clients. It is also helpful to review homework assignments at the beginning of the session. Was the assignment accomplished? If not, why not? A brief review of medication, its effectiveness, and its side effects is also helpful. It's often very useful for the therapist to be in periodic contact with the prescribing physician to share observations regarding medication. Then the therapist should ask the client what issues he or she would like to address during the session. If both therapist and client write these topics down, the session becomes more structured. At the end of the session, a brief review of topics and strategies that have been discussed, followed by a new homework assignment, sends the client on his or her way with a focused approach for the week ahead.

## Collaborating with an ADHD Coach

Distractibility, poor follow-through, and faulty memory sometimes combine to render weekly therapy sessions only moderately effective. With such clients, I sometimes engage the support of a trained ADHD coach who can contact the client for brief phone sessions during the week to reinforce the strategies we have been working on. This can be especially helpful when a client with ADHD is engaged in a complex, multistep task, such as working on a dissertation, applying to college or graduate school, or engaging in a job search. Thrice-weekly, and at times even daily, contact with a coach can help keep them moving forward, taking some step every day to move them closer to accomplishing their goal. It is important to find a coach who is welltrained and experienced in working with adults with ADHD and who has a clear sense of the appropriate boundaries between coaching and psychotherapy. Since most coaching takes place via telephone and/or e-mail, it is not necessary that the coach live in the same area as the therapist and client. Brief communications between the therapist and coach will help to coordinate their efforts.

## Use of Professional Organizers and Time Management Technologies

The single most common complaint of adults with ADHD has to do with disorganization, including time management, household management, and money management. It is extremely helpful for therapists who specialize in treating adults with ADHD to remain abreast of new technologies and tools that can aid their clients in becoming better organized, such as computer software, electronic reminders, and time management systems. Engaging a professional organizer when a client expresses feeling completely overwhelmed by disorganization in the home, in paperwork, or at the office can often be extremely useful. A professional organizer can assist the client in digging out from under chronic chaos. Then the therapist and/or coach can assist the client to develop better habits that can help maintain better organization. Many adults with ADHD find it so difficult to remain organized that they may need to budget for biannual visits from a professional organizer as one of their ADHD coping mechanisms.

## Expanded Clinical Skills Called For in Treating ADHD in Adults

Psychotherapists who seek to become a specialist in treating adults with ADHD need to develop a broad skill base that allows them to assist with the "neurocognitive" issues as well as the more familiar psychological issues of anxiety, depression, low self-esteem, and relationship problems. Although adults with ADHD come with an enormous variety of abilities, family backgrounds, and life circumstances, there seems to be a core set of issues with which most of these adults typically struggle, including problems with daily life management, time management, decisionmaking, and workplace functioning.

- *Self-esteem issues* may plague adults with ADHD, especially women, throughout their lifetime. Even though some may have reached high levels of achievement, adults with ADHD often feel they have not lived up to their potential, that they are "imposters" struggling to hide inadequacies from family and coworkers, and may characterize themselves as lazy, disorganized, immature, and unreliable.
- *Underdeveloped life management skills*, or a sense that the management of daily life causes great stress and often a feeling of being "out of control," include the following.
- *Thing management*—the ordering and maintenance of the household and the objects it contains (e.g., filing papers, keeping personal objects in remembered retrievable locations)
- *Time management*—the ability to be on time, to remain appropriately aware of the passage of time, and to predict accurately how much time should be allocated to specific daily tasks.
- *To-do management* (prospective memory)—the ability to keep in mind, or to recall at the appropriate time, specific acts that should be undertaken at some future time (e.g., remembering to take necessary papers to school or the office, running errands at specific points en route, keeping appointments)
- *Money management*—the ability to track expenditures, to accurately assess whether one can afford new expenditures, to control impulsive spending, to keep track of and pay bills in a timely manner, to maintain records necessary to file accurate tax returns
- *Relationship problems*, which are often related to poor communication patterns, including monologuing, interrupting, becoming distracted during conversation, not knowing "when to stop," and emotional overreactions.
- *Workplace problems*, such as feeling highly stressed at work, feeling unable to successfully meet some of the demands of one's current job, questioning whether one has made an appropriate career choice in view of the challenges of ADHD

Childhood ADHD specialists wouldn't dream of saying that they couldn't deal with daily behavioral issues or school-related concerns for a child. Yet as adult specialists, we haven't yet mastered the equivalent skills to help adults with daily life management and workplace concerns. As children with ADHD mature and leave their school years behind, the workplace, rather than the classroom, becomes the area of greatest challenge. The things we do at work are comparable in many ways to schoolwork. At work, most of us must read, write, make calculations, organize and carry out projects, meet deadlines, learn new information, and pay attention during meetings and lectures. The challenges that adults with ADHD face in the workplace deserve the same attention that has been focused on the academic functioning of children and adolescents with ADHD.

## TREATING ADHD ACROSS THE ADULT LIFE SPAN

### Transition to Independence in Young Adulthood

Let's consider the types of issues and problems that must typically be addressed as young adults with ADHD begin to make the transition to independent adult living.

First, consider approaches that have proven effective for children and how they might be appropriately applied as children transition to adulthood. Sam Goldstein and Michael Goldstein write in the Preface to their recent, comprehensive text, *Managing Attention Deficit Hyperactivity Disorder in Children* (1998) that "successful treatment of ADHD requires a balance between symptom relief and building in protective factors that enhance resilience, defined as the capacity to recover from stress and lead children to successful transition into adulthood" (p. xv). The protective factors to which the Goldsteins refer include those related to (1) school, (2) friends, and (3) family. In working with young adults, all three of these factors remain relevant. In addition, a fourth set of protective factors, relating to the workplace, become critical.

Although for many individuals with ADHD in adulthood there is symptom reduction and the development of coping strategies, adult life also brings a great increase in demands on the individual for judgment, organization, self-control, and long- range planning. The very psychological traits that one normally associates with maturity—the ability to delay immediate gratification in order to achieve long-term benefit, the ability to act based on reason rather than on immediate emotional impulse, the ability to make plans and to carry through on those plans—are all among the most challenging traits for individuals with ADHD.

When children with ADHD become teens and then young adults, many of the protective factors that have supported them will gradually, or even suddenly, fall away. Their lives are less structured by parents and teachers. There is no one available to make sure that medication is taken as prescribed, or taken at all. The transition from adolescence to independent adult living is fraught with challenges that require knowledge that has not yet been acquired and a planning ability that is inadequately developed. They must suddenly be able to manage money, successfully make job applications, make choices as to career direction, sign leases, apply for automobile insurance, file income tax returns, and keep up with the routine maintenance activities of daily life—getting adequate sleep, providing themselves with regular meals and clean clothes, and maintaining their living space. As one mother of an adolescent boy with ADHD voiced, with reason for concern, "He's not able to make his bed. How's he going to make a life?"

As they struggle to cope with the lack of structure in their lives, young adults with ADHD may make decisions that only increase their sense of being overwhelmed. For example, one young man found himself uninterested in the limited jobs available to him as a high school graduate. He reasoned that if he purchased an expensive automobile the large monthly car payment would motivate him to get up in the morning and maintain regular employment. Instead, as might have been predicted, this decision only led to financial overextension that caused him to break the lease on his apartment, whose rent payments he could no longer afford. Soon he was sleeping on the couch of a friend, sinking into depression as his barely established independence crumbled.

As psychotherapists, how can we best help young adults with ADHD as they struggle to make the successful transition to independent adult life? Somehow, we need to help the young adult with ADHD seek, develop, or create the same sorts of protective factors that support children with ADHD. These protective factors include things such as an environment that promotes structure and predictability, a work or school environment that is supportive and that reasonably accommodates ADHD traits, and the social support of friends and family who accept the negative and appreciate the positive in them.

## ADHD-Friendly Lifestyle

One overarching concept essential in the treatment of all adults with ADHD is that of an

ADHD-friendly lifestyle. It is critical that the therapist have a clear sense of what factors might constitute an ADHD-friendly lifestyle for each client. The therapeutic task, then, is to convey this to clients in a constructive manner that helps them to identify the "unfriendly" factors in their current lifestyle as well as to identify ways they can make choices and changes to move toward a more ADHD-friendly living environment. This ADHD-friendly lifestyle is built, in part, from the "protective factors" discussed previously. The therapist and client, together, must work to identify situations that tend to worsen ADHD patterns: poor sleep patterns, poor nutrition, lack of exercise, substance abuse, high stress level, too little or too much stimulation, social relationships that encourage ADHD-unfriendly behaviors, and career choices that require the client to operate in areas of relative weakness, among others.

## ADHD-Informed Life Choices

One of the great advantages of seeking treatment as a young adult is that the most important defining life choices are still ahead. With the help of therapy, such choices can become informed by the concept of building an ADHD-friendly life. Typically, as a young adult, one has not yet chosen a life partner, has not become a parent, and has not made great commitments of time or money toward any single career or profession. Understanding oneself—one's strengths, weaknesses, interests, and passions—within the framework of ADHD can help make those choices beneficial ones that can have a positive impact on ADHD.

## Appropriate Treatment Rather Than "Self-Medication"

Another important concept to introduce to the young adult with ADHD is the common pattern of self-medication. The therapist can help the young adult better understand his attractions to alcohol, marijuana, excessive caffeine, carbohydrates, cigarettes, or other substances, and can perhaps minimize patterns that can, if left untreated, rapidly lead to very destructive addictions and dependencies.

## Increased Choices Beyond High School

Many young adults with ADHD have just passed through some of the most ADHD-unfriendly years of their life as they exited high school and entered their young adult years. High school is often a demoralizing experience for teens with ADHD. Suddenly they are bombarded with increasing academic demands. Their native intelligence is often no longer enough to support them as reading and writing assignments lengthen in high school. They can't get by just by paying occasional attention in class and hurriedly scribbling homework assignments on the bus. During high school years there is relatively little choice available to students with ADHD. They must conform to the standard curriculum and must sit and listen for many hours every day. Once they graduate from high school, however, an enormous range of choices opens up. The clinician working with young adults with ADHD should take an active role to make them aware of the many choices available and should help them carefully consider the choices they make in view of creating an ADHD-friendly life.

## Decreasing Structure and Support

If they have been fortunate, young adults with ADHD have had parents who worked to provide them with an ADHD-friendly environment as they have been growing up—an environment that is structured and predictable, with regular routines that support the completion of daily activities necessary for a healthy, productive life. Such predictability has probably eroded as the teens with ADHD have struggled to assert their independence. Now the teens have become young adults and routines may be almost nonexistent, even if they are still living in the family home.

One young man, whom we'll call Chris, was brought to therapy by his parents as a last-ditch effort before evicting him from their home. He had been a struggling student in high school, but had attended fairly regularly until he was injured in an automobile accident. This injury suddenly eliminated normal routines from his life. After a several-month recovery, during which his classmates completed the school year, he chose not to return to school because he would have been required to repeat his junior year while all of his friends would be seniors. A series of short-lived minimum-wage jobs followed. Chris gradually sank into despondency as he recognized that he had few options without a high school diploma and as his social isolation increased.

Eventually he fell in with a group of other young men whose situations were similar—school dropouts with marginal employment. They stayed up all night, smoking marijuana and drinking beer, and slept until noon. Frequent arguments with parents occasionally motivated them to make a minimal effort to find employment, and severe conflict with parents led these young men to seek refuge, periodically, on the basement couch of another friend in the group. As Chris was brought for therapy he was facing a similar eviction notice from his parents—go to work, go to school, or get out. In a family session Chris expressed a fear that if he complied with his parents' demands he would have to shift to a daytime existence and would lose the only emotional support he had—the all-night gatherings with his going-nowhere buddies. "If I do what *you* want, then I won't have *any* friends!"

Chris, like many young adults with ADHD, was highly influenced by his immediate environment. Also, like many with ADHD who have struggled with school and have experienced little success in other arenas, he harbored enormous self-doubt and low self-esteem. The challenge in therapy was to help him find a more constructive support system and a plan for the future that encouraged rather than threatened him.

## Collaborative Work with Parents of Young Adults with ADHD

The central challenge facing all parents of young adults with ADHD is how to provide constructive support while at the same time promoting the young adult's independence. To this end, Chris' parents were involved in his treatment, both joint and collateral sessions—a pattern that may seem inappropriate if viewed from the perspective of more traditional psychotherapy, where autonomy and confidentiality may take precedence over parental concern and involvement, especially for a client 18 years of age. The parents' sessions focused on gaining a better understanding of their son's ADHD and how it affected him at this point in his life. The parents had vacillated between enabling his self-destructive dependence and angrily demanding that he leave their home and fend for himself. They were aware of the precarious, even dangerous situations that his peers found themselves in after ejection from the family home, and their fears led them to back away from the angry ultimatums they had repeatedly delivered. Therapy with the parents focused on ways to gradually and systematically support Chris in becoming more functional and independent.

## Engaging Community Resources as Protective Factors

Just as clinicians working with young children with ADHD should be aware of community resources that can support parents in finding the help they need for their child, the same is true for young adults; however, the resources generally come from different agencies and educational institutions. Chris was referred to the Department of Rehabilitative Services, where he was encouraged to learn that he was eligible for their services and could receive assistance in a variety of job-training programs—for jobs that paid triple the minimum wage or greater. Chris was also referred to the local community college, where there were many two-year-certificate vocational programs available that might interest him. All he needed to do was to take his GED exam and earn a passing grade.

## Tutoring for Young Adults with ADHD

Chris began to discuss the need to earn his GED in order to be eligible for job training. His parents, also feeling more hopeful, were willing to pay for private tutoring to help Chris prepare for his GED. One-on-one tutoring was strongly suggested due to Chris' academic anxiety, poorly developed self-discipline, and need for structure. Because Chris had missed most of the last two years of high school and had not been a strong student, it seemed unlikely that he could adequately prepare for the GED without the support of an individual tutor. Clinicians should be aware that even in the case of much stronger and more accomplished students, it is often helpful, if not mandatory, that the adult with ADHD work individually with someone to adequately prepare for licensing or professional exams.

## Success Breeds Confidence, Which Leads to Success

As Chris prepared for the GED, his self-confidence began to increase. A friend he had encountered by chance told him of a job in a record store at the nearby mall. To his parents' surprise he went to the mall without their prodding, applied for the job, and was hired. He began to become friendly with other teens who worked at the mall, whose lives were more structured and functional than his previous group of friends. In therapy he began to talk in a different way about his group of unemployed friends, questioning where their lives were going. Conflict at home with his parents greatly decreased. His parents felt they had a blueprint for helping Chris to become self-sufficient, and they could see the concrete steps that Chris was taking to achieve independence.

## Importance of Short-Term, Reachable Goals

Therapy began to focus on financial management as Chris began to bring home a regular paycheck. A concrete, highly desired goal for Chris was the purchase of a car. Chris decided to give his parents 25% of each paycheck to save for a down payment. His more mature attitude toward money encouraged his parents, who agreed to help him with a car purchase if he saved a predetermined amount of money. Passing the GED three months later led to an enormous sense of achievement. Rather than spending the summer partying and going to the beach with friends, he decided to work full time so that he could purchase a car in September and be ready to enroll in a computer technician class at the local community college.

## Continuing Collateral Parent Education

Collateral therapy sessions with parents helped them to better understand the slower maturity rate of their son and assisted them in developing realistic expectations. Rather than nagging or exploding, they learned to help Chris solve problems. After six months in therapy Chris was taking responsibility for his own medication and coming to treatment in the car he had purchased with his parents' help, and was enrolled in a course of study that gave him an optimistic sense of his ability and his future.

It is readily evident, in examining the role of the therapist in Chris' treatment, that there are strong parallels between the role of a therapist with a child with ADHD and with a young adult. Parent education and guidance was a critical component of the treatment, with a focus on helping the parents to understand and help create an ADHD-friendly environment for Chris, an environment that offered structure, emotional support, and short-term incentives more motivating than their earlier admonition that Chris was "throwing away his future." The therapist was active in making referrals to other service providers—a tutor as well as the DRS counselor. The tutor was engaged in recognition of Chris' learning disabilities and his need for structured, one-on-one learning. Therapy was focused on:

1. Concrete problem solving (developing an ADHD-friendly environment)
2. Assisting Chris in recognizing the strong influence his environment had on him and the critical importance of changing his social and physical environment (recognizing that his current environment was ADHD unfriendly)
3. Helping him to discover and develop areas of competence (a practical approach to combating the low self-esteem so common in young adults with ADHD)
4. Helping him to recognize the importance of planning and consistency and guiding him in developing more constructive patterns—saving money, recording appointments, getting himself to appointments on time, and changing sleep patterns so that he could function constructively during the day (developing compensatory strategies as well as habits to promote an ADHD-friendly lifestyle)

A more traditional therapist might have involved the parents little, if at all. A more traditional therapist might have focused the therapy on talking about his anger and despair rather than on taking actions that would reduce those feelings. A focus in therapy should be on the simple, concrete notion that success breeds success. Chris and his parents were guided to find concrete ways to achieve small degrees of success that would make later successes more likely.

Later sessions would focus on helping Chris develop the skills necessary for successful independent living as an adult. These skills could be learned in the relatively protective home environment and then later tested in a more challenging, independent living situation. Career-oriented counseling would come later as well. It was a great step forward for Chris to have employment at all. In the future, it will become critical to help Chris better understand his interests and abilities as well as his needs for structure and support in a work environment so that he will be more likely to find employment in which he can be successful.

Let's consider the case of a young adult at the opposite end of the ability spectrum. A young man whom we will call Nick had been in gifted programs throughout his years in public high school, but, despite very high intelligence, his grades had only been mediocre. He had strongly resisted taking medication during his high school years and had scraped by, relying on his native ability. Instead of going on to the top colleges that most of his friends would attend, Nick had his choices limited by his academic record. His final selection was a large southern state school, better known for its social and athletic life than for its academics. His parents were skeptical but had always raised Nick to "make his own decisions," not realizing that such respect for autonomy might have disastrous consequences. Nick's family was filled with academic professionals. An older brother had attended an Ivy League college. Nick, according to his parents, was the brightest of all of their children. They were disappointed in his choices and baffled about how best to help him.

Following a disastrous freshman year that ended with academic probation, Nick was home for the summer, at his parents' insistence. Nick's preference had been to take a road trip out west with a close friend, but his parents reined him in. They insisted that he seek counseling and treatment over the summer in order to reach a decision about whether to return to the same university in the fall. In addition to academic concerns, Nick showed signs of depression. He had fallen intensely in love with a young woman at school who had a serious struggle with depression herself. Together they had gone in a downward spiral of frequent fighting, making up, sinking into mutual dependency and increasing depression.

## Parental Involvement in the Treatment

Nick first came to therapy with his mother, at my request. (Due to work pressures, Nick's father was not available regularly.) Talking with both of them together, I pieced together the history of his first 18 years. His mother was able to provide the family history and early childhood history that Nick would be unable to provide in detail. As elementary, middle, and high school years were discussed, Nick entered fully into the discussion. The history taking was structured to be the beginning of the therapeutic process for Nick—to help him begin to think of the situations and circumstances in which he had functioned well or had functioned poorly over the years.

The immediate assessment was that Nick needed much more structure and supervision—something that went against the grain of his mother's parenting style and certainly went against the grain of Nick's late adolescent desires for autonomy and independence. In other words, I wanted Nick and his family to reintroduce more of the "protective factors" under which he had prospered during his elementary school and middle school years. The goal was for Nick to reach and accept this conclusion during the summer and for his parents to understand his need for more hands-on parenting, even at the age of 19. Although I was seeing Nick individually, helping him to monitor the stimulant and antidepressant medication that he had agreed to take once more, I also continued to see him with his mother for joint sessions. The focus of the joint sessions was on accessing information about Nick's behavior from an outside source, but also engaging in ADHD, education as a family. The typical pattern of delayed maturity in many young adults with ADHD, as well as the need for structure and support, was discussed. I told stories about other young adults with ADHD who had failed but who, with critical changes, had later become very successful. I often find this type of storytelling helpful and therapeutic in treating adults with ADHD.

## Practical Interventions

In a more practical vein, I suggested that Nick enroll in two courses at the local community college during the summer. I recommended that his family engage the services of a tutor or coach to make sure that Nick did well in those summer courses, enhancing his chances of being able to return to school in the fall. I talked to Nick of the kinds of supports he could access from the student disability support office—priority registration, extended time on tests, note takers in class, and reduced course load. When he had left for college in his freshman year he completely denied his need for treatment or support. After failing, he was somewhat more open to such possibilities. With weekly therapy and biweekly tutoring sessions during the summer, Nick earned two A's in summer school. In response to this success, and with the help of antidepressants, Nick's mood lifted and he became better able to engage in more constructive planning for his future.

Nick slowly came to recognize that the completely unstructured living situation at the university he had attended, as well as his denial of his need for treatment or supports for ADHD, had led to his academic failure. His girlfriend's decision not to return to the university in the fall probably helped Nick decide to stay at home and apply as a transfer student to the state university a few miles away. Despite his poor grades as a freshman, the A's he had earned in summer school convinced the local university to allow him to enroll.

## Shifting Focus to Longer-Term Goals

Our focus in therapy now shifted to helping Nick think about future career goals. Testing was done to measure academic strengths and weaknesses. Interest testing as well as the Myers-Briggs Inventory were completed as well. All the results were considered together, and Nick began to explore various college majors from this more informed viewpoint. The Myers-Briggs not only suggested several possible career directions, but also highlighted Nick's extremely extroverted personality. This was interpreted to Nick, and it was suggested that he might enjoy his studies and be more successful in them if he organized study groups rather than attempting to hole up in his room to study silently and alone.

## More Structure and Practical Problem Solving

Nick's natural ability to bring people together meant that soon he had organized study groups for each of the four classes in which he was enrolled. His strong needs to socialize were now being met in a much more constructive context. Nick continued to work with his tutor/coach throughout the fall semester and ended with honor roll grades, despite some last-minute paper writing and studying for exams. Nick began to understand his tendencies to procrastinate and to underestimate how long an assignment might take and his need for external structure. Rather than resenting living at home, he began to appreciate the fact that, when he needed it, he had a calm, quiet environment in which to rest and study—something that had not existed in his dorm life the previous year.

By the end of Nick's second semester at home he was in top form. He recognized the benefits that stimulant medication gave him, but felt he needed it only during class and study time. Nick's depression had lifted, and after a year of taking antidepressants he was directed by his psychiatrist to gradually reduce and finally stop taking the medication. By summer he no longer took the antidepressant medication. During his second year in college, through guidance in therapy Nick had come to identify environmental protection issues as a strong interest. He took a course in environmental science and, after speaking with an uncle, began to think of longer-term plans—perhaps law school after college, with a focus on environmental law. Such a career would accommodate his need for extroverted social interaction and would allow him to focus on an issue in which he had a growing, passionate interest. Rather than the unplanned road trip he had wanted to take the previous summer, Nick, with encouragement in therapy, did some advanced planning and applied for a summer internship with the National Park Service to give him more hands-on experience in an environmental area.

## Ready to "Fly"—Not Just Leap Out of the Nest

After a year in treatment, Nick felt ready to leave ongoing therapy. He had gained a better respect for the potential destructive influence of living an impulsive, unstructured life. He recognized that he thrived with more structure, both at home and in school, and that he could find a way to combine his extroversion needs and his need to study in a very constructive fashion by forming study groups. Testing and therapy had given him a much clearer sense of strengths, weaknesses, and interests. Nick's family also learned that the "hands-off" approach they had taken in raising his older brother wasn't, perhaps, the best approach for Nick. Both Nick and his parents realized that as he, appropriately, left home again in the next year or two that he would need to think seriously about building "protective factors" into his independent life—through careful choices of where he lived, how he lived, and with whom he lived. Nick was ready to try his wings, and this time his flight was less likely to end in a crash landing.

## THE CHALLENGES OF THE MIDDLE ADULT YEARS

Once the initial challenges of leaving home are past, the adult with ADHD has many challenges ahead. He or she also has a huge range of critical choices to make—of career, of lifestyle, of life partner, of parenthood—that can either worsen or reduce ADHD symptoms. As discussed earlier, an essential role for the therapist to take in working with young adults is to help them learn to make ADHD-friendly life choices. However, in working with adults in their 30s and beyond, I have discovered that most have already made these critical life choices before they seek treatment and before they are introduced to the concept of the "protective factors" of an ADHD-friendly lifestyle.

Unfortunately, many of them have made decisions that are decidedly ADHD unfriendly, for example, a mother of five children under the age of 8, who sought a diagnosis of her own ADHD following the diagnosis of her twin 7-year-olds. She had already made irrevocable choices that would be daunting for anyone but close to impossible for her, with the challenges of ADHD. Other choices, however, aren't irrevocable, although they may be very costly to change. For example, one man choose to earn a law degree—after much hard work—only to realize later that his ADHD and learning disabilities would make the pursuit of this profession continually exhausting and unrewarding. Another family had chosen to purchase an older home that was in much need of repair and maintenance, without taking the husband's ADHD into account. The therapist can be most helpful to the client by regularly focusing on the stress level in the client's life, problem solving with the client about feasible ways to reduce stress, and teaching the client to consciously building into life some of the "protective factors" that parents typically provide for children with ADHD.

## Selecting a Partner

Perhaps one of the most important protective factors is the choice of a life partner, or conversely the choice not to have a life partner, for those for whom relationship issues are particularly stressful or daunting. Many adults with ADHD choose a partner whose strengths lie in their areas of weakness—organization, planfulness, and attention to detail. Such a choice can be very wise if the partner with ADHD does not allow him, or herself to become overly reliant and dependent, leading to inevitable resentment on the part of the non-ADHD spouse. In some instances, however, the more organized partner also tends to be impatient and critical, leading to chronic stress and low self-esteem in the ADHD spouse—a very poor choice indeed if one is trying to build in protective factors.

Others with ADHD go to the opposite extreme, choosing a partner who has more severe ADHD patterns than they do. This may be a defensive choice, after the experience of rejection by a more organized but critical partner. Such a partnership can be an exciting roller coaster ride, but is often fraught with crises. The ideal choice is a more organized partner who appreciates the ADHD spouse for the liveliness, spontaneity, creativity, interest, and stimulation they bring to the relationship, while not being overly distressed by the ADHD patterns of forgetfulness and disorder that are inevitable to some degree.

The psychotherapist working with a single ADHD client or one going through separation and divorce can provide very helpful counsel as the client ventures into the world of dating. An adult with ADHD, whether already in a committed relationship or just entering into new relationships, needs guidance from the therapist about how to introduce the topic of ADHD and how to educate the significant other about the challenges of ADHD while retaining full responsibility for managing the challenges of ADHD him- or herself. The client can also greatly benefit from considering the pros and cons of each newly emerging relationship from the vantage point of whether it will be likely to worsen or lessen his or her ADHD patterns.

## Career Choices and Changes

As mentioned earlier, it is critically important for the ADHD specialist to develop the skills to address a range of career issues that typically challenge the adult with ADHD. Workplace issues related to ADHD are among the most common difficulties that bring adults for treatment. To warrant calling ourselves adulthood ADHD specialists, we must develop a set of skills that allow us to address these issues, just as a childhood ADHD specialist must address educational issues. We need not become career counselors, but we should be able to advise our clients on ADHD-friendly career choices, and we should have intimate knowledge of typical workplace dilemmas and the types of strategies needed to overcome them.

We need to familiarize ourselves with the laws pertaining to disabilities and how they apply (or don't apply) to our clients. Very importantly, we need to be able to advise our clients whether it is in their best interest to disclose their disability at work and whether they should formally request accommodations or work on compensatory strategies without any formal assistance from their employer. There is currently much debate about what constitutes a disability and who qualifies for accommodations. In most workplace situations, however, I have found that official disclosure and accommodations are not often called for, except in extreme circumstances. We need not become disability law experts to assist our clients, but we certainly should become familiar with current case law and be able to advise our clients about the most effective approaches to take in dealing with workplace difficulties related to their ADHD.

## Other Critical Issues

Although beyond the scope of this chapter, there are other critical issues that the adulthood ADHD specialist should be prepared to deal with. The therapist should be aware of gender-specific issues for women with ADHD, including the impact of premenstrual syndrome (PMS), perimenopause, and menopause on the cognitive functioning of women with ADHD. It is not uncommon, for example, for PMS to severely impact a woman with ADHD and thus to need to be treated actively as a comorbid condition. Parenting issues also pose a great challenge for most adults with ADHD. They are likely to have children with ADHD and to experience intensified struggles because they have difficulty with the very issues for which their children need assistance. Single parenting, faced by many women with ADHD, poses an even greater set of challenges because there is no partner to share the burden and provide a counterbalance. And finally, ADHD can pose unique challenges in the later adult years, when the support and structure provided by a career and/or a spouse may be lost.

## TREATING ADULTS WITH ADHD IN THEIR MIDDLE YEARS

The following case history is intended to illustrate the multiple levels on which the ADHD specialist must work in treating adults. I have chosen a female case history in order to provide a balance, since the preceding two case histories are of young males. Although fewer females than males are diagnosed ADHD, the ratio among adults is changing rapidly, approaching a more equal ratio of males to females.

The case also involves multiple diagnoses, including alcoholism and depression, offering a good example of dealing with related comorbid conditions. And a major issue involved in this woman's treatment related to employment, allowing discussion how a clinician can approach career issues from an ADHD perspective. Lastly, since the woman I'll be discussing has earned not one but two graduate level degrees, it allows us to address the issue of whether an adult can legitimately be diagnosed with ADHD while being able to reach this level of achievement.

Cecile was a single woman in her early 40s with a long history of depression and alcoholism when she was referred to me for evaluation for possible ADHD. Despite years of medication and psychotherapy, her life remained in complete disorder. A bright woman, she had earned degrees in counseling and in law, although she had never been able to pursue either profession. Financial problems had kept her from paying off student loans so that she could receive her transcript from grad school and apply for licensure as a counselor. Law school had been completed in an alcoholic haze. She graduated at the bottom of her class and had never studied consistently enough to pass the bar exam.

Despite being in recovery for over seven years, she continued to struggle with huge financial problems. Bills were paid late, her apartment was in a permanent state of chaos, and she had recently quit her job due to stress, overwhelming paperwork, and a difficult, demanding supervisor. Cecile was an attractive, but overweight, soft-spoken woman who invariably arrived late for our appointments—anywhere from 10 to 30 minutes. Sometimes she missed the appointment altogether, having overslept. Despite antidepressants, despite successful recovery from active alcoholism, Cecile was unable to take charge of her life. Her psychiatrist began to suspect that ADHD might play a part in her problems with life management.

First, let's briefly address the issue of whether Cecile warrants a diagnosis of ADHD. She reports a family history in which ADHD seems very likely in her father (although never diagnosed). Early childhood academic history is one of a bright child who chronically underachieved. She was very disorganized and forgetful and a chronic procrastinator. Consistency and follow-through have eluded her throughout her life; however, high ability has allowed her to pass from one academic level to the next, albeit barely in many instances. When compared to her peers (i.e., others with counseling and law degrees) she shows marked dysfunction. Cecile offers us a good example of a highly capable individual who is unable to meet her potential due to a complex cluster of psychiatric difficulties, one of which is ADHD.

## Neurocognitive Treatment Approaches

Remember, in approaching any client from a neurocognitive perspective we are trying to assist the client to: (1) function better cognitively—i.e., to focus, concentrate, plan, and evaluate, better; (2) to develop compensatory strategies that will decrease the ADHD tendencies; and (3) to change the environment so that it is more supportive, more ADHD friendly.

### Improve Cognitive Functioning

**Medication** Psychostimulant medication is one of the most immediate and powerful ways to improve cognitive functioning for adults with ADHD. In Cecile's case, the medication issue was complicated by her history of alcoholism. Her psychiatrist, inexperienced in treating adults with ADHD, was understandably reluctant to prescribe potentially addictive stimulant medication to Cecile in addition to the antidepressants she was already taking. Often alcohol and/or marijuana are attempts at self-medication for ADHD, and psychostimulant medication could provide the ability to focus and accomplish goals that would lower her frustration level and therefore reduce the likelihood of relapsing. With the understanding that we would both closely monitor Cecile, the psychiatrist agreed to continue her antidepressant medication and to begin to prescribe a stimulant as well. At my urging, however, and in view of her eight years of sobriety, the psychiatrist cautiously began to prescribe Adderall®. Cecile functioned well on Adderall and found that she felt more alert and able to remain focused on a task.

**Exercise** Successfully engaging an adult with ADHD in regular exercise, given a history of lethargy and depression and given a lifelong difficulty with consistency and follow-through, is difficult. While exercise was guiltily avoided for many months after commencing treatment, several factors suddenly came together (a new job, spring weather, lowered depression) to lead to Cecile's positive response to a notice in the newspaper. No-fee training sessions were offered to adults who were out of physical condition to help them prepare for a marathon, to be held in six months. Cecile, to her own amazement, contacted a friend and together they signed up, relegated to the slowest group. Even more to her amazement, in response to the structure and group support, Cecile took her training seriously and ran or exercised five or more days a week. As the spring days lengthened and the pounds gradually melted away, her motivation was maintained. She reported increased energy and focus at work after several weeks of regular exercise.

**Adequate Sleep and Nutrition** Poor sleeping and eating habits are very common among adults with ADHD. They are, as a group, typically night owls who chronically sleep-deprive themselves and have difficulty rising on time in the morning. Recent surveys have shown that women with ADHD, in particular, tend to crave carbohydrates and to resort to binge eating, leading to low energy and highly variable blood sugar levels. Although with less success than with exercise, our treatment regularly focused on her sleeping and eating habits.

**Compensatory Strategies**

The second prong of the three-pronged neurocognitive approach is to help the client develop compensatory strategies to cope better with the challenges of everyday life. The first compensatory strategy challenge was for her to arrive on time for her appointments. Late arrival seemed a function of both depression and ADHD. She had difficulty sleeping, which led to enormous reluctance to rise when her alarm sounded early in the morning. We focused on night patterns that might improve sleep, dual alarm clocks, and ways to streamline her morning routine. Success was mixed, but gradually improved. We worked on a number of such strategies: developing a regular place to put bills and important paperwork until she took care of them; self-calming strategies before bedtime, to try to achieve an earlier bedtime; setting aside a regular evening at home to clean and organize her apartment; learning to use a day timer to plan her days and her weeks.

Another practical theme was never far from our sessions—the urgent, practical need to better manage her money and her enormous debt load. Until she could either earn her counselor's license or pass the bar exam, her job potential and earning power were significantly limited. Both of these projects required money—paying off an overdue student loan and saving the money to pay for the review class, preparatory to taking the bar exam. We examined her typical ADHD pattern of "leaking" money—spending small and medium sums of money frequently, sums she could ill afford—cab fares when she was late, expensive coffee and pastries when she was needing a psychological pick-me-up, purchasing lunch because she hadn't been organized enough to bring lunch from home, etc. Because detailed record keeping is typically difficult for adults with ADHD, we established a weekly cash allowance. She would go to an ATM machine each Friday, withdraw a set, affordable amount, and then make her cash expenditure decisions for the week based on how much cash she had in her wallet. That way, each day she made very concrete decisions—would I rather spend $2.50 for a specialty coffee several days or eat lunch out with a friend on Saturday? If I need to buy cosmetics at the drug store, then I'd better pack my lunch for the rest of the week.

### Environmental Changes

**Workplace**  The biggest "environmental" issue facing Cecile was her unemployment. In a typically ADHD fashion, she had quit a highly stressful job without having found another position, assuming she would have little trouble finding employment. As bills mounted and depression and anxiety rose, she felt less and less able to organize herself for a job search. At the time she entered therapy for her ADHD she had been unemployed for two months, had mounting debts, and depended increasingly on her mother for moral support and financial bailouts—a pattern she deplored but had reverted to repeatedly throughout her adult life.

We analyzed her work history, pinpointing aspects of jobs that she had enjoyed as well as factors that had been her downfall in previous jobs. Cecile's self-esteem was low and her sense of discouragement was great. Meanwhile, she had a weekly assignment from me to scan the Sunday paper for job possibilities, to circle those for which she wanted to apply, and to bring the job descriptions to each session so we could analyze them in terms of ADHD friendliness and her specific interests, strengths, and weaknesses. Understanding her need for structure and support, she engaged the help of both a friend and her mother in tailoring her résumé and completing applications for each job that seemed appropriate. Within several months, Cecile was successfully re-employed.

Now she faced the day-to-day reality of how ADHD affected her on the job. We strategized ways to reduce distractions in her crowded office environment by shifting the position and direction of her desk. This was not done as a formal "accommodation" but simply in response to her request and initiative. (Such unofficial "accommodations" are often the most effective way to arrange the work environment to better suit an individual with ADHD.) She also requested permission to work at home on days when she had an intensive writing project. Procrastination patterns re-emerged, and she engaged in several all-night marathons at work doing last-minute preparations for a conference. We focused on ways to improve this pattern through partnering with others and by setting intermediate deadlines.

## Co-Morbid Anxiety, Depression and Alcoholism

Cecile had been sober for eight years. With my encouragement, she continued to be active in Alcoholics Anonymous, which continued to support her sobriety and offered her a structured, constructive social outlet.

From the very beginning of our work together, the practical "neurocognitive" approaches just outlined were woven together with a focus on more "psychological" issues. Cecile struggled with both loneliness and a tendency to withdraw when she was depressed. We focused on how both depression and ADHD could contribute to social isolation. I advised her that making social plans is typically difficult for individuals with ADHD and suggested that she look for regularly occurring social activities that she need not plan but only need attend. She joined a singles group at church and began to participate in a weight-loss support group as well.

Cecile was also troubled by dysfunctional patterns within her family, and we focused on these as various issues arose with her mother, brother or sister. She explored her patterns of dependency and worked on developing a different, more adult relationship with her mother.

As her emotional health increased, Cecile remarked that she felt her social isolation had a different character now. She no longer felt such a strong urge to withdraw, but found that she was less satisfied with the relationships she had formed when she was much more dysfunctional. I talked to her about this as a sign of health and personal growth. She began to think about ways she could meet different people, outside of the context of the self-help groups that had been her main social outlet for many years.

After a year in treatment, Cecile continued to face huge challenges—she had far to go to eradicate her debt, she needed to pay off student loans in order to obtain her counseling license or to pay for the prep course to take the bar exam. She had, however, pinpointed a good career direction that would allow her to use her clinical and legal skills together by working with abused children. She continued to train for her marathon and continued to work on developing better spending habits that would allow her to take better control of many aspects of her life. She was actively seeking a more gratifying personal life. In general terms, she was learning to stay the course. The intermediate gains that she had made gave her greatly increased confidence that she could meet longer-term goals. Cecile had come to understand the concept of building "protective factors" into her life and to recognize the circumstances that had repeatedly led to ADHD crises and depression in the past. The coping strategies that she had learned helped her to recognize the signs of depression or of encroaching ADHD patterns and to take active steps to keep herself from sinking again into serious dysfunction.

## SUMMARY

There are many parallels between the types of interventions and clinical skills necessary to be effective in treating children and adults with ADHD. For children, the necessary "protective factors" that can minimize ADHD are provided by adults—by parents, teachers, coaches, tutors, and others. As clinicians working with adults, we need to introduce the concept of these "protective factors"—of creating an ADHD-friendly lifestyle—and help adults with ADHD build such protective factors into their adult life.

Because ADHD is a neurobiological condition, we need to be prepared to work with adults clients on a neurocognitive level, supporting improved cognitive functioning through medication and better health habits, teaching coping skills and compensatory strategies, and helping the client to develop a more supportive environment, including the workplace environment. At the same time, we must treat the secondary anxiety and depression that are so frequently found in adults with ADHD, as well as the commonly comorbid conditions. As a result, both the diagnosis and treatment of adults with ADHD is complex and calls for a broad set of clinical skills.

Because the workplace is the environment in which our adult clients spend the majority of their waking hours, we need the skills to help them identify and find jobs appropriate to their strengths and weaknesses. We also need to help them define workplace problems related to their ADHD as well as to develop strategies to reduce any negative impact that ADHD may have on their job performance.

In addition to this specialized set of ADHD-focused clinical tools, we must, in the final analysis, function as sensitive and supportive clinicians, seeing our clients as the complex human beings they are and never treating them in a formulaic or simplistic fashion as a person defined by their ADHD.

## REFERENCES

Goldstein, S., & Goldstein, M. (1998). *Managing attention deficit hyperactivity disorder in children: A guide for practitioners.* New York: Wiley.

# 7

# Changing the Mindset of Adults with ADHD

## Strategies for Fostering Hope, Optimism, and Resilience

Robert B. Brooks, Ph.D.

Several years ago I received a poignant letter from a man in his mid-40s who knew that I was collecting life stories from children and adults with ADHD. He was diagnosed with ADHD as an adult and noted, "When I found out about my ADHD I felt no relief. The depth of my anger and hurt surprised my therapist.... I've had lots of rejections: loves lost, great jobs blown. I take all of this personally so all these rejections mean they're my fault. Then the diagnosis comes, and it confirms what others have said about me: that something was wrong, that I'm defective, or just plain no damn good."

He continued, "My time has past.... I wish you well on your research. You can't help me but I'm willing to be used as a 'bad example' for those younger than me.... Because for them, perhaps, there's still some hope."

The pain, distress, feelings of hopelessness, and honesty of this man were evident throughout his letter.

In contrast, a number of years ago I worked with an adolescent with ADHD who described his condition in the following way:

I sat in the red chair, listening behind the old unbreakable desk, while the teacher rambled out our next in-class assignment, listening, focusing on the words as they came from her lips. Her lips stopped, and I reached for my math book, setting it down on my desk, my pencil in my right hand, ready to work. But wait a minute! What was the assignment? I turned to the classmates on both sides, but they were already working away, scratching the graphite into numbers on the standard gray sheet of paper.

ADD haunted me in everything I did. I did not know how to react to the situations around me.... In fifth grade the kids would slide down the ice-covered hill, like toboggans on the slope. I would join in, but what at first seemed to be fun turned into an abusive and painful experience. The kids would try to hit me as they slid down, their bodies crashing into mine, knocking the wind out of me, leaving me gasping for breath amongst my assailants, frozen in fear against the next onslaught. Yet each day, I returned.... Yet these experiences of pain have led me to my interest in others. Whenever I see a child being teased, I remember. I want to rush in and defend, to annihilate the inhumanity of harassment.

The young man who wrote these words, who committed himself to helping others, who turned despair into optimism, realized his dream and is a physician today.

Two men, each diagnosed with ADHD, and yet each views himself and the world so differently. Each possesses a different mindset or assumptions about his condition and his future. One is filled with hope, the other with hopelessness and despair. One is resilient, the other cannot even entertain the notion that things might improve.

What factors contribute to these very different mindsets? In this chapter I will review how the major characteristics of adults with ADHD, evident since childhood, shape the mindset of these individuals, a mindset often permeated with negative thoughts and feelings. I will examine how this negative mindset often prompts coping behaviors that turn out to be counterproductive and self-defeating, intensifying rather than relieving sadness. Finally, I will describe the features of a positive mindset and what we can do as clinicians to reinforce these features in adults with ADHD.

## THE CHARACTERISTICS OF ADULTS WITH ADHD

Adults with the diagnosis of ADHD are not a homogeneous group. Their cognitive styles and behaviors that led to being diagnosed with ADHD do not define their entire functioning or existence. However, there are certain core behaviors that many possess that distinguish them to a greater or lesser degree from individuals without ADHD. These behaviors elicit responses from others, responses that contribute to the formation of their mindset. Unfortunately, in far too many instances the mindset of individuals with ADHD is filled with negativity. The following represent a selected list of those behaviors that exert the strongest impact on their lives.

### Impulsivity

One of the most prominent characteristics of individuals with ADHD is their impulsivity. They are often described as acting before they think, of failing to consider the consequences of their behaviors. As children they are likely to blurt out answers in a classroom, or push their peers out of the way to be first in line, or place their finger in a light socket to see what happens, or climb a tall tree without considering the dangers. Adults will remind them how to behave in certain situations and they will agree. However, moments later they seemingly forget what they have just been taught, behaving in ways that are in stark contrast to what they have been told. It is easy to interpret their behaviors as manipulative or oppositional, but as Barkley (1995) and others observe, it is not that they don't know what to do, but rather that they are so impulsive they don't use what they know.

One observes similar patterns of behaviors in adults with ADHD. They may rush through tasks, or fail to demonstrate social skills by saying things that others experience as abrasive, or engage in risk-taking activities. I recall a couple I worked with in therapy. The husband with ADHD constantly interrupted his wife because he had important things to say. At the beginning of one session, his wife was furious. Earlier that day he had impetuously quit his job when his supervisor asked him to make some modifications on a project. Apparently, he told his supervisor that he knew more than the supervisor and that the latter should "get off his back or he would quit." The supervisor accepted his offer to quit.

As these examples suggest, impulsivity is often reflected in a lack of self-discipline or self-control. Goleman (1995) has highlighted self-discipline as a major ingredient of emotional intelligence, which he defines as "being able to motivate oneself and persist in the face of frustrations; to control impulse and delay gratification; to regulate one's moods and keep distress from swamping the ability to think; to empathize and to hope" (p. 34). Goleman's definition of emotional intelligence has direct bearing on other features of adults with ADHD as well.

## Low Frustration Tolerance

Closely linked to an impulsive style is how quickly adults with ADHD become frustrated and angry. This frustration is evident in many situations. If a task is difficult and not very interesting, they are quick to give up. If someone doesn't respond to what they want, they are quick to anger. One man with ADHD had a 10-year-old son with the same disorder. Instead of being empathic and appreciating his son's struggles with homework, he would shout, "Just try harder! You always give up! Do you want to be a loser in life?"

Adults with ADHD have difficulty tolerating their own shortcomings as well as the shortcomings of others. It is not unusual for them to cast blame on others when things do not go well. They often expect others to change but may not be as willing to change themselves. On the surface this unwillingness may appear as a statement that they are right and others wrong, but often their reluctance to change is rooted in feelings of helplessness. As one woman with ADHD told me, "I just felt I couldn't change my angry outbursts at my kids. I felt terrible but I blamed them and told them that if they met their responsibilities and treated me with more respect, I wouldn't have to shout at them or spank them. But I didn't take any responsibility for my own behavior." Her insight was to be the first step toward change.

## Moodiness

Many adults with ADHD are burdened by fluctuations in mood. One moment they may feel happy, only to have feelings of sadness dominate a few moments later. Some clinicians contend that the depression is primarily biologically based, while others feel that it is in response to years of frustration and failure. As with any affective disorder, most likely both biology and environment interact to different degrees with different individuals to contribute to the moodiness and depression. These shifts in mood are burdensome not only to adults with ADHD but also to those who interact with them. As one 9-year-old boy told me about his father with ADHD, "I never know how he's going to feel or act. It's scary sometimes."

## Disorganization

One of the most frequent complaints about individuals with ADHD is their difficulty with organization. As children and adolescents, they are the ones whose desks in school look as if a tornado has struck, whose three-ring binders that appeared so neat the first day of school quickly fall prey to different subjects being mixed together, who fail to complete homework assignments, who finally finish assignments that somehow are lost or misplaced on the way from home to school (for many of these children it seems that a black hole exists between home and school, sucking up assignments and papers with great regularity), and who constantly search for lost socks, shoes, coats, and book bags.

This pattern typically follows them into their adult years. They lose things, forget where they placed their keys, cannot locate bills to pay, neglect to jot down an important appointment in their book, or fail to complete a project at work because they have misjudged the time required or become distracted with two other projects. Needless to say, their time management skills leave much to be desired. As one man with ADHD sadly related, "I feel I have no control of my life. I can't keep track of things. I can't keep track of my schedule. I spend all of my energy trying to keep things in order, but you would never know it from the outcome."

## Rigidity, Inflexibility, and Insatiability

The other side of the coin of impulsivity and disorganization is the lack of flexibility that many adults with ADHD demonstrate. Someone observing their behavior might be puzzled how someone can be so impulsive and disorganized at one moment and so rigid the next. On the one hand this rigidity may exemplify, in part, a desperate attempt to cope with the disorganization and lack of control in one's life, but it also seems to be another example of a failure of self-regulation.

Children will manifest this pattern by having difficulty with transitions. Thus, in school they take a great deal of time to get started with an activity. When the teacher informs the class it is time to stop this activity and begin a new one (e.g., shifting from reading to math), they will not want to stop the first activity until they have completed it. If they are involved with a game or task at night, they do not want to go to bed until they have finished it, much to the frustration of their parents. Relatedly, I recall a number of youngsters with ADHD whom I would remind with at least 10 minutes left in our therapy session that our meeting would be over in 10 minutes. Even with this reminder, some would plead or argue for another few minutes to finish a drawing or a game.

This characteristic of inflexibility will frequently be manifested in the difficulty children with ADHD have in accepting "no" as an answer to a request (demand?) they have made. Their cognitive style does not leave room for compromise. They believe that their requests are reasonable and that when adults do not comply, the adults are being unfair and arbitrary. They frequently perceive only one solution to the problem, namely, that others comply with their wishes, and when this does not occur they often experience meltdowns, with accompanying tantrums (Greene, 1998).

A feature closely linked to inflexibility and a failure to compromise is what might be labeled "insatiability." I have been impressed by the number of parents who have described their children with ADHD as "impossible to please." One mother tearfully said, "From the moment my son was born, I felt I could not satisfy him. He always seemed to want more and more and more. As he got older, no toy was good enough for him, even if we had given him a choice of what toy he could buy. I thought I must have done something really wrong to have a child who never seemed satisfied or grateful."

This inborn feeling of insatiability, which is not easily quenched, leads to the perception that the world is unfair. When insatiability, inflexibility, and rigidity become interwoven into a cognitive and emotional tapestry, which is not unusual in children with ADHD, the end result are children who are demanding, unhappy, difficult to soothe, and unable to compromise. While this may seem an overly bleak picture, it is found in many youngsters with so-called "difficult" temperaments (Brooks & Goldstein, 2001; Chess & Thomas, 1987). Children with ADHD typically fall under the category of temperamentally "difficult."

In adults, insatiability and inflexibility are displayed in many aspects of their lives. They are seldom satisfied even when they succeed. Enjoyment is fleeting at best. In couples therapy, when one member of the couple has ADHD, it is not surprising to hear the other describe his or her spouse as difficult to please, unhappy, always seeing the glass as half empty, possessing an intense need to be right, perceiving compromise as giving in, and frequently not paying attention. Often, the spouse with ADHD minimizes these descriptions by saying he or she would feel fine if other people were more giving and considerate. In their parenting roles, the inflexibility may be expressed in an authoritarian style replete with anger. It is little wonder that tension and friction become dominant features of families where one or more members have ADHD.

## A Dearth of Empathy

Many individuals with ADHD struggle to be empathic. While this difficulty with empathy is closely linked to the characteristics I have already described, I believe that given its importance in our day-to-day interactions it deserves special mention. Goleman (1995) has highlighted empathy as a major ingredient of emotional intelligence.

In simple terms empathy may be defined as the capacity to put oneself inside the shoes of other people and to see the world through their eyes. Empathic people are able to take the perspective of others, even when they disagree with these others. They attempt to understand how their words and deeds are experienced and how others would describe them. They reflect upon and take responsibility for their behavior. They are able to realistically assess and appreciate the "social scene."

Cognitive and emotional skills are necessary for empathy to develop. If one examines the characteristics of children and adults with ADHD, one can appreciate why empathy is often compromised. It is a great struggle to take the perspective of another when we are impulsive, frustrated, or moody, when we quickly interpret the actions of others as withholding or unfair, when we believe that others are not listening to us, and when we feel we are being cheated. A man with ADHD I worked with in therapy for several years summed up his improvement with the following insightful statement: "It wasn't until I could slow down and realistically separate what I was feeling from the intention of others that I could become a more empathic person."

In contrast to this comment was one offered by a young adult with ADHD during a discussion of empathy. He argued, "Why should I really care about how I come across to others or how others see me? If I think too much about that, if I act too nice, they might take further advantage of me." This young man's definition of empathy was much different. He viewed empathy as a weapon for manipulation rather than as a skill to foster more satisfying relationships. As long as he maintained this perspective it would be difficult for him to engage in comfortable, satisfying relationships.

## THE UNFORTUNATE MINDSET OF ADULTS WITH ADHD

If impulsivity, low frustration tolerance, moodiness, disorganization, rigidity, inflexibility, insatiability, and a lack of empathy are the possible manifestations of the biological underpinnings of ADHD, as we have already seen, these characteristics will impact on almost all aspects of a person's life. They will serve as a major influence in determining the ways in which we respond to others, how they respond to us, and how successful we are in the many personal and professional activities in which we engage.

From childhood, the particular style of many individuals with ADHD as just described results in poor peer relationships as well as compromises in school and subsequent work performance. Slowly, negative assumptions or perceptions about oneself and others take shape, becoming an integral part of an individual's mindset. In turn, this mindset plays a powerful role in determining one's behaviors in a wide spectrum of situations, generating a cycle of negative beliefs, a loss of hope, and self-defeating behaviors.

The following are several of the main interrelated features of this negative mindset, with suggestions at the end of this section of ways that clinicians might assess this mindset via interview questions. Also, questionnaires such as Seligman's (1990) "learned optimism" scale may be used in conjunction with interview material to evaluate the positive or negative qualities of an individual's mindset.

## I Do Not Have a Great Deal of Control of My Life

One of the hallmarks of a positive mindset is feeling a sense of control over what transpires in one's life, together with a realistic appraisal of those areas over which one has control and those that are beyond one's influence. As Covey (1989) has eloquently noted, all people have "circles of concern," but effective people recognize and use their time and energy to focus on their "circles of influence"; that is, they are proactive rather than reactive. Stress is frequently linked to the belief "I have little say or control over the important things that occur in my life."

The very nature of the characteristics of ADHD contribute to a feeling of not being in control. For example, if one behaves impulsively without considering the consequences, negative results are likely to follow that are often interpreted as a lack of control of one's actions. As one woman told me, "I always yell at my kids. I tell myself not to, but then when they don't do what I want them to do I get so frustrated so quickly that I scream. I feel terrible afterwards." A man with ADHD said, "No one really listens to me. Nothing I do seems to work."

Or as another example, if one is insatiable, constantly seeking unobtainable gratification, then continued hunger and frustration are the likely outcome, as is the feeling that "nothing I do is enough to get what I want" or "people won't give me what I deserve."

## When I Am Successful It Is Based on Luck or Chance

Whether we are aware of it or not, when we succeed or fail at things in our life we offer ourselves different explanations for these successes and failures. As suggested by attribution theory (Weiner, 1974), these explanations are linked to our self-esteem and sense of optimism. Attribution theory has been studied relative to individuals with attentional and learning problems as a target population (Brooks, 1999; Canino, 1981; Licht, 1983). Children and adults with high self-esteem perceive their successes as based in great part on their own efforts or abilities. These individuals assume realistic ownership for their achievements. They believe they are active participants in their own success.

In contrast, individuals with low self-esteem typically attribute success to things outside of their control, such as luck, chance, or fate. One child with ADHD told me that his good grade on a test was "pure luck." Another said, "The teacher made the test easy." An adult with ADHD vividly said that her success in life was like "a house made out of cards." She added, "I feel that if any kind of wind comes along, my entire facade of success will crumble."

If you believe that your success is not rooted in your resources and effort but rather in luck or chance or things beyond your control, then it is difficult to be confident about experiencing success in the future. In such a case, a loss of hope becomes a dominant feature of one's life.

## Failure Indicates My Inadequacy as a Person

Just as attribution theory highlights differences in how individuals understand the successes in their lives, so too does it clarify how failure is perceived. Children and adults with high self-esteem typically believe that mistakes are experiences from which to learn rather than feel defeated. Mistakes are attributed to variables that can be modified, such as a lack of adequate effort when engaged in reaching a realistically attainable goal or the use of ineffective strategies when studying for a test. A child requesting assistance to learn the strategies involved in solving math problems or an adult registering for a computer course in response to struggles to master the computer represent examples of taking positive action to confront mistakes.

In contrast, individuals with low self-esteem, which is often present in ADHD, are vulnerable to thinking that they cannot correct the situation or overcome the obstacle. They view mistakes as a consequence of factors that are not modifiable, such as a lack of ability or intelligence, and this belief breeds a feeling of helplessness and hopelessness. They begin to believe that regardless of what they do, few, if any, positive outcomes will appear. The probability of future success is diminished because these people expect to fail and, thus, retreat from the challenges at hand. I have seen this pattern with a number of adults with ADHD.

## I'm Less Worthy Than Others

If one encounters many failure situations, it is not difficult to understand how self-esteem is adversely affected. True self-esteem, or what Lerner (1996) calls "earned self-esteem," is based on realistic accomplishment. Each success serves as a step up the ladder of future success. However, when mistakes, failure, and negative feedback are major parts of a person's landscape, there is little room for high self-esteem or confidence.

Self-doubts appear early in the lives of many children with ADHD and continue into their adulthood. Sentiments such as "I can't do that, it's too tough" or "This is stupid" (the child in fact feels stupid) are voiced by children as young as 5 and 6. Just as each success serves as the foundation for future success, so too does each setback serve as a reinforcement of the idea "I am not very capable."

A man with ADHD said to me, "If I have any doubts about my ability to do something, these doubts quickly multiply and interfere with my ever being able to succeed. I see myself as klutzy and I have trouble concentrating. The other day I went to assemble a toy we had bought for my son. The moment I saw the number of parts and the directions I told myself, 'I'll never be able to do that. I can't understand directions. I bet I'll have pieces left over.' And guess what? When I finished, the toy didn't work and I had pieces left over." With much insight he added, "The moment I told myself I couldn't do it, the outcome was no longer in question."

The man mentioned at the beginning of this chapter described these feelings of low self-worth when he wrote to me, "Then the diagnosis comes, and it confirms what others have said about me: that something was wrong, that I'm defective, or just plain no damn good."

As we shall see, these negative feelings of low self-worth trigger coping strategies that often exacerbate rather than improve the situation.

## The World Is Unfair

Individuals with ADHD often believe that situations and people are unfair. The characteristics of ADHD noted earlier, such as insatiability, inflexibility, and low frustration tolerance, reinforce the feeling that things are not fair. This belief was vividly and directly captured by a boy who wrote to me, "Why did I have to be born with ADHD? It's not fair."

The sense of unfairness is manifested in other ways during one's youth. One middle school boy with ADHD was angry with a teacher who gave him a D grade for the semester. On five tests he had received three F's, one D, and one B. In actuality, the teacher might have been justified in giving him a failing grade. The boy complained that he deserved a B as a grade since one of his test scores was a B. When I pointed out that the teacher was probably basing the grade on all five tests, the boy persisted, "But I got a B on a test!"

At first I thought that he realized that he did not deserve a B but was attempting to convince himself or me that he did. However, I soon appreciated that his seeming distortion of the situation actually reflected a couple of the characteristics associated with ADHD. One, he was conditioned to perceive things as unfair when he did not get what he wanted, and two, his cognitive style was to view situations in a rigid, black-and-white fashion, not allowing him to assume another perspective. Once he felt he deserved a B, there was no room for a different view.

This feeling of unfairness, which becomes an ongoing, emotional strain, is also apparent in adults with ADHD. They harbor constant complaints about employers, spouses, and salespeople they believe are unfair. While at times there may be justification to these complaints, frequently they represent anger at feeling misunderstood and not having demands met.

## People Seem Angry with Me

Closely related to this last point but deserving separate mention is the sense that others are angry with you. This perception, although exaggerated at times, does have some basis in reality. People do not find it easy to be with someone who comes across as self-centered, impulsive, demanding. Annoyance and frustration often pervade relationships, contributing to the feeling that the other people are angry with me. Unfortunately, if empathy is lacking, the response to this feeling is to become angry rather than attempt to resolve the conditions that are reinforcing the anger.

A woman with ADHD told me that her brother and sister were always "ganging up" on her and calling her "inconsiderate" and "selfish." She said that she let them know in "no uncertain terms" that they were the selfish ones and should go see a therapist. She was unable to consider the possibility that her siblings were accurate about her behavior, instead feeling that they were angry because of their "personality problems" and their "jealousy" of her talents.

## I Have Little, If Anything, to Offer the World

A sense of self-esteem and dignity is nurtured when individuals feel that they are making a contribution to their world, that their actions makes a positive difference (Brooks, 1999; Brooks & Goldstein, 2001). This hypothesis was supported by narrative research I conducted when I asked adults to identify one of the most positive moments they ever had in school. The most frequent answer I received concerned when they were asked to help out in some manner (e.g., painting a mural on the wall, watering plants, tutoring younger children). The act of assisting others typically reinforces the belief "I am worthwhile, I have something positive to offer others." The second man I described at the beginning of this chapter is an example of someone who found a way of turning his hurt into helping others, namely, by becoming a physician.

Many adults with ADHD who possess a negative mindset view themselves as adding little, if anything, to the lives of others. The first man I mentioned at the beginning of this chapter, who gave me permission to use his story as an example to others, emphasized the negative in doing so ("My time has past.... I wish you well on your research. You can't help me but I'm willing to be used as a 'example' for those younger than me.... Because for them, perhaps, there's still some hope").

The belief that one has little to contribute to others lessens feelings of competence and a sense of worth and dignity. One man I saw with ADHD summed up his feelings when he told me with great honesty, "I think the only thing I have ever given others is heartache."

## I Am Pessimistic That Things Will Improve

This feature of a negative mindset is also understandable given the other beliefs that many individuals with ADHD hold. It is difficult to be optimistic when people feel little control of their lives, when they have difficulty taking ownership for success, when they believe people are unfair and angry, and when they are unable to see any ways in which they make a positive difference in their world. Pessimism about future success and happiness often results in a self-fulfilling prophecy for failure. If you expect that you will continue to experience unhappiness and failure, subtly or not so subtly your actions will lead to these expectations being realized. An ongoing cycle of expected failure and actual failure is a very powerful force in contributing to a pessimistic outlook that is devoid of a sense of hope.

This sense of pessimism and loss of hope was poignantly reflected in the writings of a young man with ADHD explaining why he dropped out of high school. "My alarm goes off and I awake to a new day. At 7:00 in the morning my stomach is queasy and my head hurts. 'Oh God, another day of school.' Too sick to eat breakfast, I stand in the shower saying, 'Maybe it will be a good day,' but deep inside I know it will be the same." Given these strong beliefs it is little wonder that he perceived that his only way of coping was to leave school.

## ASSESSING THE MINDSET OF INDIVIDUALS WITH ADHD

It is important to emphasize that while not all adults with ADHD develop a negative mindset, many appear to possess some if not all of these characteristics. Before examining the coping strategies used by adults with ADHD and the ways in which a clinician can help replace a negative mindset with a mindset that is filled with more positive and resilient beliefs, it may be helpful to articulate the kinds of questions that clinicians can raise to assess the mindset of individuals with ADHD.

While paper-and-pencil procedures have been developed to evaluate a person's self-esteem, sense of competence, and optimism or pessimism, as a clinician I have found that interview questions remain the best resource for obtaining revealing information. Interview questions permit a more in-depth view of an individual's perspective, and they allow you to follow up and elaborate on particular points. The following represent a sample of questions that may be raised (see Table 7.1). It is important to remember that many of these questions serve as a springboard to further questions and discussion, helping us to understand the mindset of adults with ADHD.

All of these questions tap into the views that people have of themselves, of others, of their competencies and vulnerabilities, of their relationships, of their hopes for the future, of their beliefs if they can bring about change. In essence, the answers to these questions represent a mindset, or a set of assumptions about oneself and others.

## COPING STRATEGIES: HELPING OR EXACERBATING THE PROBLEM?

We all rely upon a variety of coping strategies to deal with stresses and challenges in our lives. Some coping strategies appear to be effective, helping individuals to deal successfully with the challenges

**TABLE 7.1  Sample Assessment Questions**

How does having ADHD affect your life?
What are the negative and positive aspects of having ADHD?
What things would you like to see changed in your life?
What have you attempted to do to change any of these things?
In what areas have you been successful?
Why do you believe you have been successful?
In what areas have you been unsuccessful?
What do you think has contributed to your not being successful?
When you are not successful at a certain task, what is your usual response? Give a few examples.
Are there people who are trying to be of help to you?
Who are they?
How do you know they are trying to be of help?
What is one of the most helpful things someone did for you?
Are there any people who actually seem to be interfering with your chances for success?
In what way are they behaving to keep you from being successful?
What is one of the least helpful or even hurtful things someone did to you?
If you could change one or two things about yourself beginning tomorrow, what would they be?
How would you start?
Looking a year or two ahead, how do you see your life changing?
For things to improve, do you think others have to become more tolerant of your having ADHD, or do you feel you have to begin to make some changes, or is it a combination of the two?

they face. Other coping behaviors may afford temporary or illusory relief, but not only do they fail to resolve the problem, they actually worsen the situation. One of the questions raised in the last section is an attempt to gather information about the ways in which a person copes: "When you are not successful at a certain task, what is your usual response? Give a few examples."

The question of what differentiates an effective from an ineffective coping strategy does not always invite an easy answer. Paradoxically, what I might consider to be an ineffective coping strategy may actually diminish stress for at least a certain period of time more than what I would perceive to be an effective coping strategy. As one example, imagine you were invited to give a presentation at a local organization and you are fearful of public speaking. One way of coping with the anxiety would be to offer the excuse that you are busy and unable to accept the offer. The immediate feeling is typically relief. One might argue that this way of coping was effective since it lessened stress. However, as a clinician I have found that eventually what replaces this relief is regret. Regret at having fled away from a challenge.

For example, a woman with ADHD whose main coping behavior was to avoid situations that she felt could lead to mistakes and embarrassment came to see me. She said that she was constantly telling her two children to "stick with things and not give up" but that she felt like "a hypocrite" since she had spent much of her life "running away from things that might lead to failure and humiliation." She noted, "When I say no to a certain request, I feel okay for a few minutes, but then I hate myself for being so scared and always avoiding tough things. But then I keep running from things."

Now imagine that instead of immediately offering an excuse not to speak, this woman said yes and then considered ways to cope with the anxiety she was experiencing. She listened to a tape or read a book about lessening the anxiety of public speaking. She practiced her speech using a tape recorder or in front of a trusted friend or relative. As she coped in this way, she might remain anxious, but most likely her preparation would lead to a more than satisfactory performance. The fact that she did not back away from the challenge, but rather faced it directly, would be one of the strongest determinants of feeling a sense of self-worth. If she took this route, although her coping behavior might not at first diminish her distress, I believe that eventually it would, since she faced rather than fled from a problematic event.

A coping behavior may be deemed effective when individuals confront challenging situations rather than retreat from them, when coping leads to emotional growth and greater feelings of self-worth, and when coping helps people to experience a sense of control of their own lives, when they believe they are masters of their own fate. The factors that contribute to whether an individual uses effective or ineffective ways of coping appear to be based on an ongoing, dynamic interaction between inborn temperamental factors and environmental conditions (Brooks, 1984).

Since a major feature of the mindset of many individuals with ADHD is their belief that they are not very competent, that they are destined to fail, and that they do not control their own destiny, they are likely to recruit coping strategies that prove self-defeating and do not result in emotional growth or in success.

There are some common ineffective coping strategies I have observed with adults with ADHD. As clinicians we must remember that these strategies, although self-defeating, originally served a protective purpose. They were called upon in an attempt to avoid the possibility of further failure, humiliation, and embarrassment. If we keep this purpose in mind we will recognize that our task is to help adults with ADHD feel less vulnerable so that they are more secure and better able to replace ineffective means of coping with effective strategies. The following represent some of these self-defeating coping behaviors, several of which can occur at the same time.

## Avoiding

This coping behavior is represented by the actions of the woman described earlier who turned down a speaking request. People will usually avoid a task that they believe will lead to failure. I worked with one man with ADHD who described himself as "klutzy and unathletic." When friends asked him to join in a relatively noncompetitive local softball or basketball game, he always said no. Yet a number of other people who also were not athletically inclined did participate. In the course of therapy this man reflected, "I spend more time and energy avoiding things than I do trying things. I guess I'll never know what I'm capable of doing, but I hate to look foolish."

## Quitting

This coping style is similar to avoiding but is used to describe people who begin a task and then quit as soon as they encounter difficulty. Often this pattern is established early in children's lives, continuing into their adulthood. I have heard many examples of children with ADHD who start a musical instrument or join a sports team, only to leave in a short time with some excuse. A woman I knew had quit college. When she returned several years later to take courses, her style was to drop certain courses, either saying they were boring or required too much work given her busy schedule. However, her quitting was truly rooted in her feeling that she could not succeed at the task.

## Rationalizing

This strategy is frequently used by adults with ADHD. It involves offering excuses for perceived difficulties and failure rather than accepting responsibility. The woman who quit college because the courses were too "boring" provides an example of the use of rationalization. A man I saw in therapy refused to go for a job interview for a new position, saying he was certain it would not be a challenge. He offered this opinion even before he had obtained all of the details of the new job. In fact, he was quite frightened of taking on new challenges, which he saw as eventuating in failure.

At times, rationalization assumes the form of *externalizing*, that is, blaming other people or external events for unsatisfactory outcomes. Examples include a woman with ADHD who explained her poor interpersonal relations by contending that other people were unfair to her for no reason or a man who blamed his boss for his own poor work performance. He told me, "My boss knows I have ADHD, but yet he gives me very detailed work to do, more detailed than my coworkers get." When I wondered why his boss would do this, he answered, "He just doesn't like me. He's unfair." However, as our therapy work progressed, he was able to acknowledge that the work his boss expected of him was no different from that of other employees. He was able to realize that blaming his boss was a way of coping with his own feelings of inadequacy and also represented the mindset that the world is unfair.

## Controlling

As noted earlier, a number of adults with ADHD feel little, if any, control of what occurs in their lives, so a sense of helplessness is not an uncommon result. In response, some individuals attempt to take command and become dictatorial, telling others what to do or how to run their business or their lives. This coping behavior is typically reinforced by problems with empathy and poor social skills. A man with ADHD lost several jobs as he fell into the pattern of telling his manager how the department should be run. On a couple of occasions he did not fulfill certain responsibilities that he felt "made no sense." He also was free with advice to his colleagues about how they might do a better job.

A woman with ADHD who felt "overwhelmed" by the requirements of parenting resorted to micromanaging everything her 10- and 8-year-old sons did. Her need to control their lives was based, in part, on her feelings of inadequacy as a parent as well as a need to "keep the household in order."

## Aggressive Behavior

Closely tied to several other counterproductive coping behaviors, such as externalizing and controlling, is being aggressive and striking out at others. If people feel that others are unfair or that the task is too difficult, some may respond by avoiding the situation, while others may resort to angry outbursts bordering on bullying. The specific coping behavior that is used will often be influenced by an individual's temperament as well as his or her life experiences. I have found that a number of adults with ADHD will manifest being aggressive with a heavy dose of rationalization; that is, they will rationalize their aggressive behavior by arguing that their actions were justified given the ways in which the other person behaved toward them.

A rather driven president of an engineering company was diagnosed with ADHD. While brilliant in his scientific work, he had difficulty accepting vulnerabilities in himself or in others; his ability to be empathic was limited at best. He had an intense need to be in control, which his position in the company permitted him to do. He left college after his junior year with a transcript filled with "incompletes," feeling that many of the requirements to complete a class were "stupid." He then quit his first two jobs after arguments with his supervisors. He began his own company to show his professors "I don't need a college degree to be successful" and to show his former employers that if they "listened to me, their companies would be much more successful."

A downturn in his own business resulted in symptoms of anxiety, and he was referred to a psychiatrist for a medication consultation. The psychiatrist completed an evaluation and made a diagnosis of ADHD as well as an anxiety disorder. This man was placed on medication and referred to me. As he became more comfortable in therapy, he shared his disappointment at not having finished college and added, "It's not a good example for my teenage son and daughter."

He then discussed his relationship with his employees, especially since many of his middle managers were leaving the company. As he described his interactions it was obvious that he demanded perfection, rooted, in part, in a driving force to prove his professors and former employers wrong. When something did not work out, rather than discuss it rationally with his staff, he would become angry and say some hurtful things. At one meeting he shouted, "What a dumb thing to do!" while at another he asked one of his managers, "Are you using your brains?" He justified these outbursts by saying, "I get angry when people fall short of what their performance should be, and it's good to let them know how disappointed I am."

Given his lack of empathy and his need to be in control, he had little awareness of how this form of motivation was counterproductive; it basically motivated his staff to avoid him or leave the company. Much of the emphasis of our therapy was to help him become more accepting of his own vulnerabilities and more empathic toward other people in his life.

## Acting Impulsively by Rushing Through Things

Although impulsivity is a major characteristic of ADHD, it may also represent a way of coping. It is not unusual for some adults to want to finish a challenging task or burdensome chore as quickly as possible "to get it over with." The obvious problem is that the more quickly and impulsively the task is done, the more likely that the final product will be riddled with mistakes and flaws. A negative cycle is established, since these mistakes reinforce for adults with ADHD that they are not very competent, and to deal with these feelings they resort to one or several of the self-defeating coping behaviors that have been described in this section. Success becomes more and more elusive, while a negative mindset becomes increasingly entrenched.

## STEPS FOR CHANGING NEGATIVE INTO POSITIVE MINDSETS

As clinicians, one of our main roles when working with individuals with ADHD burdened by a negative mindset and accompanying self-defeating coping behaviors is to help them to replace their negative feelings and thoughts with an optimistic, positive outlook and more adaptive ways of managing stress and pressure. We must serve as a catalyst to generate a positive cycle in which the individual engages in activities that lead to fulfillment, satisfaction, and success. As each success chips away at negative feelings, realistic risk taking and the confronting of challenges are likely to follow. As noted earlier, success breeds success.

## 1. Demystifying Mindsets

An initial step in changing negative mindsets is to help individuals define and understand (a) the assumptions that they have about themselves (including ADHD) and others and (b) how these assumptions prompt certain behaviors and coping strategies that may be self-defeating. In essence, this first step emphasizes the strengthening of self-awareness, which Goleman (1995) views as a basic component of emotional intelligence.

As examples, the two men described at the beginning of this chapter had different understandings of ADHD. The first man, who was diagnosed as an adult with ADHD, had already suffered years of humiliation and failure. In his case, the despair and hopelessness were apparently such entrenched features of his mindset that the diagnosis did not help to demystify what had occurred all of these years. Rather, the diagnosis was quickly incorporated into his negative mindset as a confirmation "that something was wrong, that I'm defective, or just plain no damn good."

In contrast, the man who became a physician learned of his ADHD earlier in his life. His parents and doctors explained what it meant and how it manifested itself. Understanding his condition helped to demystify it, so it was not as foreboding. While he experienced pain and rejection, he also was helped to see that one could learn ways of coping with ADHD, that it was not a sentence for lifelong misery. Even when upset, he could see a light at the end of the tunnel and could appreciate that he could learn from his experiences. He could harness the pain into a positive force of understanding and helpfulness, eventuating in his becoming a physician.

The questions I outlined earlier to assess the mindset of adults with ADHD can serve as the catalyst for demystifying ADHD and promoting greater self-awareness. As an example, when I asked a man with ADHD to describe both a successful and an unsuccessful experience from his life, his answers were very revealing. It was almost as if he had read and decided to adhere to the tenets of attribution theory. The successful experience he recounted was of a tennis match against a friend who was a good tennis player. He won the match and told me in therapy, "I was lucky. My friend didn't play at his best. I even wondered if he was trying to let me win since he had beaten me so often."

As an unsuccessful experience, he recalled an incident from college when he failed the initial exam given in a mathematics course. His first thought was, "I'm really stupid in math. I'll never pass." He dropped the class. He then confided in me, "After I dropped the class, I started to blame the teacher and thought, 'If the teacher were a better teacher, I would have been able to handle the material in the class and pass it.'" He used two main coping strategies to deal with his sense of failure, the first was *quitting* and the next was *rationalizing/externalizing*.

Although it may seem very obvious to the reader that this man with ADHD had a negative mindset, that he was unable to take credit for his success and felt like he would never learn from his failure, he was unaware of his assumptions and how they affected his life. In therapy he offered a number of other examples of this way of thinking. To assist him to become more cognizant of these negative assumptions and to begin to challenge him to change, I borrowed a technique described by solution-oriented therapists, namely to elicit "exceptions" to typical ways of behaving and thinking. Exceptions pertain to situations in which certain problems do not occur or occur less frequently (de Shazer, 1991; Murphy, 1997).

I have modified to some extent the "exception" technique by asking individuals to think of times that they were successful in a certain domain rather than focusing on when the problem did not occur. I asked this man with ADHD to reflect upon times that he was successful and attributed his success to his own resources and of times he made mistakes and was able to learn from those mistakes.

He struggled at first to think of examples but with some encouragement was able to do so. Both illustrations involved the actions of a coach. He recalled as a young teenager playing in a youth basketball league; he almost single-handedly won a playoff game by making two steals and three baskets in the last minute. "When the game was over and my coach congratulated me, I said, 'I was really lucky.' My coach said really strongly, 'It wasn't luck, it was your determination and skill.' The way he said it made me believe him."

He also recalled that from the first day of practice this coach actually told the team that if they thought their success was based on luck, they did not realize the benefits of practice, hard work, and teamwork. "I also remember when I had a bad game and was really feeling down. The coach put his hand on my shoulder and said even the pros have bad games. He reminded me of my good games and then pointed out how I wasn't following through on my shot. I wish I could have remembered this coach's lessons. During the year he was my coach I felt more confident than ever before, but unfortunately the feeling didn't last long."

He then described the coach he had the following year, who "believed in sarcasm and put-downs and never seemed to offer encouragement." He continued:

> I remember one game where we were losing by one point. A teammate threw the ball to me with a few seconds to go and it went off my hands and out of bounds. We lost the game. I don't know if the throw to me was too hard or I was just too anxious to get it and shoot. I felt terrible and then even worse when the coach said in front of everyone that I missed the ball because "I didn't have good hands." Can you imagine that? I wasn't that secure to begin with, and his remark made me feel like I would never be good. After that, anytime someone threw the ball to me, I felt uncomfortable. I'm still upset with myself that I let his remark have such a negative impact on me.

These examples, especially the "exceptions" to his current mindset, helped him to appreciate and understand the assumptions that directed his way of thinking and behaving and set the stage for the second step involved in developing a more positive mindset, namely, articulating the components of this mindset. This articulation provides clinicians with a compass in guiding interventions to nurture a resilient mindset.

## 2. Defining The Main Components of a Positive, Resilient Mindset

In many ways the features of a positive mindset are the mirror image of the earlier description of a negative mindset. They include the following.

**a. I will learn to distinguish what I have control over from that which I do not. I will focus my time and energy over those things over which I have control, since I am the author of my life.** As was noted earlier, one of the hallmarks of effective people is their belief that they are masters of their own destiny. Research focusing on successful adults with learning and attentional difficulties found that they did not adhere to a martyr role. They never asked, "Why me?" but instead believed, "I had no control of being born with ADHD, but what I do have control over is how I deal with ADHD."

Gerber, Ginsberg, and Reiff (1992) studied the ways in which successful adults with learning disabilities view themselves (I believe the same is true for adults with ADHD) and emphasize the importance of feeling in control when they write, "Control is the key to success for adults with learning disabilities.... Control meant taking charge of one's life and adapting and shaping oneself in order to move ahead.... Control was the fuel that fired their success" (p. 479).

The sense of being in control is associated with the attitude that if changes are to occur in my life, I must take responsibility for these changes and not wait for others to come to my rescue or immediately satisfy my needs. Such a perspective not only lessens the sense that the world is unfair and ungiving but also places responsibility for change within oneself.

**b. Success can be based on my own strengths and resources.** This feature of a resilient mindset is closely aligned with feeling a sense of control of one's life. While effective people will give credit to individuals who contributed to their success, they also believe that their success rests largely on their own efforts. In essence, they assume ownership for what occurs in their lives.

A woman with ADHD constantly downplayed any of her accomplishments, an attitude that not only diminished her enjoyment when she succeeded, but also lessened the probability of future achievement. Adhering to a negative script, she had the following knee-jerk reaction to success: "I was lucky this time. It probably won't happen again." Each success elicited the same thoughts. In her case, she segregated one success from the next, so they did not build on each other to change her negative mindset. As she became more aware of this self-defeating attitude, she was able to adopt a realistic outlook in which she could say, "I did well because I planned what I was going to do and worked hard."

**c. I have "islands of competence."** We all have areas of strength, or what I refer to as *islands of competence*. However, as we have seen, a number of adults with ADHD fail to acknowledge or appreciate their strengths. People with a more positive, resilient mindset are able to identify their islands of competence. It is for this reason that in my clinical work I ask my patients to tell me directly what they view as their strengths and how they use these strengths in their daily lives. It is also why I use the technique of searching for "exceptions" when people respond that they don't feel they are very good at anything. I want to begin to plant the seeds that will flower into areas of competence.

**d. I believe that mistakes are opportunities for learning and growth.** No one is really thrilled when they make mistakes or fail. However, as clinicians we recognize that one of our most important tasks is to help people feel less intimidated by mistakes. When mistakes are viewed as situations from which to learn, people are more willing to take realistic risks rather than backing away from challenges. They do not expend an inordinate amount of time and energy fleeing from possible setbacks. Rather, their efforts are directed toward developing plans of action to succeed; if they do not succeed, they reflect upon what they have learned and what they can do differently next time. Their outlook is optimistic.

**e. I make a positive difference in the world.** A basic component of emotional well-being appears to be the belief that one's actions benefit others (Brooks & Goldstein, 2001). As a therapist I have witnessed countless examples of individuals, many with ADHD, who engage in activities that make a positive difference (e.g., being involved in a charity, serving as a coach in a youth sports league, helping at a senior citizen center); in the process their own sense of dignity and self-worth is enhanced, and the roots of a resilient mindset are secured.

## 3. Developing a Plan of Action for Change

Once clinicians help adults with ADHD gain a clearer picture of what ADHD entails, and once these adults can appreciate the assumptions that characterize their mindset and guide their behaviors, the next step is to articulate a problem-solving model for change. The model I predicate my interventions upon, developed by psychologist Myrna Shure for children and adolescents, appears equally relevant for adults (Shure, 1994, 2000). My modification of Shure's basic model includes the following components, all of which I believe have a commonsense, achievable quality to them.

**a. Articulate both short-term and long-term goals for change**. If adults with ADHD have developed a negative mindset that offers little hope for the future and we have helped them to understand that mindsets can be changed, a first step is to have them begin to articulate the changes they would like to see occur in their lives. It is often a help to divide these changes into short-term and long-term goals, with the short-term goals contributing to the realization of the long-terms goals.

**b. Select a few goals to address**. I have discovered that while some adults with ADHD struggle to articulate goals (as therapists we can help them to do so), others are able to generate a long list. However, sometimes their impulsivity and low frustration tolerance prompt them to begin to work on all of these goals at once, almost a certain prescription for failure. Instead, as therapists we must assist them to prioritize their goals and to select one or two on which to give initial focus (O'Hanlon, 1999). We want to maximize the probability that the goals they have selected are achievable so that success will be more likely. Once we have selected the areas they wish to address, we can help to articulate both the short-term and long-terms components of these goals.

As an example, in my sessions with adults with ADHD I take out a sheet of paper and ask them what they would like to see change in their lives. We write down their responses and then select one or two areas on which to focus. The very exercise of examining and selecting these one or two areas serves several purposes. It helps to define precise and realistic goals. In addition, it serves to challenge and modify various components of a negative mindset, such as feelings of low self-esteem and not having control over one's life.

I once worked with a man with ADHD who defined as two of his goals "strengthening his marital relationship" and "focusing on his physical health" (he was overweight). We discussed both of these goals, which at first were cast in somewhat general terms. While describing his marital relationship, aspects of a negative mindset were immediately apparent. He initially placed responsibility for change on his wife contending that "she was not as supportive and loving as she could be" and he also felt that she was unfair in what she expected him to do around the house.

The characteristics of a negative mindset, especially the sense that he had little, if any, control of his life, were also operating when we discussed the issue of his physical health. He complained that he had a "poor metabolism," noting that "I can just smell food and I put on weight." He also said that his job demands made it almost impossible to engage in a regular exercise routine.

In essence, he was erecting obstacles to the achievement of goals before they were well defined and planned. He externalized responsibility by arguing that his wife needed to be more supportive and that she should not expect too much of him since he had ADHD; he blamed his poor fitness on his metabolism and job schedule. While there might be some truth in all of these assertions, if he continued to adhere to these obstacles to success, it would keep him from asking the following question: "Even given these obstacles, what is it that I can do to slowly begin to deal with the problems at hand?"

In my role as a therapist, I pointed out, in an empathic way, the self-defeating patterns he had established, and we reframed his goals in the following way.

- Improving his marital relationship was set as his long-term goal. Short-term goals were to spend more time with his wife, be less critical of her, and fulfill two designated household responsibilities on a regular basis.

- Improving his physical fitness was set as his long-term goal. His short-term goal was to go on a healthy diet, begin exercising on a regular basis, and lose a pound each week until he had shed 20 pounds.

**c. Develop realistic, achievable plans to reach designated goals**. Given the impulsivity, poor planning skills, and low frustration tolerance evident in even medicated adults with ADHD, the importance of designing a realistic plan of action is of paramount importance. For example, I once worked with a woman with ADHD who, similar to the man in the last example, wanted to lose weight through diet and exercise. However, she was in such a "rush" to do so that she went on what could be seen as a starvation diet and she immediately started doing several hours of exercise a day, having done little exercise previously. She began to lose weight quickly, but her initial exuberance and feeling of success were soon replaced by exhaustion and not feeling well physically. Before long, she resorted to her old habits, asserting, "This diet and exercise stuff really doesn't work." As obvious as it may appear to the reader that this woman's approach was doomed to failure, the possibility of failure was not at first evident to her.

Returning to the man whose goals were to develop a better relationship with his wife and to become more physically fit, once he accepted his role in making changes, we explored the actions he could take to reach his goals. We discussed sharing with his wife his wish to spend time with her and their setting aside a time each week to be together with no distractions. While some may wonder why this couple could not just discuss things on a spontaneous basis, the issue of time management for many adults with ADHD is poor. Thus, establishing a set time to chat was important for this man.

We also considered different topics that he wanted to discuss with her. But as he described them to me, many seemed critical of his wife and were certain to lead to increased tension in their relationship. I wondered how often he gave his wife positive feedback; it was not easy for him to offer an example. Consequently, we discussed his finding opportunities throughout the week (not just at a "scheduled" meeting) to compliment his wife. In essence, we were searching for ways for him to change the "negative scripts" that had become entrenched in his style of relating (Brooks & Goldstein, 2001).

Concerning the goal of becoming more fit, he thought it would be easier if he and his wife consulted a nutritionist. He felt it was important for his wife to be present since she often bought the food and prepared the meals in the house. He told me, "Her support will be crucial." Also, he joined a local health club. But before he started an exercise regimen, he met with one of the staff and they developed a realistic and achievable plan for him. A course of action that may come easily for an adult without ADHD often requires specific input and feedback for adults with ADHD.

**d. Have criteria for evaluating the success of a plan of action**. Another key issue involved when developing a strategy to reach one's stated goals is the criteria to use to assess whether the plan is working effectively. In some instances, the criteria are very concrete, such as weight loss and greater fitness (e.g., losing a certain amount of weight in a specified time period or being able to jog two miles within a month). In other instances, an assessment of effectiveness may require more work in defining criteria for success, such as when the goal is "an improved relationship with one's spouse." This man did monitor that he and his wife were meeting at the time they had agreed upon and that they were discussing issues in the marriage that both judged to be important; he even found it helpful to keep a record for himself of the number of times he complimented his wife. He said, "At first I thought it would seem artificial, but it soon became a more natural part of my new script." The evaluation of the effectiveness of any intervention should also include realistic time limits.

**e. Consider possible obstacles to the goals being achieved as well as how these obstacles will be handled.** In addition to developing criteria to assess the effectiveness of different strategies, I have found that it is important to discuss openly the possibility that a plan may not work. It is not unusual for me to say after we have considered a plan, "What if it doesn't work?" This comment is not offered as a self-fulfilling prophecy for failure, since I then add, "Some plans seem great in my office but they don't work outside the office. So let's think of possible backup plans should the first one prove ineffective."

I believe that is it important in advance to acknowledge that some courses of action will prove ineffective but that we can learn from these. I found that when I did not discuss the possibility of failure, the reaction of many adults with ADHD to a plan that proved unsuccessful was to view it as another indication of their ineffectiveness. It lowered even further their sense of self-worth, triggered feelings of sadness, prompted anger toward themselves or toward me as their therapist, and reinforced a more pessimistic view of what they could accomplish to change their lives. However, by proactively considering possible obstacles as well as subsequent strategies, these adults were less vulnerable to feelings of failure and better equipped to handle disappointments. By possessing backup plans they also felt more in control of their lives rather than victims or martyrs.

The man we have been discussing learned that if at times his wife did not want to talk, instead of getting angry at her, he would simply say, "That's okay, we can find another time." In terms of exercising regularly, when he began to find it "boring" to go to the gym, he made plans with a friend who was also using the same gym to go together, in effect supporting and encouraging each other (apparently his friend also struggled with following through on things).

Given the negative mindset of many adults with ADHD that assumes the worst and takes each failure as an indication of how unworthy they are, it is critical to build in this step of anticipating that interventions may not work and designing alternative strategies.

**f. Change the goals if repeated efforts at success do not work.** If our strategies to reach particular goals continue to lead to failure, it is often a signal that the goals may need to be changed. Goals that appear reasonable may actually turn out to be too ambitious, or other, unanticipated factors may interfere with their success. When this occurs, it is important to review and modify the original goals.

A woman with ADHD set as one of her goals to spend a half-hour each evening playing the piano, an activity she not only enjoyed but that helped to relax her. In our sessions she decided that if this goal of playing piano a half-hour each evening didn't work, her backup plan was to practice every other evening. Given her other responsibilities, she found it difficult to set aside a half-hour every evening to play piano. She resorted to the backup plan, namely, to practice every other evening. She discovered, much to her dismay, that she began to miss some of her practices every other evening. She said to me, "Another example of my not being able to follow through on things."

I asked what she thought would help her find time to play the piano, especially since it was an activity that brought her enjoyment. At first she fell prey to a negative mindset and contended that "probably nothing would work. I can't even succeed at something I enjoy doing." However, with some encouragement she offered an interesting observation, together with a revised goal. "A half-hour doesn't seem like much but maybe it is. I wonder what would happen if I began by setting aside 15 minutes each evening."

While some may judge this modification of a goal as simplistic, I viewed it as a major step forward in terms of indicating that she was altering her negative mindset. The very task of contemplating and implementing a new goal was a reflection that she was moving beyond the feeling that she was helpless, that the situation was hopeless, and that she did not have the resources to find an alternative solution. She discovered, much to her delight, that 15 minutes of practice a night was achievable for her. Not surprisingly, she frequently extended the 15 minutes to 20 or 25 minutes once she was seated at the piano. She perceived this additional time as a "bonus."

**g. As goals are reached, add new goals to reinforce a positive mindset, and be aware of the negative thoughts that may serve as obstacles to future growth.** After one month of practicing piano for 15 minutes a night, she moved to her next goal—playing 20 minutes each evening. The seemingly small accomplishment of playing 15 minutes a night was like climbing Mt. Everest for her. She found that true success is based on realistic accomplishment and that each success reinforces a positive mindset, thereby setting the stage for future success. Feeling more confident, she added a new goal, namely, taking piano lessons once a week to strengthen her skills. She felt that she had achieved a certain level of discipline and commitment to take these lessons.

I will never forget the session we had when she came in and said, "My piano teacher feels I have real talent." In the past, she might have added, "I think the teacher is just saying this to be nice." However, her attributions about success had changed. She could now accept the piano teacher's appraisal. Given her greater self-assurance I could even joke and ask, "Now, you're certain that your accomplishments are not just because of luck or that somehow your fingers just moved across the piano without any direction from you?" She laughed and said, "No, it's me in charge." That statement had great meaning on both a figurative and a literal level. For one of the first times in her life she felt a sense of ownership for her accomplishments.

**h. As new goals are added, continue to develop more effective ways of coping that will help to maintain a positive mindset and strengthen the gains that have been made.** Replacing a negative mindset takes ongoing work and effort. As a clinician I have discovered that until a more positive mindset is firmly rooted, there will be many occasions when the old mindset rears its ugly head and begins once again to be a dominating force.

It is for this reason that I spend time helping adults with ADHD to recognize (a) the feelings and beliefs that signal the possibility that a negative mindset is taking hold (e.g., believing "I am stupid" or "I am worthless" or "I will always fail" or, as the woman I described earlier told me, her success in life was like "a house made of cards. I feel that if any kind of wind comes along, my entire facade of success will crumble"), (b) the different coping strategies that are being used to manage these feelings and which ones are actually counterproductive, (c) the need for more realistic goals and plans of action, and (d) the acceptance of one's strengths and vulnerabilities.

## CONCLUDING THOUGHTS ABOUT TWO MEN

Returning to the stories of the two men at the beginning of this chapter, I believe that the one who went on to become a physician was aided by an early diagnosis, ongoing support from his parents and therapists, discovering his islands of competence (e.g., helping others), and learning as much as he could about ADHD (he even volunteered as a research assistant during one summer on a project related to ADHD). He increasingly gained a feeling of control over his life.

In contrast, the other man did not "discover" his condition until he was in his 40s. Unfortunately, by then his negative mindset was so entrenched and so hardened that all of his life experiences were filtered through this mindset. The pain of continuous failure made it difficult for him to find a new path, although I believe even individuals trapped in such a negative mindset can change. They typically require the input and support of therapists and others who can help them to learn about and follow the ideas outlined in this chapter.

As clinicians, we must be empathic and understand the world of adults with ADHD. We must provide realistic hope by offering strategies for success. We must strive to replace a negative mindset with a mindset filled with optimism and promise. This is one of our greatest gifts to individuals with ADHD. When this gift is realized, it offers us a great source of satisfaction as well.

## REFERENCES

Barkley, R. (1995). *Taking charge of ADHD: The complete, authoritative guide for parents.* New York: Guilford Press.

Brooks, R. (1984). Success and failure in middle childhood: An interactionist perspective. In M. D. Levine & P. Satz (Eds.), *Middle childhood: Development and dysfunction* (pp. 87–128). Baltimore: University Park Press.

Brooks, R. (1999). Fostering resilience in exceptional children: The search for islands of competence. In V. Schwean & D. Saklofske (Eds.), *Handbook of psychosocial characteristics of exceptional children* (pp. 563–586). New York: Kluwer Academic/Plenum Press.

Brooks, R., & Goldstein, S. (2001). *Raising resilient children.* Chicago: Contemporary Books.

Canino, F. J. (1981). Learned-helplessness theory: Implications for research in learning disabilities. *Journal of Special Education, 15*, 471–484.

Chess, S., & Thomas, A. (1987). *Know your child.* New York: Basic Books.

Covey, S. R. (1989). *The 7 habits of highly effective people.* New York: Simon & Schuster.

de Shazer, S. (1991). *Putting difference to work.* New York: Norton.

Gerber, P. J., Ginsberg, R., & Reiff, H. B. (1992). Identifying alterable patterns in employment success for highly successful adults with learning disabilities. *Journal of Learning Disabilities, 25*, 475–487.

Goleman, D. (1995). *Emotional intelligence.* New York: Bantam Books.

Greene, R. (1998). *The explosive child.* New York: Harper/Collins.

Lerner, B. (1996). Self-esteem and excellence: The choice and the paradox. *American Educator, 20*, 14–19.

Licht, B. G. (1983). Cognitive-motivational factors that contribute to the achievement of learning-disabled children. *Journal of Learning Disabilities, 16*, 483–490.

Murphy, J. J. (1997). *Solution-focused counseling in middle and high schools.* Alexandria, VA: American Counseling Association.

O'Hanlon, B. (1999). *Do one thing different and other uncommonly sensible solutions to life's persistent problems.* New York: William Morrow.

Seligman, M. (1990). *Learned optimism: How to change your mind and your life.* New York: Pocket Books.

Shure, M. B. (1994). *Raising a thinking child.* New York: Holt.

Shure, M. B. (2000). *Raising a thinking preteen.* New York: Holt.

Weiner, B. (1974). *Achievement motivation and attribution theory.* Morristown, NJ: General Learning Press.

# 8

# A Model of Psychotherapy for Adults with ADHD

Susan Young

This chapter examines psychotherapy for adults with ADHD. Stimulant medication is likely to help individuals with ADHD to make more effective use of psychological intervention. The chapter first reviews the specific problems individuals with ADHD contend with in adulthood and how psychological therapy may help them with these problems. Four vignettes illustrate how the heterogeneity of ADHD leads to vast individual differences in the expression and sequelae of the disorder. These problems are not restricted to individuals with symptomatic ADHD. ADHD adults in partial remission, as well as those in total remission, may also experience relative difficulty in adaptive functioning. Cognitive-behavioral therapy (CBT) is proposed as the most appropriate therapy for individuals with ADHD in adulthood (Young, 1999). This may be applied on an individual or group basis. Therapy should include a psychoeducative component in order to help the individual better understand the disorder as well as to improve family stability and cohesion. Specific CBT interventions are outlined for the development of time management and organizational skills; planning and problem-solving skills; impulse control; interpersonal skills; and the treatment of anger, anxiety, and depression. Contextual factors (e.g., age, employment, and marital status) are likely to influence whether an individual will benefit most from individual, group, and/or family work.

The clinical management of adults with ADHD has focused almost exclusively on stimulant medication, yet psychological therapy can play a vital role in addressing their problems (Young, 1999; Young & Harty, 2001). The aim of this chapter is to consider how an individual may best be supported with psychological intervention and to provide guidelines to this end. The aim of psychological therapy for adults with ADHD is twofold: (1) to adapt the environment around the individual in an attempt to make it one in which he or she can achieve success; and (2) to help the individual develop the skills to achieve set goals and develop constructive coping strategies to deal with life challenges and stress. These goals are consistent with Goldstein's (1997) treatment model of environmental interventions to reduce the consequences of symptoms combined with strategies to reduce the symptoms.

## WHO ARE ADULTS WITH ADHD AND WHAT ARE THEIR PROBLEMS?

Adults with ADHD have difficulties attending to tasks and activities and inhibiting their impulses. They have poor concentration for short, focused work and poor ability to sustain attention over a long period. They act without thinking, which often results in reckless and impetuous behavior. Impulsiveness may be an important defining characteristic of ADHD in young adulthood (Young, Toone and Tyson (in submission). Although they do not necessarily present with the overactive behavior frequently seen in children, they feel subjectively restless. This means an individual may act without reflection or consideration for the consequences of action. They may be disorganized and forgetful and have planning deficits and poor time management skills. Impetuous, novelty-seeking behavior may result in criminal acts, substance misuse, and dependence.

A comprehensive empirical review of the long-term outcome ADHD is presented in Young (2000) but briefly summarized here. Children with ADHD often have language deficits and school problems and experience academic failure. Many become conduct disordered and have dealings with the police from a young age. These problems often continue into adulthood, when they have antisocial behavior problems and frequent police contact (Hechtman & Weiss, 1986; Satterfield, Hoppe, & Schell, 1982; Satterfield, Swanson, Schell, & Lee, 1994). An increasingly antisocial trajectory is likely to be a significant risk factor for criminal behavior (even in the face of remitting symptoms), and by young adulthood individuals may become indoctrinated into a criminal culture.

Adults with ADHD often have problems in their work lives, becoming underemployed in their occupations relative to their intelligence and their education and family backgrounds. They frequently experience a high turnover of jobs and/or unemployment. Individuals often report feeling they possess ability yet, unlike their siblings, are unable to achieve positive outcomes. They often deviate from family expectations of job status by being employed in significantly lower-ranking jobs than those of their siblings. This may reflect the heritability of hyperactivity (Swanson et al., 1998), with ADHD siblings also being impaired by dimensional features of ADHD. Employers of adults with ADHD have reported that they have poor levels of work performance, are poor in task completion, lack independent skills, and have poor relationships with supervisors (Weiss & Hechtman, 1986).

Interpersonal relationship problems are also present, with individuals reporting difficulties maintaining relationships personally, socially, and with work colleagues. ADHD adults are more likely to become divorced or separated (Biederman, Faraone & Chen, 1993). They may vent frustration on close family members. Aggression may be directed toward loved ones (verbal and/or physical) or the destruction of property.

Our research has shown that individuals with ADHD have an early onset of behavioral problems requiring multiple presentations to childhood psychiatric and educational services (Young et al (in submission). Yet despite these frequent contacts with clinical and educational services, the diagnosis of ADHD may not have been made until after repeated clinical contacts. Adults with ADHD are likely to have internalized academic and social failure and to have developed problems with self-esteem. Anxiety, depression, and suicidal ideation are common comorbid problems (Biederman, Faraone & Kieley, 1996; Brent et al., 1988; Young et al., 2001), and poor impulse control may be a determining factor, with individuals being unable to inhibit suicidal ideation and attempts. Individuals diagnosed in adulthood (as opposed to having their problems recognized in childhood) may feel that they have been unfairly treated by a system that has not only failed to identify their problems but in some cases labeled them as "untreatable" (Young & Harty, 2001). They may feel angry and bitter and lack trust in service providers.

As one moves from adolescence into adulthood the sum of these problems can seem insurmountable (Lomas & Gartside, 1999). It may be easier to give up trying than to fail again. A longstanding history of failure is likely to result in low self-esteem and demoralization. Comorbid anxiety and depression will lead individuals to avoid certain situations, anticipate failure, lack confidence, and feel misunderstood by others. Borderline and/or antisocial personality problems may develop as individuals become rigid and inflexible in thought and behavior, in addition to having long-term interpersonal relationship problems.

It is important to emphasize that not every person with ADHD will present with all of the problems just discussed. It is vital to identify at the beginning of therapy an individual's strengths and successful adaptive strategies. Indeed many individuals have developed strategies to overcome their problems (e.g., they become self-employed owners of small businesses), reflecting a preference for personal autonomy outside of structured work settings that have expectations of performance and achievement and require appropriate interaction with colleagues and people in authority (Mannuzza, Klein, Bessler, Malloy, LaPadula, 1993). It is important that therapy emphasize the clients' strengths and resources. People with ADHD, just as everyone, possess positive qualities that can be built upon. By minimizing the negative effects of the disorder, it is hoped to improve the overall quality of life experienced by adults with ADHD and thereby enhance their sense of control and self-efficacy.

## Individual Differences

Many of the problems and difficulties that all individuals face are shared by people with ADHD. Nevertheless there are some fundamental differences that need to be acknowledged by the therapist in order that therapy can be adapted and tailored to the clients' needs. Particular consideration should be given to the age of the individual and the context of his or her presentation. For example, problems will differ between a single 17-year-old student and an unemployed 32-year-old man living with his partner and two young children.

Gender differences have been shown to be present in core symptomatology: In childhood, boys display greater levels of motor activity and aggressive and antisocial behaviors, while diagnosed girls tend to display higher rates of cognitive impairment, language dysfunction, and compromised neurological status (Berry, Shaywitz & Shaywitz, 1985; Biederman, Faraone, & Mick, 1999; James & Taylor, 1990; Kashani, Chapel, Ellis & Shekim, 1979). Females with ADHD also tend to show greater brain metabolism abnormalities than males (Ernst et al., 1994; Zametkin et al., 1993). Thus gender as well as age must be considered in understanding the pathophysiology of ADHD. Gender differences in outcome is a severely neglected issue in the literature. Outcome findings in ADHD have traditionally been based on research on males and then sometimes erroneously generalized to include both sexes. But males have different rates of maturity. The impact of puberty may be quite different between genders. Males' and females' socialization and styles of interaction are also disparate. It cannot be assumed that the implications of the ADHD syndrome are the same for both sexes. ADHD is more prevalent in men, by a ratio of approximately 3:1 (Heptinstall & Taylor, 1996), leading many clinicians to operate from a male paradigm. Lability may be the most important construct when considering the emotional functioning of females with ADHD. Emotional instability characterized by fluctuating anxiety, depression, and sudden mood swings is commonly reported by ADHD females, and the self-regulation of their emotional state may be a primary problem (Nadeau, Quinn, & Littman, 2000; Solden, 1995). In the case of females, therefore, therapy may need to prioritize skills that monitor self-regulation of mood and affect. Men, on the other hand, are more likely to require help with verbal and physical aggression. They are more likely than females to engage in antisocial and criminal behaviors, which are often opportunistic and unplanned. Thus they may become engaged in an increasingly antisocial trajectory. Developing skills in anger management, problem solving, and impulse control is likely to be a priority target for therapy.

## ADHD Graduates

It is reported that many people with ADHD will gradually experience an improvement in some symptoms with maturation (for review see Goldstein, 1997; Chapter 3 in this book). Traditionally, "graduates" of childhood ADHD have not been routinely offered psychological therapy, for they are no longer considered symptomatic. Yet such individuals often feel that they are "survivors" of a syndrome that has left them with significant personal, social, and occupational consequences. It may be that they are no longer symptomatic—indeed, their ability to attend to information and remain on task may have improved. But they are likely to retain a learned sense of helplessness, reinforced by years of failure.

This "hangover" of ADHD needs to be addressed therapeutically in order to generate change in an individual's life. Clinicians may be unsympathetic and attribute current difficulties to motivational and attitude problems, with little appreciation that these stem from a sense of insecurity and lack of confidence. Cognition precedes behavior, and graduates of ADHD are likely to need help reappraising their place in life, their capabilities, and their opportunities. Negative assumptions and expectations about the ability to succeed or simply cope in a given situation are likely to lead individuals to avoid situations and exercises they perceive as anxiety provoking or unmanageable. Therapy should be supportive and constructive, for example, making use of modeling and graded exposure techniques. One of the most difficult aspects of therapy will be improving self-efficacy, because the negative experiences of adults with ADHD (whether symptomatic or not) are long term and deep rooted. Failure has been repeatedly reinforced by more failure. Successes are often minimized, if recognized at all. In other words, they no longer believe in themselves.

## PSYCHOLOGICAL THERAPY

Adults with ADHD present with multiple problems and complex histories. Their strengths may be buried under a mountain of negative thoughts and experiences. They require structure in terms of personal organization and social boundaries. They achieve best in an environment where there are clear rules and expectations of behavior.

Cognitive-behavioral therapy is the most appropriate therapy for adults with ADHD because it is a collaborative and structured model. This is not to say, however, that other models will be inappropriate. For example, marital and systemic therapy may well be required before individual work can commence, for the most pressing issue may be troubled family relationships. Adults with ADHD may well become parents of children with ADHD and are often ill equipped to deal with a hard-to-manage, disruptive child. Young adults may well still live at home with parents and siblings, and family therapy may be required to reduce cycles of negative reciprocity and conflict within the family. This could be achieved by identifying different points of view and acknowledging the impact of ADHD on the feelings and motivations of others. It is not difficult to imagine how traits of disorganization, poor motivation, and aggressive and impulsive behavior have a negative impact on family dynamics. Excessive alcohol and substance abuse are also likely to exacerbate existing problems in families that often lack the usual avenues of social support.

Marital dissatisfaction is not uncommon, and non-ADHD partners may have little understanding about the disorder and complain that their partner fails to listen to them, that he or she is unreliable, insensitive, argumentative, or irresponsible. Marital therapy should encourage couples to reexamine their relationship from an ADHD perspective, to stop blaming each other and reduce conflict.

## Psychoeducation

Adults with ADHD often feel misunderstood by their partners, friends, and family. They may feel isolated and alone. It has commonly been reported that they have always felt different in some way from others, even as young children. In spite of the developing understanding and font of knowledge about ADHD, it is still often considered a disorder of childhood. A psychoeducational component to therapy is essential in order to dispel erroneous lay beliefs and provide information to explain the etiology, prognosis, and associated factors of the ADHD syndrome. Understanding that their problems have an underlying neurodevelopmental basis will be an important step in repairing the self-esteem of people who have long believed themselves to be stupid and/or who have been labeled as lazy by others. Furthermore, by understanding their limitations, individuals can develop realistic expectations for performance. This will be especially important when applied to psychological therapy; for example, patience is unlikely to be characteristic of adults with ADHD, and information about the disorder can help individuals appreciate that learning new strategies requires ongoing practice until a new skill becomes automatic and routine. Thus individuals may stick with a program for longer and not give up at the first hurdle.

Education about the disorder, its prognosis, and its management may facilitate understanding and reduce feelings of anger and frustration often experienced by family members. And CBT is likely to be more beneficial if family members are supportive, develop a working understanding of ADHD, and its associated problems and support the efforts the individual is making to effect change. Family members may learn to appreciate the strengths and limitations of an adult with ADHD and develop realistic expectations of behavior. In this way subtle changes in the environment could be achieved that make it easier for an adult with ADHD to function. For example, partners could learn to give clear, concise instructions that are easy to follow and understand; to write down specific and important instructions; to break down tasks into small, achievable steps rather than set general goals that may be perceived as unobtainable. Partners should also be encouraged to give consistent and immediate positive feedback in order to encourage an individual to remain on task.

## A Cognitive-Behavioral Therapy Model

A cognitive-behavioral approach is likely to be most effective for adults with ADHD, whether applied on an individual or a group basis, because it is structured. It should focus on self-management strategies, although, as discussed, the context in which strategies are offered will vary according to presentation. The clinician will need to adapt the therapy to the individual's needs at that time. A central tenet of cognitive-behavioral therapy is collaboration. It is vital to engage and motivate an individual by setting agendas and goals of therapy together. This approach is likely to have face validity for individuals who may feel ambiguity over engaging with (yet another) clinician. It will be vital that they have confidence in the therapist and perceive that the therapist understands their problems and the prognosis of ADHD in adulthood.

Cognitive-behavioral therapy is usually time limited, with an average of 12–15 sessions. But adults with ADHD may require extended therapy and support, up to 30 sessions, in order to address their multiple problems. A therapist should not attempt to address everything at once. It is better to focus on agreed, specific issues. The aim is to empower the individual to develop self-efficacy and the confidence that change can be achieved. This will require education about the disorder, cognitive restructuring, and reframing of the past. Thus an individual should be taught to challenge negative automatic thoughts, self-monitor performance, recognize errors in thinking, and evaluate cognitive distortions and misattributions. In addition to cognitive interventions, the therapist should employ a variety of behavioral techniques, such as graded task assignments, modeling, and role play. Whenever possible, it will be important to elicit core beliefs the individual holds about him/herself, other people, and the world. This will help the therapist to understand how the individual perceives the world.

The application of CBT to people with ADHD is discussed in the following sections, which focus specifically on treatment to help individuals develop time management and organizational skills; planning and problem-solving skills; impulse control; and interpersonal skills. Cognitive-behavioral therapy for anger management, anxiety, and depression is also discussed. These problems are illustrated using examples from four case vignettes (Anne, Peter, Jane, and Michael) which appear in the Appendix at the end of this chapter.

## Time Management and Organizational Skills

A primary complaint of adults with ADHD is that they possess poor time management and organizational skills. Individuals describe themselves as forgetful, resulting in their being late for appointments. They forget to bring necessary items to meetings, such as important papers and work equipment. They have difficulty organizing themselves, both on a daily basis and more generally when making long-term plans, for they tend not to think ahead and anticipate potential problems. Setting goals and developing strategies to complete goals is likely to be an important focus of therapy for these difficulties.

Such problems can be addressed by introducing notebooks, a diary, or an appointment book and by posting visual reminders in strategic locations. The introduction of cues and reminders means a person can make an immediate note of an idea, before a new stimulus distracts them. Individuals should be taught to make lists of things to do and then to prioritize their tasks for the day or week. Jane found this particularly helpful because weekly tasks appeared more achievable when broken down into smaller items to be completed each day. Day lists can be further broken down and prioritized into those items that are imperative to do and those that are less important. Small, immediate rewards should be introduced once imperative items are completed and again for the completion of less important tasks. Small rewards can in turn be aggregated to earn a greater reward. Jane was able to attend additional exercise classes in the time that opened up from her more efficient time management. Achievements, or learning to complete sets of tasks, may well be rewards in themselves (even if tasks are perceived as monotonous), because individuals with ADHD may not have developed a sense of ending or completion from their tendency to start lots of different things and never finish any of them.

## Planning and Problem-Solving Skills

The cognitive deficits of adults with ADHD, in addition to their poor impulse control, are likely to result in inadequate problem-solving skills. Adults with ADHD describe having difficulty following through a train of thought in a logical fashion. This may be complicated by difficulty with self-expression. They also tend to make rapid decisions, based on inadequate or inappropriate information, resulting in fundamental errors of attribution and judgment. This may cause multiple long-term problems because they then have to live with the consequences of an overly rapid and ill-informed decision-making process. This, together with a tendency to catastrophize situations, may result in the perception that they have made a total mess of their lives and that nothing ever goes right for them.

Therapy should be solution focused and also prepare the individual for future events by outlining a blueprint for coping with new problems. However, it is likely that adults with ADHD may list nonspecific, overarching problems. Peter cited his problems to be "I have difficult motivating myself, I'm lonely, I have difficulty expressing myself." In such cases the therapist will need to help the individual break these difficulties down and identify core problems that can be worked on therapeutically. This can be achieved by asking the client to give specific examples of each difficulty. Therapy should focus initially on immediate problems that are relatively easy to solve and then progress to long-term aims and goals. A review of progress should regularly be introduced as an opportunity for positive feedback. In Peter's case, by attending art therapy sessions he found a peer set to refer to; by developing his creative skills he participated in an activity that was of interest to him and was able to express himself in his artistic work. Longer-term goals became possible with the prospect of Peter's taking formal qualifications in the subject as he progressed in his classes.

Adults with ADHD have often learned to live with their problems and may have adopted strategies that have successfully helped them overcome problems in the past. These strategies should be identified and the individual encouraged to apply them to current problems. It will be very common, however, for individuals to perceive numerous obstacles that bar their path to achievement. These must be dealt with by systematically breaking them down into smaller, manageable obstacles and generating various solutions to overcome them. Barriers to this process and difficulties they may have in exploring appropriate solutions (both cognitive and practical) should also be addressed.

**Impulse Control**

Difficulty with impulse control will lead individuals to act without thinking. Adults with ADHD do not think ahead or consider the consequences of their action. Their search for thrills and novelty may stem from an excessive attraction to immediate reward. They may also have difficulty inhibiting the impulse to avoid aversive tasks and/or situations. Their decision-making processes may also be impulse driven, with an individual making important choices rapidly and without careful consideration or planning. A model therapy should aim to teach self-regulation (e.g., to "stop and think"), consider consequences of action, and generate appropriate alternatives (Barkley, 1997).

Core deficits in attention and concentration are likely to cause adults with ADHD to act spontaneously and without consideration of small details or planning. This may lead individuals, like Peter, to get into trouble with the police should they become increasingly involved in antisocial and criminal behavior. Offenses are most likely opportunistic and unplanned. Peter was very entrenched in perceived failure. He could not hold down a job and he stole on impulse to fund his drug habit. Even as a petty criminal he was unsuccessful, and he had a long list of criminal convictions. It was not easy to elicit his strengths or to get him to take a positive perspective. Peter reported he had been a good artist in school, and once this interest had been identified I worked with prison staff to develop a rehabilitation program that initially focused on his creative abilities. This represented an area in which he was most likely to obtain a sense of achievement. One problem was getting Peter to engage in sessions at the Art Therapy Center on a regular basis. Peter believed it was a waste of time and that he would not do well in the classes. Peter's assigned prison officer encouraged him to attend initially for short periods, and gradually he engaged with the center. It was hoped that by completing pieces of work and finding satisfaction in the work he produced, he would learn the feeling of achievement. This was a turning point in his rehabilitation. His tutors recommended that he apply for a place in an Art Foundation course when he left prison (which would give him access to attending a university course) but this was too distant (or difficult) for Peter to envisage. By breaking down the goal into smaller, achievable steps, or "minigoals," this became more realistic to Peter (e.g., completing a piece of work that would be required for his application). Thus his focus was more immediate and did not get lost in a perceived hopeless and distant aim.

**Anger Management**

Adults with ADHD are often hyperaroused individuals with a tendency toward temper or violent outbursts. Cognitive-behavioral techniques can be applied to teach an individual to consider the consequences of angry outbursts and to manage the inappropriate expression of anger. There are two ways to manage anger: (1) to bottle it up inside and (2) to direct it toward self or others. Excessive expression by either method is dysfunctional. Adults with ADHD may well express anger both ways. They may have a "short fuse," meaning they quickly respond with anger in the face of minimal provocation (as was the case for Michael), or they may build up frustration over a long period of time (as was the case for Jane). Individuals with ADHD may vent their frustration and angry feelings by lashing out at others (both strangers and loved ones) and/or by damaging property. Their difficulty with stress intolerance was one of the first symptoms described to differentiate between children and adults with ADHD (Bellak, 1979). Loved ones may feel they are walking a tight rope.

Within the therapeutic environment, the distinction between escalating anger and bottling up anger should be explored. The therapist should always be cautious when treating volatile individuals who may well overrespond in the face of perceived threat. However, when appropriate the most effective intervention is likely to be achieved when the therapist models the dysfunctional expression of anger and the client role-plays the appropriate expression of anger with the therapist. Various methods of appropriately managing anger should be introduced into the therapy (e.g., talking problems over with friends; walking away from provocation; cognitively restructuring an event). However, individuals with ADHD may not have the available social support to draw on for personal problems. Most people can talk things over with someone or seek out advice, but people with ADHD may not have developed a social network to draw on in this respect. Often, close questioning about social relationships reveals that a nominated "best friend" is the equivalent of an acquaintance by normal standards. In such cases clients need to be wary about revealing thoughts and attributions to acquaintances because this may be perceived as overfamiliarity and may be thus met with rejection.

It is important for the therapist to acknowledge the clients' feelings of deep distress and emotional turmoil. This will be especially important when inviting them to cognitively reframe a situation. Individuals with ADHD have often learned that the world may be a threatening place and that people are unkind or even hostile. It may not be easy to encourage the client to take a different perspective in the face of challenging situations. Clients should be taught to stop and think (e.g., control the impulse to jump to a conclusion about underlying intent). Negative automatic thoughts are likely to be "people hate me" and "people provoke me." These cognitive distortions should be challenged and alternative perspectives generated (e.g., the person may have a lot on his mind, have personal problems, and/or be exceptionally busy). Thus the client makes fewer personal attributions in favor of more general attributions. It will be important that clients are taught to self-monitor and regulate their emotions, identifying the point at which they start to become overaroused and need to engage in a counterstrategy. Specific methods can be taught to interrupt the dysfunctional cognitive process, such as distractive techniques like mental arithmetic (i.e., counting backwards from 500 by subtracting 7). It may be difficult to apply the techniques learned in therapy to situations in the outside world. When aroused, people often become less rational and forget to apply learned coping mechanisms. Michael found it helpful to keep a card on which he listed useful strategies generated in therapy to help him remain calm when feeling provoked. He carried this card with him so that if he found himself in a situation he could not cope with, he was able to refer to the card and adopt some of the strategies, as opposed to "going blank" and feeling helpless and unable to control his anger and rage.

**Interpersonal Skills**

It may be that adults with ADHD are unaware of the impact of their behavior on others, with cognitive deficits causing them to misappraise social situations. There is evidence that their self-report lacks validity when reporting interpersonal relationship problems in the family setting (Barkley, Fischer, Edelbrock & Smallish, 1991). Adults with ADHD frequently report difficulties interacting with others and maintaining relationships. This may stem from an underlying problem in communication skills. An adult with ADHD may not perform well in situations that demand rapid shifts in style or topic of conversation. This may be especially apparent in small-group environments. Inattention and distractibility may be perceived by others as an inability to listen or as a lack of interest. Impulsivity may be interpreted as rudeness if a person makes untimely and inappropriate interruptions to conversation. Failure to follow instructions, mood swings, and an unpredictable temperament may be perceived by others as obnoxious behavior, and individuals may ultimately become ostracized socially and/or withdraw from social situations. This was the case for Michael. Work colleagues viewed him as unable to participate on a team. He did not act appropriately with authority figures, such as his managers, because he would not accept direction and advice, saying he would not be "told what to do." Michael solved the problem by adapting his occupational environment to meet his needs. He withdrew from forms of employment defined by a linearly structured line-management format in preference to long-distance driving work. In this type of work he was largely self-employed and relatively autonomous in the organization of his day. Michael said he never became bored with the work because he found stimulation in the changing scenery. No two days were the same.

Michael's adaptive lifestyle meant, however, that he spent long periods alone on the road. He avoided social interaction and the development of social relationships. In such cases individuals with ADHD may possess inadequate and/or underdeveloped social skills. They certainly appear to display difficulties in the production of appropriate social behavior and tend to show disproportionate rates of socially noxious behavior. Empirical studies, however, suggest that there are few deficiencies in rates of social interactions, in social cognitive problem-solving skills, or in their ability to perceive social situations accurately (Whalen & Henker, 1985, 1992). It may be that people with ADHD have difficulty modifying social behavior in accordance with shifting situational demands. Hyperactive youngsters tend to persist in social roles calling for assertion and dominance even when the situation shifts to call for more deferent or accommodating behavior (Grenell, Glass, & Katz, 1987; Landau & Milich, 1988; Whalen, Henker, Collins, McAuliffe & Vaux, 1979). They may possess social agendas that differ from those of their peers (e.g., by valuing sensation-seeking or social disruption at the expense of smooth interaction as desired goals). Appropriate goals of therapy therefore need to be determined and agreed on at the outset.

It is possible that an attention deficit causes individuals to be slow to recognize vital social cues. They have inadequate knowledge of social rules, roles, and routines (Landau & Milich, 1988; Whalen & Henker, 1992). They may be deviant in their understanding of the fundamental "rules" of friendship patterns and social interaction. For Michael, initiation of friendships was less problematic than the maintenance of friendships. He was also poor at negotiating interpersonal conflict. His impulsive and restless nature meant he engaged in limited activity with peers to whom he most likely appeared distracted and unfocused as he constantly moved on sharply to new stimuli. These are common social problems for ADHD adults, who in turn are viewed by others as unreliable and fickle.

Social skills training aims to equip the individual with the behavioral responses necessary for successful outcomes in social situations. For adults with ADHD, therapy needs to focus on both microskills (e.g., maintaining eye contact, appropriate voice volume and tone, body positioning) as well as macroskills (e.g., giving compliments and constructive feedback, turn-taking and listening skills). An important issue is likely to be the misinterpretation of social cues. Individuals should be taught basic social perception skills enabling them to recognize and engage in appropriate social behavior. This can be achieved by role-playing familiar social circumstances and modeling an appropriate response.

### Anxiety

Worry, as well as clinical anxiety, is a frequent comorbid problem for adults with ADHD (for review see Chapter 2 in this book). Individuals like Anne may develop social phobia in addition to generalized anxiety, resulting in avoidance of anxiety-provoking situations. Such individuals may well have had extensive prior contact with mental health services for their comorbid problems, which may have been considered primary, so their underlying attention deficit disorder would have gone unrecognized and untreated. Therapy should aim to reduce anxiety by teaching individuals how to identify, evaluate, control, and modify their negative, danger-related thoughts and associated behaviors. This will include giving information about the model of anxiety and the relationship between thoughts, feelings, and behavior. If appropriate, the cognitive model of panic should also be explained, setting out how individuals tend to interpret a range of bodily sensations in a catastrophic way. Anne found it difficult to believe at first that she could experience such debilitating physical symptomatology from a psychological phenomenon. Gradually, however, she began to accept the possibility. This was achieved through hypothesis testing and the accumulation of evidence-based information collected from set homework tasks. Anne practiced progressive relaxation techniques and introduced relaxation into her daily routine. She learned to identify early signs of anxiety and to apply the learned cognitive-behavioral techniques to reduce anxious feelings.

Cognitive-behavioral therapy is therefore very appropriate for adults with ADHD whose primary motivation is immediate gratification. The therapist should set up immediate, small, achievable goals, so achievement is reinforced by success. A graded hierarchy of anxiety-provoking situations should be determined by the individual and, starting with the least threatening (and most achievable), the therapist should use these in homework tasks. Individuals should be encouraged to keep a diary of their thoughts and feelings when attempting to complete homework tasks; through the diary, clients can be helped to identify negative thoughts. These are errors in processing through which perceptions and interpretations of experience become distorted. For example, Anne thought people were looking at her and thinking "she's stupid." They can then learn that they can control their feelings of anxiety by employing various distraction techniques and/or cognitive challenges of automatic and irrational thoughts (Therapist: "What is the evidence that those two men in the bar thought you were stupid?"). Eventually, through exposure to feared situations, Anne learned to cope with her feelings of anxiety and to exercise control over them.

Common thinking distortions for adults with ADHD are that they tend to think in all-or-nothing terms, complicated by the fact that they make snap decisions and jump to conclusions. Thus if something does not *immediately* go very well (and often on the first attempt), then they give up and do not try again. They may also make negative interpretations, even though there are no definite facts. Thus they become "mindreaders" predicting the outcome of events. Another common distortion is that they set unrealistic or unobtainable standards for themselves and become anxious when they are unable to achieve them. Adults with ADHD often possess an awareness that they are underperforming relative to their potential. In response, they may set unrealistic goals. Efforts to assist in breaking larger goals into smaller steps may be resisted and viewed as menial. In these situations individuals may perceive that they are being treated as "stupid" by the therapist, unwittingly reinforcing a negative underlying assumption.

### Depression

A longstanding history of internalized failure combined with a tendency to self-regulate and overmonitor performance is likely to result in low self-esteem and demoralization, anticipated failure, poor self-confidence, and feeling misunderstood by others. Low self-esteem affects not only self-perception and self-image but the ability to succeed in our achievement-oriented society. The cognitive model of depression should be explained to the individual, because developing a practical understanding of problems is likely to facilitate the individual's ability to overcome them. A problem list should be generated that categorizes various problems (e.g., poor self-expression, feelings of inferiority, symptoms of depression). This can be used to focus on specific problems collaboratively. A daily diary of thoughts and feelings will help to identify such problems. Homework assignments should be set for between sessions (and follow logically from each session). These should have a self-help and motivating focus. Once the individual has learned to identify negative automatic thoughts, he or she can be taught to challenge them.

Common underlying schemas are "I can't cope" and "I'm useless." Individuals with ADHD may tend to catastrophize or overexaggerate negative experiences, focusing only on the negative and not viewing things from a positive perspective. When depressed, adults with ADHD may be at greater risk for attempting suicide due to poor impulse control. Thus they may struggle to inhibit the impulse to act out a suicidal ideation (Brent, Perper, Goldstein, et al., 1988).

A positive reward system should be set up that represents an "immediate" reward system, for adults with ADHD are unlikely to delay positive reinforcement for long periods. For example, "If I finish the daily household chores each day for the entire week, then I'll go swimming on the weekend" is unlikely to gratify adults with ADHD who favor immediate small rewards over a single longer-term and greater reward. A more immediate reward, such as telephoning a friend that evening, is likely to offer greater incentive. It is important that reward be matched to reflect value to the individual. Activity scheduling may be helpful. Jane found that intense periods of stimulation served as a reward for the completion of mundane tasks, especially because this represented time out from her family for herself. A daily schedule or timetable was structured so as to intersperse regular periods of high stimulation (such as physical activity) in order to avoid boredom and distractibility.

## Group Therapy

Adults with ADHD may feel socially isolated and misunderstood by others. A group forum provides the opportunity to meet people with similar problems. The psychological interventions discussed in this chapter are described elsewhere as efficacious when offered in a group format (Morgan, 2000). Many adults with ADHD have never had contact with fellow ADHD sufferers. A group format therefore offers the opportunity to share information and to learn how others cope with their difficulties. Individuals are likely to feel less isolated and alone. The group provides a supportive environment for acquiring and rehearsing key skills such as communication and anger and stress management. Group CBT treatment usually includes approximately ten individuals. It has a time-limited, semistructured format with target goals and themes for each session. Optimally, the group should balance didactic instruction with time for open-ended discussion.

Weekly sessions, however, whether individual or group, may not be the optimum format for adults with ADHD, due to significant problems with organization and time management. Adults with ADHD are likely to have difficulty making a regular commitment to a therapeutic process they perceive as lengthy and drawn out, thus not satisfying their desire for immediate gratification. In order to avoid client disengagement, therapists should consider capitalizing on the individual's natural enthusiasm by organizing one-day group therapy work shops. This format is very attractive to individuals with ADHD because they offer an intensive, interactive environment that is perceived to be fast-track learning and that requires minimal commitment. Topics can include all those described in this chapter, but can also be extended to include medication issues, decision making, stress reduction, work/vocational issues, and the development of personal coping strategies. These could be offered in the form of a progressive series of group therapy workshops, starting with an introductory "Living with ADHD."

## CONCLUSIONS

This chapter has proposed a cognitive-behavioral model of psychotherapy for adults with ADHD that emphasizes the importance of invoking change from the outside in (change the environment) as well as change from the inside out (change the individual). Historically, treatment for ADHD has been predominantly stimulant medication, but long-term prognosis and adaptive functioning are likely to improve with psychological therapy. A variety of techniques may be adapted to match individual needs. An important component, however, must be an educative factor in order that family members, as well as the affected individual, develop an understanding of the disabling effects of ADHD in addition to its long-term implications. This information is likely to facilitate the development of appropriate, realistic expectations for behavior and potential achievement. Pragmatic cognitive-behavioral therapy is likely to be the most effective therapeutic model because it focuses on the development of self-management skills. And CBT can be applied within either a one-to-one or a group setting. One-day group workshops are likely to be especially attractive to clients with ADHD because they represent fast-track learning and treatment.

The therapy required will be determined not only by an individual's presentation but also by his or her sex, age, and place in the life course. An important determining factor of treatment outcome is likely to be whether ADHD was identified and treated in childhood or whether it was missed or misdiagnosed in childhood and not identified until adulthood. In the latter case, individuals may feel resentment and anger toward "the system" and their clinical care providers. The therapist needs to be aware that a potential outcome of treatment is that the client become more reflective, resulting in increased rumination over life's failures. The risk of depression may increase. Adults with ADHD in partial remission and ADHD "graduates" should not be dismissed with their remitting sympotmatology. They may well have much to contend with— maladaptive coping strategies, anticipated failure, poor self-confidence, low self-efficacy, and negative core beliefs about themselves, other people, and the world.

Finally, adults with ADHD have many strengths that should always be emphasized and applied therapeutically. With help, they have choice and opportunity to develop these talents and adapt the environment to suit their personal needs. What they often lack is the vision and courage to do so.

## APPENDIX

## Vignettes

**Anne**

I met Anne, an attractive young woman, when she was 28 years old. She suffered with ADHD and comorbid anxiety. As a child she succeeded relatively well academically, probably reflecting that she was not educated in a mainstream school but in the private sector, which provides smaller class sizes, more structure, and individual one-to-one tuition. Nevertheless, Anne believed she was identified by teachers as more vulnerable than her peers and as requiring more attention and support in her academic work. Teachers said that she had the potential but that she was lazy and unmotivated to complete school work. Anne said she tried very hard but something always went wrong. Either she did not understand the basic concepts, or she would find it difficult to study for long periods of time. Sometimes she would forget what she had to do, and she frequently lost relevant school books and materials. She recalled feeling humiliated when she would turn up at the wrong classroom because she had gotten mixed up about where she should be.

Anne became very anxious over her inability to get things right; the more she tried, the more everything seemed to go wrong. She described experiencing panic attacks from the age of 12 years. Anne was bullied by her peers, who called her names such as "stupid" and "backward." She recalled spending a lot of time in the playground feeling lonely and watching the children play. She recalled always being the last to be chosen for team sports. Although she struggled with academic work, Anne worked hard and left school with average grades and went to university.

It was at university that she met Roger, her first boyfriend. They dated for about two years, and at this stage in her life Anne reported beginning to feel more settled. She felt she had the potential to achieve academically and socially. Roger ended the relationship when he met someone else. Anne knew this person and perceived her to be confident and outgoing. Anne felt rejected and worthless, and her self-worth became a measure of how other people perceived her. To Anne this meant she had to be perfect. Whenever she had to go anywhere, she would leave hours before her appointment time in order to ensure that she arrived at the correct place and on time. This meant that she frequently arrived early at her location. She would while away time in coffee bars.

Anne had a memory of being in one coffee bar when two young men kept looking at her and smiling. One of them offered to buy her a coffee. She could remember getting very red in the face and feeling very stupid. Her cognitions were that the men must know that she is stupid and that they were offering to buy her a coffee because they felt sorry for her. After that Anne became increasingly uncomfortable whenever she went into coffee bars. If anyone looked at her, especially if they were young men, her hands would start to shake and she became frightened that she would spill her coffee. A few months later, when out with friends in a bar, she had a similar experience when a man she did not know started to talk to her. Anne started to avoid using long-stemmed wine glasses because she was afraid she would spill the contents. This later became a problem in restaurants, especially if they were brightly lit when her hands would start to shake and she would feel that she could not breathe.

On several occasions she had such extreme feelings of panic that she left the social event and went home. Eventually Anne realized that she needed help with her social phobia and sought help. Within the therapy she identified her underlying negative schemas as "I am unlovable" and "I am stupid." These stemmed from her early childhood experiences of getting things wrong in school and her peer relationship problems. Anne believed that no man could ever love someone so stupid.

## Peter

I first met Peter when he was 20 years old. He was diagnosed with ADHD and antisocial personality disorder. He was born and brought up in London and was one of three children. His parents separated when he was 4 years old and resulting in sporadic contact with his father. As a child he was hyperactive, disruptive, and conduct disordered. When he was 7 years old, he was seen by an educational psychologist on two occasions for his behavior. Peter was educated at a special school for children with behavioral difficulties. In later years he missed a lot of schooling through truancy. Peter was expelled from four schools due to his behavioral problems and eventually left school when 14 years old, with no qualifications. He had never been employed.

Peter had a history of contact with the police from the age of 12 years. He had approximately 50 convictions, most involving impulsive acts of theft (usually alone), criminal damage, and possession of class B drugs. His criminal behavior was usually opportunistic and not well thought out or planned. He had been a polydrug user since the age of 14 years and tended to offend to fund his drug habit. He had spent a significant proportion of his youth and young adulthood in young offenders' institutes or prison, usually for stays of a few months in duration. As a child and as an adult he had significant problems with interpersonal relationships. He had no longstanding friends because he believed that people would let him down if he got too close to them. He said he found it difficult to trust people. In later years, he saw his mother rarely and reported having a poor relationship with her.

Peter was very difficult to engage, and he was unreliable in his clinic attendance. A pattern developed whereby he would comply with medication when in prison but disengage once in the community. Eventually he received a five-year prison sentence and started to take stimulant medication regularly. His medical officer noted a significant decrease in his aggressive and oppositional behavior and an increase in his ability to concentrate and control his impulses. He was described as being calmer and more manageable. Peter's motivation and self-esteem improved to the point that, with encouragement, he was participating in further education classes and was making progress in a literacy class. Peter also attended art therapy sessions, and his artistic talent was such that it was felt that a long-term goal would be to enroll him in a Art Foundation University course.

A striking aspect was his developing insight into his cognitive and hyperactive behavioral problems. He said that at first he had felt very angry that, despite having had numerous contacts with child and adolescent services, his ADHD had been missed. His improved concentration, lower threshold of distractibility, and better impulse control, however, led him to ruminate and think about how different his life might have been had his problems been better recognized in childhood. He contemplated his broken relationship with his mother and his dysfunctional upbringing. It was felt that he was at risk for becoming depressed and that he required individual therapy to help him adjust to the changes in his personal functioning, how he saw himself, and how he saw the world in a different way. The interactions of others became more positive toward him, and his problems were better understood by those around him. In the course of his psychotherapy Peter developed better insight into his psychological problems and substance dependency. He expressed concern that he would again abuse street drugs when in the community, and it was arranged for him to attend substance-misuse group therapy sessions. Rehabilitation became possible within a shorter time than expected.

## Jane

Jane is 35 years old. She is a mother with ADHD with two children with ADHD, boys ages 9 and 7 years. Her ADHD was diagnosed and treated in adulthood when the clinicians involved in her childrens' care noticed that she also had ADHD symptomatology. Jane would frequently be late for appointments with pediatricians, and sometimes she would turn up on the wrong day. She seemed to have difficulty following instructions and advice and would frequently lose track of the conversation. She was objectively observed to be restless, and she seemed to be overly rapid in her behavior, making careless mistakes. Jane often felt exhausted and drained by her sons, who learned that there were wide differences between their parents in terms of boundary setting. Their father, Jack, was very consistent and set clear boundaries, whereas their mother was very inconsistent in her management of the children. She was volatile, haphazard, and disorganized, and her mood swings determined her parenting style. For example, sometimes Jane would allow the children to stay up late at night watching television and playing in their bedrooms. Other times she made them go to bed very early. Jack, who worked a night shift, was very clear and consistent in what they could and could not do in the day time. The children generally obeyed Jack but were challenging and oppositional toward their mother.

Jane often experienced feelings of anger and frustration, and she would vent her feelings on Jack and the children. She often felt that she could not cope. Her relationship with Jack became increasingly strained, and they frequently argued over the children. Family therapy initially helped the couple examine their different parenting styles and the impact these had on their children. Gradually Jane learned to be firmer in her boundary setting with the children and to be more consistent. It was important to Jane to have her feelings of frustration and helplessness acknowledged, for she had always felt like the least important person of the family, who simply provided for everyone else's needs. Diagnosis and treatment with stimulant medication of her ADHD meant that she was able to focus on her own difficulties and put those into context with her relationship with her family.

With therapeutic support, Jane set aside "time out" for herself on a daily basis. She organized for Jack to have the children for an hour before he went to work while she did aerobics with a neighbor in her local church hall. She started to structure her time better by making a week-ahead plan and then generating a list of priorities. These techniques helped Jane to impose order in her day, and this helped her feel more in control and able to cope. She started to use a diary that she kept in her handbag, as opposed to jotting rushed, illegible notes on pieces of paper that were eventually lost. This meant that she began to settle bills on time (twice her telephone had been disconnected for nonpayment), and the children had the appropriate items required for school on the correct day (such as sportswear). Jane interspersed her day with frequent periods of reward. These ranged from small rewards, such as a short rest over a cup of tea, to larger rewards, such as half hour to read a magazine or book.

### Michael

When I met Michael he was 38 years old, divorced, and with no children. He was a proud man who tended to deny his problems and painful emotions. Although he had suffered all his life with ADHD symptomatology, he had no idea that these were problems that could be diagnosed and treated. His mother told me that by age 3 he was frequently involved in reckless and dangerous escapades, such as climbing out of windows and disappearing from the house. He was referred to a child psychologist when he was 6 years of age for disruptive behavioral problems. As is the case for most children with ADHD, he had struggled in school and was expelled from two schools for disruptive and oppositional behavior. He could not read or write until he was 8 years old. It was not until he attended a special school for children with learning and behavioral problems, with smaller class sizes and greater structure, that he began to progress academically.

Michael left school at 16 without taking any formal examinations. He had difficulty settling into any particular employment and tended to work in temporary unskilled agency work (e.g., laboring, warehousing, driving, retail, lifeguard, catering). Michael was of average intelligence and perceived this work to be beneath his abilities. He become quickly bored and was either fired or left jobs when he fell out with line management because he "did not need to be told what to do when employed in menial tasks." Psychosocially Michael had been an aggressive child who did not relate well to same-age peers. In adulthood he was frequently involved in verbal altercations with friends, acquaintances, and work colleagues. He was challenging toward others, which made him lose friendships. When unemployed he became frustrated, bored, and depressed. He had feelings of uselessness and inferiority.

Michael had a low threshold for boredom, requiring employment that offered him high stimulation, frequent opportunity for positive feedback, and immediate gratification. Such employment was difficult to find, especially for someone with no qualifications and a poor job record. Michael took a tractor trailer driving course when he was 29 years old. He enjoyed driving because it offered greater stimulation and responsibility, since he was not in the same environment all day and every day, and he had the opportunity to structure his time according to his needs. With driving, Michael successfully adapted his working environment to meet his needs. For example, he was able to make frequent stops at different places; driving on the European continent offered changing scenery; to a certain extent he could manage his own time and structure his day; he could vary his routes; different jobs and destinations offered relief from monotony and boredom, and he did not have to relate to line management or colleagues on a daily basis.

Six years later, he sustained a serious knee injury, making it unlikely that he would be able to continue vocational driving for much longer. Alternative working opportunities were limited by his age and his untreated ADHD; e.g., he was unable to take a job operating machinery because this might endanger himself or others. Michael's self-esteem and confidence were closely related to his occupation, which represented one of the few areas in which he had achieved and succeeded in life. He required psychological therapy to help him with impulse control and to adjust to a significant change in occupational status. It became an important factor in preventing him from becoming depressed. Therapy also focused on the development of interpersonal relationship skills, anger management techniques, time management, and organization skills.

## REFERENCES

Barkley, R. A. (1997). *The nature of self-control.* New York: Guilford Press.

Barkley, R. A., Fischer, M., Edelbrock, C., & Smallish, L. (1991). The adolescent outcome of hyperactive children diagnosed by research criteria — III. Mother–child interactions, family conflicts and maternal psychopathology. *Journal of Child Psychology and Psychiatry, 32*(2), 233–255.

Bellak, L. (1979). *Psychiatric aspects of minimal brain dysfunction in adults.* New York: Grune and Stratton.

Berry, C. A., Shaywitz, S. E., & Shaywitz, B. A. (1985). Girls with attention deficit disorder: A silent minority? A report on behavioral and cognitive characteristics. *Pediatrics, 76,* 801–809.

Biederman, J., Faraone, S. V., & Chen, W. J. (1993). Social Adjustment Inventory for Children and Adolescents: Concurrent validity in ADHD children. *Journal of American Academy of Child and Adolescent Psychiatry, 32*(5), 1059–1064.

Biederman, M. D., Faraone, S. V., & Kieley, K. (1996). Comorbidity in outcome of attention-deficit/hyperactivity disorder. In L. Hechtman (ed.). *Do they grow out of It? Long-term outcomes of childhood disorders* (p.39). London: American Psychiatric Press.

Biederman, J., Faraone, S., & Mick, E. (1999). Clinical correlates of ADHD in females. *Journal of the American Academy of Child and Adolescent Psychiatry, 38,* 966–975.

Brent, D. A., Perper, J. A., Goldstein, C. E., et al. (1988). Risk factors for adolescent suicide victims with suicidal inpatients. *Archives of General Psychiatry, 45,* 581–588.

Ernst, M., Liebenauer, L. L., King, C., Fitzgerald, G. A., Cohen, E. A., & Zametkin, A. J. (1994). Reduced brain metabolism in hyperactive girls. *Journal of the American Academy of Child and Adolescent Psychiatry, 33,* 858–868.

Goldstein, S. (1997). *Managing attention and learning disorders in late adolescence and adulthood: A guide for practitioners.* New York: Wiley.

Grenell, M. M., Glass, C. R., & Katz, K. S. (1987). Hyperactive children and peer interaction: Knowledge and performance of social skills. *Journal of Abnormal Child Psychology, 15*(1), 1–13.

Hechtman, L., & Weiss, G. (1986). Controlled prospective fifteen-year follow-up of hyperactives as adults: Non-medical drug and alcohol use and anti-social behavior, *Canadian Journal of Psychiatry, 31*, 557–567.

Heptinstall, E., & Taylor, E. (1996). Sex differences and their significance. In S. Sandbury (ed.). *Hyperactivity Disorders of Childhood*. Cambridge University Press. New York.

Hill, J. C., & Schoener, E. P. (1996). Age-dependent decline of attention deficit hyperactivity disorder. *American Journal of Psychiatry, 153*(9), 1143–1146.

James, A., & Taylor, E. (1990). Sex differences in the hyperkinetic syndrome of childhood. *Journal of Child Psychology and Psychiatry, 31*, 437–446.

Kashani, J., Chapel, J. L., Ellis, J., & Shekim, W. O. (1979). Hyperactive girls. *Journal of Operational Psychiatry, 10*(2), 145–148.

Landau, S., & Milich, R. (1988). Social communication patterns of attention-deficit-disordered boys. *Journal of Abnormal Child Psychology, 16*, 69–81.

Lomas, B., & Gartside, P. (1999). ADHD in adult psychiatric outpatients. *Psychiatric Services, 5*, 705–717.

Mannuzza, S., Klein, R. G., Bessler, A., Malloy, P., & LaPadula, M. (1993). Adult outcome of hyperactive boys. *Archives of General Psychiatry, 50*, 565–576.

Morgan, W. D. (2000). Group treatment of adults with ADHD. In J. White & F. Freeman (Eds.). *Cognitive behavioral group treatment with specific problems and populations*. Washington, DC: American Psychological Association Books. (pp. 227–248).

Nadeau, K., Quinn, P., & Littman, E. (2000). *Understanding girls with AD/HD*. : Advantage Books.

Satterfield, J. H., Hoppe, C. M., & Schell, A. M. (1982), A prospective study of delinquency in 110 adolescent boys with attention deficit disorder and 88 normal adolescent boys. *American Journal of Psychiatry, 139*(6), 795–798.

Satterfield, T., Swanson, J., Schell, A., & Lee, F. (1994). Prediction of antisocial behavior in attention-deficit hyperactivity disorder boys from aggression/defiance scores. *Journal of American Academy of Child & Adolescent Psychiatry, 33*, 185–190.

Solden, S. (1995). *Women with attention deficit disorder: Embracing disorganization at home and in the workplace*. Grass Valley, CA: Underwood Books.

Swanson, J. M., Sergeant, J. A., Taylor, E., Sonuga-Barke, E. J. S., Jensen, P. S., & Cantwell, D. P. (1998). Attention-deficit hyperactivity disorder and hyperkinetic disorder. *The Lancet, 351*, 429–433.

Weiss, G., & Hechtman, L. (1986). *Hyperactive children grown up: Empirical findings and theoretical considerations*. New York: Guildford Press.

Whalen, C. K., & Henker, B. (1985). The social worlds of hyperactive (ADDH) children. *Clinical Psychology Review, 5*, 447–478.

Whalen, C. K., & Henker, B. (1992). The social profile of attention-deficit hyperactivity disorder: Five fundamental facets. *Child and Adolescent Psychiatric Clinics of North America, 1*, 395–410.

Whalen, C. K., Henker, B., Collins, B. E., McAuliffe, S., & Vaux, A. (1979). Peer interaction in a structured communication task: Comparisons of normal and hyperactive boys and of methylphenidate (Ritalin) and placebo effects. *Child Development, 50*, 388–401.

Young, S. J. (1999). Psychological therapy for adults with attention deficit hyperactivity disorder. *Counseling Psychology Quarterly, 12*(2), 183–190.

Young, S. J. (2000). ADHD children grown up: An empirical review. *Counselling Psychology Quarterly, 13*(2), 1–10.

Young, S. J., & Harty, M. A. (2001). Treatment issues in a personality-disordered offender: A case of attention deficit hyperactivity disorder in secure psychiatric services. *Journal of Forensic Psychiatry, 12*, 158–167.

Young, S. J., Toone, B., & Tyson, C. (2001). Comorbidity and psychosocial profile of adults with attention deficit hyperactivity disorder manuscript submitted for publication.

Zametkin, A. J., Karoum, G., Rapoport, J. L., et al. (1984). Phenylethylamine excretion in attention deficit disorder. *Journal of the American Academy of Child Psychiatry, 23*, 310–314.

# 9

# Pharmacotherapy of Adult ADHD

Jefferson B. Prince, M.D., Timothy E. Wilens, M.D.

## INTRODUCTION

Originally conceptualized as a disorder of childhood (Laufer, Denhoff, & Solomons, 1957), attention deficit hyperactivity disorder (ADHD) is increasingly recognized in adults. ADHD is estimated to affect 2–9% of school-age children and up to 5% of adults (Bauermeister, Canino, & Bird, 1994; K. Murphy & Barkley, 1996). Although some investigators question the persistence of ADHD in adulthood (Hill & Schoener, 1996), long-term controlled follow-up studies of young adults diagnosed with ADHD in childhood demonstrate persistence of the syndrome in up to 60% (Weiss & Hechtman, 1986; Mannuzza, Klein, Bessler, Malloy, & LaPadula, 1993). While some clinicians remain skeptical of adult ADHD (Shaffer, 1994), evidence supports the descriptive, face, predictive, and concurrent validity of the syndrome in adults (Spencer, Biederman, Wilens, Faraone, & Li, 1994; Spencer, Biederman, Wilens, & Faraone, 1998a). Adults with ADHD present with a developmental derivation of symptoms similar to those of children, notably inattention/distractibility followed by hyperactivity-impulsivity. Comorbidity with mood, anxiety, substance use, and antisocial disorders are common in adults with ADHD.

Like children, pharmacotherapy is a mainstay of treatment for ADHD in adults. Despite the large amount of data on pharmacotherapy of ADHD in children, there is a limited number of medication studies in adults with the disorder. Most controlled investigations in adults with ADHD have studied the stimulants. As with children, there tends to be a dose-related improvement in ADHD symptoms with the stimulant medications in adults. This literature supports the stimulants as the most effective available treatment for ADHD symptoms in adults. Several nonstimulant alternatives have been investigated. Although these data are limited, medications with catecholaminergic activity appear to have efficacy, whereas those with predominately serotonergic properties appear ineffective in the treatment of core ADHD symptomology. In cases with psychiatric comorbidity, residual symptoms, or adverse effects, clinical experience, coupled with a small literature, supports combining medications, such as the stimulants and antidepressants. Often, cognitive/behavioral-based psychotherapies are necessary in conjunction with medication in order to fully address executive function deficits, dynamic issues (within individual and family), residual symptomatology, as well as comorbid psychopathology in adults with ADHD. Future controlled studies applying stringent diagnostic criteria and outcome methodology are necessary to enhance the range of pharmacotherapeutic options for adults with ADHD.

## OVERVIEW OF THE NEUROBIOLOGY AND GENETICS OF ADHD

The Neurobiology and genetics of ADHD includes the following characteristics.

- Highly familial disorder with heritability estimated to be 0.8
- Primary disturbance of catecholamine neurotransmission
- Anterior cingulate, frontal cortex, basal ganglia, corpus callosum, and cerebellum manifest decreased size in ADHD
- Variations in genes that code for dopamine transporter protein (DAT) and dopamine D4 receptor (DRD4) associated with distinct ADHD subtypes
- No current role for neuroimaging or genetic testing in diagnosis of ADHD in clinical practice (but stay tuned)

The pharmacotherapy of ADHD is related directly to our understanding of its the pathophysiology. Although the exact neural and pathophysiological substrate remain unknown, an emerging neuropsychological and neuroimaging literature supports our understanding of ADHD as a disorder involving dysregulation of the frontal networks and/or frontostriatal dysfunction. The neurochemical dysfunction in ADHD appears to be mediated by dopaminergic and adrenergic systems, with little direct influence by the serotonergic systems (Zametkin & Liotta, 1998). Stimulants, the most effective treatment for ADHD, block the reuptake of dopamine and norepinephrine presynaptically and simultaneously increase the release of these monoamines into the extraneuronal space (Elia et al., 1990; Wilens & Spencer, 1998, 2000). Similar pharmacodynamic effects are reported with those antidepressants (tricyclic antidepressants and bupropion) effective for ADHD. While recent reports using data from animal models speculate on a role for serotonin in the pathophysiology of ADHD (Quist & Kennedy, 2001), serotonergic dysregulation does not appear integral in the pathophysiology of ADHD. Additionally, medications, which increase serotonin, have not been shown to be useful for core ADHD symptomatology. Although cholinergic modulation of temporal memory has been investigated (Meck & Church, 1987), the effects of cholinergic-enhancing agents on ADHD, as well as dopaminergic and other neurotransmitter systems, are currently under investigation (Wilens, Biederman, Wong, Spencer, & Prince, 2000; De Fockert, Rees, Frith, and Lavie, 2001). Regions of the brain, including the anterior cingulate, frontal cortex, basal ganglia, corpus callosum, and cerebellum, all show diminished size when individuals with ADHD are compared to individuals without the disorder. Similarly, functional-imaging studies in adults with ADHD demonstrate reduced global metabolism in catecholamine-rich areas of the brain (Zametkin & Liotta, 1998). Contributions from family, adoption, and twin studies strongly support the neurobiological basis of ADHD and suggest that genetic risk factors are operant in this disorder (Faraone et al., 1992; Faraone, Tsuang, & Tsuang, 1999). Recent work form molecular genetics focuses on the association of ADHD with various genes, including rare mutations in the human thyroid receptor-β gene on chromosome 3 (Hauser et al., 1993), the D4 receptor gene on chromosome 11 (LaHoste et al., 1996; Faraone et al., 1999), as well as the dopamine transporter gene on chromosome 5 (Cook et al., 1995; Daly, Hawi, Fitzgerald, & Gill, 1998). Conversely, increased density of presynaptic dopamine transporter proteins (DATs) has been associated with certain subtypes of ADHD, especially in patients with significant hyperactivity and impulsivity (Waldman et al., 1998; Swanson, Flodman, & Kennedy, 2000). This increased density of DATs appears to be a trait that is transmittable across generations. Thus, ligands specific for DATs (e.g., Altropane and TRODAT–1) are being actively investigated. A recent letter describes significantly increased DAT density in a group of six adults with ADHD compared to controls. Similarly, Krause et al., using single photon emission tomography (SPECT) with the ligand TRODAT–1, demonstrated increased striatal DAT density in adults with ADHD, which was normalized using methylphenidate (Krause, Dresel, Krausse, Kung, & Tatsch, 2000). These exciting developments have implications for our understanding and identification of various subtypes of ADHD, in the diagnosis of ADHD, and perhaps as an a priori method of identifying the best medication for individual patients. However, at this time the use of genetic testing and neuroimaging is not necessary in clinical practice.

## CLINICAL FEATURES OF ADHD IN ADULTS

Adults with ADHD typically present with the following clinical picture:

- Problems with regulating attention and concentration
- Disorganization, failure to plan ahead, forgetfulness
- Poor time management skills
- Difficulty initiating and completing tasks
- Difficulties in job, parenting, marriage
- While adults with ADHD usually can be relied on to accurately report their symptoms, additional informants often helpful

Adults with ADHD usually describe symptoms of poor attention, lack of concentration, easy distractibility, shifting activities, daydreaming, and forgetfulness (Millstein, Wilens, Biederman, & Spencer, 1997). They often begin one task and then find themselves in the middle of several projects. These patients appear to have a poorly developed sense of time and are often harried and late. They lose or misplace important personal items, such as keys and work and family projects. They usually avoid tasks that require high levels of concentration and patience, such as balancing a checkbook, filing tax returns, and helping children with homework. Projects are often put off until the last minute, at which time they often are highly motivated and are able to hyperfocus. Often these patients are drawn to novel stimuli, usually at the expense of the designated object of their attention. Their boredom or intrusiveness often compromises conversations with.25 coworkers, spouses, or children. Others frequently view adults with ADHD as either flighty or egotistical. Adults with ADHD seem to have difficulty regulating their attention, which leads to repeated problems as they attempt to manage affairs at work, home, or with friends.

Additionally, these patients report symptoms of impulsivity, impatience, boredom, fidgetiness, and intrusiveness (Millstein, Wilens, Biederman, & Spencer, 1997). These symptoms are often evident in the context of social situations. Frequently, adults with ADHD have long histories of social impairment and are often perceived as aloof (because they become easily bored) or as self-centered (because they interrupt or make socially inappropriate comments). Others are quite gregarious and talkative, "the life of the party," almost an adult equivalent of the class clown. Adults with ADHD have a sense of urgency and immediacy to their lives and have little tolerance for frustration, delay, or planning. They are easily irritated while waiting in lines and often make decisions without proper consideration of alternatives. Collaboration with others is often a mutually frustrating experience. Also, young adults with ADHD experience increased rates of traffic accidents, traffic violations, and license suspensions (Barkley, Murphy, & Kwasnik, 1996; Barkley, Murphy, DuPaul, & Bush, in press). Finally, symptoms of overt hyperactivity may be diminished, for many patients have developed compensatory strategies to diminish these symptoms. Recent data support the clinical observation that symptoms of hyperactivity-impulsivity decline over time while symptoms of inattention persist (Biederman, Mick,

& Faraone, 2000). Overall, these investigators note that most patients with ADHD continue to struggle with a substantial number of symptoms and a high level of impairment.

Adults with ADHD are thought to have deficits of working memory, as exemplified by less ability to attend to, encode, or manipulate information (Seidman, Biederman, Weber, Hatch, & Faraone, 1998). Such deficits in working memory have recently been shown to decrease the ability to filter out distractions, and may contribute to symptoms of inattention in adults with ADHD (De Fockert et al., 2001). Although less defined within ADHD, organizational difficulties and procrastination also appear common.

Like children with ADHD, adults with the disorder may be stubborn and demoralized and have low self-esteem (Biederman et al., 1993; Biederman, 1998). Relationships with family, friends, and employers are often conflicted, which may contribute to high rates of separation and divorce, as well as to the academic and occupational underachievement characteristic of these adults (Weiss & Hechtman, 1986; Mannuzza et al., 1993). Compared to their non-ADHD peers, adults with ADHD have increased rates of anxiety, depression, and substance use disorders (Weiss & Hechtman, 1986; Biederman et al., 1993; Biederman et al., 1995).

## ASSESSMENT AND DIAGNOSIS OF ADHD IN ADULTS

The assessment and diagnosis of ADHD in adults has the following features.

- DSM-IV is the gold standard.
- Several available scales and available to aid assessment, including the Brown Attention Deficit Disorder Scales, Conners Adult Attention Deficit Scale, DuPaul ADHD Rating Scale, and the Wender Utah Rating Scale.
- Recent reports validate the reliability of data collected from adults with ADHD.
- There is a potential for use of neuroimaging and genetic testing to identify certain subtypes of ADHD.
- Disentangling comorbidities and associated impairments (e.g., executive functions) are a prime clinical challenge.

ADHD can be diagnosed in adults by carefully querying for developmentally appropriate criteria from the DSM-IV (American Psychiatric Association, 1994), attending to a childhood onset of symptoms, persistence through adolescence, and current presence of symptoms as well as impairment. Self-report scales, such as the Brown-ADD Scale (Brown, 1996) and the DuPaul scale (DuPaul, 1990), may assist in the evaluation and monitoring of ADHD in adults. Recently, the Conners Adult ADHD Rating Scale (CAARS) demonstrated high sensitivity and specificity, with an overall diagnostic efficiency of 85% (Conners, Epstein, & Erhardt, 2000). These instruments have generally sound psychometric properties and may be used to aid in diagnosis as well as to assess treatment response. The Wender Utah Rating Scales may be used to aid diagnosis rather than to monitor treatment (Ward, Wender, & Reimherr, 1993). A variety of issues arise in the assessment and diagnosis of ADHD in adults. First, the appropriate diagnosis of ADHD in adults relies on the accurate recall of childhood symptoms and a reliable account of current symptoms and their impact. Some clinicians have questioned the reliability of adults with ADHD to accurately report this information (Shaffer, 1994). Recently, Murphy and Schachar evaluated correlation of symptoms between adults with ADHD and other informants (Murphy & Schachar, 2000). Diagnostic information is obtained from the patient and, whenever possible, from significant others, such as partners, parents, siblings, and close friends. If ancillary data are not available, information from an adult is acceptable for diagnostic and treatment purposes, because adults with ADHD, as with other disorders, are appropriate reporters of their own condition. Careful attention should be paid to the childhood onset of symptoms, the longitudinal history of the disorder, and a differential diagnosis, including medical/neurological as wellpsychosocial factors contributing to the clinical presentation. Neuropsychological testing should be used in cases in which learning disabilities are suspected or when learning problems persist in the presence of a treated ADHD adult (Barkley, 1990, 1997, 1998).

## Differential Diagnosis

A variety of medical and psychiatric conditions should be considered as part of the evaluation of ADHD within adults. Such conditions include sleep disorders, headaches, visual and auditory disorders, seizure disorders, endocrine disorders; hepatic function; use of illicit substances as well as herbal remedies, impact of concurrent medications on cognition (e.g., anticholinergic or antihypertensive medications). Laboratory tests, such as thyroid studies, EEG, baseline EKG, and baseline hepatic function tests, are generally not necessary unless indicated by the patient's symptoms or family history. Additionally, clinicians should obtain a history of anxiety disorders (including trauma), mood disturbances (including bipolar disorder), current and past substance use, aggression and impulse control problems, legal involvement, psychosis. In addition, current stresses as well as issues involving the patient's adherence are important to the overall treatment plan.

## Disentangling Comorbidities

In adults with ADHD, issues of comorbidity with learning disabilities and other psychiatric disorders need to be addressed (Biederman et al., 1993, 1995). Since alcohol and drug use disorders are frequently encountered in adults with ADHD (Wilens, Spencer, & Biederman, 1995a), a careful history of substance use should be completed. A Patient with ongoing substance abuse or dependence should generally not be treated until appropriate addiction treatments have been undertaken and the patient has maintained a drug and alcohol free period. Our experience attempting to treat adults with ADHD and ongoing substance use disorders indicates the necessity of addressing the comorbid substance use first and then reassessing and treating the ADHD. Other concurrent psychiatric disorders also need require evaluation. In subjects with ADHD plus bipolar mood-disorders, for example, the risk of mania needs be addressed and closely monitored during the treatment of the ADHD. In cases such as these, the conservative introduction of anti-ADHD medications along with mood-stabilizing agents should be considered.

Since learning disabilities do not respond to pharmacotherapy, it is important to identify such deficits to help define remedial interventions. For instance, this evaluation may assist in the design and implementation of an educational plan for the adult who is considering returning to school, or serve as an aid for structuring the current work environment. Appropriate remedial strategies should be employed to address the morbidity of these factors at work and in school.

## GENERAL PRINCIPLES OF PHARMACOTHERAPY OF ADHD IN ADULTS

Despite increased recognition that children with ADHD commonly grow up to be adults with the same disorder, the treatment of this disorder in adults remains under intense study. In addition, complicating the diagnostics and treatment strategy, many adults with ADHD have depressive and anxiety symptoms as well as histories of drug and alcohol dependence or abuse (Tarter, McBride, Buonpane, & Schneider, 1977; Eyre, Rounsaville, & Kleber, 1982; Wood, Wender, & Reimherr, 1983; Biederman et al., 1993; Wilens et al., 1995a). Thus, with the increasing recognition of the complex presentation of adults with ADHD, there is a need to develop effective pharmacotherapeutic strategies.

In the following sections, guidelines for pharmacotherapy will be delineated, the available information on the use of medications for adult ADHD reviewed, and pharmacologic strategies suggested for the management of ADHD symptoms with accompanying comorbid conditions.

Pharmacotherapy should be part of a treatment plan in which consideration is given to all aspects of the patient's life. Hence, it should not be used exclusive of other interventions. The administration of medication to adults with ADHD should be undertaken as a collaborative effort with the patient, with the physician guiding the use and management of efficacious anti-ADHD agents. The use of medication should follow a careful evaluation of the adult, including medical, psychiatric, social, and cognitive assessments.

## STIMULANTS IN THE TREATMENT OF ADULTS WITH ADHD

Stimulant treatment of adults with ADHD can be characterized as follows.

- Stimulants represent the first-line pharamcotherapy for ADHD in adults.
- The two main types of stimulants, methylphenidate and amphetamine compounds, have different effects and are metabolized differently.
- Methylphenidate does not show up on urine drug screens.
- Stimulants are not effective for comorbidities within ADHD.
- Stimulants generally have few medication interactions (except with MAOIs)

Stimulant medications remain the mainstay treatment in children, adolescents, and adults with ADHD. In comparison to the more than 200 controlled studies of stimulant efficacy in pediatric ADHD (Spencer et al., 1996), there are only two open and nine controlled stimulant trials in adults with ADHD (Wood, Reimherr, Wender, & Johnson, 1976; Wender, Reimherr, & Wood, 1981; Mattes, Boswell, & Oliver, 1984; Gualtieri, Ondrusek, & Finley, 1985; Wender, Reimherr, Wood, & Ward, 1985a; Shekim, Asarnow, Hess, Zaucha, & Wheeler, 1990b; Spencer et al., 1995; Iaboni, Bouffard, Minde, & Hechtman, 1996; Spencer et al., 1999b) (Table 9.1). In contrast to consistent robust responses to stimulants in children and adolescents of approximately 70% (Wilens & Biederman, 1992; Wilens & Spencer, 2000), controlled studies in adults have shown more equivocal responses to stimulants, ranging from 25% (Mattes et al., 1984) to 78% (Spencer et al., 1995a) of adults responding to treatment. Controlled trials of methylphenidate (MPH)) (Wood et al., 1976; Mattes et al., 1984; Gualtieri et al., 1985; Wender et al., 1985a; Spencer et al., 1995a) and mixed amphetamine compound (Adderall) (Spencer et al., 1999a), demonstrate more robust response compared to pemoline (Wender et al., 1981; Wilens et al., 1996b). At this time there are no available studies in adults of extended-release preparations or new delivery systems of methylphenidate or dextroamphetamine.

Variability in the response rate appears to be related to several factors, including the diagnostic criteria utilized to determine ADHD, varying stimulant doses, high rates of comorbidity, and differing methods of assessing overall response. Dosing of the stimulants, for example, appears to effect outcome. Controlled investigations using higher stimulant dosing ($> 1.0$ mg/kg/day) resulted in more robust outcomes (Spencer et al., 1995; Iaboni et al., 1996) than those using lower stimulant dosing ($<0.7$ mg/kg/day) (Wender et al., 1981; Mattes et al., 1984). In addition, dose-dependent response to stimulants was found in three studies of adults with ADHD (Spencer et al., 1995; Wilens et al., 1997a; Spencer et al., 1999b). Although commonly used, the utility of dextroamphetamine for ADHD in adults remains unstudied. Although long-term data are generally lacking, preliminary data from one controlled trial of 117 adults suggests that the response to MPH is sustained at six-month follow-up (Wender et al., 1995).

## TABLE 9.1  Studies of Stimulant Pharmacotherapy in Adult ADHD

| Study (year) | N | Design | Medication | Duration | Total Dose (Weight-corrected) | Response rate | Comments |
|---|---|---|---|---|---|---|---|
| Wood et al. (1976) | 15 | Double blind | MPH | 4 weeks | 27 mg 0.4 mg/kg* | 73% | Dx criteria not well defined, low doses of Pemoline; mild side effects |
|  |  | Open | Pemoline | 4 weeks | 37.5–70 mg (0.5–1.0 mg/kg)* | 33% |  |
| Wender et al. (1981b) | 51 | Double blind Placebo crossover | Pemoline | 6 weeks | 65 mg (0.9 mg/kg)* | 50% (childhood onset) | Dx criteria not well defined, high rates of dysthymia; moderate effects |
| Mattes et al. (1984) | 26 | Double blind Placebo crossover | MPH | 6 weeks | 48 mg (0.7 mg/kg)* | 25% | Moderate rate of comorbidity; mild side effects |
| Wender et al. (1985a) | 37 | Double blind Placebo crossover | MPH | 5 weeks | 43 mg (0.6 mg/kg)* | 57% | 68% dysthymia, 22% cyclothymia; mild side effects |
| Gualtieri et al. (1985) | 8 | Double blind Placebo crossover | MPH | 2 weeks | 42 mg* (0.6 mg/kg)* | 70% | Problematic outcome measures |
| Shekim et al. (1990b) | 33 | Open | MPH | 8 weeks | 40 mg (0.6 mg/kg)* | 70% | Problematic outcome measures |
| Spencer et al. (1995) | 23 | Double blind Placebo crossover | MPH | 7 weeks | 30–100 mg 0.5, 0.75, & 1.0 mg/kg | 78% dose relationship | No plasma level associations; no effect gender or comorbidities |
| Iaboni et al. (1996) | 30 | Double blind Placebo crossover | MPH | 4 weeks | 30–45 mg (0.6 mg/kg)* | Moderate | Improvement in neuropsych. & anxiety |
| Wilens, et al. (1996b) | 42 | Double blind Placebo crossover | Pemoline | 10 weeks | 150 mg 2 mg/kg | 61% | 35% reduction in all symptoms; moderate effects >2 mg/kg |
| Spencer et al. (1996b) | 27 | Double blind Cross over | Adderall | 7 weeks | 30 mg BID | 70% Response rate | Dose–response relationship |
| TOTAL | 292 | Double blind; N = 9; open: N = 2 | MPH, Adderall, & Pemoline | 2–10 weeks | 40 mg (MPH) (0.6 mg/kg)* 105 mg (Pem) (1.5 mg/kg)* 30 mg BID (ADD) | Variable | Dx not well defined; high rate of comorbidities; side effects in 30%; apparent dose–response relationship |

Duration of medication trial includes placebo phase. Abbreviations: MPH = methylphenidate, DX = diagnosis.
*Weight-normalized dose using 50th percentile weight for age.

## Pharmacokinetic Issues in Stimulant Treatment

Plasma levels of the stimulants have not been shown to correlate with response in ADHD in adults (Gualtieri, Hicks, Patrick, Schroeder, & Breese, 1984; Spencer et al., 1995). Moreover, comorbidity with ADHD and gender has not been associated with variable response (Spencer et al., 1995; Wilens et al., 1996b); however, sample sizes have not been large enough to adequately address this issue.

## Pharmacodynamics of Stimulant Treatment

The effects of the stimulants in the brain are variable. Preclinical studies have shown that the stimulants block the reuptake of dopamine and norepinephrine into the presynaptic neuron and that both drugs increase the release of these monoamines into the extraneuronal space (Elia et al., 1990; Wilens & Spencer, 1998). While not entirely sufficient, alterations in dopaminergic and noradrenergic function appear necessary for clinical efficacy of the anti-ADHD medications, including the stimulants (Zametkin & Rapoport, 1987). There may be differential responses to the chemically distinct available stimulants because each may have a different mode of action. For example, although methylphenidate (MPH) and amphetamines alter dopamine transmission, they appear to have different mechanisms on release of dopamine from neuronal pools (Elia et al., 1990; Wilens & Spencer, 2000). The different mechanisms of actions of the amphetamines may explain why adults not responding to one stimulant may respond favorably to another. Moreover, given the differing mechanism of action, it is empirically reasonable, although unstudied, to consider combining methylphenidate with amphetamine in refractory patients.

## Initiation of Therapy and Dosing Guidelines

Given the limited controlled data on the use of stimulants in adults with ADHD, there are limited data available to guide dosing parameters in this population. FDA guidelines for dosing reflect general cautiousness and should not be the only guide for clinical practice. For instance, absolute dose limits (in mg) do not adequately consider a patient's height or weight and may result in underdosing. Although adults were not included in the MTA study, many clinicians extrapolate these results in their treatment of adults (Group, 1999). Other clinicians may turn to the Texas Medication Algorithm Project for guidance (Pliszka et al., 2000). Doses should be individually titrated based on therapeutic efficacy and tolerability. The overall clinical picture, taking into account all the variables of the patient's current presentation, should guide selection of an initial stimulant.

Many patient's respond equally well to either methylphenidate or amphetamine compounds (Greenhill & Osman, 1999). Treatment should be started with short-acting preparations at the lowest possible dose. Initiation of treatment with once-daily dosing in the morning is advisable until an acceptable response is noted. Treatment generally starts at 5 mg of methylphenidate, dextroamphetamine, or amphetamine compound once daily and is titrated upward every three to five days until an effect is noted or adverse effects emerge. Repeat dosing through the day is dependent on the duration of effectiveness, wear-off, and side effects. Typically, the half-life of the short-acting stimulants necessitates at least twice-daily dosing, with the addition of similar or reduced afternoon doses dependent on breakthrough symptoms.

Treatment with stimulants appears to be moving in the direction of longer-acting delivery systems. For instance, the new OROS system found in Concerta delivers methylphenidate for approximately 8–9 hours and thus has a behavioral life of between 10 and 14 hours. Concerta can be initiated at 18 mg and increased in weekly increments as tolerated to an effective dose. Typical adult dosing of methylphenidate is up to 30 mg three to four times daily, amphetamine 15–20 mg three to four times a day, and pemoline 75–225 mg daily. If an adult with ADHD symptoms is unresponsive or experiences significant side effects to the initial stimulant, consideration of an alternative stimulant or class of agents is recommended.

## Monitoring Treatment with Stimulants

Once pharmacotherapy is initiated, monthly contact with the patient is suggested during the initial phase of treatment to carefully monitor response to the intervention and adverse effects. Given that many adults with ADHD have comorbidites, once a successful regimen of medications is identified, the clinician must monitor for symptoms of comorbidity. For instance, some concerns have been raised about the anxiogenic properties of Adderall, and thus patients with comorbid anxiety disorder should be closely monitored (Horrigan & Barnhill, 2000). If issues of substance use are present, then consider the use of urine screens or hair sampling. Remember that methylphenidate will not be identified on the urine screen as amphetamine since it is metabolized primarily to ritalinic acid (Wilens & Spencer, 1998).

## Side Effects of Stimulants

The side effects of the stimulants in ADHD adults have been reported to be mild, with the following side effects most frequently reported: insomnia, edginess, diminished appetite, weight loss, dysphoria, obsessiveness, tics, and headaches (Wilens & Spencer, 2000). No cases of stimulant-related psychosis at therapeutic doses have been reported in adults (Wilens & Spencer, 2000). Likewise, despite the theoretical abuse potential of the stimulants, there have been no reports of stimulant abuse in controlled or retrospective studies of adults with ADHD (Langer, Sweeney, Bartenbach, Davis, & Menander, 1986). Although concerns about adverse cardiovascular effects of stimulants have been raised (Werry & Aman, 1975), effects appear benign, with minimal elevations of heart rate and blood pressure weakly correlated with dose (Brown, Wynne, & Slimmer, 1984; Kelly, Rapport, & DuPaul, 1988). Studies of stimulants in normotensive adults demonstrate elevations of 4 mm Hg of systolic and diastolic blood pressure as well as increases in heart rate of less than 10 beats per minute (Spencer et al., 1995; Wilens et al., 1997a; Spencer et al., 1999a).

While these studies are reassuring in normotensive adults, long-term data are lacking, as are data in adults with borderline hypertension. It is recommended that clinicians inquire about familial hypertension, regularly follow patient's blood pressure, and proceed with caution in patients with borderline hypertension. The addition of low-dose beta-blockers (i.e., propanolol at 10 mg up to three times daily) or busipirone (5–10 mg up to three times daily) may be helpful in reducing the edginess/agitation associated with stimulant administration (Ratey, Greenberg, & Lindem, 1991).

Although not observed in short term studies of pemoline in ADHD adults (Wilens et al., 1996b), elevated liver function tests remain a concern when using this medication, and the FDA recommends liver enzyme tests every two weeks. While the benefit of biweekly liver function tests is debatable, discussion and close observation of hepatitis symptoms, including change in urine/stool characteristic, abdominal pain, persistent flulike symptoms, or jaundice are useful in monitoring for hepatic dysfunction with pemoline. Pemoline may have a role in the treatment of ADHD and comorbid substance use disorders.

## Medication Interactions

The interactions of the stimulants with other prescription and nonprescription medications are generally mild and not a source of concern (Wilens & Spencer, 2000). Whereas coadministration of sympathomimetics (i.e., pseudoephedrine) may potentiate both medication effects, the antihistamines may diminish the stimulant's effectiveness. Excretion of amphetamines can be enhanced by acidification of the urine, and thus in some cases clinicians may need to limit the amount of citrus juices patients drink at the time they take their medications. Extreme caution should be exercised when using stimulants and antidepressants of the monoamine oxidase inhibitor (MAOI) type because of the potential for hypertensive reactions with this combination. The concomitant use of stimulants and TCAs is common practice, with a recent study indicating no significant drug interactions [(Cohen et al., 1999).

## New Stimulant Preparations

As already discussed, several new delivery systems for methylphenidate are available. Similarly, clinicians can expect several other stimulant preparations to be available soon. These include SlI381, a once daily formulation of Adderall. This compound utilizes the Micotrol delivery system employed in Carbatrol (a long-acting form of carbamazepine). Recent trials in children and adolescents have been published and are promising (McGough, Greenhill, & Biederman, 2000).

Despite the increasing use of stimulants for adults with ADHD, up to 50% do not respond, have untoward side effects, or manifest comorbidity that stimulants may exacerbate or be ineffective in treating (Taylor et al., 1987; Shekim et al., 1990b; Biederman et al., 1993). Reports of nonstimulant treatments for ADHD adults have included the use of antidepressants, antihypertensives, and amino acids (Table 9.2).

TABLE 9.2  Management of Common Stimulant-Induced Side Effects

| Adverse effects | Management |
| --- | --- |
| Anorexia, nausea, weight loss | Administer stimulant with meal<br>Use caloric-enhanced supplements (discourage forcing meals)<br>Change preparations |
| Insomnia, nightmares | Consider adjunctive treatment (nortriptyline, pergolide)<br>Administer stimulants earlier in the day<br>Change to short-acting preparations<br>Discontinue afternoon or evening doses<br>Assess sleep hygiene<br>Consider adjunctive treatment (clonidine, mirtazapine, melatonin, antidepressants) |
| Dizziness | Reduce dose<br>Monitor blood pressure<br>Change to longer-acting preparation |
| Rebound symptoms | Overlap stimulant dosing<br>Change to longer-acting preparation<br>Consider alternative or adjunctive treatment (small dose of short-acting stimulant; clonidine, antidepressant) |
| Irritability | Assess timing of symptoms (during peak or offset phase)<br>Reduce dose or change to long-acting preparation<br>Evaluate comorbid disorders (anxiety, mood, substance use)<br>Consider alternative or adjunctive treatments (antimanic agents, antidepressants) |
| Growth impairment | Attempt weekend or vacation holidays<br>If severe or persistent, consider alternative treatments |

## NONSTIMULANT MEDICATIONS IN THE TREATMENT OF ADULTS WITH ADHD

Here are some important points regarding nonstimulants in the treatment of adults with ADHD.

- Tricyclic antidepressants and bupropion are second-line therapies.
- Antidepressant dosing of the agents appears necessary for ADHD efficacy.
- Serotonergic medications do not appear effective in the treatment of core ADHD symptoms but may be useful for comorbid anxiety and depression.
- Cholinergic-enhancing medications may have a role in improving areas of inattention, but data are limited.
- There is an empiric role for antihypertensives in aggression and tic disorders.
- Empiric use of combinations may be appropriate in refractory and comborbid patients.

## Antidepressants

### Tricyclic Antidepressants

Within the past two decades, the tricyclic antidepressants (TCAs) have been used as alternatives to the stimulants for ADHD in pediatrics (Spencer et al., 1996). Despite an extensive experience with children and adolescents (Spencer et al., 1996), there are only two studies of these agents in adult ADHD. Compared to the stimulants, TCAs have negligible abuse liability, once-daily dosing, and efficacy for comorbid anxiety and depression.

An initial chart review indicated that desipramine or nortriptyline, often in combination with other psychotropics including stimulants, resulted in moderate improvement that was sustained at one year (Wilens, Biederman, Mick, & Spencer, 1995b). A controlled trial of desipramine with a target dose of 200 mg daily resulted in significant reductions in ADHD symptoms in adults (Wilens et al., 1996a). In that study, response was noted during the initial titration at two weeks, which continued to improve at the six-week endpoint. Whereas a minority of subjects responded to <100 mg daily, the majority required more robust dosing (mean of 150 mg daily) for efficacy.

Generally, TCA daily doses of 50–250 mg are required, with a relatively rapid response to treatment (i.e., two weeks) when the appropriate dose is reached. Tricyclic antidepressants should be initiated at 25 mg and slowly titrated upward within dosing and serum level parameters until an acceptable response or intolerable adverse effects are reported. Common side effects of the TCAs include dry mouth, constipation, blurred vision, weight gain, and sexual dysfunction. While cardiovascular effects of reduced cardiac conduction, elevated blood pressure, and heart rates are not infrequent, if monitored they rarely prevent treatment. Because serum TCA levels are variable, they are best used as guidelines for efficacy and to reduce CNS and cardiovascular toxicity.

### Bupropion

Recently, the atypical, stimulant-like antidepressant bupropion (Wellbutrin®) has been reported to be moderately helpful in reducing ADHD symptoms in children (Casat, Pleasants, & Fleet, 1987) and adults (Wender & Reimherr, 1990). In an open study of 19 adults treated with an average of 360 mg of bupropion for 6–8 weeks, Wender and Reimherr (1990) reported a moderate-to-marked response in 74% of adults in the study (five dropouts), with sustained improvement at one year noted in 10 subjects. Despite the small numbers of adults studied, bupropion may be helpful in ADHD, particularly when associated with comorbid mood instability or in adults with cardiac abnormalities (Gelenberg, Bassuk, & Schoonover, 1991). Bupropion should also be started at very low doses (37.5 mg) and titrated upward weekly to a maximal dose of 450 mg per day. ADHD adults may benefit from the long-acting bupropion preparation. Bupropion appears to be more stimulating than other antidepressants, and it is associated with a higher rate of drug-induced seizures than other antidepressants (Gelenberg et al., 1991). These seizures appear to be dose related (>450 mg/day) and elevated in patients with bulimia or a previous seizure history. Bupropion has also been associated with excitement, agitation, increased motor activity, insomnia, and tremor.

**Monoamine Oxidase Inhibitors (MAOIs)**

The monoamine oxidase inhibitor antidepressants have also been studied for the treatment of ADHD. Whereas open studies with pargyline and deprenyl in adult ADHD showed moderate improvements (Wender, Wood, Reimherr, & Ward, 1983; Wender, Wood, & Reimherr, 1985b), a more recent controlled trial of selegeline (Deprenyl) yielded less enthusiastic findings (Ernst et al., 1996). Ernst et al. reported dose-dependent improvements in ADHD symptoms on selegeline, which were not significant when compared to a high placebo response. Although a pilot child-based study demonstrated efficacy of the reversible monoamine oxidase inhibitor moclobemide, data of its effectiveness for ADHD are not available in adults. The monoamine oxidase inhibitors may have a role in the management of treatment-refractory, nonimpulsive adult ADHD subjects with comorbid depression and anxiety, who are able to comply with the stringent requirements of these agents. The concerns of diet- or medication-induced hypertensive crisis limit the usefulness and safety of these medications, especially in a group of ADHD patients vulnerable to impulsivity. Additionally, other adverse effects associated with the monoamine oxidase inhibitors include agitation or lethargy, orthostatic hypotension, weight gain, sexual dysfunction, sleep disturbances, and edema, often leading to the discontinuation of these agents (Gelenberg et al., 1991).

Serotonin-reuptake inhibitors (SRIs). The selective serotonin-reuptake inhibitors do not appear to be effective for ADHD (Spencer et al., 1996); however, venlafaxine, an antidepressant with both serotonin and noradrenergic properties, may have anti-ADHD efficacy. In three open studies totaling 41 adults, 75% of adults who tolerated venlafaxine had a measurable reduction in their ADHD at doses of 75–150 mg daily (Adler, Resnick, Kunz, & Devinsky, 1995; Findling, Schwartz, Flannery, & Manos, 1995; Reimherr, Hedges, Strong, & Wender, 1995). Although further controlled trials are necessary to determine its optimal dosing and efficacy, venlafaxine is generally titrated from 25 mg daily to more typical antidepressant dosing of between 150 and 225 mg daily for ADHD control. Side effects to venlafaxine in adults include nausea, gastrointestinal distress, anorgasmia, and concerns of elevated blood pressure at relatively higher dosing. Patients may experience discontinuation symptoms if the medication is stopped rapidly. Venlafaxine is often used conjointly with stimulants for control of ADHD in adults.

## Antihypertensives

The antihypertensives clonidine and guanfacine have been used in childhood ADHD, especially in cases with a marked hyperactive or aggressive component (Spencer et al., 1996). However, because of a lack of efficacy data and concerns of their sedative and hypotensive effects, their use in adults remains dubious. Beta-blockers may be helpful in adult ADHD but remain unstudied under controlled conditions (Mattes, 1986; Ratey et al., 1991). One small open study of propranolol for adults with ADHD and temper outbursts indicated improvement in both the ADHD symptoms and outbursts at daily doses of up to 640 mg/day (Mattes, 1986). Beta-blockers when added to stimulants have also been reported to be helpful for ADHD in three adults (Ratey et al., 1991), although it may be that this combination was helpful by reducing the stimulant-induced adverse effects.

## Amino Acids

Trials with the amino acids were in part undertaken with the assumptions that ADHD may be related to a deficiency in the catecholaminergic system and that administration of precursors of these systems would reverse these deficits. The results of open studies with L-DOPA and tyrosine and controlled studies of phenylalanine in adults with ADHD have generally been disappointing, despite robust dosing and adequate trial duration (Table 9.3) (Wood, Reimherr, & Wender 1982, 1985; Reimherr, Wender, Wood, & Ward, 1987). In these studies, transient improvement in ADHD was lost after two weeks of treatment.

## Cholinergic Agents

More recently, the relationship of nicotine and ADHD has attracted attention, including findings of higher-than-expected overlap of cigarette smoking in ADHD children (Milberger, Biederman, Faraone, Chen, & Jones, 1997) and adults (Pomerleau, Downey, Stelson, & Pomerleau, 1995). One small study of two days' duration showed a significant reduction in ADHD symptoms in adults wearing standard-size nicotine patches (Conners et al., 1996). Moreover, the authors have observed the efficacy of the nicotine patch in reducing ADHD symptoms in smokers who report the emergence of ADHD symptoms with cigarette cessation. Donepezil, a cholinesterase inhibitor, increases the bioavailability of acetylcholine and has been found to improve memory and attention in Trisomy–21 and traumatic brain injury (Whelan, Walker, & Schultz, 2000; Kishnani, Spiridigliozzi, & Heller, 2001). Data on donepezil in ADHD are limited to case series in children and adolescents (Wilens et al., 2000). ABT–418 is a selective and potent nicotinic cholinergic agonsit. In the one published study, symptoms of inattention improved preferentially over symptoms of impulsivity and hyperactivity. The effect was more gradual than with methylphenidate and it was associated with some dizziness. Although compelling, the role of cholinergic medications in treatment of ADHD remains to be further defined.

## Modfanil

Modfanil is a nonstimulant medication used in the treatment of narcolepsy. Its main effects appear to be on the hypothalamus rather than on central dopaminergic or noradrenergic pathways. Despite anecdotal reports of its usefulness in ADHD, initial trials demonstrated no benefit over placebo, and manufacture-sponsored trials were discontinued. It may have a role in cases of refractory ADHD.

## Medications Under Investigation

Tomoxetine, an investigational antidepressant with selective noradrenergic-reuptake inhibitor properties, is under study for the treatment of ADHD in children, adolescents, and adults (Heiligenstein et al., 2000). In one controlled trial with adults, average daily doses of 76 mg were well tolerated and moderately effective in reducing core ADHD symptomology. Full therapeutic benefit may have been compromised by the short duration of the study (Spencer et al., 1998b). Although time to response with tomoxetine appears longer compared to the stimulants, it will likely provide an excellent alternative to the stimulants in patients with comorbid mood, anxiety, and/or substance use disorders. Reboxetine, a highly selective noradrenergic-reuptake inhibitor, is expected to be available in the United States soon. Although it has not been formally studied for the treatment of ADHD, clinicians may consider using it as an alternative for the treatment of ADHD with comorbid mood, anxiety, and substance use disorders. The investigational antidepressants

TABLE 9.3 Studies of Nonstimulant Pharmacotherapy in Adult ADHD

| Study (year) | N | Design | Medication | Duration (weeks) | Dose (mean) | Response | Comments |
|---|---|---|---|---|---|---|---|
| Wood et al. (1982) | 8 | Open | L-DOPA (+ carbidopa) | 3 | 625 mg | No benefit | Side effects: nausea, sedation; low doses |
| Wender et al. (1983) | 22 | Open | Pargyline | 6 | 30 mg | 13/22 moderate improvement | Delayed onset; brief behavioral action |
| Wender et al. (1985) | 11 | Open | Deprenyl | 6 | 30 mg | 6/9 responded, 2 dropouts | Amphetamine metabolite |
| Wood et al. (1985) | 19 | Double-blind crossover | Phenylalanine | 2 | 587 mg | Poor | Translent; mood improvement only |
| Mattes (1986) | 13 | Open Retrospective | Propanolol | 3–50 | 528 mg | 11/13 improved | Part of "temper" study |
| Reimherr et al. (1987) | 12 | Open | Tyrosine | 8 | 150 mg | Poor response, 4 dropouts | 14-day onset of action; tolerance developed |
| Shekim et al. (1989) | 8 | Open | Nomifensine maleate | 4 | < 300 mg | 18/18 responded, reduction in ADHD Sxs | Immediate response; one patient with allergic reaction |
| Shekim et al. (1990a) | 8 | Open | S-Adenosyl-L-methionine | 4 | <2400 mg | 75% of patients responded | Mild adverse effects |
| Wender & Reimherr (1990) | 19 | Open | Bupropion | 6–8 | 360 mg | Moderate response, 5 dropouts | 10 subjects with improvement at 1 year |
| Wilens et al. (1995) | 37 | Retrospective | Desipramine Nortriptyline | 50 | 183 mg 92 mg | 68% response rate, response sustained | Comorbidity unrelated to response, 60% on stimulants |
| Adler, et al. (1995) | 12 | Open | Venlafaxine | 8 | 110 mg | 10/12 responded | 4 subjects on other meds |
| Reimherr et al. (1995) | 20 | Open | Venlafaxine | | 109 mg | 8/12 responded | Side effects led to 40% dropout rate |
| Spencer et al. (1995) | 22 | Double-blind crossover | Tomoxetine | 7 | 76 mg | 52% response rate | Adrenergic agent, well tolerated |
| Findling et al. (1996) | 9 | Open | Venlafaxine | 8 | 150 mg | 7/9 responded, reduction in ADHD | Improved anxiety scores |
| Ernst et al. (1996) | 24 | Double-blind parallel | Selegeline | 6 | 20 & 60 mg | Mild improvement; 60-mg dose better | High placebo response, mild side effects |
| Wilens et al. (1996a) | 43 | Double blind parallel | Desipramine | 6 | 147 mg | 68% response rate | Comorbidity or levels not related to response |
| TOTAL | 287 | 4 controlled 10 open 2 retro-spective | Mixed | 2–50 | Moderate | Variable response | Side effects common, often loss of effect, inconsistent ADHD Dx |

Duration of medication trial includes placebo phase. Abbreviations: Sxs = symptoms, Dx = diagnosis.

*S*-adenosylmethionine and nomifensen have also been shown to be effective for ADHD in adults, although they remain unstudied under controlled conditions (Shekim, Masterson, Cantwell, Hanna, & McCracken, 1989; Shekim, Antun, Hanna, McCracken, & Hess, 1990a). GW320659 is a relatively short-acting noradrenergic/dopaminergic-reuptake inhibitor under study for ADHD in children and adolescents (Swanson et al., 2000; Deveaugh-Geiss, et al., 2000). Although it remains unstudied in adults with ADHD, Phase II trials demonstrated reductions of 20% in Conners Teachers Rating Scales and a half-life of 7 hours with linear pharmacokinetics.

## CLINICAL STRATEGIES FOR THE PHARMACOTHERAPY OF ADHD IN ADULTS

Basic clinical strategies for the pharmacotherapy of adults with ADHD include the following.

- Set clear, realistic treatment goals with the patient.
- Stimulants are the first-line medications.
- If the first stimulant is not effective or tolerated, consider an alternative stimulant.
- When comorbidites are present, prioritize treatment.
- Use additional therapies to support and complement the effects of medication.
- Use remedial services to support the patient in work and educational settings.

Once you have established the diagnosis of ADHD as the primary current problem, patients should be familiarized with the risks and benefits of pharmacotherapy, the availability of alternative treatments, the likelihood of adverse effects, as well as the prognosis both with and without medications. Patient expectations need to be explored and realistic goals of treatment defined. Likewise, the clinician should educate the patient that each medication trial requires adherence to the dosing regimen as well as using clinically meaningful doses of the medication for a reasonable duration of time. Patients with substantial psychiatric comorbidity, who have residual symptomatology with treatment, or who report psychological distress related to their ADHD (i.e., self-esteem issues, self-sabotaging patterns, interpersonal disturbances) should be directed to appropriate psychotherapeutic intervention with clinicians knowledgeable in ADHD treatment.

Stimulant medications are considered the first-line therapy for ADHD in adults (see Table 9.4). Given the high variability in effective dose, stimulants are typically started at low doses (e.g., Ritalin 5 mg, Concerta 18 mg, Metadate 10 mg, Adderall 5 mg, Dexedrine 5 mg) in the morning and gradually titrated up. Tolerance of the medication as well as the time of effect should be noted by the patient. It is often clinically helpful for the adult to ask for observations from significant others regarding the effects of the medication; however, if no one is available, data from the patients can be relied on (Murphy & Schachar, 2000). Decisions on how many doses a day and how many days of the week to take the medication should be tailored for each patient (Zametkin & Ernst, 1999). Consideration of another stimulant or class of agents is recommended if an ADHD adult is unresponsive or has intolerable side effects to the initial medication. The use of TCAs and bupropion can improve anti-ADHD response to the stimulants, whereas the SRI and other antidepressants can be used adjunctly for comorbid depression, anxiety, or obsessive-compulsive disorder. The effect of age, long-term adverse effects, and stimulant use in substance abusing subgroups of ADHD remains unstudied. Monitoring of routine side effects, vital signs, and the misuse of the medication is warranted.

The antidepressants, namely, TCAs and bupropion, are less well studied, appearing useful for stimulant nonresponders or adults with concurrent psychiatric disorders, including depression, anxiety, and active or recent substance abuse (Wender & Reimherr, 1990; Wilens et al., 1996a). Comparative data between the antidepressants and stimulants coupled with studies in children support that

**TABLE 9.4  Strategies in Difficult ADHD Cases**

| Symptoms | Interventions |
|---|---|
| Worsening or unchanged ADHD symptoms | Change medication dose (increase or decrease) |
| Inattention, impulsivity, hyperactivity | Change timing of dose<br>Change preparation, substitute stimulant<br>Evaluate for possible tolerance<br>Consider adjunctive treatment (antidepressant, alpha-adrenergic agent, cognitive enhancer)<br>Consider adjusting nonpharmacologic treatment (cogntiive/behavioral therapies or coaching or reevaluating neuropsychological profile for executive function capacities) |
| Intolerable side effects | Evaluate if side effect is drug induced<br>Assess medication response vs. tolerability of side effect<br>Aggressive management of side effect (change timing of dose; change preparation of stimulant; adjunctive or alternative treatment) |
| Symptoms of rebound | Change timing of dose<br>Supplement with small dose of short-acting stimulant or alpha-adrenergic agent 1 hour prior to symptom onset<br>Change preparation<br>Increase frequency of dosage |
| Development of tics or Tourettes Syndrome (TS), or use with comorbid tics or TS | Assess persistence of tics or TS<br>If tics abate, rechallenge<br>If tics are clearly worsened with stimulant treatment, discontinue<br>Consider stimulant use with adjunctive anti-tic treatment (haldol, pimozide) or use of alternative treatment (antidepressants, alpha-adrenergic agents) |
| Emergence of dysphoria, irritability, acceleration, agitation | Assess for toxicity or rebound<br>Evaluate development or exacerbation of comorbidity (mood, anxiety, and substance use, including nicotine and caffeine)<br>Reduce dose<br>Change stimulant preparation<br>Assess sleep and mood<br>Consider alternative treatment |
| Emergence of major depression, mood lability, or marked anxiety symptoms | Assess for toxicity or rebound<br>Evaluate development or exacerbation of comorbidity<br>Reduce or discontinue stimulant<br>Consider use of antidepressant or antimanic agent<br>Assess substance use<br>Consider nonpharmacologic interventions |
| Emergence of psychosis or mania | Discontinue stimulant<br>Assess comorbidity<br>Assess substance use<br>Treat psychosis or mania |

Adapted from Wilens & Spencer, 2000.

stimulants are generally more effective in reducing ADHD symptoms (Spencer et al., 1996). In addition, the response to the stimulants is rapid (Wood et al., 1976; Spencer et al., 1995), while antidepressants demonstrate improvement up to four weeks after titration (Wilens et al., 1996a). Although some adults may respond to relatively low doses of the TCAs (Ratey, Greenberg, Bemporad, & Lindem, 1992), the majority of adults appear to require solid antidepressant dosing of these agents (i.e., desipramine >150 mg daily). Selegiline, a short-acting MAO-B inhibitor used primarily for Parkinson's disease, has some potential benefit in adults with ADHD. Monoamine oxidase inhibitors are mildly effective and are generally reserved for treatment-refractory adults who can reliably follow the dietary requirements. The antihypertensives may be useful in adults with ADHD and aggressive outbursts (Mattes, 1986), tic disorders, impulse control disorders, or bipolar disorder or those with adverse effects to first- and second-line medications. The amino acids have not been shown effective, and the cholinergic-enhancing compounds remain to be studied comprehensively in ADHD adults.

## COMBINED PHARMACOTHERAPY

Although systematic data assessing the efficacy and safety profile of combining agents for ADHD in adults are lacking, empiric use of combination treatment may be necessary in those who have residual symptomatology with single agents or psychiatric comorbidity. For example, in a recent naturalistic report on TCAs for adults with ADHD, 84% of adults were receiving additional psychoactive medications, with 59% receiving adjunctive stimulants (Wilens et al., 1995b). These findings are similar to controlled data in juvenile ADHD, in which the combination of methylphenidate and desipramine improved the ADHD response more than either agent singly (Rapport, Carlson, Kelly, & Pataki, 1993). The use of methylphenidate conjointly with fluoxetine has been reported to be well tolerated and useful in improving depression in ADHD adolescents (Gammon & Brown, 1993) and appears useful in adults with the same comorbidity. In cases of partial response or adverse effects with stimulants, the addition of low-dose SRIs, TCAs, or beta-blockers has been reported to be helpful (Ratey et al., 1991; Gammon & Brown, 1993). While the stimulants appear to be well tolerated with TCAs and SRIs (Cohen et al., 1999), clinicians should consider potential drug interactions as have been described between TCAs and some SRIs (Aranow et al., 1989).

## Managing Suboptimal Responses

Despite the availability of various agents for adults with ADHD, there appears to be a number of individuals who either do not respond or are intolerant of the adverse effects of medications used to treat their ADHD. In managing difficult cases, several therapeutic strategies are available (Table 9.4). If adverse psychiatric effects develop concurrent with a poor medication response, alternate treatments should be pursued. Severe psychiatric symptoms that emerge during the acute phase can be problematic, irrespective of the efficacy of the medications for ADHD. These symptoms may require reconsideration of the diagnosis of ADHD and careful reassessment of the presence of comorbid disorders. For example, it is common to observe depressive symptoms in an ADHD adult that are independent of the ADHD or treatment. If reduction of dose or change in preparation (i.e., regular vs. slow-release stimulants) does not resolve the problem, consideration should be given to alternative treatments. Neuroleptic medications should be considered as part of the overall treatment plan in the face of comorbid bipolar disorder or extreme agitation. Concurrent nonpharmacologic interventions such as behavioral or cognitive therapy may assist with symptom reduction.

## Combining Psychotherapies with Medications

Although the efficacy of various psychotherapeutic interventions remains to be established, a retrospective assessment of adults with ADHD indicated that traditional insight-oriented psychotherapies were not helpful for ADHD adults (Ratey et al., 1992). A cognitive therapy protocol adapted for adults with ADHD has been developed (McDermott, 1999) that preliminary data suggest is effective when used with pharmacotherapy (Wilens, McDermott, Biederman, Abrantes, & Spencer, 1997b).

## SUMMARY

The aggregate literature supports the notion that pharmacotherapy provides an effective treatment for adults with ADHD. Effective pharmacological treatments for ADHD adults to date have included the use of the psychostimulants and antidepressants, with unclear efficacy of cognitive enhancers. Structured psychotherapy may be effective when used adjunctly with medications. Groups focused on coping skills, support, and interpersonal psychotherapy may also be very useful for these adults. For adults considering advanced schooling, educational planning and alterations in the school environment may be necessary. Further controlled investigations assessing the efficacy of single and combination agents for adults with ADHD are necessary, with careful attention to diagnostics, symptom and neuropsychological outcome, long-term tolerability and efficacy, and use in specific ADHD subgroups.

## REFERENCES

Adler, L. A., Resnick, S., Kunz, M., & Devinsky, O. (1995). Open label trial of venlafaxine in adults with attention deficit disorder. *Psychopharmacology Bulletin, 31,* 785–788.

American Psychiatric Association. (1994). *Diagnostic and statistical manual of mental disorders IV.* Washington, DC: American Psychiatric Association Press.

Aranow, R. B., Hudson, J. L., Pope, H. G., Grady, T. A., Laage, T. A., Bell, I. R., & Cole, J. O. (1989). Elevated antidepressant plasma levels after addition of fluoxetine. *American Journal of Psychiatry, 146,* 911–913.

Barkley, R. A. (1990). *Attention deficit hyperactivity disorder: A handbook for diagnosis and treatment.* New York: Guilford Press.

Barkley, R. A. (1997). *ADHD and the nature of self-control.* New York: Guilford Press.

Barkley, R. A. (1998). *Attention deficit hyperactivity disorder: A handbook for diagnosis and treatment* (2nd ed.). New York: Guilford Press.

Barkley, R. A., Murphy, K. R., DuPaul, G. J., & Bush, T. (in press). Driving knowledge, performance, and adverse outcomes in teens and young adults with attention deficit hyperactivity disorder.

Barkley, R. A., Murphy, K. R., & Kwasnik, D. (1996). Motor vehicle driving competencies and risks in teens and young adults with attention deficit hyperactivity disorder. *Pediatrics, 98,* 1089–1095.

Bauermeister, J. J., Canino, G., & Bird, H. (1994). Epidemiology of disruptive behavior disorders. In L. Greenhill (Ed.), *Child and adolescent psychiatric clinics of North America* (pp. 177–194). Philadelphia: W.B. Saunders.

Biederman, J. (1998). Attention-deficit/hyperactivity disorder: A life-span perspective. *Journal of Clinical Psychiatry, 59,* 1–11.

Biederman, J., Mick, E., & Faraone, S. V. (2000). Age-Dependent decline of symptoms of attention deficit hyperactivity disorder: impact of remission definition and symptom type. *American Journal of Psychiatry, 157(5),* 816–818.

Biederman, J., Faraone, S. V., Spencer, T., Wilens, T. E., Norman, D., Lapey, K. A., Mick, E., Lehman, B., & Doyle, A. (1993). Patterns of psychiatric comorbidity, cognition, and psychosocial functioning in adults with attention deficit hyperactivity disorder. *American Journal of Psychiatry, 150,* 1792–1798.

Biederman, J., Wilens, T., Mick, E., Milberger, S., Spencer, T., & Faraone, S. (1995). Psychoactive substance use disorder in adults with attention deficit hyperactivity disorder: Effects of ADHD and psychiatric comorbidity. *American Journal of Psychiatry, 152(11),* 1652–1658.

Brown, R. T. (1996). *Brown Attention Deficit Disorder Scales.* San Antonio, TX: The Psychological Corporation.

Brown, R. T., Wynne, M. E., & Slimmer, L. W. (1984). Attention deficit disorder and the effect of methylphenidate on attention, behavioral, and cardiovascular functioning. *Journal of Clinical Psychiatry, 45(11),* 473–476.

Casat, C. D., Pleasants, D. Z., & Fleet, J. V. W. (1987). A double-blind trial of bupropion in children with attention deficit disorder. *Psychopharmacology Bulletin, 23,* 120–122.

Cohen, L., Bierderman, J., Wilens, T., Spencer, T., Mick, E., Faraone, S., Prince, J., & Flood, J. (1999). Despramine clearance in children and adolescents: Absence of effect of development and gender. *Journal of the American Academy of Child & Adolescent Psychiatry, 38(1),* 79–85.

Conners, C. K., Epstein, J., & Erhardt, D. (2000). A new self-report rating scale for ADHD adults. In (Ed.), *Scientific Proceedings of the 47th Annual Meeting of the American Academy of Child and Adolescent Psychiatry* (p. 59). New York: American Academy of child & Adolescent Psychiatry.

Conners, C., Levin, E. D., Sparrow, E., Hinton, S., Erhardt, D., Meck, W., Rose, J., & March, J. (1996). Nicotine and attention in adult attention deficit hyperactivity disorder. *Psychopharmacology Bulletin, 32,* 67–73.

Cook, E. H., Stein, M. A., Krasowski, M. D., Cox, N. J., Olkon, D. M., Kieffer, J. E., & Leventhal, B. L. (1995). Association of attention-deficit disorder and the dopamine transporter gene. *American Journal of Human Genetics, 56,* 993–998.

Daly, G., Hawi, Z., Fitzgerald, M., & Gill, M. (1998). Attention deficit hyperactivity disorder: Association with the dopamine transporter (DAT1) but not with the dopamine D4 receptor (DRD4). *American Journal of Medical Genetics, Neuropsychiatric Genetics, 81,* 501.

DeFockert, J. W., Rees, G., Frith, C. D., and Lavie, N. (2001) The role of working memory in visual selective attention. *Science 291*(5509), 1803–1806.

Deveaugh-Geiss, J., Conners, C. K., Sarkis, E. "Efficacy of GW320659 in children with attention-deficit/hyper-activity disorder (ADHD)" Abstract p29, scientific proceedings of the 47th Annual meeting of the American Academy of Child and Adolescent Psychiatry. New York City, USA (2000).

DuPaul, G. (1990). *The ADHD Rating Scale: Normative data, reliability, and validity.* Unpublished manuscript, University of Massachusetts Medical Center, Worcester, MA.

Elia, J., Borcherding, B. G., Potter, W. Z., Mefford, I. N., Rapoport, J. L., & Keysor, C. S. (1990). Stimulant drug treatment of hyperactivity: Biochemical correlates. *Clinical Pharmacological Therapy, 48,* 57–66.

Ernst, M., Liebenauer, L., Jons, P., Tebeka, D., Cohen, R., & Zametkin, A. (1996). Selegiline in adults with attention deficit hyperactivity disorder: Clinical efficacy and safety. *Psychopharmacology Bulletin, 32,* 327–334.

Eyre, S. L., Rounsaville, B. J., & Kleber, H. D. (1982). History of childhood hyperactivity in a clinic population of opiate addicts. *Journal of Nervous and Mental Disorders, 170,* 522–529.

Faraone, S. V., Tsuang, D., & Tsuang, M. T. (1999). *Genetics and mental disorders: A guide for students, clinicians, and researchers.* New York: Guilford Press.

Faraone, S. V., Biederman, J., Chen, W. J., Krifcher, B., Keenan, K., Moore, C., Sprich, S., & Tsuang, M. T. (1992). Segregation analysis of attention deficit hyperactivity disorder. *Psychiatric Genetics, 2,* 257–275.

Faraone, S. V., Biederman, J., Weiffenbach, B., Keith, T., Chu, M. P., Weaver, A., Spencer, T., Wilens, T., Frazier, J., Sakai, J., & Cleves, M. (1999). The dopamine D4 gene—repeat allele is associated with attention deficit hyperactivity disorder in families ascertained through ADHD adults. *American Journal of Psychiatry, 156*(5), 768–770.

Findling, R. L., Schwartz, M. A., Flannery, D. J., & Manos, M. J. (1995). Venlafaxine in adults with attention-deficit / hyperactivity disorder: An open clinical trial. *Journal of Clinical Psychiatry, 57(5),* 184–189.

Gammon, G. D., & Brown, T. E. (1993). Fluoxetine and methylphenidate in combination for treatment of attention deficit disorder and comorbid depressive disorder. *Journal of Child and Adolescent Psychopharmacology, 3(1),* 1–10.

Gelenberg, A. J., Bassuk, E. L., & Schoonover, S. C. (1991). *The practioner's guide to psychoactive drugs* (3rd ed.). New York: Plenum Medical.

Greenhill, L. L., & Osman, B. B. (1999). *Ritalin: Theory and practice.* New York: Mary Ann Liebert.

Group, M. C. (1999). A 14-month randomized clinical trial of treatment strategies for attention-deficit/hyperactivity disorder. *Archives of General Psychiatry, 56,* 1073–1086.

Gualtieri, C. T., Hicks, R. E., Patrick, K., Schroeder, S. R., & Breese, G. R. (1984). Clinical correlates of methylphenidate blood levels. *Therapeutic Drug Monitoring, 6(4),* 379–392.

Gualtieri, C. T., Ondrusek, M. G., & Finley, C. (1985). Attention deficit disorder in adults. *Clinical Neuropharmacology, 8,* 343–356.

Hauser, P., Zametkin, A., Martinez, P., Vitiello, B., Matochik, J., Mixson, A., & Weintraub, B. (1993). Attention deficit-hyperactivity disorder in people with generalized resistance to thyroid hormone. *New England Journal of Medicine, 328(14),* 997–1001.

Heiligenstein, J. H., Spencer, T. J., Faries, D. E., Biederman, J., Kratochvil, C., & Conners, C. K. (2000). Efficacy of tomoxetine vs. placebo in pediatric outpatients with ADHD. *Scientific proceedings of the 47th Annual Meeting of American Academy of Child and Adolescent Psychiatry.* New York: American Academy of Child & Adolescent Psychiatry.

Hill, J., & Schoener, E. (1996). Age-dependent decline of attention-deficit hyperactivity disorder. *American Journal of Psychiatry, 153*(9), 1143–1147.

Horrigan, J. P., & Barnhill, L. J. (2000). Low-dose amphetamine salts and adult attention-deficit/hyperactivity disorder. *Journal of Clinical Psychiatry, 61,* 414–417.

Iaboni, F., Bouffard, R., Minde, K., & Hechtman, L. (1996). The efficacy of methylphenidate in treating adults with attention-deficit/hyperactivity disorder. *Scientific Proceedings* of the 43rd Annual Meeting of the American Academy of Child and Adolescent Psychiatry, Philadelphia, PA.

Iaboni, F., Bouffard. R., Minde, K. Hectman, L. "The efficacy of methylphenidate in treating adults with attention-deficit/hyper-activity disorder." *Proceedings from the 43rd Annual meeting of the American Academy of Child and Adolescent Psychiatry*, 1996, Philadelphia, PA.

Kelly, K. L., Rapport, M. D., & DuPaul, G. J. (1988). Attention deficit disorder and methylphenidate: A multi-step analysis of dose–response effects on children's cardiovascular functioning. *International Clinical Psychopharmacology, 3(2)*, 167–181.

Kishnani, P. S., Spiridigliozzi, G. A., & Heller, J. H. (2001). Donepezil for Down's Syndrome. *American Journal of Psychiatry, 158*, 143.

Krause, K. H., Dresel, S. H., Krausse, J., Kung, H. F., & Tatsch, K. (2000). Increased striatal dopamine transporter in adult patients with attention deficit hyperactivity disorder: Effects of methylphenidate as measured by single phot emission computed tomography. *Neuroscience letters, 285*, 107–110.

LaHoste, G., Swanson, J., Wigal, S., Glabe, C., Wigal, T., King, N., & Kennedy, J. (1996). Dopamine D4 receptor gene polymorphism is associated with attention deficit hyperactivity disorder. *Molecular Psychiatry, 1*, 121–124.

Langer, D. H., Sweeney, K. P., Bartenbach, D. E., Davis, P. M., & Menander, K. B. (1986). Evidence of lack of abuse or dependence following pemoline treatment: Results of a retrospective survey. *Drug and Alcohol Dependency, 17*, 213–227.

Laufer, M. W., Denhoff, E., & Solomons, G. (1957). Hyperkinetic impulse disorder in children's behavior problems. *Psychosomatic Medicine, XIX(1)*, 38–49.

Mannuzza, S., Klein, R. G., Bessler, A., Malloy, P., & LaPadula, M. (1993). Adult outcome of hyperactive boys: Educational achievement, occupational rank and psychiatric status. *Archives of General Psychiatry, 50*, 565–576.

Mattes, J. A. (1986). Propanolol for adults with temper outbursts and residual attention deficit disorder. *Journal of Clinical Psychopharmacology, 6*, 299–302.

Mattes, J. A., Boswell, L., & Oliver, H. (1984). Methylphenidate effects on symptoms of attention deficit disorder in adults. *Archives of General Psychiatry, 41*, 1059–1063.

McDermott, S. P. (1999). Cognitive therapy of attention deficit hyperactivity disorder in adults. *Journal of Cognitive Psychotherapy, 13(3)*, 215–226.

McGough, J. J., Greenhill, L., & Biederman, J. (2000). PK/PD analyses of SLI381 in pediatric AHD. In (Eds.) *Scientific Proceedings of the 47th Annual Meeting of the American Academy of Child and Adolescent Psychiatry*. New York: American Academy of Child & Adolescent Psychiatry.

Meck, W., & Church, R. (1987). Cholinergic modulation of the content of temporal memory. *Behavioral Neuroscience, 101(4)*, 457–464.

Milberger, S., Biederman, J., Faraone, S., Chen, L., & Jones, J. (1997). ADHD is associated with early initiation of cigarette smoking in children and adolescents. *Journal of the American Academy of Child and Adolescent Psychiatry, 36*, 37–43.

Millstein, R., Wilens, T., Biederman, J., & Spencer, T. (1997). Presenting ADHD symptoms and subtypes in clinically referred adults with ADHD. *Journal of Attention Disorders, 2(3)*, 159–166.

Murphy, K., & Barkley, R. A. (1996). Prevalence of DSM-IV symptoms of ADHD in adult licensed drivers: Implications for clinical diagnosis. *Journal of Attention Disorders, 1(3)*, 147–161.

Murphy, P., & Schachar, R. (2000). Use of self-ratings in the assessment of symptoms of attention deficit hyperactivity disorder in adults. *American Journal of Psychiatry, 157(7)*, 1156–1159.

Pliszka, S. R., L. L., G., Crimson, M. L., Sedillo, A., Carlson, C., Conners, C. K., McCracken, J. T., Swanson, J. M., Hughes, C. W., Llana, M. E., Lopez, M., & Toprac, M. G. (2000). The Texas children's medication alorithm project: Report of the Texas consensus conference panel on medication treatment of childhood attention-deficit/hyperactivity disorder. Part I. *Journal of the American Academy of Child and Adolescent Psychiatry, 39(7)*, 908–919.

Pomerleau, O., Downey, K., Stelson, F., & Pomerleau, C. (1995). Cigarette smoking in adult patients diagnosed with attention deficit hyperactivity disorder. *Journal of Substance Abuse, 7*, 373–378.

Quist, J. F., & Kennedy, J. L. (2001). Genetics of childhood disorders: XXIII. ADHD, part 7: The serotonin system. *Journal of the American Academy of Child and Adolescent Psychiatry, 40(2)*, 253–256.

Rapport, M. D., Carlson, G. A., Kelly, K. L., & Pataki, C. (1993). Methylphenidate and desipramine in hospitalized children: I. Separate and combined effects on cognitive function. *Journal of the American Academy of Child and Adolescent Psychiatry, 32*, 333–342.

Ratey, J. J., Greenberg, M. S., Bemporad, J. R., & Lindem, K. J. (1992). Unrecognized attention-deficit hyperactivity disorder in adults presenting for outpatient psychotherapy. *Journal of Child and Adolescent Psychopharmacology, 2(4)*, 267–275.

Ratey, J. J., Greenberg, M. S., & Lindem, K. J. (1991). Combination of treatments for attention deficit disorders in adults. *Journal of Nervous and Mental Disease, 176*, 699–701.

Reimherr, F. W., Hedges, D. W., Strong, R. E., & Wender, P. H. (1995). An open trial of venlafaxine in adult patients with attention deficit hyperactivity disorder. In (Eds.), *New clinical drug evaluation unit program 35th annual meeting* (pp. poster no. 81). Orlando, FL: American Academy of Child & Adolescent Psychiatry.

Reimherr, F. W., Wender, P. H., Wood, D. R., & Ward, M. (1987). An open trial of L-tyrosine in the treatment of attention deficit hyperactivity disorder, residual type. *American Journal of Psychiatry, 144*, 1071–1073.

Seidman, L. J., Biederman, J., Weber, W., Hatch, M., & Faraone, S. (1998). Neuropsychological functioning in adults with attention-deficit hyperactivity disorder. *Biological Psychiatry, 44(4)*, 260–268.

Shaffer, D. (1994). Attention deficit hyperactivity disorder in adults. *American Journal of Psychiatry, 151(5)*, 633–638.

Shekim, W. O., Antun, F., Hanna, G. L., McCracken, J. T., & Hess, E. B. (1990a). S-Adenosyl-L-methionine (SAM) in adults with ADHD, RS: Preliminary results from an open trial. *Psychopharmacology Bulletin, 26*, 249–253.

Shekim, W. O., Asarnow, R. F., Hess, E., Zaucha, K., & Wheeler, N. (1990b). A clinical and demographic profile of a sample of adults with attention deficit hyperactivity disorder, residual state. *Comprehensive Psychiatry, 31*, 416–425.

Shekim, W. O., Masterson, A., Cantwell, D. P., Hanna, G. L., & McCracken, J. T. (1989). Nomifensine maleate in adult attention deficit disorder. *Journal of Nervous and Mental Disease, 177*, 296–299.

Spencer, T., Biederman, J., Wilens, T., & Faraone, S. (1998a). Adults with attention deficit hyperactivity disorder: A controversial diagnosis. *Journal of Clinical Psychiatry, 59*(Suppl. 7), 59–68.

Spencer, T., Biederman, J., Wilens, T. E., Faraone, S. V., & Li, T. (1994). Is attention deficit hyperactivity disorder in adults a valid diagnosis? *Harvard Review of Psychiatry, 1*, 326–335.

Spencer, T., Wilens, T. E., Biederman, J., Faraone, S. V., Ablon, S., & Lapey, K. (1995). A double blind, crossover comparison of methylphenidate and placebo in adults with childhood-onset attention deficit hyperactivity disorder. *Archives of General Psychiatry, 52*, 434–443.

Spencer, T., Biederman, J., Wilens, T., Harding, M., O'Donnell, D., & Griffin, S. (1996). Pharmacotherapy of attention deficit disorder across the life cycle. *Journal of the American Academy of Child and Adolescent Psychiatry, 35(4)*, 409–432.

Spencer, T., Biederman, J., Wilens, T., Prince, J., Hatch, M., Jones, H., Harding, M., Faraone, S., & Seidman, L. (1998b). Effectiveness and tolerability of tomoxetine in adults with attention deficit hyperactivity disorder. *American Journal of Psychiatry, 155(5)*, 693–695.

Spencer, T., Biederman, J., Wilens, T., Prince, J., Girard, K., Parekh, A., Doyle, R., Kagan, J., & Bearman, S. K. (1999a). Efficacy and tolerability of adderall in adults with ADHD. *Scientific Proceedings of the American Academy of Child and Adolescent Psychiatry*. (Eds.), Chicago: American Academy of Child & Adolescent Psychiatry.

Spencer, T., Wilens, T., Biederman, J., et al. (1999b). Effectiveness and tolerability of Adderall for ADHD in adults. *Scientific proceedings of the American Psychiatric Association* pp. 101–141. Washington, DC: The association.

Swanson, J. M., Flodman, P., & Kennedy, J. (2000). Dopamine genes and ADHD. *Neuroscience Biobehavioral Review, 24*, 21–25.

Tarter, R. E., McBride, H., Buonpane, N., & Schneider, D. U. (1977). Differentiation of alcoholics. *Archives of General Psychiatry, 34*, 761–768.

Taylor, E., Schachar, R., Thorley, G., Wieselberg, H. M., Everitt, B., & Rutter, M. (1987). Which boys respond to stimulant medication? A controlled trial of methylphenidate in boys with disruptive behaviour. *Psychological Medicine, 17*, 121–143.

Waldman, I. D., Rowe, D. C., Abramowitz, A., Kozel, S. T., Mohr, J. H., Sherman, S. L., Cleveland, H. H., Sanders, M. L., Gard, J. M., & Stever, C. (1998). Association and linkage of the dopamine transporter gene and attention-deficit hyperactivity disorder in children: Heterogeneity owing to diagnostic subtype and severity. *American Journal of Human Genetics, 63(6)*, 1767–76.

Ward, M. F., Wender, P. H., & Reimherr, F. W. (1993). The Wender Utah Rating Scale: An aid in the retrospective diagnosis of childhood attention deficit hyperactivity disorder. *American Journal of Psychiatry, 150*, 885–890.

Weiss, G., & Hechtman, L. T. (1986). *Hyperactive children grown up*. New York: Guilford Press.

Wender, P. H., & Reimherr, F. W. (1990). Bupropion treatment of attention deficit hyperactivity disorder in adults. *American Journal of Psychiatry, 147*, 1018–1020.

Wender, P. H., Reimherr, F. W., & Wood, D. R. (1981). Attention deficit disorder ("minimal brain dysfunction") in adults: A replication study of diagnosis and drug treatment. *Archives of General Psychiatry, 38*, 449–456.

Wender, P. H., Reimherr, F. W., Wood, D., & Ward, M. (1985a). A controlled study of methylphenidate in the treatment of attention deficit disorder, residual type, in adults. *American Journal of Psychiatry, 142*, 547–552.

Wender, P. H., Wood, D. R., & Reimherr, F. W. (1985). Pharmacological treatment of attention deficit disorder residual type (ADD, RT, "minimal brain dysfunction," "hyperactivity") in adults. *Psychopharmacology Bulletin, 21*, 222–230.

Wender, P. H., Wood, D. R., Reimherr, F. W., & Ward, M. (1983). An open trial of pargyline in the treatment of attention deficit disorder, residual type. *Psychiatry Research, 9*, 329–336.

Wender, P., Reimherr, F., Czajkowski, L., Sanford, E., Rogers, A., Gardner, L., & Eden, J. (1995). A long-term trial of methlphenidate in the treatment of ADHD adults: A placebo-controlled trial and six-month follow-up. Journal of the American College of Neuropharmacology 21, 209–228. Puerto Rico:

Werry, J. S., & Aman, M. G. (1975). Methylphenidate and haloperidol in children. *Archives of General Psychiatry, 32*, 790–795.

Whelan, F. J., Walker, M. S., & Schultz, S. K. (2000). Donepezil in the treatment of cognitive dysfunction with traumatic brain injury. *Annals of Clinical Psychiatry, 12,* 131–135.

Wilens, T. E., & Biederman, J. (1992). The stimulants. In D. Shafer (Eds.), *The psychiatric clinics of North America* (pp. 191–222). Philadelphia: W.B. Saunders.

Wilens, T. E., Biederman, J., Mick, E., & Spencer, T. (1995b). A systematic assessment of tricyclic antidepressants in the treatment of adult attention-deficit hyperactivity disorder. *Journal of Nervous and Mental Disease, 184,* 48–50.

Wilens, T. E., Biederman, J., Wong, J., Spencer, T. J., & Prince, J. B. (2000). Adjunctive donepezil in attention deficit hyperactivity disorder in youth: Case series. *Journal of Child and Adolescent Psychopharmacology, 10,* 217–222.

Wilens, T., McDermott, S., Biederman, J., Abrantes, A., & Spencer, T. (1997b). Combined cognitive therapy and pharmacotherapy for adults with attention deficit hyperactivity disorder: A systematic chart review of 26 cases. Manuscript submitted for publication.

Wilens, T., & Spencer, T. (1998). Pharmacology of amphetamines. In R. Tarter, R. Ammerman, & P. Ott (Eds.), *Handbook of substance abuse: Neurobehavioral pharmacology* (pp. 501–513). New York: Plenum Press.

Wilens, T. E., & Spencer, T. J. (2000). The stimulants revisited. *Child and Adolescent Psychiatric Clinics of North America, 9(3),* 573–603.

Wilens, T., Spencer, T., & Biederman, J. (1995a). Are attention-deficit hyperactivity disorder and the psychoactive substance use disorders really related? *Harvard Review of Psychiatry, 3,* 260–262.

Wilens, T., Biederman, J., Prince, J., Spencer, T., Schleifer, D., Harding, M., Linehan, C., & Hatch, M. (1996a). A double blind, placebo controlled trial of desipramine for adults with ADHD. *American Journal of Psychiatry, 153,* 1147–1153.

Wilens, T., Frazier, J., Prince, J., Spencer, T., Bostic, J., Hatch, M., Abrantes, A., Sienna, M., Soriano, J., Millstein, R., & Biederman, J. (1996b). A double-blind comparison of pemoline in adults with ADHD: Preliminary results. *Scientific proceedings of the American Academy of Child and Adolescent Psychiatry* (p. 121).

Wilens, T., Frazier, J., Prince, J., Spencer, T., Bostic, J., Hatch, M., Abrantes, A., Sienna, M., Soriano, J., Millstein, R., & Biederman, J. (1997a). A double-blind comparison of pemoline in adults with ADHD. *Paper presented at the American Academy of Child and Adolescent Psychiatry Annual Meeting.* Toronto, Canada.

Wood, D., Reimherr, J., & Wender, P.H. (1982). Effects of levadopa on attention deficit disorder, residual type. *Psychiatry Research, 6,* 13–20.

Wood, D. R., Reimherr, F. W., & Wender, P. H. (1985). The treatment of attention deficit disorder with D,L- phenylalanine. *Psychiatry Research, 16,* 21–26.

Wood, D. R., Reimherr, F. W., Wender, P. H., & Johnson, G. E. (1976). Diagnosis and treatment of minimal brain dysfunction in adults. *Archives of General Psychiatry, 33,* 1453–1460.

Wood, D., Wender, P. H., & Reimherr, F. W. (1983). The prevalence of attention deficit disorder, residual type, or minimal brain dysfunction, in a population of male alcoholic patients. *American Journal of Psychiatry, 140,* 95–98.

Zametkin, A. J., & Ernst, M. (1999). Problems in the management of attention deficit hyperactivity disorder. *New England Journal of Medicine, 340(1),* 40–46.

Zametkin, A. J., & Liotta, W. (1998). The neurobiology of attention-deficit/hyperactivity disorder. *Journal of Clinical Psychiatry, 59*(Suppl. 7), 17–23.

Zametkin, A. J., & Rapoport, J. L. (1987). Neurobiology of attention deficit disorder with hyperactivity: Where have we come in 50 years? *Journal of the American Academy of Child and Adolescent Psychiatry, 26,* 676–686.

# 10

# Career Impact:

# Finding the Key to Issues Facing Adults with ADHD

Rob Crawford, M.Ed., Veronica Crawford, M.A.

## INTRODUCTION

Perhaps it is best said up front that *everyone* struggles with trying to make the correct decision on what kind of career is "right" for them. However, there is a difference between those who struggle and eventually find their way into the light and those who struggle and seem to stumble endlessly through the night. There is a quote that identifies quite well the reason so many individuals with hidden disabilities seem to struggle more than necessary: "We never know how high we are till we are called to rise and then, if we are true to plan, our statures touch the skies" (Dickenson, 1870).

If one thinks about this statement in relationship to individuals who have hidden disabilities such as attention deficit hyperactive disorder (ADHD), it becomes clear where the complications begin. If one has not had opportunities to "be called" or if past experiences have not been positive, self-esteem may be low. When low self-esteem is combined with a lack of a clear picture of what can realistically be achieved, individuals with ADHD may not easily recognize opportunities when they arise.

To be able to be called on, each of us has to know what we can do, to understand what constitutes our strengths and weaknesses, and to relate these to the real world. Over the years, our work with adolescents and adults with ADHD and related disabilities has allowed us to see patterns of difficulties, many of which are avoidable and predictable. In this chapter, we outline some strategies that will assist the clinician to: (1) understand aspects of the therapeutic process involved in job development and career planning for individuals with ADHD; and (2) assume the role of advisor, mentor, and guide for individuals who are seeking to find their place in the world of work.

## BARRIERS TO REALISTIC CAREER DECISION MAKING

Developing meaningful clinical and practical insight into what happens to adults with hidden disabilities is something that must be considered as a work in progress. Much of what will be discussed is taken from research and practice. Although these issues have not been adequately explored in adults with ADHD on individuals with learning disabilities (LD), much of the literature referring to LD in the workplace is relevant to adults with ADHD concerns (Nadeau, 1995). Individuals with LD, ADHD, and related hidden disabilities express similar concerns, frustrations, and workplace difficulties.

In essence, the very issues associated with career planning and job development for adults with ADHD are the same core issues for adults with LD (Nadeau, 1995). Some of these areas adversely impacting employment success are most often due to the lack of understanding supervisors or coworkers expectations, choosing an inappropriate career, and lacking the sense of self-competence to deal with these predicaments that challenge adults with ADHD in the workplace.

Self-esteem is a critical part of one's ability to make informed and realistic life choices. Recent literature studying successful adjustment in adults with LD with other, comorbid conditions showed that healthy self-esteem is based on self-confidence derived from personal mastery, the experience of having been able to undertake and accomplish personally chosen tasks (Wren & Einhorn, 2000). Individuals with hidden disabilities frequently have difficulty developing healthy self-esteem because of the daily frustrations they often face.

Many struggle with self-blame and are overcome with guilt. Oftentimes, they misunderstand the basis of their difficulties, which results in immature, passive-aggressive, or self-defeating patterns of problem-solving strategies (Nadeau, 1995). Difficulties additional to the disability may contribute to adjustment problems in the workplace—specifically low self-esteem. Further, Wren and Einhorn (2000) suggest that "pathological" self-esteem is self-esteem as an end in itself. They contend that pathological self-esteem occurs when people try to make children feel good about apart from their accomplishments or behaviors. This pattern, starting in early life, can ultimately interfere with healthy self-esteem development in adults with disabilities.

Although family members, teachers, and counselors may be well intended and supportive, there is a careful balance as to what information is provided to developing children so that they can develop an accurate sense of who they are as human beings. In other words, even though people have disabilities, it is unnecessary to "protect them from reality," because the outcome when they enter adulthood will be far too demoralizing. Professionals often see this sort of outcome, where adults suffer because they have not developed an accurate sense of who they are as human beings. The therapeutic process needs to start here so that the career-decision-making process is realistic and has a chance for success.

The following discussion focuses on a variety of problems the therapist might see in clients seeking career counseling. Although clients with ADHD may present with these difficulties, adults with various other disorders may have similar issues.

## No Awareness of Weaknesses

This means a lack awareness and possibly not understanding that "healthy human balance" entails the notion that everyone has a weakness. The next step in therapy is to understand how these weaknesses impact occupational or career adjustment, to develop coping strategies, and to work on improving or bypassing relevant weaknesses that can't be changed. Without this type of selective process, clients may pursue unrealistic career goals or focus exclusively on jobs they consider respectable, that pay well, or that are "fun."

## Unwillingness to See Weaknesses

An unwillingness to see weaknesses may be an attempt to protect from the devastating notion that "I'm not good at anything." Denial of weakness may set in and may lead to unrealistic career goals. Or worse, the individuals may be choosing a career because they are fearful someone will identify their weaknesses. These clients may choose careers that are less challenging than they can handle.

## Perseveration

Some clients may perseverate, get fixated, or appear to make connections with everything. Career decision making in these situations becomes complicated, and anxiety can be high. In this instance, it may be too cumbersome for clients to look at their strengths, weaknesses, interests, and values. These individuals may be unable to stay on task, complete assignments, or persevere with decisions they make regarding careers.

## Dependency

Clients may become overly dependent on family members when they have been overprotected or have not had many autonomy experiences. Career decisions may be difficult for these individuals, and family members may stay overinvolved. Fear of making the wrong decisions may persist. The therapist may address these fears and help the client make more autonomous decisions.

## Egocentricity

Some clients may appear egocentric. Feelings of inadequacy may be at the root. Clients may need lots of reassurance to develop a more positive self-image. Becoming more aware of this balance between strengths and weaknesses, without destroying safety nets, may decrease egocentric thinking. Other strategies for reconciling egocentric behaviors are presented later in the chapter.

## Insecurity

Clients who feel insecure and lack confidence in their decision-making abilities will need support from the therapist. Informed career decision-making can be nurtured with a compassionate, involved therapist. More directive techniques may be helpful here, and clients who feel insecure may be quite successful when matched with a job developer. Paraprofessionals may be used to assist the client in gathering information about career options and when "trying on" new roles or job identities.

## Lack of Awareness

These clients have not been exposed to "choices." Most of them don't even realize they have other choices. These clients do very well when they are shown they have skills that transfer to the job and are provided examples of how those skills can be cross-utilized in other careers.

## Perfectionism

Working with a perfectionist can be very trying. Adults with ADHD who have perfectionist tendencies are generally never satisfied with how things are being handled, either by the therapist or themselves. They often overlook their accomplishments or strengths, and focus on weaknesses, inconsistencies, or failures. In many instances, they need permission to be human—to be less than perfect. Perfectionistic individuals may need high levels of structure and may respond best when methods for selecting a career are made explicit. Written-down career options, career goals, and ways to measure satisfaction or success are generally helpful. Written plans may help perfectionistic clients with ADHD visualize their options and feel more in control of the process, and may assist them in monitoring their progress in meeting career goals. The written plan may need to include strategies for attending to successes as well as setbacks.

## STARTING OUT WITH A REALISTIC PICTURE

By addressing these general behaviors and personality traits, the therapist sets the stage for career counseling. In many instances, adults with ADHD and/or LD don't fully understand their own unique processing strengths and deficits. This lack of awareness may lead to over- or underestimating one's talents and one's ability to perform satisfactorily in a particular job (Wren & Einhorn, 2000). Clinicians can help their clients by investigating these issues in a supportive therapeutic environment prior to the onset of community-based career exploration. By helping the adult with ADHD become more aware of how the disorder affects the world of work represents an important initial step. A careful review of background history will assist in developing a realistic picture.

Hidden disabilities like ADHD may pose extreme career challenges on a daily basis. Gerber and Reiff (1994) found that many adults with LD did not benefit from counseling and vocational guidance because of unrealistic goals that were set too high. The authors hypothesize that a lack of trial-and-error experiences in childhood places individuals with disabilities at risk. Two types of experiences appear salient: (1) overprotection in childhood; (2) repeated failures that were demoralizing. In the latter instance, individuals did not experience failure as a temporary condition, as a necessary part of the learning curve.

We are not suggesting that the therapist should further demoralize the client by "bursting the bubble." We are suggesting that to be successful, career counseling must include a realistic picture of what a job entails, what abilities are needed, and the overall job requirements, such as occupational training and skills (Gerber & Reiff, 1994). With a realistic picture in place, the adult with ADHD can begin to see whether the career is a good personal fit or a mismatch.

The following is an example of unrealistic decision making in a young man named Joe. Joe wants to go to college, and the reason is that the rest of his family went to college. His family members are doctors, lawyers, college professors, and business professionals. Joe didn't want to go to just any college, but only to the right university. In order to measure up to his family, Harvard and Yale universities were on his short list. If he had to go a state college, then the University of California at Berkeley was his only pick. After all, he reflected, he had to be realistic, and he might not be able to get into other schools. Joe had been encouraged throughout his lifetime and was constantly told he could do anything he wanted if he would just put his mind to it.

Despite having borderline intellectual functioning and ADHD (inattentive type), Joe was not aware of how his strengths and weaknesses matched his college goals. He did not have a good sense of what was required from highly competitive universities, and he did not have a backup plan if he was unsuccessful.

In this instance, a therapist could assist Joe by exploring his functional assets and matching these to his goals. The following questions could be used to help him make a more informed decision: What is required to be admitted to Harvard or Yale? Do my grades and test scores meet the minimum requirements? What course of study would I pursue? What careers are related to my program of study? What prerequisite academic skills do I need? Is this what I really want to do, or do I feel pressure to live up to someone else's expectations? This process does not preclude Joe from pursuing a college education, but it does help him get a better match because he now has a more realistic picture of himself. In this situation, he might select an alternative education setting that might give him a sense of ownership and pride of accomplishment.

Some clients decide that because their mother or father is in a particular profession, they should follow the same path. Little or no consideration may be given to environmental factors, the occupational demands of the job, interpersonal skills that are needed, technology requirements, and workplace factors that constitute career viability. Let's assume for a moment that a client named Jane comes to you for appropriate career counseling. Jane has a diagnosis of ADHD (primarily hyperactive type). Jane is gifted mathematically and demonstrates an amazing capacity to understand computer software applications without needing to read a manual. She seems to be a perfect candidate for college. Jane gets her degree in accounting, believing that one day she will take over the family accounting firm. Jane shares with the clinician that she finds it hard to sit in one place for any length of time, and hates to go over documents that take any longer than 10 minutes to review.

A background check of Jane's college record reveals that she was successful when using allowed reasonable accommodations and medication for inattention. Jane spent so much extra time trying to finish her college education that there was no time left over to work part time. Besides, why should she need to work? She would soon be a partner in the family business, as everyone had planned her whole life. Jane comes to see you, anticipating great things will happen immediately, but she quickly realizes the unanticipated obstacles to her goals. The kind of career she has selected forces her to do just what is most difficult for her to achieve: sustain concentration, sit for extended periods of time, and review numerous lengthy legal documents. Jane and her family are taken completely by surprise They had not anticipated this mismatch and were at a loss to explain why she was having difficulties and performance failures.

Clients with job problems are often poorly matched for their jobs. They rarely fail because of incompetence or poor ability. In fact, most have great strengths and high potential if they find the right job that maximizes their personal assets (Nadeau, 1995). It is essential when young people begin to explore career options, especially those with ADHD and other hidden disabilities, that they be carefully guided along the way. Making informed decisions that are based on their capabilities, interests, and values and their sustainability to do what is required both in preparing for and working in the chosen field is crucial to success.

There are ample reasons someone with ADHD may make unrealistic career decisions beyond jumping into something because someone else is doing it. Most of the clients we have served either want to go into careers that are well below their capabilities, or they seek careers that are highly unachievable. Here are some of the comments that clients with both LD and ADHD repeatedly state in sessions:

I can do anything I want—I just don't want to.
My parents have money, so I really don't need to worry.
I'm still young—I don't really need to make up my mind until I am 30.
Lots of people change careers many times—if I don't like this one, I'll just switch.
So what if I had trouble in high school? Things are different now—I just didn't try.
ADHD goes away when people become adults—this won't impact my career.
I believe the right job is out there. No need to worry—it will find me eventually.
I should just follow my dreams—do what I love and the rest will fall into place.
The most creative people in the world have ADHD. Look out world, here I come!
There are thousands of jobs out there—I'll just get the one that pays top dollar.
I'm going to go to college—get a degree and then go to work and do something neat.
My parents do great, and they didn't get any education or training.
I saw a job sign on a telephone poll: "Work from home, earn up to $5000 per week." I am going to be in demand in a few years because of all my diverse experience.
I want to have lots of different jobs so I can decide which is best for me.
So what if I have been fired from ten jobs this year? It was their fault, not mine.
Look, I have ADHD—employers need to understand I don't do well in the morning.
I can't do any other type of work—it's too hard to learn new skills.
Go to school? No way! My experience with school in the past has been horrible.
No one can tell me what to do—they aren't me. how do they know what I need?

Though some of these examples appear humorous, what frequently lays behind these statements are themes of inadequacy, fear, frustration, confusion, and sadness. Realistically speaking, most of these clients have a great desire to be successful at something they will enjoy. Unfortunately, they mask or hide these desires because they have been repeatedly hurt by real or imagined failure, or have not had enough practical experience in life to know what it takes to succeed in the long run.

## REFRAMING AND INVOLVEMENT

There are some steps that can make the difference in what is done to prepare adolescents and adults for making well-thought-out career decisions. Strategic planning and directed action can begin in the school and home environments. One effective method contributing to successful planning is to work on reframing the minds of these young people. Vogel and Reder (1998) contends that career goodness-of-fit (i.e., choosing employment that maximizes strengths and minimizes weaknesses) correlates directly with self-understanding and awareness.

Reframing is the initial critical step to helping young people understand themselves. Doing so helps them to become clearer about what they want out of life and how to get there. The process of reframing is especially applicable to those with disabilities. Gerber and Reiff (1994) suggest that it is necessary to:

1. Recognize the disability. Its impossible to overcome a disability unless it is recognized.
2. Accept the condition—both negative and positive ramifications of the disability.
3. Understand the situation—the disability and all its implications.
4. Act. All recognition, acceptance, and understanding in the world is irrelevant without consciously deciding to take specific action toward goals.

Professionals must begin to pull the pieces of the disability puzzle together for these young people. First, stress efforts to understand oneself as a total person (including that part of oneself that has a disability). The intent is to make sure that individuals do not view or define themselves only from a disability or disorder perspective. Simply providing a diagnosis is not enough and will actually harm clients if they do not understand the implications of those symptoms and are not provided with strategies on how to self-manage or, in extreme cases, how and when to ask for reasonable accommodations. Inaccurate and unhealthy notions about future prospects should be reframed in a more positive and hopeful light so that patients can begin to rebuild their self-esteem and believe successful treatment is possible (Nadeau, 1995).

Reframing can also help in the process of career decision making. In order to realize its full value as a practiced tool, reframing preparation should begin during the formal educational years, commencing no later than age 14. Too often clinicians see clients who are unprepared or who lack knowledge about how to identify or discuss their desires, needs, and goals as adults. They have not been given opportunities or practice in becoming self-determined (advocating for themselves). For a successful transition into adulthood, communication and life planning responsibilities should be done at the beginning of high school to better prepare for the variety of adult issues they will face.

Typical adult communication requirements, such as problem ownership, is a basic requirement for competent decision making. Effective problem-solving skills give students a positive presence or enable them to learn how to cope, to effectively advocate for themselves, and to negotiate in a non-confrontational manner when they do eventually go to work. Rehearsing and practicing social skills usually increases the likelihood that students will experience social acceptance on the job.

Students who can participate in team building enhance their ability to gather support for a career from other people and resources in a school-based ecosystem (peers, family, community, teachers, etc.) and transfer them into an adult ecosystem (peers, family, coworkers, employers, community, rehab professionals, etc.). Implementing ecosystematic interventions early and routinely diminishes the need for ongoing support, with the services of external trainers and advocates eventually fading out (Rusch & Chadsey, 1998). In summary, these prerequisite skills must be developed for clients to have a more self-assured and realistic view of their future. Without this type of involvement in school and family settings, they find themselves unprepared for making informed and independent decisions about their futures. The desire to succeed fuels the engine, and goal orientation sets the direction. But a practiced ability to reframe experience ultimately empowers individuals to utilize behaviors that will determine successful employment outcomes (Vogel and Reder, 1998). Those who have had these experiences are more aware and informed and have fewer difficulties in achieving their goals.

## CLIENT INVOLVEMENT AND DEVELOPING SELF-DETERMINATION

The concepts of self-determination and becoming self-determined are not new. It is a critical component of treatment plans in the disability field. Structured opportunities, plans, lessons, or experiences with self-determination are essential. Older adolescents or adults who demonstrate self-determination skills usually have had experiences in advocating for themselves, such as participating in individualized education plan (IEP) meetings, discussions with teachers and counselors, and securing their own employment or volunteer experiences in high school.

In reviewing the literature regarding techniques leading to enhanced self-determination, it is clear that educators and individuals with disabilities must become partners, both having important roles to play (Field, Hoffman, St. Peter, & Sawilowsky, 1992). Self-determined individuals are not as likely to be overprotected by their families. Insulating and shielding children all too frequently leads to fostering dependency later in life. Young adults don't need to learn to determine their own future, because everyone else (e.g., family) is in charge of his or her life decisions.

Instead, if children are to become self-determined adults, the family must allow the children to make mistakes so they can learn from them, allow them to be involved in decisions about themselves. The family can act as a guide to children, gradually giving them a bigger part in advocating for themselves as they mature. Self-awareness offers a sure rudder for keeping career decisions in harmony with an individual's deepest values (Goleman, 1998).

Over the years, an adult with ADHD can begin to understand and accept himself because of these experiences. In short, what is done for a child with hidden disabilities should be the same as for any other child—every person is going to experience difficulties, it is the natural order of life. Everyone involved with this individual should be helping her to become independent, and although additional difficulties mitigated by the condition will arise, making the individual with ADHD an active part of solving those problems is the key to success.

Many adults exiting therapy or career counseling lack the basic skills of self-determination when starting treatment. There are many ways in which a person can become self-determined. If the client is to learn how to apply these skills to the adult world, specifically in making an informed career decision, several things need to occur. One particularly useful model for setting up a system of self-determination skills for adults with ADHD is posited by Campeau and Wolman (1993), Field, Hoffman, St. Peter, and Sawilowsky (1992), Halpern (1993), and Mithaug (1991). These can be combined with earlier action steps on reframing, and include six major steps:

1. The individual identifies and expresses his or her own needs and interests.

2. The individual sets expectations and goals to meet his or her needs and interests.
3. The individual makes choices and plans to meet goals and expectations.
4. The individual takes action to complete plans.
5. The individual evaluates results of actions.
6. The individual adjusts plans and actions until the goal is achieved.

These six steps can be integrated into educational, family, community, and rehabilitation areas. Developing program and therapeutic consistency is critical for the individual, who will need to receive similar messages from all areas. Developing expectations and timeliness, with client input, allows the individual to feel empowered and in charge of setting the therapeutic/life direction.

According to Gerber and Reiff (1994), the extent to which adults with LD shape their own lives, within their interests and capacities, seems to figure prominently in their overall resilience. This resilience develops only when adults feel they can help themselves or know who to go to when they need help. Without these skills, the individuals may give excuses, try to lie to protect themselves, and appear to be "unmotivated."

If the primary treatment objective is to help create personal consistency and promote increased involvement from clients, professionals must provide them project-specific information as reference points to work from. It is best if there are specific tasks associated with each stage of information processing. An example of this type of staging is to provide objective sources of information regarding what skills are sought by employers. Exploring the natural application of these skills and how to build them into education, training, work, family, and rehabilitation models will reinforce the competency messages.

An excellent starting point is to use the resources developed by the U.S. Department of Labor's (1992) *Secretary's Commission on Achieving Necessary Skills* (SCANS); "Learning a Living, A Blueprint for High Performance." These materials list the competencies and skills needed by *all* workers and define the know-how and application of the concepts to workplace issues that are likely to arise.

The professional, mentor, therapist, or counselor plays an important role in the process of helping the client to become more self-determined. The therapist and client could work together to: investigate and understand the client's background (e.g., school records, work experience); identify the presenting problems (e.g., unproductive behaviors and attitudes); specify and understand the employer-identified career skills needed for the job; and investigate the SCANS blueprint.

## THE ROLE OF THE PROFESSIONAL AS MENTOR AND FACILITATOR

Career counselors work to help a person select a career choice based on multiple vocational, personality, and academic evaluations. For average persons, an array of assessment data can be very useful, because they can independently take the information, explore it, and make a decision on their own if they wish to pursue it.

The most effective methods for adults with ADHD are those that integrate a number of professionals who can help the clients make an informed decision. The usual role of a career counselor involves an evaluation of: (1) interests, (2) strengths and skills, (3) temperament and personality type, and (4) values and needs. This information helps to guide the individual to a better sense of "career self" (Nadeau, 1995). When the career counselor focuses on these areas alone, issues surrounding the disability and the functional impact it might have on work performance are often ignored.

Therapists need to be familiar with the community resources that are available for remedial compensatory education, because the cognitive organizers used in therapy may not be sufficient (Gerber & Reiff, 1994). For example, a counselor is working with a 25-year-old male who has recently been diagnosed with ADHD (inattentive type). The counselor asks questions to determine the type of career he is considering. It is likely that the client with ADHD may not have a good sense about career options, so career education may be a helpful first step. A knowledgeable professional will know about local services and adult agencies available for career awareness options. Further, a referral can be made to the Department of Vocational Rehabilitation (DVR). There the young man can speak with a counselor and determine if he might qualify to get service support in college.

The DVR counselor will even help him (if accepted) to make an informed career decision through local vendors, private professionals, or other adult agencies specializing in career decision making and having a background in working with individuals who have disabilities. Some of these individualized services would include: providing vocational preparation (such as internships), on-the-job training, and other networking opportunities with area employers. Without appropriate support and referral to other agencies (e.g., One-Stop Centers, Mental Health), the young man with ADHD might pursue unrealistic career options and embark on a career path that leads to more frustration.

A therapist plays a critical and central role not only in giving pointers on where to go for help and how to get it, but also in helping the client become more self-aware of career realities. To cope more effectively, the client must be motivated to become more realistic about priorities and alternatives. There are some basic questions that lead to client-centered career decisions.

In her book *Finding a Career That Works for You*, Fellman (2000) poses these questions:

1. What are my passions...those interests that really "light me up"?
2. What have been my accomplishments thus far?
3. What personality factors contribute to my ease of handling life?
4. What are specifics that feel as natural and automatic as writing with my dominant hand?
5. What are my priority values that must be considered to feel good about myself?
6. What are my aptitude levels that maximize success?
7. What is my energy pattern throughout the day, week, month?
8. What are my dreams, and how do they relate to the real world of work?
9. What are my pieces of jobs that always attracted me, and how can those pieces be threatened together?
10. How realistic are my related options in terms of today's job market needs?
11. How much do I really know about the related options?
12. How can the options be tested out, rather than tried out, with the possibility of failure?
13. What special challenges do I have?
14. How do my challenges impact me?
15. How might my challenges impact the work options?
16. How could the challenges be overcome by appropriate strategies and interventions?
17. How great is the degree of match between the option and the real me?
18. Can I test out the degree of match before pursing the field?
19. How could I enter and sustain the chosen work environment?
20. What supports can be put in place to ensure long-term success?

This list is not meant to form the entire therapy process, but it does help the client and the therapist to identify important information that will be needed for making informed career decisions. The questions also provide a framework for exploring career options, for solving problems, and for helping the client to become more self-determined. Once this process begins, the client will have a greater opportunity for success, self-confidence, and self-esteem

(Nadeau, 1995). By seeking answers to these questions, the client will be less bored and will have more personal satisfaction in pursuing a career goal that is in line with his or her truer interests, personality, and functional assets/limitations.

Therapists can develop a partnership with their clients around issues related to career decision making. This partnership should focus on helping the clients become more self-determined and to exert more control over their life. Many adults with ADHD are tired of being misunderstood and have a history of having to explain themselves to others. They are tired of excuses, but they may be discouraged when they encounter setbacks, due to a lifetime of being misunderstood. When disappointments do occur, adults with ADHD may not see these as a normal part of life. They have trouble learning from these experiences, and are not sure how to avoid similar disappointments or setbacks in the future. Self-improvement may seem unreachable in these circumstances.

Practice in self-determination and reframing allows the client to walk away from a session with strategies for dealing with painful life experiences. These strategies can be used to show how painful experiences are a part of life and how to make better choices in the future.

## PRACTICAL TOOLS AND STRATEGIES FOR CAREER DECISION MAKING

### The Career Decision-Making Process

Decision making is a common problem facing many individuals, and most people don't know how to make decisions well. For the adult with ADHD, additional layers of difficulty surface in choosing between so many apparently conflicting options. You may face opposition because many adults with ADHD have trouble breaking down the key elements of decision making. The opposition is understandable because of the combination of high stakes involved with selecting an appropriate career and the potential consequences that a poor choice will result in frustration and self-defeating feelings.

Thus, the therapeutic process should address the anxiety, confusion, doubt, errors, embarrassments, and loss of past mistakes in a direct manner. Clients may alternate between self-doubt and overconfidence and exhibit stalling tactics, impulsive behaviors, and despair resembling burnout.

They are likely to become overwhelmed by the sheer volume of data, overlooking relevant information or important details that lead to flawed choices. They may focus on the wrong information or be unable to organize information into meaningful concepts. These feelings may present as "learned helplessness" and it may appear that the clients want a magical resolution to the career decision dilemma. Hammond, Keeney, and Raiffa (1999) believe that the ability to make smart choices is a fundamental life skill. They contend that it is one of the most critical determinants of how capable a person becomes in handling life responsibilities and in achieving personal or professional goals.

The next section of the chapter covers how to use critical-path decision making, combining task-oriented vocational counseling and career exploration activities. Successful career-planning outcomes depend on more than luck for success. Successful results are enhanced by deliberate reasoning, planning, and execution within the therapeutic relationship.

### Can't Make Up Your Mind? What's the Problem?

Frank is a software specialist and has been working for a variety of dot-com companies for the past nine years. By nature, these jobs have a cycle of instability, where the products or services are rapidly developed, aggressively marketed, and sold to investors in 12–18 months. The company he works for now has kept him continuously employed for almost three years. He has heard through the grapevine that the company may be acquired by a multinational corporation. While the pace of change was exciting and kept his interest in his younger years, Frank is now in his early 30s. He has two young boys in school and feels pigeonholed in his industry in a position he no longer likes. His previous work experience and family responsibilities contribute to the trapped feeling. He doesn't know how to change his life, and he is afraid his decisions will adversely affect his family.

What is the real career decision to be made? Is it "Which software design company should I work for?" Or is it "Should I work for someone as opposed to being self-employed?" How the decision-question is originally posed is vital to the outcome; it must be phrased carefully. The client and therapist work together to phrase the questions right. The way a problem is stated places boundaries around the choice to be made. Parameters can be identified, alternatives can be considered, and evaluations can be conducted within this basic framework. Adults with ADHD tend to jump to an immediate decision, selecting the first thing that comes to mind. Or they may choose the most obvious alternative without thinking about all the consequences. The therapist is there to help facilitate this process and to help the client take a fresh look as well as more carefully ponder career options.

By pointing out that this myriad of options isn't necessarily a bad situation, the therapist can begin to reframe the issues. The decision-problem can be viewed as a time to be creative, a time to be adventurous, and a time to pursue a more satisfying career that leads to greater personal achievement. Decision-problems, whether related to career or to other dilemmas, are often fueled by specific "triggers." Decision triggers are driving forces at work or in life that result in dramatic changes in personal status. For example, a young man graduating from high school is contemplating enrollment in college us a trade school. A mother of two worries that she will lose her job after an impending layoff. A talented computer specialist without a degree becomes a father. It is good to approach these highly emotionally charged situations by investigating "trigger" events. Because of a history of failure or self-doubt, many adults with ADHD have a built-in tendency to persist in self-limiting prejudices. The client may feel, "I'm not very smart, or I'd know what to do," or "I can't get a new job right now." The trigger is the most direct link to the essence of any decision-problem, career related or other. In the case of the mother who initially sees the problem trigger as losing her job due to company cutbacks might be thinking the decision problem should be phrased as "Who will hire me now?" The real problem may actually be better phrased as "What's the best way to use this situation to move up in the company?" She may not have to start sending résumés out by the basketful at all. Another alternative may be to develop an internal networking plan to solidify her value to the newly merged company workforce.

By reframing the triggering event leads to the career decision-problem, the professional should help the client state the problem as clearly as possible:

1. What assumptions does the client have about the career decision-problem? (E.g., I need a better job.)
2. What are the sources of the "triggering events"? (E.g., I read the newspaper.)
3. What are the connections between the "trigger" and the career decision-problem? (E.g., I need to increase my skills because of changes in technology.)

Most triggers come from others (work supervisor, parents) or from circumstances beyond the client's control (labor trends and market forces). Although these life changes come to the client from external sources and may seem to offer few alternatives, there is nothing to say that the client has to wait for the worst to happen. Your clients do not have to settle for whatever they can salvage from the situation. The threat of changing employment may actually be an excellent way for clients to create a new set of circumstances more to their liking.

Figure 10.1 shows the relationship between career decision making and (1) assumptions, (2) "triggers," and (3) connections and quality of life. Clarifying the decision-problem frequently takes a great deal of time. The therapist and client work together to generate an accurate statement of the problem and brainstorm various alternative problem statements. In our earlier example, Frank should consider how being self-employed could affect his quality of life and family relationships. The therapist should work with Frank to help him determine that he was as open and honest about perceived constraints. These constraints may alter the way the decision-problem is framed. If Frank changes jobs before the merger, is he missing exciting opportunities by bailing out too soon? Help Frank to create a larger canvas, to expand his vision. This allows for a broader range of potential solutions.

## GAINING CONTROL OF THE DECISION

Once the decision-problem has been identified, therapy can focus on consideration of the end result. What are the objectives? In this model, the importance of determining objectives allows for evaluation of options and other alternatives associated with them. The personal nature of deciding on objectives become clear when the client reflects on questions like "What do I honestly want and need from this decision?" This is an appropriate time to begin using available career/life values checklists and task analysis procedures to inventory specific vocational skills. Explore and examine work tasks at the job and at home for latent skills or interests. Evaluate what skills or life-enriching values are part of personal hobbies. This evaluation would include informal work done for home improvement or auto repair and spare-time activities such as Web designing for church and volunteering as math teacher for an adult education program.

Work-related behaviors should be explored. These include: punctuality, attendance, attention to tasks, quality and speed of work, work consistency, and the ability to interact with customers, peers, and supervisors. Find out about the client's learning styles and learning skill levels. Are he able to learn academic and functional work tasks? Are

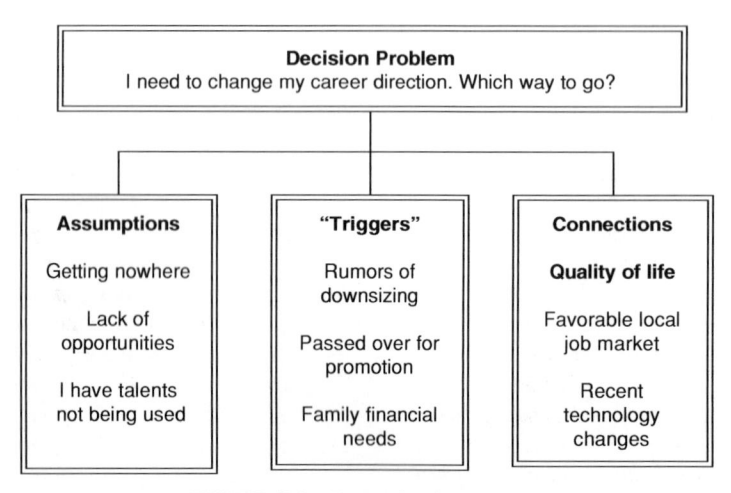

**FIGURE 10.1** Career-planning decision.

there any particular instructional or behavioral techniques that are most effective? What are typical learning strategies and the learning rate of the client. These data can come from self-report, and feedback can come from significant others, parents, employers, etc.

Interest inventories will pinpoint client preferences in work and social situations and can be used effectively to ascertain occupational awareness issues for younger clients lacking extensive work experience. It is useful to have objective functional and general academic test scores that are related to work, training, or educational demands. Personal and work temperament characteristics are important factors in determining individual values, such as environmental preferences (e.g., optimal noise and visual stimulation levels, physical demands needed to sustain attention and interest, how much supervision and authority can be handled, and coworker or customer interaction.)

By gathering this kind of additional information, the clinician and client can focus on and isolate what is relevant to the decision-problem. This information comes in handy when the client advocates for himself on the job. That is, this information can form the basis for better decision making. It can also be used to answer questions that significant others might pose; that is, "What are you going to do about your job? Where are you going to put your energy?" Family members and friends may inadvertently undermine adults with ADHD and believe those ADHD adults are rushing off without thinking things through. They may see this as another wild goose chase, such as seeking the perfect job or the perfect mate. Without meaning to, family and friends can be the harshest critics and biggest pessimists.

By having specific information, clients can begin to address these criticisms. With assistance from the therapist, they can clarify career decisions and life objectives. They can more clearly see the payoff for the time, effort, and energy they exert to achieve their goals. This is a good time to have clients write down all their hopes and dreams, to write down all the known or potential barriers to these dreams, and to begin to identify solutions to those barriers. Creative chaos and free-form thinking are good signs during this phase, indicators that the process is heading in the right direction.

At this stage, it is not necessary to get everything exactly right. Pressures to be exact may impede creativity and cause someone to eliminate a potentially great opportunity. The idea is to generate a wish list, with no possibility deemed unachievable or unworthy. The wish list should have every desirable ingredient the client could ever want from the decision. If the decision or choice is viewed as positive, then why is it so positive?

At this point in therapy, a dose of reality can be inserted into the choice consideration by having the client consider the worst possible outcome, to avoid taking any action that could lead to undesirable consequences. In Frank's case, he indicated that he should talk with his wife and children. He wanted to incorporate their input, suggestions, and perspectives into his comprehensive list. This is an important piece in the process, because many decisions do have an impact on others, and this must be taken into account. Frank may have a hard time explaining to his children that they can't go on a family vacation because his decision to start his own business makes money tight. When decisions affect others, the consequences need to be thought through with this in mind. The overall value system of the client should include these perspectives.

By refining the "what if" scenarios, fundamental objectives and goals can become organized and prioritized. Clients who present with a "if it feels good do it" perspective need to be challenged with "means–end" thinking. That is, they may need help to determine if the end justifies the means (more money but less satisfaction and less job security). Is job security and long-term stability worth less pay? Clarification at this level is very helpful, and objectives become clearer and are tied to the client's value system.

In the next step, the therapist and client explore the "refined" list of choices, questions such as "Can you live with that decision, if you have less job security?" or "Can you live with less money if you have more security?" This extra step allows clients to see if they can live with the decision. This is also the time to see if anything has been left out, if anything is unclear, or if anything has been misstated. This is the optimal time to incorporate results of any evaluations that may have been completed on the client so that a good match can be found between interests, strengths, and limitations. This will help the clients evaluate their objectives before making a final decision. Special aptitudes or abilities, the impact of the disability on the tasks involved, the ability to perform the essential functions of the career, skills or experiences that can facilitate the choice, and barriers to or skills that enhance success are explored.

During this exploration, the client should be true to him or herself. Be sure that work preferences, desires, and needs are fully considered. Identify what really matters to the client. The client should be aware of the internal and external motivating factors influencing his or her decision, including self-fulfillment, money, desire for self-improvement, authority, and the opportunity to do different job tasks.

## GENERATING REASONABLE ALTERNATIVES

The next stage of the decision-making process is brainstorming alternatives. While clients' objectives drive their decisions, there is always more than one side to every problem. The clients decision will be only as good as the best alternative, so it is important to find as many reasonable solutions or alternatives, in case there is a need for a backup plan. Therapeutic professionals need to help the client avoid limiting the full range of alternatives and, as a result, generate alternatives that are too narrowly defined to really bring passion to the vision.

Begin by having the client ask, "How can I achieve my objectives?" This should be done with each individual objective. Asking "Why?" helps bring the end into focus. Asking "How?" brings the means into focus—"How do I get there?" The client should develop a set of alternatives first, without judgment or evaluation. Keep the client's mind open during this process, and have her stay open to all kinds of ideas. Eventually, you will narrow these fluid leads to solid ones. If you see a flaw or shortcoming, don't point it out at this time to the client. Encourage the client's "stream of consciousness," which is so often a hallmark of adults with ADHD. Save the analysis and evaluation for later. This allows the client to remain in control of the process and compels them to maintain responsibility for the results.

By keeping client focused, the process is more likely to add depth to the career-planning process and is more responsive to the client's needs for access to all points of view. For example, let's look at Frank's career decision-problem again. Frank investigates labor market data specific to his career aspirations in computer technology. He is now able to look at the economic and technological trends that may affect his work environment. He begins to make a list of occupational clusters of similar or related positions based on his stated interests, abilities, and values. He can begin to study the following alternative: different computer start-up companies; registered software consultants; state and county predictions of job growth and decline; and the entry-level salary and potential for advancement in selected companies offering comparable employment.

By generating a number of viable alternatives, Frank can begin to determine whether he wants to become self-employed or whether he should pursue one of the other alternatives. Generally, the client will come to the conclusion that there is no perfect solution. This also reinforces the notion that it does no good to get too obsessive or to spend too much time worrying about the outcome. If the client can see how careful he has been and how well thought out the plan is, he can have more confidence in the decision. Table 10.1 is an example of the various objectives that Frank might identify and the alter-

TABLE 10.1  Objectives and Alternatives Related to the Career-Change Decision-Problem

| Objectives | Alternative: Pursue Employment Elsewhere |
|---|---|
| 1. Earn higher income | 1. Network with local companies for leads |
| 2. Work from home or office | 2. Look into what it takes to be independent consultant |
| 3. Training and management opportunities | 3. Find a mentor |
| 4. Paid vacation | 4. Utilize Internet, outplacement firms, and other resources |
| 5. Comprehensive benefit package | |

natives that are reasonable given his particular decision-problem.

## LIVING WITH THE CONSEQUENCES WITHOUT SUFFERING

In this section, the term *consequence* is used to describe how one evaluates competing alternatives or decisions. *Consequences* also refer to how well decisions accomplish specific objectives. The client comes to have clear understanding of the consequences inherent in choosing one career path over another. Under collaborative guidance with the therapist, he or she can begin to evaluate choices from this perspective to make sure that the choices are ones that can be lived with.

In Frank's situation, the consequences of his decisions (and alternatives) are explored. How will the decisions affect him? Frank imagines himself on a typical day, week, and month to "see" what it might be like. If he had to live out the consequences, how would he feel? This process allows Frank to consider the long-term effects of his decision and to gain a better understanding of his decision. Immediate gratification is delayed and more strategic, systematic decisions become possible. Table 10.3 summarizes the objectives he believes are essential to making a smart career choice.

The table includes the top five companies that have been researched. Frank believes these companies represent the best available and researched opportunities matching his interests, abilities, and values. By evaluating the list, Frank decides that while Job E pays more than Job A, it is more important to have flexibility in his schedule than a larger paycheck. He also decides that though Job C offers him flexibility, he couldn't live on the salary. He also sees that Job A has better benefits. The therapist employs this "comparative" strategy with the client to get him to see if any of the options clearly dominates or is clearly inferior. By comparing facts and figures (see Table 10.3), Frank analyses each row and assigns a ranking of each of the consequences. The highest values can then be compared. The retirement benefits (even with lower starting pay) in Job A are more important than the extra day of vacation pay in Job D. Job A also offers management opportunities that are not part of any other package. The therapist begins to help Frank to set up networking opportunities where he will spend one to two intense days at each company he determines are the final candidates.

By spending time in the environment, Frank can determine if the compromises he has to accept with each choice are something he can live with. The time at each work site provides a good therapist-directed project to do a situational assessment. In the situational assessment, Frank gathers information about: job descriptions; how he likes the commute; the functional use of academic skills; how instructions and training are conveyed; insights into company culture; what types of personality style are displayed by supervisors and coworkers. This on-the-job assessment will give Frank a much better grasp on what life would be like to make a commitment to a given company.

**TABLE 10.2  Consequences of Career Change Decisions**

| Objectives | Job A | Job B | Job C | Job D | Job E |
|---|---|---|---|---|---|
| Salary | $4,000 | $4,400 | $2,800 | $3,900 | $4,200 |
| Flexible schedule | Medium | Low | High | Medium | None |
| Develop talent | Supervise, computer | Computer | Operation, computer | Logistics | Time management |
| Vacation (days) | 14 | 12 | 10 | 15 | 12 |
| Benefits | Health, dental, retirement | Health, dental | Health | Health, retirement | Health, dental |

**TABLE 10.3  Ranking Alternatives on Each Objective for Frank's Career-Change Decision**

| Objectives | Job A | Job B | Job C | Job D | Job E |
|---|---|---|---|---|---|
| Salary | 3 | 1 | 5 | 4 | 2 |
| Flexible schedule | 2 | 4 | 1 | 2 | 5 |
| Develop talent | 1 | 3 | 1 | 4 | 5 |
| Vacation | 2 | 3 | 5 | 1 | 3 |
| Benefits | 1 | 3 | 5 | 2 | 3 |

## MANAGING UNCERTAINTIES AND ASSESSING RISK TOLERANCE

In the perfect world, where an adult with ADHD would know what will happen to them before they make a decision, no uncertainty would exist. As it is, a certain amount of chance and calculated risk is inherent in every decision. Frank and his therapist will only be able to know what *might* happen. Frank and his therapist decide that it would be a good idea to eliminate as much of the random unknowns as possible.

Frank reviews the two basic directions in which his original decision-problem took him: (1) to *stay* at his original job and take his chance with the new management, or (2) to *change* his job and accept the best offer of his top five companies. Some of his uncertainties with staying with his present employer are: "How secure is my present job with the current management?" "Will I have a buy-out option, get a promotion, or be laid off with new ownership?" If he moves and takes a new job, "How will I deal with the commute?" "Can I handle the responsibilities of management?" "What if I don't get along with my boss or coworkers?"

He decides to put together a risk-tolerance chart (Table 10.4). In order to decide what is most desirable among the alternatives he is considering, Frank comes up with three possible outcomes related to his uncertainties if he makes the move to a new company. He also calculates the chances that each one will happening and assigns an "odds-based" percentage to them. For this part of the chart, he has to rely on his judgment, to review everything he has

**TABLE 10.4  Uncertainties of the Career-Change Alternative**

| Outcome | Chance | Consequences |
|---|---|---|
| I get little or none of what I want—*No long-term opportunity* | Least likely, 10% | Too horrible! No results despite my best. Will have to get old job back or start over. |
| I get some of what I want—*Long-term opportunity achieved* | Most likely, 60% | Good. I would be satisfied for my first plan. More stability, room to grow. |
| I get most of what I want—*Long-term opportunity achieved/exceeded* | Somewhat likely, 30% | Excellent! Great both professionally and personally. I don't know how I would act getting everything I wanted! |

learned so far, and to get input from his family, friends, coworkers, and supervisor. In conversation with his boss, Frank finds another possible alternative: *job tryout*. He gains approval from his current employer to take an unpaid six-month leave of absence to see if his option is the right choice. His supervisor tells Frank that he might be eligible for rehire if the merger goes through. He assures Frank that he would considered for cross-training if he came back.

Frank decides to focus on the decision to move to a new company, although he could have stayed with his present employer to see what opportunities the merger might bring. He also could have sought another job while staying at his company, but he chose to keep his decision streamlined by focusing on the new opportunity. Now that the decision is made, Frank and his therapist can concentrate on any remaining details that were overlooked, including updating his résumé, evaluating his personal appearance, and working on interview techniques.

## CONCLUSION

Clinicians and practitioners can achieve consistent results with their clients who are struggling through career changes or looking for methods and strategies for making solid vocational decisions through the use of this planning technique. This approach provides a mechanism for clients to reexamine their interests and clarify what they find is truly useful and valuable to carry forward into the next phase of their working lives. It forces the clients to specify long-term goals and objectives while evaluating various trade-offs. By acknowledging that every decision has an element of uncertainty, the client must do a thorough job of analyzing and problem solving the many "what if's" that are part of making a decision.

By performing the community-based fieldwork outside of the controlled clinical setting, the client and the therapist can explore resources in the corporate, rehabilitation, and education sectors. By learning how to anticipate changes, the client develops better coping mechanisms and problem-solving skills. When problems arise the client has a strategy and method to deal with these issues. When forces are beyond immediate control, the client can still remain focused and can be empowered with his or her knowledge of how to plan and respond in a flexible manner.

The more opportunities the client has to practice these techniques, the better the quality of the decisions that will be made in the future. Clients will come to realize that tough decisions have no more than one or two decision elements. They will come to see more than one solution to a problem. By maintaining a systematic focus, clients will see how helpful it is to generate alternatives and to evaluate the consequences of each. By getting a clear description of the problem, establishing core objectives, and generating good alternatives on these difficult elements, they can resolve complex decisions with great skill and consistency. Eliminating less attractive or functional alternatives becomes easier. This step-by-step method of decision making reduces impulsive choices and increases successful outcomes that are client centered and therapist supported.

## REFERENCES

Campeau, P., & Wolman, J. (1993). *Research on self-determination in individuals with disabilities.* Palo Alto, CA: American Institutes for Research.

Dickenson, E. (1870). *Bartlett's book of business quotations* (No. 1176, St. 1). Quebec, Canada: Little Brown.

Fellman, W. R. (2000). *Finding a career that works for you.* Plantation, Fl: Specialty Press.

Field, S., Hoffman, A., St. Peter, S., & Sawilowsky, S. (1992). *Research in self-determination: Interim research report.* Detroit: Developmental Disabilities Institute/College of Education, Wayne State University.

Gerber, P. J., & Reiff, H. B. (1994). *Learning disabilities in adulthood. Persisting problems and evolving issues.* Stoneham, MA: Andover Medical.

Goleman, D. (1998). *Working with emotional intelligence.* New York: Bantam Books.

Halpern, A. S. (1993). Quality of life as a conceptual framework for evaluating transition outcomes. *Exceptional Children, 59,* 486–498.

Hammond, J., Keeney, R., & Raiffa, H. (1999). *Smart choices: A practical guide to making better decisions.* Boston: Harvard Business School Press.

Mithaug, D. (1991). *Self-determined kids raising satisfied and successful children.* Lexington, MA: DC Heath.

Nadeau, K. (1995). *A comprehensive guide to attention deficit in adults.* New York: Brunner/Mazel.

Rusch, F., & Chadsey, J. (1998). *Beyond high school: Transition from school to work.* Belmont, CA: Wadsworth.

U.S. Department of Labor (1992). *Secretary's commission on achieving necessary skills.* Washington, DC: Author.

Vogel, S. A., & Reder, S. (1998). *Learning disabilities, literacy, and adult education.* Baltimore: Brookes.

Wren, C., & Einhorn, J. (2000). *Hanging by a twig: Understanding and counseling adults with learning disabilities and ADD.* New York: Norton.

# 11

# What Clinicians Need to Know About Legal Issues Relevant to ADHD[*]

Peter S. Latham, J.D., Patricia H. Latham, J.D.

## INTRODUCTION

ADHD may prove legally relevant in a variety of contexts. It may affect education, employment, custody proceedings, criminal prosecutions, and divorce. The principal laws under which adults with ADHD may have rights are the Rehabilitation Act of 1973[1] (RA) and the Americans with Disabilities Act of 1990 (ADA).[2]

These laws are not self-executing. In order to obtain protection, individuals may be required to *document* their disabilities. Documentation for legal purposes differs from documentation for general purposes. The purpose for some reports may be to inform the individual concerning his or her disabilities, to recommend treatment, such as medication and/or counseling, and to recommend coping strategies. Documentation for *legal* purposes is organized specifically around establishing a disability that entitles the person to particular accommodations or services under the law.

There are three basic elements of disability documentation: (1) diagnosis, (2) evaluation of impact, and (3) recommendations. Together they establish the existence of a disability, the areas of functioning affected by the disability, and the specific strategies and accommodations in education, testing, workplace, and life in general made necessary by that disability. This chapter will consider when ADHD may be a disability under the law and what the proper methods are of documenting a disability and writing a report for legal purposes.

It is essential for the medical or mental health professional to understand the difference between furnishing an opinion for the purposes of *treatment* and furnishing one in support of an individual's *legal* claim for accommodation under the RA or ADA. In the first case the medical or mental health professional functions only as such; in the latter case, he or she functions as an expert witness in support of the patient's claim. That is so because the professional will almost certainly be called as a witness should the claim proceed to a lawsuit and then to trial. Thus, the medical or mental health professional may wear two hats in today's legally oriented environment: healer and potential expert

[*]The citations used in this chapter (see the Endnotes at chapter's end) refer to court cases, statutes, and regulations. The referenced materials are available at law libraries, and most can be accessed on the Internet at http://www.legal.gsa.gov/.

witness. Let's begin with an overview of the relevant laws.

## TWO STATUTES

### The Rehabilitation Act of 1973

In the mid-1970s, Congress adopted legislation whose purpose was to end discrimination against individuals with disabilities generally and to improve the educational and other services available to them. The first piece of legislation was the Rehabilitation Act of 1973 (RA), which prohibits discrimination against individuals with disabilities in federal employment as well as in government contracts and programs receiving federal financial assistance.

The RA bans discrimination by (1) the United States Government,[3] (2) contractors with the U.S. Government,[4] and (3) recipients of federal funds.[5] This last provision, popularly known as Section 504, covers all federal grant and aid recipients. Most notably, it applies to most elementary, secondary, and postsecondary educational institutions. It also served as the model for the Americans with Disabilities Act of 1990.

### The Americans with Disabilities Act of 1990

The Americans With Disabilities Act (ADA) was passed in July 1990 for the purpose of ending discrimination against individuals with disabilities in the area of employment, state and local government activities, public accommodations, and other public activities.

The ADA was intended to extend the basic disability-based civil rights set forth in the RA to virtually all segments of society. The rights and obligations created by the ADA overlap, to some extent, those of the RA. The simplest way to think of the matter is to remember that the RA follows federal dollars. It applies to most federal employment, to federal government contractors, and to grant and aid recipients. The ADA applies more broadly.

The ADA prohibits discrimination in three major areas: private employment (Title I), the activities of state and local governments (public schools, employment, licensing, public programs, etc.) (Title II), and access to privately owned places of public accommodation (private schools, except for religiously controlled schools, hotels, theaters, etc.) (Title III). The Rehabilitation Act of 1973 and the Americans with Disabilities Act of 1990 apply to most academic institutions and employers.

## INDIVIDUAL WITH A DISABILITY

### Introduction

In the text that follows we will consider whether and under what circumstances an individual with ADHD may be considered an individual with a disability under the RA and ADA. Under these laws an individual with a disability is one who "has a physical or mental impairment which substantially limits one or more of such person's major life activities."[6] Each of these requirements has been the subject of extensive judicial analysis and are discussed next.

### Physical or Mental Impairment

To be covered by the RA and ADA, an individual must first have a physical or mental impairment. The term *physical or mental impairment* includes "any mental or psychological disorder, such as mental retardation, organic brain syndrome, emotional or mental illness, and specific learning disabilities."[7]

Note that the RA/ADA definition expressly includes individuals with "specific learning disabilities." Typical of the many judicial expressions to the effect that ADHD is an impairment under the RA/ADA is the statement of the Seventh Circuit in *Davidson* v. *Midelfort Clinic, Ltd*.[8]: "There is no dispute that ADD qualifies as an impairment for purposes of the statute."

ADHD is an impairment under the RA and ADA. However, not every case of ADHD is sufficiently severe to constitute a disability under the law. *Only those cases in which ADHD substantially limits a major life activity are covered.*

## Major Life Activities

The requirement for proof of a substantial limitation to a major life activity was recognized in *Schneider v. San Francisco*[9]. There, a parts storekeeper with ADHD stated in his deposition that he was not substantially limited in any major life activity and that ADHD did not limit his ability to do the job from which he had been fired. The Court entered summary judgment for San Francisco, holding that he had no disability under the ADA.

The major life activities consist of "caring for oneself, performing manual tasks, walking, seeing, hearing, speaking, breathing, learning, and working."[10] However, the list of major life activities contained in the federal regulations is not exclusive.

The Equal Employment Opportunity Commission (EEOC) has added certain activities, including concentrating and interacting with others, to the list of major life activities its investigators will recognize. The EEOC has issued a pamphlet entitled *EEOC Guidance on the Americans with Disabilities Act and Psychiatric Disabilities* (*Guidance*). The purpose of this document is to set forth the commission's position on this topic and to provide guidance to its personnel in enforcing Title I (concerning employment) of the ADA. In it, the EEOC has added thinking, concentrating, and interacting with others, as well as sleeping, to the list of major life activities its investigators will recognize.

In *Sutton v. United Air Lines, Inc.*,[11] discussed hereafter, the Court ruled that "[n]o agency...has been given authority to issue regulations implementing the generally applicable provisions of the ADA," and therefore, the helpfulness of these regulations and guidance is questionable. Nonetheless, they have had a major impact in the administration of the RA/ADA; and because this is so, they may yet prove persuasive to the courts. We will briefly review major life activities that may be limited by ADHD and/or related impairments and that have been addressed by the EEOC and/or the courts.

### Learning

Learning is a major life activity in which many individuals with ADHD may be substantially limited. However, in order to meet the substantial limitation requirement, it is necessary to show that *learning* truly is substantially limited. In *Price v. The National Board of Medical Examiners*,[12] for example, the Court found that three medical students, who had no history of substantial academic difficulties but had been diagnosed by responsible professionals as having learning disabilities and/or ADHD, were not individuals with disabilities under the ADA because their impairments did not substantially limit them in a major life activity of learning when compared to most people. Accordingly, the Court denied them an injunction requiring additional time on the United States Medical Licensing Examination (USMLE).

The Tenth Circuit, in *McGuinness v. University of New Mexico School of Medicine*,[13] ruled that McGuinness, a medical student, had no disability because he failed to show that his mental impairment (anxiety) "impedes his performance in a wide variety of disciplines, not just chemistry and physics."

In *Leisen v. City of Shelbyville, Leisen v. City of Shelbyville*,[14] the Seventh Circuit reached a similar result. There, the Court held that Leisen, a female firefighter who was unable to complete a required paramedic course because of depression, was not an individual with a disability. Leisen never showed that her depression "substantially limited" a major life activity. The Seventh Circuit said:

> The mere fact that Leisen was having obvious difficulty in passing the course for paramedic certification does not show that she was substantially limited in the

major life activity of learning, any more than the fact that a particular individual might not be able to pass a course in physics or philosophy would allow an inference that all learning activity was substantially limited.

The Court went on to note that "Leisen successfully completed other training courses around the same time she was repeatedly failing the paramedic course; she successfully maintained her EMT certification; and she passed most of the courses in the last paramedic program even while she was suffering from all the stress she described." Thus, proof that learning is substantially limited requires a showing that learning is substantially limited in a broad sense and not just in one course or program.

### Reading and Writing

Some courts have broken learning down into components such as reading[15] and writing.[16] When learning is thus subdivided it becomes easier for one to show that one component of learning has been substantially affected. However, the Supreme Court has not indicated any inclination to break major life activities into components.

### Working

Working is treated differently from all other major life activities for purposes of considering whether an individual with an impairment is substantially limited. In order to determine whether a substantial limitation on working exists, the individual's impairment must bar him or her from significant classes of jobs and not just a particular job. Only disabilities with the former (and broader) impact are considered substantially to limit working.

In *Davidson v. Midelfort Clinic, Ltd.*[17] the Seventh Circuit addressed the application of this rule to an individual with ADHD. That case involved Barbara Davidson, a licensed psychotherapist whose employment with the Midelfort Clinic had been terminated for cause. Ms. Davidson's ADHD was described by the Court that viewed it as "a chronic psychological disability resulting from a biochemical imbalance. The disorder can interfere with one's cognitive processes, including the ability to concentrate, to learn, to organize one's thoughts, to verbalize them, and to formulate explanations."

In Ms. Davidson's case, ADHD substantially limited her ability to perform all the tasks required of a psychotherapist at the Midelfort Clinic. The Court found that therapists at the clinic were "required to dictate their patient notes for transcription by other staff members and inclusion in the patient's file." However, ADHD made it more "difficult for Davidson to organize her thoughts without first writing them down on paper," a fact that led her "to write out her notes before dictating them, an obviously time-consuming process." As a result, Ms. Davidson fell unacceptably behind in her dictation of patient notes and was fired for it. She sued under the ADA.

The Court readily agreed that ADHD was an impairment under the ADA. The Court said: "There is no dispute that ADD qualifies as an impairment for purposes of the statute." However, the Court then went on to find that Ms. Davidson's ADHD did not limit her substantially in working:

> At most, the evidence in this case suggests as a result of ADD, Davidson was unable to perform her job at Midelfort. Davidson has come forward with no evidence from which one might reasonably infer that ADD precluded her even from holding other comparable positions as a therapist. Indeed, by her own account, the principal reason for Midelfort's decision to discharge her was her slowness in completing her dictation. Whatever importance Midelfort may have attached to timely dictation, that was only one aspect of Davidson's employment with Midelfort, and the record does not suggest that ADD imposed other limitations on her ability to function effectively in her role as a counselor.... Moreover, so far as the ability to dictate her notes is concerned, Davidson has made no showing that this is a skill that other counseling positions require. It strikes us as somewhat unlikely that all employers of psychotherapists demand that one's notes be dictated for transcription by other employees, particularly with computers becoming an omnipresent fixture in the workplace. We can only speculate about that, however, because Davidson has given us no evidence on this point. She has shown only that Midelfort required her to dictate her notes and deemed her compe-

tence in that regard to be subpar. [Citations and footnotes omitted.]

The Supreme Court has viewed working (as a major life activity) with skepticism. In *Sutton v. United Air Lines, Inc.*,[18] the Court noted that, because "the parties accept that the term 'major life activities' includes working, we do not determine the validity of the cited regulations." The Court nonetheless commented "that there may be some conceptual difficulty in defining 'major life activities' to include work."

### Concentrating

An individual might be considered to have a substantial limitation in the ability to concentrate "if s/he was easily and frequently distracted, meaning that his/her attention was frequently drawn to irrelevant sights or sounds or to intrusive thoughts; or if s/he experienced his/her 'mind going blank' on a frequent basis."[19]

However, the Tenth Circuit has ruled that concentration is not a major life activity. In *Pack v. KMart Corporation*,[20] Pack, an employee for 18 years, was transferred to the job of pharmacy technician. She developed major depression, moderate to severe in nature, which caused her to make "technical errors in the pharmacy, including mislabeling prescriptions and incorrectly entering prescription data into the pharmacy computer," for which she was fired. She sued under the ADA, contending that she was substantially limited in the major life activities of concentrating and sleeping. The Court held that, while sleeping is a major life activity, Pack failed to prove that she was substantially limited in it, and concentrating was no major life activity at all. The Court said:

> In deciding whether a particular activity is a "major life activity," we ask whether that activity is significant within the meaning of the ADA, rather than whether that activity is important to the particular individual.... We hold that sleeping is a major life activity, but concentration is not. Sleeping is a basic activity that the average person in the general population can perform with little

or no difficulty, similar to the major life activities of walking, seeing, hearing, speaking, breathing, learning, working, sitting, standing, lifting, and reaching.... However, concentration is not itself a major life activity. Concentration may be a significant and necessary component of a major life activity, such as working, learning, or speaking, but it is not an "activity" itself.

In reaching this result, the Court noted that, while "the EEOC's guidance may be entitled to some consideration in our analysis, it does not carry the force of law and is not entitled to any special deference."

### Ability to Interact with Others

An individual would be considered to have a substantial limitation in the ability to interact with others "if his/her relations with others were characterized on a regular basis by severe problems, for example, consistently high levels of hostility, social withdrawal, or failure to communicate when necessary."[21] The courts have divided on the question of whether interaction with others is a major life activity.[22]

### Thinking

At least one court has held thinking to be a major life activity. In *Schumacher v. Souderton Area Sch. Dist.*,[23] the Court held that a middle school teacher would be considered an individual with a disability under the ADA if she could show that she had ADHD that substantially limited her ability to engage in "cognitive thinking," a major life activity recognized as such by the Court. In order to establish disability status, ADHD must substantially limit a major life activity, such as learning or working.

## Substantially Limited

Not every impairment that affects a major life activity is a disability under the ADA. Only those whose effects substantially limit a major life activity can be considered disabilities. The concept of *substantial limitation* has been elaborated by regulations and court decisions. The regulations provide that an individual with a substantial limitation is:

> (i) Unable to perform a major life activity that the average person in the general population can perform; or
>
> (ii) Significantly restricted as to the condition, manner or duration under which an individual can perform a particular major life activity as compared to the condition, manner, or duration under which the average person in the general population can perform that same major life activity.[24]

Questions have arisen as to when and how the limiting effects of an impairment should be measured in determining whether they are substantial in nature.

### When Measured

*When* do you measure a disability's severity? Do you measure the severity with or without considering the effects of a person's coping strategies or the effects of medication? Prior to 1999, most courts held that, under the ADA, the severity of an impairment is to be measured *without* considering the effects of a person's coping strategies, medication, or prosthetic devices. In the ADA. In *Sutton v. United Air Lines, Inc.*,[25] the Supreme Court rejected those cases.

Karen Sutton and her twin sister, Kimberly, had "severe myopia," which was correctable to "20/20 or better" with glasses or contact lenses. Without these, however, both sisters "effectively" could not "see to conduct numerous activities, such as driving a vehicle, watching television or shopping in public stores." Nonetheless, the sisters applied to United Airlines for employment as commercial pilots. The sisters met United's requirements for "age, education, experience, and FAA certification qualifications" but not United's vision standards that required "uncorrected visual acuity of 20/100 or better." When United refused to consider their employment applications, they sued under the ADA. The sisters lost in both the District Court and the Tenth Circuit Court of Appeals. They then asked the U.S. Supreme Court to hear their case.

In the Supreme Court, the sisters argued that applicable regulations, the EEOC's "Interpretive Guidance," and a "similar guideline" issued by the Department of Justice, require that "[t]he determination of whether an individual is substantially limited in a major life activity must be made on a case-by-case basis, without regard to mitigating measures such as medicines, or assistive or prosthetic devices." Applying these rules, the sisters' uncorrected vision would have been a disability under the ADA.

The Supreme Court nonetheless ruled for United Airlines, seven to two, concluding that Congress never intended the ADA to protect, as disabled, those who, like the sisters, were able to "function identically to individuals without a similar impairment," when employing "mitigating measures such as medicines, or assistive or prosthetic devices." When enacting the ADA, the Court reasoned, Congress found that "some 43 million Americans have one or more physical or mental disabilities, and this number is increasing as the population as a whole is growing older."[26]

> Because it is included in the ADA's text, the finding that 43 million individuals are disabled gives content to the ADA's terms, specifically the term "disability." Had Congress intended to include all persons with corrected physical limitations among those covered by the Act, it undoubtedly would have cited a much higher number of disabled persons in the findings. [The Court noted that, under a more liberal definition of disability, the ADA could be read to include as many as "160 million disabled.] That it did not is evidence that the ADA's coverage is restricted to only those whose impairments are not mitigated by corrective measures.

The Court then stated its ruling:

> We conclude that respondent is correct that the approach adopted by the agency guidelines—that persons are to be evaluated in their hypothetical uncorrected state—is an impermissible interpretation of the ADA. Looking at the Act as a whole, it is apparent that if a person is taking measures to correct for, or mitigate, a physical or mental impairment, the effects of those

measures—both positive and negative—must be taken into account when judging whether that person is "substantially limited" in a major life activity and thus "disabled" under the Act.

Justice Ginsburg wrote a concurring opinion. She noted that Congress' purpose in adopting the ADA was "to restrict the ADA's coverage to a confined, and historically disadvantaged, class" of individuals, specifically those who, by reason of their disabilities, had been "subjected to a history of purposeful unequal treatment, and relegated to a position of political powerlessness in our society."[27] The "inclusion of correctable disabilities within the ADA's domain would extend the Act's coverage to far more than 43 million people. And persons whose uncorrected eyesight is poor, or who rely on daily medication for their well-being, can be found in every social and economic class; they do not cluster among the politically powerless, nor do they coalesce as historical victims of discrimination."

The Supreme Court applied its reasoning in a companion case to *Sutton*, *Murphy v. United Parcel Service, Inc.*[28] There, the Court ruled, on the same grounds as in Sutton, that an individual with hypertension (high blood pressure) that was "approximately 250/160" without medication was not a disability under the ADA because, with medication, his "hypertension does not significantly restrict his activities and... in general he can function normally and can engage in activities that other persons normally do." The Court affirmed the dismissal of Murphy's claim.

The Court reached the same result with respect to compensatory strategies in a related case, *Albertsons, Inc. v. Kirkingburg*.[29]

Together, these three cases hold that the effects (both positive and negative) of prosthetic devices (*Sutton*), medicines (*Murphy*), and compensatory strategies (*Kirkingburg*) must be considered when determining whether an individual has an impairment that substantially limits a major life activity and is therefore covered by the ADA.

Lower court decisions have made it clear that the severity of ADHD must be measured after considering the positive and negative effects of medication. In *Blackston v. Warner-Lambert Co.*,[30] the Court held that a person with ADHD whose condition is corrected by medication is not an individual with a disability within the meaning of the ADA. Blackston admitted, and his physician confirmed, that Blackston's ADHD, when treated with medication, did not present in such a manner as to substantially limit him in the major life activities of thinking and working.

In *Schumacher v. Souderton Area Sch. Dist.*,[31] the Court discussed the impact of Sutton on a middle school teacher's claim that her ADHD substantially limited her ability to engage in "cognitive thinking," eating, and sleeping, major life activities recognized as such by the Court.

> Therefore, under *Sutton*, to determine whether her continuing impairment qualifies as a disability, this court must consider whether Schumacher's ability to engage in these major life activities is substantially limited by ADHD, even in its corrected state, that is, even when she properly takes her medication as prescribed.... If medication controls ADHD such that it enables Schumacher to think, sleep, and otherwise function as would the average person, just as corrective eyewear enables a person with myopia to attain 20/20 vision, Schumacher would not have a disability under [the ADA]. However, this court is unable to say, at this stage, that ADHD, controlled by medication, still does not substantially limit Schumacher's ability to perform these major life activities and still does not render her disabled within the meaning of the ADA.... The Amended Complaint alleges that Schumacher remains limited in these activities and those allegations are accepted as true for present purposes.... Schumacher sufficiently has pled a disability under [the ADA].

Considering the total effects of the impairment, together with those of the prosthetic devices, medications, and strategies, makes the ADA/RA approach much closer to that used in the Social Security Act. In *Andersen v. Apfel*,[32] for example, the Court held that ADHD that is "remedied" by medication is not an SSI disability, because, under that law, any medical condition that is remedied by surgery, treatment, or medication is not disabling. Only individuals with ADHD that substantially limits a major life activity are considered disabled under the RA and ADA. The evaluation of ADHD's impact must take into account the positive and negative effects of any medication and compensatory strategies.

## How Measured

Human attributes such as intelligence, beauty, and athletic prowess are often measured by comparing those of the individual in question with those of other people. Impairments under the ADA are also measured by comparing those of the individual against a norm. However, while there is universal agreement on this point, there are divisions among judges, attorneys, and other professionals as to just what norm an impairment should be measured against. Several methods of comparison have been used under this standard.

*Price. v. The National Board of Medical Examiners*[33] considered the request of three medical students who had no history of substantial academic difficulties but had been diagnosed by responsible professionals as having learning disabilities and/or ADHD, for an injunction requiring additional time on the United States Medical Licensing Examination (USMLE), Step 1. The Court ruled that the students were not individuals with disabilities under the ADA because their impairments did not substantially limit them in a major life activity when compared to most people. The Court described the medical students thus:

> First, each plaintiff has some learning difficulty. Second, each of the students has a history of significant scholastic achievement reflecting a complete absence of any substantial limitation on learning ability. Further, this record of superior performance is corroborated by standardized test scores measuring cognitive ability and performance. Finally, there is a complete lack of evidence suggesting that plaintiffs cannot learn at least as well as the average person. That is, these students do not suffer from an impairment which substantially limits the life activity of learning in comparison with most people.

Based on these findings, the Court concluded that the medical students were not protected under the ADA. The Court focused on comparing bottom-line performance to the average person's performance.

If the courts were to focus on bottom-line performance compared to the average person, it would be difficult, under this test, to show the requisite impact at the college level and even more difficult to do so at the graduate school level, since the average person does not complete college.

## The Average Member of the Population

Proof of substantial limitation when compared to the average member of the population is essential. Who is the "average person"? These questions are of minor importance for persons with physical impairments, such as mobility, vision impairments, and hearing impairments, which can be measured in individual cases with a high degree of reliability and statistics compiled to generate a norm. This is less so for learning, attentional, and psychiatric impairments.

In *DeMar v. Car-Freshner Corp.*,[34] the Court denied the claim of an employee with ADHD because that essential proof was not forthcoming: "Plaintiff mistakenly leaps to the conclusion that because he has ADHD, his ability to concentrate is substantially limited as compared to the average person."

*Sevigny v. Maine Education Association-National Education Association*[35] reached a similar result. The magistrate hearing the case ruled that the plaintiff had failed to establish the existence of a disability. Specifically, the plaintiff failed to show that the conditions of his life with ADHD and depression were different from those of the average member of the general population. Noting that "Plaintiff has presented evidence that these conditions affect his ability to communicate, focus, and sleep," the magistrate observed:

> It is clear that Plaintiff has had to adopt particular methods of coping with his lack of focus and communication difficulties, but he has apparently done so success-

fully. There is nothing remarkable about developing tools "about taking notes and keeping track of things using a calendar in a different way and initiate conversations more successfully," or having to use "a lot of sort of detailed trial-and-error problem solving." Quite likely Plaintiff's impairments have simply forced him to acquire skills which would benefit most people.

Most glaringly, however, Plaintiff's only attempt to compare the manner in which he has to communicate, think, or sleep with the manner in which the average person can do these things is the one paragraph stating that "[t]hinking, concentrating, and communicating are activities that the average person in the population can do with little or no difficulty." While this may be true, it says nothing about how *well* the average person does them with little or no difficulty....

Plaintiff is asking the Court to conclude from the mere fact that his conditions *affect these aspects of his life that he is substantially limited in his abilities when compared to the average person. There is no evidence in the record to support this conclusion. [Citations to the trial record omitted.]*

In *Jones v. Men's Wearhouse*[36] the Court considered the case of a former employee with ADHD who sued his employer under the ADA. The Court found against the former employee, holding that (1) the existence of some behavioral difficulties arising from ADHD and the medications that address it does not amount to a substantial limitation on the ability to care for oneself, (2) difficulty recalling some words does not amount to a substantial limitation on the ability to speak, and (3) the existence of excellent work evaluations and a high college GPA shows that the former employee experienced no substantial limitation on the ability to learn.

These cases hold that the ADA requires a comparison between the individual's performance of major life activity and that of the average member of the population. *They recognize that the average is not the perfect person and does not perform these activities in a perfect manner.* As a result, the ADA requires proof not only of a substantial limitation or deviation but of a deviation from a benchmark that itself may have significant imperfections. In evaluating the impact of ADHD, the individual's ability to perform a major life activity must be compared to that of the average member of the population, recognizing that the average member's ability to perform those activities is imperfect.

## OTHERWISE QUALIFIED

The RA and ADA do not protect all individuals with disabilities, only those who are "otherwise qualified" for the educational program, job, or license at issue.[37] However, the very facts that show that an individual is one with a disability can also show that the individual is not otherwise qualified.

In *Robertson v. Neuromedical Center*,[38] for example, the Fifth Circuit upheld the termination of a neurologist with ADHD. Holding that there was no duty to accommodate Robertson in his medical practice, the Court said:

> We agree with the district court's conclusion that "[c]onsidering the limitations on plaintiff's abilities caused by ADHD, the type of work he is engaged in, the interests of NMC in running its business, and most importantly, the safety of the patients at NMC... plaintiff cannot establish a prima facie case that he could continue in his position as a neurologist because accommodation is not possible in these circumstances."
>
> Robertson posed a "direct threat" to the health and safety of others in the workplace. Robertson's short-term memory problems had already caused various mistakes to be made in patients' charts and in dispensing medicine. Most significantly, Robertson voiced his own concerns about his ability to take care of patients, stating that it was only a matter of time before he seriously hurt someone. In light of this evidence, we agree with the district court's conclusion that any accommodations in this case would be unjustified from the standpoint of the basic medical safety of Dr. Robertson's patients.

The very proof that showed Robertson to have ADHD amounting to a substantial limitation in a major life activity also showed that he was not qualified to perform his job.

In *Bercovitch v. Baldwin School, Inc.*,[39] the United States Circuit Court of Appeals for the First Circuit held that Jason, a student with ADHD, was not entitled to "be exempted from the normal operation of the school's disciplinary code" as a reasonable accommodation under either the ADA or the RA! The proposed accommodation was that the student "only be suspended after at least three warnings, and then only for the remainder of the day." This modification would eliminate "the normal progressive discipline built into the school's code" and would have prevented the school "from suspending Jason, as it would any other student, for repeated disruptive behavior." The Court ruled that "[t]his was an alteration of a fundamental requirement of the school's academic program and as such is not required by the ADA," or the RA, which the Court viewed as "imposing parallel requirements." Jason's behaviors had rendered him not otherwise qualified to attend the school. These problems exist with respect to licensing as well.

In the Spring of 1997, the Subcommittee on the Constitution of the House Committee on the Judiciary held a hearing regarding the "Application of the Americans with Disabilities Act to Medical Licensure and Judicial Officers." Testifying on behalf of the Federation of State Medical Boards was Ray Q. Bumgarner, Executive Director, State Medical Board of Ohio.

The Federation stated that requests for medical licensure testing accommodations are skyrocketing and are based primarily on learning disabilities and ADHD. According to the Federation testimony, anyone who asks for accommodations may put his or her competence to practice medicine legitimately at issue.

The Federation had this to say about ADHD and learning disabilities:

> Many disabilities, such as LD and ADD/ADHD, are life-long conditions which impact and impair one's functioning in a pervasive way. Any expert in the fields of these disabilities will confirm that they do not limit their impact solely to the context of standardized multiple-choice examinations. An individual with ADD/ADHD, for example, may be expected to have difficulty focusing and to be easily distracted or unable to concentrate in the presence of distractions in a testing context, but would be expected to encounter these same difficulties in other contexts as well.[40]

Quoting from ADA documentation provided by applicants with ADHD and learning disabilities, the Federation advised Congress that

> it would be relevant to a medical licensing authority to know that the responding applicant needed to be tested in a room separate from other people with double the amount of testing time because she asserted that "[I]n her day-to-day work, she is quite distractible so that it is hard for her to work or study in an environment in which there are many other people," or because "[n]oise, others talking, rustling papers, extra movement around him, etc. distract him and cause him to lose focus," or because he is "often having difficulty sustaining attention in tasks (especially in the area of reading), often having difficulty organizing tasks and activities, often avoiding or reluctant to engage in tasks that require sustained mental effort, and often not responding when spoken to directly. He is very easily distracted by extraneous stimuli, and quite frequently loses things necessary for an activity."
>
> While knowledge of the need for such accommodations in a context requiring intellectual functioning and decision making should not necessarily lead to the denial of a license, it might logically lead to further and appropriate inquiry as to the setting in which the physician intends to practice and the accommodations or modifications, if any, to be made in the practice setting to enable the physician to perform the essential functions of medical practice in a safe and competent manner.[41] [Emphasis added; footnotes omitted.]

Yet some physicians with dyslexia report difficulty with heavy reading requirements that call for rapid reading of complex material but report no difficulties in their clinical work. Other physicians with ADHD report difficulty with concentration and processing lengthy written tests but report receiving excellent evaluations in performing the actual work of a physician in their residencies. Since learning disabilities and/or ADHD present in a widely different manner in different people, applying general concepts about these disorders in individual cases would be unsound. Individual performance in clinical settings provides the best evidence of competence and should be determinative. The ADA protects only qualified individuals with disabilities. A qualified individual with a disability is one who can meet academic or job-related requirements with or without a reasonable accommodation.

## THE RIGHT TO REASONABLE ACCOMMODATION

### In General

Once an individual has shown that he or she is a qualified individual with a disability, the RA and ADA mandate that the individual be provided on request with reasonable accommodations in the academic and employment environments.

Reasonable accommodations are of three general types: (1) those required to ensure equal opportunity in the process of applying for admission to an academic program or for employment, (2) those that enable the individual with a disability to perform the essential features of a course of study or a job, and (3) those that enable individuals with disabilities to enjoy the same benefits and privileges, in both academic and job situations, as those available to individuals without disabilities. The first two of these are the most important for purposes of this chapter.

### Academic Accommodations

Academic accommodations are those modifications to the nonessential features of an academic program that will give to a qualified individual the opportunity of obtaining the same educational benefits as individuals without disabilities. These may include taped texts, interpreters or other effective methods of making orally delivered materials available to individuals with hearing impairments, brailled or large-print texts or qualified readers for individuals with visual impairments and learning disabilities, classroom equipment adapted for use by individuals with manual impairments, and other, similar services and actions.[42]

### Workplace Accommodations

Workplace accommodations are those modifications to the nonessential features of a job that will enable a qualified individual to perform the essential features of that job.

The EEOC has suggested that some or all of the following may be reasonable accommodations for individuals with psychiatric disabilities. They are of particular interest to many individuals with learning disabilities and ADHD.

- Time off: Use of accrued paid leave, or additional unpaid leave for treatment or recovery related to a disability. Occasional leave (e.g., a few hours at a time, or a leave of absence may prove appropriate).
- Modified work schedules.
- Physical changes to workplace or equipment. These might include room dividers, partitions, soundproofing, or visual barriers, accommodations recommended for "individuals who have disability-related limitations in concentration." Moving the individual to a quieter location, lowering the pitch of telephones, or permitting use of headphones to block distractions are also possibilities.
- Modification of a workplace policy. The EEOC suggests that "it would be a reasonable accommodation to allow an individual with a disability, who has difficulty concentrating due to the disability, to take detailed notes during client presentations even though company policy discourages employees from taking extensive notes during such sessions."
- Adjusting supervisory methods to ensure that assignments, instructions, and training are delivered "by the medium that is most effective for a particular individual (e.g., in writing, in conversation, or by electronic mail)." Increased feedback and structure are also reasonable accommodations.
  However, employer monitoring to ensure that required medications are taken is not a reasonable accommodation.
- Job coaches. The EEOC recommends the use of a temporary job coach to assist in the training

of a qualified individual with a disability as a reasonable accommodation.
- Reassignment to a vacant position must be considered as a reasonable accommodation when accommodation in the present job would constitute an undue hardship.

## Selecting the Accommodation

The process of selecting a reasonable accommodation is an interactive one. In *Beck v. University of Wisconsin*,[43] the Seventh Circuit Court of Appeals considered the case of a secretary who "suffered from osteoarthritis and depression." Following a three-month medical leave, she disclosed her disabilities and supported them with letters from her doctor. However, she refused to sign a release allowing the university to obtain further information from her doctor and provided no further information about her need for accommodations. Adjustment to her workload was the only accommodation specifically requested by the doctor, and it was granted. Following another medical leave, the university offered her old job back. When she insisted on another job, she was fired. She brought suit under the ADA. The Seventh Circuit affirmed the trial court's decision against the secretary, reasoning that the ADA and its regulations contemplate an interactive process to identify appropriate accommodations. The employer must provide information about its facilities and equipment, and the employee must provide information about his or her disability. The Court stated: "Once an employer knows of an employee's disability and the employee has requested reasonable accommodations, the ADA and its implementing regulations require that the parties engage in an interactive process to determine what precise accommodations are necessary." The same rules apply to academic accommodations.

The *Beck* case illustrates a common dilemma. Often an individual will seek the support of his or her medical or mental health professional to obtain an accommodation without realizing that the request may require the revelation of most or all of his or her medical record. The probability of full disclosure increases as the parties approach litigation. Medical records are often required to be produced in a case in which the impairment of the individual is at issue.

Accordingly, the individual and his or her mental health professional should take the time to consider a worst-case scenario in which the claim is refused and litigation becomes necessary. Is the individual comfortable with disclosure? Is the professional comfortable with defending the accuracy and thoroughness of his or her professional judgment? Qualified individuals with disabilities are entitled to reasonable accommodations. Reasonable accommodations are of three general types: (1) those required to ensure equal opportunity in the process of applying for admission to an academic program or for employment, (2) those that enable the individual with a disability to perform the essential features of a course of study or a job, and (3) those that enable individuals with disabilities to enjoy the same benefits and privileges, in both academic and job situations, as those available to individuals without disabilities.

## THE PROFESSIONAL'S OPINION

At the beginning of this chapter we noted that there are three basic elements of disability documentation: (1) diagnosis, (2) evaluation of impact, and (3) recommendations. Together they establish the existence of a disability, the areas of functioning affected by the disability, and the specific strategies and accommodations in education, testing, workplace, and life in general made necessary by that disability.

The professional's report or opinion should include:

- Identification of the individual's physical or mental impairment, using the current version of the *Diagnostic Statistical Manual* (DSM) where possible. (While not legally required, judges and attorneys are used to referring to this volume.)

# THE RIGHT TO REASONABLE ACCOMMODATION

## In General

Once an individual has shown that he or she is a qualified individual with a disability, the RA and ADA mandate that the individual be provided on request with reasonable accommodations in the academic and employment environments.

Reasonable accommodations are of three general types: (1) those required to ensure equal opportunity in the process of applying for admission to an academic program or for employment, (2) those that enable the individual with a disability to perform the essential features of a course of study or a job, and (3) those that enable individuals with disabilities to enjoy the same benefits and privileges, in both academic and job situations, as those available to individuals without disabilities. The first two of these are the most important for purposes of this chapter.

## Academic Accommodations

Academic accommodations are those modifications to the nonessential features of an academic program that will give to a qualified individual the opportunity of obtaining the same educational benefits as individuals without disabilities. These may include taped texts, interpreters or other effective methods of making orally delivered materials available to individuals with hearing impairments, brailled or large-print texts or qualified readers for individuals with visual impairments and learning disabilities, classroom equipment adapted for use by individuals with manual impairments, and other, similar services and actions.[42]

## Workplace Accommodations

Workplace accommodations are those modifications to the nonessential features of a job that will enable a qualified individual to perform the essential features of that job.

The EEOC has suggested that some or all of the following may be reasonable accommodations for individuals with psychiatric disabilities. They are of particular interest to many individuals with learning disabilities and ADHD.

- Time off: Use of accrued paid leave, or additional unpaid leave for treatment or recovery related to a disability. Occasional leave (e.g., a few hours at a time, or a leave of absence may prove appropriate).
- Modified work schedules.
- Physical changes to workplace or equipment. These might include room dividers, partitions, soundproofing, or visual barriers, accommodations recommended for "individuals who have disability-related limitations in concentration." Moving the individual to a quieter location, lowering the pitch of telephones, or permitting use of headphones to block distractions are also possibilities.
- Modification of a workplace policy. The EEOC suggests that "it would be a reasonable accommodation to allow an individual with a disability, who has difficulty concentrating due to the disability, to take detailed notes during client presentations even though company policy discourages employees from taking extensive notes during such sessions."
- Adjusting supervisory methods to ensure that assignments, instructions, and training are delivered "by the medium that is most effective for a particular individual (e.g., in writing, in conversation, or by electronic mail)." Increased feedback and structure are also reasonable accommodations. However, employer monitoring to ensure that required medications are taken is not a reasonable accommodation.
- Job coaches. The EEOC recommends the use of a temporary job coach to assist in the training

## REFERENCES

Latham, Peter S, J. D. and Patricia H., J. D., ATTEMTION DEFICIT DISORDER AND THE LAW, 2ND ED, JKL Communications (2000).

Latham, Peter S, J. D. and Patricia H., J. D., DOCUMENTATION AND THE LAW, JKL Communications, (1998).

# 12

# Making Marriages Work for individuals with ADHD

Patrick J. Kilcarr, Ph.D.

*I speak of journeys because of course we are all of us on a journey ourselves. The comparison of life to a road is a very ancient one, and you and I are travelers along that road whether we think of it that way or not, traveling from the unknown into the unknown. When we are on a journey, what is real is not so much the role we play, the mask we wear, in the place that we are leaving, and not even the roles we will soon be called on to play when we get to the place where we are going. In other words, travel can be a very unmasking experience, bringing us suddenly face to face with ourselves—as when we are gazing out of a train window at the endless line of telegraph poles whipping by, and we find that part of what we are looking at is our own reflection.*

Anonymous

This chapter explores the journey couples undertake when they choose to enter therapy. Entering therapy is not easy, especially for distressed couples whose relationships are characterized by varying levels of outrage toward one another. Confronting the myriad problems associated with attention deficit and hyperactivity disorder (ADHD) in a relationship is, quite probably, the most difficult challenge facing a couple in therapy. Bringing couples face to face with their own issues, and challenging them to acknowledge how those issues play out in the relationship, can be a very unmasking and unnerving process.

The symptoms and behaviors associated with ADHD influence relationships in varying ways. A partner suffering with chronic depression will strain the relationship differently than a partner whose ADHD is confined largely to forgetfulness. It is essential that the therapist working with the couple understands the precise nature of the symptoms encroaching on the relationship (Christensen & Heavey, 1999). Depression, which is often a condition coexisting with ADHD in adulthood, can create a circular interaction pattern whereby the depression serves to increase martial distress, while the marital distress exacerbates the depression (Gotlib & Beach, 1995). Knowing how the couple interprets the strength of the symptoms can indicate the depth of marital dissatisfaction.

This chapter will discuss two methodologies that have shown a great deal of promise in helping couples move farther down the relationship path and closer to embracing their own reflection in what can both hurt and heal the relationship. It will focus on the couple working in tandem to reduce marital stress and improve the quality of their respective lives. Since ADHD can often have negative effects on the marital relationship, working with the couple, irrespective of individual therapy, has the potential of liberating the couple from long-standing disappointment and entrenched negative behaviors (Jacobson & Addis, 1993).

Please note that the names used in the course of the chapter, especially the anecdotal examples of therapeutic interaction, are fictitious and are not intended to represent any specific person in therapy. Additionally, although there are many models of relationships in existence, the author will refer to individuals in a relationship as "spouses" for simplicity's sake in this chapter.

## OVERVIEW

In the field of marital/couples therapy and counseling, relationships that can be objectively qualified as "successful" or "nurturing" have certain distinct and lasting characteristics. Primarily, the individuals in the relationship tend to:

- Be more separate as persons (less dependent on what the significant other says or does in order to feel prized and confident about self)
- Exhibit high levels of self-esteem and self-worth
- Be more tolerant of one another's personal foibles and regressive behavior
- Have a clear communication ritual about topics that may be emotionally sensitive or difficult to discuss
- Treat formerly "charged" issues with humor
- Have more realistic expectations of the relationship and one another
- Express deeper levels of affection and be able to discuss issues of sex openly
- Display less hostility toward one another
- Be more accepting of the natural ebb and flow of intimate relationships
- *Not* be deeply disappointed that they are not passionately "in love" every waking minute (Markman, 1979).

These characteristics are important to consider when entering into a therapeutic relationship with couples who often initially present from the opposite place—i.e., an overarching sense of personal and relational despair, mixed with very little trust and even less mutual nurturance (Novotni, 1999). Symptoms attending the presence of ADHD in a partnership can "suck the air" right out of even the most promising relationship. The following will guide the reader in moving couples away from an emotional abyss and closer to a fulfilling and loving relationship.

Although there are many "different roads to Rome," the two therapeutic approaches discussed here seem to be particularly helpful in diminishing the stored-up anger while simultaneously offering the couple a more reasoned and loving way to manage ADHD issues specifically and relationship issues in general. The chapter will also highlight the use of specific communication strategies to diminish anger. Finally, issues specific to ADHD and substance abuse will be discussed. Active substance abuse (like depression)—not uncommon for those attempting to manage ADHD-related symptoms in their lives—must be proactively addressed early in the therapeutic process. It is something the therapist must ask about directly. The frequency, intensity, and duration of substance use must be established. Even if both spouses enter therapy willingly and with high hopes, the abusive use of substances by either or both will serve to effectively undermine any real movement toward change or personal growth. Overlooking this, or downplaying its importance, wil undermine a positive therapeutic outcome (Jacob, 1988).

## FOUNDATIONS: SETTING THE INITIAL STAGES OF THERAPY

By and large, in cases where ADHD-related symptoms play a significant divisive role in the relationship, couples seeking therapeutic intervention have already tried countless strategies and methods to "change" one another's negative behavior and attitude (Markman, Floyd, Stanley, & Clements, 1993). Each demands the other spouse change, and will not yield or budge until some type of impact is evidenced. Couples initially enter therapy with the intention to do everything possible to change the other person (Olson, 1976). Of course, this serves only to tighten the emotional "airlock" even further for each spouse when acting within the relationship.

When seeking therapy, couples are often lacking in three specific areas:

1. Their arsenal of prevention skills are depleted
2. Their abilities to communicate without resorting to the expression of derailing emotion(s), particularly anger, are compromised.
3. They promote the perspective that their spouses are "acting" in a particular and deliberate way to upset them—an undercurrent similar to that felt by parents about a child with ADHD (Kelly & Luquet, 1998).

The non-ADHD spouse is infuriated with the constant disjointedness of the other, while the spouse with ADHD feels he or she can do nothing right. The more the afflicted spouse tries to assure the other that he or she is trying and that the other should "just relax and take things in stride," the more over-the-top anger develops and is directed toward the person with ADHD.

In essence, by the time a couple "darkens a therapist's doorstep," at least one of the spouses has "one foot out the door." Both are exhausted, burned out, and, in some respects, feeling hopeless. As a husband reported to the author recently, "I feel like the pilot of a 747 making one last-ditch effort before the plane goes down."

As a therapist, instilling hope is critical. However, if either spouse is not open or committed to exploring different strategies in the relationship, instilling hope will be of little consequence (Christensen & Heavey, 1999).

It has been the experience of the author that, when working with couples where ADHD is the principal culprit, an engaging, interactive, and proactive methodology is most advantageous. While insight-oriented therapy can help individual's understand why certain patterns continue to unfold in the relationship, immediately offering the couple tools to interrupt the negative patterns is critical. Seeing a couple for the first time amplifies this point, as in the following dialog.

T: So, what brings you both here today?
W: Well, we heard a lot about the work you do with people who have ADD. My husband has it; he is honest about it. We tried a therapist before who just sort of nodded as we spoke, wrote stuff down, and occasionally stated the obvious.
T: Was it helpful, talking to the therapist?
W: It was helpful to talk—getting things out in the open—but when our time was up, we just went home without any sense of real direction or what to do.
T: So there was more you were looking for. What about for you, John? Do you feel similar to your wife?
H: I think it was important, but most of the time it was my wife ragging on me about crap I hear all the time anyway.

**T:** It felt like more of the same.
**H:** Definitely.

**T:** How would you like to see things happening here?
**H:** Be more positive, build on the good stuff, learn ways to communicate better. Like that.
**W:** I like us to be able to communicate, but he has to start listening to me and taking responsibility for what he does—
**H:** See, it's all about me.

**T:** Are you both willing to see the relationship and one another differently—not only try, but *learn*, new ways of dealing with each other? I mean, practice these new things between sessions?
**H & W:** Yes.

**T:** ADHD has been part of this relationship from the beginning. Parts of ADHD that used to be fun and enjoyable may no longer be; possibly, the symptoms also may have strengthened over time and become an irritant. What I gather is you want things to be different, or you would not have tried yet another therapist. Making changes *means working together*—hearing, responding, and consistently acting differently toward one another. ADHD is not going to go away. It requires managing the symptoms and working together—and taking responsibility for individual issues.
**W:** Yes, but *I* am not the one with the problem. If *he* changes, I know I'll change.

**T:** Yes, and vice versa. As you shift your attitude and perspective, he will also shift. Changing on your own, individually, *will* change the relationship. Let's explore some ways to accomplish this.

Providing a couple with the opportunity to vent and tell their story is essential. It is the first step in providing them with a critically needed arsenal of solid skills, information about ADHD, and strategies to reshape their relationship. To be offered strategies and skills by a therapist signals hope to the couple (Halverstadt, 1998; Satir, 1964). It also offers the opportunity to quell some of the seething resentment. The following provides a template to consider during the initial interview with the couple.

*Initial Stages of Therapy*

- Acknowledge the issues for which the couple has come to you.
- Probe their understanding of ADHD-related issues.
- Define what is working in their relationship.
- Challenge them on what has *not* been working for them (i.e., more of the same behavior).
- Assist them in mutually defining what they want to have in their relationship (goals).
- Instill in them the fact that, for change to occur, it must start with each spouse individually.

## TWO THERAPEUTIC APPROACHES

The following two models used in working with couples in varying degrees of distress were chosen for the expediency with which relational change can occur. Contextual therapy and behavioral marital therapy focus on presenting the interactional sequences between spouses that result in tension, negative intent, and an overall lack of enjoyment. Very little attention is paid to the past history of either spouse individually; however, both therapies *are* interested in what has transpired in the past when the couple has tried to "fix" what they perceived to be the problem(s). Embedded in these attempts are clues that can assist the couple in realizing and actualizing a positive relationship change (Weiss, 1978).

Spouses generally continue to interact in established and entrenched behavior rituals, despite the apparent fact that the behavior is not creating a desired change in their spouses (Knudson, Gurman, & Knishern, 1980). Both therapies work to uncover these repetitive patterns and replace them with positive interactional patterns that stem from the goals that embody what they both want in the relationship. Both therapeutic approaches take the view that we humans are largely products of our conditioning; therefore, they seek to change the stimuli in order to, by necessity, change the behavior. Thus, this change occurs when spouses consistently replace their traditional problematic communication-behavior patterns with mutually satisfying exchanges in the varied situations they face (Boszormenyi-Nagy, 1978).

## Contextual Therapy

The practice of contextual therapy is based upon the understanding that certain fundamental principles guide the stability (or instability) of an intimate relationship. Boszormeni-Nagy (1978) notes that both spouses must fully understand the nature of a disorder that affects the functional health of the relationship. In the present context, both spouses must understand the impact of adult ADHD—on the person trying to manage ADHD internally and on his or her spouse. A "reciprocity" of understanding must first exist so that each spouse can fully appreciate how ADHD affects them both. This can exist only if the facts surrounding the disorder—its emotional, psychological, occupational, spiritual, and relational aspects—are known and accepted by both spouses. This is an attempt to offer explanations for certain behaviors, rather than to generate excuses for either spouse. It cannot be overstated that it is also equally critical to understand the impact of ADHD-related symptoms on the non-ADHD spouse. As one spouse once said, "I don't have ADHD, but the result of her ADHD makes me feel like I do sometimes. Everything just feels out of whack."

In the course of the first therapy appointment, once both partners have had a chance to discuss the chief complaints, a contextual therapist may ask such things as the following.

**T:** I heard you both mention that Donna has ADHD. I am wondering what role this plays in your cycle of fighting and then distancing from one another?

**H:** I am not sure what you mean by what role it plays. She takes medication, so it is basically controlled. ADD is not the cause of our problems. It's the fact that the house looks like a mess and I am tired of constantly being the one to try keeping things halfway neat.

**T:** What I mean is precisely what you just mentioned. Have you two ever had anyone actually talk to you about how ADHD can affect your relationship? One of the hallmarks of ADHD is an inability to be organized. It feels like life is one big chaotic mess. It's not that the person doesn't try to "get with it and get things done"; in many ways, it's that they need a specific type of support to help stay on task. I would like to talk a bit more about the characteristics of ADHD. Then we can talk about a way that Donna can get a different type of support through you, while you in turn feel the house is more organized and less messy.

Once the facts of adult ADHD are uncovered and discussed by the couple in the therapeutic environment, the therapist and the couple can begin to explore the influence of the disorder on each spouse. In essence, the couple will unearth the *meaning* that has been attached to behaviors of importance (Boszomenyi-Nagy, 1978). For instance, a husband forgets to stop at the store and pick up bread on the way home. Since this has happened before in many different circumstances, his wife interprets his forgetfulness (an attribute of ADHD) as a sign of profound disrespect and irresponsibility. The action (forgetting to get the bread) is thus interpreted by the wife as a signature of disloyalty; the behavior is thereby transformed into a focus of major marital stress.

The following is an example of how meaning is attached to elements of importance by a spouse and how that meaning can keep a spouse with ADHD stuck in a repetitive and unfulfilling cycle of disapproval and tension.

**W:** It never fails. I ask him to do something... something as simple as picking up a loaf of bread, and he comes home all smiles and looks at me as if I should be all happy to see him. He is clueless. I ask where the bread is, and he just stares at me with this vacant look. He doesn't even say "sorry" or anything.

**T:** You interpret this as a lack of caring?
**W:** Anybody would.

**T:** What have you done in the past to address this issue?
**W:** I tell him I ask very little of him. All I need is a loaf of bread, or the thousands of other small, simple things I have asked for and have never gotten.

**T:** Are there times where he follows through and does what you ask?
**W:** Not often enough.

**T:** Is it nice when he does follow through for you?
**W:** It's like... it's about time, you know? This is what you are supposed to do.

**T:** Taylor, how often are you in the doghouse?
**H:** When am I *not* in the doghouse? I can't do anything to please her. When I do [follow through], she's ticked because I should be doing it all the time. It really is damned if I do and damned if I don't.

**T:** What do you do then, when you feel continuously scolded?
**H:** That's it! I feel scolded like a bad dog. What do you do when you can't do anything right to please someone? I deal with it by not dealing with it. I turn away and get away from her as quickly as possible. Of course, she follows me, slinging barbs and calling me an idiot. Like she can really make me feel worse than I do! I know I forget stuff and act too much like one of the kids, or don't remember things she mentions to me, like things we are going to do. It's very hard to be me sometimes.

**W:** It's not too hard to remember basic things. You remember what you have to do at work. But when I ask things, *literally*, forget about it! It means you don't care.

This vicious cycle keeps this couple locked in an a very suffocating parent/child relationship. They have internalized, personalized, and attached negative intent to the behavior stemming from ADHD. The wife globalizes her husband's forgetfulness, while he fuels her anger by refusing to acknowledge the inappropriateness of his forgetfulness.

It is also possible for a non-ADHD spouse to feel that the spouse with ADHD is using those symptoms to align against her or him (Bowen, 1978). If the afflicted spouse either fails to take responsibility for ADHD behaviors or uses them as an excuse, the non-ADHD spouse can feel subsumed by a feeling of powerlessness. This can result in a mutually destructive interaction sequence, resulting in severe power struggles.

When a couple gets to the point where the relationship is characterized by seething anger with occasional respites (as demonstrated by the previous example), the therapist's responsibility is to invite the couple to consider the concepts of relational ethics or equitable fairness (Boszormenyi-Nagy, 1978; Boszormenyi-Nagy & Spark, 1976). These concepts measure the degree to which the couple is interested in redirecting their established negative communication and interactional patterns. The first step in beginning the process of change involves having the couple define what it would mean to have an "equitable" relationship.

Both spouses are *entitled* to have their interests and welfare considered. This process takes these values into account by defining what it would take for the couple to achieve mutual respect and trustworthiness. What would each need to see from the other person to risk shifting his or her own perspective? What would each be willing to do differently in order to achieve the results they both want?

Continuing the discussion with the previous couple will more accurately define this process.

T: All right, it is obvious you both are angry and hurt.
W: What does *he* have to be hurt about? I am not the one forgetting to do the things he asks. Maybe I should just forget to pick up the kids, or his clothes, or his mother when she calls.
T: When you get this angry and hurt, so angry you could just burst, how does it benefit the relationship?
W: I feel better. I don't feel so controlled.
T: I understand how it makes you feel. However, I am interested in how it benefits the relationship.
H: It only makes us more distant. It doesn't benefit anything.
T: Would you agree, Anne?
W: It doesn't help us. But it does make me feel better.
T: What would you like to have in your relationship? How would you like it to be?
W: I've said this a zillion times. Just listen to me, and remember something when asked by me!
T: Again, this is a bit tricky. However, I am asking how you would like the relationship to be rather than how you want to be treated.
H: I want us to be able to talk about difficult things without becoming angry or distant, for there to be enough respect to want to hear the other person and do whatever is possible to meet our needs. I want to laugh.
W: I want to be close. To rely on each other for support. To deal with anger or disappointment respectfully. Like Taylor said, to live with respect, really.
T: Part of our challenge, then, is to define what it would mean for both of you to live with and treat each other with respect. Defining the concept of *respect* is important. It begins with what are you willing to do to begin creating the type of relationship you want. Up until now, Anne, you have been waiting for Taylor to change. And Taylor, you have been waiting for Anne to be more understanding. All the while, you are both continuing to treat each other with disrespect and anger. Let's begin defining what you could do to have the type of relationship you described.

Prior to this conversation, the couple relentlessly engaged in a perilous dance, undermining the basic marital trust and perpetuating "relational stagnation" (Bowen, 1978). This pattern of interaction ignores the essential premise that basic loyalty toward one another is reinforced when fairness binds the relationship. Unlike children, who will keep trying relentlessly until their trust in their parent is utterly depleted, spouses will not instinctively show the same resiliency toward one another. Even if a couple locked in this pattern chooses (or, more accurately, *resigns*) to stay together for moral, financial, or other reasons, the level of loyalty to the relationship is profoundly weak so long as the underlying problems remain unaddressed (Jacob, 1988; Satir, 1964).

Murray Bowen (1978) noted that the process of *individuation*, or differentiation of self, occurs in a context of being responsible to and for others. To use a Biblical example, when Moses related the covenant between God and the Hebrews in the form of the Ten Commandments, he did not editorialize what he was directed to convey by saying "I will follow this commandment only if I like it" or "only if it serves my best interest." In its essence, the Ten Commandments embody the ultimate description of human responsibility. It invites everyone to "do unto others as you would have them do unto you." Each spouse's owning responsibility for his or her own behavior—regardless of their origins or of the forces that sometimes influence them—is necessary for lasting therapeutic change to occur.

If we want loyalty from those around us—especially our spouses—then we *must* assume responsibility for our behavior (Boszormenyi-Nagy, 1978; Kosten, Jalale, Seidl, & Kleber, 1987; Liberman, 1970; Markman, 1979). While we can *share* loyalty (for instance, loyalties we owe to our spouse, to our children, and/or to our coworkers), we cannot *split* loyalty. To illustrate using our example, the wife was splitting her loyalty by vacillating between her roles as spouse and as parent. This type of split creates divisiveness and confusion; in turn, this further fuels the firestorm of anger on both spouses' parts. The therapist in our example began to lead the couple on a journey toward relational integrity through self-motivation. This entails work by each spouse to redefine relational commitments and realign the balance of fairness (Jacobson & Margolin, 1979).

In order to foster such realignment, a therapist may ask probing questions, such as, "What happened after that event?" "How did you see her treat you?" "How would your spouse have described what made you so upset?" "How would you have wanted it to happen differently?" The goal of these exchanges is to get the couple to shift their intentions so that they can create an environment where they more deeply understand one another. Of course, this takes a willingness to abandon established patterns and to finding the motivation to resist allowing these "old" patterns to continue dominating their reactions and interactions (Stierlin, 1976).

The *primary shift in intentions* involves embracing a willingness to "imagine" what the other spouse may feel or experience during specific negative situations (grasping the partner's interpretations of events). An example would be for the husband in our previous example to describe what it must have been like for his wife to rely on him and ask him to do something and then for him to fail to do it. The flip side has the wife describe the feeling of being berated, even emasculated, when he forgets.

The following is example provided by a different couple.

T: All right Ben, Karen is describing what it is like for her to live with the uncertainty of not knowing if you will stay in this current job or get restless and leave for something on the spur of the moment. She says you are beginning to talk in ways that usually indicate that you are about to leave your job. Can you put yourself in Karen's shoes and describe what it would be like to live, as Karen puts it, "on the edge of an abyss?"

H: It would suck, but I am not going to do anything stupid.

T: (gently leaning in) Slow down. It is very important that you describe what it would be like to be in that position. How would it feel? What would it be like?

H: It would make me very nervous... not knowing if there would be enough money to pay the bills, maybe having to move the kids away from their friends. My father was in the service, so I know what that felt like, which was bad. You know, a job is like the foundation of a house. If the foundation is weak, the structure is in trouble. And changing jobs without talking to me about it first would make me upset. I have a right to know, especially since I am her husband. It's not a good feeling.

T: Knowing this, how can you include Karen in the decision-making process and take her feelings into account?

Along with the shift in intentions is a *description of intentionality*. This involves the wife's understanding and accepting that her husband does not intentionally neglect her input or make snap judgments despite her fears. His impulsive job changes and maneuvering are functions of his ADHD. His corresponding responsibility is to determine what skills or strategies he needs to employ to be less impulsive and to be more accommodating and inclusive of his wife (Jacobson & Margolin, 1979).

Likewise, his wife does not initially intend to get angry and belittle him; rather, her frustration and inability to understand his behavior usher forth intense anger and hurt, often resulting in extreme put-down behavior. He must realize that her outbursts are reactions to the situations and not "value judgments" as to his worth. For her part, she must determine what skills or strategies she needs to acquire in order to manage her annoyance in ways that are not damaging to her husband and by extension to the relationship (Stierlin, 1976).

Establishing new patterns of behavior and interaction requires that the therapist track the movement of the couple toward their stated goals of change in their relationship. Goal-setting outlines, in very detailed language, set out where the couple wants to be and what they are willing to do differently in order to get there (Sager, 1976; Margolin & Weiss, 1978). If they are struggling, the therapist can ask, "I wonder what more you can do at this point. You are willing to hear each other differently, yet things at home seem very similar to when you came in. What are you not doing enough of?"

Even if the couple reports failed attempts (such as "I try, but it doesn't seem to help"), the therapist can engage with follow-up questioning that will reveal the context (the backdrop to what the couple is and is not doing), for example, "What do you try, and how would you know if it was working?" (Haley, 1976). It is always essential to define the context within which the couple is attempting to make changes. The *most important* context within which the couple interacts surrounds their stated goals for change (Jacobson, 1977).

Movement by one spouse will necessarily influence the movement of the other (Halverstadt, 1998). True "neutrality" does not exist in any relationship, particularly a strained one. Therefore, a positive movement by one spouse will beget some type of shift in the other; the same is certainly true for negative behavior. The goal(s) they are working toward will provide the impetus for every instance of growth or regression (Knudson et al., 1980). If they say they have a particular goal yet are not working toward it between sessions, the therapist must develop a goal that is agreed upon *and* reinforced by action beyond the confines of the therapist's office (Gotlib & Heavey, 1999). This may be completely different than the goal they originally stated. The therapist may say, "So, this past week seemed like more of the same. Can you describe precisely what you experienced as not working? Once we determine this, let's revisit the goals you agreed upon and see how they need to be changed so you can experience success."

The foundation of contextual therapy is the relational and interactional change that occurs when the couple *chooses* to replace disruptive communication patterns with healthy interactional strategies, thus changing the context within which the relationship exists. These strategies are developed during the therapy sessions *and* are practiced between sessions.

Here is a summary of how contextual therapy with couples should work.

The Use of Contextual Therapy with Couples

- Educate both spouses on the facts regarding the impact of ADHD (on self and the relationship).
- Explore the meaning each attaches to the other's behavior. What type of behavior does this meaning ignite?
- Identify the real or perceived power alignments against either spouse.
- Define the concept of *relational ethics*, where both are entitled to have their interests and welfare considered.
- Illustrate that relationship change emerges from clear and agreed-on goals established by the couple.
- Continually refine the goals based on between-therapy behavior and interaction sequences.

## Behavioral Marital Therapy

In many ways, behavioral marital therapy is an outgrowth of social learning theory (Mahoney, 1974), which attempts to describe the pervasive effects of social influence on the development of behavior in human beings, most specifically that of verbal and nonverbal communication (Gottman, Markman, & Notarius, 1977). Each spouse brings to a relationship his or her own personal reinforcement history and an emotional ledger detailing the cost and benefits of the spousal relationship. These include ideas of very specific behaviors and interactions that are considered either positive or negative.

This discussion will strive to elucidate the behavioral ingredients embedded in a "successful" or "satisfactory" relationship. While that is defined differently for each individual (and therefore each couple), certain criteria seem to indicate the strength or health of a relationship. A relationship can be extremely gratifying to both partners during its initial stages, only to crumble when they must traverse its initial major conflict (Christensen & Heavey, 1999). The symptoms associated with ADHD can escalate this conflict in an unrelenting fashion (Kelly & Luquet, 1998).

From a behavioral perspective, "satisfaction" in a relationship is dependent on the rate of reinforcers (positive behaviors) received from the spouse. The frequency with which reinforcers are received will determine the rate of rewards the spouse is willing to return. ADHD lends itself to a dynamic wherein the spouse perceives very little consistent reward, thus becoming less willing to give in return. An individual's reinforcement history and predilections for certain reinforcers are not static or fixed. Rather, they are constantly modified by experiences in the relationship (Weiss, 1978).

These modifications are often based on the "rules" that exist in and govern the relationship. Haley (1976) noted that intimate relationships require a complex division of roles, responsibilities, and obligations in order to function smoothly. This occurs only where considerable consensus between the spouses exists regarding which behaviors are appropriate and which inappropriate in particular situations.

By their very nature, ADHD-related behaviors serve to undermine the prospect of a relied-on division of roles and responsibilities within the relationship. Normative reinforcing behavior is frequently overshadowed by the inconsistent and negative secondary effects of ADHD. If the relationship is not governed by predictable rules, mutually rewarding behaviors decrease in frequency and intensity (Weiss, 1978). The degree of satisfaction that spouses experience in the relationship depends on how the couple relate to one another with respect to the specific needs of each. If these needs are not positively addressed, satisfaction and stability decline (Patterson, 1976). Jacobson and Anderson (1980) point out that there is some evidence that, as the expectation for rewarding behavior dwindles, distressed couples notice "selectively" and attend almost exclusively to negative behavior. The following describes the interaction between a couple and a behavioral marital therapist where both spouses suggest that the "costs" of the relationship far exceed the "rewards."

T: Sheila, you mentioned you are extremely unhappy with your life right now. Have there been times in the relationship with Todd when you were more satisfied?

W: After we got married, Todd would take me out to dinner after a long day at the office. He would surprise me with a rose or some type of gift—not expensive, just something to show how much he cared. He would call me during the day and chat. Basically, he was interested in me. He showed he cared by the small things. He did them consistently, though.

T: And what changed?

W: Work and his clients became more important than me and the children. I guarantee his clients know he cares. He takes them to dinner, buys them wine during the holidays, has his secretary send out cards. The most attention I get is a "Hi, hon" when he comes home, whenever that might be.

H: What do you expect? You are nothing but a sourpuss constantly. I am tired of hearing what I am not doing for you. Yeah, I do work long hours. I know at work where I stand and how the system works. I know when I do the right thing I will get praise—not "Oh, even though you did this, you forgot to do thus and so." Come on. No one in his right mind would subject himself to this!

This couple has conditioned one another to seek out and expect the worst in the relationship. As a result, positive moments are overlooked in an attempt to identify the negative behaviors that are at the center of their unrest. Unhappy couples tend to attempt to bring about behavior change and compliance through aversive control tactics—that is, by strategically presenting punishment and withholding rewards.

As we will see, the therapist attempts to promote the notice of enhancing stability and satisfaction by linking current conflict antecedents in the couple's interaction with undesirable relational outcomes.

T: You both mentioned very specific things that bother you in the relationship. Take a moment and describe for me what leads up to the conflict and unrewarding interaction. Now Todd, when you hear Sheila describe what bothers her, what creates the problem situation? What do you hear her saying?

H: I suppose that I don't do anything right.

T: Sheila, is that accurate?

W: No. I said it [the problem] is not paying attention specifically to me. Like taking me out to a quiet, enjoyable dinner, bringing flowers occasionally, letting me know you still care.

T: When these things don't happen on occasion, what happens?

W: I get upset and try to make him feel like I feel—unappreciated.

T: So Todd, what are the things leading up to your wife's anger?

H: Not showing I care.

T: Not showing you care in very specific and predictable ways.

H: Even if I did start doing these things again, she still would find something to be angry at me about.

T: I don't know if that is true. I know that showing caring in ways that are positive for your wife will certainly change her attitude and feelings toward you. Would you agree?

H: Yes, I guess.

This same type of exploration was done with the wife. She realized, after "stepping into Todd's shoes," that she would summarily dismiss whatever he would say because she was angry and wanted to punish him or at least have him experience her frustrations. This only served to make him even more recalcitrant in his responses toward her. Choosing to hear him out would more closely approximate the type of response she has been looking (longing) for.

Changing the previously negative antecedents leading to the relationship's problems will have a positive influence on how the spouses begin to view the level of satisfaction that exists in the relationship. By increasing the reinforcement value for one another, a greater likelihood exists that those reinforcing behaviors will be applied to other areas in the relationship (Jacobson, 1977).

**Flow of Behavioral Therapy**

Several aspects of behavioral marital therapy are important—the flow of the therapeutic process and enhancing positive regard within the relationship. Behavioral therapists working with couples generally follow a specific format to achieve a level of desired behavior change within the relationship. The first part of the process entails spending very little time on the presented problem(s). The early history of the relationship is explored so the couple can refocus their energies on earlier, happier moments, with the intention of elevating the feelings of positive regard within the relationship (Jacobson & Martin, 1976). The couple is asked to reflect on how they met and on what characteristics were initially attractive about one another. Details involving the courtship are elicited in order to begin reshaping their perspective toward one another. This alone helps place their current problems in a different perspective.

The second part of the process entails exploring the types of problems each spouse experiences. As noted earlier when discussing contextual therapy, spouses enter therapy feeling victimized by the other and believe that the therapist must work aggressively to change their spouse. In practice, then, the therapist spends quite a bit of time defining the exact nature of the problem(s). This includes identifying the antecedents inciting the problem, the couple's interaction with respect to the problem, and the outcome as embodied in the couple's resolution of the problem (Robinson & Price, 1980).

In doing so, the therapist can instruct each spouse to keep a *behavior log* of the other, documenting when and what type of troubling behavior occurred between sessions. When documenting these behaviors, the spouse is not to respond but rather just to write them down and bring the notes to the following session. The therapist takes these respective accounts and converts them into language that avoids assigning blame to either spouse. The reformulated information is delivered in an objective manner and as an expert opinion. This serves to expand the couple's perspective, which, hopefully, leads to a consideration of other behavior options. The therapist facilitates their acceptance of mutual accountability and responsibility for maintaining the current distressed state of the relationship (Liberman, 1970). This is important, because distressed couples, by the time they enter therapy, often severely underutilize the repertoire of reinforcers they already have. An example of this follows.

T: Let's explore the type of interaction between you two that creates such tension in the relationship. Todd, could you give us examples of what happens between you and Sheila to create such difficulties?

H: "There's a lot. To be specific, it is when I do something that annoys Sheila and she just blows up and starts giving me grief about anything or everything I have ever done. She starts getting all upset and then I shut down. It's either that or explode.

T: I want to understand this. You do something to upset Sheila She gets annoyed and begins bringing in a lot of past behavior or hurts that were not resolved. This gets you mad and you withdraw. Is this accurate?

H: Yeah.

T: Sheila, does this sound fair to you? I sense that this is one of the major stress points for you two.

W: Yes. However, I get so frustrated because I have told him so many times it is ridiculous. He doesn't respect me. If he did, he would try to take my feelings into account and stop doing it.

T: So, you ask Todd specific things that he doesn't remember to do, or he keeps doing the same things over and over. What are those things?

W: I ask him to clean up his clothes, put away things he takes out, pick up something on the way home—these type of things. His refusal to do them shows he couldn't care less.

T: Is it true Todd? You don't care?

H: Of course I care. I just get distracted and start thinking about other things and forget, pretty much. I wish I could remember more things.

W: You seem to remember everything you need to at work. If you did at work what you do at home, you'd be fired.

H: I keep very detailed schedules at work to remember. It's hard, but I do it. I don't want to have to work that hard at home.

T: What you are saying, though, is that you have a system at work that allows you to be successful. Is there anyone at work that helps remind you of certain things you must do?

H: Yes, my secretary. She keeps my schedule and reminds me—and at times re-reminds me—of what I need to do.

T: Can you describe how she asks you? It seems she asks in such a way that you respond and are successful.

H: She just writes me a note reminding me. Or, now that I am thinking of it, she uses gentle touches on my shoulder so I look at her, and then she reminds me.

T: One of the primary issues of having ADHD is the high level of distraction that can be very annoying for both the person with ADHD and significant others. Taking models that are successful in one place, like work, and using them in other places, like home, will certainly reduce the distraction and forgetfulness that accompanies ADHD. I don't believe you will have to work harder or be a slave to lists. You both can partner with one another to be more successful. How can your wife appropriately remind you in conjunction with strengthening your commitment to following through? You already seem to have a good formula for success. Once you begin working as a team, rather than aligning yourselves as adversaries, things will change significantly. Let's describe exactly what this plan would look like.

The therapist taps into an existing positive relationship in the husband's life and suggests extrapolating this process to home and the relationship with his spouse. As in every other area of joint therapy, both spouses have to agree to work together on shifting the relationship. Enhancing the spouses' collaborative behavior involves obtaining their commitment to follow the therapist's instructions. The therapist informs the couple about what they can expect from each other if they follow this new formula. To demonstrate its practical viability, some role-playing, based on a recent incident, is initiated in the session. Once the couple has a clear sense of what to do when tension and disappointment arise, the therapist has them actually sign a contract acknowledging they will follow the instructions (Sager, 1976). When couples do this, a fairly high rate of compliance and subsequent behavior change follow (Markman, 1979).

It is also important to inform the couple that progress toward sustained relationship improvement may tend to occur in a more inconsistent, rather than linear, fashion. Reminding the couple of possible "relapses" to pretherapy behavior helps diminish feelings of failure. In fact, merely mentioning the potential of a relapse can help ward it off (Haley, 1976).

### Enhancing Positive Regard

There are several strategies the therapist can employ to enhance positive regard in the relationship, including contingency contracting and communication training.

**Contingency Contract** Weiss, Birchlerr, and Vincent, (1974) developed a tool called the *contingency contract*. This strategy is generally most effectively used by couples who find it very difficult to make any type of substantive change within the relationship without some level of assurance by their spouse that they will also shift their behavior. The contingency contract essentially states, "I will do this, if you will do that." This quid-pro-quo relationship is most effective when both sign an agreement detailing the type of behaviors that each will demonstrate.

Each session follows up on the successful completion of the contract. The contract should be equally costly (and beneficial) for both spouses. It should delineate what happens if someone does not follow through. Finally it should include how the couple should celebrate following the contract. Also, the exact nature of the contingency should be specified (that is, when, where, and how much of the behavior must occur in order to produce the partner's "reinforcer"). Lastly, the contingency contract must spell out how the exchange is to be reinstated in the event of a transgression by a spouse.

**Communication Training** A critical part of behavioral marital therapy lies in training couples to utilize effective communication strategies (Jacobson & Addis, 1993). One of the primary reasons that couples seek therapy is that they have lost the art of communicating. Communication training tends to be change oriented rather than expression oriented (Weiss, 1978). Whereas most approaches to communication training focus on the reception and expression of feelings, behavior therapy teaches couples how to communicate in order to facilitate the resolution of conflict. While the expression of feelings is important, the skills imparted to couples in therapy attempt to train them to solve future conflicts better. This consists of four basic elements: rehearsal, feedback and shaping, mirroring, and solution focus.

*Rehearsal (Practice Makes Perfect)* As couples practice the new behaviors, they move closer to achieving mastery of the new interaction skills. Rehearsal provides feedback to the therapist of the individual's competency in enacting the new skill. Corrective feedback, along with successive approximations toward the desired skill, moves the couple toward competency (Jacobson & Anderson, 1980).

*Feedback and Shaping* The couple's practice attempts receive feedback from the therapist. Therapists tend to be descriptive rather then interpretive. The therapist should therefore focus on the functional aspects of the behavior (e.g., "Is it getting you what you want?"). Thus, the therapist will point out negative behaviors that occur in session: "Did you realize you just interrupted her? This is one of the key behaviors that bothers her." The whole training process can be thought of as a type of "shaping," because it endeavors to shape the couple's behaviors to be more in line with what they want and expect (Patterson, 1976).

An essential element of shaping is being able to communicate individual needs accurately and *maintain realistic perceptions and expectations* of one another's behavior (Weinstein & Block, 1998). Individuals with ADHD have difficulty slowing down their thought processes enough to actually hear what their spouse is saying. Their thoughts barge right by the important messages the spouses is trying to impart. They are busy thinking about a variety of things, none of which immediately register with what their spouse is trying to convey. Understanding this can give way to utilizing very specific strategies to focus the spouse in on what is being said.

*Mirroring* This author uses a modified version of a *mirroring technique* in order to focus couple communication while concomitantly identifying and reducing the faulty transmission or reception of information. This requires couples to look one another directly in the eyes, say what they need to say, and wait for the spouse to "mirror" back what they heard (or thought they heard). The following passage demonstrates this technique.

T: Now I would like you both to try the mirroring technique with one another. I know it seems almost silly, having to parrot back what the other person is saying, but I think you will find it enlightening to learn what you have been missing in your conversations. Jim, you start with an issue you want to bring to Patty's attention.

H: Okay, Patty, I look forward to coming home at the end of the day. When I come home from work, I know you want me to begin pitching right in with the kids and talking with you about my day. But I need a little bit of time just to shake off the workday before I can enter into the commotion of the family.

W: You need more time to rest when you get home before I should ask you anything.

T: Is that accurate, Jim?
H: Not exactly.
T: Can you repeat to Patty what you said? Patty, can you keep your eyes directly on Jim's as he speaks? Jim, can you try to shorten it and be more concise?

**H:** I look forward to coming home at night. I need time to shake off the workday before totally engaging with you and the kids.

**W:** You look forward to coming home at night, and need time to shake off the workday before engaging with me and the children.

**T:** Was that accurate?

**H:** Yes it was.

**T:** Did you feel heard by Patty?

**H:** Yes. And while it felt kind of artificial, I know she heard me.

This type of mirroring continues for both partners around issues they want to resolve. They go back and forth, mirroring what they hear the other person saying. In the initial stages of this exercise, the spouses do not comment on what they hear. Later, they can respond to what is being mirrored (which itself is then also mirrored back). This is very effective in disrupting the common and negative process whereby neither spouse actually hears what the other is saying. This retrains the couple to slow down, to hear exactly what the other person is saying, and to acknowledge that both heard it. This is followed by a reply that is in turn also mirrored.

*Solution Focus* Spouses learn to generate solutions through the process of brainstorming (Goldfried & Davidson, 1971). Couples brainstorm by generating as many solutions to specific problems as possible, without regard to quality. The idea of this exercise is to be imaginative and not to censor the other's ideas. This is particularly helpful when the couple is stuck at the solution phase. Brainstorming can be liberating and can enhance the production of creative solutions. All solutions, however improbable, are noted in writing by the therapist and discussed in turn with the couple. Some suggestions are eliminated, the remaining suggestions are ranked, and the top solutions are chosen. A plan (the development of which requires mutuality and compromise from each spouse) is devised, with a final agreement being written down and signed by all.

Here is a summary of the main points of behavioral marital therapy.

Essential Aspects of Behavioral Marital Therapy

- Explore the early positive parts of the relationship in order to shift the focus from the negative.
- Incorporate a clear and exhaustive understanding of the exact behaviors that are seen as problematic, along with a recognition of what each spouse does when these occur.
- Identify the solutions that have been tried to ameliorate the problem(s).
- Role-play in the session. The couple brainstorms on solutions and receives corrective feedback to create mutual and lasting problem-solving strategies.
- The couple signs a contract agreeing to follow specific between-session behavior outlined by both spouses.
- Discuss the concept of *behavioral reversal*. Suggest that old behavior may creep back into the relationship, and identify methods whereby the couple can prepare for and prevent it.

## SUPPLEMENTAL INTERACTION STRATEGIES

In addition to employing the techniques and strategies of contextual therapy and behavioral marital therapy, several communication strategies are available to couples that, if used consistently, can offer opportunities to create lasting change within their relationships. Where ADHD has been a principal organizing factor, a relationship experiences less emotional and physical satisfaction the longer it lasts. Affected couples define their relationships by what they lack rather than by what they possess. Years of arguing, unfulfilled expectations, and consistent disappointment have left them feeling barren in the relationship. The following sections describes two supplemental strategies that can maximize the effectiveness of either (or both) general therapeutic approaches discussed earlier.

## Caring Days

Olson (1976) describes a couple activity he termed *caring days*. It requires that each spouse list the behaviors he or she values in the other. The therapist spends time observing the compilation, in writing, of these specific behaviors. The key is that these specific behaviors be able to occur at least once a day and preferably several times a day. Even highly distressed couples can remember behaviors they enjoyed seeing in the past, such as, "I really used to like it when he would stop by the store on the way home and surprise me with dessert." A brief sample list appears at the end of this discussion.

Creating this list is empowering for both spouses, because each now has a codified list of ways he or she can please and show appreciation for the other. Each spouse's level of caring for the other is evidenced by the presence of these behaviors. Marriage is monotonous and stale without the presence of these experiences, whereas the presence of these behaviors is a harbinger of increased commitment, stability, and satisfaction. As these behaviors increase in frequency and intensity, each spouse's motivation to be more giving and understanding will likewise increase. Coupled with the skills of active listening, such as mirroring, in-session rehearsal of specific behaviors, and the use of corrective feedback, this approach can increase the expression of affection, reduce hostility, and move the couple significantly closer to their stated treatment goals for the relationship (Jacobson, 1977).

If both spouses agree to the "caring days" exercise, they must agree to demonstrate at least ten of the documented behaviors each day. The list they have created is open-ended, allowing for new behaviors to be added on a regular basis. Each spouse is asked to demonstrate these behaviors independent of those of the other. This allows each spouse the opportunity to model for the other the depth of his or her caring and commitment. It is not tit for tat. Although the behaviors are offered irrespective of the other partner, if done consistently, a natural reciprocity will be established. Therefore, one partner's failure to display acts of caring cannot be used to justify the other's failure to do so. The therapist makes it clear that each person is committing to this exercise. While each may expect the other to forget or not follow through, the "caring days" exercise will occur because of their commitment. This countermines the tendency for each to withhold positive behaviors until positives are received and helps to neutralize the expectation that the other person must change first.

Each spouse is asked to record the number and type of caring behaviors he or she has both given and received from the other. At the end of the day, the total indicates each partner's level of commitment to the relationship. If one partner does not show the "caring days" behaviors or does so modestly, the therapist revisits the couples' goals for therapy and works with the couple to determine where the difficulties reside.

**Sample List for the "Caring Days" Exercise**

*Wife's Request:*

1. Greet me with a hug and a kiss when you come home from work.
2. Surprise me with flowers.
3. Talk with me at night for at least ten minutes.
4. Tell me I look attractive.
5. Please don't demean my having ADD.
6. Touch me gently some time during the day.

*Husband's Request:*

1. Offer to make me breakfast when you make yours.
2. Rub my back.
3. If you ask a question, give me a little time before I answer.
4. Tell me you still care.
5. Forgive my roughhousing with the boys.
6. Laugh at least once a day when you would rather scream.

## Budging Grudges

Typically, distressed couples enter therapy harboring a great deal of mistrust and past hurt with respect to their spouses. This is particularly true for those presenting with issues related to ADHD. As noted earlier, the consistent disappointment and frustration when one's needs have not been understood or recognized can create enormous *grudges* (as defined by current feelings based on past hurtful experiences). Grudges are frequently (but not universally) founded upon the differing perspectives of each spouse. These differing perspectives or meanings (which often develop into incompatible and unexpressed expectations) continue to escalate into full-blown relational fissures and impasses.

Uncovering and addressing these grudges—to allow emotionally charged feelings currently blocking the growth of the relationship to be exposed in a safe and nonthreatening environment such as therapy—is critical. Doing so in an artful and healing manner can be quite a challenge. Without a definit plan, unearthing grudges in therapy can lead to ongoing volcanic eruptions that serve only to widen the emotional gulf between spouses. Many strategies attempt to manage past hurts in a curative fashion.

The moment spouses feel hurt or threatened, they begin bringing in prior unresolved issues that are born out of being hurt. Let's look at an example often heard in therapy: "So what if I don't praise you every time you do something you are supposed to? Why don't you really show me you care by having sex once in a while? Wow, wouldn't *that* be remarkable!" One spouse's request to be praised occasionally triggered the other spouse's seething anger about the lack of demonstrated caring (as expressed in this situation by a failure to initiate physical intimacy). This is a grudge.

During the session, the therapist invites both spouses to take a piece of blank paper and prepare to write a letter. Although not specifically intended to be mailed when finished, the spouses will be encouraged to read each other's letter aloud. Each spouse is asked to remember a grudge they have not been able to let go of in the relationship. (Some approaches have the spouses initially choose a grudge they are harboring for someone other than their spouse. This lessens the initial emotional impact and prepares the couple for when they perform this exercise with each other.) The therapist clearly lays out the two ground rules: (1) Each spouse must agree to follow the specific rules (set forth by the therapist) addressing the emotionally charged information that will arise during the exercise. (2) At the conclusion of the session, unresolved negative feelings are *not* to be carried out of the therapy room. Both spouses must agree to these ground rules in advance (Bornstein & Bornstein, 1986).

When the spouses have identified their grudge, they are not to say what it is. Rather, each is to write a detailed letter to the other covering all aspects of the hurt. The hurt may be repetitive in nature, may have resulted from an isolated occurrence, or may have developed over time. The letter is to be written in the first person: "It hurt me when you did [thus and so]," or "When [this] occurred, [this] is what it felt like." Aspects to be included in the letter include the following.

Part I

1. Historical perspective: When did/does this hurtful experience occur?
2. Precise description of behavior that was hurtful: What exactly happened to create the painful experience?
3. What were the emotional feelings associated with the behavior or event?
4. How did your spouse handle the situation when he/she knew you were hurt?
5. What did you do with the feelings after the incident? How did you react?

Part II

6. What do you think was going on in your partner's life at the time?

7. What do you think your partner was feeling when he/she knew you were hurt?
8. Do you think your partner felt bad at all about hurting you? If so, how could you tell?

Part III

9. What did you need from your partner at that time that would have reduced the pain? What did you need to hear, see, or feel?
10. Describe what could have been different at that time. Rewrite the script of that experience in such a way as to have the outcome you wanted.
11. What could you have done differently at that time to make the situation less hurtful?

The therapist and couple should allow at least two hours for this exercise. After the couple finishes the narrative, the therapist inquires what the writing experience was like for each. Couples often report initially experiencing a lot of anger when reliving the experience, only to have it lessen as they honestly answer the other queries. Each is then asked to read aloud what the other spouse wrote. The writer can help interpret the writing when needed.

It is very powerful when each spouse begins reading the other spouse's account of a painful incident, accompanied by ways it could have been handled differently. The spouse who is reading is not allowed to comment on what he or she is reading. This is the other spouse's perspective, and the expression of this, uneditorialized, is what counts at that moment.

Once each spouse reads the other's narrative, the two are to move close together, hold hands, and acknowledge that this experience clearly hurt their spouse. Each then recounts from memory the reasons it was painful. At the conclusion of this part, the therapist inquires whether the spouse who related the experience in writing felt that the spouse accurately captured the essence of what was hurtful. If not, the spouse is asked to fill in what was overlooked, which is then recounted by the other spouse as well.

The narratives are then given back to the respective owners, and both are asked in turn to reread parts I and II. After the spouses read these parts of their own narratives, each discusses precisely what he or she wants out of the relationship from this point forward. They also describe in detail what they will respectively do to avoid the escalation of a future situation.

This exercise can be extremely liberating for both spouses. This exercise may have to be repeated, based on the level of emotional intensity involved. This exercise can also incorporate many of the contextual or behavioral marital therapy strategies previously discussed.

## SUBSTANCE ABUSE IN THE RELATIONSHIP

Habitually abusing (or becoming addicted to) substances has a profound negative impact on a person's personal relationships, emotional integrity and balance, and overall positive life force. The abuse of substances creates an atmosphere poisonous to relationships, leaving the abuser and his or her spouse living as if on pins and needles. Although problems coping with ADHD may bring couples to therapy, substance abuse problems may also be present or may even be the primary problem. The therapist must ask in the *initial* interview directly about the type, intensity, frequency, and duration of substance use (O'Farrell, 1993). If a substance abuse issue exists but without addressing it early in therapy as the *primary concern*, the couple will not be able to achieve the emotional closeness that is the hallmark of a healthy and balanced relationship (Kosten et al., 1987).

### Alcohol's Functions in the Marital Relationship

According to Jacob (1988), Excessive use of alcohol serves three primary functions within the marital relationship.

### Signals Stress and Strain

Drinking and/or drug use is an attempt to minimize either internal or external sources of stress. The internal source may be the individual's having to live with and manage the primary and secondary effects associated with ADHD (such as moodiness, disorganization, and/or forgetfulness). The external stress may be related to job uncertainty, marital discord, family unrest, or a combination thereof. Unwittingly, the abuse of substances adds to the level of family and marital stress and strain. The use adds ongoing unpredictability and emotional distance in the marital relationship.

This can begin to create what Beattie (1987) refers to as *codependency*. Codependency describes an interaction between a non-substance-abusing spouse and the abusing partner, whereby the actions of the nonabuser often keep the abuser locked in an abusive cycle. The nonabusing spouse ritualistically makes excuses for the abusing spouse by doing such things as calling work to tell them he or she has the flu when actually the abuser is hung over. A repetitive interaction sequence is initiated that allows the abuser to continue the abusive behavior. The codependent spouse counterintuitively supports the abuse in an effort to hold things together in the relationship and family. This often creates a role for the non abuser defined by an excessive level of caring and enabling (allowing the abuser to continue to use the substance without regard to personal responsibility). Breaking the cycle of co dependence is often a significant aspect of the marital therapy as well as the impetus for the substance abuser's entering sobriety.

### Attempts to Stabilize a Chaotic System

Paradoxically, the more tension that develops in the marital relationship due to the substance abuse, the more the abusing spouse seeks refuge in the abusive substance(s). The substance use can also function as a lightning rod for other marital problems. If the abuse remediates, then the underlying problems will surface. Oddly enough, the abuse provides predictable, albeit unhealthy, interaction patterns in an unstable environment.

### Serves to Regulate Emotional Intimacy

The substance abuse alleviates the perceived need for emotional intimacy in the relationship, fostering an emotional gulf between the couple. Creating and maintaining intimacy are often difficult issues for someone living with ADHD; when substance abuse is introduced, a lasting and impenetrable barrier to developing an intimate relationship is created. In this context, intimacy is much more broadly defined than as mere sexual activity; it entails being able to identify and share the plethora of feelings that occur on a daily basis.

Like depression, the presence (or absence) of substance abuse in the relationship needs to be accurately disclosed before genuine skill development and emotional closeness can occur. Substance abusers generally utilize immature defense mechanisms (characteristic of adolescents) in response to an increase in the level of stress within the relationship. When ADHD is layered on top of this, the relationship is injected with a potentially lethal ingredient. Before all else, the substance abuse must be addressed. If it exists yet remains hidden within the therapeutic process, the therapist must make it clear that therapy will be ineffective. Removing the impediments to intimacy is critical, first and foremost of which is the abusive use of substances.

It is also important for the therapist to ask specifically about violence within the relationship. According to Christensen & Heavey (1999), violence is often an undisclosed factor in highly distressed couples. It may occur as a function of or independent of alcohol use and depression. Due to the confusing feelings of shame surrounding spousal abuse, asking the couple directly can begin to uncover abusive behavior the abused spouse would usually not willingly volunteer.

Here are things to do when addressing substance abuse issues.

### Addressing Issues of Substance Abuse

- Ask the couple directly if either believes that alcohol or other drugs, depression or relationship violence is a problem in the relationship.
- Be candid that therapy will not work if there is an existing and unaddressed substance abuse problem.
- Ask each partner the frequency, intensity, and duration of one another's drinking patterns. This provides a potentially more accurate picture of use/abuse.
- Read body language for level of comfort or discomfort as issues of substance use are explored.
- If between-therapy assignments continue to fail and the couple is at a loss to explain why, revisit the substance abuse issue. This is often a reason for assignment failure.
- Deal directly with issues regarding codependency. The co dependent is often as dependent on his or her role as the abuser is on his or her substance.

## ASSUMING INDIVIDUAL RESPONSIBILITY

As with most things in life, the success of couples therapy depends largely on the degree to which each spouse assumes responsibility for his or her role, behavior, and attitude within the relationship. When ADHD exists in combination with another problems, such as violence, substance abuse, or depression, it is paramount that the spouse with these issues assume responsibility for addressing them outside the relationship.

An individual with ADHD who also experiences anger or rage and/or acts violently toward his or her spouse or others must seek out an anger management/violence reduction program. This program must comprehensively address the myriad issues influencing the anger as well as outline and implement effective and healthy management strategies for coping with the anger when it surfaces. The process that unfolds in an anger management/violence reduction program can be further explored between the couple in marital therapy. Any change requires making successive approximations toward a specified goal. The spouse experiencing the violent behavior must be clear about his or her personal goals in terms of mitigating the violent behaviors.

The same is true for dealing with issues of addiction and/or substance abuse. It is critical that the spouse with coexisting ADHD and addiction issues be involved in some type of outpatient or inpatient treatment program that specializes in dual diagnosis (the ADHD and the addiction). An intensive program will provide the spouse with a variety of immediate strategies to address the addiction along with either suggesting or requiring that the spouse join Alcoholics Anonymous or Narcotics Anonymous. Anonymous programs are very effective in helping those suffering from addiction to move closer toward sobriety. The nonaddicted spouse will also be encouraged to attend Alanon, which is for spouses and family members of addicts. It helps them understand better the process of addiction or abuse and supports them in taking a stand not to enable inappropriate or ongoing use/abuse behaviors.

Depression also frequently needs the support of an individual therapist or physician. It is clear that depression is often most effectively controlled through the use of both medication and cognitive-behavioral therapy. The medication is intended to positively effect the malfunctioning neuro transmitter—serotonin—in the brain, while the cognitive-behavioral therapy will help develop and reinforce the use of strategies to assist in warding off depressive moments and encourage the individual to learn to reframe negative situations, resulting in a much less depressive impact. This also can be brought into the couples therapy in terms of what type of support would be helpful from the nondepressed spouse.

## SUMMARY

This chapter has focused on specific methods proven to be clinically effective in treating distressed couples where ADHD is one of the primary presenting problems. Contextual therapy and behavioral marital therapy help couples develop specific skills and strategies to successfully navigate terrain previously thought too hostile to inhabit. Aspects of these two approaches include guiding couples through understanding the factors associated with ADHD, discussing the potential impact of living with the attending symptoms, mapping out goals indicating relationship success, and assisting couples to define their relationship anew.

In addition, two supplemental techniques were described for couples who register high on the negative relationship barometer. One reintroduces the couple to the more tender "caring days" in their relationship, while the other addresses standing grudges. The chapter concluded with a discussion of the reasons to rule out the presence of substance abuse, depression, and violence in the relationship. Substance abuse, depression (as well as other disorders), and violence can effectively and efficiently foreclose any option for the couple to achieve emotional stability and intimacy. These must be dealt with separate from those problems that arise in relationships coping with an ADHD spouse. It is recommended that individuals presenting with cooccurring conditions commit to some type of intensive therapeutic process aimed at extinguishing the other problem(s) existing along with ADHD. While couples therapy is very effective in dealing with issues specific to ADHD that is both diagnosed and being treated, it is not appropriate to rely solely on couples therapy to address individual issues that have a profound negative impact on the relationship.

The effectiveness of the skills and strategies described in this chapter are often brought to life through interactional sequences between the couple and their therapist. These techniques allow for immediate utilization in any therapist's practice, regardless of theoretical orientation. They serve to decrease negative intent while simultaneously offering the couple myriad opportunities to experience lasting success and satisfaction in their relationship.

## REFERENCES

Bandura, A. (1974). *Social learning theory*. Englewood Cliffs, NJ: Prentice-Hall.

Beattie, M. (1987). *Co-dependent no more*. Center City, MN: Hazelden Educational Materials.

Bornstein, F., & Bornstein, M. (1986). *Marital therapy: A behavioral-communication approach*. New York: Pergamon Press.

Boszormenyi-Nagy, I. (1978). Behavior change through family change. In A. Bruton (Ed.), *What makes behavior change possible?* New York: Brunner/Mazel.

Bowen, M. (1978). *Family therapy in clinical practice*. New York: Jason Aronson.

Christensen, A., & Heavey, C. (1999). Interventions for couples. *Annual Review of Psychology, 50,* 169–197.

Goldfried, M., & Davidson, G. (1971). *Clinical behavior therapy*. New York: Holt, Rinehart & Winston.

Gotlib, H., & Beach, S. (1995). A marital/family discord model of depression: Implications of therapeutic intervention. In N. Jacobson & A. Gurman (Eds.), *Clinical handbook of couple therapy*. New York: Guilford Press.

Gottman, J., Markman, H., & Notarius, C. (1977). A sequential analysis of verbal and nonverbal behavior. *Journal of Marriage and the Family, 39,* 461–477.

Haley, J. (1976). *Problem solving therapy*. San Francisco: Jossey-Bass.

Halverstadt, J (1998). *A.D.D. & romance: Finding fulfillment in love, sex, & relationships*. Dallas: Taylor.

Jacob, T. (1988). Alcoholic spouse interaction as a function of alcoholism subtype and alcohol consumption. *Journal of Abnormal Psychology, 97,* 231–237.

Jacobson, N. (1977). Training couples to solve their marital problems: A behavioral approach to relationship discord. Part II: Intervention strategies. *International Journal of Family Counseling, 5(2),* 20–28.

Jacobson, N., & Addis, M. (1993). Research on couples and couple therapy: What do we know. *Journal of Consulting Clinical Psychology, 61,* 85–93.

Jacobson, N., & Anderson, E. (1980). The effects of behavior rehearsal and feedback on the acquisition of problem solving skills in distressed and non-distressed couples. *Behavior Research and Therapy, 18,* 25–36.

Jacobson, N., & Margolin, G. (1979). *Martial therapy: Strategies based on social learning behavior exchange principles*. New York: Brunner/Mazel.

Jacobson, N., & Martin, B. (1976). Behavioral marriage therapy: Current status. *Psychological Bulletin, 83*, 540–566.

Knudson, R., Gurman, A., & Knishern, D. (1980). Behavioral marriage therapy: A treatment in transition. In C. M. Franks & G. T. Wilson (Eds.), *Annual review of behavior therapy, Vol. 7*. New York: Brunner/Mazel.

Kosten, B., Jalale, J., Seidl, H., & Kleber, H. (1987). Relationship of martial structure and interaction to opiate abuse relapse. *American Journal of Drug and Alcohol Abuse, 13*, 387–399.

Liberman, R. (1970). Behavioral approaches to family and couple therapy. *American Journal of Orthopsychiatry, 40*, 106–118.

Mahoney, M. (1974). *Cognition and behavior modification*. Cambridge, MA: Ballinger.

Margolin. G., & Weiss, R. (1978). A comparative evaluation of therapeutic components associated behavioral marital treatment. *Journal of Consulting and Clinical Psychology, 47*, 1476–1486.

Markman, H. (1979). Application of a behavioral model of marriage in predicting relationship satisfaction of couples planning marriage. *Journal of Consulting and Clinical Psychology, 47*, 743–749.

Markman, H., Floyd, F., Stanley, S., & Clements, M. (1993). Preventing marital distress through communication and conflict management training. *Journal of Consulting Clinical Psychology, 13*, 29–43.

Novotni, M. (1999). *What does everybody else know that I don't? Social skills help for adults with attention deficit hyperactivity disorder—A reader-friendly guide*. Plantation, FL: Specialty Press.

O'Farrell, T. (1993). *Treating alcohol problems: Marital and family interventions*. New York: Guilford Press.

Olson, D. (1976). An operant interpersonal program for couples. In D. Olson (Ed.), *Treating relationships*. Lake Mills, IA: Graphic.

Patterson, G. (1976). Some procedures for assessing changes in marital interaction patterns. *Oregon Research Institute Bulletin, 16(7)*.

Robinson, E., & Price, M. (1980). Pleasurable behavior in marital interaction: An observational study. *Journal of Consulting and Clinical Psychology, 48*, 117–118.

Sager, C. (1976). *Marriage contracts and couple therapy*. New York: Brunner/Mazel.

Satir, V. (1964). *Conjoint family therapy*. Palo Alto, CA: Science and Behavior Books.

Stierlin, H. (1976). The dynamics of owning and disowning: Psychoanalytic and family perspectives. *Family Process, 15*, 277–288.

Weinstein, R., & Block, M. (1998). ADHD and relationships. *Attention Magazine, 5(3)*, 44–47.

Weiss, R. (1978). The conceptualization of marriage and marriage disorders from a behavioral perspective. In T. J. Paolino, Jr., & B. S. McCrady (Eds.), *Marriage and marital therapy: Psychoanalytic, behavioral, and systems theory perspective*. New York: Brunner/Mazel.

Weiss, R., Birchler, G., & Vincent, J. (1974). Contractual models for negotiation training in marital dyads. *Journal of Marriage and The Family, 36*, 321–331.

# 13

# Families and ADHD

Thomas W. Phelan, Ph.D.

## INTRODUCTION

ADHD dramatically alters family life and tremendously complicates the job of parenting. People who live in a family with one or more parents with ADHD and perhaps one or more children with ADHD experience fundamental differences in their daily living that other families do not experience, especially when the combined type of ADHD is involved. There is more tension and arguing. Sibling rivalry can be intense and unending, and the parental response to the fighting often makes the situation worse. There is constant noise. Dinnertime is not fun, and eating out is nearly impossible. Marital conflict is seriously aggravated, and divorce and separation occur more frequently than in the rest of the population. Vacations, instead of being the carefree and fun events parents hope for, become unhappy experiences where family members feel that all they do is switch from one prison (the car) to another (the motel room).

This is no way for parents or children to live, but there are millions of families that live this way day in and day out. Statistics about ADHD tell us that when there is a parent with ADHD, it is more than likely that there will be one or more children with ADHD. The reverse is also true: When there are children with ADHD, more than likely one or both parents will also have ADHD. This combination of parents with ADHD and children with ADHD intensifies and multiplies the effects of ADHD-related problems.

The good news is that, according to current research, there are therapeutic strategies that work in aiding parents to reduce family stress. Marital counseling can aid couples who are having trouble getting along (Gottman & Silver, 1999). Medication has been shown to be useful in many ways for both adults and children with ADHD (MTA Cooperative Group, 1999; Paterson, Douglas, Hallmayer, Hagan, & Krupenia, 1999). Parent training can help moms and dads intervene more effectively with their children, enjoy their youngsters, and reduce the possibilities for child abuse (MTA Cooperative Group, 1999). Finally, cognitive therapy can help some individuals get "back to reality" and lessen emotional turmoil by thinking more clearly (Beck, 1995).

Generally speaking, there is probably not a more motivated group of therapeutic subjects in the world than the parents of young, preadolescent children. When these moms and dads have ADHD, however, the situation becomes complicated. Often the ADHD octopus is vicious, pervasive, and powerful enough to strangle attempts at workable solutions. Sensible—but often complex—proposals from bright, articulate, and sympathetic mental health professionals (from normal households) can sometimes be overwhelming for individuals and families with limited personal and economic resources. Therapies and tactics that require cognitive gymnastics and sustained effort under conditions of severe emotional overarousal often have limited success, especially when the implementers of strategies are adults with ADHD.

Two things are common in parents experiencing serious, constant emotional pain: (1) they feel hopeless, and (2) they don't think very clearly. It's hard to motivate these stressed-out adults to do something differently, because they don't think anything will work. And it's hard to get them to remember what they are supposed to be doing differently in the first place, because under emotional distress, humans—especially those with ADHD—regress to destructive forms of thought and behavior.

Yet something must be done to deal with the dreadful homelife that so many families with ADHD experience. Advice and treatment from mental health professionals can help—if the program can only be implemented. Sometimes if a family can just find a few places to start, life at home will calm down and other, more complicated but useful solutions may become possible.

Since it's one thing to make a suggestion to a family and quite another thing to get them to do what you suggest, the proposals in this chapter will share—as much as possible—several characteristics:

1. A down-to-earth understanding of ADHD households
2. Simplicity
3. Ease of application
4. More or less immediate results

This may sound like another marketing pitch to an "ADHD-ogenic" society that many people feel is already spoiled rotten and can't wait for anything. As a therapist you have to find something that parents, especially those with ADHD, will do. Lack of compliance can render even the most brilliant suggestions useless (Stine, 1994). Compliance, or what is sometimes called treatment adherence, has to come first. The suggestions in this chapter are made from the point of view of someone who is both the parent of an ADHD adult and a clinical psychologist working with families in which ADHD is present. ADHD will always have a personal, family side as well as a clinical and scientific side. To grasp the problem and deal effectively with it, you need to understand both.

Our first task in this chapter will be to take a nonclinical look at how ADHD traits—in both parents and children—conspire to affect family life in general as well as parenting in particular. Having described the problem, I'll then propose some practical, straightforward ideas for trying to minimize stress in homes affected by ADHD.

## EFFECTS OF ADHD ON HOME AND FAMILY

### Home Sweet Home

Whether they actually control it, all parents—whether suffering from ADHD or not—feel deeply responsible for the kind family atmosphere they provide. Parents want things to run smoothly at home and family members to get along. When ADHD is involved, however, family life is often characterized by conflict, anxiety, noise, and disorganization. And when anger and chaos seem to be more the norm than peace and harmony, moms and dads will blame themselves and blame each other.

**Conflict**

Since it's difficult for people with ADHD to calmly discuss and resolve differences, conflict is more frequent at home—not just conflict, but energetic conflict. Domestic battles have an intensity about them that is impossible to ignore. After two parents both had difficult days at work, for instance, they may argue about how to manage the kids, while the kids are arguing about who gets to use the computer. Because genuine give-and-take negotiation is rare, attempts at conflict resolution are characterized more by various forms of testing and manipulation. Badgering, temper tantrums, threats, pouting, and sometimes even physical aggression are the more common methods people use to get their way. Husbands and wives with ADHD not only struggle to prevent or manage interpersonal conflict, but also add to it because of their predispositions toward restlessness, impulsivity, impatience, and emotional over-arousal.

**Anxiety**

Persistent conflicts over months and years inevitably give rise to a sense of tension and anxiety at home. If a fight or argument is not occurring right at the moment, it soon will be. Everyone feels a sense of negative anticipation. At the end of the day it's hard to unwind when you feel the next bit of trouble is always right around the corner. For any single family member, it seems that the only times in which peace is guaranteed occur when nobody else is home. This kind of family atmosphere soon gets depressing, and it is the opposite of what parents generally hope for when they marry.

One beleaguered couple, for example, provided the following story. These parents had three children—two boys and one girl. The mother and one of the boys had ADHD. The couple described their evening meals. Mom and dad wanted the dinner hour to be a time when each person could talk about his or her day and there could be some positive interchange. The reality, however, was that once they all sat down, it was usually less than five minutes before one of the kids would interrupt one of the other children's stories. Then the two youngsters would proceed to argue with each other about whose turn it was to talk. Next, mom (who had ADHD) would yell at the kids to be quiet. Dad would then reprimand his wife for screaming. These parents also related an intriguing fact: If you took any one person out of the picture at dinner—either parent or any one of the kids—the family would get along just fine!

**Noise**

In addition to conflict, noise in a household with ADHD can be incredible, with regard to both its persistence and its volume. The arguing and yelling involved in interpersonal conflicts can produce a terrible racket. Some parents have described these times of family discord as "yelling contests," where it appears the object of the game is to win simply by screaming louder than your opponent. Unfortunately, if the two contestants are both children, a mom or dad with ADHD may be tempted to try to resolve the feud by roaring louder than both kids combined.

ADHD-related outbursts, of course, do not always involve anger. Adults and children with ADHD can catch others off guard with sudden explosions of excitement and enthusiasm. Although it's usually nice to see someone else in a good mood, the good mood of an individual with ADHD can be extremely irritating if it is sudden, loud, and unexpected. "Look what I just caught!" For example, the scream can be both startling and aggravating to a parent when it is accompanied by a 90-pound body bombing into a formerly peaceful living room with a dripping goldfish.

Noisy expressions of good spirits can also become tiresome if the emotions involved are kept at too high a pitch for too long. A father with ADHD can show the same exaggerated feelings about buying a new car, for example, that his son does when buying a new toy. Dad's constant chatter and high level of excitement will become very tedious to his non-ADHD wife.

## Disorganization

ADHD-related disorganization is another culprit that attacks parental hopes for a rational and orderly household. For parents wanting their house kept in reasonably decent shape, a child or two with ADHD and a spouse with ADHD will present a major test of organizational abilities. Books, tools, shoes, magazines, clothes, toys, music, games, candy wrappers, and leftover food can be found in all rooms of the house, though these items tend to concentrate in rooms where there is a television. When an ADHD child returns home from school, it is not uncommon to find a trail of debris leading from the front door to the TV set. While the frequent and repeated messes around the house may drive the parents to distraction, this sloppiness usually does not bother the children at all.

ADHD is frequently accompanied by other psychological disorders, and these other psychological disorders will add to the domestic chaos. It is not unusual to have a family where two or three children have been diagnosed with ADHD. Running the show at home may be a mother who is anxious and depressed and a father who has ADHD, is disorganized and emotionally volatile, and who drinks too much. It's not a recipe for comfort, mutual enjoyment, or family togetherness.

## Those Special Times

In families where ADHD plays a significant role, parents will encounter trouble in two kinds of situations: (1) when everyone is together and there is a specific task that needs to be done, and (2) when everyone is together and there is no specific task that needs to be done.

The first category includes activities such as getting everyone (kids and adults) up and out in the morning, homework, going to bed, and eating meals. The second category includes times such as weekends, vacations, and a good deal of the summertime.

Because of problems staying focused and problems with compliance and organization, getting things done is a major problem for parents in families with ADHD. In the morning the children would rather watch TV in their pajamas than get dressed and put their book bags together. Homework in the afternoon or evening provides the opportunity for major civil wars as parents try to coerce junior—who just spent a whole day in school—to attack the added insult of more boring academic work. Going to bed is often a problem because children with ADHD don't ever seem to want to go. But if they don't get to sleep in a timely fashion, they'll be tired in the morning and the up-and-out procedure will be chaotic again. Kids not getting to bed on time also means that parents have less downtime for themselves or for each other—less time to regenerate before the start of another day.

Even vacations can be extremely trying when ADHD comes along for the ride. In the interests of family bonding and closeness, many "experts" these days recommend family vacations. But for a family with ADHD, that advice is easier given than followed. Imagine, for example, a family of four—mom, dad with ADHD, daughter and son with ADHD—taking off in the car for a five-hour drive on the first day of their vacation. Everyone is a little nervous because they're waiting for the time when dad is going to get fed up with the whirling dervish in the back seat who just can't seem to leave his sister alone, who can't stop talking, and who keeps asking how much longer it will be till they get to their hotel. Finally, the inevitable happens: Dad yells at his son for teasing his sister again and dad reaches around in the car to try to hit the boy. Mom then yells at dad for driving carelessly, which prompts the little girl to cry. By the time the family reaches the destination, everyone is wishing to have stayed home.

Unstructured family times can also create problems for parents, because when structure is lacking, kids with ADHD can get themselves into trouble. When there is nothing else to do, for instance, many children with ADHD seem to use sibling rivalry as entertainment. What may be a pastime for the kids, however, can be torture for their parents. Riding in the car, going to church, and eating at restaurants can all become miserable experiences when the kids won't leave each other alone.

One significant—and huge—chunk of unstructured time, the long summer break, often seems to stretch out endlessly for many parents. Mom and dad just lost their best babysitter, the school. Complaints of "There's nothing to do" and "I'm bored" will be heard frequently, and a parent with ADHD will become quickly exasperated with these refrains. Children with ADHD look at mom and dad as the resident entertainment committee, because these children are usually not very good at entertaining themselves.

When ADHD is involved, family outings are fraught with danger. Most parents of children with ADHD have experienced repeated public embarrassment because of their kids' behavior. In a culture that blames parents for everything their kids do wrong, children with ADHD seem to have their parents at their mercy when they go out in public. And when you add a parent with ADHD to the mix, anything can happen. If you are a mental health professional and want parents with ADHD or non-ADHD parents to feel you understand them and what they have been through, ask them to tell you the stories of their difficult experiences at restaurants, movie theaters, family picnics, amusement parks, and stores.

Here's one example of what can happen in public when you have a child and an adult with ADHD in the same family. On a summer weekend one family of four decided to visit the zoo. The family consists of mom and dad and two kids. Two of the family have ADHD, an 8-year-old boy, who had already been diagnosed, and his father, who would be diagnosed in the future. The optimistic family parked their car in the lot, bought their tickets, and entered the zoo. Since it was about lunchtime they sought out a snack bar. Everyone selected a meal. The boy with ADHD chose a hot dog. Unfortunately, the snack bar had just run out of hot dogs. Naturally, the impatient little boy did the expected: He screamed at the top of his lungs, threw himself down on the ground, and proceeded with a full-blown temper tantrum.

Though the boy's father was no stranger to this behavior, being in public and having ADHD he also became enraged. He yanked his son from the ground, picked him up, and started to half drag and half carry him back to the car. As he was heading back with his struggling, screaming burden, a group of teenagers passed by who couldn't help but see the tussle going on. At this moment the boy —for some reason—cried out, "Help me! Help me!" Now the scene looked like a kidnapping in progress. The teens called the police, who came quickly and confronted the father. Dad was required to prove that he was, in fact, the parent of this little boy. While this was going on, the boy's sister watched in horror and his mother sobbed. (Mom said later that part of her tears were from anger at her husband for his overreaction, in addition to her own embarrassment.)

Convinced finally that no foul play was occurring, the police left. The boy's parents—in a state of shock—saw that this just wasn't their day for the zoo. Instead, they decided it might be safer to stay at home for the rest of the weekend rather than to appear again in public. As they proceeded back to their car, they were followed by the group of teens and a few other adults, who hurled insults at them for being such lousy and abusive parents.

## PARENTING AND MARRIAGE

Whatever natural instincts and abilities—or strengths and weaknesses—men or women might have for parenting, the actual parenting job they do will have a lot to do with their relationship with their spouse. Even in single-parent families, the quality of parenting done by the resident parent and the "ex" will still be affected by the relationship these two adults carry on with each other. When the picture is complicated by a husband or wife with ADHD and a child or two with ADHD, certain predictable problems will occur. These problems make both the job of staying happily married—and the job of parenting—much more difficult. It is no surprise that divorce and separation rates are higher in families when ADHD is involved.

## Complications from ADHD

There are several reasons why ADHD complicates the job of parenting: (1) ADHD and comorbid conditions in the parents, (2) the fun-to-work transition that most couples experience, (3) the effects of a child with ADHD on the marital relationship, and (4) the differences between that child's responses to mom and to dad. These four issues have many effects on a marriage, but perhaps their most important and unfortunate result is to intensify the hostility and conflicts that occur between parents. This heightened level of animosity makes the job of effective parenting much more confusing and much more difficult.

### ADHD and Comorbidity

Marriages suffer from the effects of both ADHD traits and the other psychological problems that often come along for the marital ride. The ADHD symptom of inattentiveness, for example, makes for a spouse who is not a sympathetic listener. Impulsive verbal outbursts can create irritation and hard feelings. And a trait such as general restlessness can make it hard to relax around one's mate. Parents of children with ADHD also tend to have more non-ADHD psychological problems in general than the rest of the population. There is a greater incidence of depression (especially in the mothers), substance abuse and sociopathy (especially in the fathers), anxiety, learning disabilities, and communication problems (for review see Goldstein & Goldstein, 1998). These added burdens can complicate immensely the marital relationship and the job of parenting. Imagine, for example, a depressed and anxious mother—after a long day at work—trying to discuss her son's failing grade in biology with a temper-prone dad who has also worked all day and who has just opened his second six-pack of Beer.

### Fun to work

One of the strengths of individuals with ADHD is their ability to have fun. When most couples decide to marry, that is exactly what they have been doing: dating or simply having fun. The infatuated duo then reasons something like this: "We're having this much fun now, and we're not even married. Think how great it will be once we're together all the time!"

The problem with this line of reasoning is that the decision to marry is a decision to work together—not to continue playing. Now we'll both get jobs, now we'll have kids, now we'll get the house, two cars, a snowblower, and a vacuum. Instead of dinner and a movie, there will be work, driving the kids to the doctor, cooking, cleaning, and laundry. When this new lifestyle is also complicated by a spouse with ADHD, the new agenda causes even more trouble because of problems with organization, perseverance, and boredom. After a few years (or a few months!), the couple wonders, "What happened to all the fun?"

### Effects of the Child with ADHD

The effects that a child with ADHD has on a marital relationship are also the opposite of fun. It is not fun to deal with the fourth tantrum of the day or to intervene for the twelfth time in another sibling civil war. If mom and dad want to go out, they have to either take the difficult child—a risky proposition in itself—or get a sitter. Many parents, in fact, have a long list of sitters, but over the years most of these sitters have quit.

### Responses to Mom and Dad

Children with ADHD usually respond better to their fathers than to their mothers. The greater compliance with fathers is due to the fact that dads are larger, more intimidating, less familiar, and more prone to apply physical discipline. Dad is also a male, and the troublesome child with ADHD is usually male as well. Little boys in general tend to identify with and admire their fathers more than they do their mothers. Kids with ADHD are no exception, and consequently they are more cooperative with dads.

Difficulties in the marriage are magnified by the fact that mother and father aren't aware of the four factors we just discussed. Both parents, therefore, tend to assume—at least to some extent—that mom is the worse parent and dad the better parent. Though mom may bravely defend herself at times, the two will argue frequently and attack the issue from different angles. Mom may claim, for example, that her son needs professional help. Dad may respond by saying that he doesn't have any trouble with the boy. Since neither spouse really understands the issue well, the only thing these discussions accomplish is to further damage the marriage.

## Parents and Siblings Without ADHD

Unless a child with ADHD happens to be an only child, his mother and father also have to worry about parenting his brothers and sisters. When ADHD is involved in a family, this task is certainly complicated and, again, predictable problems will occur. Siblings of children with ADHD will feel neglected, embarrassed, and abused. Many people feel that siblings in families with children with ADHD are the "silent sufferers." These children endure pain and turmoil, but they often remain silent because they believe they have no choice. Their past attempts at communicating distress to their parents not only may have been fruitless, but may also have made matters worse due to the added conflict they created. This conflict-exacerbating effect is often exaggerated when children without ADHD try to share their emotions with parents who have ADHD. The parental response often involves emotional overarousal and impulsive "discipline."

### Neglect

The child with ADHD demands so much attention, positive and negative, from the parents that siblings often feel neglected. Mom and dad have to keep after him constantly in the morning or he'll be late for school. They have to closely monitor his progress with homework or he'll never finish a thing. At the dinner table the child with ADHD doesn't ever seem to keep quiet. When he's not monopolizing the conversation, he's interrupting someone else.

### Embarrassment

Young children can also feel embarrassed by their brother or sister with ADHD. Many non-ADHD kids, for example, long ago decided not to have friends over to the house anymore, because the child with ADHD—not having a playmate of his own—insists on playing with or teasing the others. The child with ADHD can also be overly aggressive, or he may simply appear strange to other children by doing his version of the "hyper-silly" routine. To make matters worse, some parents—feeling sorry for their youngster with ADHD or perhaps not knowing what to do—insist that he be included in the activities of the other kids. The result of this strategy is that—for the siblings—a deep sense of rage will be added to the feeling of embarrassment.

### Abuse

Finally, siblings of children with ADHD are often emotionally—and sometimes physically—abused by their brothers or sisters with ADHD. This mistreatment usually happens when the child with ADHD is older, but it is not unusual even when the child is younger, especially if the older, non-ADHD boy or girl has a more placid temperament. Many kids with ADHD direct a steady stream of verbal criticism, teasing, or other types of provocation at the other youngsters in the house. It is as if the children with ADHD can't stand the very presence of another child in home—and perhaps they can't.

Neglect, embarrassment, and abuse generate a good deal of hostility in non-ADHD siblings toward their cohorts who have ADHD. Not surprisingly, this unpleasant trio of problems also produces a good deal of anger in siblings toward their parents. Children who do not have ADHD feel, often correctly, that mom and dad are just not handling the situation well. Unable to understand the notion that their parents may really have no idea what to do, these kids feel that the current state of affairs is ridiculous, unfair, and extremely discouraging.

As we have just seen, ADHD in adults and children can make the task of parenting almost overwhelming. Realistically tackling this job first requires that mom and dad complete a short lesson in straight thinking. After that they will be better equipped to try some different ways of managing and changing their stressful family life.

## GOOD PARENTING AND STRAIGHT THINKING

### Attitude Adjustment

Psychotherapists have long been aware that the corrective process known as *cognitive therapy* can be very effective in reducing emotional distress. This kind of treatment, which involves identifying and then changing disturbing thoughts, is very effective when it addresses problems like anger, anxiety, and depression. Cognitive therapy, however, does not change three of the basic symptoms of ADHD: inattentiveness, hyperactivity, and impulsivity. Why is the issue of cognitive therapy, then, being raised in a chapter on parenting and ADHD? Because parents with ADHD are usually trying to manage kids with ADHD, and so much—if not most—of the emotional pain these parents experience comes from anger, anxiety, and depression about ADHD, not from ADHD itself.

Actually, the term *cognitive therapy* is a rather stuffy, uninteresting, and somewhat inaccurate name—especially to adults with ADHD—for what the process actually involves. More appealing names include *straight thinking, back to reality*, and, perhaps best of all, *attitude adjustment*. The attitude adjustment referred to here resembles education, philosophy, and training more than it does any kind of real therapy. Sometimes this part of the counseling process is simply a sympathetic slap in the face. When adults with ADHD are the recipients, of course, the procedure has to be fairly simple and straightforward. When explained properly, though, these interventions are something that parents with or without ADHD can relate to fairly quickly.

The attitude adjustment idea consists of two basic principles: (1) Emotional upset is caused not only by what's happening to you but also (and sometimes more so) by what you think about—or what you make out of—what's happening to you, and (2) the more upset you are by something, the more likely it is that your thoughts about what's bothering you are silly or unreasonable.

Adults with ADHD often respond well to a simple example. Ask them to imagine that one morning they run into an old acquaintance whom they mistakenly address by the wrong first name. After the incident, they walk around for the rest of the day thinking to themselves, "What an idiot I am!" They are very upset. What would really be upsetting them, we ask? It couldn't be their mistake—that's already past history; that part of the problem is done. What would be upsetting them is their thoughts about—or their interpretation of—their mistake. And if they are like a lot of people, they might prolong their distress by rehashing, over and over, their thoughts about what happened.

Ask them this question: What if a sympathetic friend could convince you—based on your past history—that you're not really an idiot and that everyone is entitled to a few minor verbal errors during the course of his or her existence? If our clients could take these new ideas to heart, their thoughts would be different and their feelings would change. They would feel better—not great, but better.

The attitude adjustment proposition, then, is fairly simple: Thoughts cause feelings, and foolish or dumb thoughts can cause very upsetting feelings (with adults who have ADHD the words *foolish* and *dumb* usually make more of an impression than the overly intellectual adjective *irrational*). This is what we must teach parents with ADHD as well as non-ADHD spouses. In fact, sometimes we have to hit them over the head with the notion until they begin to get it!

Next apply the attitude adjustment notion to parenting itself. Explain that even average children can be extremely aggravating at times. Kids with ADHD are even worse, so mom and dad certainly do not need to increase their parenting burdens by entertaining ineffective thoughts about their own sons and daughters. Foolish thoughts can produce emotional upset, and that upset can get way out of hand when the parent with the dumb thought also has ADHD.

## UNSOUND THOUGHTS

Here are some of the most frequently upsetting and unsound thoughts that parents of children with ADHD experience. With each defective idea are suggestions for how these adults can change the notion in order (1) to reduce their distress and (2) to behave more reasonably as a result. Try to make it clear to parents and spouses that this change does not mean "positive" thinking; it means *realistic* thinking. The attitude adjustment involves trying to see things as they actually are, rather than trying to sweep things under the rug or to pretend that things are different from what they really are. Make it clear that changing attitudes toward children is not easy, nor will this change make all of the bad feelings go away.

### Unsound Thought 1: "Why on earth can't he behave like the other children?"

This rhetorical question reflects extreme frustration. Adults with ADHD make variations of this comment frequently about their children with ADHD. "Why can't he behave like other children?" is the same as saying "He shouldn't be doing this!" During our attitude adjustment training, we must take this rhetorical question, treat it as a real question, and then answer it. The answer to the legitimate question "Why can't he behave like the other children?" is this: This child can't behave normally (like other children) because he has ADHD. For underlying neurological reasons he is unusually restless, inattentive, excitable, and disorganized for his age. He cannot turn these tendencies on or off at will.

In other words, neither a teacher nor a parent should expect normal behavior from a handicapped child. A child on crutches is not going to run the 50-yard dash in seven seconds. But at least in that situation you can see the crutches—the sign that something isn't normal. The problem with ADHD is that the handicap is hidden. The child looks normal, so you tend to think, "Why on earth can't he behave like the other children?"

### Unsound Thought 2: "My child has ADHD because I somehow messed him up by my bad parenting."

On the contrary, research has demonstrated that ADHD is largely genetic (Barkley, 1995); kids with ADHD are born that way. Since ADHD is not learned, mom and dad could not have caused it. In fact, quite the opposite is true. ADHD happens to people and to families; it is a nasty problem that wasn't requested. A little compassion for oneself as a parent—rather than criticism—is in order.

This new thought, of course, is welcomed by most parents. (Who wouldn't welcome being acquitted of the offense of injuring your own children?) Even so, it takes a while to sink in. Many parents have automatic responses to their children with ADHD that involve extreme anger, and that anger is partly due to the fact that the child first made the parent feel guilty or stupid.

**Unsound Thought 3: "If ADHD is not caused by my faulty parenting, I'm off the hook."**

This statement is false, but adults with ADHD often do not want to hear the revision of it. Even though ADHD itself is not learned during the course of a child's growing up, non-ADHD issues as well as the entire situation can be made worse by bad parenting. Oppositional behavior in children, for example, can be aggravated tremendously by crabby parents who talk too much and are unnecessarily bossy. Other comorbid possibilities, such as anxiety and depression, can also be made worse by parents who "shoot from the hip." The unpleasant reality is this: If parents have a child with ADHD, they had better learn how to be "professional parents." For each ADHD-aggravated problem they run into, such as homework, sibling rivalry, and bedtime, parents should have a reasonably well-thought-out solution that they try to apply as consistently as they can. "I just yell a lot at the appropriate time" is not a well-thought-out solution.

**Unsound Thought 4: "Gee, I hope the kids don't fight today."**

While a wish like this is understandable, this unfounded hope is also an unfortunate setup that makes for a great deal of extra anger and aggravation during the day. When children with ADHD are involved, you must start with what you get. While a parent's goal is to work on normalizing, as much as possible, the behavior of her child with ADHD, the child must be accepted. For parents who have ADHD themselves, eliminating wishful thinking is not an easy task, since wishful fantasies are always more pleasant than realistic thoughts.

Other variations of the same theme include "Maybe he'll get up and out this morning on his own," "Maybe someone will call to invite him over," "Maybe she'll clean up her room," and the popular—but totally absurd—"Maybe he'll do his homework on his own today without being asked."

We must explain to parents that when any person's expectations are not matched by reality, that person will often get mad. In fact, he can get absolutely furious if the difference between what he had hoped for and what he obtained was large. The solution for parents with ADHD who have kids with ADHD is not to expect the impossible.

Here's an example parents often relate to well. Ask mom and dad to imagine themselves waking up on a summer morning in the middle of June. School let out a few days ago. Mom or dad rolls over in bed and thinks, "Oh no! I sure hope the kids don't fight today." To eliminate this defective thought and avoid the setup that will lead to unnecessary and extreme anger, the parent needs to change this way of thinking. The new, back-to-reality version might go something like this: "Oh no! I just lost my best babysitter! The kids will probably have 15 or 20 fights today. This is how I will manage them and, while I'm at it, perhaps I can prevent a few fights by structuring the day differently."

**Unsound Thought 5: "If my ADHD child makes a fool out of me in public and people watching think I'm a lousy parent, I'll never live it down."**

As far as an attitude adjustment goes, what adults with ADHD need here is a thickening of the skin. Parents of kids with ADHD will have plenty of bad times when they're out in public with their children. During some of these times certain onlookers will conclude that these unfortunate mothers and fathers are lousy parents.

How do you teach parents with ADHD to thicken their skin? First, these parents need to remember that they did not cause ADHD or the child's difficult behavior. Second, many parents respond well to what we call the "Law of Indifference." The Law of Indifference states that most other people do not have much time for or interest in thinking or worrying about how or what you are doing. In other words, what makes you think that you're such a big deal? People in a grocery store may think a person is a lousy parent, but these observers will usually have forgotten about whatever happened by the time they get home. And if they haven't forgotten about it by the time they get home, they will sooner or later. Few people are going to obsess about someone else's faults. We therefore encourage parents with ADHD to think that if at some point other people consider them to be a bad parent or even a jerk, it's certainly unpleasant, but it's not the end of the world. We also remind them of a fact they already know very well: This is not the last time they'll go through this experience, so they had better get used to it.

**Unsound Thought 6: "It's awful and I'm a bad parent because I don't even like my kid!"**

Many parents become very distraught when they find themselves disliking their children. Trying to manage one's own feelings toward a child with ADHD is certainly no easy task. How do you consistently teach, care for, and offer help to a child who is obnoxious and uncooperative more often than not? While no parent wants to admit that she doesn't like her own child, the fact is that there are plenty of kids with ADHD who are not liked most of the time by their parents, their teachers, or their therapists.

Parents need to admit their irritation, not feel guilty about it, and not try to cover their anger with syrupy words or behavior. We try to help parents accept the fact that it is unfortunate but perfectly normal not to like an obnoxious and uncooperative child. Managing one's feelings toward a youngster with ADHD involves accepting the fact that there never will be a time when you feel totally relaxed and perfectly fine about this youngster. These kids seem to be able to keep parents off balance more often than not, but that doesn't mean children with ADHD obliterate all the rewards of parenting.

Thinking straight helps parents with ADHD to feel better. It also helps them to be less angry and less abusive—emotionally, verbally, and physically. Some cognitive therapy for parents of kids with ADHD involves education (it's not your fault), and some of this getting back to reality simply involves a firm but sympathetic slap in the face: "Listen, look at it like this: Your child can't turn off the ADHD at will. Don't make things worse by expecting the impossible." Attitude adjustments need to be repeated and reinforced. Fortunately most parents with ADHD or without ADHD will respond to compassionate attempts to change the way they think.

## MANAGING FAMILY LIFE: WHAT TO DO

Once parents have been educated to some extent about ADHD and their thinking has become more realistic, it's easier for them to implement suggestions for reducing stress and conflict. The suggestions that follow in this chapter are not intended to constitute a comprehensive treatment program. They are merely practical and simple ideas that can be relatively easily applied and have a chance of yielding fairly immediate results, which is especially important when the parents being worked with have a good dose of the ADHD trait of impatience. These suggestions can be implemented along with a treatment program, or they can be used before treatment begins as a way to reduce conflict, make life more bearable, and provide some sense of optimism.

## Picking Your Battles

Part of the art of parenting difficult children is knowing when to act and when to let something go. Adults with ADHD who also have kids with ADHD have enough to worry about. They don't need to get upset about—or involved with—trivia. We must tell parents that we have good news for them: Their children already have their MBAs! An MBA is a "minor-but-aggravating" problem that can be quite irritating but that is really not very important or a sign of severe psychological disturbance. MBAs, therefore, do not require parental intervention, even though they do produce parental irritation. When children in a family are exceptionally troublesome and their parents are unusually excitable, it is absolutely essential that mom and dad learn exactly when their parenting efforts are needed and—just as important—when they are not.

For young children with ADHD, one good example of an minor-but-aggravating problem is a messy room. There is no research evidence that kids who keep messy rooms grow up to be professional criminals or schizophrenics or have a higher divorce rate than those who formerly kept their rooms neat. If a child with ADHD, therefore, does not make her bed or pick her pajamas up off the floor in the morning, but does get to school on time with her book bag, the morning might be considered a success. When ADHD is involved, a good piece of advice for parents regarding the child's sloppy room is "Close the door and don't look."

When these kids become teenagers, the list of MBAs becomes potentially larger. Talking excessively on the phone, appearance, musical preferences, and not wanting to go out or eat dinner with the family may all fall into the MBA category. The items just mentioned involve normal teen behavior. Parents of teens with ADHD have bigger fish to fry. The fact that a youngster has poor grades, few or no friends, or a lousy relationship with his father is more important than his unkempt dress and preference for rap music.

The same MBA notion, by the way, can apply to moms and dads who have ADHD. MBAs might include a spouse's constant complaining about work, unwillingness to go out and get the mail, unfinished projects around the house, and obsession with TV. There can be a lot of relief in learning to let certain things go.

## Noise Management

Therapists who work with ADHD in families often overlook a very important point. When you really stop to think about it, much—if not most—of the family stress connected with ADHD involves obnoxious noise of one kind or another. It's obnoxious to hear people arguing with each other for the 17th time in the same evening. It's annoying to hear the TV volume so loud all the time. It's irritating to hear someone yelling, whether it's from excitement or anger. It can be maddening to hear the dog bark every time the phone or the doorbell rings. Whether it's mechanically produced racket or human conversation, too much noise can be extremely disturbing.

From the point of view of an individual parent, two kinds of noise present problems: incoming noise and outgoing noise. With incoming noise, mom or dad is the involuntary recipient of auditory disturbances produced by someone else. When outgoing noise is involved, however, the parent is the deliberate or inadvertent producer of the uproar himself or herself. Believe it or not, with a little thought both kinds of noise can be controlled and diminished to a large extent.

### Incoming Noise

There is no law saying that a parent must always keep her ears open and sharply attuned to every possible thing that either is happening or could happen at home. One of the most comforting strategies, therefore, for parents in families when ADHD is involved is to temporarily impair or block their hearing. Though this tactic may seem like a strange approach to some people, partial deafness can be easily accomplished—without injury—in one of two ways. First of all, parents can go to their local drug store and purchase a packet of foam rubber ear plugs. These little devices are inexpensive and remarkably effective. They do not block out all sounds, so parents can still hear most of what is going on at home. Parents can still carry on a conversation with someone who is sitting close to them. But the ear plugs seem to reduce total noise by a good 50% or so, which is very comforting.

A second way to diminish incoming noise is to use earphones or a Walkman type of device. The earphones themselves help to block out other sounds while, at the same time, they transmit music, ocean waves, books on tape, or other more enjoyable fare. As with the earplugs, all noise is not obliterated. Emergencies can still be attended to and the apparatus can be removed when one must talk on the phone.

These noise-reducing strategies (at least the earplugs) are also useful in other situations. These places include movie theaters (where the sound is often too loud), airplanes, sporting events, and noisy restaurants. Earplugs can help a person sleep later in the morning when everyone else is making racket downstairs. Their usefulness is limited only by one's creativity.

**Outgoing Noise**

When it comes to outgoing noise, each parent possesses even more control. We all have control over our mouths. The advice we must give parents is quite simple: Learn to keep quiet much more often. We have parents do a simple exercise: Spend one afternoon or evening—or one day on a weekend—evaluating how much of what you say is really necessary—or even helpful—in the grand scheme of things. Most people find that at least 60% of what comes out of their mouths is either useless, conflict producing, conflict enhancing, or all of these. Here are some examples:

- "How many times do I have to tell you!"
- "Leave your sister alone!"
- "I'm so worried about her grade in math!"
- "Get down here to dinner right this minute!"
- "When I was a boy..."
- "You're not going to school looking like that, are you?"
- "How was your day?" (addressed to a sullen 16-year-old at the dinner table)

As is evident from these examples, much purposeless chatter is an expression of either anxiety or anger. An incredible amount of human conflict is mediated by—or simply caused by—human conversation. Oddly enough, psychotherapists and counselors often put themselves in the position of trying to increase the amount of conversation in a household. When parents with ADHD are the clients, this can be a dangerous strategy. Fortunately, though, these parents can learn to ask themselves two questions before they speak: (1) Is what I'm about to say necessary or helpful? (2) What is likely to be the response from the recipient of my message?

If a child's usual response, for example, to "How was your day and what did you do?" is some version of "Fine," "Nothing," or "Get off my back," perhaps the question should not be asked. If the usual response at 7 a.m. to a cheerful "Good morning!" is growling, a parent should try something else or drop the greeting altogether. We must say to parents: If you know you're going to get a negative response from a certain statement, it would appear that you are trying to start a fight or cause trouble by asking or making that statement. Why would you do this?

Often parents need to learn keep their anxiety and anger to themselves, especially if they themselves have ADHD and have kids with ADHD. Better not to keep everything bottled up inside, parents often are advised. Have thought, open mouth. But in reality what this philosophy often produces is people who are irritating and unpleasant nags. In families with ADHD the way for parents to manage outgoing noise is not to talk unless (1) they have a very good reason (the simple expression of negative feelings is not a good reason) and (2) they can reasonably anticipate that their remarks will serve some useful purpose. When these two rules are followed, the number of conflicts can be more than cut in half.

## Divide and Conquer

The first two tactics we have discussed, identifying MBAs (picking your battles) and managing noise, often go together. Obviously parents can reduce a lot of unnecessary noise by not voicing their valuable opinions about trivial issues. The next suggestion for the reduction of parenting stress takes a different approach. Divide and conquer, or D and C, is one of the most beneficial and easily applied strategies for ADHD family life. Parents will not be willing to use this procedure, however, until they have first worked through a moderate dose of disillusionment and sadness. The D-and-C routine starts with another attitude adjustment.

Some dreams die harder than others. Whether they have ADHD or not, most moms and dads—especially moms—have definite positive images of what they want their family life to be like. The first characteristic of parents' optimistic imagery is the notion of the entire family being together, and the second characteristic is the idea of mutual interpersonal enjoyment. On a typical weekend, for example, parents imagine their children happily playing together for hours on end. Parents also imagine themselves not only getting a kick out of the kids' activities, but also taking pleasure in one another's reactions. The feeling will be one of warmth, joy, and togetherness.

It certainly would be nice if this scene could be replicated consistently in families with ADHD, but it can't. In families with ADHD these little bits of interpersonal heaven are rare, and the brief pieces that do occur are often marred initially by anticipatory anxiety and then shattered later by angry explosions. These shortcomings are hard for parents to accept.

The truth, however, is the opposite of the famous "The more the merrier" cliche. When ADHD is involved, the greater the number of people who get together in one place at one time, the greater are the chances for aggravation, noise, and conflict. Kids with ADHD, for example, become more hyper and silly in groups. Sibling rivalry is worse. Parents who have ADHD are more impatient and irritable. Mom and dad, therefore, have to give up the dream of a consistently congenial, peaceful, and enjoyable family life. (Of course, if parents can honestly say that their experiences with their family have been by far more pleasant than not, perhaps they don't require the advice in this chapter.)

Being honest is a large part of the problem. Imagine a wife saying to her husband, "Wouldn't it be fun if we took the kids to Disney World?" The correct (honest and realistic) answer in a family with ADHD might really be this: "No it would not be fun. The kids would fight on the plane, in the rental car, and in the hotel room. When we'd have to decide what to do, no one would be able to agree. Sit-down meals would be a chore, and our ADHD son would want to buy everything he saw. The whole experience would make him overly excited, and his tantrums would become even more frequent than they are now. And when things weren't actually going wrong, we'd be dreading the next time they would."

Positive family dreams die hard. After a fairly miserable vacation, for example, some parents may try to remember only the fun parts. They may then use this selective memory to predict what their next vacation is going to be like. Making matters worse, magazines, radio, politicians, newspapers, and TV constantly urge families to do things together in order to prevent mental illness, drug abuse, low self-esteem, underachievement, and crime. In the family that eats together, these writers and broadcasters claim, all kinds of good things will happen.

This simply is not true when ADHD is in the picture. More than likely, when the family with ADHD eats together all kinds of conflicts ensue. The idea of family times has a sort of pseudoefficiency about it. The thought is this: "If we all get together, go out to a show and to eat afterwards, we can achieve a sense of bonding and togetherness fairly quickly and easily. Then we will have done our job and we won't have to worry about it for a while." It's impossible to guess how much harm has been done to some families by the innocent and hopeful pursuit of this impossible dream.

The bright side, though, is that positive interactions between family members are possible, but usually not when the entire family is together. With the D-and-C procedure we can help parents employ a useful and proven fact about kids with ADHD: These kids are much more manageable in one-on-one situations. We must help parents to divide the family group a good deal of the time. It may be a little saddening to have to do this, but it works.

Practical illustrations of the method are numerous. Imagine, for example, that a family of four walks into a fast-food restaurant. They have no children with ADHD. They get their food, sit at the same table, and enjoy themselves reasonably well. Now imagine another family of four comes in. In this family there is both one child and one parent with ADHD. After getting their food, one parent takes one child to one table, while the other parent takes the other child to sit at another table—preferably out of sight of the first location. Both parents and both children enjoy their meals.

Here's another simple example: at church. It's amazing how many families with two children sit like this in church: parent–child–child–parent. The two kids are in the middle, so they have a better chance to tease one another and fight. The correct, prevention-oriented disposition of bodies should be this: child–parent–parent–child. The same can be done for sitting at a table and sometimes for riding in a car. It's better not to put the kids right next to each other.

Imagine that the parents from our earlier Disney World example, in a moment of insane perversity, continue to insist on taking the family to Orlando. They can still use the method to ease their burden. On the ride to the airport, for example, one child sits in the front and one in the back. On the plane, mom and daughter sit in seats 23E and F, while dad and son with ADHD sit in seats 17A and B. Halfway to Florida, parents switch kids. In the motel room at night, both kids use sleeping bags. One child sleeps on the floor on one side of the king-size bed and the other child sleeps on the floor on the other side of the bed. While at the park, mom takes one youngster for the morning and dad takes the other. The family meets for lunch but sits at adjacent tables. Then parents and kids change partners for the afternoon.

Since this splitting-up technique is largely prevention oriented, it requires a little advance planning; it is not as effective once a squabble has broken out. To accomplish the necessary advance planning, parents must have already completed the attitude adjustment that allows them to give up, to a large extent, the dream of consistent and pleasant family togetherness. The bullheaded pursuit of that unattainable goal will never allow mom and dad to feel good about—or to implement the process of—dividing the family up for different activities. Therapists must continually remind parents that there is no state or federal law that says families have to eat together every night. Neither is anyone ordering families to watch the same movie all at the same time or always to take the same vacation. When one parent goes to the store, both children do not have to come along. The applications of the D-and-C routine are many. The potential for merciful conflict reduction is enormous.

## Technological Aids

Modern technology is a mixed blessing for most of us. It's great to have a cell phone when you get a flat tire during a snowstorm in a remote rural area.

It's not so great, though, when the person next to you in the movie theater answers a cell phone call and proceeds to carry on a conversation. Computers can fascinate, entertain, and educate children. The Internet, however, has its dark side, involving uncontrolled violence and sex. Once parents accept the idea, however, that in families with ADHD interpersonal interactions are often problematic and sometimes need to be avoided, technology can help in various ways that can be carefully supervised to assist in minimizing family stress.

Television, for example, is one of the best babysitters modern civilization has devised. The average child in the United States, though, watches far too much TV, perhaps four to five hours per day, so it is best if the children's TV watching is limited by mom and dad. One of the problems with television, however, is that people tend to gravitate toward the best TV in the house (best color, biggest screen, surround sound). There they watch their programs and there they also have the opportunity to fight with one another. Even in families with no ADHD, family members will fight about what to watch, about who gets to channel surf with the remote during commercial breaks, about where to sit, about who's chewing popcorn too loudly, and about other family matters unrelated to television.

A handy solution for parents here is to use routine. Since most families have more than one television, it can be routinely prearranged that certain people use certain TVs on certain days. Another solution is to have videotape or DVD players (not actual TVs) in other rooms of the house or actually in children's bedrooms. Portable players, such as laptops with DVD slots, are also available. With these machines a child does not have unsupervised access to TV, a parent can help determine which programs are available for viewing, and kids can have enjoyable times by themselves with no opportunity to start a fight.

One mother, for example, had a 5-year-old son with ADHD who was very difficult to manage. He was oppositional, enjoyed picking on his sister, and seemed addicted to screaming and arguing. According to his mother, however, he also loved the movie *Superman II* and could sit peacefully for hours in front of the VCR watching it. He had, in fact, seen this movie 20 times. At one point this mother, feeling sheepish about using this method for reducing the turmoil at home, asked her family counselor what she should do. The counselor's reply was "Try for 21."

The small, portable game players children use can also help reduce squabbling among brothers and sisters. These games are usually engrossing enough that kids are distracted from the temptation to start a fight, even when a sibling is fairly close by. These devices are also helpful at times when physical proximity is hard to avoid, such as car rides and doctors' offices. Parents need to think ahead, of course, and remember to leave the house armed with these preventive gadgets.

Computers, too, have a fascination that can carry people away from family conflict. But as it is with the best TV set, moms and dads and brothers and sisters can argue about who gets to use the best computer. If multiple computers are not available, rules need to be agreed on and probably written down for who gets to use the computer at what times. It is very important to emphasize that rules like these will never work unless they are routine. Attempting to renegotiate guidelines every day will lead to chaos rather than conflict reduction.

Television, videos, electronic games, and even CDs can serve another purpose for parents. They can be part of a reward program for good behavior. A certain number of the total domestic crop of videos, game cartridges, cassettes, and disks, for example, can be kept in a locked place. Kids then earn time on one of them by doing homework, getting up and out in the morning, completing chores, not fighting with or teasing one another, and a whole host of other positive behaviors. By not being constantly available to the children, these reward disks and cassettes retain their attractiveness and motivational power for a longer period of time.

## Realistic and Aggressive Medication Management

Medication treatment can provide potent, dramatic and helpful behavioral changes for most children and adults affected with ADHD. The medications used for ADHD and comorbid conditions include not only stimulants, but also antidepressants, anticonvulsants, antihypertensives, and other types of drugs. When a valid diagnosis has been made, adequate follow-up is provided for, and other interventions are also employed (education about ADHD, counseling, parent training, school interventions), medication treatment for ADHD is one of the safest and most effective interventions we have available. The ability of carefully prescribed and carefully used drugs to reduce family conflict and stress is substantial—and often nothing short of miraculous.

Not all medications, however, work equally well for all individuals. Often a period of trial-and-error learning is needed while effective doses are being determined and possible side effects are discovered and managed. However, a common problem these days is that many parents with ADHD children don't even get to this first stage of constructive experimentation with medication. These parents have been prejudiced against drug treatment for ADHD by what they have seen and heard on television and radio, read in newspapers or magazines, or found on the Internet.

Because of the same exposure to bad information, other parents (and often their physicians as well) actually try medication for ADHD and comorbid conditions, but they don't conduct the drug trials correctly because of ambivalence about medication. These parents and doctors had mixed feelings about starting medication in the first place, so they later found themselves reluctant to:

1. Try another drug when one did not work well.
2. Use two medications when one could not do the entire job.
3. Increase the amount given when a lower dose provided beneficial but partial results.
4. Use medication to help with summers, after-school times, and weekends.

The amount of unnecessary suffering and outright tragedy caused by parents who either never use medication or who are ambivalent about medication is significant. Many people don't realize that there are hundreds of carefully controlled scientific studies on medication treatment for ADHD in children and an increasing number for adults. These studies show clearly that medication treatment for ADHD is very safe and very effective, that meticulous follow-up is crucial to its success, and that all medications do not work equally well for everyone.

For parents torn by the question of drug treatment, the issue boils down to this: Where are you going to get your information about ADHD? Are you going to consider television, radio, magazines, newspapers, and the Internet not-for-profit public services that consistently provide accurate information? Or, more realistically, are you going to see these different information vehicles as for-profit, highly entertaining—and often riveting—mechanisms that emphasize controversy and bad news while showing little interest in well-founded and useful—but often boring—scientific data?

When ADHD is part of family life, aggressive, open-minded, and informed use of medication—for both the children with ADHD and the adults with ADHD—needs to be a big component of the treatment package. To ignore this potential for change is not only cruel but dangerous.

## Other Useful Thoughts

Finally, here are a few additional suggestions for parents to help themselves survive ADHD in the family. These suggestions may make Mom and Dad better parents, but they may also help them to assist others in the family to avoid excessive wear and tear from the stress of ADHD.

### Getting Away

One of the healthiest things parents of children with ADHD (and spouses of adults with ADHD) can do is to get away regularly from the entire family. A weekly escape of only a few hours can be excellent therapy. Going out with friends for an evening or part of a weekend can bring significant relief, since friends are usually good distractors who are sympathetic and make few demands. Time away from home might also mean dinner and a show alone, wandering around the mall, shopping, or just a ride in the car. Unfortunately, many parents are shy about going out by themselves, and this ill-advised policy takes its toll in the long run by making them feel chained to their families. Getting away from the family, of course, does not even have to mean leaving the house. Some parents occasionally arrange to be home when everyone else is gone. Others take their earplugs and earphones—or borrow the videotape player—and hide out in the basement for a while.

### Physical Exercise

In addition to getting away from the family, regular exercise can provide large amounts of parental stress reduction. For parents who are also adults with ADHD, strenuous physical movement can be a natural outlet for a restless and intense temperament. Emotional outbursts on the racquetball court are healthier—for parents and families—than emotional outbursts at home. Physical exercise in the form of running, tennis, swimming, aerobics, and other activities can also be a response to our last suggestion—getting away from the family. Two additional suggestions for parents with ADHD themselves who are considering exercise: Make a regular schedule for the workouts, and find a buddy to work out with. Otherwise, the "program" may not happen.

### The State of the Union

When ADHD exists in a family and mom and dad are involved in a relatively young marriage, they may still have a chance at resurrecting some—but certainly not all—of the old spark that brought them together. They need to remember that their relationship was born in mutual fun and excitement. Dating was enjoyable and their spouse-to-be was an amusing and pleasant person—back then. Now, though, parents may feel that their marriage is mired in work, aggravation, and worry. What must be done, obviously, is to put some of the fun back in the relationship—on a regular basis. Parents in families with ADHD need to have times together—without the kids—when they both take pleasure from the same thing without discussing any problems at all. Never to have fun with one's spouse is marital suicide. Couples that don't have fun together stop liking each other. If the two continue not to have fun with each other, under conditions of continual ADHD-related family stress they will at some later point conclude that their spouses are idiots. Following this phase these men and women will decide that their spouses are incredibly malicious, and after that—whether they act on the inclination or not— they will want to be separated or divorced. The somewhat ironic bottom line is this: To be good parents, mom and dad had better have regular fun together—without the kids.

What about couples who are already at the "I want to be divorced but I can't because of money, the kids, and lifestyle stage?" The first thing these individuals need is another attitude adjustment, but one that may be a bit surprising to them. First, they must learn to think and to accept the reality that it's sad—but not the end of the world—if they don't love their husband or wife anymore. Divorce statistics tell us that plenty, if not most, married people eventually wind up in that state. Second, even though the two parents don't care for each other anymore, it's OK for them to live in the same house—if they respect a few guidelines. We call this type of living arrangement *parallel lives*. It's much more common than most people realize or want to admit, and many times it's better for the children than separation or divorce. But parallel lives works only if spouses—whether they have ADHD or not—observe the following rules.

1. Expectations or hopes for a warm and loving relationship with one's spouse must be abandoned.
2. Each spouse must take at least half of the responsibility for the fact that they have fallen out of love; in other words, he or she can't treat the spouse like the "evil one who caused it all."
3. Business and children's welfare issues need to be discussed calmly and objectively between the two parents, without unnecessarily resurrecting sore points from the past.
4. No unproductive arguing in front of the kids is allowed.
5. No character assassination in front of the kids is allowed.

Parallel lives is a perfectly legitimate lifestyle, and many couples bring it off very well. In these cases, mom, dad, and the children are all the beneficiaries of a couple's ability to accept and live with reality. When kids and parents are ADHD, parallel lives is often an option that must be given serious consideration. Couples must always remember that the kind of marriage they have is going to affect their parenting.

**Siblings Without ADHD**

Finally, what can a therapist do to help parents deal with the many frustrations experienced by the siblings of kids with ADHD? As we described earlier, children without ADHD can feel neglected, embarrassed, and abused. One bit of advice is for parents to try to explain ADHD periodically to brothers and sisters, but not to expect much to come from these conversations—at least right away. Many kids who don't have ADHD will begrudgingly listen to their parent, while inside what they are really thinking is this: "She's making excuses for The Brat again!" This reaction is normal, and parents needn't try to shove information down kids' throats until the youngsters beg for mercy by pretending they understand. A second—and perhaps more fruitful—piece of advice is for parents to listen sympathetically to the siblings when they are frustrated. This is especially difficult for parents who have ADHD themselves, because their own frustration tolerance tends to be low. But all parents need to understand that it is a big mistake to always defend the child with ADHD! Mom and dad need to be reassured that they are not being disloyal by quietly hearing and trying to understand the frustrations that their other children are going through.

By far the best strategy parents can employ with their other kids is to spend one-on-one time with them doing something enjoyable. Family "fun" will not do the job! Whether mom and dad like it or not—in families with ADHD the most powerful bonding and relationship building occur not when the family is together but when just two people are together. This arrangement isn't always easy to carry out. We must ask parents to imagine the following scene: You are walking out the front door for the evening with one of your non-ADHD children. Just then your son or daughter who has ADHD comes running up screaming "Can I go, too?! Can I go?! Please!" The correct answer is "No, you can go some other time." Parent and first child then exit the house, most likely leaving a ferocious temper tantrum in their wake.

Finally, parents should never expect their children to love one another the way the parents love them. This is an all-too-common parenting mistake. Sibling rivalry is real, normal, and at times intense; with ADHD in the picture it is much worse. There is absolutely no way that children's love for their own brothers and sisters will be able to match the love that their parents have for each of them. Some parents ask: "Then when will my children finally get along?" The answer probably is "When they're not living in the same house anymore and no longer have to compete for the same resources, including you."

## SUMMARY

ADHD puts stress on parents in many different ways, and this stress is especially severe when parents with ADHD are trying to raise children with ADHD. ADHD-related family problems are both oppressive and chronic, and—much as they might like to—parents cannot magically make them disappear. There is no place for wishful thinking or unrealistic sentiment when it comes to living with ADHD. With a well-informed understanding of ADHD, some brutal honesty, and a few simple strategies, however, mom and dad can begin to minimize the turmoil and provide some relief for every member of the family.

## REFERENCES

Barkley, R. A. (1995). *Taking charge of ADHD*. New York: Guilford Press.

Beck, J. (1995). *Cognitive therapy: Basics and beyond*. New York: Guilford Press.

Goldstein, S. & Goldstein, M. (1998). *Managing attention deficit hyperactivity disorder in children* (2nd ed.). New York: Wiley.

Gottman, J. M., & Silver, S. (1999). *The seven principles for making marriage work*. New York: Crown.

MTA Cooperative Group. (1999). Fourteen-month randomized clinical trial of treatment strategies for attention-deficit hyperactivity disorder. *Archives of General Psychiatry, 56*, 1073–1086.

Paterson, R., Douglas, C., Hallmayer, J., Hagan, M., & Krupenia, Z. (1999). A randomized, double-blind, placebo-controlled trial of dextroamphetamine in adults with attention deficit hyperactivity disorder. *Australian and New Zealand Journal of Psychiatry, 33*, 494–502.

Stine, J. J. (1994). Psychosocial and psychodynamic issues affecting noncompliance with psychostimulant treatment. *Journal of Child and Adolescent Psychopharmacology, 4*, 75–86.

# 14

# Life Coaching for Adult ADHD

Nancy A. Ratey, Ed. M., ABOA, MCC

*The ideal teacher guides his students but does not pull them along; he urges them to go forward and does not suppress them; he opens the way but does not take them to the place.*

—Confucius

## CLAIRE'S STORY

Claire is startled out of her deep concentration by the ringing of the phone. Lifting the receiver, she hears a voice screaming, "Gosh Mom, the phone rang about 20 times! Are you alive? Where are you? You promised to pick me up at three o'clock!"

Claire looks at her watch—four o'clock! "Oh my gosh! I'm so sorry, sweetie! I got carried away working on my project. I'll be there right away!"

She hangs up the phone and realizes she is still in her pajamas. She runs to change into jeans and thinks to herself, "Why don't I just take a quick shower?" Thirty minutes later, Claire is showered and dressed. On her way out the door, she remembers the checks she needs to deposit and grabs them. "I have been meaning to take those in for a week now and I am overdrawn," she mutters to herself. "I might as well drop off the dry cleaning, too. It's on the way." Out of the corner of her eye, she sees some packages that she has been meaning to mail. She snatches them off the table.

By now Claire's hands are full. "Shoot! I forgot my keys and purse!" she realizes when she gets to the car. She puts some of her load on top of the car and drops the rest on the garage floor. Running back upstairs, she looks at the clock and sees it's 4:45. "I can do this! I can beat the clock!" As Claire heads down the driveway, she congratulates herself. "I'm so happy that I finally remembered to bring the checks and packages with me!" Then she gasps, as she realizes she left the packages on the roof of the car. She quickly pulls over and retrieves them.

The dry cleaners are preparing to close as Claire arrives. While waiting in line, she realizes she's forgotten her purse at home. She runs back out to the car and decides to pick up her daughter before it gets any later. She pulls up to the high school at 5:30 to find her daughter sitting on the curb, arms firmly folded across her chest, fuming. "Honey, I'm so sorry!" Claire says, as she jumps out of the car to give her a hug. But to make matters worse, Claire has forgotten to engage the parking brake, and the car starts to roll out into the street. Running back to the car with her daughter in tow, Claire wonders: "Why do I always do this? What is wrong with me? I have been working so hard to be on time and to be responsible, especially to those most important to me, and yet I blunder and do the same old same old. I am such a loser! Oh well, I'll do better. (I have said that so many times.)"

Claire says she has been disorganized and distracted since she can remember. Her husband has threatened to leave her if she does not become more responsible, and her kids have learned not to depend on her for very much. She is desperate and feels that she has tried everything. When she was initially diagnosed with ADHD she started taking medication, and it helped. If only she could remember to take it. She has been in and out of therapy for years because she feels like a failure as a professional, a wife, and a mother. She has read countless self-help books on time management and organization, yet nothing ever seems to stick.

Many of the difficulties Claire is experiencing are due to ADHD, and could be successfully addressed with the introduction of compensatory strategies. Though such strategies can be gleaned from a variety of sources, what Claire really needs is a means to incorporate these strategies into her daily life. Increasingly, individuals identifying themselves as ADHD coaches offer this assistance.

## WHAT IS PERSONAL COACHING?

The idea of hiring a coach to improve one's performance is certainly not new. Athletes, musicians and business professionals have known for years that a personal coaching partnership can be the difference between maintaining competence and achieving excellence. As any one of them could attest, the huge amount of information and skills that must be learned, sorted, assimilated, and internalized in order to achieve mastery can be overwhelming. That's why they hire a coach—to help them discover and focus on what works for them.

It's not much of a stretch to understand how personal coaching has come to be popular in today's overworked, overwrought society. Faced with increasingly burdensome demands on their time and attention, many people started searching for ways to deal with the information overload so they could make the choices that would both fulfill and honor who they were. In response to this need for better life management, an industry of one-on-one helping professionals—such as personal exercise trainers, personal organizers, and personal coaches—was born.

Personal coaching helps because it is based on a very individualized approach that always focuses on the client's goals and needs. Because each client has already developed a unique way of coping, it is up to the coach to help the client identify her or his true goals and create a strategy to work around obstacles, changing old behavior patterns and creating new ones. The personal coach is an ally, providing a safe, respectful, and supportive place from which the client can examine his life. The personal coach will never be coercive or punitive, thus giving the client opportunities to consciously make proactive changes for personal growth.

## WHAT IS ADHD COACHING?

Let's return to Claire. Like anyone else, she is experiencing an information overload that would tax the most able processing system. But she experiences this overload through the lens of ADHD. Where most people are able to take in, sort out, assimilate, and recall information at least moderately well, Claire's ability to do so is inconsistent. It's as if she's unable to stop and think. Instead of considering her actions and their subsequent consequences, she acts on all of her thoughts, all at the same time. As a result, Claire is dealing with more pieces of diffuse data than are practical or useful for the task at hand—getting out the door quickly to pick up her daughter.

Coaching for persons with ADHD operates under the same premise that personal and professional coaching does—that the client is ready, willing, and able to work in partnership with the coach and rise to the challenge of creating a better life. What is different about clients with ADHD is that it is often not a matter of being overworked and losing touch with their values that has gotten them off track; it is their biology that has claimed control over their lives. A coach can play a vital role in helping clients with ADHD clear away the daily confusion of their lives and sustain focus long enough to achieve desired goals.

## HOW COACHING HELPED CLAIRE

Due to ADHD, Claire was experiencing difficulties in a variety of different areas. With the help of a coach Claire identified three main issues to work on: (1) measuring and estimating time; (2) prioritizing tasks—namely, the ability to assign and direct her attention to the most important tasks for that day; and (3) increasing her ability to self-monitor. Together, Claire and her coach came up with ways to overcome these challenges so that Claire could progress beyond repeating the same mistakes over and over again. Here are some examples of how they worked together.

- *Measuring and estimating time*: By talking out actions and plans with her coach on a biweekly basis over the phone, Claire was able to identify and remember what her major priorities were for each day. They designated specific times to take her medication and programmed her wristwatch to beep when she needed to take her next dose. Next, they designated start and stop times for working on her priorities.
- *Prioritizing tasks*: By talking out actions and plans with her coach on a biweekly basis over the phone, Claire was able to keep in mind what her priorities were. They created accountability around completion of identified tasks through e-mail check-ins.
- *Self-monitoring*: Independent of her coach, Claire used a timer and created a "time card" for herself on her computer so she would "clock in" to work, so to speak, and "clock out" for each task. Then, in her biweekly phone calls, Claire would report events that had happened during the week and would review instances where she felt she had made bad choices—for example, attempting to run several errands on the way to pick up her daughter when she was already over an hour late! By analyzing these occurrences, Claire was able to self-reflect and talk through possible alternative courses of actions. She then "programmed" her coach to keep reminding her of her tendency to pile too much on her plate. Her coach would do reality checks with her by saying: "Remember, Claire, you tend to fool yourself into thinking that you can do everything all at once. How can you be more realistic?" Also, by tracking her medication intake more closely she was able to become more aware of how she behaved on and off medication and to be more aware of the warning signs of when it was wearing off.

Claire's direct involvement in the creation of strategies, including designing the coaching partnership itself, maintained her interest and motivated her to change her behavior.

## THEORETICAL UNDERPINNINGS OF ADHD COACHING

Coaching intervention can make a difference in how people with ADHD negotiate their own particular deficits and cope with life on a daily basis. There are five major deficit areas that can be observed playing out in the lives of persons with ADHD. The following is a discussion of these areas and of how the coaching relationship can offer successful compensatory strategies.

## Coaching Maintains Arousal

If attention is underaroused, chances are motivation will lag also, and vice versa. For instance, people with ADHD often have a hard time tending to abstract goals. Coaches seek to bring the more abstract goals to the forefront of their clients' minds by creating a false sense of a "need for survival" by making the goal more critical, keeping attention aroused long enough to meet their goals.

The coaching partnership provides a shared awareness, or mutual consciousness, of goals and their associated challenges so as to sustain the ADHD client's vigilance toward an identified goal. The coach works with the client to create deadlines, schedules, meetings, and regular phone check-ins around reaching goals. This induces a certain level of "good" stress on the client, keeping her brain aroused, vigilant, and on track to reach stated goals.

People respond differently to various levels of stress. What is a good level of stress for one client may be overwhelming for another client, thus creating "bad" stress. Certain amounts of stress can create appropriate challenges for clients, increasing their attention and clarifying thoughts. Therefore, it is the coach's job to help clients discover how to create "good stress" in order to sustain their clients' attention over the long haul.

## Coaching Helps Modulate Emotions

Shame, guilt, and fear are demons plaguing many people with ADHD. Years of being labeled "stupid," "ditzy," or "irresponsible" create an emotional burden that can startle them out of action, throw them off course, or even paralyze them, leaving them no choice but to slip back into their old avoidance tactics. A coach helps clients learn how to identify bad feelings and their triggers, and explores effective ways to modulate emotional responses. Instead of blaming themselves when the ADHD gets in their way, clients can think: "Wait a minute! I know this is my disability at work, and I know I have ways to get around it now." By isolating the behavior from the emotion, it can be broken down into parts to take the mystery out of it, giving clients a more level playing field upon which to think up strategies to contain and change the behavior, thus keeping their progress moving forward.

## Coaching Maintains Motivation and Sustains the Feeling of Reward

Motivation is often questioned in people with ADHD. Although clients may have developed the tools to sustain attention to tasks, they may still lack motivation. By reminding clients of their top priorities and of all the gains they have made, the coach provides encouragement. Self-confidence is bolstered. Having a partner in their journey of self-discovery activates and provides motivation for the clients, and in terms of coaching provides them with the feeling of reward when progress is made.

The client may underfunction in certain situations, especially when it comes to prioritizing, planning, attending to details, and following through with projects. In other instances, the client may become overwhelmed with a project, not knowing where to start, and may avoid the task. Breaking down large projects into smaller, more manageable tasks are ways coaches keep clients more focused on their goals and naturally stimulates the areas that underfunction.

## Coaching Acts as the "Executive Secretary of Attention"

The client with ADHD is challenged in his or her ability to gross prioritize—to gather and focus attention. By keeping the big picture in mind, the coach helps the client to sustain his or her attention on primary goals, pointing out distractions and helping to create strategies to deal with problems should they arise.

## Coaching Supports the Client's Ability to Self-Direct Actions and to Change Behavior

The executive functions provide the flexibility that is required for autonomous action in a dynamic world. In order to function autonomously, individuals must be able to screen out distractions, sustain their attention, and use feedback appropriately. Attentional arousal is a double-edged sword for people with ADHD. While it is usually the case that their attention needs to be aroused in order to attack certain tasks, it is also true that if their attention is *too* aroused, they can find themselves becoming "overfocused" and getting stuck in a particular activity at the cost of everything else. For example, a client with ADHD taking a short break to play a few quick games of solitaire could get stuck playing for hours on end, losing sight of the goal.

Just as they can be sidetracked by pleasurable feedback, clients can also be sidetracked by negative feedback, such as negative scripts, those "voices in the head" that continually remind one of one's inadequacies. Clients with ADHD know they have behavioral deficits—they've been reminded of them for years—and whenever a new failure occurs they're ready to chastise themselves again and again and again.

Clients with ADHD are also very adept at self-deception and forgetting the pain of past procrastination. This interrelation between memory and confabulation often leads clients astray. Clients with ADHD often get caught up in telling "honest lies" about their past. They are adept at self-deception and easily forget the pain of past procrastination.

The coach compensates for these deficits by providing daily reminders and helping the client sequence out the details of needed actions. By pressing the client to process and evaluate outcomes and consequences, the coach allows the client to develop the ability to make more proactive choices and be less reactive to the environment. Coaches also help clients develop the ability to estimate the time it takes to complete tasks by having ongoing discussions, reviewing plans for timelines, and processing out the details and sequences of tasks. In effect, the coach helps clients to observe themselves in action, by processing out events, asking questions, and providing feedback.

## THE PRECEPTS OF ADHD COACHING

Can everyone benefit from coaching? Coaching is based on a wellness model—it presumes that the client is well, has an idea of what his issues are, and is ready to devote the time to work on them, only needing the coach to draw them out. Although this new, evolving service overlaps other self-improvement services—such as counseling, mentoring, and therapy—coaching focuses on the client's *actions* and the *measurable outcomes* of those actions. Because coaching is client centered and client driven, it is the client's job to design a powerful alliance with the coach to focus on forwarding the client's own agenda. Coaches enable their clients to do this by creating a nonjudgmental space for them to reflect and question their behaviors. Through their coach's gentle probing, they discover which strategies will help them cope successfully with the demands of their daily life. Once these strategies are found, they work together to figure out how to hold the clients accountable to their plan of action. In essence, the coach is fostering a climate of support and encouragement so that clients can discover for themselves how to replace negative, defeating behaviors with positive patterns for success.

Coaching is holistic. Working alongside a coach, clients develop an overall plan to compensate for their symptoms of ADHD. This involves working on the whole human, understanding that lifestyle choices—what one eats, how much sleep one gets, how strong one's social network is, whether or not one has a spiritual life, one's satisfaction with one's job—all affect client functioning.

Coaching is a process of exploration that takes place over a period of time. Clients must be ready for coaching before they can commit to the process. Clients will know they are ready to be coached when they are able to admit they have a problem, agree to spend the time necessary to create strategies to improve their behavior, and adhere to those strategies to the best of their ability. If clients with ADHD are not ready or able to commit, then they will not benefit from coaching.

## THE PROCESS OF COACHING

A coach occupies the unique position of being able to watch a client's problems manifest within the context of daily life. They can often spot the areas in which a client will be blocked, and point them out to the client. But they don't concern themselves with *why* these things happen. Instead they ask questions that will elicit strategies and action from the client: "What can you do about it?" "How can you motivate yourself to take action toward this goal?" "When must this action be completed?" Coaches focus on *what*, *how*, and *when*—never *why*.

Coaches provide encouragement, recommendations, feedback, and practical techniques such as reminders, questions, and calendar monitoring. Strategies are developed to address issues of time management, eliminating clutter in the home or office, and becoming more effective in personal and professional life. ADHD coaching is not psychotherapy.

Regular meetings and check-ins are an essential part of the coaching process. These sessions can be done in person, by telephone, by fax, or by e-mail, whichever is preferable to the client. However, before coaching begins, the potential client and the coach must have an in-depth, one-to two-hour initial meeting to develop the step-by-step plans needed to achieve goals.

## Conducting the Initial Interview

The purpose of the initial interview, or *intake*, is threefold. First, it enables coaches to assess a potential client's readiness to be coached. Second, it addresses all administrative issues associated with the partnership. Last, it starts the process of defining the coaching partnership. This session is usually one to two hours long.

The initial interview is best done in person, if possible. If the client is not close geographically, then it will be conducted over the phone. Because there is so much ground to cover in this initial session, it is often wise to divide it into two shorter, one-hour sessions. There is no set rule for how these sessions are structured, so long as the basic issues are explored and covered.

## Agreeing on Procedures and Defining Services

The bedrock of the coaching partnership lies in setting up boundaries and making sure the client knows and understands what coaching is, how it is done, and what it can offer. This involves general administrative issues along with an agreement about what role the coach will play in his or her life. It is best when coaches set forth these parameters in a *coaching service agreement*, making it a point to go over it in the beginning of the initial interview. Here are the points a coaching service agreement generally covers:

- What issues coaching will and won't cover.
- That the coach will maintain confidentiality.
- That the client will be open and honest.
- That they both want to work together.
- That they will keep lines of communication open.
- A rate for the coach's services, and billing procedures.
- A policy regarding missed appointments.
- A statement making it clear that coaching holds no guarantees, that the client is responsible for his or her own outcomes, and that the client takes responsibility for his or her actions or lack of action.

## Assessing Overall Functioning Level of the Client

The coach also needs to develop a thorough understanding of the client's background and history. This uncovers patterns and helps her to evaluate the client's current level of functioning as well as the client's awareness of her issues. The following questions were designed to elicit the information needed to construct a plan of action.

Educational, Vocational, Avocational

1. What do you do well? not well?
2. What problems do you experience?
3. What do you enjoy?
4. Are there any patterns?

Medical History

1. Diagnosis, date of diagnosis, symptoms of disability, medications.
2. What other professionals are you seeing? Have you discussed coaching with them?

Health and Social Well-Being

1. What supports are in place?
2. Sleep pattern, eating habits, etc.
3. Habits, exercise, routines, rituals, etc.
4. What stressors are present in your life?

## HOW DOES COACHING WORK?

The success of coaching depends on the client's commitment to the coaching process. Coaching is a partnership. The coach guides the process yet does not drive it; provides structure without imposing it;

How is Coaching Done?
**The ADD Coaching Model**
*Nancy A. Rtey, Ed.M., ABDA, MCC ©*

**Structure**

*Self-Initate*
**CHANGE**

Process — Partnership

Coaching is a dynamic methodology that aims to nurture clients' ability to self-initiate change in their daily lives.

and asks questions without judgment. The following are the three core components of ADHD coaching, Model © Nancy Ratey (2000).

- *Partnership*: Client and coach coengineer a partnership to benefit the client.
- *Structure*: Client and coach cocreate strength-based strategies to provide internal and external structure in the client's life.
- *Process*: Through a process of inquiry, the coach guides the client in self-exploration and learning.

Coaching is a dynamic methodology that aims to nurture clients' ability to self-initiate change in their daily lives. Only when each of these three core components is present and interacting successfully can coaching achieve its desired end.

## Partnership: A Team Effort

When a client hires a coach, he or she takes on the responsibility of developing the coaching partnership to meet his or her specific needs. The parameters of the relationship are cocreated, or *coengineered*, by both coach and client. It is an ongoing, collaborative process that propels the client forward as he or she learns strategies to become more productive in daily life. This process requires the client to identify and utilize her or his own strengths to construct a unique environment that is "userfriendly," giving the client a safe place to change ADHD behaviors. Through this method of self-help, the client learns and builds upon essential life skills, such as: understanding more deeply the nature of the disability; isolating and altering old patterns; articulating, identifying, and clarifying needs; and learning how to self-motivate.

Oftentimes clients make the initial contact with a coach because of an ultimatum from a loved one. But for coaching to work, it must be something that the clients truly want to do. They also need to understand that it is a process that happens over time and that entails a financial commitment. Clients must understand what coaching will offer them (structure, support, and encouragement) and assess their commitment to making changes. Through this discussion, a coach can decide whether or not a particular client is someone they can help and someone with whom they would like to work. If this turns out not to be the case, then the coach would refer the individual to another coach, who might be a better match. If the person is working with or was referred by a therapist, the coach might want to make contact with the therapist beforehand (with prior written consent from the client) to see if what he or she wants and what the coach can offer are in line.

It is the client's job to tell the coach where help is needed so that the coach can deliver the service in ways that will encourage and motivate. The coach requires the clients literally to *program*, or lay out, how they want to be held accountable to their goals. This helps the clients take responsibility for their action or lack of action. Over time, and with the coach's prompting, clients will learn more about what motivates them and what doesn't and how to tweak the process as needed. This is important, since most people hire an ADHD coach because they're caught up in a *start–stop* syndrome—they frequently start a project and then lose motivation or become diverted from the goal and never succeed in finishing what they started.

### Paul's Story

Paul is working on being more financially responsible. To this end, he has "engineered" his coach to remind him to pay his bills on time, and they agree that on Mondays Paul will sit down and write checks. Monday comes and goes, and no checks are written. On Tuesday he checks in with the coach and reports that the goal was not accomplished. How should the coach respond? There are a number of options. She or he could say: "Stop what you're doing and pay the bills right now." Or the coach could talk Paul through what got in the way of completing the task. Or she or he could ask Paul to commit to another deadline without further discussion. The right answer here is the coach should respond according to whichever option Paul has programmed him or her to do, which is ultimately the option he thinks would work best to propel him into action.

Paul has programmed his coach to give a "That's okay" response. At the time he first coengineered the partnership, he felt this response would help him take action. He thought it would relieve him of the burden of guilt he's always felt over not doing what he said he was going to do, leaving him free to tackle the task once more. As it turns out, when the coach does exactly that, one more week passes and the bills are still not paid. The coach prompts Paul to rethink the coach's role. He comes to realize that a different response might be more effective. Paul takes this as a learning experience and reprograms the coach to remind him of the bigger picture, which is that in order for him to achieve his goal of becoming more financially responsible, he must learn to pay the bills on time.

Paul also programs the coach to talk him through what gets in the way of being able to write those checks. They chunk the process down to examine more closely what the obstacles are. They discover that Paul blocks himself by making the task insurmountable: He tells himself that writing checks to pay the bills is an easy task that will take little of time. This attitude creates no urgency to complete this task on a regular basis, so he continually puts it off. As the bills pile up, many of them already late, he becomes completely overwhelmed by this "easy" task. Once Paul recognizes how he is actually creating his own problem, he becomes able to reprogram the coach to remind him of this fact and help him get around it by underscoring the need to pay the bills weekly. He establishes a routine schedule for bill paying with the help of the coach and is finally able to get out of his own way and do it without prompting.

Coengineering the partnership happens over time with regular, open communication between the client and the coach. As the relationship develops, the client sets new goals and fine-tunes existing ones. At first the coach acts as an external reminder and anchor. In time, the client will begin to feel a shift, as he or she becomes increasingly able to self-motivate. With experience the client becomes proficient with programming and finds it easier to transfer these skills to other situations and relationships.

## Structure: Leveraging the Strengths of the Client

Once the relationship is established, the next piece is to identify and set up structure to put the client on the road to success. Providing structure is one of the most vital skills of coaching. Coaches help clients develop structure by providing consistency (scheduled coaching sessions), building structure into coaching sessions, and helping clients recognize the need for structure in their daily lives. Regularly scheduled check-ins set up accountability and monitor the client's progress in small, achievable increments. A sense of ownership and of being in charge of their own life comes with the experience of success; and as a history of successes is built, it can be referred to later as a way of increasing client motivation and movement forward. From this work, habits will form that will reinforce that structure in the clients.

Most people with ADHD have a love–hate relationship with structure. They perceive schedules and structures as constricting forces that require them to spend their day doing tasks that they don't like, that at times don't suit them. A successful coach helps their clients build structures that do suit them, structures that work *with* their strengths and preferences, not *against* them. By emphasizing strengths, scheduling less desirable tasks at the optimal times, and teaching clients to reward themselves with pleasurable activities when they complete difficult tasks, the structures worked out by the coach and clients act as guideposts to achievement.

Like the blinders that prevent a racehorse from being distracted or spooked by the furious activity around him, structures are blinders to help direct client energy and prevent symptoms of ADHD from sending them off course. For instance, ADHD may make it difficult for clients to gauge time, hindering their efforts to make and keep schedules or to manage projects. External structures provide guideposts that help make time more tangible. Eventually these exterior structures encourage internal structures to develop, and the clients acquire an internal sense of how to measure time more accurately and can then apply that skill to achieve other goals.

Once the coach and the client have developed an understanding of the client's learning style, organizational tools that match the client's strengths need to be identified. This will increase the likelihood that the client will use them. Examples of commonly used organizational tools include calendar systems, sticky notes, color-coded files, and electronic and voice organizers. These are instrumental in helping to reduce chaos, prioritize, sustain attention, and stay focused on goals. Part of structuring is for the clients then to integrate these tools into their life.

### Sally's Story

Sally's ADHD symptoms make it challenging for her to manage daily life. Finding her keys, getting the laundry done, and keeping food stocked in the kitchen are always nagging chores. She hires a coach to help find solutions to these difficulties.

What Sally discovers is that she needs routines. Coaching helps her set up structures such as having a "key spot" so that her keys are always in the same place. To help with weekly recurring tasks she posts a huge white eraser-board calendar in her kitchen and marks her tasks with brightly colored markers on designated days. For example, to make her laundry more manageable, she designates Wednesdays to wash white clothes and Fridays to wash colors. Grocery shopping is relegated to Saturday mornings. Every evening after supper, mail is sorted into categories by priority of necessary action, with announcements, magazine subscriptions, and junk mail being immediately thrown out. Through regular check-ins with her coach and constant reminders, these routines become life-saving techniques for managing her hectic life, and eventually she becomes able to implement them with fewer and fewer reminders.

Structuring is necessary to move forward in the coaching process. Without structure, clients are more likely to be distracted by their environment and to opt for immediate gratification. Structure keep clients focused, with the goal in plain view, and helps clients to develop both internal and external organization. Routines and rituals around planning and goal setting are used to stay on track and move forward more consistently in order to obtain their goals. This then allows them to focus on what needs to be done for that day, that moment. The coach provides the reminders to help integrate these structures and organization tools into clients' lives.

## Process: Using Guided Self-Exploration

The third essential component of coaching is to develop self-awareness through guided self-exploration. The coach must possess excellent listening skills and be in a position to maintain emotional detachment. Questions are posed to clients in a nonjudgmental, nonthreatening manner. This provides a secure environment for exploring needs, identifying possible actions for meeting those needs, and determining the next steps to be taken. The continuous feedback and discussion of plans and ideas gives the coach the space and detachment to mediate between the clients and their actions. The focus is on problem solving through guided discussion, so the coach carefully chooses the right language in order to draw solutions from the clients. Because the clients come up with their own solutions, they become empowered and can more readily take ownership of their actions. Clients must perpetually look inward to identify and articulate their needs on an ongoing basis.

Questions that ask "why" a particular action was taken or not taken are avoided in coaching because they connote judgment. Asking "Why did you do that?" can sabotage progress, because it asks clients to look back and set blame, rather than looking forward toward solutions. Asking: "How are you going to approach this problem? What options do you have?" is a more constructive approach and promotes problem-solving skills. Eventually the clients will internalize these questions and be able to process on their own.

The language we use to "talk to ourselves" can have a powerful effect on how we feel about ourselves and can govern many of our actions and decisions in life. For people with ADHD, their differences have often caused them to be misunderstood as "stupid," "ditzy," or "irresponsible." In order for clients to succeed, it is essential that they *believe* they can succeed. Therefore, it is necessary to separate them from the negative self-talk—or *negative scripts*—that hold them back. Guided self-exploration allows clients to reframe their disability. By separating themselves from their negative scripts, clients are able to look at themselves more objectively. They can now choose how to respond to the *gremlin*.

**Katlin's Story**

Katlin sought coaching to help her deal with organizational difficulties at home and in the workplace. Her diagnosis of ADHD was initially a relief to her because she was able to let go of some of the guilt and shame around her lack of abilities in certain areas. Katlin is at a point in her life where she wants to find ways to coexist with her ADHD and build on her strengths. The coaching process has been instrumental in helping her to plan and organize her life better.

She has reduced the paper clutter on her desks at work and at home. She is able to keep better track of all her appointments and other obligations. She is even creating a better track record of getting to work on time on a more regular basis. However, she has begun to doubt herself.

**Katlin:** I'm just a big screw-up. I can't do anything right. I'm always late to work!

**Coach:** Wow, I can hear how upset up you are! It must have been a very difficult week for you.

**Katlin:** Yes, it was. I was late to work two days in a row! I should just give it up. I feel like such a loser.

**Coach:** Katlin, can you identify what made you late on those mornings?

**Katlin:** Well, on Tuesday, the subway train I was on broke down. By the time they got an alternate bus for us, I was already ten minutes late for work.

**Coach:** So, in this instance it was something unavoidable that made you late, right?

**Katlin:** Yes. But I am still such a loser. Why should I keep trying?

**Coach:** How many other times have you been late over the last six weeks?

**Katlin:** I don't know. I just don't care!

**Coach:** Do you have your calendar with you?

**Katlin:** Yes.

**Coach:** Can you look back and see if you have "late" written on any days?

**Katlin:** What use is that? I know I'm a failure. Why try?

**Coach:** Katlin, remember the concept of the gremlin and negative scripts we talked about when we first met? You said your gremlin would always convince you not to try, just to give up. Do you see that's what is happening now?

**Katlin:** Well, I guess so. I can see how I have blown this out of proportion.

**Coach:** Good! I'm glad you see how your gremlin has convinced you that you could never get to work on time. What were the circumstances the second time you were late this week?

**Katlin:** On Thursday I overslept.
**Coach:** What prevented you from getting up on time?
**Katlin:** I slept through my alarm because I stayed up too late. I lost track of time talking with a friend on the phone.
**Coach:** Is there a strategy that you can implement to help you remember to get to bed on time?
**Katlin:** I don't know.
**Coach:** If you did know, what would it be?
**Katlin:** I could set a timer for 10:00 p.m. to remind me that I need to be getting ready for bed.
**Coach:** Great!

The questions are open-ended to encourage Katlin to determine for herself what got in her way and how to prevent it from occurring again. The coach also helps derail the gremlin by reminding Katlin of her accomplishments and taking the focus off blaming herself.

## DISTINGUISHING COACHING FROM OTHER SERVICES

Due to the performance-based nature of ADHD, most people with these challenges will engage the services of a variety of helping professionals at some point in their lives. Help is generally sought in a few basic areas.

- *Skill building*: To improve academic or language skills by working with a tutor, educational therapist, speech pathologist, or social skills specialist.
- *Psychological*: To understand and change behaviors and emotion-based conduct. Working with a counselor, psychotherapist, or cognitive behavior therapist can help clients learn how to destress and find new ways to uncover and move beyond destructive emotional blocks.
- *Medical/neurological*: Many people with ADHD choose to take medication to reduce the biological/medical symptoms of their ADHD or to treat associated disorders like depression, obsessive-compulsive disorder, and anxiety-based disorders.
- *Organizational*: People afflicted with ADHD executive dysfunction often take time management classes to learn organizational skills or even hire a professional organizer to help with physical clutter.

In academic settings it may be difficult to distinguish coaching from tutoring. A tutor might coach a student by acting as a personal cheerleader or by helping him develop time management strategies that are focused on improving academic performance—for example, keeping an organized study space, marking due dates on a calendar. But the tutor focuses on the academic life of the client. The coach, on the other hand, deals with the ADHD client's complete life plan. A coach would look at the whole person and develop wake-up and bedtime routines, study times, exercise periods, and free time to socialize. The coach will help the student learn how to motivate himself to start a project and follow it through to the finish. All this is beyond the scope of a skills-based academic tutor, who teaches by demonstration.

There are also surface similarities between the functions of coaches and psychotherapists. Both work to help clients better understand, accept, and work constructively with their ADHD symptoms. Both work to help their clients improve their quality of life and build their self-esteem. Both are supportive and encouraging, and both hold the clients' interests in the forefront. However, each uses distinctly different methods and tools to help clients achieve progress in these same areas, and they each bring very different training and perspectives to treatment.

One way psychotherapy differs from coaching is in terms of logistics. Therapy is done in "neutral territory," in a place without emotional triggers for the client, whereas the coach may go "on site," coming into the office or home. Psychotherapy usually takes place in face-to-face, weekly or less frequent sessions of 45–60 minutes each. For coaching there is no set model. Contacts may be brief and frequent over the phone and via e-mail or they may happen for 30 minutes once a week by telephone, or they may be weekly hourlong face-to-face meetings. There is a great deal of flexibility in how a coaching relationship is set up, with the primary focus on setting up client accountability for agreed-on actions.

Psychotherapy also differs tactically. Therapists can help clients understand the impact of their behaviors and emotions. Those with a more practical cognitive-behavioral approach can even help to develop strategies to turn that understanding into a structured plan of action. But typically, psychotherapy is less structured than coaching. So it is coaching that actually pushes the client to follow through on a structured plan of action, whether that plan is developed by the therapist or by the coach.

A therapist typically addresses the issues that are immediately pressing. In contrast, coaching is highly structured, providing a framework of routines that are consistent and predictable. While therapy *may* involve goal setting, coaching *always* involves goal setting, as well as focusing on implementing the actions, strategies, and practical solutions related to those goals. Coaches do not concern themselves with medical issues. A coach cannot diagnose ADHD or write prescriptions; but a coach can help clients create systems by which to monitor and evaluate the effects of medications and to report this information back to their doctor.

The ADHD client often presents other challenges. A coach must not only have working knowledge of ADHD and its symptoms but must also be familiar with the symptoms of comorbid conditions, such as obsessive-compulsive disorder, addictions, anxiety, and depression. Additionally, most adult clients have emotional challenges in the area of damaged self-esteem due to the years of struggling with issues of lack of success, frustration, and defeat. A coach needs to be able to recognize when these other conditions are getting in the way of goal attainment. Coaches address all of these issues from a functional outcome standpoint. The focus is on acknowledging those other problems and referring clients with them to appropriate professionals. Hence, the ADHD coach actually plays a more specialized role—because, although these issues affect the progress of clients, coaches do not consider the *why's* behind the lack of action, rather how forward movement can be achieved *despite* these issues.

In sum, a coach can help individuals with ADHD discover exactly what their present needs are by asking appropriate questions. She can then direct clients to the correct agency, specialized tutor, therapist, or counselor who will be right for them while continuing to work on coaching issues.

## THE POWER OF COLLABORATION

Often the most powerful way to help one's clients is to collaborate with other helping professionals. When issues arise that are medical in nature, or have psychodynamic roots, those clients can be referred out to those professionals who could treat those problems more effectively. Indeed, it is the job of the coach to discern when to refer out and when to help the client focus on issues related to coaching—issues that are action based, that have concrete, measurable outcomes.

But even after a referral, collaboration is a powerful tactic in the ADHD treatment arsenal, allowing professionals from different disciplines to share important information about their mutual client on an ongoing basis. The synergy created by collaboration can have a powerful affect on a client's treatment.

For instance, when a person is being evaluated for ADHD by a psychiatrist, physician, or mental health professional, clear issues of organization and persistent lack of follow-through may raise the need for a coach. If the client is prescribed medication to minimize the difficulties of ADHD, the coach can help by holding the client accountable for taking the medication as prescribed.

Psychotherapists can feel limited in their ability to assist clients with ADHD because of the overriding issues of time management, forgetfulness, and disorganization. If one can't get to therapy on time and can't recall what goals were set in therapy, then it isn't likely that therapy can be effective! A coach can help develop strategies to deal with these issues so that the therapist can make the most of valuable therapy time.

A skilled professional organizer who is aware of ADHD might refer a client to a coach to help him establish an accountability plan to maintain organization. If a client is in college and is experiencing time management difficulties and struggling with writing papers, she might need to work with both a coach and a writing tutor. Or in therapy, she could explore any emotional issues that might be hampering her success.

Looking at the big picture, it would be best if all helping professionals treating a client would consider themselves as part of a team, with all team members being aware of each other and of the issues being addressed. It is important to be clear on the roles of each member of the team and on who is handling which type of issue. For instance, some therapists are unaware of coaching or what a coach does. If this is the case, it is the coach's job to inform the therapist of the scope of the coaching relationship, the issues being addressed, and the methods used to address them.

## COACHING IS NEVER A SUBSTITUTE FOR THERAPY

Many individuals with ADHD also struggle with significant emotional issues. These issues should not be ignored or downplayed. Coaches and therapists can often work most effectively by staying in regular contact with one another, working in partnership to help their client feel and function better. For example, a coach can help therapy be more productive by helping the client develop a system, such as a notebook, in which to jot down thoughts to discuss in therapy and by setting up strategies to make it to appointments on time. Therapists can enhance the effectiveness of coaching through treating the emotional issues that can sabotage the best coaching plan.

## ISSUES THAT CAN COMPLICATE THE COACHING PROCESS

It is appropriate for the coach to put the coaching relationship on hold and refer the client to another professional when any of the following occur.

- Medical or psychodynamic issues are discovered. These issues are not always apparent at the start of a relationship; but if they do come to the surface, the client should be referred to a therapist.
- The client offers continued resistance to using simple self-management and/or organizational strategies to obtain goals, despite the coach's resources and reminders. For instance, if a client had found that part of a strategy must be to delegate work but the client resists doing so even after the coach's prompting, the client is in effect refusing to carry out the plan of action.
- Comorbid issues—such as anxiety, depression, outbursts of anger, rapid mood swings, self-defeating thoughts—are present on a repeating basis. These issues obstruct progress toward goals.
- It becomes clear that the support that is needed is really more emotional or psychological in nature—for example, a death in the family, marital separation, divorce,

serious illness—thus necessitating referral to an appropriate professional.
- The goals set forth are unrealistic and need to be totally reworked.

## FINDING AND CHOOSING A COACH

Personal coaching—a field separate from ADHD coaching—is a growing industry in the United States and abroad. The number of organizations offering their own training and credentials is on the rise. Although the field is still in its infancy, it has developed a central association. The International Federation of Coaches is establishing standards and ethics for the profession and putting structures in place to oversee the credentialing of all professional coaches. There is still a lot of work to be done in the field before we see will see any kind of rigorous regulation.

The ADHD coaching field is similar in its development. As a matter of fact, many coaches come to the ADHD coaching field trained first as a personal coach, and many ADHD coaches seek dual training as a personal coach. As in the personal coaching arena, there are numerous private organizations that offer training and certification (for a full listing go to www.nancyratey.com) or that have established ethical guidelines and standards of conduct. However, no central organization or governing body exists to oversee the field or offer licenses to ADHD coaches. In light of this, the Attention Deficit Disorder Association (ADDA) has sponsored a group of coaches to define the core competencies and guiding principles of ADHD coaching to help consumers and professionals better understand what coaching is, who can be a coach, and what coaching can offer clients with ADHD.

Because the opportunities for training available to ADHD coaches are not as abundant as those for personal coaches, many ADHD coaches are first seeking out training as personal coaches; but it is imperative for them to have additional training in coaching clients with ADHD.

## CREATING THE RIGHT MATCH

Once a list of coaches has been compiled, they should be interviewed. But first the client must take stock of his or her own needs.

1. Is it important that the coaching sessions be face-to-face? If so, the client should look for a coach who is geographically close and offers this as part of the service package. Many coaches conduct the initial session in person and then do weekly check-ins by phone and/or e-mail. If in-person contact is not an issue, then a coach could be chosen from anywhere in the nation.
2. Would the client prefer to be coached by a man or a woman?
3. Should the coach be someone with a background in business, academia, gender issues, or the like?
4. Is the client looking for someone who has a special interest or expertise in an area, such as clutter management or family issues?
5. Does the client want someone who has a lot of energy, or someone who has a more subtle approach?
6. Is a sense of humor important in the coach? Or would a more serious person make a better match?

Another quality to look for in a coach is his or her involvement in and commitment to the field of ADHD coaching. Because coaching is a developing field, in order to be successful coaches need to be engaged in ongoing education. The prospective client should be sure to ask these questions.

1. How many clients with ADHD have you coached?
2. Have you attended conferences on coaching?
3. Have you taken any of the available coaching courses?
4. Are you involved in local professional coaching groups?

Some of the following questions are suggested by The American Coaching Association.

1. What percentage of your practice is devoted to individuals with ADHD?
2. How long have you been doing ADHD coaching?
3. What are your fees?
4. What professional organizations are you a member of (coaching and ADHD)?
5. Are you familiar with medication issues as they relate to ADHD?

## QUALITIES TO LOOK FOR IN A COACH

The coach should be the following.

*Knowledgeable about ADHD*: An ADHD coach must have some educational background or experience in working with persons with ADHD. They must be familiar enough with symptoms and effects so as to help their clients develop a deeper understanding and appreciation of their own ADHD and stop their self-blaming. The skilled coach will foster clients' self-acceptance, understanding, ability to forgive themselves, and ability to draw more from their strengths and to maneuver around and create bridges over their weaknesses.

*Effective*: A good way to gauge the effectiveness of the potential coach is to notice how well he or she understands the client in that very first call. The client should ask himself: "Is this coach using a type of approach I feel comfortable with? Is the coach able to listen to me and identify my needs? Does the coach ask questions that clarify issues and help me feel more empowered? Is the coach intuitive? Can she pick up on what I am saying and help move me along in the conversation?" At this level of contact, it is the coach's job to help the prospective client understand his own readiness and provide information about the coaching process that is important for him to know and understand, even if he has not thought to ask for it.

*Empathic*: Many coaches who enter the field of coaching have ADHD themselves and can understand the difficulties that a client might have. They make some of the best coaches for this very reason. Potential clients might feel an immediate connection and rapport; however, it is important that they remember they need someone who is more than just a friend or someone who can understand them. They also need a skilled person who can reroute them out of old patterns and facilitate the learning of new ones.

*A good listener*: The coach must be a good listener, able to hear and understand the client's struggles. She must be able to hear the patterns that entangle the client in order to help him undo the confusion.

*Nonjudgmental*: It is essential that the coach be nonjudgmental and that she help the client feel safe and accepted. If this is not the case, then the client is likely to give only an edited version of reality to his coach and defeat the process.

*Working on the* Client's *agenda*: For coaching to be successful, the coach must support the client in establishing his or her own agenda and then in working toward reaching those goals. The coach does not allow his or her own personal values or goals to creep into the coaching process.

*Encouraging*: Most clients who enter the coaching process have already experienced some frustration and failure. The coach is there to celebrate their success and help them find the courage to try again when they fail.

*Able to facilitate*: When a client needs direction, the coach must to be able to step in with suggestions and yet hold the client to his agenda. The coach's direction should minimize the feeling of being overwhelmed. Good direction from a coach helps the client to focus and get back on track.

*Empowering*: Everyone has thoughts like "I can't do that" or "Nothing ever goes right for me." These negative scripts are especially loud and pervasive for people with ADHD. The coach should help them recognize the ways they discourage themselves so that they can practice hearing positive scripts like "Good for me for trying!" or "I'm doing better now than before."

*Able to "forward the action"*: Forwarding the action is the process by which the coach keeps the client on track. The coach will help develop strategies the client will one day implement on her own when she finds she is not moving forward.

## CONCLUSION

The field of personal and professional coaching is gaining recognition as a way to help individuals become more purposeful and proactive in today's fast-paced world. Now coaching for people with ADHD is becoming a powerful tool in the arsenal of ADHD treatment. Coaching is about developing a partnership that motivates the client to move forward in a deliberate and structured manner. A large part of the client's motivation stems from the fact that it is his responsibility to forge a partnership with the coach.

Many people with ADHD see a number of professionals in other helping disciplines, with each professional (therapist, medical doctor, tutor, professional organizer, etc.) focusing on a particular area of difficulty (mental, medical, academic, organizational) of the client. A coach, however, focuses on the "what, how, and when." What are they having difficulty with in their daily lives? What goals can they set to work around those difficulties? How are they going to motivate themselves to follow the plan? When would it be reasonable to consider goals accomplished?

# 15

# Lifestyle Issues

Arthur L. Robin, Ph.D.

Adults with ADHD often have major lifestyle impairments with organization, follow-through, money management, parenting, household management, balancing work and home responsibilities, and relationships. This chapter is meant to provide the practitioner with a step-by-step guide for conducting behavioral/psychological interventions to help adults with ADHD cope effectively with their lifestyle issues. Two patient examples are described below and specific treatment steps highlighted for these individuals throughout the chapter.

## Case One

Dr. Bennett is a 42–year-old family physician, diagnosed with ADHD combined subtype, who works at an HMO. He has become increasingly depressed in recent months because his life seems like an endless treadmill. He is unable to meet his HMO's productivity demands, and his supervisors are hinting that they may not renew his contract. Although his patients are satisfied with his care, they complain bitterly about waiting one to two hours to see him because he is chronically behind schedule. He is always the last physician to leave the clinic, driving up overtime support staff costs. He spends evenings and weekends at home keeping up with his charts and paperwork, leaving little time for his wife and kids. Mrs. Bennett criticizes him daily for failing to do his share of the parenting and household chores, and failing to pay enough attention personally to her.

## Case Two

Thirty-four-year-old divorced Rhonda Clark is unable to organize her house, manage her finances, consistently parent her 8-year-old ADHD son and 6-year-old daughter, and hold down her job as a secretary. She feels overwhelmed by the multiple demands of her life. Her house has piles of papers everywhere, a sink full of dirty dishes, open cabinets and food strewn around the kitchen, and clothes everywhere. Bills go unpaid until Rhonda receives utility cutoff notices or collection agency calls. Checks are overdrawn, and Rhonda wastes a lot of money taking the kids out for fast food because she cannot get organized to buy groceries and cook meals. The kids are often late for school, don't have their homework done, look dirty and disheveled, and get away with a lot of mischief. Rhonda is often late for work. In the past few months she has gained 20 pounds, has stopped exercising, and has no time even to think about a social life or dating again. After seeing a television show about ADHD, Rhonda sought out an evaluation and was diagnosed as having ADHD, inattentive subtype.

## THEORETICAL UNDERPINNINGS

Research indicates that biological/genetic factors involving brain anatomy, physiology, and biochemistry underlie the attentional and self-regulatory problems constituting the core of ADHD (Tannock, 1998). Adults with such attentional and self-regulatory problems exhibit behavioral deficits and excesses negatively impacting their ability to carry out daily responsibilities at work and at home. The negative feedback received for repeatedly failing to carry out their responsibilities erodes their self-esteem, causing distorted cognitions, and adversely impacting their marriages and family life.

A comprehensive therapeutic model must address these cognitions and their effect on interpersonal relationships, in addition to addressing neurobiology and general behavior.

At the outset of intervention, the adult with ADHD needs to seek out a biological correction for underlying neurobiological deficits through the prescription of stimulant and/or nonstimulant medications. Then the therapist must address cognitive factors by: (1) instilling hope that change can take place, (2) imparting knowledge about ADHD and its specific impacts on the individual, and (3) developing reasonable expectations for change.

Many adults with ADHD expect failure as a natural consequence of their efforts (Murphy & Levert, 1995). Life experiences have reinforced this belief, leading to "learned helplessness," e.g., giving up because whatever they do doesn't matter (Seligman, 1975). The therapist must challenge these cognitions of helplessness and instill hope, optimism, and motivation, to empower the individual to change lifelong maladaptive habits and overcome the impairments caused by ADHD (Murphy & LeVert, 1995).

The therapist provides the patient with a contemporary understanding of ADHD as a neurobiological disorder rather than as a character defect or moral weakness. The therapist helps the patient examine specific examples of past failure, reframing these failures as consequences of an inherited deficit in brain functioning rather than as "laziness," "not caring," or "stupidity." The therapist instills hope by providing knowledge about ADHD and describing success stories of similar ADHD adults who overcome impairments.

The therapist guides the individual to project realistic expectations for change, with an understanding that stimulant medication will not be a panacea to cure all of their ills.

Behavior change is central to treatment of ADHD in adults. The therapist coaches the patient to: (1) define specific target behaviors to be increased or decreased; (2) arrange positive reinforcement for increasing desired behaviors; (3) modify the environment to selicit target behaviors; and (4) acquire new behaviors through instructions, modeling, rehearsal, shaping, and feedback.

Because of the ADHD adult's poorly self-regulated behavior and inconsistent follow-through, relationships and marriages flounder, parenting efforts go awry, and friends are alienated. The therapist must consider the impact of ADHD upon the family system and engage the afflicted family members in couples and family-oriented interventions to help them reframe maladaptive cognitions about ADHD and change negative interaction patterns.

## LIFESTYLE MANAGEMENT MODEL

The remainder of this chapter is organized according to the circular model outlined in Figure 15.1, which depicts the sequence of steps taken to help adults with ADHD cope with their lifestyle issues. This model is circular because each step naturally leads to the next, and eventually back to the first. Guidelines in Chapters twelve and thirteen reviewed strategies and methods to nature relationships and will not be discussed in this chapter.

There are six major areas of focus in treatment of the ADHD adult:

1) Understand strengths and weaknesses. Through the use of checklists and verbal discussion, the individual is prompted to catalog his or her strengths and weaknesses, review the ways ADHD applies to him or her, identify and challenge faulty perceptions and unrealistic expectations, and develop a realistic hope for change in the future.

2) Maximize medication. After the patient has been referred to a competent physician for a trial on medication, the therapist teaches the individual what to look for from medication and how to systematically monitor the effectiveness of medication.

3) Achieve balance and plan long-term goals. Coping with ADHD requires the adult to achieve a balance in life among work, play, relationships, and health-related pursuits such exercise, nutrition, and sleep. The individual is prompted to examine the amount of time, effort, and energy currently expended in each of these domains, and to consider modifications to his or her lifestyle that would create a better balance. Long-term goals should be established to reflect the individual's values, character, and desired accomplishments.

4) Use a planner to navigate towards your goals. The therapist teaches the individual how to use a day planner to proactively translate long-term goals into monthly, weekly, and daily action plans. The individual learns to use the day planner to manage time effectively, manage memory effectively, and move planfully toward his or her goals rather than living reactively from one crisis to the next.

5) Organize "things" effectively. After time management, clutter management is the second major

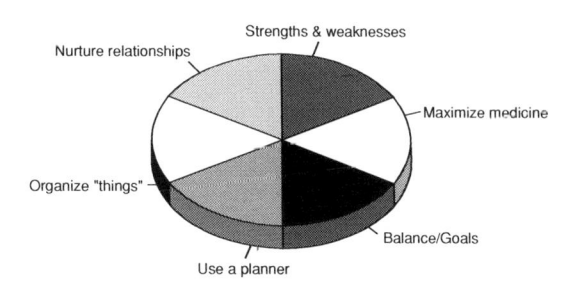

**FIGURE 15.1** Lifestyle management model.

challenge in planning for adults with ADHD. The therapist teaches the individual how to creatively organize, and keep organized, his or her home, office, and car.

6) Nurture Relationships. Achieving intimate relationships and meaningful friendships is central to maintaining a sense of balance in life. The therapist meets with the ADHD adult and his spouse or significant other, analyzes their specific relationship problems, establishes goals for change, and conducts conjoint couples sessions helping them cope with ADHD and achieve their goals. The most common areas in which ADHD impedes relationships involve expectations and attributions about ADHD-mediated behaviors, communication, sexuality, household management, and parenting. A detailed discussion of ADHD, marriage, and intimate relationships goes beyond the scope of this chapter, but can be found in *ADD and Romance* (Halverstadt, 1998).

## UNDERSTANDING STRENGTHS AND WEAKNESSES

The first step in coping with lifestyle issues is to understand the ways in which ADHD impacts the individual's current lifestyle management techniques. The therapist begins the discussion by asking the individual to give his or her personal definition of ADHD. The therapist should validate the patient's definition and/or correct any misperceptions or inaccuracies. Then, the therapist should ask the individual to discuss how ADHD symptoms of inattention, impulsivity, and restlessness impact the individual's life at work and at home. The therapist should introduce contemporary models of ADHD, such as Barkley's response inhibition theory (1997) and Brown's executive functioning model (2000), to help the adult better understand his or her own experiences. The therapist should also touch on any positive aspects of having ADHD, e.g., creativity and that a high energy level permits the person to keep going when others wear out.

The patient should complete the checklist in Figure 15.2. The therapist should review this questionnaire with the patient, collaboratively building a picture of the individual's strengths and weaknesses with regard to maximizing medication, achieving balance, establishing goals, planning,

### Understanding My Strengths and Weaknesses

This questionnaire is designed to prompt you to review your strengths and weaknesses with regard to lifestyle management skills, particularly those that may be affected by ADHD. Your therapist will use your responses to collaboratively plan interventions to compensate for your weaknesses and to maximize your strengths. Read each item and indicate whether it does or does not apply to you.

| | | | |
|---|---|---|---|
| YES | NO | 1. | I am getting the most I can out of my medication. |
| YES | NO | 2. | I rate myself in writing on specific target behaviors to see if my medication is helping me improve those behaviors. |
| YES | NO | 3. | I can tell whether my medication is helping me. |
| YES | NO | 4. | I have a good balance between work and play in my life. |
| YES | NO | 5. | I exercise regularly as part of my daily/weekly routine. |
| YES | NO | 6. | I eat in a healthy manner. |
| YES | NO | 7. | I get enough sleep each night. |
| YES | NO | 8. | I am satisfied with my close relationships (marriage, significant others, friends, family). |
| YES | NO | 9. | My wife/significant other is satisfied with his/her relationship with me. |
| YES | NO | 10. | I know what I want out of life. |
| YES | NO | 11. | I have clear goals for the future in my job/career. |
| YES | NO | 12. | I have clear goals for the future in my personal life. |
| YES | NO | 13. | I have clear financial goals for the future. |
| YES | NO | 14. | I have tried to use a paper-and-pencil day planner or an electronic planner such as a Palm organizer. |
| YES | NO | 15. | I have been successful in using a day planner/electronic planner. |
| YES | NO | 16. | I use a day planner or electronic planner regularly to keep track of my schedule. |
| YES | NO | 17. | I make a "to do list" regularly and use it to guide my actions. |
| YES | NO | 18. | I use my day planner/electronic planner to organize my day. |
| YES | NO | 19. | I use my day planner/electronic planner to plan my week. |
| YES | NO | 20. | I write long-term goals in my day planner/electronic planner. |
| YES | NO | 21. | I try to make my weekly and daily plans consistent with my long-term goals. |
| YES | NO | 22. | I am able to stick to my plans and complete tasks that I start. |
| YES | NO | 23. | I do not make spur-of-the-moment decisions about important things. |
| YES | NO | 24. | I am able to keep my office and home well organized. |

**FIGURE 15.2** Lifestyle management checklist.

organizing things, and nurturing relationships. This picture will guide the therapist and patient in collaboratively deciding which areas of lifestyle management to emphasize throughout the intervention.

## MAXIMIZING MEDICATION

Although stimulant medication may have a global, positive impact on a handful of individuals with ADHD, in most cases the effects are much more modest. Controlled research indicates that approximately 78% of patients who have gone through a careful diagnostic evaluation for ADHD show improvement on stimulant medication (Weiss, Hechtman, and Weiss, 1999).

The primary goal is to maximize the impact of stimulant medication on specific aspects of functioning. In doing so the therapist should assist the patient to (1) develop realistic knowledge about the effects of medication, (2) define specific target behaviors to be impacted by medication, (3) develop a simple system to measure the effects of medication, (4) collect data on the effectiveness of different doses or types of medication, and (5) provide accurate information to the physician so that medication dosages can be fine-tuned.

It is realistic for the patient to expect stimulant medication to enhance performance on tasks that require planning, organization, prioritization, time management, sustained attention, working memory, attention to detail, repetition and monotony, and resisting distraction. It is also reasonable to expect stimulant medication to enhance performance in interpersonal interactions that require frustration tolerance, anger management, tact, patience, consistent follow-through, waiting one's turn, sensitive listening, intimate communication, attending to subtle social cues, managing restlessness, and generally any other type of inhibitory control. Several examples of target goals follow for the two individuals introduced earlier.

Dr. Bennett
1. Stick to patient concern topics when talking to patients; do not engage in tangential conversations.
2. Write up patient charts for 2 hours, without distraction.

Rhonda Clark
1. Do the dishes within 30 minutes after dinner.
2. Sort and file papers and pay bills on Saturday mornings for two hours.

The list should include at least one *benchmark behavior*, (e.g. a behavior that the majority of adults with ADHD perform poorly and that is known to be positively affected by stimulant medication). The inclusion of such a benchmark dramatically increases the chances that the patient will notice a positive stimulant medication effect. The therapist should also discuss the timing of the stimulant medication and the target behaviors. Medication must be timed so that the individual is "covered" during the time when the target behavior is to be performed.

A simple measurement system needs to be developed for the individual to assess the daily effect of stimulant medication on the target behavior. A written record is preferable to a verbal report because of the notorious forgetfulness, inconsistent reporting, and subjective biases of adults with ADHD. Figure 15.3 presents a simple form for recording daily ratings of the effectiveness of medication.

The patient should bring the data to each therapy session and review the results with the therapist. The therapist should advise the patient to provide feedback to his or her physician regarding the effectiveness of each dose of stimulant medication on the target behaviors.

## ACHIEVING BALANCE AND ESTABLISHING LONG-TERM GOALS

The therapist's next task is to help the individual consider "the big issues" in life before moving on to

## MAXIMIZING MEDICATION—SELF-REPORT FORM (MMSR)

Name _____    Week of ___  _____

Medications _____    Doses & Times _____

Rating Scale:   0—Very poor   1—Poor   2—Marginal   3—Good   4—Very good

| Goals | Day__ | Day__ | Day__ | Day__ | Day__ | Day__ | Day__ |
|---|---|---|---|---|---|---|---|
| A |  |  |  |  |  |  |  |
| B |  |  |  |  |  |  |  |
| C |  |  |  |  |  |  |  |

## MAXIMIZING MEDICATION—OBSERVER FORM (MMOR)

Name of person being rated _____ Week of _____

Your Name _____

Rating Scale:   0—Very poor   1—Poor   2—Marginal   3—Good   4—Very good

| Goals | Day__ | Day__ | Day__ | Day__ | Day__ | Day__ | Day__ |
|---|---|---|---|---|---|---|---|
| A |  |  |  |  |  |  |  |
| B |  |  |  |  |  |  |  |
| C |  |  |  |  |  |  |  |

**FIGURE 15.3**   Forms for Recording Medication Responses.

planning, time management, and organization. Often, adults with ADHD get so caught up in the overwhelming exigencies of their work or home lives that they do not take time to examine the major aspects of their lives. Work, play, relationships/family, and health (nutrition, sleep, exercise) are the major dimensions to be balanced. Many adults with ADHD *hyperfocus* on one or two of these dimensions, to the exclusion of the others. Eventually, such an imbalance results in negative behavioral, emotional, or medical consequences.

The therapist should describe the need for achieving some balance among work, play, relationships/family, and health. The individual should be asked to estimate and record in writing: (1) what percentage of his or her time and effort is currently devoted to each dimension, and (2) what percentage of time and effort should ideally be devoted to each dimension. The discrepancies between the current and the ideal balance become the starting point for projecting long-term goals for change. Figure 15.4 provides a long-term planning worksheet to be used in conjunction with this step. Long-term goals should specify who the person wants to be (character), what the person wants to do (achievements), and what the person wants to have (possessions) (Covey, 1989). Using the long-term planning worksheet of figure 15.4, the therapist should review the analysis of balance in the

**Long-Term Planning Worksheet**

1. In the column labeled "Current", estimate the percentage of your overall time and effort that you currently devote to each area of your life. In the column labeled "Ideal", estimate the ideal percentage of your overall time and effort you would like to devote to each area of your life. Subtract the current percentages from the ideal percentages in order to determine what changes you need to make.

   |  | Current | Ideal | Discrepancy (Ideal minus Current) |
   |---|---|---|---|
   | Work | ____ | ____ | ____ |
   | Play | ____ | ____ | ____ |
   | Health (exercise, sleep, nutrition) | ____ | ____ | ____ |
   | Spouse/significant other | ____ | ____ | ____ |
   | Family | ____ | ____ | ____ |
   | Friends | ____ | ____ | ____ |

2. What would have to change in your life for you to achieve your ideal percentages of activities?
3. What do you want to accomplish/do in your professional life, career, and/or job?
4. What do you want to accomplish/do in your personal and/or family life?
5. What kind of person do you want to be?
6. What things, possessions, and/or objects would you like to have in your life?

Using the answers to the preceding questions, list your long-term goals for change:

1. _____
2. _____
3. _____
4. _____
5. _____

**FIGURE 15.4** Worksheet for long-term planning.

individual's life, prompt the patient to answer the questions, and assist the patient in translating the answers into a written list of long-term goals.

For example, Dr. Bennett estimated the following percentages of time to be devoted currently to different areas of his life (his ideal reallocations are given in parentheses): (1) work 80% (55%); (2) play 2% (5%); (3) health 3% (8%); (4) his wife 5% (15%); (5) his children 10% (15%); and (6) his friends 0% (2%). He was very unhappy with this situation, but could not find any ways to work more efficiently so that he would have a greater percentage of time for the other areas of his life.

After reviewing the questions in Figure 15.4 with his therapist, Dr. Bennett listed the following long-term goals, which he felt would put his life in better balance: (1) Search for a different type of job within medicine involving less patient contact and more teaching/ research/ administration; (2) increase his efficiency at writing patient charts; (3) analyze the factors that were slowing him down during patient contacts; (4) try to cover more of his salary from research grants, concentrating on a single research area; (5) creatively build more time with his wife and children into his weekly schedule; (6) find ways to exercise during the day at the medical center; and (7) improve the magnitude of his stimulant medication effect.

## PLANNING TO ATTAIN GOALS: THE DAY PLANNER

After the adult with ADHD has been coached to generate long-term goals, the next step is to become pro-active. Planning to attain long-term goals involves translating them into yearly, monthly, weekly, and daily goals and managing time effectively to work towards these goals. A day planner facilitates this process.

The behaviors involved in using a day planner need to be broken down into small, manageable chunks and taught through a step-by-step shaping program (Nadeau, 1995, 1996). The therapist should briefly assess the individual's past experiences with day planners, express empathy for the pain, shame, criticism, and hopelessness associated with these experiences, and clearly explain that the current experience will be different because the individual will have the therapist as a guide. The therapist will creatively tailor the steps to the patient's particular ADHD-related impairments and life circumstances and will stick with the patient until the habits involved in using the day planner are thoroughly established.

The therapist should shape the behavior for using a day planner in accordance with the program outlined in Table 15.1, moving on to the next step only when the adult has mastered the previous step. Several steps may be combined, or sub-divided into smaller steps, as needed, depending upon the skills and attitudes of the patient. Not all adults with ADHD will master all of these steps, and individuals will move through them at different rates.

1. Select a compatible day planner. At a minimum, a day planner is a device that includes a calendar, space to write to-do lists, and space to write telephone numbers, addresses, and other basic identifying/reference information. It can be a paper-and-pencil notebook or binder. The therapist should help the individual select a day planner

**TABLE 15.1  Steps for Learning to Use a Day Planner**

1. Select a compatible day planner—paper-and-pencil variety or electronic organizer.
2. Find a single, accessible place to keep your day planner.
3. Enter the basics in to your day planner: addresses, phone numbers, and vital reference information.
4. Carry your day planner at all times.
5. Refer to your day planner regularly.
6. Use your day planner as a calendar, writing in appointments and time-locked activities.
7. Construct a daily to-do list and refer to it often.
8. Prioritize your daily to-do list and act in accordance with your priorities.
9. Conduct daily planning sessions.
10. Break your long-term goals into small, manageable chunks, and allocate those chunks to the monthly and weekly task lists and planning sessions.
11. Establish monthly goals and conduct a monthly planning session.
12. Establish weekly goals and conduct a weekly planning session.

compatible with his or her learning style and personal characteristics. Computer-oriented individuals may select electronic devices; others will find paper and pencil day planners easier to master. Electronic devices offer some advantages, in that they can provide audible reminders, can sort, organize, and exchange information with cell phones, web sites, e-mail, and office home computers.

2. Find a single, accessible place to keep the day-planner. After selecting a planner, the next step is to start keeping it in a single, accessible location at home and at work. The location should be designed to maximize the chances of noticing it, remembering to use it, and transporting it everywhere the patient goes. The therapist should assign the task of leaving the planner in the designated locations at home and at work for a week and not losing it. If the patient was unable to keep the planner in the designated locations at all times, the therapist explores alternative strategies.

3. Enter the basics in the day planner. The individual should bring the planner to the therapy session. Then the patient should be coached to make the first few entries in the planner while the therapist observes. The therapist should prompt the individual to consider what vital information might be helpful to have in the planner—birthdays and anniversaries, etc.. The therapist then assigns the individual the task of entering the remaining names, addresses, phone numbers, and other information over the next week.

4. Carry the day-planner at all times.

The therapist asks the patient to carry the day-planner with him or her at all times. The therapist and patient define "at all times."

5. Refer to the day-planner regularly. The therapist should teach the individual the habit of referring to the planner regularly; a minimum of three times per day—once in the morning to plan/review the day's upcoming events, once in the middle of the day to make any midcourse corrections and/or refresh memory about the remaining day's events, and once in the evening to plan/review the next day's events. At this stage, the therapist should assign as homework looking at the planner in the morning, at midday, and in the evening.

Three approaches will help the individual remember to look at the planner. First, alarm wrist watches or alarms on electronic planners could be set to go off and remind the adult to look at the planner. Second, looking at the planner could be associated with high-probability activities that are already ingrained habits, (e.g. eating meals, getting dressed in the morning or ready for bed at night, entering or exiting the office). Third, the individual could leave reminder notes in strategic locations (on the desk in the office, on the mirror in the bathroom at home, on the dashboard or door handle of the car) to remind him or her to look at the planner.

6. Use the day planner as a calendar, writing in appointments and time-locked activities. When the adult with ADHD has mastered the habit of referring to the planner regularly, the next step is to learn to use the planner as a calendar. The individual is instructed to write all appointments in the appropriate time slots on the pages of the planner for the relevent days. The individual is instructed to review the scheduled appointments for that day each time he or she checks the planner. The individual is also instructed to write additional appointments into the planner as soon as they are scheduled. The therapist assigns the task of using the planner as a calendar for the next week.

7. Construct a daily to-do list and refer to it often. After the individual is successfully referring to the planner regularly and using it as a calendar, the therapist introduces the daily to-do list. Most planners have a place to put to-do lists adjoining the calendar for each day. During a session the therapist prompts the adult to make a list of everything that he or she needs to accomplish that day. Behaviors that are already deeply ingrained habits (eat meals, go to the bathroom, etc.) don't belong on the list unless the adult is trying to change these habits.

The number of items that are realistic for a particular patient will vary. To increase the chances of a successful learning experience, the therapist should limit individuals to no more than five to seven items on the list initially and later encourage him or her to increase numbers of items as all of the tasks on the shorter list are successfully completed.

After making the list, the individual should decide when to do *time-locked* tasks (e.g., require action at a particular time of the day). These items should be written into the daily planner and scheduled in the time block when they will be executed. The therapist should point out that the patient is more likely to complete the task if he or she has made a commitment to do it at a particular time.

The patient should make a daily to-do list, to be completed during the first or last time of the day when he or she refers to the planner. Some prefer to make the list in the evening for the next day; others prefer to make the list in the morning.

The individual should be instructed to refer to the list often throughout the day, checking off any completed items and reviewing the remaining items to be completed.

At the end of the day during the last review of the planner, the individual should be instructed to assess the percentage of listed items not completed. A small number of items that remain to be completed can be moved forward to the next day's list. However, if the individual is regularly unable to complete many items on the list, then the therapist needs to help the individual analyze whether he or she has unrealistic expectations for how much can be done, and then scale back his/her expectations or find other approaches to getting tasks done (e.g., delegate, streamline, eliminate.).

8. Prioritize the daily to-do list and act in accordance with your priorities. After the individual has been successfully using a daily "to-do" list for at least two weeks, the therapist should introduce the concept of prioritizing the items on the list. There are many ways to prioritize a to-do list. All of the items on the list can be numbered in order of decreasing priority. Alternatively, the items can be classified into one of three categories: "Essential, must do," "Important," and "Do only if I have extra time." The individual should prioritize at least one to-do list in the therapist's presence, and then plan how each item will be accomplished.

Several methods or strategies can be used to combat interference with task completion. Stimulant medication helps adults with ADHD to persist in completing tasks as prioritized on a to-do list. Cognitive self-instructions also help increase adherence to priorities.

The therapist should assign the patient the task of prioritizing the daily "to-do" list and acting in accordance with the priorities. It may take a number of weeks or months before the patient develops the habit of adhering to his/her priorities, and some adults with ADHD may never completely achieve this step.

9. Conduct daily planning sessions. The therapist should ask the patient to plan the upcoming day's activities and develop a plan of attack to carry them out. In addition to listing priorities and reviewing schedules, the planning session is the time to consider exactly how each task will be accomplished. What materials will be needed? What individuals will have to be consulted? What obstacles are likely to be encountered? How can these obstacles be overcome?

10. Long-term planning. Some patients will be able to translate the long-term goals established earlier in treatment into monthly and weekly plans for action. The therapist should coach the patient to break down each long-term goal into a set of measurable and attainable monthly and weekly goals. The patient should schedule brief planning times at the beginning of each month and week. During these planning times, the patient should schedule time in the daily calendar to work on these long-term goals.

## ORGANIZING "THINGS"

Most adults with ADHD have made many attempts to organize their work and home environments but have either become overwhelmed and abandoned their efforts or have been unable to maintain their improved organization for any length of time. They typically make attempts to organize their possessions when the clutter has reached an extreme point and their significant others are threatening to throw it all out or file for divorce. Being impulsive, at such times their knee-jerk reaction is to attack the piles first and ask questions later—just to dive in and do whatever they can to gain control over the clutter quickly. Rarely do they systematically analyze the factors promoting clutter and carefully plan an organizational strategy that will result in permanent improvements. As a result, their organizational attempts are short-lived, ultimately failing because they do not reflect the larger picture of their lifestyles, personalities, or preferences.

Morgenstern (1998) has outlined an approach to creating a carefully thought-out, proactive organizational system. She refers to her calls her approach "organizing from the inside out" because the individual plans an organizational approach based upon his or her personal characteristics and needs rather than impulsively binge-organizing in reaction to external pressures. Her approach has three steps: (1) *Analyze*—take stock of the current organizational situation by defining where you are, where you are going, what's holding you back, and why it is important to get there; (2) *strategize*—create a plan of action for the physical transformation of your space, including a realistic schedule for carrying it out; and (3) *attack*—methodically dive into the clutter, sorting and arranging things to reflect the way you think and act, and monitoring progress over time. An overview of these steps will be given here; the therapist should consult Morgenstern (1998) for more details.

## Analyze the Problem

The therapist guides the individual patient to examine four questions: (1) What aspects of my organizational efforts are currently working? (2) What aspects of the my organizational efforts are not working? (3) What obstacles are standing in the way of getting organized? (4) Why do I want to get organized?

### What Is Working?

Most adults with ADHD can point to a small area of their homes, offices, or cars that is at least partially organized, an island of neatness in a sea of clutter. The therapist needs to probe for such islands of neatness so that the individual can be given credit for his or her accomplishments, boosting his or her confidence and demonstrating that it is possible for the patient to deal with clutter.

### What Is Not working?

The therapist should have the individual describe every relevant physical space in his or her life that is disorganized, including the individual's home, office, car, and any other relevant physical spaces. Then the therapist should help the individual draw up a list of which rooms or spaces will be organized first, second, etc. The list should be in the form of a hierarchy, from easiest to most difficult to organize, reflecting spaces that are most important to the patient, since it may not be possible to organize everything within a reasonable amount of time.

### What Are the Obstacles to Organizing?

Next, the therapist should prompt the patient to analyze what obstacles are holding him or her back from organizing more effectively. Such obstacles might include: (1) items may not have a home, (2) the storage location is inaccessible, (3) the storage system is too complex, (4) life transitions interfere with organization, (5) discarding possessions is traumatic, (6) the individual is forgetful, as well as many others (Morgenstern, 1998).

### Increasing Motivation: Why Do I Want to Get Organized?

To overcome learned helplessness and build motivation, the therapist should prompt the adult with ADHD to brainstorm a list of all of the reasons for getting organized. Such reasons might include:

1. Spend less time looking for things.
2. Be a positive role model for the children.
3. Reduce feeling internally chaotic or overwhelmed.
4. Be more productive in less time.
5. Make more money.
6. Improve a marriage or other intimate relationship.

This list should be posted in a prominent location and reviewed daily.

Second, the therapist should prompt the individual to develop a reinforcement system for completing the various steps of organizing. A list of favorite activities should be made; a reinforcement schedule making favorite activities contingent upon completing each step of organization should be developed, and spouses and family members can be enlisted to help administer the reinforcements. The use of photographs documenting before, during, and after may also prove motivating to some patients. Finally, working with a buddy or friend may make the job go smoother.

## Strategize: Create an Organizational Plan

The therapist should help the individual create a plan of action for transforming the space according to the kindergarten classroom model (Morgenstern, 1998). A kindergarten classroom is divided into activity zones such as Reading Corner, Dress-Up, Building Blocks, Snack, Arts and Crafts, and Music. Each zone is well defined and self-contained; everything the child needs for an activity is within the zone, easily accessible to the child, because it is stored at the point of use. There are clear boundaries between zones. It is therefore easy for the child to focus on one activity at a time; nothing else distracts the child, and the child does not have to leave the zone to locate the materials necessary for the activity. Furthermore, each item in an activity zone has a clear, well-labeled home in a container that is the correct size to hold it. It is easy for the child to put the objects away efficiently, keeping the zone orderly.

The therapist helps the individual divide the room to be organized into activity zones and draw a picture of the reorganized room. For example, Rhonda needed to re-organize her den. Together, she and her therapist decided that there were five predominant activities that she did in the den: listen to music, work on the computer, sew, read, and do personal paperwork. Rhonda drew a picture of the re-organized den with a zone for each of these activities. She included storage space for all the equipment and supplies for each activity in it's zone. Then, she went home and moved things around in the den to approximate the new zones; this helped make her vision concrete. At her next session, her therapist helped her plan when she was going to do the final re-organization, scheduling times in her day planner.

## Attack the Clutter: Implementing the Plan

Morgenstern's (1998) step by step approach to implementing an organizational plan is coded in the pneumonic, SPACE: (1) **S**ort; (2) **P**urge; (3) **A**ssign a home; (4) **C**ontainerize; and (5) **E**qualize. *Sorting* involves going through each possession in the room, categorizing it, and deciding whether to keep it or discard it. *Purging* involved discarding those possessions that are not needed, then assigning the remaining items a home within one of the zones of the room. *Containerizing* involves putting items into clearly labeled containers so that it is easy to retrieve them. *Equalizing* involves monitoring the success of the new organizational plan over time and fine-tuning it to eliminate minor problems which could not easily have been anticipated.

Rhonda decided to work on her den, one hour at a time, three days per week. She scheduled times over four weeks to sort, purge, and containerize. She scheduled these times to be two hours after taking a dose of Concerta. Slowly, over a month, she successfully reorganized her den. At a follow-up session one month later, however, she verbalized that she also liked to talk on the phone in the den, and she needed a phone zone; this illustrates the importance of equalizing the organizational plan over time. After she added the phone zone, the room organizational plan worked well for her.

## CONCLUSION

After reviewing the methods by which the therapist can help the adult with ADHD cope effectively with a variety of lifestyle issues, it would be appropriate to review the research on the effectiveness of these methods. Unfortunately, no such published research exists. In fact, medication is the only intervention for adults with ADHD that has been subjected to controlled research (Weiss et al., 1999).

Instead, this chapter will conclude with an appeal to the readers to conduct the research needed to demonstrate the effectiveness of lifestyle interventions with ADHD adults and their families. Medication researchers need to move beyond the usual double-blind, placebo trials to studies designed to teach adults with ADHD how to maximize their own medication regimens using everyday activities as dependent measures. The interventions outlined in this chapter for organizing clutter and learning to use a day planner need to be tested in controlled investigations with appropriate dependent measures. Research is needed to determine the impact of ADHD on relationships and how to tailor marital therapies to the unique difficulties created by ADHD in the family.

Meanwhile, while researchers explore these topics, clinicians need to meet the growing demands for help from adults who are discovering that they have the neuro biological disorder known as ADHD. The suggestions in this chapter, while not empirically tested, are grounded solidly in behavioral theory, which has been proven to lead to effective treatments for many other disorders. Clinicians are advised to creatively apply these ideas in their daily practices.

## REFERENCES

Barkley, R. (1997). *ADHD and the nature of self-control.* New York: Guilford Press.

Brown, T. E. (Ed.). (2000). *Attention deficit disorders and comorbidities in children, adolescents, and adults.* Washington, DC: American Psychiatric Press.

Covey, S. R. (1989). *The 7 habits of highly effective people.* New York: Simon and Schuster.

Halverstadt, J. S. (1998). *A.D.D. & romance: Finding fulfillment in love, sex, and relationships.* Dallas, Tx: Taylor.

Morgenstern, J. (1998). *Organizing from the inside out.* New York: Henry Holt.

Murphy, K., & LeVert, S. (1995). *Out of the Fog.* New York: Hyperion Press.

Nadeau, K. G. (Ed.) (1995). *A comprehensive guide to attention deficit disorder in adults: Research, diagnosis, and treatment.* New York: Brunner/Mazel.

Nadeau, K. G. (1996). *Adventures in fast forward: Life, love, and work for the ADD adult.* New York: Brunner/Mazel.

Seligman, M. E. P. (1975). *Helplessness: On depression, development, and death.* San Francisco: Freeman.

Tannock, R. (1998). Attention deficit hyperactivity disorder: Advances in cognitive, neurobiological, and genetic research. *Journal of Child Psychology and Psychiatry, 39,* 65–99.

Weiss, M., Hechtman, L. T., & Weiss, G. (1999). *ADHD in adulthood: A guide to current theory, diagnosis, and treatment.* Baltimore: John Hopkins University Press.

# Index

Note: Page numbers followed by f or t refer to the figure or table on that page, respectively.

## A

ABT-418, 177
Abuse, 247–248
Academic performance, 6–7. *see also* Education
  and adaptive functioning, 55–57
  and adult outcome, 15, 29–30
  and gender, 9
Academy of Child and Adolescent Psychiatry, 77
Accommodations
  academic, 215
  case study, 99–105
  and disability documentation, 205
  for medical licensure, 214
  types of, 215
  in work and educational settings, 63–64
  in workplace, 215–216
Adaptive functioning
  in academic setting, 55–57
  in adulthood vs. childhood, 45
  definition, 43
  and degree of impairment, 44
  and employment, 57–58
  and intelligence, 6
  and interpersonal relationships, 57
  and motor vehicle operation, 58–59
  as predictor of adult outcome, 16
  and psychotherapy, 147
  self-care, 55
  unstudied domains, 61
Adderall. *see* Stimulant medication
Adolescence
  characteristics of ADHD, 11–14
  and development of self determination skills, 192
  and Inattentive Type ADHD, 65
  prevalence of ADHD, 19
  prognosis for adulthood, 38
  transition to adulthood, 113–114
Adoption studies, 2
Adult ADHD
  associated problems, 148–149
  challenges of middle years, 121–126
  characteristics, 14, 128–131
  characteristics vs. adolescent ADHD, 12t
  clinical features, 167–168
  cumulative effects, 14–15
  difficulties in diagnosis, 71
  domains of adaptive functioning, 45
  evidence for, 165
  factors affecting outcome, 37–39
  health risks, 72
  impact on daily functioning, 72
  mindset, 131–134
  outcome, 27–28
  in parents of ADHD children, 108
  prevalence, 19
  psychological/emotional outcomes, 28–29
  research, 26
Affective disorders, 47–49
Age
  and hyperactivity, 8
  and individuality of treatment, 149
  and inhibitory control, 5
  and psychotherapy, 158
  requirement for symptom onset and diagnosis, 75–76
Aggression
  comorbidity into adulthood, 15
  as coping strategy, 137–138
  and gender, 9, 149
  as predictor of adult outcome, 38
  risk factors, 11
Aging, and differential diagnosis, 76, 81
Alcoholism
  and cerebral atrophy, 4
  conductivity disorder as predictor, 47
  as health issue, 64
  impact on family life, 150
  in marital relationship, 236–238
  as self-care issue, 55
Alerting/arousal network, 3

American Psychiatric Association. *see* DSM IV-TR diagnostic criteria
Americans with Disabilities Act
  about, 206
  and correctable disabilities, 210
  as legal statute, 205
  and reasonable accommodations, 216
  and test accommodations, 99
Amino acids, 176
Amphetamine compounds. *see* Stimulant medication
Anger
  managing through psychotherapy, 154–155
  and marital relationships, 238
  and perception of interpersonal relations, 133–134
  and relationships, 220
  and self-regulation, 54
Antidepressants, 165, 166, 175–176
  clinical strategies, 179
  investigational, 177, 179
Antidiscrimination, 99
Antihypertensive medication, 176, 181
Antisocial behavior, 7
  and comorbid disorders, 17
  incidence in adults with ADHD, 32
  persistence into adulthood, 27
Antisocial personality disorder (ASPD)
  case study, 160
  comorbidity, 47
  in first degree relatives, 15
  level of comorbidity, 76
Anxiety
  addressing with psychotherapy, 156–157
  in adolescence, 13
  in families, 243
  and gender, 9
Anxiety disorders
  comorbidity, 47
  in first degree relatives, 15
  incidence in adults with ADHD, 28

## A

Assessment, 37. *see also* Diagnosis
  challenges of, 85
  importance of objectivity and independence, 90
  of mindset, 135
  practice parameters, 77–78
Attention Deficit Disorders Evaluation Scale (ADDES), 9
Attentional networks, 3–4
Attitude adjustment, 248–249
  and marital stress, 258–259
Auditory attention, 26
Autonomy, 265
Avoidance, 136
Axis I and II disorders, 80

## B

Barkley's response inhibition theory, 282
Basal ganglia, 5
Behavior
  benchmark, 283
  influence on relationships, 219
  isolating from emotions, 264
  and parenting, 249
  work-related, 198–199
Behavior problems
  in adults with ADHD, 148
  and Americans with Disabilities Act, 214
  changing with cognitive-behavioral therapy, 152
  in clinic-referred adults, 56
Behavioral marital therapy
  brainstorming, 233
  communication training, 232
  contingency contract, 231
  essential aspects, 233
  feedback and shaping, 232
  flow of therapeutic process, 229–231
  mirroring technique, 232–233
  rehearsal, 232
  shifting focus on negative behaviors, 228–229
  and social learning theory, 227–228
Behavioral maturity, 16
Benchmark behavior, 283
Beta-blockers, 176
Biogenetic findings, 2–3
Biopsychosocial disorder, 2
Bipolar disorder
  in adolescence, 13
  case study, 91–95
  and gender, 9
  incidence in adults with ADHD, 28
Brain
  abnormalities, 166
  anomalies in ADHD, 4–5
  structures and functions, 3
Brain metabolism, 4, 15, 149, 166
Brown Attention-Deficit Disorders Scales, 80, 168
Brown's executive functioning model, 282
Bupropion, 166, 175–176

## C

Career choices, 122. *see also* Employment
  barriers to realistic decision making, 187–189
  client role in self-determination, 193–194
  common client statements, 191–192
  control of decision, 198–200
  decision making process, 198 f
  Department of Vocational Rehabilitation (DVR), 195
  *Finding a Career That Works for You*, 195
  and interest inventories, 199
  living with the consequences, 201
  practical tools and strategies, 196–198
  realistic picture, 189–192
  reality and worst-case scenarios, 199
  and reasonable alternatives, 200–201
  reframing, 192–193
  risk tolerance, 202–203
  role of professional, 194–196
  triggering events, 197
Caring days, 234
Case studies
  ADHD with substance dependence and conduct disorder, 95–99
  Anne (ADHD and panic disorder), 159
  bipolar disorder and ADHD, 91–95
  career choices (Frank), 196–198, 200–202
  Cecile (middle aged woman), 122–126
  Chris (young adult), 116–118
  Claire (disorganized mother), 261–262
  Dr. Bennett, 279, 285
  incorrect diagnosis, 86–91
  Jane (35 yr. old mother), 160–161
  Katlin (coaching and organization), 270–271
  Michael (employment and self-esteem), 161–162
  Nick (young adult), 119–121
  Paul (coaching), 268–269
  Peter (ADHD and antisocial personality disorder), 160
  Rhonda (divorced mother), 279–280, 290
  Sally (structure through coaching), 269–270
  SCANS blueprint, 194
Catecholaminergic medication, 165, 166
CBT. *see* Cognitive-behavioral therapy
Cerebral atrophy, 3
Characteristics
  in adolescence, 11–14
  in childhood, 10
  difference between adults and adolescents, 12t
  gender differences, 9
Child abuse, 247–248
Child rearing. *see* Parenting
Childhood ADHD
  academic adjustment, 6–7
  age of symptom onset for adult diagnosis, 75–76
  behavioral/psychosocial findings, 7
  biogenetic findings, 2–3
  and brain abnormalities, 4–5
  characteristics, 10
  cognitive functioning, 6
  comorbid disorders, 10–11
  executive functioning deficits, 5
  gender and symptoms, 149
  gender differences, 9
  long-term outcome, 148
  MRI (magnetic resonance imaging) data, 4
  neurobiological and environmental factors, 6
  prevalence, 165
  as risk factor for adult adjustment difficulties, 1
  self-regulation, 8
  types and prevalence, 8
  underreporting of symptoms, 79
Children's Attention and Adjustment Scale, 9
Cholinergic agents, 177, 181
Chronic nature of ADHD, 14–15, 72
  and treatment planning, 63
Cigarette smoking, 31

# Index

and anticholinergic agents, 177
as health issue, 64
and olfactory functioning, 54
Clinician's role. *see also* Treatment
and client readiness, 108
developing goals, 142
focus of therapy, 107
shift to neuropsychological issues, 107
skill needed for ADHD adult treatment, 113
using the "exception" technique, 139–140
Coaching, 112
about, 262–263
and arousal, 264
and autonomy, 265
case study, 263
client match, 275
client readiness, 265–266
collaboration with other professionals, 273
complicating issues, 274
defining client/coach roles, 266–267
desirable qualities, 275–276
distinguishing from other services, 271–272
and emotional regulation, 264
and functional level, 267
initial interview, 266
and motivation, 264–265
as a partnership, 267
professional development within field, 274
and recognition of comorbid conditions, 273
and structure, 269–270
using guided self-exploration, 270
Cognitive-behavioral therapy
anger management, 154–155
anxiety management, 156–157
appropriateness, 147, 150
depression, 157
interpersonal skills, 155–156
and lifestyle change, 280
organizational skills, 152
and parenting, 248–249
and problem-solving skills, 152–153
structure and goal setting, 151–152
time management, 152
Cognitive functioning, 6–7
in adults with ADHD, 29
defects, 49

improving through medication, 122–123
improving through treatment, 110
as major life activity, 209
mental impairment as disability, 206–207
Cognitive maturity, 16
Collaboration, 273
Combined Type ADHD, 65
comorbidity, 11
differentiation from Inattentive Type, 65
incidence, 8
Communication
and behavioral marital therapy, 227–228, 232
developing through marital counseling, 221–222
as source of conflict, 253
Community resources, 116–117
for remedial education, 194–195
Comorbidity, 7, 10–11
in adolescence, 13
affective disorders, 47–49
anxiety/depression/alcoholism case study, 125–126
apparent vs. real, 46–47
bipolar disorder and ADHD, 91–95
case study (bipolar disorder), 91–95
case study (CD and substance dependence), 95–99
common disorders, 46–47
as confounding factor for diagnosis, 72
definition, 43
and differential diagnosis, 76–77, 76–77
disentangling from ADHD, 169
excluding as explanation for EF deficiency, 55
externalizing disorders, 47
with Inattentive Type ADHD, 65
and parenting, 246
as predictor of adult outcome, 27
premenstrual syndrome, 122
psychiatric disorders, 16
and role of coach, 273
seasonal affective disorder, 29
social disability (SD), 14
and treatment planning, 63, 111
Compensatory strategies, 167. *see also* Coping strategies
clinician's role in developing, 110, 124–125

and legal definition of disability, 211–212
Compliance, 242
Computers as distraction, 256
Concentration, 209
Conceptual fluency, 51
Conduct disorder (CD), 7, 10–11
and adult antisocial personality disorders, 29
case study, 95–99
comorbidity, 46, 47
in first degree relatives, 15
as predictor of adult outcome, 38
risk of comorbidity in adolescents, 13
Confidence, 117
and career choices, 189
and coaching, 264
Conflict
in families, 242–243
through communication, 253
Conners Adult ADHD Diagnostic Interview, 78–79, 168
Conners continuous performance task (CPT), 50
Contextual therapy, 223–227
Contingency contract, 231
Continuous Performance Test, 11, 80
Contributing factors, 6
Control
and anger management in relationships, 225
in career planning decisions, 198–200
Coping strategies, 113
aggression, 137–138
avoidance, 136
controlling, 137
developing effective, 135–136
discovery through coaching, 265
encouraging with cognitive-behavioral therapy, 153
impulsivity, 138
quitting, 137
rationalizing, 137
Corpus callosum, 4
Cortico-striatal-thalamo-cortical (CSTC) circuit, 3, 5
Counseling. *see* Marital counseling; Psychotherapy
Criminal activity, 7, 148
addressing with psychotherapy, 153–154
incidence in adults with ADHD, 32

Cultural context, 8
Cumulative effects, 14–15
Cyclothymia, 93

## D

Daily living. *see* Functioning
Data analysis
  driving record results, 46
  problems with, 26
  symptoms in adults, 32–35
  unreliability of self-perception, 44
Day planner, 286–288
Department of Vocational Rehabilitation (DVR), 195
Dependency
  and career choices, 189
  and relationships, 220
Deprenyl, 176
Depression
  addressing with psychotherapy, 157
  in childhood, 10
  comorbidity, 46, 48, 49
  differential diagnosis, 37
  in first degree relatives, 15
  and gender, 9
  incidence in adults with ADHD, 28
  influence on relationships, 220
  level of comorbidity, 76
  within marital relationship, 238
Developmental history
  and adult ADHD diagnosis, 78–79
  age of symptom onset for adult diagnosis, 75–76
  parent rating scale, 79
Diagnosis
  and age of symptom onset, 75–76
  basis for, 71
  and brain imaging data, 5
  criteria, 35–37, 168–169
  criteria for case study, 88–89
  criteria worldwide, 73
  DSM IV-TR, 73–77
  as executive functioning data, 62
  guarding against overdiagnosis, 81–82
  incomplete, 109
  incorrect, case study, 86–91
  as multimodal process for adults, 78–81
  and number of symptoms, 75
  problems with symptoms as basis, 45–46
Differential diagnosis, 73, 169
  complicated nature, 85

Disability
  clinician's role in understanding, 122
  definition, 99
  definition with corrective measures, 210
  documentation to establish, 205, 216–217
  hidden and career choices, 188, 190
  and impairment, 206–207
  measuring, 212
  and reasonable accommodations, 216
  and Social Security Act, 211–212
  substantiation, 100
Discrimination, 206
Disinhibition, 5
Disorganization, 129
  case study, 261–262
  and family life, 244
Distractive techniques
  for anger management, 154–155
  for anxiety management, 156
Divorce rate, 57
Documentation
  case study (accommodation), 104–105
  and diagnosis of ADHD, 89–90
  and establishing a disability, 100, 205, 216–217
Donepezil, 177
Dopamine transporter protein (DAT), 166
Driving incidents, 7, 30–31
  and adaptive functioning, 58–59
  in ADHD vs. control group, 60t
  data interpretation, 46
  reduction with treatment, 39
  and treatment, 64
Drug use. *see* Substance abuse
DSM-III criteria, 8
DSM-IIIR, 26
DSM-IV
  comorbidity of clinical psychiatric disorders, 48t
  diagnostic criteria, 71, 168
  types of ADHD, 8
DSM-IV symptoms
  Conners Adult ADHD Diagnostic Interview, 78–79
  for Inattentive Type ADHD, 74
  incidence in normal adults, 44
DSM IV-TR diagnostic criteria, 73–77, 90
DuPaul ADHD Rating Scale, 168
Dyslexia, 214
Dysthymia
  comorbidity, 49
  differential diagnosis, 37

## E

Education
  accommodation case study, 99–105
  accommodations, 63–64
  achievement levels, 6–7
  and adaptive functioning, 55–57
  choices beyond high school, 115
  clinician's role, 108
  coaching vs. tutoring, 272
  community resources for remedial work, 194–195
  Landmark School, 101
  level vs. general population, 29, 56
  practical interventions, 119–120
  realistic college goals, 190
  regarding limitations and realistic expectations, 151
  and self-determination skills, 194
  tutoring, 117
Egocentricity, 189
Emotional regulation, 154
  and thought control, 248–249
  through coaching, 264
Empathy, 130–131
Employment, 15. *see also* Career choices
  accommodations, 63–64, 215–216
  and adaptive functioning, 57–58
  ADHD friendly, 125
  and Americans with Disabilities Act, 206
  and boredom, 162
  difficulties in adults with ADHD, 148
  as major life activity, 207, 208–209
  and self-esteem, 161–162
  vocational outcome for adults, 30–31
  and vocational training/career guidance, 108
Encephalographic (EEG) studies, 4
Environmental factors, 2, 73
  and clinician's role, 108
  interaction with neurobiological influences, 6
  and social restructuring, 110
Equal access, 99
Equal Employment Opportunity Commission (EEOC), 207
Equitable fairness, 224
Evaluation criteria, 35–37
"Exception" technique, 139–140

# Index

Executive function
  Brown's model of, 282
  deficits, 26–27, 29, 49
  definition, 49
  diagnostic use of test data, 62–63
  disinhibition, 5
  emotional self-regulation, 54
  flexibility/fluency, 51
  inhibition, 50
  interference control, 50
  as model for impact of ADHD symptoms, 62
  and neurobiological basis of ADHD, 3
  response organization, 51–52
  sense of time, 52–54
  test results, 52t
  working memory, 50–51
Exercise, 123
  and family stress, 258
Externalizing disorders, 47

## F

F-A-S test, 51
Family adversity
  addressing with psychotherapy, 150
  and adult outcome, 17
  as predictor of adult outcome, 15, 16, 38
Family stress. *see also* Parenting
  and anxiety, 243
  and conflict, 242–243
  and disorganization, 244
  distinguishing important and unimportant issues, 252
  and medication, 257
  and noise, 243
  parenting styles, 247
  and psychoeducation, 151
  sibling distress, 247–248, 259–260
  technological aids, 255–256
  therapy strategies, 241–242
  and time away, 258
  and unstructured time, 244–245
Financial management, 61
  through coaching, 268–269
*Finding a Career That Works for You*, 195
Flexibility, 129–130
Flexibility/fluency, 51
Frontal cortex, 5
Frustration, 129
Fun, 246
Functioning
  assessing prior to coaching, 267

  global impairment caused by ADHD, 61–62
  impairment and adult diagnosis, 76

## G

Gambling, 72
Gender
  and adult outcome, 38
  and brain metabolic abnormalities, 4
  and genetic heritability, 3
  and impulsivity, 8
  and manifestations, 9
  and persistence of symptoms into adulthood, 27
  and prevalence, 9
  and psychotherapy session structure, 158
  and seasonal affective disorder, 29
  and symptoms during childhood, 149
Genetic link, 2–3, 73, 166
Glucose metabolism, 4
Goals
  and changing mindset, 142
  of cognitive-behavioral therapy, 151–152
  identifying through coaching, 264
  importance of flexibility, 144–145
  for lifestyle change, 281
  long term, 120
  long-term, 283–286
  for marital counseling, 227
  of psychotherapy treatment, 147
  realistic plans for reaching, 143, 153–154
  short term, 117
  through coaching and psychotherapy, 272
Grudges, 235–236

## H

Health considerations, 64
Health risks, 72
History
  and adult diagnosis, 85
  and bipolar disorder diagnosis, 91–92
  and diagnosis of ADHD, 87–88
HMO policies, 47
Household responsibilities, 61
Hyperactive-Impulsive Type ADHD, 74
  comorbidity, 11
  symptoms, 75
Hyperactivity
  and adult diagnosis, 73

  in childhood, 10
  data on adults, 32–35
  decline with age, 167
  genetic and environmental components, 3
  incidence in adults with ADHD, 28
  and type of ADHD, 8
Hyperactivity Type ADHD, 8
Hyperfocus, 284
Hypo-/hyperthyroidism, 36
Hypomania, 93

## I

Imaging studies, 3–5, 166
Impairment
  and adult diagnosis, 76
  clinically significant, 85
  domains, 76
  global nature, 61–62
  and legal definition of disability, 206–207
  and major life activities, 207–209
  measuring, 212
  professional documentation, 216–217
  and selecting accommodation, 216
  and substantial limitation, 209–213
Impulsivity
  addressing with psychotherapy, 153–154
  and adult outcome, 38
  in adults with ADHD, 128
  and age, 5
  in childhood, 10
  as coping strategy, 138
  decline with age, 167
  as defining character of ADHD, 148
  and gender, 8, 9
  genetic and environmental components, 3
Inattention
  and adult diagnosis, 73
  and adult outcome, 38
  in childhood, 10
  and coaching, 265
  data on adults, 32–35
  DSM-IV symptom, 74
  and executive function, 50
  genetic and environmental components, 3
  incidence in adults with ADHD, 28
  persistence into adulthood, 167
  and type of ADHD, 8

Inattentive Type ADHD
  assessment, 77–78
  comorbidity, 11
  diagnostic criteria, 74
  prevalence, 8
  research about, 65
  symptoms, 74–75
Individuality
  and cognitive-behavioral therapy, 151–152
  and differences in symptoms, 149–150
  and medical licensure, 214
  and suboptimal response to pharmacotherapy, 181–182
Individuals with Disabilities Education Act, 99
Individuation, 225
Inhibition
  disruption of inhibitory mechanisms, 5
  as executive function, 50
  and neurobiological basis of ADHD, 3
Insatiability, 129–130
Intelligence test scores
  case study (accommodation), 100–101
  case study (bipolar disorder), 92–93
  and comorbid disorders, 17
  discrepancy with adaptive functioning, 16
  as predictor of adult outcome, 16, 38
  results with ADHD, 6–7, 49
  substance abuse case study, 87
  WAIS-R, 51
Interference control, 50
Internet, 256
Interpersonal problems, 7, 148
  and adaptive functioning, 57
  addressing with psychotherapy, 155–156
  and emotional self-regulation, 54
IQ. *see* Intelligence test scores
Islands of competence, 141

**J**

Job stress, 15

**L**

Language difficulties, 10
Learning disabilities (LD), 6
  accommodation case study, 100–101
  and career choices, 188
  common, 10

  and definition of major life activities, 207–208
  and legal definition of disability, 206–207
  level of comorbidity, 76
  nonverbal, 30
  as predictor of adult outcome, 38
  reading disability, 11
  remedial interventions, 169
  risk with ADHD, 29
  and self determination, 194
Legal cases
  *Albertsons, Inc. v. Kirkingburg*, 211
  *Andersen v. Apfel*, 211
  *Beck v. University of Wisconsin*, 216
  *Bercovitch v. Baldwin School, Inc.*, 213–214
  *Davidson v. Midelfort Clinic, Ltd*, 206–208
  *DeMar v. Car Freshner Corp.*, 212
  *Jones v. Men's Wearhouse*, 213
  *Leisen v. City of Shelbyville*, 207
  *McGuinness v. University of New Mexico School of Medicine*, 207
  *Murphy v. United Parcel Service, Inc.*, 211
  *Pack v. KMart Corporation*, 209
  *Price v. The National Board of Medical Examiners*, 207, 212
  *Robertson v. Neuromedical Center*, 213
  *Schneider v. San Francisco*, 207
  *Schumacher v. Souderton Area School District*, 209, 211
  *Sevigny v. Maine Education Association*, 212–213
  *Sutton v. United Air Lines, Inc.*, 207, 210
Legal issues
  accommodations, 215–216
  Americans with Disabilities Act, 206
  defining a disability, 206–207
  difference between ADA and IDEA, 99
  and major life activities, 207–209
  otherwise qualified, 213–214
  Rehabilitation Act of 1973, 206
  role of professional, 205
  substantial limitation, 209–213
  Web site, 205
Lifelong treatment, 18, 63
Lifestyle, 114–115
Lifestyle management
  day planner, 286–288
  long-term goals, 283–286

  strength/weakness evaluation, 281–283
Limitations vs. symptoms, 44
Lithium, 91

**M**

Major life activities, 207–209
  comparison to average abilities, 212–213
MAOIs, 174, 176
Marital counseling
  behavior log, 230
  behavioral therapy, 227–233
  brainstorming, 233
  caring days, 234
  communication training, 232
  contextual therapy, 223–227
  contingency contract, 231
  cost/reward relationship, 228–229
  developing respect, 225
  equitable fairness, 224
  goal setting, 227
  grudges, 235–236
  and individual responsibility, 238
  individuation, 225
  initial stages of therapy, 221–222
  intentionality, 226
  meaning attached to behavior, 223–224
  mirroring technique, 232–233
  overview, 220–221
  rehearsal, 232
  relational ethics, 224
  split loyalty, 225–226
Marital satisfaction, 57, 72
  counseling treatment, 64–65
  and fun, 246
  and parallel lifestyle, 258–259
  and partner selection, 121–122
  and psychotherapy, 150–151, 161
Maturity, 122
  behavioral and outcome prediction, 16
  cognitive, 16
  gender differences, 149
Medical conditions
  with ADHD vs. normal population, 64
  and differential diagnosis, 77
  as predisposing factors, 73
Medical history
  age of symptom onset for adult diagnosis, 75–76
  assessing prior to coaching, 267
Medical licensure, 214

# Index

Medication. *see also* Pharmacotherapy; Stimulant medication
  amino acids, 177
  antidepressants, 175–176
  antihypertensives, 176
  cholinergic agents, 177
  and correctable disabilities, 210
  currently under investigation, 177, 179
  as early treatment, 18
  and family stress, 257
  for improved cognitive function, 122–123
  maximizing impact, 283
  modfanil, 177
  as predictor of adult outcome, 38
  reminders through coaching, 263
  response record, 284f
  and treatment planning, 63–64
  types of, 165–166
Memory. *see also* Working memory
  and cholinergic-enhancing agents, 166
  and psychotherapy session structure, 111–112
Metabolism
  abnormalities of brain, 4, 15, 149, 166
  as predisposing factor, 73
Methylphenidate, 16, 167
Mindset issues
  assessing, 135
  changing negative to positive, 142–145
  control, 131–132
  demystifying, 139–140
  directed anger, 133–134
  failure and inadequacy, 132
  pessimism, 134
  positive mindset, 140–141
  success based on luck, 132
  unfairness, 133
  worthiness, 132–133
Minor-but-aggravating (MBA) problems, 252
Mirroring technique, 232–233
Misdiagnosis, 86–91, 109
Modfanil, 177
Monoamine oxidase inhibitors, 174, 176, 181
Mood disorders, 13
Mood shifts, 72, 129
Motor skill development, 25
Motor vehicle operation. *see* Driving incidents
MRI (magnetic resonance imaging) data
  of children with ADHD, 4
  and diagnosis of ADHD, 5
  and neurobiological basis of ADHD, 3
Multimodal treatment, 19

## N

Neurobiological basis, 3–4, 73, 166–167, 280
  and clinician's role, 109–110
  interaction with environmental factors, 6
Neuropsychological tests, 37
Nicotine patch, 177
Noise, 243, 252–254
Nonverbal learning disability, 30
Not Otherwise Specified (NOS) Type, 74
Nutrition, 73, 123

## O

Obsessive-compulsive disorder (OCD), 48
Olfaction, 52t, 54–55
Oppositional defiance disorder (ODD), 7, 10–11
  comorbidity, 46, 47, 49
  in first degree relatives, 15
  as predictor of adult outcome, 38
  risk of comorbidity in adolescents, 13
Optimistic mindset, 140–145, 280
Organizational skills, 152
  analysis of problem, 289–290
  developing effective, 281
  developing through coaching, 270–271
  developing through tools, 269, 286–288
  inside out approach, 288–289
  SPACE plan for, 290
  and time management classes, 272
Orienting/shifting network, 3
Otherwise qualified, 213–214
Outcome
  and academic performance, 29–30
  in adults with ADHD, 27–28
  and aggression in adolescents, 13–14
  and antisocial/criminal behavior, 32
  and cognitive deficits, 29
  and early treatment, 17–18
  factors affecting, 37–39
  predictors, 16
  psychological/emotional predictors, 28–29
  resiliency factors, 16–17
  and substance abuse, 31–32
  vocational, 30–31

## P

Panic disorder
  case study, 159
  incidence in adults with ADHD, 29
Parent rating scale, 79
Parenting, 61
  and attitude adjustment, 248–249
  and comorbid disorders, 246
  dealing with other people's reactions, 250–251
  distinguishing important and unimportant issues, 252
  divide and conquer technique, 254–255
  expectations vs. reality, 250
  and finding solutions to behavior problems, 250
  and medication, 257
  noise management, 252–254
  role in treatment of young adults, 116, 117–118, 119
  and stress reduction through exercise, 258
  and time away, 258
  unsound thoughts, 249–251
Pargyline, 176
Pemoline, 170
Perfectionism, 189
Persistent ADHD
  and comorbidity of psychiatric disorders, 16
  genetic link, 3
  predictors, 15
  research about, 72
Personal relationships. *see also* Marital satisfaction
  and adulthood, 15
  difficulties in adults with ADHD, 72
  and major life activities, 209
  and partner selection, 121–122
  supportive environment and outcome, 97
Pessimistic mindset, 127, 131–134, 280
  changing negative to positive, 140–145
PET (positron emission tomography) scan, 4
Pharmacotherapy. *see also* Medication
  clinical strategies, 179–181
  combination treatment, 181
  combined with psychotherapy, 182
  general principles, 169–170
  nonstimulants, 178t

## Index

Pharmacotherapy. (*Continued*)
  stimulant effectiveness, 170–171
  suboptimal responses, 181–182
Physical impairment, 206–207
Predominantly Hyperactive-Impulsive Type. *see* Hyperactive-Impulsive Type ADHD
Predominantly Inattentive Type. *see* Inattentive Type ADHD
Premenstrual syndrome, 122
Prevalence worldwide, 8
Prioritizing tasks, 263, 288
Problem-solving skills, 152–153
Propranolol, 176
Protective factors, 115
  and partner selection, 121–122
  using community resources, 116–117
Psychiatric conditions
  comorbidity, 47–49, 75–76
  differential diagnosis, 35–37
  ruling out prior to treatment, 66
Psychoeducation, 151
Psychosocial problems, 7
  in childhood, 10
Psychotherapy. *see also* Marital counseling
  addressing emotional problems, 110–111
  approaches, 150–151
  collaboration with coaches, 274
  combined with pharmacotherapy, 182
  distinguishing from coaching, 272
  goals, 147
  group sessions, 157–158
  structure of session, 111–112

### Q
Quantitative encephalograph, 4

### R
Race, 9
Rating scales, 9, 168
  Brown Attention-Deficit Disorders Scales, 80
  as part of assessment, 79
  results for case study, 88
Reading disabilities, 11, 208
  dyslexia, 214
Reboxetine, 177
Referral bias, 47
Reframing career decisions, 192–193, 197
Rehabilitation Act of 1973, 205, 206

Relational ethics, 224
Relationships. *see* Personal relationships
  learning to nurture, 281
Relaxation techniques, 156
Remission, 15, 16
  likelihood, 25
Resiliency
  factors affecting, 38
  fostering factors leading to, 19
  moderating factors, 16–17
Respect, 225
Response organization, 51–52
Rey-Osterrieth Complex Figure Drawing, 51
Rigidity, 129–130
Risk, 15–18
  disease as accumulation of, 73
  of Ritalin with bipolar disorder, 94
Risk factors for subtypes, 11
Ritalin, 86, 90, 94, 97
Routine tasks. *see* Functioning

### S
SCANS blueprint, 194
Seasonal affective disorder, 29
Section 504, 206
Selegeline, 176
Self-care, 55
Self-determination skills
  and career choices, 193–194
  development in adolescence, 192
Self esteem
  and ADHD graduates, 150
  and career choices, 187–188
  in children, 10
  and coaching, 264
  and confidence, 117
  and positive mindset, 140–141
  and relationships, 220
Self-exploration, 270
Self-regulation, 8
  addressing with therapy, 280
  and coaching, 263
  as executive function, 54
  as explanation for ADHD, 27
Self-reported symptoms
  in normal adults, 44
  as part of assessment, 79
Serotonergic medication, 165, 166, 176
Serotonin, 238
Sexual activity, 7, 59–61
  counseling treatment, 65

Sibling distress, 247–248, 259–260
  divide and conquer technique, 254–255
Simon Game, 51
Sleep, 123
Smell (sense of), 54–55
Smoking. *see* Cigarette smoking
Social disability (SD), 14
Social isolation
  and adulthood, 15
  and anger management, 154
  and group psychotherapy, 157–158
Social problems, 7
  and gender, 9
  phobias, 156–157
  restructuring environment, 110
Social Security Act, 211–212
Social skills training, 18
  addressing with psychotherapy, 155–156
  and career choices, 192
Socioeconomic status (SES), 15, 17
SPACE organizational plan, 290
Spouse. *see* Marital counseling
Stimulant medication, 165, 166
  clinical strategies, 179
  delivery systems, 174–175
  dosing guidelines, 172
  effectiveness, 170–171
  interactions, 173–174
  maximizing impact, 283
  pharmacodynamics of treatment, 172
  pharmacokinetic issues, 171
  side effects, 173, 174t
  study results, 171t
Strength/weakness evaluation, 281–283
Stress
  appropriate amount, 264
  environmental, as risk factor, 73
  in families, 242
  job-related in adults, 15
  trauma and course of outcome, 16
Stroop Color-Word Test, 50
Structure
  and family vacation, 244–245
  and practical problem solving, 120
  of psychotherapy session, 111–112
  through coaching, 269–270
  and transition to adulthood, 115–116
  and tutoring for young adults, 117
Substance abuse
  in adolescence, 13

# Index

and adult outcome, 17
in adulthood, 28
case study, 95–99, 160
conductivity disorder as predictor, 47
differential diagnosis from ADHD, 87–88
as health issue, 64
impact on family life, 150
incidence in adults with ADHD, 31–32, 37
level of comorbidity, 76
in marital relationship, 236–238
and relationships, 220–221
treatment and ADHD diagnosis, 169
Substantial limitation
definition, 210
measuring, 212–213
Subtypes, 65
comorbidity, 11
DSM IV-TR diagnostic criteria, 74
incidence, 8
and presynaptic dopamine transporter proteins, 166
Success
based on luck, 132
in career planning decisions, 196
control over, 141
Suicidal ideation, 148, 157
Symptoms
of adult ADHD, 167–168
adult education concerning, 79
daily impact, 62
data on adults, 32–35
developmental differences, 75
and diagnosis of ADHD, 26, 35–37
for Hyperactive-Impulsive Type ADHD, 75
impact on non-ADHD spouse, 223
of Inattentive Type ADHD, 65
and incorrect diagnosis, 86
influence on relationships, 219
vs. limitations, 44
in normal adults, 34–35, 88
number required for diagnosis, 75
persistence into adulthood, 25, 27
primary and secondary, 81
reduction with treatment, 38
underreporting in childhood, 79

## T

Technological aids, 255–256, 286–288
Television as distraction, 256
Temper, 72
managing through psychotherapy, 154–155
Temperament, 73
Therapy. *see* Psychotherapy
Time management, 61, 281
addressing with psychotherapy, 152
and coaching, 263
day planner, 286–288
technologies for, 112
Time (sense of), 52–54
Tomoxetine, 177
Tower of Hanoi (TOH), 11
Transactional model, 2–6
Trauma, 16
Treatment. *see also* Case studies;
Cognitive-behavioral therapy;
Lifestyle management;
Pharmacotherapy; Psychotherapy
of ADHD as global functional impairment, 61–62
ADHD coach, 112
ADHD-friendly lifestyle, 114–115
appropriate vs. self-medication, 115
areas of focus, 281
based on developmental perspective, 18–19
of comorbid conditions, 63, 111
and driving problems, 64
effect on adult outcome, 17–18
group psychotherapy, 157–158
and impact of ADHD symptoms, 62
as lifelong endeavor, 18
neurotherapy, 109–110
as predictor of adult outcome, 38
professional organizers, 112
psychoeducation, 151
psychotherapy, 110–111
role of parents, 116, 117–118, 119
structure of psychotherapy session, 111–112
Tricyclic antidepressants, 166, 175
Triggering events, 197
Twin studies, 2
and brain imaging data, 5
Types of ADHD, 11

## U

U.S. Department of Labor, 194
Utah Criteria, 73, 80, 168

## V

Vacation stress, 244–245
and divide and conquer technique, 254–255
Venlafaxine, 176
Verbal fluency, 51
Videos as distraction, 256
Violence. *see also* Anger
child abuse, 247–248
within marital relationship, 237, 238
Visual tracking, 26
Vitamin deficiency, 36
Vocational outcome, 30–31

## W

WAIS-R intelligence test, 51
Web sites
assessment practice parameters, 77
legal documents, 205
Wender Utah Rating Scale, 168
Weschler Coding subtest, 11
Wisconsin Card Sort test, 11
as measure of flexibility, 51
Wisconsin Selective Reminding Test, 11
Work performance, 6–7
substantial limitation and disability, 208–209
Working memory, 50–51, 168
definition, 53
Writing disabilities, 208

Printed in Great Britain
by Amazon.co.uk, Ltd.,
Marston Gate.